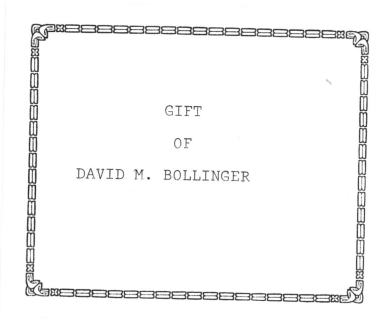

GIFT

OF

DAVID M. BOLLINGER

The Therapist's Handbook

Treatment Methods of Mental Disorders

SECOND EDITION

The Therapist's Handbook

Treatment Methods of Mental Disorders

SECOND EDITION

Benjamin B. Wolman, Ph.D., Editor

Stephen DeBerry, Ph.D., Associate Editor

In collaboration with

Richard Abrams, M.D.
Michael S. Aronoff, M.D.
Rogelio D. Bayog, M.D.
Gertrude Blanck, Ph.D.
Ewald W. Busse, M.D.
Morris E. Chafetz, M.D.
Richard D. Chessick, M.D.
John F. Clarkin, Ph.D.
Stephen DeBerry, Ph.D.
James W. Dykens, M.D.
Jack R. Ewalt, M.D.

Patricia L. Ewalt, M.S.W.
Marshall F. Folstein, M.D.
Allen Frances, M.D.
Sol L. Garfield, Ph.D.
Thomas R. Garrick, M.D.
Sanford Goldstone, Ph.D.
Daniel N. Hertz, M.D.
Chase P. Kimball, M.D.
Milton V. Kline, Ed.D.
Samuel B. Kutash, Ph.D.
David B. Larson, M.D.

Arnold A. Lazarus, Ph.D.
Stanley Lesse, M.D.
Paul R. McHugh, M.D.
Barry B. Perlman, M.D.
Max Rosenbaum, Ph.D.
Itamar Salamon, M.D.
Arthur H. Schwartz, M.D.
Marshall Swartzburg, M.D.
Alan D. Whanger, M.D.
G. Terence Wilson, Ph.D.

Foreword by **Bertram S. Brown, M.D.**

VNR **VAN NOSTRAND REINHOLD COMPANY**
NEW YORK   CINCINNATI   TORONTO   LONDON   MELBOURNE

Published by Van Nostrand Reinhold Company Inc.
135 West 50th Street, New York, N.Y. 10020

Van Nostrand Reinhold Publishing
1410 Birchmount Road
Scarborough, Ontario M1P 2E7, Canada

Van Nostrand Reinhold
480 Latrobe Street
Melbourne, Victoria 3000, Australia

Van Nostrand Reinhold Company Limited
Molly Millars Lane
Wokingham, Berkshire, England

15 14 13 12 11 10 9 8 7 6 5 4 3 2 1

Library of Congress Cataloging in Publication Data

Main entry under title:

The Therapist's handbook.

    Includes indexes.
    1. Psychotherapy.   2. Mental illness—Treatment.
I. Wolman, Benjamin B. [DNLM: 1. Mental disorders—Therapy.
2. Psychotherapy.   WM 420 T398]
RC480.T445 1982   616.89'14   82-8404
ISBN 0-442-25616-7   AACR2

Contributors

Richard Abrams, M.D.   Professor and Vice Chairman, Department of Psychiatry and Behavioral Sciences, UHS/The Chicago Medical School, North Chicago, Illinois.

Michael S. Aronoff, M.D.   Associate in Clinical Psychiatry, Columbia University; Associate Psychiatrist, Presbyterian Hospital; Adjunct Psychiatrist, Lenox Hill Hospital, New York.

Rogelio D. Bayog, M.D.   Chief, Alcohol and Drug Program, Brockton VA Medical Center, Brockton, Massachusetts; Instructor in Psychiatry, Harvard Medical School.

Gertrude Blanck, Ph.D.   Curriculum Director, Institute for the Study of Psychotherapy, New York.

Ewald W. Busse, M.D.   Associate Provost and Dean, J.P. Gibbons Professor of Psychiatry, Duke University Medical Center.

Morris E. Chafetz, M.D.   Director, National Institute on Alcohol Abuse and Alcoholism, National Institute of Mental Health, Department of Health, Education and Welfare, Washington, D.C.

Richard D. Chessick, M.D., Ph.D.   Professor of Psychiatry, Northwestern University Medical School, Evanston, Illinois; Senior Attending Psychiatrist, Evanston Hospital, Evanston, Illinois; Adjunct Professor of Philosophy, Loyola University of Chicago.

John F. Clarkin, Ph.D.   Associate Professor of Clinical Psychology in Psychiatry, Cornell University Medical College and Director of Psychology, Westchester Division—New York Hospital, White Plains, New York.

Stephen DeBerry, Ph.D.   Assistant Clinical Professor of Psychiatry, Albert Einstein College of Medicine; Director, Soundview Throgs-Neck CMHC Geriatric Clinic.

James W. Dykens, M.D.   Chief of Staff, Brockton VA Medical Center, Brockton, Massachusetts; Associate Clinical Professor of Psychiatry, Harvard Medical School.

Jack R. Ewalt, M.D.   Bullard Professor and Chairman, Executive Committee, Department of Psychiatry, Harvard Medical School, Cambridge, Massachusetts.

Patricia L. Ewalt, M.S.W.   Assistant Chief, Social Service, Framingham Youth Guidance Center; Clinical Assistant Professor, School of Social Work, Boston University, Boston, Massachusetts.

Marshal F. Folstein, M.D.   Assistant Professor of Psychiatry, University of Oregon, Portland, Oregon.

Allen Frances, M.D.   Associate Professor of Psychiatry, Cornell University Medical College and Director of the Outpatient Department, Payne Whitney Clinic—New York Hospital, New York, New York.

Sol L. Garfield, Ph.D.   Professor of Psychology, Washington University.

Thomas R. Garrick, M.D.   Assistant Professor of Psychiatry, University of California at Los Angeles and Assistant Director, Psychiatric Liaison Consultation Service, Wadsworth Veterans Administration Medical Center, Los Angeles, California.

Sanford Goldstone, Ph.D.   Professor and Head, Psychology Division, Cornell University Medical College; Head, Community Consultation Services, Payne Whitney Psychiatric Clinic, New York.

Daniel N. Hertz, M.D.   Assistant Clinical Professor of Psychiatry, Cornell University Medical College; Attending Psychiatrist, New York Hospital-Cornell Medical Center, and St. Vincent's Hospital, New York.

Chase P. Kimball, M.D.   Professor of Psychiatry and Medicine, Division of Biological Sciences and Professor in the College, University of Chicago, Chicago, Illinois; Director, Psychiatric Liaison-Consultation Service, University of Chicago Hospitals and Clinics.

Milton V. Kline, Ed.D.   Director of the Institute for Research in Hypnosis and Psychotherapy and Editor Emeritus of the *International Journal of Clinical and Experimental Hypnosis.*

Samuel B. Kutash, Ph.D.   Director, New Jersey Division, New York Center for Psychoanalytic Training.

David B. Larson, M.D.   Assistant Professor of Psychiatry, Duke University Medical Center, Department of Psychiatry, Durham County General Hospital, Durham, North Carolina.

Arnold A. Lazarus, Ph.D.   Professor of Psychology, Graduate School of Applied and Professional Psychology, Rutgers University, Piscataway, New Jersey; Executive Director, Multimodal Therapy Institute, New Jersey, New York.

Stanley Lesse, M.D.   Editor-in-Chief, *American Journal of Psychotherapy;* President, Association for the Advancement of Psychotherapy; Associate Attending Neurologist, Columbia-Presbyterian Medical Center, New York.

Paul R. McHugh, M.D. Professor and Chairman, Department of Psychiatry, University of Oregon Medical School, Portland, Oregon.

Barry B. Perlman, M.D. Director of Psychiatry, St. Joseph's Medical Center, Yonkers, New York and Assistant Clinical Professor of Psychiatry at the Mount Sinai School of Medicine of the City University of New York, New York, New York.

Max Rosenbaum, Ph.D. Clinical Professor, Adelphi University; Co-Director of American Short-Term Therapy Center, New York, New York.

Itamar Salamon, M.D. Associate Clinical Professor of Psychiatry, Albert Einstein College of Medicine; Director, Soundview Throgs-Neck CMHC.

Arthur H. Schwartz, M.D. Associate Professor of Psychiatry, Mount Sinai School of Medicine, The Mount Sinai Medical Center, New York, New York.

Marshall Swartzburg, M.D. Associate Professor of Psychiatry at the College of Medicine and Dentistry of New Jersey-Rutgers Medical School, Piscataway, New Jersey.

Alan D. Whanger, M.D. Professor of Psychiatry and Chief, Duke Geriatric Psychiatry Service, Duke University Medical Center.

G. Terence Wilson, Ph.D. Professor of Psychology, Graduate School of Applied and Professional Psychology, Rutgers University, Piscataway, New Jersey.

Benjamin B. Wolman, Ph.D. Professor Emeritus, Doctoral Program in Clinical Psychology, Long Island University and Editor-in-Chief of the *International Encyclopedia of Psychiatry, Psychology, Psychoanalysis, and Neurology.*

Foreword

Throughout the remainder of this decade, more than three million individuals in this country will seek the assistance of a mental health professional each year, if current patient episode rate remains the same. The brunt of this national caseload will be borne by the four mental health core disciplines: psychiatry, psychology, psychiatric social work, and psychiatric nursing. Additional vital services will be provided by medical, educational, correctional, pastoral and other human service professionals and paraprofessionals. The multidisciplinary team approach will become increasingly imperative within a diverse population of nearly a quarter billion persons.

Only a century ago, the study of mental health and illness was the stepchild of general medicine and neurology. Prior to that time, "treatment" was found, more often than not, in dungeons, torture, and even exile or death. The era of scientific psychiatry, as we know it today, is a relatively recent phenomenon, founded on an exponentially increasing knowledge of the nature, causes, treatment, and prevention of mental disorder and of the course of normal development.

This volume reflects the major schools of thought and approaches to treating mental illness which comprise the mental health armamentarium today. The distinguished contributors, all authorities in their fields, represent both the traditions and trends in treatment. Such a dynamic approach is inherent to a field where even the definition of our subject is ever open to discussion.

The Handbook represents, also, the interrelationship of research, training, and service which is so essential to continued progress in our field. In any science, but perhaps particularly in ours, a compilation such as this provides fresh insights to evaluative needs and, in turn, to research directed toward the development of refined techniques.

Twenty-five years ago, Freudian psychoanalysis was the most highly developed form of psychosocial treatment. The major somatic treatments were electro-convulsive therapy, insulin "shock," and prefrontal lobotomy. Treatments for central nervous system syphilis and psychosis associated with pellagra were also available. Behavior modification, on the other hand, had not yet emerged from the laboratory. Few psychoactive drugs were known, and these typically were used to manage rather than treat mental patients.

Today, as we see in the first section of this volume, the scene has changed vastly. The full range of mental and emotional disorders is treated by a panoply of techniques ranging from chemotherapy and classical and modified psycho-therapy to behavior therapy and physical manipulation.

Part Two of the Handbook portrays even more strikingly the advancement of our knowledge base over the past quarter century. Specialized treatments for the major and more severe disorders have been made possible through a vastly increased understanding of the biological, biochemical, psychological, and social bases of behavior. Furthermore, chapters on the treatment of antisocial behavior and narcotic and alcohol addictions bring to mind the changing social attitudes with respect to human problems which are more frequently acknowledged to fall within the purview of the mental health practitioner.

Because the contributing authors of this volume need no introduction and because their papers speak well for themselves, I would like to use this space to summarize briefly certain of the events which have led us to these treatment methods and to question where they will lead from here. This overview is based on a major review and analysis by the National Institute of Mental Health of the Institute's contributions to the nation's mental health research effort since passage of the National Mental Health Act in 1946. The full review — *The Report of the Research Task Force: Research in the Service of Mental Health* — is available through the NIMH.

During the first half of the twentieth century, psychotherapeutic treatment, particularly psychoanalysis, was felt to be the only effective form of treatment, and the somatic techniques were held in low esteem. In the late 1940s psycho-analytic emphases were beginning to shift from id to ego psychology and to the study of interpersonal relationships. Rogerian and neoanalytic therapies gained impetus and were supplemented by a number of new adjunctive approaches which included art, music, drama, and play therapy. Also at that time, in part because of the scarcity of trained therapists, a shift in emphasis from individual to group settings was just being explored, a shift that was to de-velop into the most significant modification of psychotherapy during this period.

A major turning point, from any number of perspectives, occurred in the early 1950s with the introduction of psychotropic drugs in the treatment of mental illness. Somatic therapies — based on the recognition that behavior, thought, and feeling are linked to biochemical and neural mechanisms — are, of course, firmly rooted in scientific psychiatry. These include a variety of drug and convulsive therapies. With the development of the psychoactive agents, the treatment of the severe mental disorders has changed dramatically. Whereas schizophrenic patients formerly were likely to spend years in a mental hospital, many are now treated in general hospitals or as outpatients. Patients are discharged into the community to their families, halfway houses, or foster families. Treatment of the affective disorders has been influenced similarly by the new medications. Today, with the usefulness of drugs proven in the control of acute disorders, the researcher's attention is turned toward investigations of the prophylactic action of psychotropic drugs as well as the reduction of drug side effects.

Because the drug-treated patient is more accessible to other forms of treatment, we are also witnessing a resurgence of psychosocial treatment for even the most seriously ill patients. These events have enabled mental hospitals to continue to move from a custodial philosophy to the modern practice of the traditional "moral treatment."

In fact, the psychotherapies — with their focus on treating the "whole person" through verbal and symbolic techniques — have been an area of tremendous growth in recent years. As group therapy qua therapy demonstrated its effectiveness, the way was open for the development and refinement of group approaches applied to such units as the family, the hospital ward, and the community. The number of individual psychotherapies, the variety of techniques, and the number of therapists — both authorized and self-appointed have also grown steadily, matched by the number of consumers — professionally and self-diagnosed. A recent survey of psychosocial modalities revealed more than 130 therapies reported in the literature.

As psychotropic drugs and these concomitant developments were emerging as major forces in the treatment of mental illness, principles of operant and classical conditioning were providing a foundation for the experimental and clinical development of behavior therapy. Essentially a form of psychosocial treatment, behavior therapy has as its goal alteration of principal presenting problems rather than a direct therapeutic focus on personality, character structure, or underlying conflicts. In the view of the behavior therapists, maladaptive responses obey the same laws of learning and conditioning as do "normal" responses and are amenable to change through the application of what is known about learning and behavior modification. Introduced in hospital wards in the 1950s, behavior therapy offered an alternative to orthodox psychotherapeutic techniques. Within ten years, behavior modification techniques were extended from the back wards of institutions to home settings, classrooms, rehabilitation wards, prisons, nursing homes, and other settings. Behavior therapy has become a frequently used treatment, particularly for managing institutional populations and children's behavior problems.

Even this brief summary of highlights serves to distinguish the major categories of treatment — psychosocial, somatic, and behavioral — available to the mental health practitioner. Such a categorization, however, may tend to oversimplify the types of treatments a given client might receive. An individual's behavior is the result of complex interactions involving the biological and physiological bases of behavior, interpersonal relations, and social environment. In selecting a treatment, the therapist must have some conception of what produces, interacts with, aggravates, or sustains the problem to be treated. Does he view the manifest symptomatology as a product of disordered brain function, intrapsychic or interpersonal conflicts, learning deficits, environmental factors, or, as is likely the case, an interaction among all these factors? Overriding considerations must be given to making the treatment fit the unique needs of the individual client. Perhaps in no other branch of medicine are the subjective needs of the patient as paramount as in the treatment of mental and emotional disorders. Thus any of these three major categories of therapy, each with its respective subsets, might be used in succession, in combination, etc.

At the same time that therapeutic approaches are multiplying, "problems of living" are being brought to mental health practitioners in ever-increasing numbers. Consequently, one of the greatest continuing needs of the treatment field is improved therapy evaluation methods. Evaluation is difficult, particularly in the psychosocial area with the many interpersonal variables which must be taken into account. Yet the identification of which therapies are most effective with which groups of patients under what conditions constitutes the matrix from which future therapies will be formulated.

As an immediate result of improved treatment techniques and faster hospital population turnover, we are currently experiencing a need for more effective rehabilitative and follow-up, or maintenance, therapies. Without adequate post-discharge programs — as much an issue of service delivery as treatment efficacy — little is gained in the long run by returning patients to the community.

On a long-range scale, we are witnessing a shift of emphasis, among practitioners and policymakers, from psychological illness to psychological health. In part, this reflects an optimistic attitude toward the possibility of enhancing functioning rather than merely ameliorating distress. This shift is due to both the economics of health care and the realities of effective preventive mental health measures. Continuing research suggests that early identification of emotional problems particularly among children, may permit appropriate intervention, arrest and reversal of processes that could produce serious problems more resistant to change later in life.

The papers presented in this volume provide a base for further modification and revision as we continue to build on our present knowledge and improve our ability to treat mental and emotional disorders.

BERTRAM S. BROWN, M.D.
Director
National Institute of Mental Health

Preface

Almost seven years have passed since the first edition of the *Therapist's Handbook* went to press. The enthusiastic reception of the Handbook by psychiatrists and psychologists has inspired the publisher, the editor, and the authors to closely follow the ever changing approaches to the treatment methods of mental disorders. The present, second and revised edition of the Handbook faithfully reflects these changes.

Fourteen chapters out of the twenty-three chapters of the present edition are new, especially written for the Handbook. Five out of the fourteen new chapters cover areas not dealt with in the first edition, namely: (1) The patient-doctor relationship, (2) Brief psychotherapies, (3) Hypnotherapy, (4) Interactional psychotherapy, and (5) Research in psychotherapy.

It gives me great pleasure to express my profound gratitude to Eugene Falken, Vice President and Publisher of Van Nostrand Reinhold, for his cordial and most encouraging attitude. I am deeply indebted to Mrs. Alberta Gordon, Managing Editor of Van Nostrand Reinhold, for her most efficient work on this Handbook. I am also indebted to Dr. Stephen DeBerry, my former disciple and presently most successful colleague, for his unswerving help in putting together the second edition of the Handbook.

BENJAMIN B. WOLMAN

Contents

PART TWO: SPECIALIZED TECHNIQUES

The Therapist's Handbook

Treatment Methods of Mental Disorders

SECOND EDITION

Part One
General Techniques

1 The Patient-Doctor Relationship

Benjamin B. Wolman

Several years ago I taught resident psychiatrists in a postdoctoral program in a university hospital. The young physicians treated the in- and outpatients, and we, the senior staff members, supervised them. This was an intensive training program, and the residents received one hour of supervision for two hours of their work with patients, in addition to lectures, seminars, case presentations and so on.

At a certain period I decided to watch the young doctors at work. It was not that I distrusted the residents or disbelieved what they communicated in supervision sessions; I simply decided to learn more about the doctor–patient interaction process. I chose a close ward. I took a leave of absence from my other responsibilities, and for a few weeks I spent all days and a few nights with the patients.

I took my meals with the patients and sat with them in the daytime room, listening to their conversations, playing cards with them (I always lost), watching TV and so on. I did not interfere with the hospital routine, for this was supposed to be a nonparticipant observation. For a day or two the patients wondered whether I was one of them, but the nurses told them that I was a research professor who did not treat patients but helped the doctors to become better doctors.

Pretty soon my passivity and friendly attitude broke the ice. The patients related to me in a friendly manner and some of them began to confide to me, and described what was going on in therapeutic sessions with the young psychiatrists. I had listened to the doctors' stories, and now the patients' stories portrayed the other side of therapy, from the recipients' vantage point.

Listening to the patients in this nontherapy setting and the direct, on-the-spot, nonparticipant observation taught me a lot about the therapist–patient interaction. Several times a day I witnessed patient–doctor verbal and nonverbal interaction.

At one point I noticed the difference between the way two resident psychiatrists related to the same elderly lady-patient. Both doctors had excellent academic records, they had graduated from the best medical schools, and both were gifted young men. But the first psychiatrist talked down to the elderly patient and gave her an order to take the medication, whereas the second took a chair next to her, talked for a while about her son, volunteered to invite him to visit her and explained the need for the medication.

I believe that the second doctor will become a better therapist, but can one scientifically prove or disprove my hypothesis?

PRAXIOLOGY

All scientific propositions can be divided in five classes, as those that describe 1) observable data, 2) introspectionistically observable data, 3) inferrable date, 4) empirical generalizations, and, finally, the 5) nondescriptive hypothetical propositions used for theory formation. All these propositions are used by empirical sciences including the science of human behavior.

However, psychiatrists and clinical psychologists must go beyond empirical science. Every therapist engages in a certain *action* aimed at cure or remedy of mental health. Such an action, called treatment, therapy and so on, does not form a part of any empirical science, and the study of such actions does not belong to the empirical science. It belongs to *praxiologies.*

Praxiology is a science of action. Praxiological sciences set *goals* and propose *means* toward achievement of those goals. The propositions describing goals belong to praxiological *teleology;* those dealing with means belong to praxiological *technology.*

Psychotherapeutic systems are not the only existing praxiology. There are several other sciences of action, such as education, medicine, ethics, agriculture, political science and so on. The aim of praxiological sciences is to *guide, direct* and/or *improve* human actions. Praxiologies are applicable to practically every aspect of goal-directed human behavior.

Empirical sciences study things as they are. Their propositions are either true or false, are open to verification. Praxiological propositions do not deal with things as they are. They deal with "what should-be-done" (teleology) and "how-it-should-be-done" (technology).

The study of human behavior, normal and abnormal alike, can be divided into *descriptive* (empirical) science as long as the investigators describe and interpret objects and facts, and *praxiologic* (normative) science when they set goals and means for human actions.

How do praxiologies proceed in setting goals?

It is not easy for scientific inquiry to set goals for what-should-be-done. The word "should" defies scientific classification. It sounds like a whimsical order given by a self-righteous parent or teacher, and it is not related to objective standards set by empirical sciences. Small wonder that many authors believe that education, surgery and psychotherapy are not sciences at all but some sort of poorly defined "art."

Were this true, one would have to arrive at the sad conclusion that all the research conducted by surgeons, educators, psychotherapists and other experts is senseless and futile, and all the above-mentioned fields should be left to crooks and quacks who perform miraculous pieces of art.

Obviously, this is not the case, and although science cannot set goals, it can examine the reasons *why* people choose certain goals. *Science can study the decision-making process and analyze the causes that make people choose certain goals.* Instead of dealing with *what* "should-be-done," the praxiological sciences study the reasons for the "should-be." The knowledge of reasons for a "goal-setting" enables one to know what goals should be set.

As a rule, people make their choices in accordance with their *needs.* Individual needs may be contradictory and subjective. Social groups *objectify* and *generalize* those needs, set up norms and define values. The norms, values and aims originate from *the needs of the respective society. Socially approved* needs are the reasons for goals set up by society. They may be right or wrong, or they may *seem* to be right or wrong to some, but nobody can have the right to claim infallibility. There may be some gradation of truth as well as of ethics. Newton's theory is narrower than Einstein's; national ethics is narrower than international. Probably the all-embracing truth as the all-embracing ethics is still unknown, and nobody can be sure that it is knowable at all. Humanity seems to be progressing on a hyperbolic line, approaching the point asymptotically but never reaching it.

For a definite society, the question of goals can be reasonably answered. Consider educational systems. Every society expects that the new generation will join the existing institutions and support them; thus every society sets its educational goals in accordance with its needs — and the basic need is continuity of its way of life, and of its norms, rules and institutions. The very *survival* of a society depends on the behavior of generations to come. Obviously the question of "what should be" is being converted into a *causal* question: What are the causes that make a given society choose a particular educational pattern? Why did the ancient Spartans stress military education? Why is democracy the aim of American education?

In education one can distinguish between the universal, built-in, immanent *biological goal* of helping the child to grow and mature, and the changing transcendent *sociocultural* goal of adjustment to a certain society in which the growing child will have to live. Contemporary educators in the United States and the Soviet Union share the same *immanent* goal of helping the child to reach maturity, but the *transcendent* concepts of sociocultural adjustments are certainly different in these countries.

Psychotherapeutic methods, whether Freudian, behavioristic or any other, have a lot in common in that their goal is mental health. The *immanent* goal of therapy is to restore mental health, but the transcendent goals must take into consideration the changing sociocultural factors, and so specific transcendent therapeutic goals must be set.

THE CONCEPT OF MENTAL HEALTH

A group of psychiatrists and sociologists headed by Dr. Srole undertook a survey of mental health in Manhattan (Srole *et al.,* 1962). They came to the astonishing conclusion that 81.5% of the population is somewhat emotionally disturbed. How then could the 18.5% undisturbed people take care of the 81.5% disturbed ones?

Overinclusions have their spectacular precedent in the Middle Ages, when tens of thousands of women were believed to be practicing witchcraft, and witch-hunting was the favorite pastime of monks and theologians. The famous Benedictine abbot Trithemius (believed to be a great scholar and a very gentle person) regretted that there were not enough inquisitors to punish the witches. He wrote the following:

> There is no part in our body that the witches would not injure. Unfortunately, the number of such witches is very great in every province; more than that, there is no locality too small for a witch to find. Yet inquisitors and judges who could avenge these open offenses against God and nature are few and far between. Man and beast die as a result of the evil of these women and no one thinks of the fact that these things are perpetrated by witches.

In 1487, two great theologians, Sprenger and Kraemer, published the book *Malleus Maleficarum* (The Witches' Hammer), in which they recommended, "The witch should be stripped of her clothes, her wounds and marks of torture exposed, her head and genitals shaven so that no devil could conceal himself in her hair, and led into court backwards so that her evil eyes might not rest on the judge and bewitch him" (quoted after Zilboorg and Henry, 1941).

In 1587, the judge Boguet estimated that under King Charles IX, France had 300,000 witches and sorcerers. The witch-hunts continued in Europe well into the eighteenth century, and the last witch was executed in Glarus, Switzerland in June 1782. Even the more liberal people, such as the British physician Willis, suggested that "Nothing is more necessary and more effective for the recovery of these people than forcing them to respect and fear intimidation. By this method, the mind held back by restraint is induced to give up its arrogance and wild ideas . . . . This is why maniacs recover much sooner if they are treated with torture and torments in a hovel instead of with medicaments."

Judged against this background, Dr. Pinel's work was indeed revolutionary. On September 11, 1793, Dr. Pinel was appointed director of the mental asylum of Bicêtre. He declared that the mentally sick, far from being guilty people deserving of punishment, are *sick people* whose miserable state deserves all the consideration that is due to suffering humanity.

Diseases are caused by external forces, and one cannot be blamed for being sick. By calling Bicêtre inmates "sick," Pinel gave them a new status — the status of innocent, helpless victims of unknown diseases. There is no doubt that the change from "madman" to mentally "sick" caused a revolution in the treatment of mental disorders. One may torture people without knowing anything about them, but one cannot cure diseases without understanding them. According to Pinel, mental disorders were diseases of the central nervous system caused by heredity and unfortunate experiences.

THE FIRST PSYCHIATRIC REVOLUTION

Viewing mentally disturbed people as such individuals made them into mental "patients" and, as such, exposed them to medical treatment. However, in the vast majority of cases, none of these medical methods worked, and the crossroads of the nineteenth and twentieth century witnessed a growing feeling of skepticism concerning the possibility of curing mental diseases.

Freud's discovery of unconscious motivation opened new vistas in dealing with emotionally disturbed people. Freud maintained that the majority of mental disorders are not of organic origin and thus not related to the nervous system. Although Freud's terminology is rooted in medical phraseology, he strongly objected to the idea that psychoanalysis should ever become a chambermaid to psychiatry.

Small wonder that Freud's ideas met with stern opposition by his contemporaries. Hysteria was believed to be a disease of the uterus (*hysterus* in Greek) which wandered around the human body in search of moisture. Hysterectomies were often performed on women in order to cure hysteria. When Freud proposed that hysteria is caused by emotional conflicts in childhood and occurs in men also, he was widely criticized and ridiculed.

Whether one subscribes to Freud's ideas concerning disturbed behavior or not, one must admit that the shift of emphasis from the medical model to emotional factors has certainly brought a better understanding of what makes people act in a disturbed manner, thus permitting a more rational approach to the treatment of their irrationality. However, many scientists and practitioners, leaning on Freud's ideas, went beyond Freud and discovered additional factors in the so-called mental disorders. The sexual aspects of emotional life are certainly a relevant factor in human behavior but by no means the only one, and today not the most important one. While some of Freud's faithful disciples and dissidents have modified his teachings to include other aspects of human life, some experts have gone even further and rejected the notion of mental disease as such, and recently some researchers have introduced new ideas concerning disturbed behavior.

MENTAL DISEASES OR HUMAN TRAGEDIES

It seems doubtful that one can draw a sharp dividing line between the so-called normal and abnormal people. Hardly anyone can be consistently well-balanced, rational, aware of what to do — in short, always in perfect mental health. Everyone has periods of elation and depression, sociability and alienation, bouncing energy and passivity, thus experiencing periods or moments of irrational behavior.

There are certain cases of clear-cut mental disease in the organic sense of the word. For instance, paresis caused by syphilis, Kirchoff disease caused by alcoholism, Down syndrome (mongolism) caused by an additional chromosome and so on, are diseases of the nervous or glandular systems. But the vast majority of the so-called mental diseases are *human tragedies* caused by a variety of factors, some related to a particular sociocultural climate.

The difference between so-called normal and abnormal behavior is a matter of degree. Every human being is occasionally irrational; some people are more often so than others. Some people are so irrational that they need help in adjusting to life.

Whereas Freud's patients talked mainly about sexual problems, today's patients' main complaints are insecurity and depression. After World War II and the Holocaust, in times of the proliferation of nuclear weapons, no one can feel secure. Automation, inflation and economic crises have made everyone's livelihood vulnerable, and the decline of family ties and traditional values contributes to the feeling of alienation and loneliness. Thus, in addition to the immanent mental health criteria of reasonable success, emotional balance, cognitive functions and social adjustment (discussed below), new transcendent criteria must be added.

IMMANENT CRITERIA OF MENTAL HEALTH

One of the most relevant criteria of mental health is the relationship between one's *achievements* and one's *potentialities*. All other factors such as physical health and objective opportunities being equal, the greater the discrepancy between promise and fulfillment, the more severe is the disorder.

There are, however, gifted individuals who function well in their business and professional lives as executives, scientists and creative artists, while unable to act in a balanced and rational manner in their personal lives and interindividual relations. Apparently, their poorly integrated personality structure permits adequate functioning in the conflict-free ego spheres, but it fails in conflict-laden areas.

The second criterion of mental health is *emotional balance*. The reactions of healthy individuals are typically in accordance with the nature and magnitude of stimuli. Normally we react with pleasure and joy to situations that enhance our well-being. Happiness is generally attained when one's wishes come true, whereas grief is the reaction to failure or loss.

Normal emotional reaction is *proportionate* to the stimulus. Let us consider the case of a man who has lost money. Assuming that he is emotionally well-balanced, his reaction will be appropriate to the fact of loss and *proportionate* to its magnitude and to the ensuing financial hardship. The more money lost, the greater the degree of upset; if the loss is only a small fraction of his possessions, this worry will be mild and of short duration. A well-balanced individual will do whatever is possible to regain the loss and to prevent the recurrence of losses in the future. A rational, balanced and mentally healthy individual reacts with disappointment to failure — his reaction is proportionate to the damage incurred, and his actions lead to reduction or alleviation of past troubles, and prevention of future ones. In short, normal emotional behavior is *appropriate, proportionate* and *adjustive.*

Disturbed individuals tend to persist in mourning and perpetuating their depressed or aggressive moods instead of compensating for past losses and preventing future misfortunes. Because their emotional balance cannot be easily restored, the depressed or agitated anxiety states are likely to occur again and again. The failure in coping with hardships often leads to increasing irritability, each new frustration adding to the difficulty in restoring emotional balance. It becomes apparent that mental disorder is a dynamic process with a distinct tendency toward deterioration.

The third criterion of mental health is related to the validity of *cognitive functions.* An erroneous perception, an oversight of danger, an inability to distinguish fantasy from reality seriously jeopardize one's chances for survival and adjustment.

In most mental disorders, the perception of the outer world is disturbed, but not as a result of some malfunction of the sensory organs as is the case in sight or hearing impairments. Nor is the reduced ability to perceive, compare and reason a function of mental deficiency as is true of the retarded. The mental apparatus is, in most cases of mental disorder, fully or partly preserved, but it seems that the mentally disturbed individual is unable to properly utilize his mental capacities because of a malfunction in the realm of feelings.

The more one is disturbed, the poorer is his contact with reality. We all make an occasional perceptual error, but, as a rule, we are accurate and capable of correcting our errors. In mentally disturbed individuals, this ability is impaired or nonexistent.

The situation can become quite serious when the picture of the outer world is distorted. An individual who consistently misconstrues or misinterprets what he perceives is said to be *delusional.* For example, when a mentally disturbed individual flees a policeman who simply wants to check his driver's license, in fear that the policeman will arrest him for a noncommitted crime, or when he ascribes hostile feelings to his friends who are loyal and trustworthy, his reality testing is practically nonexistent. Whereas delusions are distorted perceptions, hallucinations are creations out of nothingness. Hallucination is perception without external stimulation, such as seeing ghosts and hearing voices. A hallucinating patient is unable to distinguish his inner fears, wishes and dreams from the outer world. His ability in reality testing is lost.

The fourth criterion is social *adjustment*. People live in societies. They interact with one another in cooperation and competition, love and hate, peace and war. The term "social life" denotes both the friendly or cooperative and the hostile or competitive aspects of human interaction.

There are no ideal societies. Every social group has its share of the constructive life-preserving and cooperative factors, as well as the disruptive, destructive and antisocial forces. However, when the forces of hate prevail, life and society perish. No society can afford a free display of hostile and disruptive forces. If these forces are innate, they must be checked; if they are learned patterns of behavior, they must be unlearned at least to a point where they do not threaten the survival of men. There is a great diversity in the prohibitive actions of social groups; some are more, some less restrictive; some limit their "thou shalt not kill" restraint to the members of their own group only. Judeo-Christian civilization believes in the sanctity of human life, but even the most primitive societies did not tolerate unlimited intragroup hatred and belligerence.

The fourth criterion of mental health is, as stated above, the ability to cooperate with other individuals. Mentally healthy individuals are capable of living on friendly terms with other members of their group. They are capable of cooperation and are willing to enter into social relations based on mutual respect, agreement and responsibility. Normal adults accept and make commitments that they can honor. They may disagree with associates and understand why others may disagree with them. They may occasionally feel hostile, but their actions are generally kept under rational control. They may, however, fight in self-defense and in a manner approved by their cultural group.

TRANSCENDENT CRITERIA: SEARCH FOR IDENTITY AND PURPOSE

Today, some people have sexual problems, but many more people are afflicted with the feeling of futility, lack of purpose and inability to determine who they are and what they want. Many people seek therapeutic help hoping to find out the meaning and purpose of life.

I believe that the training of clinical psychologists and psychiatrists should take into consideration the changing nature of the patient population; sociological, socio-psychological and philosophical issues should be included in the training of clinicians; and the problems of personality integration and purposeful behavior must be given adequate consideration. Quite often patients ask, "Who am I?" and "Where am I going?" and the therapists cannot ignore the perplexing problems. For if realistic perception of the world is the most important criterion of mental health, this also applies to the way *one sees oneself*. Individuals who do not perceive themselves correctly may run into tremendous difficulties in life.

If they overestimate their abilities, they may do things that will bring frustration and defeat. If they underestimate their own abilities, they may be afraid to do useful things that present no threat.

Awareness of oneself does not imply an unconditional acceptance of one's faults and shortcomings. *Awareness of oneself is the awareness of the fact that here are the cards that one got from heredity and experience, and one must play these cards the best one can.*

One may realize that if he or she tends to be belligerent, that belligerence should be used for an active life, as, for instance, in conquering disease and not necessarily for fighting people. The individual must not accept all aspects of his or her own personality, nor need one experiment with all possibilities. The individual must make selective choices among the various possibilities and set his or her own course in life.

POWER AND SELF-ESTEEM

The fundamental, innate, *basic* necessities are oxygen, water, food, rest, shelter, sex and so on. The *acquired* needs are to be accepted, protected, loved, respected and so on. Power is the ability to satisfy needs, but no human being is omnipotent. Weakness makes one totally dependent on others at infancy and less independent in adulthood. The more power one has, the less one depends on others.

Self-esteem depends on awareness of one's power. An individual who perceives him- or herself to be physically healthy, attractive, intelligent, influential or outstanding in any form or shape has the feeling of power, defined as the ability to satisfy needs. An individual who is materialistic and has a good income or substantial possessions has the feeling of "money-power."

People whose self-confidence was built up in childhood have increased courage and independence, as a result. One's own abilities, efforts and achievements gradually count more than whatever other people's opinions may be. Well-adjusted people are aware of the fact that not everyone is going to like them. *Dependence upon one's own judgment is a crucial ingredient in personality integration and mental health, provided it is based on a realistic estimate of one's own potentialities and environmental opportunities.*

Courage to be oneself is a highly important element of self-esteem. Courage implies faith in oneself. It represents the belief that one has the power to stand up and be counted. True courage is related to a realistic estimate of one's own power and the power of the threatening forces. Mature and well-adjusted men and women take necessary precautions and make responsible decisions.

MENTAL DISORDERS: FALLEN ANGELS

Some mental disorders are caused by organic, genetic and/or natal or postnatal factors, but apparently most mental disorders are a product of harmful interpersonal relationships. While parents could not always be blamed for their children's difficulties, nor could all parents be so indicted, I distinguished three patterns of noxious parental interference with the mental health of their children. These patterns are the overdemanding, rejecting and inconsistent parental attitudes.

Some parents act as if they were the children who need to be loved, and demand the kind of love and affection from the child that would more properly be expected to come from their own parents. In such families, the parents' attitude toward the child is overdemanding, and the child is forced too early into an overanxious and oversubservient attitude toward his parents. The child, in effect, is robbed of his childhood and forced prematurely to worry about his parents. His parents, disappointed in one another, expect him to compensate for all the love and affection they failed to obtain from each other. The child is not allowed to express his dissatisfaction. Exposed to immature and overdemanding parents, he is expected to become a *model child* who renounces his own desires in order to please his parents. These model children feel sorry for their parents and feel responsible for their parents' true and imaginary misfortunes. In many instances, this reversal of social roles confuses the child, destroys his self-esteem and deprives him of the ability to become an independent adult. The parents expect the child to act like an angel, but there is a limit to how far one can go in suppressing one's own impulses. When the self-controls break down, the angels go beserk and a full-blown schizophrenia develops. Thus, I called schizophrenics "fallen angels."

INNOCENT CRIMINALS

Children need love and security and, if deprived of both, they may develop the mentality of a hunted animal, a combination of extreme selfishness, hostility and suspicion. They feel that they are alone in a cold and hostile world; it is either devour or be devoured, destroy or be destroyed. Some of these selfish and hostile people come from underprivileged classes and extreme cases of poverty and despair conducive to a "sink or swim" mentality. However, I came across children of upper class families who developed a similar mentality of selfishness, lack of consideration and hostile attitude toward the world. These children have received plenty of money but no affection or guidance.

Typically these people are the extreme opposite of the "fallen angels." While schizophrenics are guilt-ridden individuals who fear their own hostility, children of rejection believe that they are innocent even when they exploit and hate other people. In my book *Call No Man Normal* (1973), I called these people "innocent criminals" because they themselves are unaware of their extreme lack of consideration for other people.

DR. JEKYLL AND MR. HYDE

Individuals with extreme shifts of mood belong to the third category of disturbed people. Traditional psychiatry calls them manic-depressives. I believe that the shifting moods of elation and depression are merely the smoke, while love and hatred are the fire. Some parents reject their child and even hate him, but when the child is seriously ill, the same parents, torn by guilt feelings, shower the child with affection. The prevailing atmosphere of rejection with occasional outbursts of affection makes the child hate and love the rejecting parent and wish to suffer in order to win affection. The moods shift from hatred toward those who don't love him and hatred toward himself (depression) for not being loved, to brief periods of elation when he feels loved by others and therefore loves himself. He becomes a love-addict, willing to suffer in order to gain love. In his shifting moods of euphoric love and kindness, he resembles the kind Dr. Jekyll; in the prevailing mood of rejection and depression, he is as full of hatred as Mr. Hyde.

The severity of social maladjustment usually corresponds to the severity of mental disorder, although it is not a simple one-to-one relationship. Uncontrollable hostility is, however, a definite sign of serious disturbance. Social adjustment must not be confused with conformity. The former is the ability for a peaceful and friendly interaction with other individuals, while the latter implies unconditional acceptance of certain social norms and mores. Were conformity identical with social adjustment, all ethnic, religious and political minorities could be considered maladjusted. Every inventor, original scientist, creative writer, political reformer and nonconformist, and all pioneers of social, religious or scientific progress could be branded as maladjusted.

What then is mental health? Probably a precarious and unstable state of mind when human emotions are somehow balanced and one can relate to himself and others in a wholesome way. When the disbalanced emotions prevail and a person is unable to restore the balance himself, he needs help. Many people occasionally need some help; some people need a prolonged period of help.

POWER AND ACCEPTANCE

Any process of treatment, whether it is surgical, dental or psychological, involves two parties, namely the helping professional and the help-seeking public. The patients come to the therapists because they need help. A patient suffers from and is aware of shortcomings or malfunctions of his bodily structure, sensory apparatus or mental functioning. He looks for somebody qualified and licensed to provide the appropriate treatment for diseases, ills, handicaps and disorders. This patient–therapist relationship, like any other social relationship, can be presented in two dimensions. The first dimension is the dimension of power — power being defined as the ability to satisfy needs. People who can satisfy the needs of themselves and others are strong; those who cannot are weak. The peak of power is omnipotence, and human beings ascribe omnipotent features to their gods. The bottom of power is the zero point of death; corpses have no power.

The concept of power originates in the physical strength of muscles and jaws, for the primitive man and subhuman species satisfy their fundamental needs such as food, water, shelter, by using their physical strength. With the development of higher nervous functions, the human species has developed and learned to use other elements in order to survive, for survival is the arch-need of all needs.

While the lower levels of power are often activated in struggle for survival, most human beings have to learn to use other strengths in addition to and in preference to their muscles and jaws. Most human beings procure their food, water and shelter not through physical fighting, but through work. The use of working tools, technology and the skills for producing, providing, exchanging, shipping and storing goods have become far more important aspects of power than the initial, archaic physical strength.

Power, defined as the ability to satisfy needs, applies also to the practitioners in the fields of physical and mental health. People who have certain innate abilities and have developed these abilities by training and experience, have acquired the power to heal other people's wounds, ills and shortcomings. They are the competent and skilled helpers, called surgeons, dentists, psychiatrists or psychologists, according to their particular training and skill.

Power can be used in more than one direction. Power can be used to help satisfy needs or to prevent their satisfaction. Thus, the interaction between individuals can be presented on quasi-Cartesian coordinates, with the vertical line presenting power, starting with omnipotence at the top and at the bottom, the zero point of power, death. The horizontal line toward the right represents the friendly attitude and toward the left, the hostile attitude. People can be friendly or hostile, friendly meaning willing to satisfy needs, hostile meaning preventing their satisfaction. Let us call these two dimensions of strong-weak and friendly-hostile power and acceptance, respectively.

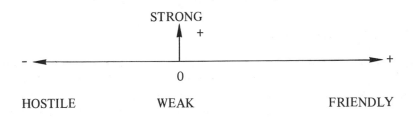

Obviously, when one has a toothache, he looks for somebody who has the power to heal his tooth, that is, a competent, skilled and experienced dentist; and at the same time, the patient looks for someone who is friendly, or willing to heal him. The dimension of power implies competence; the dimension of acceptance is indicated by integrity, devotion to the profession and conscientious work with patients.

People interact with one another not on the basis of how things are, but how they perceive them. Imagine someone who has migrated from another country to the United States. Suppose that in his home country, he was well known as a highly experienced dentist, and people flocked to his office, seeking his help. But in the new country, people don't know how good he is, and therefore they may not seek his help. The same reasoning applies to the dimension of acceptance. People choose a professional man or woman not on the basis of what he or she is, but by reputation, that is, public opinion. When the consensus is that a particular psychiatrist or surgeon or dentist or psychologist is exceptionally gifted and highly competent, then he is believed to be powerful. If he has the reputation of being devoted and conscientious, then he is believed to be friendly, and people will seek his help.

PATIENT-THERAPIST RELATIONSHIP

Treatment of mental disorders often resembles the child-parent relationship. Adult men and women go to someone who is not always wiser, not necessarily better established, more influential, or more powerful than themselves. People seek therapy because they are unhappy, and they don't know how to manage their lives. Most of them are unable to adequately cope with their jobs, their families and the whole complexity of life. Some think about quitting life altogether. Many are in despair; all are in pain. People usually have valid reasons when they decide to seek help, be it chemotherapy or psychotherapy. They go to someone who they believe can help.

Putting one's faith and fate in the therapist makes one much more dependent than one usually is in regard to one's physician, dentist or lawyer. In the patient-therapist dependency, one develops an infantile regression, called "transference" by Freud. When under stress one tends to develop regressive moods and to transfer emotions onto the person who takes care of him. Freud noticed it first, but transference, which is the transfer of emotions in a state of regression to infancy, takes place in all kinds of psychotherapy.

This kind of emotional regression creates a patient-doctor relationship unheard of in any other type of treatment. The dependence on the psychotherapist goes to the gut level. It deals with the deepest human emotions and elicits emotions that are not necessarily related to the here-and-now, factual relationship. I had men and women in treatment who were wiser, more competent, more influential and much richer than I. A dentist asked me how to deal with his patient; an internist consulted me about how to make a diagnosis; a lawyer sought my advice in complex business contracts. It was rather amazing, although not surprising, that these people asked me for advice in areas in which they were far more competent than I was, and expected me to give them advice as if they were little children and I their parent.

Most patients develop affection, admiration and even love for their doctor. This love has the infantile element of demanding reciprocation — children expect their parents to love them, to care for them, to take care of them. Quite often, this love has sexual undertones, and patients, both male and female, develop heterosexual or homosexual crushes on their therapist. Many a patient, despite the fact that he pays the fees to his doctor in private practice or the society pays the fees in a clinic or hospital, ascribes to himself a position of total dependence and craves the doctor's affectionate attitude. Sometimes transference takes a negative turn, and the patient uses his therapist as a target for his hostile feelings. Past grievances against parents and other significant adults are redirected against the therapist, who may be unfairly blamed for whatever miseries the patient has experienced in his life.

The patient versus therapist attitude can be presented on two levels. One level is the here-and-now relationship, and the patient is aware of the fact that he goes to a doctor whom he pays or who is paid by society, and who is supposed to help him to relieve his tensions and resolve his inner conflicts. But on the other level, a great many irrational feelings are directed against the therapist, who serves as a target for the patient's emotional onslaughts.

THE TASK OF THE THERAPIST

Serving as a target for frequent onslaughts of human emotions is a mental health hazard. Small wonder that psychiatrists have a high incidence of suicide, and some of Freud's early associates, who were inadequately psychoanalyzed, suffered mental breakdowns. It is therefore self-evident that whoever intends to deal with the emotional problems of other people must put his own house in order and undergo his own analysis. In order to save drowning lives, one must be a good swimmer, well-prepared to do the job of lifesaving.

There are three main ingredients that make a good therapist: 1) his own aptitude, 2) his training and 3) his experience. A therapist's aptitude includes his total personality because the total personality is the tool one uses in helping other people. Psychotherapists, like all other human beings, go through the wear and tear of life; they may fall in love and be disappointed; they may get physically ill or suffer car accidents; they may lose somebody very dear to their hearts; and they may react like all other human beings. However, one expects that even in their personal lives, they are at least as good as the patients they have cured, which means that they act as rational human beings. They should be able to retain rational and self-controlled reactions, irrespective of whatever upheavals they may experience. A therapist who carries his personal troubles to his office does injustice to his patients; thus one of the main criteria for a good therapist is a strong ego, which implies an objective, calm, realistic attitude. Severely disturbed people drown in their unconscious. A good psychotherapist is like a good diver; he should be able to join his patients in their unconscious journey, but he always comes back. He must be able to empathize, that is, be capable of receiving nonverbal messages from his patients.

A good therapist must get involved with his patients without getting involved with them. The psychotherapist must get involved with the patient's cause; he is determined to help his patients. His mind is set on helping people who are in trouble, and he is ready to do so. But on the other side, he must not become personally involved with patients or get caught in the murky waters of morbid countertransference feelings. To be dependable and yet not involved — this is the task of the therapist. Moreover, the therapist's attitude toward his patients is a giving attitude. He must enable them to go through corrective emotional experiences to remedy their past bad experiences and correct their personality deficiencies. However, in order to do that, he must be reasonably independent and serve the needs of the patient and not his own narcissistic needs. If one tries to take a shortcut in defining psychotherapy and asks what its aim is, I guess its aim is to make itself superfluous. A good psychotherapist works in such a way that his work becomes unnecessary. When he helps the patients to grow up, then they don't need him anymore — their dependence on him is terminated while they become more independent in their lives and able to make their own rational decisions.

THE PITFALLS OF PSYCHOTHERAPY

While the psychotherapeutic situation fosters regression in the patient who looks up to the therapist as if the therapist were his parental figure, the therapist may succumb to the illusion of infantile omnipotence. One of Freud's early associates, Ferenczi (1950) noticed that infants hallucinate omnipotence as their wishes are fulfilled by loving parents. Quite often, younger colleagues came to me for supervisory sessions with a glowing feeling of success because their patients expressed love and admiration for them. The beginning therapists often take the expression of transference love as a sign of therapeutic success.

Megalomania seems to be the main mental health hazard of psychotherapists. Many a psychiatrist or psychologist develops the illusion of omnipotence because the patients' glowing remarks and admiration can make him believe that he possesses superhuman powers. Such an illusion of omnipotence is certainly a sign of regression, for mature men and women know the limits of their power. In that atmosphere of omnipotence, the therapist may lose some of his professional standards and self-restraint.

Disinhibition is very much in vogue today, and some psychotherapists seem to have fallen prey to the climate of license and decline of self-discipline. Often in meetings of psychiatrists and psychologists, one hears self-praising stories indicative of an impaired sense of reality. Some psychotherapists seem to believe that their ideas are unquestionably the best ones. This self-righteous attitude represents a violation of the rights of the patients. While the patients come to us in need of help to grow, the imposition of the therapist's ideas on them may prevent growth, and, in a way, it unnecessarily perpetuates the infantile dependence of the patient on the therapist.

Sometimes this relaxation of self-discipline and regression into infantile behavior goes quite far. In August 1973, I chaired some sessions at the Congress of

Group Psychotherapy in Zurich. Some colleagues reported that they treated patients as "human beings"; they went with them to bars, slept with them and related to them in an atmosphere of complete freedom. It is my conviction that this kind of freedom is not permitted by professional ethics. People come to us not because they want to drink beer or go to bed, but because they need help. I asked my colleagues in these sessions why sexual relations with somebody with a Ph.D. or M.D. degree who practices psychotherapy is more therapeutic than with somebody who has a Ph.D. or an M.D. in ophthalmology. Moreover, I wondered why the treatment of alcoholism is best conducted in a bar.

I don't believe that psychotherapists, whatever their degrees are, are necessarily superior human beings. Sleeping with a patient comes quite close to statutory rape because patients in psychotherapeutic interaction necessarily regress to an infantile stage and their defenses are lowered, they can be easily carried away by their moods, and they may act as a minor would. Furthermore, since in a transference situation patients tend to see the therapist as a parental substitute, to accept their sexual advances seems tantamount to incestuous behavior.

Unless the psychotherapist exercises a great deal of self-discipline and rational self-control, he is unfit to perform his duties. Unfortunately, not all therapists are properly qualified for their jobs. Some of them act like insecure parents, unable to go through the process of weaning. Insecure therapists unnecessarily prolong treatment even when the treatment is going nowhere. Quite often I have had referrals of patients by therapists who did not know what to do next with a patient, or by the desperate patients themselves, who felt that after five, six or seven years they were still at their starting point.

THE RIGHTS OF PATIENTS

Suffering people have the right to seek help or to refuse help. There is no way to force anyone to go to a dentist even if he has several rotten teeth. No one forces a man with a broken foot to go into surgery. It is an integral part of civil rights to be free to determine whether one is interested in getting well. Moreover, the patient has the right to decide into whose hands he would put his fate. The patient chooses who is going to be his surgeon or dentist. Of course, the patient may seek advice from a local professional organization if he wishes to do so. He may consult with professionals in the same or related fields about the reputation of the therapist to whom he intends to go, but ultimately, it is the patient who determines whether he will seek help and whom he will choose as his therapist.

This basic human freedom is not always preserved in the field of mental health. In most countries there are laws that make possible forced hospitalization and, implicitly, permit forced treatment of confined mentally disturbed individuals. This involuntary treatment raises grave moral and legal issues. In my practice, I have had several cases where husbands, wives and relatives insisted on the hospitalization of a member of their family. Their intentions concerning the patient were not necessarily noble. Once I had in treatment a paranoid schizophrenic woman whose husband had a girlfriend. He wanted to put his hands on a quite substantial inheritance that belonged to his wife. He demanded that I take the necessary steps and hospitalize his wife. In addition to the legal problems (which I could have solved with the help of my colleague psychiatrists and administrators in the hospital where I was the supervisor of psychiatry at the time), the issue presented grave moral problems. This woman undoubtedly was a menace to the well-being of her husband. Whether she would go so far as to try to put an end to his life, I wasn't sure, but I could not exclude such a possibility. Moreover, her overt hostility and paranoid accusations impaired her husband's personal freedom and his rights to a minimum of human happiness. What should one do in such a case?

In some cases I had decided to hospitalize the patient. Once, a colleague psychiatrist called me and requested that I see a young woman who developed postpartum psychosis. She was hallucinating and, to the best of his knowledge, suicidal. Since I had been working with schizophrenics for years with some degree of success, he recommended this young woman to me for ambulatory treatment. The young woman was brought to my office by her mother, brother and husband. The woman was in bad shape; she was incoherent, hallucinated and had garbled speech. However, after talking with her for half an hour, I felt that I had a reasonably good chance of successful treatment. Her initial reaction toward me was friendly, and it seemed to me that we could develop good rapport, and I could eventually resolve her emotional conflicts. I called in the mother and told her that although not enthusiastic about it, I was willing to take care of her daughter. In the beginning I had to see the young woman every day, seven days a week; this was a sort of sacrifice on my part for I work five days a week and hate to work on weekends. Moreover, I told her mother that I would be responsible for her daughter for one hour out of every twenty-four hours, and the family must make sure that somebody else would keep an eye on her for the remaining twenty-three hours a day. I explained to the mother that her daughter had strong suicidal tendencies, and I must establish a watchdog over her with a sort of hot-line to my office and to my home. The mother replied with a barrage of accusations directed against the ungrateful daughter. She said that because of her daughter, her husband had left her and didn't want to come home. She blamed her daughter for breaking up the family, for causing disorder, grievances and hostility in the family. She resented the fact of the girl's birth, hated the newborn grandchild and wished to get rid of both of them.

Certainly, the mother was not the best guardian for this severely sick girl. I invited the brother into my office for a talk while the other members of the family waited in the waiting room. The brother was in worse shape than the patient. He told me hallucinatory stories about his sister. He was apparently a very disturbed young man with a tenuous contact with reality. Certainly, I could not leave this poor girl under the supervision of her brother, who needed treatment no less than she did. Finally, I invited the husband. The husband was a youngish-looking, charming man in his early thirties. He told me about his studies and his great successes in graduate school. When I asked him about his wife, he told me that she was a little nervous, somewhat quarrelsome and occasionally unpleasant, but otherwise she was all right. He was busy with his studies and did not intend to spend much time with her, especially when she would make a nuisance of herself.

It became obvious that there was no one who could be responsible for the poor girl. I called in all the members of the family to my office and told them that I could not treat her on an outpatient basis, and I advised them to take her to a hospital. If they wished it, I could call the director of a private hospital whom I knew and trusted. I suggested that they go straight from my office to the hospital because I wouldn't leave the sick girl with them even for one day. Her husband remarked that she didn't have pajamas and therefore they would not take her to the hospital.

What should be the criterion for involuntary confinement? I recommend confinement only in the case of acute danger of suicide or homocide. But whereas on the issue of genocide most people would agree with me, on the issue of suicide there is a great deal of controversy.

Thomas Szasz (1971) believes that every individual has the right to his own life and no psychiatrist has the right to "save" a person's life against that individual's wishes. The moral issue is quite complex because a person may act on impulse, or in a state of severe depression; or he may be unaware of what he is doing, or be unable to use judgment about his situation in life (Schneidman *et al.*, 1970). But even when a person is a menace to others, the issue is not perfectly clear. What does it mean to be a menace to others? One may recall the case of the young man at the University of Texas who told his psychiatrist, "I feel like killing." According to the newspapers, the psychiatrist told him, "Please come next week." Certainly such a conversation makes one doubt whether good judgment could be exercised in regard to all mental cases. There is a country where people are being forcibly hospitalized in mental hospitals whenever they are perceived by the rulers to be "enemies of the people." Many years ago, Henrik Ibsen wrote a play entitled *The Enemy of the People.* Ibsen described an honest physician who tried to defend the rights of the patients against the greedy fathers of his town. Today, in the Soviet Union, people who disagree with the system and express ideas critical of the leadership are often thrown into mental hospitals and declared insane.

Quite often, in a conversation or an argument, we call neurotic, moron or insane those who express opinions contrary to our own. As long as this is merely a figure of speech, there is no severe threat to the basic human freedoms. But when labeling people as mentally sick becomes a matter for the police, the issue may become quite grave. Certainly in the Soviet Union and, in certain instances, in other countries, some people are forced to undergo treatment that they may not wish to get.

However, even in a democratic society, the issue is far from simple. Should we allow mentally irresponsible people to be at large and jeopardize the lives of others? What should be done in a case when the freedom and the civil rights of one individual clash with the freedom and rights of other individuals?

The question of the rights of mental patients hinges upon the definition of mental health.

REFERENCES

Ferenczi, S. *Selected papers,* vol. 1. New York: Basic Books, 1950.

Jahoda, M. *Current concepts of mental health.* New York: Basic Books, 1958.

Shneidman, E.S., *el al. The psychology of suicide.* New York: Science House, 1970.

Srole, L., Angner, T.S., Michael, S.T., Opler, M.D. and Rennie, T.A. *Mental health in metropolis.* New York: McGraw-Hill, 1962.

Szasz, T. The etics of suicide. *The Antioch Review.* **31** (1971).

Wolman, B.B. *Call no man normal.* New York: International Universities Press, 1973.

Wolman, B.B. *Being, lasting, becoming.* (In press)

Zilboog, G. and Henry, G.W. *A history of medical psychology.* New York: Norton, 1941.

2 Psychopharmacology and ECT

Richard Abrams

The biological therapies in psychiatry consist of a variety of pharmacologic, convulsive and other somatic treatment methods. Insulin coma therapy, psychosurgery and convulsive therapy were introduced one after another during the 1930s and provided the first successful and reliable methods for treating patients with major psychoses who, until then, had received only custodial care.

The neuroleptic drugs introduced in the early 1950s provided the first effective chemical therapy for psychiatric patients and were responsible — along with more progressive mental health laws — for the subsequent continued annual decrease in mental hospital populations and for the establisment of an increasing number of acute treatment psychiatric units in general hospitals.

Antidepressant drugs, first used in the United States in the late 1950s, were effective in treating many depressed patients in and out of the hospital. These drugs are now well-established in clinical psychiatry, although the initial hope that they would replace convulsive therapy in the treatment of depressed patients remains unfulfilled.

Lithium therapy for manic-depressive illness was made available in this country in 1972 and is the only truly prophylactic treatment in psychiatry. Lithium is also the first psychiatric treatment to have been fully tested and demonstrated to be effective prior to its distribution for general clinical use.

In addition to the clinical advances of the biological therapies, the investigation of their mode of action has accelerated progress in neuropharmacology and neurophysiology and provided many hypotheses to be tested concerning the etiology of the major psychoses.

The present chapter includes a discussion of psychopharmacologic and convulsive therapies. The more specialized somatic methods, such as psychosurgery and insulin coma therapy, are not available to most practitioners and will not be considered here.

Psychopharmacology

GUIDES TO THERAPY

Psychiatry shares with other medical specialties the basic principles of clinical pharmacology. Successful drug therapy results from administration of active compounds, in sufficient doses, of suitable preparation, by an effective route of administration and for an adequate period of time.

Dose.   The correct dose of a psychoactive drug will yield the desired clinical effect without producing excessive side-effects. The dose should be increased rapidly to the desired level or until side-effects supervene. Manufacturers' recommended doses of psychoactive drugs are often inadequate, particularly for neuroleptics, and one must frequently exceed the "maximum" suggested in order to treat patients successfully.

Preparation and Route of Administration.   Parenteral administration guarantees drug intake at the most rapid onset of action and the highest blood levels. For orally administered medication, the highest blood levels for the greatest duration occur with liquid concentrates which have the added advantage of being difficult for the patient to sequester. Tablets are intermediate in duration of action and multi-pellet "timed-release" capsules least effective in providing adequate blood levels for sustained periods of time. For adequate absorption, oral preparations should be given one-half hour before or two hours after meals, and hospital medication schedules should be adjusted accordingly.

Duration of Treatment.   This will vary with the clinical response, diagnosis, severity and chronicity of the illness, and the prior pattern of response to drug therapy. It is unwise to change drugs within the same class in less than two weeks unless side-effects are pronounced or persistent. The necessity for changing drugs can usually be avoided by increasing the dose of the original drug or changing the preparation or route of administration.

In the past, the desirability of long-term administration of neuroleptic drugs was widely stressed, especially for the treatment of patients diagnosed as having chronic schizophrenia. However, such therapy entails the risk of permanent skin and eye changes and the persistent brain changes underlying tardive dyskinesia, and should be interrupted every six months to be reinstituted only if warranted by the reappearance of symptoms. Diagnoses also require periodic reevaluation, as many patients receiving chronic neuroleptic drug therapy for what was originally diagnosed as a schizophrenic illness will now be found to satisfy criteria for an affective disorder and to benefit from prophylactic lithium therapy, with many fewer long-term side-effects.

Side-Effects. Therapeutic doses of active drugs often produce side-effects that provide evidence that the dosage is adequate. If patients show neither therapeutic effects nor side-effects at doses presumed to be sufficient, they should be suspected of not taking their medication or of being resistant to standard dosages for idiosyncratic reasons. Such patients will often be found to be receiving oral drug preparations, and a change to the parenteral route will frequently yield sudden improvement.

Drug Combinations. In the absence of proven synergism or potentiation, drug combinations generally complicate treatment and multiply unwanted side-effects. There is no evidence that combinations of neuroleptic drugs (e.g., chlorpromazine plus trifluoperazine) are superior to single drugs given in equal doses for the same period of time. Combinations of neuroleptics with tricyclic antidepressants are designated "irrational" by the American Medical Association Council on Drugs, as no specific evidence for their efficacy exists. Moreover, they expose depressed patients to the risk of tardive dyskinesia without any justification. One combination that is often justified is that of lithium plus a neuroleptic drug, described below in the section on lithium therapy.

NEUROLEPTIC DRUGS

These compounds produce sedation without sleep, emotional quieting and affective indifference. They are all capable of inducing the extrapyramidal syndrome of parkinsonism, dystonia and akathisia, and produce dopamine receptor blockade in various animal species. The five main classes of neuroleptic drugs are shown in Table 2-1. The rauwolfia alkaloids are a sixth class, no longer used in psychiatry.

To date, all effective neuroleptic drugs available in the United States are capable of blocking dopamine in various cerebral systems. Dopamine blockade in the nigrostiatal system produces extrapyramidal side-effects and in the tuberoinfundibular system, hormonal side-effects (e.g., secondary to prolactin release); and it is hypothesized that such blockade in the mesolimbic/corticolimbic systems is related to antipsychotic effects.

Clinical Indications. Neuroleptic drugs reduce excitement, agitation and overactivity, remove hallucinations and delusions, and improve formal thought-disorder. Paranoid-hallucinatory syndromes and psychotic excitement states are most rapidly responsive to neuroleptic drug therapy. Such phenomena may occur in patients with diagnoses of mania, schizophrenia, paranoid states and a variety of organic brain syndromes such as those occurring secondary to cerebral arteriosclerosis, intoxications and altered metabolic states.

Excitement and Overactivity in Acute Mania. Excitement, agitation, restlessness and overactivity are a principal object of neuroleptic drug therapy. Required neuroleptic drug dosages are usually high in psychotic excitement states, and parenteral therapy is the rule (e.g., haloperidol, 20 mg intramuscular, b.i.d.). A majority of patients will respond to such a treatment regimen over a 24–72-hour

TABLE 2-1 NEUROLEPTICS.

	Usual 24-Hour Dosage Range in mg	
	Acute	Maintenance
TRICYCLICS		
Phenothiazines		
Chlorpromazine (Thorazine)	300–2000 oral	200–600 oral
	50–75 I.M.	
Trifluopromazine (Vesprin)	100–200 oral	50–150 oral
	60–150 I.M.	
Acetophenazine (Tindal)	40–80 oral	20–40 oral
Butaperazine (Repoise)	15–100 oral	5–15 oral
Carphenazine (Proketazine)	25–400 oral	25–75 oral
Fluphenazine (Prolixin, Permitil)	20–60 oral	5–20 oral
	5–30 I.M. (Hydrochloride)	
	25–75 I.M. (Enanthate, weekly/biweekly)	
Perphenazine (Trilafon)	16–80 oral	8–16 oral
	5–30 I.M.	
Piperacetazine (Quide)	40–160 oral	20–50 oral
Prochlorperazine (Compazine)	30–150 oral	15–75 oral
	30–100 I.M.	
Thiopropazate (Dartal)	30–100 oral	15–30 oral
Trifluoperazine (Stelazine)	10–45 oral	5–15 oral
	6–12 I.M.	
Thioridazine (Mellaril)	300–800 oral	100–300 oral
Mesoridazine (Serentil)	50–400 oral	25–200 oral
	25–200 I.M.	
Thioxanthenes		
Chlorprothixene (Taractan)	100–600 oral	50–200 oral
Thiothixene (Navane)	10–60 oral	5–15 oral
	6–12 I.M.	
Dibenzoxazepines		
Loxapine (Loxitane)	150–250 oral	100–150 oral
BUTYROPHENONES		
Haloperidol (Haldol, Serenace)	15–80 oral	10–30 oral
	15–40 I.M.	
DIHYROINDOLENES		
Molindone (Moban)	125–225 oral	75–125 oral

period. If four to five days of such high-dose parenteral therapy fails to control an acutely excited patient, it is wise to discontinue drugs and start ECT. This is especially the case for those patients who become febrile and dehydrated and present the risk of a fatal outcome in a psychotic exhaustion state.

Paranoid-Hallucinatory States. Patients with mania, schizophrenia or toxic psychoses may display multiform persecutory delusions often associated with auditory hallucinations and experiences of influence and alienation (first-rank symptoms). If excitement is not marked and patients will accept oral therapy, excellent results can be obtained if treatment is continued for adequate periods of time. A typical regimen might be fluphenazine concentrate increased rapidly to a dose of 40–60 mg/day and maintained at this level for two to four weeks. Thought-disorder, whether in the form of flight-of-ideas or acutely fragmented speech ("word-salad"), accompanying such paranoid hallucinatory states also responds to neuroleptic drugs.

Emotional Blunting and Formal Thought-Disorder. These phenomena occur together in patients who satisfy criteria for "process" or "nuclear" schizophrenia, and who have an extremely poor prognosis regardless of treatment. Even prolonged high-dose neuroleptic drug therapy may have only a modest effect in such patients, who often receive the diagnosis of hebephrenia. Their response to ECT is also poor.

Catatonic Stuporous States. Catatonic posturing, rigidity, mutism, negativism and stupor rarely respond satisfactorily to neuroleptic drugs and may occasionally be aggravated by them. Intravenous or intramuscular sodium amobarbital is temporarily useful to differentiate catatonic schizophrenia from manic or depressive stupor or to permit stuporous patients to eat (e.g., sodium amobarbital, 250–500 mg intramuscular, one-half hour before meals). ECT rapidly removes the catatonic state, frequently with only one or two treatments, but therapy must be continued with additional seizures, neuroleptics or lithium, according to clinical diagnosis.

Neuroleptic Drug Selection. Extensive collaborative studies by the Veterans Administration and the National Institute of Mental Health have not revealed important therapeutic differences among the various neuroleptic drugs in the treatment of psychotic patients. Two exceptions are promazine and mepazine, which were found less effective than other neuroleptics and are not included in this discussion.

The main criteria for choosing one over another neuroleptic are differences in individual patient tolerance to side-effects, the availability of various preparations and the physician's experience with the different compounds.

Drug Administration. Patients who are acutely ill require rapid symptom-control, which is best achieved with parenteral medication as frequently as every four hours. Stepwise dosage increments are needed until clinical improvement occurs or side-effects supervene. For such patients, parenteral therapy is best continued for 48–72 hours even if their abnormal behavior is controlled earlier, for a rapid change to oral medication frequently results in a relapse. When oral medication is substituted, an increased dose of a concentrate should be given in one or two daily divided doses. There is no reason to prescribe tablets for hospitalized patients if a concentrate is available. Extrapyramidal side-effects may first appear when a parenteral is changed to an oral route of administration. They may result from a somewhat different metabolism of the oral medication, which must initially traverse the portal circulation and liver before entering the general circulation and the brain ("first-pass" effect).

Duration of Therapy. The dose required to achieve full symptom remission should be continued for two to four weeks and then gradually reduced to a maintenance level. If patients remain symptom-free for three months or so after the first-onset of an acute psychotic illness, their medication should be discontinued for an observation period. If symptoms rapidly recur, this suggests merely a suppressive action of the neuroleptic drug, and a course of convulsive therapy should be considered. Patients who were chronically or recurrently ill prior to initiation of drug therapy should receive longer courses of treatment, perhaps from six to eight months, but they also deserve a drug-free observation period. Symptoms will recur in about 40% of such patients, and therapy ought then to be resumed with neuroleptic drugs, as convulsive therapy is rarely effective in chronically ill patients.

Indefinite continued administration of neuroleptic drugs not infrequently produces permanent structural brain changes accompanied by involuntary choreiform movements (tardive dyskinesia), and the need for such chronic therapy must be clearly demonstrated.

Side-Effects, Precautions and Contraindications

Central Nervous System. The extrapyramidal syndrome of parkinsonism, dystonia and akathisia occurs early in treatment and most frequently with the piperazine tricyclics and haloperidol. The individual components of the syndrome may occur alone or in combination and are a function of the total drug dose and its rate of increase. Patients often adapt to the extrapyramidal syndrome after two or three weeks of treatment, but if it remains distressing or disabling, antiparkinson medication (Table 2-2) or dose reduction will be required. Akathisia is most disturbing to the patient and may simulate psychotic agitation or a worsening of the clinical state, leading the physician to erroneously increase rather than decrease the drug dosage. The extrapyramidal syndrome occurs least frequently with thioridazine, probably owing to its potent anticholinergic properties.

Acute dystonia is a dramatic and sometimes alarming occurrence, but it carries no morbid risk and responds rapidly to parenteral benztropine, 1-2 mg, or diphenhydramine, 25-50 mg. Convulsive seizures may occur with very large

TABLE 2-2 ANTIPARKINSON DRUGS.

	Usual 24-Hour Dosage Range in mg			
	Acute		Maintenance	
Anticholinergics				
Procyclidine (Kemadrin)			5–30	oral
Biperiden (Akineton)	2.5–5	I.M.	4–8	oral
Cycrimine (Pagitane)			2.5–15	oral
Trihexyphenidyl (Artane)			4–10	oral
Antihistaminics				
Diphenhydramine (Benadryl)	25–50	I.M./I.V.	50–150	oral
Orphenadrine (Disipal, Norflex)	15–30	I.M.	100–200	oral
Anticholinergics/Antihistaminics				
Benztropine (Cogentin)	1–2	I.M./I.V.	2–6	oral
Ethopropazine (Parsidol)			30–300	oral
Dopaminergics				
Amantadine (Symmetrel)	100–300	oral	100–200	oral

doses of neuroleptic drugs (e.g., chlorpromazine in doses over 2,000 mg/day), but they are quite rare and respond to dose reduction.

About 25–50% of patients receiving long-term neuroleptic drug therapy develop a syndrome of involuntary choreiform movements that persists after the drugs are discontinued (tardive dyskinesia). The symptoms differ from those of the acute extrapyramidal triad and include periodic tongue-protrusion and lip-smacking, puffing and chewing movements of the mouth, athetoid hyperextension of the fingers and a restless shifting of weight from leg to leg. A comparative study of autopsy material from patients with the syndrome of tardive dyskinesia demonstrated histopathological changes in midbrain structures. The biochemical alterations are believed to be either excessive dopamine accumulation in the basal ganglia, or an increased dopamine receptor sensitivity. The treatment of tardive dyskinesia is unsatisfactory; antiparkinson agents aggravate the syndrome and should not be used. Cerebral amine-depleting agents (reserpine), cholinergic agents (diethylaminoethanol, physostigmine, choline, lecithin) and GABA-ergic agents (sodium valproate, baclofen) have all been reported effective in scattered, small clinical trials, but no methodologically adequate studies have shown any of them to be unequivocally (and substantially) more effective than placebo.

Reinstitution of other neuroleptic drugs, particularly the potent dopamine-blocker haloperidol, also reduces the syndrome, but such therapy is clearly unsatisfactory in the long view.

Tardive dyskinesia has now been reported to occur after only brief (three- to four-month) courses of neuroleptic drug therapy, and for this reason such drugs should be reserved exclusively for the treatment of severely ill or psychotic patients. Their use in mildly ill, depressed or neurotic patients cannot be justified, and their use in children and pregnant women should be avoided whenever possible.

Cardiovascular System. Neuroleptic drugs, especially chlorpromazine, thioridazine and chlorprothixene, produce orthostatic hypotension which is dose-related and occurs more frequently in older patients and with parenteral administration. Adaptation to this phenomenon often occurs over a week or two, and patients should be warned to rise slowly from lying or sitting positions. For high-dose parenteral neuroleptic therapy, the more potent neuroleptics (e.g., haloperidol, fluphenazine, thiothixene) are to be preferred, as they have little hypotensive effect. Epinephrine should not be used to treat neuroleptic drug-induced hypotensive collapse, as the alpha-adrenergic blocking properties of the neuroleptic will leave the hypotensive action of epinephrine unopposed. In such an event, the pressor amine of choice is norepinephrine.

Repolarization abnormalities of the electrocardiogram (EKG) are frequently seen with neuroleptics, particularly thioridazine and mesoridazine. Flattening, notching, splitting and inversion of T-waves, prolongation of P–Q and Q–T intervals and S–T segment depression may all occur. These EKG changes are related to drug-induced myocardial potassium depletion and are reversed by oral potassium replacement. Neuroleptics should be used cautiously in patients with myocardial disease, as there is a suspected relation between the EKG abnormalities and the rare instances of autopsy-negative sudden death in patients receiving these drugs.

Hematopoetic System. Agranulocytosis is a rare and dangerous idiosyncratic allergic response to neuroleptic drugs that occurs in the first weeks of therapy at doses exceeding 150 mg/day of chlorpromazine or the equivalent. Frequent white cell counts are ineffective in the early detection of this syndrome, which is most successfully prevented by clinical vigilance. Painful oropharyngeal infections and fever are the usual presenting complaint, and these may occur within 24 hours of a normal white count. The complaint of sore throat or mouth, or the occurrence of fever in a patient receiving neuroleptics requires that medication be withheld until a white blood cell count is obtained. If there are less than 2,000 neutrophiles per cubic millimeter (40% of a 5,000 total white count), the patient must be seen by a medical consultant without delay. If the white count is adequate, drug therapy may be continued.

Autonomic Nervous System. The antiadrenergic and anticholinergic properties of the neuroleptic drugs are responsible for their most commonly described side-effects. Dry mouth, stuffed nose, impaired taste, blurred vision, constipation and urinary retention are all dose-related, and if severe or persistent, respond only to dose-reduction. Antiparkinson agents with their own anticholinergic effects merely aggravate these symptoms. Inhibition of ejaculation is an anti-adrenergic phenomenon seen most frequently with thioridazine and mesoridazine.

Skin and Eye. Photosensitivity is reported by patients receiving neuroleptics, and painful sunburn may result from only brief exposure. Patients should be warned of this possibility and advised to use a suntan preparation to prevent it. Ocular photosensitivity also occurs and can be prevented with sunglasses.

Long-term effects of phenothiazine neuroleptics include a characteristic blue-gray pigmentation of the skin, and the development of stellate lenticular and corneal opacities visible only on slit-lamp examination. These changes have no known clinical sequelae but seem to be permanent. They are a function of the total lifetime dose of medication received and have been reported most often after chlorpromazine therapy.

Pigmentary retinopathy leading to blindness has occurred in patients receiving more than 1,200 mg/day of thioridazine, and no more than 800 mg/day of this drug should be given. For this reason, if high-dose neuroleptic drug therapy is anticipated, thioridazine is a poor initial choice.

Liver. Benign intrahepatic cholestatic jaundice occurred during the early years of chlorpromazine use and is now a rare complication of neuroleptic drug therapy. Mildly abnormal liver function tests often occur in patients receiving neuroleptics, but their significance is obscure, and no untoward results occur if treatment is continued.

Hormonal Changes. Impaired glucose tolerance with elevated fasting blood sugars often occurs with neuroleptics, more commonly in women than in men. There is no known clinical significance for this, and no treatment is recommended. A temporary pseudopregnancy syndrome (due, in part, to increased prolactin secretion) may also occur in women, with amenorrhea, lactation, breast swelling and false-positive pregnancy tests. Gynecomastia has also been reported in men receiving neuroleptics.

Fatalities. Sudden death in patients receiving neuroleptic drugs has various etiologies. Autopsy-negative deaths in psychiatric patients were well-known before the introduction of neuroleptic drugs, and patients who died in febrile/dehydrated states were described as having lethal catatonia, "Bell's mania," or manic exhaustion. Altered temperature regulation secondary to the anticholinergic effects of neuroleptics and the oft-prescribed antiparkinson agents has produced hyperpyrexic deaths during the hot summer months. Asphyxiation by food bolus has been discovered at autopsy in some patients, but these deaths cannot readily be attributed to a drug therapy being received. Fluoroscopic examination of patients receiving neuroleptics does show impaired swallowing, but no more so than in chronic patients not receiving drugs. Hypotensive deaths have also been reported, and some deaths have been ascribed to drug-induced cardiac arrhythmias.

Psychiatric Complications. Depression may occur during or after neuroleptic drug therapy, most commonly when the acute phase of the illness is over.

Antidepressant drug therapy or ECT may be required, as there is a risk of suicide in such cases. This is most often seen in acute manics, and it is unclear whether the depressive state is drug-related or simply that which frequently precedes or follows a manic attack even without drug therapy (mislabeled "post-schizophrenic depression").

Contraindications. True contraindications to neuroleptic drugs are rare. Narrow-angle glaucoma is one and pronounced prostatic hypertrophy another. Caution should be employed in prescribing these drugs for pregnant women.

ANXIOLYTIC DRUGS

These compounds share the sedative, hypnotic, central muscle-relaxant, anticonvulsant, central depressant and addicting properties of the barbiturates. Sudden cessation of these drugs after chronic high-dose administration in man may be followed by convulsive seizures.

Clinically, these drugs are widely prescribed and have replaced barbiturates for anxiety reduction and nighttime sedation in neurotic patients. They are also extensively used in the treatment of delirium tremens and epilepsy. Anxiety responsive to the action of these drugs occurs in patients with neurotic disorders often with associated phobias, depersonalization, hypochondriasis, neurasthenia, obsessions and depression.

Some characteristic drugs, dose ranges and available preparations are given in Table 2-3. There is little hard evidence that one or another of these drugs is to be preferred for any specific clinical use, and the choice among them depends on the availability of different preparations and the familiarity of the physician with them.

Oral therapy is the usual mode of administration for anxiolytics, and where parenteral therapy is needed, as in the treatment of delirium tremens, injectable preparations are available only for the benzodiazepines. In such cases, the intravenous route should be used, as absorption is poor after intramuscular injection. Because tolerance develops rapidly to the antianxiety effects of these drugs, they are useful only for short periods of continuous administration. If unusual circumstances require their administration beyond several weeks, drug-free intervals may be required to avoid a regular stepwise increase in dosage. One advantage of the anxiolytics over barbiturate and nonbarbiturate sedatives (e.g., glutethimide) is their lower respiratory depressant effect and consequent diminished lethal potential in suicide attempts. Another is their reduced tendency to suppress REM (rapid eye movement) sleep.

Clinical Indications

Acute Anxiety States. Patients with diagnoses of anxiety neurosis, hypochondriacal neurosis, hysterical neurosis and other related syndromes are frequently

TABLE 2-3   ANXIOLYTICS.

	Usual 24-Hour Dosage Range in mg			
	Acute		Maintenance	
Benzodiazepines				
Clorazepate (Tranxene)	30–60	oral	15–30	oral
Chlordiazepoxide (Librium)	30–100	oral	10–30	oral
	150–400	I.M./I.V.		
Diazepam (Valium)	15–60	oral	10–30	oral
	15–30	I.M./I.V.		
Flurazepam (Dalmane)	15–30	oral	15–30	oral
Oxazepam (Serax)	30–120	oral	20–60	oral
Substituted Diols				
Meprobamate (Miltown, Equanil)	1200–2400	oral	600–1200	oral
Tybamate (Tybatran)	750–3000	oral	500–1000	oral

subject to sudden attacks of intense fear or dread, accompanied by shortness of breath, sweating, pressure, pain and pounding in the head and chest, and numbness and tingling of the extremities. Oral anxiolytics are effective in such attacks, and high doses may be needed (e.g., chlordiazepoxide, 25–50 mg; diazepam, 15–30 mg), which should be rapidly tapered off and discontinued over several days.

Chronic Anxiety States.   Patients with chronic, disabling, anxiety may have associated insomnia, depression, phobias, obsessions/compulsions, depersonalization/derealization, hypochondriasis or somatic symptoms, and are extremely difficult to treat. They are often made worse by the neuroleptic drugs or convulsive therapy they receive from physicians who label them "pseudoneurotic schizophrenics," and they frequently abuse alcohol and sedative/hypnotics. Anxiolytic drugs are unsatisfactory as they temporarily relieve symptoms but require increasing doses to maintain the status quo as adaptation occurs. Monoamine-oxidase inhibiting drugs (MAOI's), although classed as antidepressants, are sometimes unusually successful in the treatment of such neurotic patients (see section on antidepressant drugs below).

Delirium Tremens.   This alcohol withdrawal syndrome is characterized by visual and auditory hallucinations, restless agitation, disorientation, shifting consciousness, tremor, vomiting and a history of recent relative or absolute reduction in alcohol intake. A standard treatment is chlordiazepoxide, 100 mg intravenous every four to six hours. Neuroleptics such as chlorpromazine or promazine have been recommended in the past, but they only increase the morbidity and mortality rate.

Nighttime Sedation.   The anxiolytics are effective hypnotics and are widely prescribed for this purpose. One compound in particular, flurazepam, is intensively advertised for this purpose, but there is no evidence that it is any more effective than an equivalent dose of diazepam or chlordiazepoxide. The benzodiazepines have an advantage over the older hypnotics in that they exhibit less suppression of REM sleep.

Side-Effects, Precautions and Contraindications

Drowsiness, ataxia, confusion and stupor may occur with increasing doses of the anxiolytics, and patients receiving these medications should be warned against driving automobiles or operating complex machinery. The combination of alcohol and anxiolytic sedatives presents a lethal risk for patients who will not refrain from driving. Unintended "suicides" have also occurred with this combination.

Transient excitement states may occur when older or extremely agitated patients are treated with low doses of anxiolytics. There is nothing "paradoxical" about these reactions; as for the barbiturates and many other drugs, low doses may be excitatory and high doses inhibitory. If excitement occurs, the drug should be either increased or discontinued.

Withdrawal seizures can occur in patients whose long-term high-dose anxiolytic drug therapy is abruptly stopped. As for other addicting drugs, these compounds should be withdrawn gradually.

LITHIUM

The lithium ion is unrelated to any other class of psychopharmacologic agent, and is active exclusively in patients with manic-depressive illness. The antimanic action of lithium is more specific than that of neuroleptics or convulsive therapy, which are also effective in a variety of other illnesses. About 80% of manic patients achieve full remission or are much improved with lithium therapy, and the prophylactic effect of continued lithium administration against future manic attacks is extremely well documented. The depressive phase of manic-depressive illness is also less frequent in patients receiving maintenance lithium therapy, as are recurrent episodes of unipolar depression. A direct antidepressant effect of lithium in unipolar and bipolar depressive illness has also been reported.

Lithium is given orally as the carbonate in 300 mg tablets or capsules. The usual starting dose for manic patients is 1,200 to 1,800 mg/day in three or four divided doses, with twice-weekly monitoring of serum lithium levels during the initial few weeks of therapy. (A "prolonged action" preparation is marketed for b.i.d. administration, but has no advantage over giving the standard formulation at the same frequency.) Therapeutic blood levels for acutely ill patients range around 1.5 mEq/L, and when this level is stable, the lithium dose can usually be reduced to 900 to 1,200 mg/day, assuming a satisfactory therapeutic response. Serum lithium levels exceeding 2.0 mEq/L may be associated with toxic effects although older patients can become lithium-toxic at lower levels. For safety and clinical control, maintenance lithium serum determinations are usually made at monthly intervals to maintain serum levels around 1.0 mEq/L.

Although lithium is the preferred treatment for mania, many manics initially refuse oral medications, and even if they accept them, there is a 5–7-day lag before the onset of therapeutic effects. For this reason, treatment must often be initiated with a parenteral neuroleptic (usually haloperidol) to control the acute state. After this has been achieved, and the patient accepts oral medications, lithium can be instituted, continuing neuroleptic therapy until stable lithium levels in the therapeutic range are achieved. At this point the neuroleptic can be tapered off and discontinued, as it is in the patient's best interest to be treated with lithium alone.

A 1974 report of irreversible neurotoxicity with the lithium/haloperidol combination has never been confirmed, although this combination of drugs has been widely prescribed for many years. There is no specific evidence that the toxicity of combined therapy is qualitatively different from that seen with neuroleptic drugs alone. It may be that lithium potentiates the neuroleptic-induced extrapyramidal syndrome in some especially sensitive patients, and it is prudent to discontinue lithium in any patient who appears to be developing unusually severe parkinsonism on combined therapy.

Side-Effects, Precautions and Contraindications

During the initial week or so of therapy, patients may experience a fine tremor, mild fatigue or drowsiness, nausea, abdominal fullness, increased thirst and polyuria. These symptoms are no indication to reduce dosage and usually remit when stable blood levels are achieved. Vomiting immediately after ingestion of lithium sometimes occurs and can be avoided by instructing patients to take their lithium with food. Genuine toxicity rarely appears below serum lithium levels of 2.0 mEq/L, and is characterized by profuse vomiting or diarrhea, slurred speech, ataxia, coarse tremors, lethargy, myoclonus, stupor and coma. Atypical neurologic syndromes may occur, with unilateral focal signs mimicking a stroke. Treatment of moderate lithium toxicity is supportive. The drug is stopped, fluids are forced, and an adequate food (and salt) intake is encouraged. No specific antidote is yet available for lithium toxicity.

Renal dialysis is the only known method for actively removing lithium from the body. Although insufficient data have been accumulated for a definitive statement on its efficacy, dialysis should be instituted in the presence of severe lithium toxicity (e.g., patient in coma; renal elimination of lithium inadequate; serum lithium level > 4 mEq/L). In addition, standard supportive procedures are instituted (parenteral fluids, prophylactic antibiotics, frequent turning in bed, airway maintenance).

Lithium should be used with extreme caution in patients with impaired renal function, employing low doses (e.g., 150 mg b.i.d. or t.i.d.) and frequent serum lithium determinations. Caution should be observed in cardiac patients as well, as EKG repolarization abnormalities occur with lithium. This drug should not be prescribed for patients receiving diuretics or a low sodium diet, as severe lithium poisoning may rapidly occur in salt-depleted patients. (An exception is the use of chlorothiazide, described below.)

As an inhibitor of cyclic-AMP/adenylcyclase, lithium impairs the function of two major hormones mediated by this system: antidiuretic hormone (ADH) and thyroid hormone (T3/T4). The effect on ADH is to prevent its action on the kidney, producing a nephrogenic diabetes insipidus–like syndrome (which is, of course, ADH-resistant), manifested by a large output of dilute urine. With such a large urine volume it becomes difficult to maintain adequate serum lithium levels, and therapeutic results may suffer. In such cases, chlorothiazide is indicated in order to reduce urine volume and increase serum lithium levels. There may be long-term effects related to this syndrome as well. Several reports have appeared in the literature of patients with this syndrome who demonstrate glomerular changes on renal biopsy. Often, there has been a history of severe lithium toxicity as well. Follow-up studies have not shown significant long-term impairment in renal function in patients maintained on lithium, and no case has yet been reported of end-stage renal disease in a patient on maintenance lithium. However, it is prudent to reduce or discontinue lithium whenever possible in patients who develop the diabetes insipidus–like syndrome.

The antithyroid effect of lithium results in a few patients receiving long-term maintenance lithium therapy who develop nontoxic goiters that shrink with discontinuation of lithium or the addition of small doses of thyroid. The patients are usually clinically euthyroid, but signs of hypothyroidism may occur. The T3/T4 levels are often reduced, and there is an increased uptake of radioactive iodine.

The safe use of lithium in pregnant women is not established, and sporadic reports of possible teratogenic effects continue to accumulate. Lithium is excreted in mother's milk, and mothers on lithium therapy should bottle-feed their babies. Excessive weight gain and acneiform eruptions are frequent troublesome side-effects of lithium that respond to dose reduction.

There are no specific guidelines on the duration of lithium maintenance therapy. Patients who have remained well on such a regimen for years may relapse in a week's time when lithium is discontinued. The duration of therapy will depend largely on the number, rate and severity of prior attacks of illness.

As noted in the section on neuroleptic drugs, manic episodes are frequently followed by depression. This pattern also occurs in patients receiving lithium, and it is unclear whether the drug increases the frequency of the pattern. If depression occurs, lithium should be continued and the appropriate antidepressant therapy started (e.g., a tricyclic antidepressant or ECT).

ANTIDEPRESSANT DRUGS

There are two main classes of antidepressant drugs, the tricyclics and the monoamine oxidase inhibitors (MAOI's). Recently, a modification of the tricyclic structure has yielded the tetracyclics as well. The tricyclics and MAOI's have different structures, chemical properties and clinical indications, and they will be discussed separately. Psychostimulant drugs such as the amphetamines and related compounds have no true antidepressant properties and will not be considered.

Tricyclic Antidepressants

These drugs, which are minor chemical modifications of chlorpromazine, were introduced as potential neuroleptics. The prototype drug of this group, imipramine, was immediately found to have antidepressant properties without significant antipsychotic effects. A variety of modifications of the tricyclic prototype have been introduced for the treatment of depressed patients, and these drugs are listed in Table 2-4.

Clinical Indications and Treatment Results. The best results with tricyclic antidepressants are obtained in patients with endogenous depressions. Indeed, the scientific differentiation of endogenous from reactive depression derives largely from a study of the effects of imipramine in a group of unselected depressed patients. Imipramine-responders displayed a cluster of symptoms that are now subsumed under the rubric of endogenous depression, whereas the nonresponders manifested the phenomena associated with reactive depression. These syndromes are described in more detail in the section on convulsive therapy below. Briefly, the clinical indications for tricyclic antidepressants are the same as for convulsive therapy in depression.

The response rate to tricyclic drugs for patients with endogenous depression is about 60-70%, significantly lower than that for convulsive therapy but often higher than for placebo. The presence of hallucinations or delusions in patients with endogenous depression is often associated with an inadequate response to tricyclics or even a worsening of the illness. It is typically the late-onset unipolar depressive patient who displays such psychotic symptoms and who is often diagnosed as having involutional melancholia or an agitated depression. Such patients fare poorly with the antidepressants but do well with ECT.

TABLE 2-4   ANTIDEPRESSANTS.

| | Usual 24-Hour Dosage Range in mg. | | | |
	Acute		Maintenance	
Tricyclics				
Imipramine (Tofranil)	200–300	oral	150–200	oral
Amitriptyline (Elavil)	200–300	oral	150–200	oral
Desipramine (Norpramin, Petofrane)	150–300	oral	100–150	oral
Nortriptyline (Aventyl)	75–125	oral	50–100	oral
Protriptyline (Vivactil)	30–60	oral	15–30	oral
Doxepin (Sinequan, Adapin)	200–300	oral	150–200	oral
MAOI's				
Tranylcypromine (Parnate)	30–40	oral	20–30	oral
Phenelzine (Nardil)	60–90	oral	45–60	oral
Tetracyclics				
Maprotiline (Ludiomil)	200–300	oral	150–200	oral

Choice of Drugs.   Imipramine and amitriptyline are the most widely used tricyclics, and for the most part their effects are interchangeable. One study showed amitriptyline to be somewhat superior to imipramine for older, agitated depressives, and imipramine more successful in younger, retarded depressives. Amitriptyline is more sedating than imipramine and may therefore be useful in agitated patients or those with severe insomnia.

The chemical derivatives of imipramine and amitriptyline are widely touted as the active metabolic products of the parent drugs. However, most studies have shown the parent compounds to be equal or superior to their derivatives in antidepressant activity, with an equal or faster onset of effect. Side-effects are frequently more pronounced with the desmethylated derivatives, and some patients experience insomnia or an unpleasant sense of "activation" with them. An exception is nortriptyline, which has reduced cardiovascular side-effects, especially in older patients.

Drug Dosage.   Adequate dosage is a critical variable for successful tricyclic antidepressant therapy. For imipramine and amitriptyline, the starting dose is 100–150 mg/day, increasing to 200–300 mg/day by the end of four to five days. A daily dosage of either drug below 200 mg is usually ineffective except in older patients, who also poorly tolerate the side-effects of higher doses. For most patients, the entire dose can be taken at bedtime without increased side-effects and with a duration of activity equal to that achieved with multiple daily divided doses.

Plasma Level Monitoring.   Bioavailability of tricyclics, which is now believed to be the most important variable determining treatment response, is estimated by determining plasma levels of these compounds. This method is not yet widely available, and technical problems still impair the reliability of such estimates; but there is no doubt that before long, plasma level monitoring of tricyclics will be as standard as that for lithium therapy. Two tricyclics, imipramine and nortriptyline, have provided most of the relevant data for plasma levels. The dose-response curve for imipramine is relatively linear, with increased levels associated with an increased therapeutic response. The minimum therapeutic plasma level for imipramine is 250 ng/ml. The dose-response curve for nortriptyline is curvilinear, requiring a more precise adjustment of dosage due to a fall-off of therapeutic effect at higher blood levels. Nortriptyline plasma levels should be maintained between 75 and 125 ng/ml.

Duration of Therapy.   It is often stated that there is a two-week lag in the onset of action of the tricyclics, but, in fact, most studies show the greatest proportion of total improvement occurring during the first two weeks of therapy. For this reason, if a patient has shown no significant improvement after two weeks of tricyclic antidepressant therapy at therapeutic levels, there is little reason to persist with this form of treatment.

Once symptom remission has been achieved, the drugs should be continued at the same dosage or blood level for one to three months or for the duration of the usual depressive episode, if known. The duration of therapy will also vary with the number and severity of prior attacks. Continued administration of tricyclic antidepressants beyond that required for the particular episode is not known to prevent future attacks of illness.

The onset of clinical effects of imipramine and amitriptyline is accelerated in women by combined therapy with thyroid hormone. The regimen consists of the addition of liothyronine, 20–40 µg/day, to the tricyclic drug. The onset of clinical improvement is hastened, and there may also be an improved overall therapeutic effect.

Methylphenidate has been used to increase blood levels of tricyclic antidepressants, owing to its inhibitory effects on hepatic microsomal enzymes. There is no evidence that this method is more effective than simply increasing the dosage of the tricyclic.

Patients with endogenous depression often require nighttime sedation in addition to tricyclic therapy. Barbiturates are a poor choice for such sedation, as their enzyme-inducing properties have been associated with reduced blood levels of tricyclic antidepressants. Sedatives without enzyme-inducing activity, such as the benzodiazepines, should be used instead.

Side-Effects, Precautions and Contraindications.   The tricyclic antidepressants share many side-effects of the tricyclic neuroleptic parent drugs, but have more pronounced anticholinergic properties. Thus, postural hypotension, EKG changes, dry mouth, blurred vision, heartburn, constipation, adynamic ileus and urinary hesitancy and retention all occur. An extrapyramidal syndrome is absent, however, and there are no reports of tardive dyskinesia consequent to tricyclic antidepressants. A troublesome, persistent fine tremor does occur, similar to that in thyrotoxicosis. It is resistant to antiparkinson agents and does not diminish over time. Dose reduction may be required, but when this is not advisable, the beta-adrenergic blocking agent propranolol may be used with some success in doses of 10-30 mg/day.

EKG alterations are more frequent with the tricyclic antidepressants than their parent compounds, and there is a significant incidence of unexplained sudden death in cardiac patients receiving these drugs for the treatment of depression. For this reason, ECT is a more conservative method than the use of tricyclic antidepressants for the treatment of depressed patients with myocardial disease.

Hematologic abnormalities also occur with the tricyclics, and a case of near-fatal total aplastic anemia has occurred with imipramine. Jaundice is also reported as a rare idiosyncratic response to amitriptyline.

Profuse sweating frequently occurs with the tricyclics, particularly imipramine, a phenomenon not observed with the neuroleptics.

The tricyclics may induce mania in bipolar patients receiving these drugs for depression, a response also observed with ECT. The occurrence of mania or hypomania in a depressed patient without prior history of such suggests that he suffers from bipolar disease.

Overdosage with tricyclic antidepressants can induce a toxic psychosis. This anticholinergic delirium is characterized by confusion, disorientation, clouding of consciousness, dilated pupils, dry skin and a history of tricyclic drug ingestion. It is responsive to the cholinesterase-inhibitor physostigmine, 1-2 mg intravenously, which may be repeated in 15 minutes and again in half an hour.

Narrow-angle glaucoma and severe prostatic hypertrophy are contraindications to tricyclic antidepressants, a subject discussed more fully below.

Tetracyclic Antidepressants

Chemical modifications of the tricyclic nucleus have yielded new antidepressants classed as monocyclic, bicyclic and tetracyclic. Of these, only the tetracyclic maprotiline (Ludiomil) is available for use in this country. This compound is very similar to the tricyclics, having only the potential advantage of reduced cardiovascular side-effects. As far more data exist in support of tricyclic efficacy, and as there already exists an effective tricyclic with reduced cardiovascular side-effects, there is little reason to prescribe maprotiline.

Monoamine Oxidase Inhibitors (MAOI's)

These compounds are traditionally listed as antidepressants, although most studies show them to be only partially effective in the treatment of patients with endogenous depression. Their activity has always been purportedly greatest in patients with "atypical" depression, which usually describes neurotic or reactive depressives with associated phobic, obsessional, hypochondriacal or depersonalization symptoms. Until recently, little scientific evidence had been adduced in support of these clinical observations. However, reports are now accumulating that clearly show that this class of drugs is effective in neurotic patients whose anxiety or depression is associated with the various symptoms that are noted above and in the section on anxiolytic drugs. Patients with agoraphobia or the "phobic anxiety-depersonalization syndrome" may be particularly responsive to MAOI's.

Choice of Drugs. There are two therapeutically active MAOI's available to American psychiatrists, phenelzine and tranylcypromine. The two are structurally similar but the closer resemblance of tranylcypromine to amphetamine is reflected in its initial amphetamine-like stimulating properties, not present with phenelzine. Because of the greater incidence and severity of "cheese" reactions with tranylcypromine (see below), this drug is usually reserved for the more severely ill, therapy-resistant patient. Although the manufacturer recommends that tranylcypromine be reserved for hospital use, it is nonetheless well tolerated by outpatients if they adhere strictly to their dietary proscriptions.

Clinical Indications. These have been described above and are not more precise simply because they are still evolving. Severe neurotic symptoms combined with anxiety or depression and in the absence of a diagnosis of one of the major psychoses constitute the main indication for MAOI's. The diagnosis of "pseudo-neurotic" schizophrenia, although purportedly that of a psychosis, often augurs well for a therapeutic response to MAOI's. These severe obsessional patients with multiple neurotic symptoms and anxiety have been more aptly designated "pseudoschizophrenic" neurotics. If severely crippled by their symptoms, these patients may be referred for psychosurgery, and they should always have a full and fair trial with an MAOI before the decision to operate is made.

Drug Dosage and Duration of Therapy. The dose of phenelzine is 60–90 mg/day in two or three divided doses, and that of tranylcypromine 30–40 mg/day. There is a delayed onset of action with both drugs, which may be as short as a week and as long as three or four weeks. As most patients referred for MAOI therapy have chronic illnesses that have been unresponsive to other treatments, it is wise to continue therapy for four weeks at therapeutic doses before declaring failure. Patients should be warned not to expect any clinical improvement for at least two weeks lest they become discouraged and discontinue treatment prematurely. The initial amphetamine-like stimulation with tranylcypromine may be advantageous in patients whose fatigue and inertia threaten imminent loss of employment. If anxiety is severe, the benzodiazepines may be safely prescribed during the initial period before the MAOI's become effective. There is some potentiation of the anxiolytic effect of these compounds, and smaller doses are usually required.

The response rates to MAOI's are still poorly defined, but perhaps half of such chronically ill therapy-resistant patients respond to treatment. When a response occurs, it may be dramatic, and patients characteristically remark that the medication gives them a "different" feeling from any ever before experienced in their lives. Therapy should be continued for two or three months and followed by gradual dose reduction. For many patients, this will result in a recrudescence of symptoms, necessitating resumption of the original dose. Nonetheless, it is prudent to attempt dose reduction at six-month intervals, although for many this will prove unfeasible.

Side-Effects, Precautions and Contraindications.   The principal side-effect of MAOI's is the dangerous hypertensive crisis that may occur in patients who eat foods with high tyramine content. This "cheese" reaction (so called because ripened cheeses have been associated with a majority of the severe reactions) may range from a sudden, throbbing headache to a paroxysmal hypertensive crisis with subarachnoid hemorrhage and, rarely, death. It results from failure of the body to metabolize the ingested pressor amine tyramine due to inhibition of monoamine oxidase, for which tyramine is a substrate. Treatment of the hypertensive crisis requires an alpha-adrenergic blocking agent, and parenteral phentolamine is the standard (5 mg intravenous). Many physicians provide their patients on MAOI's with 100 mg tablets of chlorpromazine to take immediately for its alpha-adrenergic blocking action should a "slip" occur in dietary observance.

Foods that have been associated with severe headache or paroxysmal hypertension include cheese (except cottage or cream cheese), pickled herring, liver (especially chicken liver), raw yeast or yeast extracts such as "Bovril" or "Marmite," beer and wine (especially Chianti wine) and Italian broad beans (fava beans). Despite these caveats, there are data to show that even if the dietary proscriptions are occasionally transgressed, serious or fatal reactions are quite rare. Patients must not take any medications with adrenergic properties, including amphetamines and related compounds, or cocaine. Central nervous system depressants are potentiated by MAIO's, and alcohol, opiates and barbiturates should be used with caution. Chlorothiazide diuretics are to be avoided. Patients should be instructed to "clear" any over-the-counter medications with their physician, as many such preparations contain pressor amines for their decongestant action. Phenylephrine and ephedrine are contained in many nosedrop preparations and should not be used. If dental procedures are contemplated, local anesthetics without epinephrine should be employed.

For many years it was asserted that tricyclics and MAOI's should never be combined because fatal reactions had ensued from such treatment. However, a detailed review of all such cases failed to demonstrate a convincing negative drug interaction, and a number of reports on the safety of such combined therapy have appeared in recent years. Unfortunately, there are no data from controlled trials at adequate dosages demonstrating the superiority of such combined therapy over either compound given alone.

Autonomic side-effects are similar to those of the tricyclics and include postural hypotension, blurred vision, dry mouth, constipation, paralytic ileus and urinary retention. Increased libido is experienced by some, and transient impotence has also occurred in men receiving tranylcypromine. Some patients with personality disorders abuse tranylcypromine because of its amphetamine-like properties. Patients are usually instructed not to take MAOI's within four hours of bedtime, as insomnia occasionally results. Increased dreaming has been reported with MAOI's, and some patients complain of frequent nightmares. This class of drugs, however, suppresses REM sleep.

An amphetamine-like psychosis can occur with the MAOI's, especially tranylcypromine. This toxic psychosis occurs in a clear consciousness, unlike the delirium of tricyclic drug overdosage, and is treated with neuroleptic drugs.

ECT

In 1935, Meduna first induced therapeutic generalized convulsions with injections of camphor in oil as a treatment for schizophrenia. Based on an erroneous theory of an incompatibility of epilepsy and schizophrenia and the observation that spontaneous seizures relieved symptoms in mental patients, the treatment was effective. Later observations showed it to be even more effective in patients with depressive illness. The uncertainty of inducing seizures with camphor and the frequent occurrence of repeated seizures led to trials with pentylenetetrazol (Metrazol). These seizures were more dependable although they were associated with intensely unpleasant sensations of impending death just prior to the onset of the convulsion.

In 1938, Cerletti and Bini refined the technique by applying alternating electric current to the temples, inducing instantaneous unconsciousness followed by a grand mal seizure. This method was safe and dependable and became the standard for convulsive therapy.

CLINICAL INDICATIONS

The Affective Disorders.   The best results with convulsive therapy are obtained in patients with affective disorders, especially endogenous depression. This syndrome is characterized by terminal insomnia, anhedonia, inability to cry, depression worse in the morning, guilty ruminations, anorexia, weight loss, and retardation or agitation. Patients with reactive depressions (depressive neurosis) may fare poorly with convulsive therapy and display initial insomnia, difficulty arising, mood worse in the evenings, fluctuating course, emotional reactivity and lability, and self-pity. The terms "endogenous" and "reactive" have no etiological implications and merely define certain clinical syndromes. The presence or absence of a precipitating event does not differentiate the two syndromes.

Results in Depression. Improvement with ECT in patients with endogenous depression ranges from 80 to 100%. A full remission in a psychotically depressed patient is frequently induced with four or five seizures, but if treatment is terminated at this point, relapses commonly occur. For this reason, six to eight seizures are most commonly given. Successful therapeutic outcome may vary inversely with the severity of the depression, and patients without hope, preoccupied with ruminations of guilt and worthlessness and reduced to a depressive stupor often show the best treatment results.

Compared with Drugs. Convulsive therapy is clearly superior to the antidepressant drugs in the treatment of depressed patients. The older and more psychotic the patient, the less likely is he to respond to drugs. In one study of tricyclic antidepressants, there was a group of older, deluded patients who failed drug treatment only to recover with ECT.

Combined with Drugs. The use of antidepressant drugs in combination with convulsive therapy has been advocated in order to shorten the treatment course. The suggestion has not been objectively studied, but it is worth noting that by the time antidepressants demonstrate clinical effects, most depressed patients have already recovered with a course of convulsive therapy.

Patients given maintenance antidepressants following a successful course of convulsive therapy have fewer relapses. Such maintenance therapy is extremely important as the relapse rate following convulsive therapy for depressions ranges from 25 to 50% within a six-month period. A typical maintenance regimen is amitriptyline, 200 mg q.h.s. for three or four months. Lithium may also be used.

Results in Mania. In the treatment of mania, lithium or the neuroleptics are effective and reliable in about 80% of patients, but the remainder will need convulsive therapy. Acute mania, often characterized by overactivity and psychotic excitement to the point of exhaustion, requires more intensive treatment than depression. Seizures are usually given twice daily for two to three days until psychomotor overactivity is controlled. Lithium may then be introduced or the remainder of the treatment course continued with convulsive therapy at the usual rate of three seizures each week.

Schizophrenia. ECT is no longer considered a useful treatment for schizophrenic patients diagnosed according to modern, operational, criteria (e.g., DSM–III). In the past, many reports were published extolling the virtures of ECT in schizophrenic patients, but it is now clear that most such ECT-responders would have satisfied modern criteria for affective disorder. Thus, acute, catatonic and schizoaffective schizophrenics were always considered prime candidates for ECT. There is now abundant evidence, however, showing that most patients with such diagnoses actually suffer from an affective illness. The motor symptoms of catatonia, especially stupor/mutism/negativism, are often dramatically responsive to ECT, even after only a few treatments. As such symptoms are frequently seen in very severe endogenous depression, the prognosis for sustained recovery is good. When catatonia (which is diagnostically nonspecific) is a manifestation of schizophrenia, however, the prognosis for recovery will be very poor, even though the motor symptoms remit.

Organic Psychoses.   Of practical and theoretical interest is the successful use of convulsive therapy in acute organic psychoses such as stupor secondary to head trauma; bromide psychosis; the delirium of alcohol withdrawal, meningitis, pneumonia, encephalitis, rheumatic fever and uremia; and the dysphoria of epileptic clouded states. The antipsychotic effect is nonspecific, as the exogenous psychosis may remit without a change in the underlying disorder.

Neuroses and Character Disorders.   Convulsive therapy is of no merit in patients with neuroses and character disorders and may make such patients worse by producing myriad side-effects, real and imagined, that form a nidus for hypochondriacal and obsessional ruminations.

Affective and Paranoid Psychoses of the Senium.   Many elderly patients receive the erroneous diagnosis of "organic brain syndrome" when they present with affective or paranoid symptoms in association with disorientation and impaired memory. The affective or paranoid coloring is prognostically favorable in such geriatric patients even in the presence of evidence for concurrent arteriosclerosis (e.g., hypertension, angina, retinal changes, diminished pulses). Many of these patients live alone, and their personal hygiene and nutritional state deteriorate, yielding a high mortality rate when untreated. These patients with depressive pseudodementia may respond dramatically to convulsive therapy, and their poor physical condition is an indication, not a contraindication, for such treatment.

True organic senile or arteriosclerotic psychoses without productive symptoms do not respond well to convulsive therapy. Such patients have characteristic severe cognitive defects and neurological signs of cerebral dysfunction.

TREATMENT METHODS

General Considerations

Pretreatment Examinations.   No laboratory test is an absolute prerequisite for convulsive therapy, and in an emergency, treatment may be given immediately. Ordinarily, a medical history and complete physical examination are obtained, and the routine laboratory tests include a urinalysis, hemogram, chest film and an EKG in patients over forty or those with a history of cardiovascular disease.

An EEG, skull films and dorsal spine films are not routine screening tests. Determination of plasma pseudocholinesterase levels is not useful, owing to the overwhelming number of false-positive results.

Premedication. Atropine, 0.4 mg subcutaneous, is administered 30 minutes prior to treatment to prevent excessive tracheobronchial secretions. If a vagal blocking dose of atropine is needed, as in a patient with a supraventricular arrhythmia or bradycardia, a minimum dose of 1.2 mg is required, and this may be given intravenously immediately prior to seizure induction.

Anesthesia and Muscle-relaxant. For several patients treated in one session, an intravenous infusion is rapid and convenient. The anesthetic and muscle-relaxant are prepared in separate sterile bottles and connected by plastic tubing to a three-way stopcock that, in turn, has a single disposable tube and needle for administering the drugs.

Methohexital (Brevital) is the anesthetic agent of choice and causes fewer cardiac irregularities than the older sodium thiopental (Pentothal). The induction is more rapid, the duration of action is shorter, and there is less post-anesthesia confusion as well. A 0.2% (2 mg/ml) solution is given as rapidly as possible until the patient no longer responds to questions (50–80 mg).

Succinylcholine (Anectine, Quelicin, Sucostrin) is the muscle-relaxant of choice. A 0.2% infusion is given rapidly immediately following the methohexital and continued until inhibition of the patellar reflex, or until the fasciculations of the first stage of the succinylcholine effect disappear in the muscles of the feet (40–80 mg).

If only one or two patients are to be treated, methohexital, 50–80 mg, may be given by syringe, followed immediately by 40–60 mg succinylcholine through the same needle but using a different syringe.

Oxygenation. Ventilation with 100% oxygen is begun when the patient falls asleep and continued throughout the procedure until spontaneous respirations return. An airway is seldom required. In edentulous patients or those with a full complement of healthy teeth, the jaw is merely held shut at the time the seizure is induced. In patients with poor dentition, a rolled 4×4 gauze sponge should be inserted between the molars just before treatment is given. Well-fitting dentures or bridges should be left in place, but ill-fitting ones must be removed and the sponge bite used.

Post-ictal Care. With the return of regular respirations, the patient is taken to a recovery area and observed until he awakens and is able to walk. Patients occasionally require tracheal suction or the administration of oxygen, and the required equipment should be available.

Emergence deliria occur in about 10% of patients in the immediate post-ictal period. These acute excitement states are extremely difficult to control once they have begun, and several staff members are usually required to restrain the patient while the delirium runs its usual 10–15 minute course. Patients who once develop a delirious state usually have it after each treatment; however, it is readily prevented by an intravenous injection of diazepam, 10–15 mg, at the termination of the seizure.

Ambulatory Convulsive Therapy. Outpatient convulsive therapy is useful for depressed patients with low suicide potential, for those who must continue to work during a course of treatment, and for patients who are to receive maintenance treatment. Outpatients are included in the same treatment schedule with inpatients. It is advisable to have a relative or other responsible person take the patient home (about one hour after he awakens), but if this is not possible, patients should remain in a waiting area until examined and cleared for release to their own care by a physician. Relatives should be warned to keep confused or amnesic patients away from friends who might incorrectly assess their mental capacities. Such patients should not enter into business or legal arrangements until amnesia and confusion have disappeared.

Maintenance convulsive therapy is frequently useful in patients who do not tolerate the side-effects of tricyclic antidepressants or who relapse rapidly after treatment in spite of maintenance drug therapy. Such outpatient maintenance convulsive therapy is given at the rate of one or two treatments each month and rarely causes significant memory difficulty. Prophylactic lithium therapy has greatly reduced the number of patients who require maintenance convulsive therapy. There is little justification for continuing maintenance ECT beyond six months.

Specific Techniques

Bilateral ECT. This is the standard mode of induction of therapeutic generalized seizures and is the most frequently used method for convulsive therapy. In bilateral ECT, a generalized seizure is induced by passing a current between bitemporal electrodes. Treatments are initially given three times a week, and are reduced to twice a week if amnesia and confusion become prominent. As the post-ECT memory loss with bilateral ECT is directly related to the amount of current delivered, it is advisable to use the lowest treatment apparatus setting that will yield a full grand mal seizure.

Unilateral ECT. In this method, the treatment electrodes are applied to one side of the scalp only, over the nondominant hemisphere, in order to avoid the direct passage of current through the speech and verbal memory areas of the dominant temporal lobe. With adequate current, a generalized seizure is obtained. Post-ECT amnesia and confusion do not occur with nondominant unilateral ECT, and treatments may be given daily or several times a day without the appearance of these troublesome side-effects. The therapeutic effect of unilateral ECT is also less than that for bilateral ECT, and longer courses with unilateral ECT may be required to achieve the usual remission. For some patients, four to six unilateral ECT will induce a full remission, but this is infrequent. More often, recovery will not be complete without the addition of two or three bilateral ECT.

Choice of Unilateral or Bilateral ECT.   The lack of post-treatment confusion and memory loss argues in favor of an initial trial with unilateral ECT whenever possible. If there is no clinical urgency, such as suicidal risk, overactivity or refusal to eat, unilateral ECT may routinely be given an initial trial of four to six treatments, changing to bilateral ECT if significant improvement does not occur. Where time is a factor, as for patients who have a limited number of insurance-paid days in hospital or who must return to their work by a specific time, or when illness severity is marked (e.g., psychosis, suicidal ruminations), it is advisable to initiate treatment with bilateral ECT.

Regressive ECT.   This technique induces a state of temporary dementia by the administration of one to three bilateral ECT each day until total disorientation, urinary and fecal incontinence, dysarthria and the need for spoonfeeding occur. This acute organic brain syndrome is transient, and recovery of cognitive and physiological functioning is complete two to three weeks after the final treatment. Therapeutic outcome in the chronic cases treated is asserted to be superior to that achieved with treatments administered at the standard rate. No controlled study supports this contention, however, and the putative success of regressive ECT may as well be attributed to the increased total number of ECT received as to any induced "regression."

Side-Effects, Precautions and Contraindications

Memory Changes.   The immediate post-ictal confusion is transient and results from the anesthesia, the seizure and the effects of the electric current. For bilateral ECT there is also an anterograde and a retrograde amnesia, with the retrograde amnesia most pronounced for recently learned items and least for those learned in more remote times. The retrograde amnesia results from impairment in the retrieval process and not from interference with stored material. The span of retrograde amnesia shrinks rapidly after a single treatment and is eventually limited to about 30 seconds immediately prior to the seizure, the "consolidation time" for newly registered material. The anterograde amnesia is for events subsequent to the seizure and results from faulty registration of new material. For this reason, it is permanent and accounts for the frequent statement of patients who have received ECT that their hospital stay is "a complete blank." Permanent alterations of the memory process itself do not, however, occur with convulsive therapy, and this has been amply demonstrated over the past thirty years by a variety of investigators.

Nondominant unilateral ECT does not produce any clinically important anterograde or retrograde amnesia, and is followed by a shorter period of post-ictal confusion than occurs in bilateral ECT.

EEG Changes. Induced convulsions reflect the cerebral generalized seizure discharges occurring during treatment and are followed by EEG changes that persist during the interseizure period. These changes are those of slowing, increased amplitude and increased rhythmicity. They appear all over the head and are a function of the number and frequency of seizures, the age of the patient and the location of the treatment electrodes. The EEG abnormalities fade progressively after the final treatment and are unrelated to treatment outcome.

Other Side-effects. With the introduction of succinylcholine muscle-relaxation, fractures are extremely rare, and no special precautions are required. The use of succinylcholine introduces the rare complication of prolonged apnea due to a reduced serum pseudocholinesterase level, probably as a genetic variation. Treatment requires continued artificial respiration, usually with intubation, until whatever pseudocholinesterase is present metabolizes the succinylcholine. If apnea is prolonged beyond 30 minutes, fresh whole blood can be given to provide exogenous pseudocholinesterase.

Nausea and vomiting in the post-ictal phase can be prevented by dimenhydrinate, 50 mg intramuscular at the termination of the seizure.

Organic psychotic reactions to ECT occasionally occur. These paranoid-confusional states arise during the course of treatment and may be misdiagnosed as "uncovered schizophrenia." They usually resolve with continued ECT and are no reason to discontinue treatment. Less commonly, they occur immediately following the last treatment of a series and may then be treated with a brief course of neuroleptics until spontaneous resolution occurs. An EEG taken during the height of these organic paranoid psychoses will show dominant, high-voltage, theta and delta activity.

Contraindications. Caution should be observed when combining convulsive therapy and neuroleptic drugs. As noted above, reserpine should not be administered in combination with convulsive therapy, and it is best to withhold treatment for a week in a patient who has received reserpine or its congeners for the treatment of hypertension.

It is often stated that brain tumor is a contraindication to convulsive therapy. However, a few patients with psychosis secondary to brain tumor have been reported to show psychiatric improvement with ECT without sudden neurological deterioration.

Patients with cardiovascular disease should be treated with caution and their cardiac state carefully defined. The possible deleterious effects of seizures must be weighed against the severe effects of the illness itself in a patient with compromised cardiac status. In such cases, the balance will usually weigh in favor of giving ECT. Cardiovascular conditions are thought to be responsible for the mortality rate with convulsive therapy, but this is quite small, probably less than .001% of treatments given. Successful ECT has been reported for patients with recent myocardial infarction, open-heart surgery and major arterial graft procedures.

Age is no contraindication to treatment, and some of the most rewarding results with convulsive therapy are obtained in the elderly debilitated patients, described above, whose primary affective or paranoid disorder masquerades as senile or arteriosclerotic dementia.

When one is considering indications and contraindications for convulsive therapy, the suicidal potential of the patient must be carefully evaluated. This will often take precedence irrespective of the physical condition. A determined patient may commit suicide despite stringent precautions and constant surveillance. Once ECT is started, however, suicide is extremely rare.

3 Principles of Psychotherapy

Michael S. Aronoff and Stanley Lesse

"Psychotherapy," in Western cultures, has many meanings. It usually refers to a strategy or series of strategies, each of which is supported by an explicitly stated, or implicitly implied, theoretical base. The strategies are designed to bring about changes in attitudes, behaviors and life-styles in a group of self-selected people who experience their "life's problems" in the form of recognizable and identifiable emotional reactions. An assumption underlying all forms of psychotherapy is that human behavior is understandable and alterable. Each particular strategy (or "therapy") takes place within a context involving a designated helper, authority or "therapist."

The different technologies represented by different forms of psychotherapy, therefore, are processes by which one may extend his knowledge of himself (in the context of another person's presence), in an attempt to initiate new behaviors and to incorporate them within one's repertoire. Therapists, regardless of their school of thought, listen for expressions of underlying meaning, which are beyond the patient's awareness. These are embodied in symptoms, thought content and associations, fantasy productions, paraverbal and nonverbal cues, and stylistic variations in presentation. That which follows, by way of corrective, explicative, or readjustment maneuvers, depends upon the basic theoretical model of behavior, personality and etiology of behavioral problems, as well as upon the concept of normalcy, held by the particular therapist.

The range and spectrum of psychotherapies is broad and, at superficial glance quite varied. The psychotherapies are categorized according to underlying theory, primary activity undertaken, or any one of a number of specific structural features of the process, goals desired, or types of problems addressed. The spectrum encompasses psychoanalysis, behavior therapies and group therapies. It includes strategies falling under categories such as client-centered therapy, Gestalt therapy, Adlerian and Jungian therapy, transactional analysis, integrity therapy, reality therapy, logotherapy, milieu therapy, primal therapy, hypnotherapy, desensitization. flooding/implosion therapy, aversion therapy, Morita therapy, biofeedback, meditation, psychodrama, dance therapy, occupational therapy, art therapy, poetry therapy, family therapy, conjoint therapy, encounter groups, self-help groups (e.g., Alcoholics Anonymous, Synanon), and so forth (Wolberg, 1967).

The list seems endless and constantly expanding. Each variety of psychotherapy tends to persist once it has been established. The extent to which each persists, however, often depends upon the current vogue and the proselytizing of its advocates.* It seems that although there may be many schools of psychotherapy, the different types of therapy are limited in number and have certain features in common. Each strategy of psychotherapy begins with a procedure of systematic and sequential observation of behavior. The therapist notes historical material and recurring or persistent patterns in the patient's behavior. He then begins an additional interaction with the patient in order to educate the patient and/or redirect certain attitudes or behavior patterns. The therapist, finally, evaluates the apparent effectiveness of his maneuvers to alter the patient's original response pattern. The entire process requires a "working alliance" between the patient and therapist, involving values such as trust, rapport and reality, and based upon a matrix of expectancies (Zetzel, 1956: Greenson, 1965: Goldstein, 1962).

There are, of course, differences among various schools of psychotherapy, based upon the type of technique used, the nature of the goals, and the mutual expectations of both the practitioner and the patient. The goals may be to focus on a specific symptom, or to attempt to increase self-awareness or to reorganize one's life-style. Various schools of therapy propose different goals which, once designated, are then explicated by certain processes. All psychologic problems may be treated, with varying success, by psychotherapeutic processes.

Therapies, depending upon the setting and the nature of the relationship between practitioner and patient, may be brief, time-limited or open-ended. They may vary with different types of patient, depending upon such diverse factors as socioeconomic background, diagnosis, verbal ability, age, sex, etc. They attract different types of practitioners, and may vary in their public appeal. The activities of different schools of psychotherapy are diverse. However, the question is whether the basic principles underlying the techniques utilized are significantly different.

---

*It sometimes appears as if different schools of psychotherapy are in competition for adherents. Unfortunately, the advocates often are not the practitioners but the patients. The different schools then can lend themselves to the politics of personal ambition, professional competition or cultism.

PROCESSES OCCURRING DURING PSYCHOTHERAPY
AS SEEN BY DIFFERENT THEORISTS

Strupp states that "a primary purpose of psychotherapy is the acquisition of self-control, mastery, competence, and autonomy . . . inner controls are often guided by central processes, such as beliefs, assumptions about oneself and others. many of which are implicit and highly symbolic. One of the tasks of psychotherapy is to make these symbolic processes explicit." (Strupp, 1973, p. 118.) It might be suggested further that, by making certain processes and representations conscious, they are transformed into less powerful guiding forces that permit the patient greater flexibility in his choice of modes of interaction while attempting to increase his adaptational capacities.

There are, of course, alternative metaphors available for the conceptualization of the processes and goals of psychotherapy. From an adaptational point of view, emotional disorders might be thought of in terms of a disorder in the homeostatic regulation of psychic equilibrium and integration, with faulty feedback loops resulting from distorted central guiding processes or the faulty assimilation of images, affects and thoughts. The goal of psychotherapy, from this vantage point, is the readjustment of the feedback loops. Different methods or processes for obtaining this goal (e.g., insight, imitation, direct retraining) represent possible distinguishing points among the different therapeutic strategies.

Frank (1974) has recently written that the primary function of all psychotherapies is to combat "demoralization." He proposes that anxiety and depression are derivative reactions to this demoralization. Earlier, Frank (1961) was one of the first to emphasize a central role of "persuasion" in all successful psychotherapies. Haley (1963) subsequently emphasized the struggle for control between therapist and patient which is acted out in the communicative interaction between the two, and which the therapist must win for the psychotherapeutic transaction to be successful. Within this framework, the therapist responds to the patient's behavior in a double-binding way, thereby forcing the patient, if he is to continue his relationship with the therapist, to change his mode of interaction.

Orne (1962) also emphasized the importance of the techniques of persuasion and covert coersion in the psychotherapeutic situation — a "persuasion" or control that may be delivered in varying gradations of directness and activity. Bibring and Freud, although they thought that persuasion is a necessary component underlying factors which lead to clinical change in the psychotherapeutic situation, did not believe it to be of so fundamental importance. For, although in psychoanalysis indirect suggestion occurs at all levels of the interaction between patient and practitioner, the resultant insight gained must be applied actively in ongoing situations in the patient's life. In the use of this insight, a new affect is experienced which then offers different controlling properties. What results then, may be a sense of conviction, permitting access to new behaviors, and perhaps, new rewards.

Abroms (1968) takes issue with any theory implying that psychotherapy heals primarily by persuasion. He states that this view does not represent an empirical hypothesis and that neither persuasion nor insight are at the core of healing. Both, instead, provide a stage-setting by means of which new functional linkages can be established which would then lead to the incorporation of behavior changes. For example, in psychoanalysis this is performed via the process of working through, and in certain behavioral therapies via systematic desensitization.

The goal of psychoanalysis is structural personality change. This refers to internal personality change such as the removal of particular defenses, or the conversion of defense mechanisms to coping mechanisms (e.g., intellectualization becoming intellectuality). The goal is not symptomatic change nor the rechanneling of conflicts (e.g., via displacement). Structural change, however, is inferred and not actually experienced as a specific process. This is presumed to be achieved through insight into transferences and resistances, and genetic (or historical) reconstruction of previous inputs to one's behavioral repertoire. Other schools of psychotherapy argue that this type of theory and therapeutic procedure is unnecessary. They believe that a narrower focus of attention can lead to broader gains through stimulus generalization.

The analyst offers himself as a consistent object with a consistent attitude toward the patient. What hopefully results is a secure situation in which the patient has to *tell* rather than *do* things. Then the practitioner can deal with the inherent meanings of the verbal (and nonverbal) presentations. Interpretations are used to further the analytic situation and to stimulate the formation of insight. The analyst neither condemns nor encourages, but highlights certain recurrent patterns. This focusing is thought to encourage insight which then hopefully leads to the desired structural change.

The goals and processes of psychoanalytically-oriented psychotherapy are somewhat different from those of classical psychoanalysis (Rangell, 1954). The assumption that behavioral symptoms are the resultant distillate of an internal conflict remains the same. Here, however, therapeutic tasks include the strengthening of defenses and the clarification of the transference, alerting the patient to individual displacements and classes of misidentifications. The "transference cure" may be the means by which the patient may institute constructive life changes. In this instance, regressive defenses, based on unconscious dependent connections in the form of the so-called magical transference, now substitute for the more pathological defenses previously operative.

Various types of behavior therapy, including logotherapy, employ maneuvers of counter-conditioning using principles of: 1) reciprocal inhibition (the systematic utilization of responses that are inimical to anxiety in the presence of anxiety-producing stimuli), 2) operant conditioning (rewarding the consequences of certain behaviors), and 3) aversive conditioning (punishing the consequences of certain behaviors and thereby attempting to supply a stronger alternative countermotive). "Flooding," as found in implosion therapy, the use of paradoxical intention, and the catharses of psychodrama and primal therapy, operate through the mechanism of sudden and protracted confrontation with an anxiety-provoking stimulus presented in a supportive setting. The suddenness and intensity of the presentation is what distinguishes flooding from desensitization and from the more prolonged procedure of extinction.

Existential therapy offers still another apparently different approach. Existential therapists do not deal with isolated components of behavior. In fact, they do not deal with "health" or "adaptation," but rather with "authenticity." They purportedly take things "as they are" without reducing them to underlying theoretical construction. Gestalt and transactional analysis therapies, in somewhat related traditions, develop tactics to uncover fixed, stereotyped interpersonal interactions ("games") and attempt to free impounded feelings by the use of "play" as an exercise in trying out new roles.

PROCESSES COMMON TO MOST PSYCHOTHERAPIES

Discussion, explanation, relaxation, exploration, catharsis, support, and drawing connections between internal experiences and external events or responses are techniques employed in different psychotherapies. These interactive techniques are then related to the "nonspecific" effects of the psychotherapies (for instance, mood change) which occur in addition to the general aim of supplying the patient with an organized system for self-understanding and control. How these various processes are conceptualized and utilized leads to the variations involved in the different therapeutic methodologies and their associated descriptive metaphors. While the metaphors associated with the various therapies often reflect the bias of the particular advocate or practitioner, in reality the procedures may not differ significantly from each other. In fact, the stimulus properties of the setting of each form of psychotherapeutic technology may represent variations on a common theme.

One of the factors common to all psychotherapies is the patient's explicit or implicit desire for help. The procedures are conceived of as being voluntary and based on a mutuality of goals. Each form of therapy, in one way or another, explores the beginnings and the extent of the disorder for which the patient seeks help. They all attempt to establish a helping situation with a therapist and, in fact, utilize active processes by which the therapist engages and involves the patient in a working relationship. Thereby, a therapeutic alliance is actively, although perhaps not fully consciously, begun. This is accomplished by history-taking, evaluation, and the completion of a diagnostic process. The therapist then attempts to stimulate the development of new learning and/or a new behavior pattern.

The prerequisites for the establishment of an effective therapeutic setting include a permissive, relaxed sanctuary in which a societally-sanctioned therapist has the trust and confidence of the help-seeker because of his competence and his demonstration of interest and understanding. The therapist, employing a theoretical construct to explain the patient's problems, determines what therapeutic techniques are to be employed. He then creates a therapeutic aura which includes positive expectations. He points out the possibility of a larger spectrum of adaptive options available to the patient, and provides an environment in which "secrets" may be revealed, distorted perceptions may be corrected and symptoms may be ameliorated. In addition, a sense of mastery and restoration of order may be experienced, new perspectives can be attained, and more mature behavior can be practiced.

Eclectic therapists use different maneuvers at different stages during the evolution of a patient's treatment, and their choice of technologies is guided, in part, by the patient's needs and responsiveness. Hopefully each strategic variation has a rational basis and is well-directed. Certainly each strategy is dependent in part upon the cultural role assigned to the various therapies (Frank, 1959) and the mutual expectations held by both the patient and the therapist (Goldstein, 1962; Frank, 1968). Bromberg (1965) stated that the "underlying precontent premises of the therapist and patient" are the basic part of the therapeutic relationship. He hypothesized that they preceded the development of transference or countertransference issues within a developing therapeutic situation. With this in mind, the psychotherapies could be viewed as a psychological means of "influence" with a trusting relationship with a designated therapist acting as an impetus for change.

Bibring (1954) has described a hierarchy of operations which the practitioner uses to induce change in the intensive therapies which are designed to restructure mental contents (e.g., altering symbolic frames of reference, freeing impounded affects). These include suggestion, abreaction, manipulation, and clarification and interpretation. Transactional therapists hold that what occurs in therapy is the exchange of persuasive messages (i.e., "suggestion" is the common denominator of different therapies). "Abreaction," in which an affective experience is evoked by proxy (e.g., in encounter groups, primal therapy, child play) has played major roles in some religious cures, aspects of psychodrama and family therapy, aspects of hypnotherapy, and in narcosynthesis previously used in the treatment of war neuroses. "Manipulation" refers to learning from experience, where a new experience is presented to a patient in order to provide him with a different self- and world perspective. This is involved in corrective-emotional-experiences, behavioral modification therapy, client-centered and milieu therapies, and group therapies. Learning from experience is not necessarily the agent for change, however, and it remains to be seen to what extent a verbal statement itself may become an agent of change or solution of a problem. "Clarification" and "interpretation" both represent steps in the explanation to the patient of things about which he is unaware. Clarification attempts to make the patient aware of how he appears to others. Interpretation attempts to tie in the forgotten past with the now-clarified present. The aim of both is to broaden understanding. They form the basis of therapy which uses insight as a means to change. All five of these operations are used, to a greater or lesser extent, in the treatment of a broad spectrum of patients, with or without the adjunctive use of organic and pharmacologic regimens.

We can say, in summary, that "psychotherapy" is not one particular, unitary process (Strupp, 1973). One determinant of the degree of balance among the various operations within a particular psychotherapeutic strategy, or of the use of that particular form of strategy in the first place, is the evaluation of the role played by intrapsychic defense versus intrapsychic defect (i.e., distortions in cognitive-perceptual systems based on motivational factors versus constitutional factors) in the development and support of a patient's symptom-complex. Every form of psychotherapy seems to have an underlying, at times, unspecified, theory of personality. This theory serves at least two functions. It determines, in part, how the therapist will view the development and integration of behavior. It will also serve as the rationale from which his therapeutic interventions spring. Ideally, his therapy meshes with his theory. Here, we are bypassing the personality-theory matrices in which different psychotherapies are embedded, to look cross-sectionally at the phenomena involved in the structured psychotherapies.

FACTORS UNDERLYING APPARENT DIFFERENCES AMONG THE VARIOUS PSYCHOTHERAPIES

Differences among what psychotherapists do, within the context of different theoretical approaches, include variations on the themes of: 1) methods (e.g., free association and the interpretation of dreams as compared with systematic relaxation and desensitization); 2) aims (e.g., that of psychoanalysis involving the restructuring of personality via the resolution of the transference neurosis and emphasis on understanding the unconscious determinants of behavior, as compared with focusing more on overt behavior, symptoms and the reality situation of the patient); and 3) kinds of results sought (e.g., reconstructive results as compared with improvement in symptoms, as a measure of progress).

Differences among the different psychotherapies may be more quantitative than qualitative. Emphasis can be directed toward rational or irrational operations, and unconscious factors may be stressed or ignored. Varying degrees of emphasis may be placed upon psychological understanding, ideals, attitudes, or on interpersonal relations. Various aspects of the particular psychotherapeutic procedure (e.g., introduction, engagement, conclusion) may be modified; time commitments, financial arrangements, and the structuring and demand characistics (Orne, 1962) of the therapeutic situation may all be altered and have their own accompanying rationale and putative therapeutic impact. Procedures may be continued beyond the point of symptomatic relief because of belief that: 1) better results will be obtained with the patient then able to resume his own growth; 2) the symptoms *per se* are not the prime problem; and 3) retrogressive displacements, in the form of symptom substitution, will be avoided.

In terms of specific techniques and processes, there are different degrees to which and modes by which different therapists attempt to restructure the cognitive representations of their patients. For instance, emphasis may be placed on the "real" relationships with therapist and on environmental influences, with the explicit encouragement of specific behaviors and a replication of an aspect of the environment for role playing. Alternatively, the transference relationship may be emphasized with the "analysis" of transference and resistance assuming the larger operative role, as opposed to the "use" of the transference solely as a tool. Other examples of different areas where technical focus and thrust may vary among different therapeutic strategies include the extent to which feelings accompanying change are examined, the degree of uncovering done with respect to developmental distortions, and the particular emotional tone chosen to be created within the psychotherapeutic situation. All of these factors are found, however, in the procedures performed by all therapists. Additionally, each therapist evaluates various adjunctive maneuvers for use, based on a number of factors including the following: the interplay among the structural qualities of the particular form of psychotherapy, the patient's expectations, and the patient's ability to use emotionality and verbal communication; the particular area(s) of psychopathology to be worked with; the level of patient sophistication, development and need; and the ability of the patient to work with the therapist at multiple levels, such as real/fantasy, conscious/unconscious, ego-observing/fantasy-participating (G.A.P. Report, 1969). The majority of psychotherapies emphasize the central role of the interpersonal relationship (Snyder, 1961; Murray, 1963) but the specific characteristics of the factors supporting this phenomenon remain to be elucidated.

The differences among the various forms of psychotherapies, with their resultant outcomes, are contingent upon the factors just mentioned, but should also be viewed in terms of the qualities of the patient and the therapist as individuals and as a working, interdigitating team (Singer, 1965; Meltzoff and Kornreich, 1970; Weisskopf-Joelson, 1968). Existentialists such as Buber and Rogers view the therapist as an "authentic presence" in the therapeutic encounter. The role of the therapist in strategies emphasizing learning paradigm is that of a shaper and supervisor. The qualities present in an effective therapist include judgmental and clinical skills, the ability to instill hope, to encourage relaxation, and to provide a warm, tolerant and receptively responsive atmosphere. Most theorists emphasize the importance of the therapist's capacity for empathy and responsiveness (Brady, 1968). A situation is set up whereby the therapist provides a model for imitating as well as participating in the direct retraining or shaping of behavioral responses. But these previously mentioned factors are also very much a part of any doctor-patient relationship.

In its broadest application, psychotherapy refers to an interaction and interrelationship among individual psychodynamics, interactional dynamics, and sociodynamics. In order to be an effective therapist, particularly within a rapidly changing societal matrix, one must be aware of these components and their relationship to each other. One of the thrusts of the administrative strategy called community psychiatry is to make interaction between psychotherapeutic issues of symptom, conflict and ego capacity, on one hand, and environmental inputs on the other, more explicit and substantive in the therapeutic strategy.

EFFECTIVENESS OF PSYCHOTHERAPY

How then is one to organize one's thinking about the different forms of therapy? How is one to judge the efficacy of differing procedures and the validity of the differing claims of various advocates? Meltzoff and Kornreich (1970), using a broad definition of what constitutes psychotherapy, amply document the effectiveness of such procedures in terms of outcome. However, the criterion of outcome with its subcategories of symptomatic and adjustment improvement, and the relative lack of specificity of patient populations treated, create problems in evaluating different therapeutic regimes. Certainly not all therapists can treat all patients and not all forms of therapy are acceptable to all cultures or subcultures.

Luborsky (1972) has reviewed published studies of the effects of various psychotherapies on adult, mainly nonpsychotic, patients in controlled comparative studies. His findings are as follows: a) in twelve studies comparing individual psychotherapy with group psychotherapy, similar gains were reported for each type: b) seven studies comparing time-limited versus unlimited individual psychotherapy reported similar gains for each; c) in a review of eleven studies evaluating the outcome of psychotherapy as practiced by different traditional schools (e.g., psychoanalysis, client-centered therapy, Adlerian therapy), Luborsky reported that both data and controls in any one category were insufficient to draw conclusions about a particular form of therapy (although there was evidence suggesting that different schools of psychotherapy may provide different benefits for different patients); d) in twelve studies reviewed with respect to the comparison of individual psychotherapy with behavior therapy (excluding treatment of specific "habit" disturbances), if sufficient treatment time was allowed, there seemed to be no significant difference in the benefits to patients between these two forms of therapy. The only exceptions seem to be for mild and circumscribed phobias and agoraphobia, in which desensitization or implosion is better (Bandura, 1971; Boulgouris et al, 1971); e) in thirty-five studies comparing psychotherapy and pharmacotherapy in nonschizophrenic patients, pharmacotherapy was judged better than psychotherapy, and both of them together was better than either psychotherapy or pharmacotherapy alone. The studies with schizophrenic patients show that pharmacotherapy leads to more indicators of improvement than psychotherapy alone; f) in ten studies comparing psychotherapy with other treatments for psychosomatic conditions, all showed overwhelming support for the effectiveness of psychotherapy (with or without attendant medical regimes). Luborsky's conclusions are that; 1) a high proportion of patients who go through therapies make gains (exclusive of psychosomatic conditions and situations utilizing pharmacotherapy); 2) generally, the type of patient probably makes more difference than the type or form of psychotherapy; and 3) although rates of improvement may be similar for different types of therapy, what is considered to be the criteria of improvement may not necessarily be the same.

Exclusive of psychosis, psychosomatic disorders, and perhaps severe character disorders, it would seem that outcome differences for different forms of therapy are more related to the qualities of the therapist and the patient, separately and together.   Circumscribed phobias and agoraphobia may be exceptions to this conclusion.   In its monograph on psychotherapy (1969), the Group for the Advancement of Psychiatry delineates certain assumptions felt to be implicit in all psychotherapies: a) distress and deviancy can and should be ameliorated; b) learning plays a role in the development of a patient's disturbance; c) this disturbance is amenable to relearning; d) the human relationship, within the therapeutic situation, is an important effector; e) training can improve the necessary abilities of both the therapist and the patient; and f) processes within the therapeutic situation are lawful, however differently they may be conceptualized.   They go on to suggest a series of continua along which various processes of the therapeutic operation may be seen to vary when compared cross-sectionally among different strategies of therapy.   These are trusting-mistrusting, gratifying-frustrating, revealing-concealing, encouraging fantasy-testing reality, regressing-progressing, and reliving-new experiencing.

Other studies of outcome, as mentioned before, with attendant problems of criteria, control, patient selection and theoretical bias, have reported varying results. Those without a specific cross to bear clearly suggest the effectiveness of psychotherapeutic interventions. We would emphasize that psychotherapy is an effective series of strategies, the specific details of which remain to be delineated. Some theories emphasize the "nonspecific" features of different forms of psychotherapy to account for their effectiveness. Obviously "nonspecific" means not-yet-specifiable or not-yet-particularized.   Certainly the subtlety of the interaction and the elusiveness of the factors supporting the interaction do not make the factors involved in psychotherapy "nonspecific."

A further problem in the understanding of the complexity of the factors involved in the psychotherapeutic interaction which may initiate and support behavioral change, is that multiple levels of discourse are used to talk about observed process — from the holistic, man-in-action, I-thou perspectives to the close scrutiny and microdissection of operantly reinforced verbal and nonverbal behaviors.   The various approaches to psychotherapy not only offer different specific technologies, but also offer different metaphoric formulations of what might be a similar underlying interpersonal process.   In any case, Luborsky's findings provide the basis for looking at similarities and differences cross-sectionally among different psychotherapies and for relating such observations to the empirical evidence, in terms of outcome. It would seem that the "schools" of psychotherapy, *per se,* are not essential features important to outcome. Instead, "outcome" may be related to other factors, alluded to but not as yet sufficiently explained.

REFERENCES

Abroms, G.M. Persuasion in psychotherapy. *Amer. J. Psychiat.* **124** : 1214 (1968).

Aronson, H. and Weintraub, W. Certain initial variables as predictors of change with classical psychoanalysis. *J. Abn. Psychol.* **74** : 103 (1969).

Bailey, K.G. and Sowder, W.T. Audiotape and videotape self-confrontation in psychotherapy. *Psychol. Bull.* **58** : 143 (1961).

Bandura, A. Psychotherapy as a learning process. *Psychol. Bull.* **58** : 143 (1961).

Bandura, A. Psychotherapy based upon modeling principles. In : Bergin, A.E. and Garfield, S.L. (Eds.), *Handbook of Psychotherapy and Behavior Change,* Wiley, New York, 1971.

Begley, C.E. and Lieberman, L.R. Patients: expectations of therapists' techniques. *J. Clin. Psychol.* **26** : 113 (1970).

Benfari, R.C. Relationship between early dependency training and patient-therapist dyad. *Psychol. Rep.* **25** : 552 (1969).

Bergin, A.E. and Garfield, S.L. (Eds.) *Handbook of Psychotherapy and Behavior Change, An Empirical Analysis.* Wiley, New York, 1971.

Betz, B. Validation of the differential treatment success of "A" and "B" therapists with schizophrenic patients. *Amer. J. Psychiat.* **119** : 883 (1963).

Bibring, E. Psychoanalysis and the dynamic psychotherapies. *J. Amer. Psa. Assoc.* **2** : 745 (1954).

Bierman, R. Dimensions of interpersonal facilitation in psychotherapy and child development. *Psychol. Bull.* **72** : 338 (1969).

Birdwhistell, R.L. *Kinetics and Context: Essays on Body Motion and Communication.* University of Pennsylvania Press, Philadelphia, 1970.

Boulgouris, J.C., Marks, I.M. and Marset, P. Superiority of flooding (implosion) to desensitization for reducing pathological fear. *Behav. Res. Ther.* **9** : 7 (1971).

Boulware, D.W. and Holmes, D.S. Preferences for therapists and related expectancies. *J. Consult. Clin. Psychol.* **35** : 269 (1970).

Brady, J.P. Psychotherapy by a combined behavioral and dynamic approach. *Comp. Psychiat.* **9** : 536 (1968).

Bromberg, W. The nature of psychotherapy. *Trans. N.Y. Acad. Sci.* **28** : 102 (1965).

Bruche, H. Activity in the psychotherapeutic process. *Current Psych. Therapies* **2** : 69 (1962).

Cahoon, D.D. Symptom substitution and the behavior therapies: a reappraisal. *Psychol. Bull.* **69** : 149 (1968).

Caracena, P.F. and Vicory, J.R. Correlates of phenomenological and judged empathy. *J. Couns. Psychol.* **16** : 510 (1969).

Chartier, G.M. A-B therapist variable: real or imagined? *Psychol. Bull.* **75** : 22 (1971).

Chessick, R.D.   Psychotherapeutic interaction. *Amer. J. Psychother.*   28 : 243 (1974).

Collingwood, T., Hefele, T.J. Muehlberg, N. and Drasgow, J.   Toward identification of the therapeutically facilitative factor. *J. Clin. Psychol.*   26 : 119, (1970).

Cross, H.   The outcome of psychotherapy: a selected analysis of research findings. *J. Consult. Psychol.*   28 : 413 (1964).

Dewald, P.A.   The clinical assessment of structural change. *J. Amer. Psa. Assoc.*   20 : 302 (1972).

Dyrud, J.E. and Holzman, P.S.   The psychotherapy of schizophrenia: does it work?   *Amer. J. Psychiat.*   130 : 670 (1973).

Ellis, A.   Requisite conditions for basic personality change. *J. Counsel. Psychol.*   23 : 538 (1959).

Eron, L.D. and Callahan, R. (Eds.)   *The Relationship of Theory to Practice in Psychotherapy.*   Aldine, Chicago, 1970.

Fiedler, F.   Factor analyses of psychoanalytic, nondirective and Adlerian therapeutic relationships. *J. Consult. Psychol.*   15 : 32 (1951).

Fiske, D.   Strategies in the search for personality changes.   *J. Exp. Res. in Personal.*   5 : 323 (1971).

Forizs, L.   Some common denominators in psychotherapeutic modalities.   *Dis. Nerv. Syst.*   27 : 783 (1966).

Frank, J.D.   The dynamics of the psychotherapeutic relationship. *Psychiatry.*   22 : 17 (1959).

Frank, J.D.   *Persuasion and Healing: A Comparative Study of Psychotherapy.*   Johns-Hopkins Press, Baltimore, 1961.

Frank, J.D.   Therapeutic factors in psychotherapy. *Amer. J. Psychiat.*   131 : 271 (1974).

Frank, J.D.   Psychotherapy: the restoration of morale. *Amer. J. Psychiat.*   131 : 271 (1974).

Frankl, V.E.   Paradoxical intention: a logotherapeutic technique. *Amer. J. Psychother.*   14: 520 (1960).

Friedman, P.   Limitations in the conceptualization of behavior therapists: toward a cognitive-behavioral model of behavior therapy. *Psychol. Rep.*   27 : 175 (1970).

Fromm-Reichman, F.   *Principles of Intensive Psychotherapy.*   University of Chicago Press, Chicago, 1950.

Gallagher, E., Sharaf, M. and Levinson, D.   The influence of patient and therapist in determining the use of psychotherapy in a hospital setting. *Psychiatry.*   28: 297 (1965).

G.A.P. Report (Group for the Advancement of Psychiatry), Psychotherapy and the dual research tradition, Volume 7 (#73), October, 1969.

Gardner, G.G.   The psychotherapeutic relationship. *Psychol. Bull.*   61 : 426 (1964).

Garduk, E.L. and Haggard, E.A.   Immediate effects on patients of psychoanalytic interpretations. *Psychol. Issues,* Vol. 7, Monograph 28, 1972.

Garfield, S.L. and Bergin, A.E.   Therapeutic conditions and outcome. *J. Abn. Psychol.*   77: 108 (1971).

Goldman, R.J. and Mendelsohn, G.A.   Psychotherapeutic change and social adjustment: a report of a national survey of psychotherapists. *J. Abn. Psychol.*   **74** : 164 (1969).

Goldstein, A.P.   *Therapist-Patient Expectancies in Psychotherapy.*   MacMillan, New York, 1962.

Goldstein, A.P.   *Psychotherapeutic Attraction.*   Pergamon Press, Elmsford, N.Y., 1971.

Greenson, R.R.   The working alliance and the transference neurosis. *Psychoanalytic Quart.*   **34** : 155 (1965).

Gunderson, J.C.   Controversies about the psychotherapy of schizophrenia. *Amer. J. Psychiat.*   **130** : 677 (1973).

Haley, J.   *Strategies of Psychotherapy.*   Grune and Stratton, New York, 1963.

Harway, N.I. and Iker, H.P.   Content analysis and psychotherapy. *Psychother. Theory Res. Pract.*   **6** : 97 (1969).

Hertel, R.K.   Application of stochastic process analyses to the study of psychotherapeutic processes. *Psychol. Bull.*   **77** : 421 (1972).

Hill, J.A.   Therapist goals, patient aims and patient satisfaction in psychotherapy. *J. Clin. Psychol.*   **25** : 455 (1969).

Hoehn-Saric, R., *et al.*   Systematic preparation of patient for psychotherapy: I and II. *J. Psychiat. Res.*   **2** : 267 (1964).

Honigfeld, G.   Nonspecific factors in treatment. *Dis. Nerv. Syst.*   **25** : 145 (1964).

Houts, P.S., MacIntosh, S. and Moos, R.H.   Patient-therapist interdependence: cognitive and behavioral. *J. Consult. Clin. Psychol.*   **33** : 40 (1969).

Karush, A.   Working through. *Psychoanalyt. Quart.*   **36:**   497 (1967).

Kelley, J., Smits, S.J., Leventhal, R. and Rhodes, R.   Critique of the designs of process and outcome research. *J. Couns. Psychol.*   **17** : 337 (1970).

Kiesler, D.   Some myths of psychotherapy research and the search for a paradigm. *Psychol. Bull.*   **65** : 110 (1966).

Knupfer, G., Jackson, D.D. and Krieger, G.   Personality differences between more and less competent psychotherapists as a function of criteria of competence. *J. Nerv. Ment. Dis.*   **129** : 375 (1959).

Lazarus, A.A.   Behavioral rehearsal vs nondirective therapy vs advice in effecting behavioral change. *Behav. and Ther.*   **4** : 209 (1966).

Lennard, H.L. and Bernstein, A.   *The Anatomy of Psychotherapy.*   Columbia University Press, New York, 1960.

Lorion, R.P.   Socioeconomic status and traditional treatment approaches reconsidered. *Psychol. Bull.*   **79** : 263 (1973).

Lorr, M., *et al.*   Frequency of treatment and change in psychotherapy. *J. Abn. Soc. Psychol.*   **64** : 281 (1962).

Luborsky, L.   Comparative studies of psychotherapies — is it true that everybody has won and all must have prizes?   Paper presented at 3rd Ann. Mtg. of Soc. for Psychother. Res., June 6, 1972, Nashville.

Luborsky, L., *et al.*   Factors influencing the outcome of psychotherapy: a review of quantitative research. *Psychol. Bull.*   **75** : 145 (1971).

Malan, D.H.   The outcome problem in psychotherapy research. *Arch. Gen. Psychiat.*   **29** : 719 (1973).

Meltzoff, J. and Kornreich, M.   *Research in Psychotherapy.*   Atherton Press, New York, 1970.

Miller, R.L. and Bloomberg, L.I.   No therapy as a method of psychotherapy. *Psychother. Theory Res. Pract.* **6** : 49 (1969).

Moos, R.H. and MacIntoch, S.   Multivariate study of the patient-therapist system. *J. Consult. Clin. Psychol.* **35** : 298 (1970).

Murray, E.J.   Learning theory and psychotherapy: biotropic vs sociotropic approaches. *J. Counsel. Psychol.* **10** : 250 (1963).

Nacht, S.   The curative factor in psychoanalysis. *Int. J. Psa.* **43** : 206 (1962).

Nurnberger, J.I. and Hingtgen, J.N.   Is symptom substitution an important issue in behavior therapy? *Biol. Psychiat.* **7** : 221 (1973).

Offenkrantz, W.   Psychoanalytic psychotherapy. *Arch. Gen. Psychiat.* **30** : 593 (1974).

Orne, M.   Implications for psychotherapy as derived from current research on the nature of hypnosis, *Amer. J. Psychiat.* **118** : 1097 (1962).

Parsons, T.   On the concept of influence. *Publ. Opin. Quart.* **27** : 44 (1963).

Patton, M.J.   Attraction, discrepancy and response to psychological treatment. *J. Couns. Psychol.* **16** : 317 (1969).

Piper, W.E. and Wogan, M.   Placebo effect in psychotherapy. *J. Consult. Clin. Psychol.* **34** : 447 (1970).

Rangell, L.   Similarities and differences between psychoanalysis and dynamic psychotherapy. *J. Amer. Psa. Assoc.* **2** : 734 (1954).

Sargent, H.D.   Intrapsychic change: methodological problems in psychotherapy research. *Psychiatry.* **24** : 93 (1961).

Schacter, S.   *The Psychology of Affiliation.*   Stanford University Press, Palo Alto, 1959.

Singer, E.   *Key Concepts in Psychotherapy.*   Random House, New York, 1965,

Snyder, W.U.   *The Psychotherapy Relationship.*   MacMillan, New York, 1961.

Strupp, H.H.   *Psychotherapy, Clinical Research and Clinical Issues.*   1973.

Strupp, H.H.   On the technology of psychotherapy. *Arch. Gen. Psychiat.* **26** : 234 (1972).

Strupp, H.H. and Bergin, A.E.   Some empirical and conceptual bases for coordinated research in psychotherapy. *Int. J. Psychiat.* **7** : 2 (1969); and critical evaluations of "Some empirical and conceptual bases for coordinated research in psychotherapy." **7** : 3 (1969).

Strupp, H.H. and Williams, J.V.   Some determinants of clinical evaluations of different psychiatrists. *Arch. Gen. Psychiat.* **2** : 434 (1966).

Suomi, S.J., Harlow, H.F. and McKinney, W.T.   Monkey psychiatrists. *Amer. J. Psychiat.* **128** : 927 (1972).

Tower, L.   Countertransference. *J. Amer. Psa. Assoc.* **4** : 224 (1956).

Truax, C.B., *et al.*   Effects of therapist persuasive potency in individual psychotherapy. *J. Clin. Psychol.* **24** : 359 (1968).

Wallach, M.S. and Strupp, H.H.   Dimensions of psychotherapeutic activity. *J. Consult. Psychol.* **28** : 120 (1964).

Wallerstein, R.S.   The problem of assessment of change in psychotherapy. *Int. J. Psa.* **44** : 31 (1963).

Weiss, J.   The emergence of new themes: a contribution to the psychoanalytic theory of therapy. *Int. J. Psa.* **52** : 459 (1971).

Weisskopf-Joelson, E.   The present crisis in psychotherapy. *J. of Psychol.* **69** : 107 (1968).

Wolberg, L.R. *The Technique of Psychotherapy.*   Volumes I and II, Grune and Stratton, New York, 1967.

Wolberg, L.R.   Contemporary problems in psychotherapy. *Canad. Psychiat. Assoc. J.*   **16** : 387 (1971).

Wolff, H.H.   The therapeutic and developmental functions of psychotherapy. *Brit. J. Med. Psychol.*   **44** : 117 (1971).

Wolpe, J., Brady, J.P., Serber, M., Agras, W.S. and Liberman, R.P.   The current status of systematic desensitization. *Amer. J. Psychiat.*   **130** : 961 (1973).

Yeats, A.J.   Symptoms and symptom substitution, *Psychol. Rev.*   **65** : 371 (1958).

Zetzel, E.   Current concepts of transference. *Int. J. Psa.*   **37** : 369 (1956).

Zuk, G.H.   Family therapy during 1964 – 1970. *Psychother. Theory Res. Pract.* **8** : 90 (1971).

4 Psychoanalytic Technique

Gertrude Blanck

Freud's monumental discoveries have captured the interest of many who hitherto felt baffled by the intricacies of the mind. Some, whose defenses became mobilized, were forced to reject the new science altogether; others first seized upon it as messianic, but later reached a predictable moment when overidealization and grandiose expectation led to disappointment. The former group never accepted psychoanalysis as a science; the latter became its detractors. There remained, fortunately, a third group who welcomed psychoanalysis and who became the hard-working scientists who studied Freud's work the better to be able to extend, elaborate and build upon it. Especially in the current era of theory construction we are indebted to the ego psychologists — Hartmann, Kris, Loewenstein, Anna Freud, Greenacre, Mahler, Jacobson and Spitz — who, as gifted and serious thinkers, ventured beyond the master to explore new ground, thereby providing a body of knowledge unsurpassed as a psychology of normality and pathology.

Psychoanalysis is tripartite — a theory of human behavior, a research tool and a therapy. While this discussion will be restricted to the technique of psychoanalysis, i.e., to that aspect which represents psychoanalysis as a therapy, technique can only exist as a valid treatment procedure when it is solidly based on conceptual ground. To begin, therefore, some historical notes about psychoanalytic theory are in order. Rapaport (1959) divided psychoanalytic theory into four historical eras. "The *first phase* of the history of psychoanalytic ego psychology coincides with Freud's prepsychoanalytic theory; it ends with 1897, the approximate beginning of psychoanalysis proper (Freud, 1887-1902, pp. 215-218). The *second phase*, which ends in 1923, is the development of psychoanalysis proper. The *third phase* begins with the publication of *The Ego and the Id* (1923), and encompasses the development of Freud's psychology, which extends to 1937. The *fourth phase* begins with the crucial writings of Anna Freud (1936), Hartmann (1939), Erikson (1937), Horney (1937), Kardiner (1939), Sullivan (1938,1940) and extends to the present day. The general psychoanalytic psychology of the ego based on the foundations laid by Freud began to evolve in this phase (p. 6)."

This brief historical survey will aid in the understanding of how technique follows theory and will help to indicate which techniques are still pertinent to modern practice, which have been superseded, as well as which have had to be added by the dictates of contemporary theory. The final discussion will show how technique appears on the frontier, that is, as current theory provides rationale for approaches to the formerly baffling pathology of the borderline and narcissistic states. Psychoanalysis as a treatment modality nevertheless remains the treatment of choice for neurosis, and the main burden of this description of technique refers, therefore, to the neuroses.

It is well known that Freud's first technical tool was hypnosis. While he abandoned this technique early, for reasons which shall be explained shortly, it is interesting to observe how some of the "new" nonanalytic procedures involve several which Freudians no longer employ. These include, in addition to hypnosis, suggestion, ventilation, abreaction, and confrontation, among others. They appear and reappear periodically in different guises, such as the variations of conditioning, behavior modification, primal therapy and the like, but in their essence, they represent elaborations on the same themes. Freud began as he did because he thought at first of all pathology as hysteria and of all defense as repression. The ego, in his early definition, was the conscious part of the mental apparatus. Hysteria was the illness resulting from repression of a sexual (usually incestuous) fantasy. He used hypnosis to retrieve the repressed memory in order to make it conscious, that is, to unite it with the rest of the ego, then regarded as already conscious. He later found hypnosis to be ineffective for reasons which only became fully clear when he formulated the structural theory in 1923. By then he knew that not all of the ego is conscious and not all defense is repression. The structural theory explains more fully why hypnosis, suggestion and their modern variations are not theoretically tenable. Simply stated, the theoretical fallacy is that they bypass the ego. The synthetic function (Nunberg, 1931) and the defensive function (A. Freud, 1966) are inoperative in such technique, as are other ego functions. Insight cannot be gained when the ego, the very instrument for its attainment, is bypassed. Without interpretation of defenses they remain intact; countercathexis may even become intensified as behavior is altered; symptoms may take another form and even the character structure may be invaded. Thus, not only is there no cure, but there even exists the danger that pathology may be exacerbated.

These matters are stressed in order to dramatize the importance of the structural theory, the new direction it provided for technique and, particularly, to emphasize that poststructural-theory techniques differ markedly from those which, in the prestructural era, were thought to be effective. The structural theory also provided a new direction for theory building. Its impetus continues to carry theory forward to this day and, predictably, beyond. Shortly after proposing the structural theory, Freud (1959) revised his theory of anxiety, now regarding anxiety as the affective consequence of conflict with which the ego has to deal. This states simply the concept of intersystemic conflict, a theoretical cornerstone upon which traditional psychoanalytic technique is based. Neurosis is, by definition, a pathological solution to the oedipal conflict, arrived at by an ego which employs defenses against anxiety and guilt produced by tension between ego and id or superego and id or superego and ego. Compromise is reached between these conflicting institutions, resulting in symptom formation or, if ego syntonic, in character alteration. Traditionally, therefore, analysis has as its purpose dealing with defense (analysis of resistance) on the one side of the compromise, and uncovering the id wish (making the unconscious conscious) on the other side. The major portion of any psychoanalytic endeavor still pursues this purpose. After the structural theory and the revision of the theory of anxiety, it fell to Freud's heirs to pursue theory construction. Anna Freud (1966) dealt with the defensive function of the ego and contributed immeasurably to technique by pointing out that, since it is clear that defense and resistance are unconscious ego functions, it is as important for the analyst, in listening to the patient's free associations, to concern himself with the functioning of the ego as with the derivatives of the id, formerly regarded as the analyst's sole concern. In fact, it has become a prime tenet of technique that *defense is to be interpreted before content* (Fenichel, 1941). It will later be shown how ego psychological theory modifies still further the prestructural emphasis upon id content alone. The major technical tools of psychoanalysis as they have developed since the structural theory and are practiced today will be described briefly. They are so adequately treated in the standard texts on the technique of psychoanalysis that little would be served in repeating at length what the authors of these texts (Freud, 1958; Glover, 1958; Fenichel, 1941; Sharpe, 1950; Menninger, 1958; Greenson, 1967) have already presented.

Free association, while at first devised by Freud to eliminate the analyst's influence upon the direction of the patient's thought, has a broader purpose — that of loosening cathexis of the secondary process so that primary process thought, not ordinarily operative to such a high degree in the waking state of the individual with an intact ego, will, in the analytic process, break through, providing access to the unconscious, especially when resistance is at a low level. Free association is often described as the basic rule of psychoanalysis in that it is the main analytic obligation of the patient.

Interpretation is the basic tool of the analyst. For heuristic purposes, Eissler (1953) proposed that an ideal analysis may be conducted using no technique other than interpretation, but he does not extend his argument to insist that, practically, this is possible. Interpretation, formerly regarded as of id content only, may now be of ego as well. On the ego side, one may interpret defense and resistance (A. Freud, 1966) and support may be provided for purposes of strengthening even the intact ego, by interpretation of adaptation (Hartmann, 1958; Blanck, 1966). In its fundamental feature, interpretation disturbs an equilibrium established by the synthetic function (Nunberg, 1931), by introducing a heretofore unconscious element into consciousness, necessitating a new synthesis for the re-establishment of a new equilibrium which now must absorb the added (interpreted) feature. In order to understand the theory of interpretation thoroughly, it is necessary to take into account Waelder's (1936) enunciation of the principle of multiple function in which he enumerated eight aspects of the psyche to be satsified for equilibrium to be maintained. While it would take us too deeply into metapsychology to discuss the principle of multiple function thoroughly here, it is necessary to indicate that theoretical understanding of how interpretation operates in depth adds immeasurably to technical artistry.

At first, theorists of technique (Freud, 1958; Glover, 1958; Fenichel, 1941) cautioned that interpretation is not to be made before the transference neurosis is established and before transference (especially positive transference) becomes resistance. It is now feasible, with the backing of contemporary theory, to begin interpretative work early in analysis. Interpretation is made, not only of resistance, but of the broader and more conscious aspects of the neurosis, paving the way for deeper approach to these same matters later in the analysis. An example is presented here which illustrates both how early interpretation is made and the importance, diagnostically and technically, of the first dream. A woman in analysis with a female analyst dreams that she is in a car with a man who is driving at a dangerous speed and that another woman (understood to represent the analyst, but not yet so interpreted) is in the back seat and tells the man to slow down. This dream informs the analyst that the protection of the pre-oedipal mother is sought against heterosexual anxiety. It indicates the point of fixation and regression and provides the analysis with a direction. The defensive need for the preoedipal mother will have to be analyzed before the positive oedipal conflict may be resolved.

Interpretation is hardly ever a single pronouncement by the analyst. It is to be thought of, rather, as taking place in a series of "incomplete" interpretations (Glover, 1958, pp. 357-358), the totality of which constitutes *the* interpretation. One may envision it as a pyramid with the narrowest, most general, preconscious, partial interpretation beginning at the apex. Intermediary and ever-deepening partial interpretations proceed over many sessions often interspersed with other matters, because free association rather than compulsive analytic zeal propels the treatment. The final, fullest interpretation of the unconscious, completing those that preceded it, constitutes the base of the pyramid. In the case illustrated, the first interpretation was simply, "The woman protects you." The series then proceeds over many sessions in close connection with the patient's associations and leads the patient ever more deeply toward the realization of how she clings to the analyst for protection. For example, she brings her marital problems into the sessions, seeking the analyst's advice about her husband's behavior. When the transference neurosis ensues, the interpretation may be altered to, "You need *me* to protect you." When resistances have been interpreted, such as the attempt to use the analyst in taking sides against the husband, and when genetic material and sexual fantasies have been provided, the interpretation is reduced to the genetic, "You needed your mother to protect you." This is still an incomplete interpretation. The patient is left to wonder why. As associations proceed, she may herself link anxiety about her sexual fantasies to the defense of maintaining a strong libidinal tie to the preoedipal mother. This illustrates not only how interpretation is made in a series of incomplete interpretations, but also how the patient is led to make self-interpretations — how the ego is encouraged to function in the analytic situation. It begins the explanation, to be elaborated upon, of change in technique regarding the division of labor dictated by the theoretical advances in the present era of psychoanalytic theory construction. This description and illustration of the technique of interpretation is also closely related to another technical concept, *working through*. Briefly, working through refers to repeated interpretations from different facets, depending upon the material provided, until the genetic conflict is understood in its entirety. Again, the principle of multiple function is of value in understanding how working through deals with each of the eight aspects of multiple function.

In the United States, *frequency of analytic sessions* is preferably five days a week, minimally four days a week. (Freud saw his patients six days.) The daily succession of sessions propels analytic work because that which is begun in one session is quickly followed up in the next as the stream of associations continues to flow and as the ever-deepening contact with the unconscious is uninterrupted, except for the weekend when the analyst needs to recover his own resources. As an example, a partial (incomplete) interpretation made in a given session may constitute the day residue for a dream that night, which adds new material, so that interpretative work proceeds and deepens. Even without a remembered dream, the unconscious continues its work in the twenty-four hour interval and carries the analytic work forward the next day. Greenacre (1954), in describing the disadvantages of brief therapy and infrequent sessions, shows that long intervals between sessions tend to thicken resistance, allow for re-repression of material already interpreted, and especially permit the negative aspects of transference to be covered over.

The *use of the couch* is misunderstood in unsophisticated quarters because Freud's remark that he did not like to be stared at has been so much overstressed at the expense of the more profound reasons for this procedure. Lying in a relaxed position, without being able to see the analyst, the patient is better able to fantasy and to regress, to project and displace upon the analyst feelings and attitudes toward figures from the past — that is, to form a transference. The supine position also minimizes motor activity, thus encouraging *verbalization* rather than action. Freud (1958) described acting-out as substituting for remembering. Verbalization is now valued, not only because it facilitates remembering, but is understood also to consist of a complex of ego functions which includes symbolization and semantic communication (Spitz, 1957) and is condusive to ego-building, to neutralization and to the establishment of higher levels of object relations. Acting-out, on the other hand, blocks remembering by bypassing the ego, thus lessening opportunity for insight; it permits temporary discharge without therapeutic gain; it obscures the conflict and even reinforces infantile gratification at the risk of rendering the conflict unanalyzable.

There is a form of action on the part of some patients which is to be distinguished from acting-out. This refers to enactment of preverbal affect and experience. Especially from the observational studies (Mahler, 1963, 1965, 1968, 1971; Spitz, 1957, 1965), we have become familiar with the richness of affectivity between mother and child in the early weeks and months of life and of the essential nature of this dyadic relationship for ego development. These studies have also made us aware of the inner life of the child before the acquisition of speech. Spitz (1957) designates 18 months as the average age when speech (semantic communication) begins. But it is not until approximately seven years of age (Piaget, 1955) that capacity for abstract thought develops. Therefore, there is much unsaid in the child's emotional life which results in the adult analysand's relative incapacity to verbalize that which had been experienced outside the verbal realm. One of the newer techniques derived from ego psychological theory is that of enabling the patient to cathect with words those preverbal experiences which otherwise tend to lead to action. Technically, both acting and acting-out, although differently determined, are dealt with by encouraging verbalization; in the instance of acting-out, it is the repressed that is to be verbalized; in acting, we have a more difficult technical task because that which had never been cathected to language must now be cathected retroactively.

Regression is facilitated by the use of the couch. Thus regression, primarily a mechanism of defense, becomes secondarily a deliberate part of the technical repertory; regression to the point of fixation leads the analysis to revival of infantile conflict now to be interpreted and resolved. In the present era of psychoanalytic theory-building, it is essential to stress that the intact ego of the analyzable patient rarely regresses unless "in the service of the ego" (Kris, 1952), that is to say, reversibly. Regression is, in the main, along the psychosexual line of maturation only. With little or no danger of ego regression, it is a valid analytic tool; in the psychoanalytically oriented psychotherapy of the less intact ego, regression is to be employed with more caution, if at all. It is this analytic tool that causes many an analyst technical difficulty because misdiagnosis of the structure of the ego, an understandable error made sometimes by even the most experienced diagnostician, leads to the use of regression as a technique when it is contraindicated because the ego, too fragile to tolerate such stress upon it, regresses along with the id. With the loss of ego function, there may be decompensation.

Regression, frequency of attendance and the supine position with freedom to fantasy without the interference of the analyst's appearance in reality, all serve to facilitate the onset of *transference* and *transference neurosis.* Transference is a phenomenon which occurs in everyday life as well as in psychoanalysis. Persons, especially those in positions of authority and nurturing — teachers, doctors, dentists, nurses, policemen, judges, even relatives and friends — are objects of transference. Only the psychoanalyst, however, uses the transference and transference neurosis deliberately and with full awareness of their therapeutic potentialities. Transference neurosis is distinguished from transference in that, when the transference neurosis sets in, there is no longer merely casual repetition of feelings and attitudes from the past displaced and projected onto the person of the analyst, but the totality of the neurosis is revived and relived within the analytic situation. Glover (1958) is very precise about indications that the transference neurosis is beginning to take hold. The drift of associations centers more and more around the analyst's possessions, clothing, office furnishings and, ultimately, upon the analyst himself. Before the transference neurosis proper ensues, that is, in the beginning phase of analysis, the analyst's efforts are devoted to providing the climate within which analysis may best flourish. Along with regression and fantasy formation — in fact, an inherent part of those processes — is promotion of the transference which will lead, shortly after the opening phase, to the transference neurosis. The word *promotion* is not used here in the active sense. The analysand regresses because of his need for the analyst, reviving childhood dependence upon parental guidance and love. There are innumerable instances of such transference dependency being exploited in nonanalytic situations for the advantage of the authority figure. It is one of the proudest features of psychoanalysis that the analyst, conscious of his responsibility for cure, uses the transference entirely for the benefit of the patient. In the contemporary period, Greenacre's (1954, 1959) discussions of the value of guardianship of the patient's autonomy in the transference add an important dimension to the concept of transference as an analytic tool and elaborate on the analyst's responsibility for ensuring that the patient will never become inextricably dependent upon the analyst, although he must become dependent for the purpose of reliving and thereby working through his residual dependency needs to true independence. Greenacre also provides useful clarification of the heretofore black and white consideration of negative and positive transference. She notes that transference shifts and changes, sometimes within the same analytic session. She prefers, therefore, to speak of "active transference-neurotic manifestations" (Greenacre, 1959, p. 486) which describe more fluidly the varying feelings of the analysand toward his primary figures as they shift and change within the transference.

In the contemporary era, distinction is made not only between transference and transference neurosis, but between those phenomena and the real relationship with the analyst. It is now recognized that the analyst cannot altogether constitute the "blank screen" that was earlier thought to be desirable. He has a personality which inevitably reveals itself to the discerning analysand; his office furnishings, clothing, mannerisms and the like give some indication of how he is in reality. His responses to the patient cannot be the same as those of any other person. So, much as he tries to keep personal information at a minimum for the purpose of encouraging fantasy, the patient gains some assessment of him as a person and responds to that. To the extent that he is kind, respectful, empathic and helpful, an alliance is formed which carries the analytic work forward. The patient's contribution to the analytic situation is some capacity to form realistic object relations in the present as well as to transfer from the past. The realistic aspects of his relationship to the analyst have been termed the *therapeutic alliance* by Zetzel (1956) and the *working alliance* by Greenson (1967). Both these rather similar distinctions between transference and a real relationship expand Sterba's (1934) concept of the therapeutic split into an experiencing and an observing ego. In Sterba's terms, the observing ego allies itself with the analyst in their mutual task and goal; the experiencing ego relives in the transference. Usually, except for moments in every analysis when the power of the affective experience causes the ego to lose, temporarily, its capacity to distinguish present from past, the competent ego of the analytic patient is divided in the way that Sterba has described. Reality testing and a good level of object relations lead him not only to ally himself with the analyst in their common goal, but to know that he is a real person. That is not to be relied upon in the treatment of the more disturbed patient. In the analyzable patient, however, his perception of the reality aspects of the analyst as a person increases in value as the analysis proceeds to termination and aids in the dissolution of the transference.

Particularly pertinent to the issue of the capacity to experience the analyst as real as well as an object for transference are the contributions of Jacobson (1971) and Loewald (1962). Jacobson shows how selective identification, normally, is a developmental process. One of the technical implications of her position is that, toward the end of analysis, when distorted self and object representations have been corrected, selective identification with the analyst inevitably takes place. Loewald elaborates on this aspect of the analytic process, describing how termination of analysis involves a mourning process and how identification operates to facilitate giving up the object. Both of these authors move away from the formerly held concept of identification as a defense only (A. Freud, 1966) and point up that it can also be developmental and adaptive. None of the Freudian authors who recognize that there is a real relationship with the analyst in addition to the transferential one implies that this real relationship involves personal friendship or reciprocity in the ordinary sense. They abide by the abstinence rule which is designed to protect the patient from antitherapeutic involvement with the analyst and his personal life.

Transference and transference neurosis were rediscussed at a Panel of the 28th International Congress of Psycho-Analysis held in Paris in July, 1973. At the Panel, Loewald summed up the definition and description of transference by pointing out that it is both interpersonal and intrapsychic and that, by and large, it restructures infantile object relations. Valenstein, another panelist, asserted that the classical definitions of transference and transference neurosis apply to the symptom neuroses only.   Currently, he stressed, we are concerned with preoedipal features — that is, the earliest experiences which determine transference.   Van der Leeuw added to Valenstein's statement that the narcissistic patient, as contrasted with the neurotic, does not see the analyst as a person in his own right, but only as a need-satisfying object.   This follows the theoretical views of Jacobson (1971) and Mahler (1968).   Jacobson's formulation that, in the early months of life self and object representations are undifferentiated, coincides with Mahler's observations that, upon emergence from the objectless state of autism, the infant enters into symbiosis with the maternal object.   Both these positions lead logically to the conclusion that experiences derived from that period of life cannot be transferred to an object because self and object are one.   Arlow, as Chairman of this same Panel, raised questions about the division of transference into positive and negative.   It was generally agreed to by the Panel that these are not useful concepts, but surprisingly omitted from that discussion was Greenacre's (1959) proposal that the term *active-neurotic transference manifestations* more accurately describes the fluctuation in feeling that takes place within the transference.   Also at the same Panel, Greenson exceeded Fenichel's (1941) parsimonious definition of transference as mistaking the present for the past.   Greenson defined transference as a distortion in time.   He described the ideal patient as one who is capable of engaging in both transference and a working alliance.

Discussion of transference is not complete without reference to *countertransference.*   Orr (1954) dealt with this subject in great detail.   Strictly defined, countertransference refers to the unconscious feelings, both libidinal and aggressive, which are incurred by the analyst in reaction to the attitudes and productions of the analysand.   Some consider that the only way that the analyst can deal with these feelings is by means of self-analysis.   Sharpe (1950), for example, said that it is desirable to analyze one's own dreams about a patient before attempting to deal with the patient in the next session.   This does not imply that Sharpe restricted consideration of countertransference to the phenomenon of the dream, but only that she presented this method as an illustration of how to cope with countertransference if it should happen to present itself in the analyst's dream.

Some analysts employ a broader definition of countertransference, including within it not only unconscious but also conscious personal response to the patient. They do not, as do some non-Freudian therapists, advocate using the countertransference in direct interpersonal transaction with the patient.   The emphasis is rather upon understanding one's own feelings toward the patient, to engage in self-analysis in order to know why they have occurred, and, if possible, to trace them to their infantile origins and to the analyst's neurotic residua.   If countertransference reactions do not yield to self-analysis, or if they are extreme, or if they follow a repetitive pattern, it is desirable for the analyst to seek the help of another analyst.   When thoroughly understood by the analyst as not stemming from his own infantile or neurotic responses, countertransference reactions can be useful technical tools. When the analyst is certain that it is not he who is responding inappropriately, but that the patient is unconsciously stimulating a particular response in him, then it is technically proper to interpret what the patient is doing. This is perhaps one of the most delicate areas of technique because the analyst must be very well analyzed and must be quite certain that his response is indeed initiated by the patient's unconscious neurotic behavior before he ventures such an interpretation. Otherwise, it becomes all too easy to "blame" the patient for one's own neurotic responses. This would constitute a technical error of immeasurable magnitude and, if not corrected, could cause irreparable damage to an analysis. Such errors may be distinguished qualitatively and quantitatively from the more ordinary, readily correctable errors in interpretation which every analyst makes on occasion. For example, a misinterpretation of a dream fragment in one session may be corrected in the next session by a new dream or an additional association which informs the analyst that he saw the matter incorrectly in the previous session. These kinds of ordinary misinterpretations are not even to be regarded in the realm of error and are certainly not of the same magnitude as are persistent misinterpretations based on countertransference.

Resistance is defined as the use of defenses in the analytic situation. Fenichel (1941), among others, cautioned that resistance is always to be interpreted before content. Analysts have long been familiar with the so-called abuse of free association, whereby a form of pseudo free association takes place without, however, providing interpretable analytic material. Dreams and memories can also be used in the service of resistance sometimes so subtly that even the most skilled analyst may be temporarily deceived by the patient's unconscious use of defense in this way. A classic example of resistance in the transference is the presentation of material to intrigue the analyst. The correct order of interpretation is first of the wish to please, seduce or otherwise interest the analyst, later of the content and of the infantile antecedents. In order to understand the resistances for interpretative purposes, the analyst listens actively to the associations to determine how to begin to interpret them. Contrary to logical expectation, resistance does not diminish in consistently descending levels of intensity with interpretation. Rather, interpretation of resistance leads to new unconscious pathways which the resistance had defended. This, in turn, touches upon new conflict, which results in intensification of defense against increased anxiety. Thus, interpretation of resistance does indeed prepare the way for new content, but the experienced analyst is then prepared to deal with ever-intensified resistance until the entire resistant structure crumbles. In an analysis, the occurrence of increased levels of resistance, although apparently paradoxical, constitutes in fact a confirmation that the analysis is proceeding properly. That resistance tends to thicken is understandably baffling to the patient whose lack of such technical knowledge leads him to think that the analysis is stalemated when, in fact, progress is good.

In modern technique, although the analyst does still deal interpretatively with the resistances as they occur and, as described, proceeds to deeper layers of conflict, his objective is broadened. No longer is he principally interested in the single resistance or even in the series of deepening levels of resistance which stand in the way of uncovering content. His overall objective is the dissolution of a resistant structure (Kris, 1956), following upon which the patient becomes able to take over his own interpretative work and to approach termination of his need for the analyst. This kind of redistribution of the work of the analysis takes place in the context of employment of the aggressive drive in its neutralized mode in the service of independence. Kris compares this with the unneutralized aggression of the patient who indicates no need for the analyst as a defensive rather than an adaptive measure.

The thrust of the position that countertransference is usually a matter for self-analysis, and is to be revealed to the patient interpretatively only when it is the result of the patient's unconscious instigation (R. Blanck, 1973) leads logically to consideration of the *abstinence rule*. This much misunderstood technical device is, nevertheless, one of the most important in the technical repertory because it is designed to assure that the analysis will be solely in the service of resolving the patient's conflicts. Abstinence means nothing more than that the analyst safeguards the analysis by abstaining from gratifying infantile needs, for the purpose of avoiding reinforcement of fixation. Misunderstandings about abstinence include failure to engage in appropriate human response, maintenance of unnecessary and often cruel silence, and the converse of these — provision of too much gratification and self-revelation in order to prove that one is a "human being." In fact, the analyst is obliged to provide a great deal. Above all, his task is to provide interpretation or to facilitate the patient's capacity for self-interpretation. Human response, if distinguished from neurotic response, self-gratification, and gratification of the patient's infantile wishes, is never contraindicated.

To correct another misconception, the analyst is neither inactive nor silent. His activity consists of maintaining free-floating attention, formulating diagnostic hypotheses, considering when to intervene in the stream of free association, and the like. That he may have to remain silent while this kind of activity is going on is not the equivalent of passivity. He is required also to speak at the appropriate time and with the appropriate wording, and also to think before he speaks. He must actively avoid responding to provocation, seduction and the like except in the manner that will be most helpful to the patient, that is to say, interpretatively. Some regard such procedure as impairing spontaneity. Often this is a rationalization for inappropriate outbursts which gratify the analyst. An analyst who has acquired secondary autonomy (Hartmann, 1958) in his professional role uses himself with pleasurably tinged discipline instead of indulgent self-gratification which would be damaging to the analysis.

A seeming contradiction to this liberal definition of the abstinence rule is posed when the patient, in the throes of the transference neurosis, becomes greatly interested in the analyst as a person. In such circumstances, personal questions are not answered. But neither need they be met with stony silence. After one or two statements such as, "If I answer that question it will impair our work," the competent ego of the analytic patient understands the technical purpose of encouraging fantasy instead of shutting it off with facts about the analyst's personal life. This illustration serves also to illuminate one of the ways in which the therapeutic alliance is called upon and strengthened. Now, patient as well as analyst lend themselves knowledgeably to the same technical purpose without heavy-handed burdening of the patient with technical rules. The analyst has enlisted the patient's reasonable ego in the joint endeavor. This is one of the more important purposes of the abstinence rule — to keep the reasonable ego functioning separate from the experiencing one. Advice-giving also contravenes the abstinence rule because it infantalizes the patient. The analyst's narcissism has to suffer, too, from the fact that analysts are not especially competent in knowing how others should conduct their realistic business. The analyst's expertise lies in the use of a trained (analyzed) personality combined with knowledge of theory and technique to help the patient understand and work through his conflicts. When the ego is relatively freed of conflict, increased adaptive functioning will be available for the patient to employ in arriving at his own reality solutions.

There is some historical justification for the misunderstanding that abstinence is synonymous with silence and, in all fairness, this must be considered. Before contemporary ego psychology, and especially before Kris (1956) made his exceptional contributions to contemporary technique, the division of labor between patient and analyst was thought to be such that the patient was the provider of material and the analyst the interpreter. Under such arrangement, the analyst awaited the emergence of material and the development of the transference neurosis. He was not to interpret the positive transference, nor even other material until transference became resistance (Glover, 1958 ; Fenichel, 1941). Therefore, he was left with not much to say and so silence was, perforce, the practice of that earlier era. The ego psychological approach dictates redistribution of the division of labor. Indeed, it is now thought that the former position encouraged too much dependency upon the analyst as omniscient interpreter and made, ultimately, for difficult termination of analysis. Now active interventions are made at the outset for the deliberate purposes of dealing with initial resistance, promoting transference and transference neurosis, encouraging free association, establishing a therapeutic alliance and allowing regression to proceed along the psychosexual line of maturation to the fixation point.

The concept of *autonomy* also lends itself to misunderstanding. It does not mean that the patient is permitted to do as he pleases, but only that the analyst refrain from usurping ego functions in those areas where the patient's ego is competent — that is, not involved in conflict. In conflict-bound areas, the patient may not have his way because this would result in acting-out, indulgence in infantile gratification, or in errors in judgment. Although we no longer establish, at the outset, a list of rules about what the patient may not do in the course of analysis, neither do we abandon him to the dangers of conflict-bound decisions that would be lastingly disadvantageous. As an example, we might consider that Freud told his single patients not to marry during analysis. But, in those days, analysis was of short duration and long-term engagements were the mores of the times. Now, when analysis can take many years, we do not prohibit marriage.   Adult patients in their child-bearing years cannot reasonably be expected to wait until the possibility of having children is over. That we do not prohibit, however, does not mean that we abandon the patient to unwise choices. One might say, for example, if the proposed marriage is not well-enough understood analytically, "If this is going to be a valid marriage, it will be just as valid six months from now. Let us use the time to try to understand more about it." Again, this appeals to the reasonable ego, protects the patient from the omnipotence of the analyst and, simultaneously, from his own conflict-bound ego function of judgment.

The theory, but not necessarily the technique, of *dream interpretation* is based upon Freud's discovery of the construction and meaning of the dream (Freud, 1953). He used his own dreams to describe in detail the nature of the dream work — how the latent content becomes concealed beneath the manifest content. Modern science and instrumentation has made possible experimentation beyond that which was available to Freud in 1899, the year he wrote *The Interpretation of Dreams,* first published in 1900. From recent experimentation (Fisher, 1965) much has been learned about the physiology and psychology of the dream.   These experiments tend to confirm Freud's findings in many respects; none refute them. By and large, Freud did not intend the analyses of his own dreams to demonstrate the technique of dream analysis. However, so formidable were his discoveries that few have ventured to write further on dream theory and technique.   Among those that did are Sharpe (1937) and, more recently, Altman (1969) and Bergmann (1966). Bergmann adds a new feature to dream theory and especially to the technique of working with the dreams of the so-called borderline or narcissistic personalities.   He calls attention to the communicative aspects of the dream, an important consideration in understanding why the patient who is not in analysis proper tells the psychotherapist his dream.   In the area of technique, Brenner (1969) has argued that avenues provided by material other than dreams diminish the importance of the dream as the "royal road" to the unconscious.   Greenson (1970) has refuted this view, upholding the special position of the dream in the psychoanalytic process. Waldhorn (1967) is spokesman for the widely held position that both dreams and material provided by free association are of equal importance to the analysis; therefore, the analyst's technical interest should be evenly distributed.

It is incontestable that dreams (and parapraxes) can provide quick access to the unconscious. A rather neglected aspect of technique, however, is the question of when and under what circumstances such rapid access is desirable. Following Waldhorn's (1967) view that dream analysis is one aspect of the totality of the analytic process, it is not necessarily the aspect which occupies the analyst's attention at all times. Contemporary modification of technique provides the analyst with even more scope. When uncovering of the unconscious is desirable, one travels the royal road. At other times, however, it may be more pertinent to a particular phase of an analysis to deal with the dream differently. The analyst may choose to work with the ego aspects only, whether these be defense, resistance or adaptation; or he may deem it desirable to deal with the transferential aspects; or he may treat the entire dream as a resistance if, in his judgment, it is proffered unconsciously to that end; or he may decide to bypass the dream altogether because other material is of greater importance at a given phase of the analysis. On the whole, the technique of dream analysis should not follow too literally the method Freud employed in *The Interpretation of Dreams* (Freud, 1953) in associating to each element in an orderly fashion. It has already been indicated that his purpose was the presentation of a dream theory. In the everyday practice of psychoanalysis, one relies upon the patient's random associations to the dream elements, preferably at his selection. Because the associations are free, selection is unconsciously determined. This fact provides leverage for dream analysis in that those elements which are chosen by the patient have a particular significance, probably exceeded, when there is heavy resistance, by the significance of those elements which are overlooked by him.

Symbolism in dreams is, by this time, common knowledge. Yet, there are relatively few reliable standard symbols. The analysis of dreams is far more precise if guided by the unique associations of the patient rather than by the analyst's Procrustean notions about the symbols and even about the dream as a whole. Some dreams, nevertheless, are rather transparent to the experienced analyst, especially if he knows the patient well. In such circumstances, shortcuts may be taken, eliminating the laborious process of seeking associations. Better still, as Kris (1956) has pointed out, it is desirable for the patient to learn to interpret his own dreams with increasing independence from the analyst.

It is already clear that modern technique is influenced by ego psychology. These conceptualizations and the techniques derived therefrom arise from the seminal work of Hartmann (1958) who carried forward the psychology of the ego from Freud's introduction of the structural theory in 1923. The position of the ego as one of a tripartite psychic system and its redefinition as a coherent organization of mental processes (Freud, 1961) led logically to the development of an ego psychology. While Anna Freud (1966) worked on the defensive function of the ego, Hartmann (1958) contributed his theories about the origin and development of the ego and about the adaptive function. His chief contributions are briefly listed here because they constitute the foundation upon which subsequent theorists and technicians proceeded to build. The concept of *primary autonomy* describes what is to be relied upon in each individual in terms of innate equipment; the concepts of the *conflict-free sphere* and of *secondary autonomy* as the result of *change in function* help the analyst distinguish between defense and adaptation; the arrival of the infant with *inborn ego apparatuses* into an *average expectable environment* explains the dyadic relationship and its effect upon structuralization, internalization, and the development of object relations.

Much in the arena of controversy these days is Freud's concept of psychic energy in general and Hartmann's (1952) concept of *neutralization* in particular. Appelgarth (1971), Holt (1965) and others argue that psychoanalytic energic concepts need to be updated in accordance with modern physics and neurophysiology. Parens, on the other hand, has recently (1973) elaborated on the clinical value of the concept of psychic energy in general and of neutralization in particular, with emphasis upon its relevance to aggression. For the clinician, neutralization, which is concerned with transfer of energy from id to ego is indispensable, at least until a better theory is brought forward. Recently, Sandler (27th and 28th International Congresses of Psycho-Analysis, Vienna, 1971, and Paris, 1973) has proposed, in theory, how the concept of neutralization, which he finds merely descriptive, may be eliminated. The technical applicability of Sandler's position and its superiority over that of Hartmann await further clarification.

Hartmann's work, as a whole, was further developed by him in collaboration with Kris (Hartmann and Kris, 1945) and Loewenstein (Hartmann, Kris and Loewenstein, 1946). Contingent upon these important theoretical origins of ego psychology are the further conceptualizations of Jacobson (1971), Mahler (1968) and Spitz (1957, 1965). An integrated presentation of the theories of these major ego psychologists is by Blanck and Blanck (1974). Hartmann is also credited with addition of the concept of intrasystemic conflict to the traditional dynamic view of intersystemic conflict. This has become increasingly useful in dealing with the adaptive function of the ego, whereas the intersystemic concept alone enabled the analyst to deal with dynamic processes only. Examples of intrasystemic conflict are: conflict between two defense mechanisms; between defense and adaptation; between two ego functions, one of which might be more highly developed than the other.

Two papers on ego psychological technique contributed by Kris (1956) alter traditionally held views about some major aspects of technique. He pointed out that we are no longer very interested in the rapid uncovering of the id, but that the patterning of childhood memories and the promotion of the patient's ego capacities in the form of encouraging him in the direction of performing his own analytic tasks now supersede uncovering. His presentation of ego building techniques complements that aspect of Greenacre's (1954, 1959) work which emphasizes guardianship of autonomy. Elaborating upon technique by interrelating it with new theoretical development Kris discusses the value of knowledge about childhood development in understanding the genetic aspect of metapsychology. This came at a time when the observational studies of Mahler (1968) and Spitz (1959, 1965) were providing important insights about preoedipal development.

But it was Hartmann who was the first to write on "The technical Implications of Ego Psychology" (1951). With the accumulation of the ongoing work of the ego psychological theorists, G. Blanck (1966) summarized some of the

further implications of ego psychological theory in the treatment of the analyzable patient, pointing up that while a patient with a competent (neurotic) structure may be successfully analyzed in the traditional way, ego building techniques
refine and deepen the analysis. In the treatment of borderline structures, where
ego building is essential, ego psychological theory and the techniques that are
derived from it are indispensable and even make it possible, in some cases, to
bring the ego of the borderline or narcissistic patient to the point of analyzability.

On the whole, modern psychoanalytic technique tends more toward promoting growth and independence than did the earlier analytic techniques. Concepts
such as the employment of the aggressive drive in the service of ego building
(Spitz, 1953; Mahler, 1968; Jacobson, 1964) alter formerly held views about
aggression and especially about the resistances of the anal phase when stubborn-
ness, withholding, negativism and the like predominate. The technical problems
of this psychosexual stage, coinciding as it does with enormous expansion of the
ego, are now surmounted by the understanding that the instinctual drives of the
anal phase, when neutralized, serve growth. This is of great technical advantage
in dealing with the anal character and with obsessional neurosis. Interpretation
of the characteristic resistances of these patients has always been a delicate and
sometimes ineffective procedure.   If, however, the interpretations are first
directed toward the ego building features of the anal phase – the acquisition of
the capacity of say "No," (Spitz, 1957) for example, a background is provided
for interpretation of the drive aspects and of the defenses against them. That
order of interpretation helps the patient understand his aggression not solely as
hostility and anal sadism, but rather as aggression in the service of development.
This is at once more palatable to the patient, more effective and more correct
technically.

Currently, analysts are turning more and more to consideration of the technical problems posed by the so-called borderline and narcissistic patients – that
is, those whose ego development has not arrived fully at the level of structuralization where purely neurotic solutions to conflict are possible. When Eissler (1953)
introduced his concept of the *parameter,* he still had the analyzable patient in
mind. Therefore, he posited four requirements that were to be fulfilled by the
parameter. He said (p. 111):

> We formulate tentatively the following general criteria of a parameter if it
> is to fulfill the conditions which are fundamental to psychoanalysis: (1)
> A parameter must be introduced only when it is proved that the basic
> model technique does not suffice; (2) the parameter must never transgress
> the unavoidable minimum; (3) a parameter is to be used only when it
> finally leads to its self-elimination; that is to say, the final phase of the
> treatment must always proceed with a parameter of zero.

To this he added a fourth requisite (p. 115):

> . . . in order to delineate the conditions which a parameter must fulfill if
> the technique is to remain within the scope of psychoanalysis: the effect

of the parameter on the transference relationship must never be such that it cannot be abolished by interpretation.

By 1954 the psychoanalytic world was becoming more concerned with the less-than-neurotic structures that were presenting for treatment, and a panel on "The Widening Scope of Indications for Psychoanalysis" was held in that year. Much of the trend, to this day, is in the direction of widening the scope of analyzability. Thus, Kohut (1971) has presented a broad theory and technique for treatment of the *narcissistic personality disturbance.* Theoretically, he differs considerably from the ego psychologists whose developmental theories tend to regard narcissism as a normal developmental phase. Jacobson (1964) is particularly informative on this issue. Mahler (1968) believes that the two stages of development that observational discoveries have revealed — autism and symbiosis — are two different levels of narcissism. Her subdivision is of special technical value because it indicates, by its very exposition, that problems having their origin in failure of development in the autistic stage are quite different from problems arising from impaired development in the symbiotic phase. Kohut disagrees sharply with Jacobson and Mahler in theory and also disputes Mahler's methodology. His own view is that narcissism follows two distinctly different developmental lines: (1) from autoerotism to narcissism to object love and (2) from autoerotism to narcissism to higher forms and transformations of narcissism. In the development of the *narcissistic personality disturbance,* a cohesive self has been established and this cohesion distinguishes such patients from the borderline states and renders them analyzable. Thus, Kohut, remaining very much within the theoretical and technical philosophy of "the widening scope" school of thought, believes that analysis of the narcissistic patient proceeds in the traditional way, with deviations only designed to heal the narcissistic fixations.

Kernberg (1967, 1968, 1970, 1971), another contemporary investigator into borderline and narcissistic problems, accepts more readily that these patients are to be treated by psychotherapy as distinguished from psychoanalysis. He differs with Kohut, theoretically as well as technically, employing more of ego psychological theory, especially that of Jacobson, in his schema. His concept of the *borderline personaltiy organization* is that, in these structures, the "good" self and object representations are separated from the "bad" self and object representations by defensive employment of a mechanism of splitting — this for the unconscious purpose of preventing the aggression against the "bad" self-object representations from destroying that as yet undifferentiated unit.

Blanck and Blanck (1974) deal with the "widening scope" issue by asserting that it dilutes psychoanalysis as a technique to extend it to an ever - widening scope of pathology because, in severe pathology, the necessary parameters (Eissler, 1953) reach a point where the least possible deviation from standard technique is, nevertheless, quite large. It is doubtful in such circumstances, whether Eissler's requirement, that the parameter be eliminated before treatment can be successfully terminated, is possible to fulfill. Rather than stretch psychoanalysis to the breaking point, it seems wiser to reserve it for the analyzable neuroses and to devise psychoanalytically oriented psychotherapy, based on the same theory but different in technique from psychoanalysis proper for the borderline and narcissistic states. Since the fixations and regressions of the less structured personalities have their roots in phases of development earlier than the oedipal, and since it is these phases that the combined work of the ego psychologists illuminate so well, an integrated theory of psychoanalytic developmental psychology is indispensable for elaborating techniques for the treatment of these patients. This is especially important because, until the advent of ego psychology, the progression of psychosexual maturation was the only developmental theory available in psychoanalysis. To that may now be added the vast knowledge about structuralization which enables the analyst to devise techniques which are likely to bring success in dealing with preoedipal developmental lesions.

Pathology, in the less structured personality is in essence, pathology of object relations. This vital ego function progresses through graduated stages in its development to the final stage of object constancy. At first, the neonate is objectless; after some weeks, he becomes dimly aware of an "outside" which is experienced as part of the self. Gradually, self and object representations accumulate and then differentiate. The infant moves from the position of regarding the maternal object as part of himself, to viewing her as a gratifier of his needs, to valuing her for her function (Edgecumbe and Burgner, 1973). Ultimately, he acquires the capacity to love and to value the object regardless of his state of need (Hartmann, 1964). Those patients designated as borderline or narcissistic are usually fixated on the object relations developmental line (A. Freud, 1963), at the level of need gratification (Hartmann, 1964). They need therapeutic intervention to help them attain higher levels of object relations. Diagnostic designations of these borderline and narcissistic states still suffer from unclarity, and recent attempts (Kohut, 1971; Kernberg, 1970) at nosological classification of certain clinically presented symptom clusters have not been altogether successful. It leaves more scope, at this stage of our knowledge, to employ description of the various developmental lines as they appear in a given individual to identify pathological areas of development and to know, thereby, where to address treatment. These lines of development are: *psychosexual maturation; taming of the drives* (neutralization, fusion, sublimation); *object relations; levels of anxiety* (from fear of annihilation, to fear of loss of the object, to fear of loss of the object's function, to fear of loss of love and, finally, to fear of the superego). According to Mahler's scheme (1968) they are autism, symbiosis, separation-individuation in four subphases — differentiation, practicing, rapprochement, object constancy. According to Spitz (1965) they are the organizers of the psyche, indicators of which are the smiling response, stranger anxiety, semantic communication; and according to Jacobson (1964), *internalization,* which includes selective identification and superego formation; *defensive organization; adaptive function.*

The borderline and narcissistic personality has failed in some of the early, primitive stages of development, usually along more than simply one or two developmental lines. This suggests that many of the techniques of psychoanalysis proper are not used in these less structured cases, or are used differently qualitatively and in timing. Transference, for example, can only exist when there is sufficient differentiation of self from object representations to make it possible for the patient truly to transfer from a past figure to the analyst. While self and object representations are experienced as undifferentiated, as is the situation in borderline and narcissistic personalities, there can be no transference; therefore, other means of working with the patient who experiences the analyst as part of himself have to be employed. With patients who have experienced excessive, or as Mahler (1968) has termed it, parasitic symbiosis, it is not desirable to enter into a symbiotic transference-like relationship. This is especially so when symbiosis, in the course of development, has been carried on into periods of life later than a phase-specific time. Mahler (1968) has said that the infant needs adequate, phase-specific symbiotic experience in order to proceed into the separation-individuation phase. From that, one can conclude that it is not usually useful to yield to the adult patient's insistence upon continuation of symbiosis because it would seriously impair progress to later developmental phases. In other words, the analyst is constrained to avoid reinforcing fixation. But here one is dealing, not with the better known psychosexual fixations of the pre-ego psychological era, but with fixation in ego development. For the patient who has been severely deprived in phase-specific symbiotic experience, however, there is a need for him to repair some of the shortcomings of that phase in reliving it with the analyst. It is in this regard that Kohut's (1971) technical procedures are of inestimable value because, although there is some controversy about his theoretical formulations, there is no doubt that for some patients, carefully selected diagnostically, there is need for reliving in the therapeutic relationship in order to repair developmental damage. Then development can proceed, this time under the guidance of the growth-producing analyst.

There is also some controversy about whether the relationship with the analyst in such cases can rightfully be regarded as transference. Kohut (1971) believes that it can, but acknowledges that he is extending the definition. No controversy exists, however, about the fact that there usually cannot be transference neurosis in a non-neurotic case. Therefore, by definition, transference neurosis does not often ensue in borderline and narcissistic structures, although it may come about later in treatment, when the ego has been helped to develop to the point where it approaches neurotic structure. In such an eventuality, one deals with the transference neurosis as in the psychoanalysis of neurosis. More likely, but also more dangerous, in impaired or undeveloped structures, is transference psychosis — the belief that the analyst actually *is* the primary object, which comes about by combination of intense need for an undifferentiated partner and of poor reality testing.

Free association is not a "basic rule" in the treatment of the borderline and narcissistic structures because there is danger that too much primary process thinking already exists. Therefore, allowing the patient to speak at random, as in the treatment of neurosis, often means allowing non-therapeutic discharge. It is preferable that the analyst be available for helping the ego structure itself, rather than wander with the patient in the ramblings of the primary process. Therefore, in such type of treatment, the analyst takes a more active role in supplementing ego functions until they can stand on their own.

Interpretation is used, but consists in the main, of interpretation on the ego side, at least until the ego has been strengthened so that it can cope with the drives. Here again, the concept of neutralization is useful. For example, one can offer interpretations such as that the patient experiences the analyst as part of him; that he would like to be understood without words; and similar aspects of nondifferentiation (Jacobson, 1964) or symbiosis (Mahler, 1968). As the patient begins to realize that the analyst is a separate person, he is also likely to become aware that it is his own aggression that causes him to fear his and the analyst's separateness lest they both be destroyed in the process. This, too, can be interpreted for the purpose of encouraging venture in the direction of separation, this time by an aware ego which can take the risk with diminished fear of the destructive consequences of aggressive wishes. When the patient has been informed interpretatively that his aggression is not destructive but can serve growth, neutralization is thereby encouraged and the aggressive drive can more comfortably be employed for growth promoting rather than for destructive purposes. This illustrates how the aggressive drive is used in ego building and how, if approached from the ego side, aggression can be neutralized, that is, transferred to the ego to be used for its benign purposes.

Regarding frequency of therapeutic contact, the less-than-neurotic patient is, by practice, usually seen less frequently than the analytic patient. This, however, is often a matter of convenience and finances rather than a technical decision based upon the sound reasoning that has been established for frequency of contact in the analytic case. Because treatment procedures for the less structured personality are currently in the process of being elaborated (Kernberg, 1968; Blanck and Blanck, 1974), there are, as yet, no hard and fast rules about frequency. Possibly such rules can never be established because the structures of such cases are far more diverse than is neurotic structure. One might, for example, see some such patients as frequently as one would an analytic case; others would be treated on a less frequent schedule; still others would be seen more frequently at times of crisis and less so when the crisis abates. Jacobson (1971) warns against seeing depressed patients too frequently after the suicidal danger has passed, lest continued frequent contact hold out promise of gratifications impossible to fulfill.

The more disturbed patient is usually not treated on the couch because he needs to see the analyst in order to experience reality rather than to lose himself in fantasy. This procedure avoids the already discussed danger of transference psychosis because, in contrast with the better structured ego of the neurotic, these patients do not possess an observing ego to differentiate between fantasy and reality. Here, too, however, there are no hard and fast rules, and many analysts do use the couch with such patients while exercising careful control to prevent loss of contact with reality. Contraindicated is the procedure whereby the patient alternates too frequently between chair and couch. It seems more desirable to keep him seated until one is certain that he can function therapeutically on the couch without danger. Otherwise one is likely to enter into a jumping jack kind of procedure with the result that neither chair nor couch is used effectively, nor is the patient constrained to stretch his capacity to tolerate frustration and anxiety if change in position offers too ready relief.

Dream analysis, too, differs somewhat from classical psychoanalytic technique when one is treating borderline and narcissistic structures. This does not imply that dreams are to be avoided. Usually, if they are approached from the side of the ego, there is no contraindication for their use with the more disturbed patient. In fact, they may be especially helpful in discovering adaptive processes of which the patient is unaware or does not appreciate. As an example, a patient may have an anxiety dream of such intensity that, lacking adequate defensive function of the ego, he wakens. This can be used to point out to him that his ego does function, at least in that he does not allow the dream to proceed to a frightening and disastrous conclusion. This is particularly important because these types of impaired egos lack the capacity to distinguish clearly dream from reality. This illustration also serves to describe a manner of providing ego support — that is, support of the capacity to function, no matter how limited, so that that functioning can be appreciated and improved upon.

Regression is not usually encouraged because such patients are already severely regressed or fixated and because regression of ego functions is a danger to be avoided in these kinds of structures, as contrasted with the more structured ego of the neurotic patient which rarely regresses irreversibly. In the borderline states, ego regression can result in decompensation. Therefore, it is of technical importance to prevent regression below the already regressed state of the ego. Regression along psychosexual lines is equally undesirable because of the ego's incapacity to cope with the drives and the resultant danger that impulses will be acted on without adequate control.

Resistance, too, presents a different problem than in the treatment of neurosis. It is more likely to take the form of fear of closeness, engulfment, loss of identity. In other words, fear of closeness is a defense against the wished-for symbiotic merger. However, there too, the growth promoting features of developmental theory suggest technical devices. If it is realized that any form of resistance is indicative of an ego that functions to some degree, then this can be turned to technical advantage. Again, by means of ego interpretation, the ego can be supported by helping the patient to understand the adaptive value of his stance. Thus, we do not controvert his defenses, but rather support them in a very specific manner. Specificity is stressed here because it has been found by experience that blanket support is usually ineffective. Statements such as, "You have done well," have little value now, when we have a theoretical body of knowledge available for understanding exactly how the patient has done well. "You withdrew when you were overwhelmed by your father's rage because that was the best way, at the time, to protect yourself and him from your own anger," is the type of interpretation of adaptation which touches directly upon a specific experience in the patient's life.

Verbalization is most necessary in this type of treatment and must be encouraged to the utmost because it exercises ego function, interposes thought before action and builds object relations. Spitz (1957) designates the acquisition of speech as a crucial organizer of the psyche, requiring of the child that he engage in semantic communication as the vehicle which carries him toward higher levels of object relations. To the normally developing infant, this means that he can no longer enjoy the blissful oneness of being understood without words. For the borderline patient who has not conquered this developmental phase, the analyst, aware that verbalization is essential to growth, assiduously avoids the appearance of intuitive and omniscient understanding. Because of the deeper levels of fixation and regression, these patients tend to act rather than to verbalize. It is necessary, technically, to search out and to help the patient cathect his preverbal experiences with words, especially if they have been traumatic. This is a difficult and slightly risky procedure — difficult because the patient cannot remember, and risky because one can be mistaken and make adultomorphic speculations. When correct, however, the results of such a procedure are likely to be dramatically effective. It is a milestone in the building of object relations when, for example, the patient who never telephones the analyst at times of stress, anxiety or depression, begins to understand that he early gave up crying for relief because none arrived for him.

The foregoing is not an exhaustive itemization of techniques for the treatment of the severe pathologies, but is intended to be illustrative of the trend in technique dictated by the most recent discoveries in ego psychology. These techniques are still in the pioneering stages and only time and experience will indicate whether they are evolving in the right direction. Mahler proposed recently (Pre-Congress Panel of the Association for Child Analysis, Paris, 1973) that the rapprochement subphase of the separation-individuation phase is crucial not only in the etiology of the so-called borderline states, but contributes either favorably or pathogenically, depending upon the nature of the experience at that subphase, to the capacity to deal with the oedipal conflict when that arises. This postulate contains vast and as yet altogether unexplored implications for the treatment of neurosis as well as for borderline and narcissistic states. Thus, a new theoretical frontier appears even before the end of the pioneering era of consolidation of the conceptualizations of the ego psychologists, and also before extrapolation of techniques from these conceptualizations has been completed and tested in large enough sampling to provide as much assurance of their validity as now exists for the classical psychoanalytic techniques. Nevertheless, there is no doubt that we are now in the era when patients formerly regarded as untreatable — those designated by Freud as suffering from "narcissistic neuroses" — are now being treated with a modicum of success with techniques derived from ego psychology. Some reach the level of structuralization which renders them analyzable. However, for the time being, until more refined theory and technique becomes available, it remains accurate to state that the goal of psychoanalysis of the neuroses is that of resolution of the oedipal conflict while the goal of treatment of the borderline and narcissistic structures is resolution of the separation-individuation crisis, with consequent acquisition of identity and object constancy.

REFERENCES

Altman, L.L. *The Dream in Psychoanalysis.* New York: International Universities Press, 1969.

Appelgarth, A. Comments on aspects of the theory of psychic energy. *Journal of the American Psychoanalytic Association.* 19: 379–416 (1971).

Bergmann, M.S. The intrapsychic and communicative aspects of the dream. *International Journal of Psycho-Analysis.* 47: 356–363 (1966).

Blanck, G. Some technical implications of ego psychology. *Internatonal Journal of Psycho-Analysis.* 47: 6–13 (1966).

Blanck, G. Crossroads in the technique of psychotherapy. *The Psychoanalytic Review.* 56: 498–510 (1970).

Blanck, G. and Blanck, R. *Marriage and personal development.* New York: Columbia University Press, 1968.

Blanck, G. and Blanck, R. Toward a psychoanalytic developmental psychology. *Journal of the American Psychoanalytic Association.* 20: 668–710 (1972).

Blanck, G. and Blanck, R. *Ego Psychology: Theory and Practice.* New York: Columbia University Press, 1974.

Blanck, R. Countertransference in the treatment of the borderline patient. *Clinical Social Work Journal.* I: 110–117 (1973).

Brenner, C. Some comments on technical precepts in psychoanalysis. *Journal of the American Psychoanalytic Association.* 17: 333–352 (1969).

Edgecumbe, R. and Burgner, M. Some problems in the conceptualization of early object relationships: Part I. The concepts of need-satisfying relationships. *Psychoanalytic Study of the Child.* 27: 283–333 (1973).

Eissler, K.R. The effect of the structure of the ego on psychoanalytic technique. *Journal of the American Psychoanalytic Association.* 1: 104–143 (1953).

Fenichel, O. Problems of psychoanalytic technique. New York: *Psychoanalytic Quarterly,* 1941.

Fisher, C. Psychoanalytic implications of recent research on sleep and dreaming. *Journal of the American Psychoanalytic Association.* 13: 197–303 (1965).

Freud, A. The ego and the mechanisms of defense. In: *The Writings of Anna Freud,* 2. New York: International Universities Press, 1966.

Freud, A. The concept of developmental lines. In: *The Psychoanalytic Study of the Child,* 28: 245–265. New York: International Universities Press, 1963.

Freud, S. *The Standard Edition of the complete psychological works of Sigmund Freud,* J. Strachey *et al.* (Eds.). London: The Hogarth Press, 1953–64.

Freud, S. The interpretation of dreams. *Standard Edition.* 4 and 5: 339–621 (1953).

Freud, S.   Papers on technique. *Standard Edition.*   **12**:   89–171 (1958).

Freud, S.   The ego and the id.   *Standard Edition.*   **19**: 12–59 (1961).

Freud, S.   Inhibitions, symptoms and anxiety. *Standard Edition.*   **20**:   87–156 (1959).

Glover, E.   *The technique of psychoanalysis.*   New York: International Universities Press, 1958.

Greenacre, P.   The role of transference. *Journal of the American Psychoanalytic Association.*   **2**:   671–684 (1954).

Greenacre, P.   Certain technical problems in the transference relationship. *Journal of the American Psychoanalytic Association.*   **7**:   485–502 (1959).

Greenson, R.R.   The exceptional position of the dream in psychoanalytic practice.   *The Psychoanalytic Quarterly.*   **29**: 519–549 (1970).

Greenson, R.R.   *The technique and practice of psychoanalysis.*   New York, *Hallmark Press,* 1967.

Hartmann, H.   *Ego psychology and the problem of adaptation.*   New York: International Universities Press, 1958.

Hartmann, H.   The mutual influences of the development of ego and the id. *The Psychoanalytic Study of the Child.*   **7**: 9–30 (1952).

Hartmann, H.   Notes on a theory of sublimation. *The Psychoanalytic Study of the Child.*   **10**:   9–29 (1955).

Hartmann, H.   Contribution to the metapsychology of schizophrenia. *Essays on Ego Psychology,* pp. 215–240.   New York: International Universities Press, 1964.

Hartmann, H.   Technical implications of ego psychology.   *The Psychoanalytic Quarterly.*   **20**: 31–43 (1951).

Hartmann, H. and Kris, E.   The genetic approach in psychoanalysis.   *The Psychoanalytic Study of the Child.*   **1**:   11–30 (1945).

Hartmann, H., Kris, E. and Loewenstein, R.M.   Comments on the formation of psychic structure. *The Psychoanalytic Study of the Child.*   **2**:   11–38 (1946).

Hartmann, H., Kris, E. and Loewenstein, R.M.   Notes on the theory of aggression. *The Psychoanalytic Study of the Child.*   **3** and **4**:   9–36 (1949).

Holt, R.R.   Ego autonomy re-evaluated. *International Journal of Psycho-Analysis.*   **46**:   151–167 (1965).

Jacobson, E.   *The self and the object world.*   New York: International Universities Press, 1964.

Jacobson, E.   *Depression.*   New York: International Universities Press, 1971.

Kernberg, O.F.   Borderline personality organization. *Journal of the American Psychoanalytic Association.*   **15**:   641–685 (1967).

Kernberg, O.F.   The treatment of patients with borderline personality organization.   *International Journal of Psycho-Analysis.*   **49**: 600–619 (1968).

Kernberg, O.F.   Factors in the psychoanalytic treatment of narcissistic personalities. *Journal of the American Psychoanalytic Association.*   **18**: 51–85 (1970).

Kernberg, O.F.   A psychoanalytic classification of character pathology. *Journal of the American Psychoanalytic Association.*   **18**:   800–822 (1970).

Kernberg, O.F.   Prognostic considerations regarding borderline personality organization. *Journal of the American Psychoanalytic Association.*   **19**: 595–635 (1971).

Kohut, H. *The analysis of the self.* New York: International Universities Press, 1971.

Kris, E. *Psychoanalytic explorations in art.* New York: International Universities Press, 1952.

Kris, E. On some vicissitudes of insight in psychoanalysis. *International Journal of Psycho-Analysis.* **37:** 445–455 (1956).

Kris, E. The recovery of childhood memories. *The Psychoanalytic Study of the Child.* **11:** 54–88 (1956).

Loewald, H.W. Internalization, separation, mourning and the superego. *The Psychoanalytic Quarterly.* **31:** 483–504 (1962).

Mahler, M.S. On the significance of the normal separation-individuation phase. In: Schur, M. (Ed.) *Drives, Affects and Behavior,* pp. 161–168. New York: International Universities Press, 1965.

Mahler, M.S. Thoughts about development and individuation. *The Psychoanalytic Study of the Child.* **18:** 307–324 (1963)

Mahler, M.S. *On human symbiosis and the vicissitudes of individuation.* New York: International Universities Press, (1968).

Mahler, M.S. A study of the separation-individuation process: and its possible application to borderline phenomena in the psychoanalytic situation. *The Psychoanalytic Study of the Child.* **26:** 403–424, (1971).

Menninger, K. *Theory of psychoanalytic technique.* New York: Basic Books, 1958.

Nunberg, H. The synthetic function of the ego. *International Journal of Psycho-Analysis.* **12:** 123–140 (1931).

Orr, I.W. Transference and countertransference: a historical survey. *Journal of the American Psychoanalytic Association.* **2:** 621–670 (1954).

Parens, H. Aggression: a reconsideration. *Journal of the American Psychoanalytic Association.* **21:** 34–60 (1973).

Piaget, J. *The language and thought of the child.* New York: Meridian Books, 1955.

Pre-Congress Meeting of the Association for Child Analysis, Paris, 1973.

Rapaport, D. Introduction to Erikson, E.H. *Identity and the Life Cycle.* Vol. I, pp. 5–17, Monograph number 1 of *Psychological Issues.* New York: International Universities Press, 1959.

Ross, N. An examination of nosology according to psychoanalytic concepts. *Journal of the American Psychoanalytic Association.* **8:** 535–551 (1960).

Sharpe, E.F. *Collected papers on psycho-analysis.* London: The Hogarth Press, 1950.

Sharpe, E.F. *Dream analysis.* London: The Hogarth Press, 1937.

Spitz, R.A. Aggression: its role in establishment of object relations. In: Loewenstein, R.M. (Ed.), *Drives, Affects, and Behavior.* New York: International Universities Press, 1953.

Spitz, R.A. *No and yes.* New York: International Universities Press, 1957.

Spitz, R.A. *The first year of life.* New York: International Universities Press, 1965.

Spitz, R.A. *A genetic field theory of ego formation.* New York: International Universities Press, 1959.

Sterba, R.   The fate of the ego in analytic therapy. *International Journal of Psycho-Analysis.* **15:** 117–126 (1934).

Stone, L.   The widening scope of indications for psychoanalysis. *Journal of the American Psychoanalytic Association.* 2: 567–594 (1954).

Twenty-seventh International Congress of Psycho-Analysis, Vienna, 1971.

Twenty-eighth International Congress of Psycho-Analysis, Paris, 1973.

Waelder, R.   The principle of multiple function. *The Psychoanalytic Quarterly.* 5: 45–62 (1936).

Waldhorn, H.F.   The place of the dream in clinical psychoanalysis. *Kris Study Group Monograph II,* pp. 96–105 (1967).

Zetzel, E.R.   An approach to the relation between concept and content in psychoanalytic theory. *The Psychoanalytic Study of the Child.* **11:** 99–121 (1956).

5 Modified Psychoanalytic Therapies

Samuel B. Kutash

It is a truism that the practice of psychotherapy in the treatment of mental disorders requires the continual modification of the practitioner's systematic approach or methodology in accordance with the needs and problems of each individual patient. This would imply that the underlying personality theory to which the practitioner subscribes is altered and changed as a result of his practice. Since this is a *Handbook for Practitioners* we will deal in this chapter with modifications in the *practice* of psychoanalysis and psychoanalytically-oriented psychotherapies.

As experience with patients accumulates, various modified psychoanalytic therapies emerge which have superior usefulness and specific value for the kinds of patients and problems for which they were developed. The originator of psychoanalysis, Sigmund Freud, developed the classical psychoanalytic method mainly working with patients in Victorian Vienna and particularly with hysterical patients from the upper middle classes. He himself exemplified the readiness to modify his personality theory and methodology as new data emerged with other kinds of patients. His early clinical experiences with hysterics nevertheless remained central to his treatment. As the editor of this *Handbook* has stated in a recent article (Wolman, 1971), "Freud never hesitated to modify his theory whenever new empirical data suggested that such a modification might be advisable. Freud never bent facts to fit into a theory; he was never an orthodox Freudian. Must we be?"

To this statement may be added that, above all he never forced patients to fit his system of treatment and his theory but rather discarded treatment techniques that did not "do the job." The prime example of this flexibility was when he discarded hypnosis in favor of free association as a technical tool of psychotherapy.

Freud, however, preserved his *system* of classical psychoanalysis but on an evolving basis while adding to and changing the technical tools of his treatment.

SYSTEMS AND TECHNICAL TOOLS OF THERAPY

Before describing and discussing the various modifications in psychoanalytic therapies we need to distinguish between systems of psychotherapy and the technical tools or specific techniques which may be used in the framework of some, any, or all of the systems. A given system may have its favorite or preferred technical tools. Thus, the system of Freudian classical psychoanalysis utilizes such technical tools as free association, dream interpretation, use of the couch, analysis of transference and resistance, working through, the abstinence rule, interpretation and construction, and the rule against "acting out."

A complete system of analytic psychotherapy includes, as a minimum, a therapeutic relationship, catharsis or abreaction, insight (both emotional and intellectual), working through and reality testing or the application of the insights and their translation into changed and more effective behavior and living. A system also is based on a well-worked out theory of personality development and of neurosis as well as a *theoretical rationale* for the treatment. These phases of the therapeutic process may be called by different names in the different systems. For example, in classical psychoanalysis and in the most analytically-oriented psychotherapies, the relationship is termed the *transference* while in the Sullivanian system of interpersonal analysis (the "cultural" school) it is referred to and defined as *parataxic distortion.*

Some of the modifications and variations of psychoanalytic therapy represent the development of alternative systems while some consist of the development of different technical tools. In some instances the variation involves the intensive emphasis of one phase of therapy so that it becomes the "complete" therapy in itself (Relationship Therapy, Primal Scream Therapy, Rational Therapy, Reality Therapy). Modifications have also resulted from shifting the emphasis of the focus of the therapy from the id to the ego and superego. We thus have therapeutic methods based on ego psychology as differentiated from the id emphasis of bringing unconscious material into consciousness.

The earliest modifications in technique and treatment resulted from the development of different theoretical systems growing out of ideological and interpersonal disagreements between Freud and his close associates. These included Alfred Adler's system of *individual psychology* (Adler, 1927), Carl Jung's system of *analytical psychology* (Jung, 1920) and Otto Rank's (1945) system of *will therapy.* To these were added the systems of Karen Horney's "holistic" approach (Horney, 1937), Harry Stack Sullivan's (1953) and Erich Fromm's (1955) "Cultural" school, and Wilhelm Reich's (1945) *character analysis.* These are examples of modified psychoanalytic systems of therapy although like E.K. Schwartz (1965) and Lewis (1958) one might question whether the systems of Adler and Jung are basically analytic in the sense of sufficiently recognizing the importance of unconscious processes and the phenomena of transference, the role of infantile sexuality, and the other factors which Freud considered central to his system of psychoanalysis. The basic assumption in this chapter is that the psychoanalytic method of Freud has influenced all subsequent treatment of mental disorders. A variety of the modifications such as the developments in ego psychology and the use of *ego boundary theory* in relation to choice of treatment strategy, and the new orientations toward transference like Heinz Kohut's conceptualizations with reference to the treatment of narcissistic character disorders, represent modifications and extensions of psychoanalytic technique which take into account the cultural changes, changes in life-style and the newest developments in psychodynamic thinking.

Since we are concerned here with the treatment of mental disorders, we will be guided in our presentation of modified psychoanalytic therapies by the practical considerations relating to the treatment of patients rather than a historical review of changes in psychoanalytic thinking. As Harry Guntrip (1973) wrote "to care for people is more important than to care for ideas." We are convinced that each of the systems, methods, and approaches described has made important contributions to the treatment of the kinds of patients for whom they were developed, and in the milieu in which they were elaborated. There is always the question of what is the treatment of choice or variation in technique for the particular patient in his specific circumstances. As Munroe (Munroe, 1955, p. 507) has said, "All good analytic work is actually centered around the patient, not around a theory. The various therapeutic techniques are flexibly applied in accordance with the special requirements of each case and are somewhat modified by each analyst in accordance with his own temperatment." The modifications, variations, and modernization of techniques and systems are now so numerous, we must first classify them and then discuss them around the central themes of therapeutic practice. To cover all the variations, individually, would fill a volume in itself. It is hoped that practitioners will be enabled to select those techniques and variations in method that fit best the patient they are treating, and their own skill and temperament.

CLASSIFICATION OF MODIFICATION IN PSYCHOANALYTIC THERAPY

The modifications and variations of psychoanalytic therapy can best be understood in terms of purpose.

I. Alternate Systems of Analytic Psychotherapy based on Theoretical or Ideological Differences from Freudian Classical Analysis.

    1. The non-Freudian systems
        a. The *individual psychology* of Alfred Adler.
        b. The *analytical psychology* of Carl Jung.
        c. The *Will therapy* of Otto Rank.

2. Neo-Freudian Systems based on the Cultural Emphasis.
    a. The *holistic* approach of Karen Horney.
    b. The *interpersonal relations* school of Harry Stack Sullivan.
    c. The *cultural* approach of Erich Fromm.

II.   Attempts to Streamline, Abbreviate and Speed Up the Process of Psychoanalytic Therapy.
    1. Stekel's *active analytic* psychotherapy.
    2. Ferenczi's experiments with *active* techniques.
    3. The Chicago school of *brief psychoanalytic therapy.*

III. Expansions of Freudian Classical Analysis in Various Directions.
    1. The "Object-Relations Approach" of Guntrip, Winnicott, Fairbairn, and the British School.
    2. The "Eight Stages of Man" and Erikson's extension of Freud's theory of character development.
    3. Character Analysis of Wilhelm Reich.
    4. Kohut's approach to the treatment of narcissistic character disorders.

IV.   Modifications Based on the Shift in Emphasis to Ego Psychology.
    1. Federn's ego psychology and the psychotherapy of the ego boundaries.
    2. Wolman's Interactional Psychoanalytic Therapy.

V.   Attempts to Combine Psychoanalytic Therapy With Experimental Psychological Findings.
    1. Mowrer's learning theory approach.
    2. Dollard and Miller's interpretation of learning theory and psychoanalysis.
    3. Ittelson and Kutash's integration of perceptual psychology and psychoanalytic therapy.

VI.   Modernization and Changes in Technical Tools of Psychoanalytic Therapy Applicable to All Systematic Approaches.

VII. Analytic Group Therapy.

VIII. Analytic Play Therapy.

CHANGES IN THE ANALYTIC SETTING

The original technical tools of psychoanalysis included the use of the couch with the analyst sitting behind the patient with the lights dimmed so that the patient could concentrate on his inner thoughts and associations with a minimum of distraction. This format has been altered by most of the newer schools of analysis and in insight-oriented psychoanalytic psychotherapy. Most psychotherapy is now conducted on a face-to-face basis and the interaction between patient and therapist receives greater emphasis. Analytic therapy has been extended to a greater variety of patients in addition to the hysterics and obsessive-compulsive neurotics and is now in use with borderline psychotics, character disorders, and people who aim to actualize their unused potentials and develop a richer experience in living.

Frequency of sessions may be geared to the productivity of the patients and no longer do analysts adhere to the tradition of five sessions a week. It is recognized by more therapists that the intensity of and depth of therapy is not necessarily related to the frequency of sessions. For some patients therapy may be on a "superficial" level, four or five times a week, while for others, great depth can be reached in two or three sessions a week. Many patients get good results with visits once a week. The cultural schools generally advocate seeing patients less frequently than four or five times a week.

There are also definite changes in some of the traditional customs of analytic therapy. The previously strict rules about the therapist having no contact with the patient outside the office if he should encounter him by chance have been relaxed. Analysts will now greet their patients and may also, on a selective basis, have communication with members of the patient's family with the patient's consent. This has resulted from a better understanding of the phenomena of transference and countertransference. For example, it is recognized that counter-transference may be present even if the therapist observes all the older rules, and that the overriding consideration is the therapist's awareness of his feelings in relation to the patient and to analyze and be aware of the patient's transference to him as distinguished from the real relationship between patient and therapist which may provide a corrective emotional experience.

Group psychoanalysis and analytic group therapy are now generally accepted as important new additions to the analytically-oriented modalities of treatment. Therapists now more often work with more than one member of a family as in marital therapy and there is a significant new development in working with the entire family in family therapy. (Bell, 1962; Fitzgerald, 1973; Greene, 1965; Rosenbaum and Berger, 1963; Wolf and Schwartz, 1962.)

CHANGES IN TECHNIQUES

Freud originally adopted the technique of *free association* as a basic method of psychoanalysis and adherence to the fundamental rule was paramount. The rule is now translated into merely requiring that the patient speak freely without censoring or holding back pertinent material. We all know how difficult it is for the patient to achieve truly "free" association. Sullivan questioned early the value of this technique. His patients were, of course, more schizoid and autistic and he felt that patient and therapist tended to indulge in parallel autistic reveries which too often did not meet in truly therapeutic contact (Munroe, 1955). Sullivan, like most of the other neo-Freudians, pointed out the need for and therapeutic value of genuine *communication* between patient and therapist. Free association is now used only occasionally and for a special purpose by many analysts. Horney and Fromm relied more on focused discussion rather than free association.

While all the schools of analysis and most analysts consider dreams to be "the royal road" to unconscious processes, there are marked differences in the interpretive methods and the use made of dreams in the analytic process. Where-as Freud used dreams primarily to help bring unconscious and preconscious material into consciousness in a timely fashion, when the non-Freudians interpret dreams, they do so in relation to the patient's actual current life problems and conflicts. While Freudians use the manifest content to get to the latent content through associations, the neo-Freudians often relate the material to the conflicts and anxieties of the patient in the here and now. A major contribution to more efficient and effective use of dream material has been made by Gutheil (1951) who was a disciple of both Freud and Stekel.

To the major technical tools of free association and dream interpretation, modern analysts and analysts from the non-Freudian and neo-Freudian schools have added and adapted a host of additional techniques some of which are derived from the classical method and many from the modified approaches. The communications from patients do not only consist of verbal free association, the relating of dreams, and the spontaneous expressions or slips of the tongue that were emphasized by Freud. There is now an arsenal of techniques that have been adopted and incorporated into the psychoanalytic therapeutic systems.

Thus, nonverbal communications and behavior within and outside the sessions are now reacted to and taken into account by the analyst. Langs (1973, p. 327) states in his two-volume work *The Technique of Psychoanalytic Psychotherapy,* "Such behavior constitutes a relatively important, although infrequently directly useful, source of data. It includes, for example, in-session rhythmic movements, playing with or pulling hair, biting or picking at fingernails, smoking, getting up from the chair, pacing, sitting away from the therapist, not looking at him, and unusual forms of dress. It may take the form of silences and instances of acting in-disturbed behavior directed toward the therapist. Such matters as requests for matches or Kleenex, leaving the session to go to the bathroom, and the offer of a gift include many nonverbal dimensions, as do many neurotic symptoms."

Attention is also paid to nonverbal cues in the patient's associations. "This includes his tone of voice, mood and affects, phrasing, language and ideas, richness or shallowness of thought, and other such dimensions."

Freud originally treated highly verbal patients who were quite repressed. As experience developed with other varieties of patients, attention to body language, nonverbal communication, and "acting in" behaviors and symptoms as commun-ications began to be incorporated in the psychoanalytic systems of treatment. For example, Adler would ask, "What does the symptom prevent you from doing?" Wilhelm Reich began to analyze "character armor," muscular tension, and character defenses expressed as silence and rigid postures. Rank gave atten-tion to manifestations of will while Ferenczi and Stekel analyzed such phenom-ena as procrastination and delay. Today, most psychoanalysts utilize all the forms of communication — body language, postures, verbalizations, behavioral communications, etc., within the framework of their system of analytic therapy.

There has developed a large body of techniques for arriving at interpretations and the trend among the neo-Freudians and the eclectic psychoanalysts is to draw from the various technical tools those they consider most applicable to a particular patient. Thus, there is a trend away from the heavy emphasis mostly on past historical material, in the direction of analysis of current events and behaviors which are considered to be representative of the past reaction pattern or what Freud called the repetition compulsion. As Langs (1973, p. 331) says, "References to current events and behavior on the part of the patient and others .... constitute a substantial part of the content of most sessions."

Of course the "depth" analysts working with a patient with sufficient ego strength will search for and bring into focus the latent meaning and this becomes a good source of insight. At the same time, the cathartic discharge takes place in the context of a corrective emotional experience. The analyst helps the patient correlate these insights with reality situations.

In modified psychoanalytic therapy the more flexible individualized interpretation of the significance of acting out has been fostered. Some analysts appraise its significance in terms of whether it does the patient harm or good. Thus, Fine (1971, p. 154) in discussing *acting out* states, "In discussion groups of analysts it frequently becomes apparent that what is acting out for one person is normal release of emotion for another. The meaning of sexuality in the therapist's own life plays a powerful role in his theoretical views on the subject. A decisive question is whether the activity does the person harm or good." In general, the current views range from the original Freudian injunction known as the rule of abstinence while in therapy, to the permissive approach that regards acting out as a communication and piece of behavior that should be analyzed. Acting out can subvert the therapy in some instances but enhance it in others depending on its specific significance. In general, the cultural schools are more likely to work with it in terms of its "here and now" significance.

The concept of acting in is well defined by Langs as "the living out of feelings and fantasies directly toward the therapist in the session, and often has both verbal and nonverbal aspects. It may take the form of direct attempts to seduce or attack the therapist, leaving the session, and pacing about. It usually indicates some kind of neurotic problem, and may convey latent content when viewed in proper context. Such behavior is not uncommon in borderline patients and when disruptive to treatment and the therapeutic alliance, merits prompt exploration and resolution. Nondisruptive forms of this behavior may require both verbal and nonverbal tolerance and response by the therapist."

THE RELATIONSHIP BETWEEN PATIENT AND THERAPIST

When examining the therapist-patient relationship we must recall that the transference and its utilization as a major agent of the analyst's therapeutic work is one of Freud's most original and creative discoveries. Its crucial importance is recognized by most practicing analysts and psychotherapists but dynamic changes and new developments have taken place in this dimension of analytic treatment. Many modern psychoanalysts have made major contributions to this subject.

Almost every book on the subject deals with this as a major facet of effective therapy.   As an example, we might cite Kohut's discussion of the "mirror" transference in narcissistic patients (Kohut, 1971).

Freud's definition of the transference was a very precise one. He viewed it as a repetition of those attitudes and affects toward the parents that existed during the oedipal period of childhood.   This resulted in neurotic patients concerning themselves more with the analyst thus neglecting their problems. Patients sought the analyst's love while others developed a hostile attitude resenting the analyst's authority and becoming competitive.   Freud interpreted these in terms of the oedipal situation which was consistent with his sexual theory of neurosis. Classical analysts and those who adhere to the traditional view still regard the transference as a reliving of the oedipus situation with the analyst.

With the greater use of face-to-face therapy and more direct communication between patient and therapist it became less and less possible for the therapist to conceal his real personal characteristics.   The patient's attitude began to be seen more and more as a blending of transference and realistic appraisal.   The unreal and symbolic emphasis became less prominent except in traditional classical couch psychoanalysis. The limitations of the early view and his precise definition of the transference lead Freud to assume that some patients such as narcissistic persons were incapable of transference. Today, Kohut has found that narcissists form a *mirror* transference in which the analyst is seen as a reflection of the patient. This is in line with the patient's self-love.

Freud's concept of transference led to the conclusion at first that only hysterics, obsessive-compulsive neurotics and phobic patients were susceptible to analytic treatment which required ability to form a transference.

All subsequent schools of therapy as they attempted treatment of other varieties of patients extended the concept of transference.   Thus, Reich (1945) extended the idea of transference so that it took into account defensive character traits and repetitive life patterns and applied not only to the libidinous situations of the oedipal period, but to induced long standing habitual patterns of behavior developed in relation to the parents at all other periods particularly the pre-oedipal ones.   He attributed the same irrational quality to these as the other transference phenomena.

Sullivan (1953) began to refer to these phenomena, which now included a variety of distortions, as *parataxic distortions*.   He regarded these as reaction patterns taken from the past and applied indiscriminately to the present situation even though they were no longer appropriate.   The therapist's task became one of helping the patient become aware of these as he acts them out, thus learning his true role in his interactions and problems and thus dropping his self-defeating archaic patterns.

Sullivan's great contribution was his therapeutic breakthroughs with psychotic and borderline patients.   He demonstrated that narcissists and pre-genital characters were capable of transference. As Thompson (1950) has stated, "The indifference or distrust so frequently shown toward the analyst by psychotics is just as truly a repetition of earlier patterns as the hysteric's "love" or "competitiveness."

The neo-Freudian analysts built upon the original idea that the relationship was not one-sided or unilateral and that countertransference was not just an error in treatment, but was always present. The therapist's awareness of his countertransference and the interpersonal transactions enables him to elucidate the patient's problems and to relieve his maladaptive symptoms.

Horney (1939) called attention to the bilateral nature of the analytic interaction. Some analysts, such as Reich (Munroe, 1955) advocated role playing as a means of re-enacting early experiences with the parents and resolving the conflict. The role playing or paradigmatic technique reached its most explicit development in Moreno's technique of *psychodrama* (Moreno, 1946).

One of Horney's major contributions was her novel interpretation of the repetition compulsion. She regarded the phenomena encompassed by this term as more than automatic repetitions of early childhood situations and felt that these did not occur in a compulsive manner. The mother transference was not an exact reproduction of the patient's attitude toward her mother at the age of four. The original basal attitude has been added to and modified in the course of growing up by subsequent experiences with mother figures. The current or final transference is thus the culmination of the accumulated experiences. According to Horney, psychological vicious circles within the person growing out of the neurotic defenses, complicate the transference which then includes a complicated defensive system that must be unwound.

Ferenczi also came to the conclusion that transference is not "a specific type of behavior peculiar to the doctor-patient relationship but, on the contrary, is generally applicable to social intercourse . . . . For Ferenczi, transference is simply a displacement . . . . or as Freud himself put it, 'a wrong connection.' But whereas transference is quite harmless in a healthy person, the neurotic's passion for transference, which prevents him from recognizing objective connections, actually makes him sick" (Wyss, 1973, p. 173).

Of interest as a forerunner of the "here-and-now" analytic therapists are the modifications in technique introduced by Rank. As stated by Thompson (1950, pp. 176-177), "Rank instituted three modifications of technique. The first was, like Jung's and Adler's, placing the chief emphasis on the present situation in the analysis in contrast to Freud's emphasis on the past, while treating reactions to the analytic situation as resistance. For Rank the therapeutic process involves a 'new experiencing,' not merely a re-living of the infantile past." The other modifications were the mother transference emphasis arising out of Rank's stress on the birth trauma, and the setting of a definite time limit for treatment and "considering the patient's reaction to that the most important material to be discussed." Making the analysis a living experience in the present with the analyst is considered Rank's most valuable modification.

Fromm (1947) among his numerous elucidations of analytic therapy, distinguished between rational and irrational authority. Rational authority is based on competence and genuine ability while irrational authority is based on a neurotic need for power. In competent therapy the analyst is a rational authority.

There seem to be as many interpretations and definitions of transference as there are systems of therapy. In the system of Melanie Klein and in terms of object relations theory, "transference is the phenomenon of the patient involving the therapist, who is part of his outer world in the conflicts that constitute his inner world, and its analysis reveals the kind of interaction that is going on between his inner and his outer worlds, mainly by projection and introjection" (Guntrip, 1973, p. 65).

NEW CONCEPTIONS OF THE ANALYST'S ROLE

Modification in the role of the analyst as conceived by today's psychoanalytic therapists reflect accurately the sweeping sociocultural and historical changes that have taken place. The original "neutral" analyst who tried to preserve anonymity by sitting behind the patient who reclined on the analytic couch on the theory that in this way the relatively uncontaminated transference would manifest itself, has in the modified current approaches, given way to the analyst who faces the patient and recognizes the importance of interactional relatedness and the reality of the therapist's person and characteristics. And as the movement toward more and more revealing and active therapists develops and persists in our activist culture, we begin to have "experiential" therapists who share their feelings and conflicts with the patient. The "experiential" school advocates that the therapist tell the patient how the patient makes him feel and what his concerns are (Whitaker and Malone, 1953). Representative schools of thought that involve greater activity on the part of the therapist are such currently popular techniques and orientations as: *transactional analysis* (Harris, 1973; Berne, 1961, 1964), *Gestalt therapy* (Perls, *et al.,* and Polster and Polster, 1973). *group analytic therapy, group process experiences, and encounter groups* (Bach, 1954; Foulkes and Anthony, 1965; Lieberman, Yalom, and Miles, 1973).

The essential and most relevant problem for the analyst today is how to maintain a suitable and flexible balance between listening, reacting, interacting and control of the process. Flexibility and sensitivity to the patient's needs determine when he reacts and with what mixture of warmth, affects and intellectual resourcefulness. To what extent does the therapist aim to fill the role he is placed in and to what extent is he himself? The view that the analyst must at all costs be himself seems to be appropriate not only with the dictum, "To thine own self be true," but with the current emphasis on "telling it like it is." Truth and reality are stressed by most of the here-and-now approaches. Many modern analysts have adopted and merged in with their system some brand of existentialism. (May, Angel and Ellenberger, 1958). Here, the philosophy of the analyst, his concern with the human condition and the essence of existence, the meaning of life and the promotion of "beingness" become prominent. Some of this can be compared with Adler's, "What life should mean to you" and Maslow's "process of self-actualization."

In non-Freudian methods it is recognized, but in different degrees, that neither the analyst nor the patient can maintain the degree of passivity originally advocated as an ideal by Freud and the classical analysts. As Schwartz (1965) has stated, Tarachow (1963) in presenting the Freudian viewpoint takes the position that, "to the extent that the analyst becomes an object for the patient treatment is not psychoanalytic." Schwartz (1965) goes on to say, "Since it is patently impossible for the patient to remain totally oblivious, totally unaware, and totally unknowing of any reality concerning the analyst, it is futile to hope to attempt ever to achieve such an idealized model for treatment. Analysis in this sense may never occur, may never be experienced." Most non-Freudians of all schools of thought and to a certain extent, the modern Freudian ego psychologists and most notably the object relations school (Guntrip, 1973), regard the analyst as always becoming an "object" for the patient so that they aim at his being a *real being* and along with Adler, Sullivan, etc. emphasize the educational activity of the analyst.

The Freudian ego psychologists such as Erikson (Evans, 1967), Hartmann (1958), Kris (1945), and Lowenstein (1951) certainly emphasize a reality orientation in the therapist's role as does Melanie Klein (1960) in her object relations approach. Hartmann and Kris (1945) developed the concept of the *autonomous ego development* and Hartmann included in his theory of *adaptation* a generalized theory of reality relations which stressed the special role of social relations. It remained for Erikson to build on the theory of reality relationships (1945) and especially to elaborate the theory of the role of social reality (1950) culminating in a *psychosocial* theory of development. This had a far-reaching impact on the analyst's role as did the work of Melanie Klein. The analyst did indeed become an object and in accordance with Erikson's concept of mutuality (1950) an important part of the analytic task is to analyze the ego and promote its strengthening, growth, and healthy development, through restoring healthy object relations. Certainly in helping the patient to resolve such basic conflicts as those involved in patients who have not reached a satisfactory homeostasis in each or in some of the eight stages or phases of the life cycle that Erikson postulates, the anaylst must allow himself to be an object and to analyze the conflicts involved.

Thus, in treating the conflict between *basic trust* and *mistrust* which stems from the earliest Freudian oral stage, the analyst must be capable of being the medium through which the patient can develop the optimal proportion between trust and mistrust. This needs to be accomplished in the *relationship* or *transference* through the analyst's responses and reactions to the patient's unconscious and contrived "tests" of the analyst's reliability. Certainly, this applies to the treatment of those patients whose conflict is between *autonomy* and *shame* and *doubt*.   Autonomy has meaning only in a relationship with another person or people — otherwise it is isolation. The active role of the therapist in all of the pre-oedipal stages, such as in dealing with the conflict between *initiative* and *guilt* in the patient, is of paramount importance in analysis of the ego. Kohut (1971) makes the analyst a mirror through which the patient can become aware of himself to the end that he can eventually relate to the therapist as an object.

Most non-Freudian analysts, with the possible exception of Jung, do not aim to promote regression in the patient as part of the analytic process. This is also related to the change from the couch to the face-to-face treatment. Yet, Hartmann's concept of regression in the service of the ego has restored some of the values of regression as a reinforcement of the ego as an antidote to the passivity of the patient leading to apathy, isolation, and alienation. The flexible analyst will work toward helping poorly-controlled, impulse-ridden patients to inhibit so that they can reflect upon and gain a preview of the possible consequences of acting without thinking or feeling.   Thus, with the hysteric or the behavior disorder patient he may encourage looking inward and becoming more aware of inner processes; while with the obsessive patient, the *passive* and *apathetic* patient, and the depressed, he may not only encourage activity, but aim to help them develop the outward look into the world around them and to act decisively and assertively.

An important distinction is often made between the classical psychoanalysts and the neo-Freudian and non-Freudian analysts in terms of *choice of patients.* As recently as 1965, E.K. Schwartz stated, "The more classical analyst justifies his treatment model by restricting psychoanalysis to neurotic patients . . . . The non-Freudians are not so exclusive in the choice of patients, and they treat the more severe neurotics, such as the obsessive, the character-disordered, and the varieties of psychotic patients.   Sullivan, like Fromm-Reichmann, saw schizophrenia as a human process to be understood, participated in, and healed."

The extensions of Freudian theory and practice by the ego psychologists, the child analysts, and the object relations school have, to some extent, enabled Freudian analysts to treat, both through new modifications of classical analysis and through analytic psychotherapy, a greater variety of patients than Freud originally contemplated although he conceived of the possibility of these later developments. Thus, Guntrip (1973) presents a plausible case for his view that analysis should include a regression beyond the limits called for by the classical Freudian school He facilitates the patient's regression beyond the oedipal to the pre-genital stages.   "Being accepted and understood in the schizoid position enables the patient to feel hopeful and to be born again" (Witenberg, p. VI, in Guntrip, 1973).

An interesting example of a modern modified psychoanalytic approach to the analyst-patient relationship. is *Interactional Psychoanalytic Psychotherapy*, introduced by Wolman (1965). Wolman divides all human relations according to the aims of the participants, depending on whether their main purpose is the satisfaction of their own needs (instrumental) or their partner's need (vectorial) or both (mutual or mutual acceptance). A normal or well-adjusted individual is seen as balanced in his social interactions. That is, he is instrumental in the struggle for survival, mutual in relationships with friends and family, and vectorial in regard to children and to those who need help. He is reasonably selfish (instrumental), reasonably mutual, and reasonably vectorial.

Mentally disturbed individuals have difficulty or are unable to preserve this balance. They are either *hyper-instrumental*, displaying infantile selfishness and parasitism as their major mode of relatedness, or they neglect themselves and worry constantly about others in a morbid *hypervectorialism* or they exaggerate in giving and taking in shifting moods of *paramutualism.*

In this conceptualization, the psychotherapeutic process involves an inter-action or exchange of cathexes. The analyst's role becomes one of restoring the healthy balance between the three types of relatedness. Wolman (1959), in his work with psychotic patients, regarded transference phenomena as true emotional involvements and as such, used greater caution in treatment. The therapist has the primary attitude of "vectorial" giving to the patient within limits set by the therapeutic situation. There is a resemblance between Wolman's mutual type of relatedness and Erikson's concept of *mutuality* which specifies that there is a crucial mutual coordination between the developing individual and his human (social) environment. Erikson's theory postulates a *cogwheeling of the life cycles.* The representatives of society, the caretaking persons, are coordinated to the developing individual by their specific inborn responsiveness to his needs and by phase-specific needs of their own (Erikson, 1959).

UNCONSCIOUS VERSUS CONSCIOUS PROCESSES

Classical psychoanalysis had the basic aim of bringing unconscious material into consciousness thus making the previously repressed conflicts available to the ego so that they can be resolved. The techniques utilized are primarily methods of making *unconscious* processes and material *conscious.* Hence, the use of dream interpretation, free association, and slips of the tongue, predominate and are emphasized in the treatment.

The deviations and departures from this basic aim are of several types. One direction is that exemplified by the schools that placed even greater emphasis on the unconscious processes even to the extent of postulating and utilizing the concept of collective unconscious, archetypes, and transcendental ideas (Jung, 1933). More modern derivatives along this line are the various brands of existen-tial analysts and the analysts who utilize the methods of Ferenczi.

At the opposite pole are those analysts and approaches that emphasize the world of outer reality, cultural and environmental influences, and interpersonal transactions and processes. Starting with Adler and Rank, we can also include the adherents of Horney, Sullivan and Fromm. A development within the

Freudian group itself is in the direction of greater emphasis on conscious processes (ego psychology).

Jung extended psychoanalytic principles to subjects with which he was intrigued, namely, the material gathered from myths, legends, fables, stories from the classics, and poetic fantasies. He also demonstrated the resemblance between dream psychology and the psychology of myths, and between the fantasies of the ancients, as expressed in myths and legends, and the thinking of children (Jung, 1920). Eventually Jung discarded Freud's causal approach and felt that mental life could be better understood by adding a *teleological perspective.* Jung thus became the inspiration for the "inspirational" movements in psychotherapy. However, Jung based his approach on a system of psychotherapy with a theoretical rationale as the basis for personality change through treatment. By contrast, the existential analysts whose general philosophical and humanistic values have much in common with Jung, nevertheless stress the phenomenology rather than unconscious processes. This has been labeled "a poorer psychology" with less clear-cut procedures by Wolf and Schwartz (1958, 1959).

Jung's intense preoccupation with the unconscious and his emphasis upon the intrapsychic "led him to the position that, 'Man's unconscious likewise contains all the patterns of life and behavior inherited from his ancestors, so that every human child; prior to consciousness, is possessed of a potential system of adapted psychic functioning (Jung, 1933, p. 184)' " (Schwartz, 1965). Schwartz concludes, "The unconscious perceives, has purposes and intuitions, feels, and thinks as the conscious mind does. Jung claims that there is sufficient evidence for this from psychopathological or clinical experience as well as from the investigation of dream processes. Consciousness is transient, whereas unconscious processes are transcendental or eternal. Reality is not objective or external, but rather internal" (Schwartz, 1965).

The cultural analysts, in contrast to Jung, place much greater emphasis on the conscious processes than he and Freud did. Horney adopted a holistic approach. Her followers deal with the entire activity of the patient, his view and outlook on life, and his conscious existence. Most of the current analysts, Horney, Fromm, Sullivan, and the "here-and-now" schools, consider consciousness to be the central problem of treatment. From this standpoint, the therapist's function has a strong educational aspect. For Adler, and his school in particular, the unconscious was the less understood portion of the personality. Adler emphasized outer reality and social values. He used educational techniques and placed primary emphasis on the role of the ego. He advocated an active attack on the patient's overt difficulties. His method was a didactic one — a form of re-education (Thompson, 1950).

Of particular significance are the changing usages with reference to dreaming and dream interpretation in relation to conscious and unconscious processes. As Green, Ullman and Tauber (1968) have stated, "Freud's self-analysis led to his investigation of his own dreams and childhood memories. His libido theory was based on the ideas he elaborated from these investigations . . .   In the end he focused on the infantile sexuality that he believed was concealed and disguised by the manifest dream content." Freud aimed at discovering and interpreting the latent content of the dream from the patient's associations to the unconscious processes and particularly oral, anal, phallic, and other instinctual strivings.   In classical analysis, the dream, like symptomatic behavior, the communication between analyst and therapist, slips of the tongue, and free associations is used to learn about and bring into consciousness, the *unconscious content* that is not in the patient's awareness.

After withdrawal from the Freudian group, Jung and Adler each developed their distinctive approaches to dreams.   Jung focused on his concern with the collective unconscious and archaic images (Jung, 1933) while Adler used dreams to reveal the "content of his theoretical preoccupation with the social and contemporary strivings of the individual" (Ullman, 1962).   Rather than review the individualized contributions to dream interpretation of Rank, Horney, Sullivan, and the experiential and existentialist schools, each of whom use dreams in a manner that fits their theoretical viewpoint, the more recent developments of the "ego psychologists" who focus more on the conscious processes and the *participation of the ego in dreams* and other unconscious processes will be emphasized.   Freud went from the conscious to the unconscious-manifest content to latent content.   The ego psychologists go from the unconscious manifestations to the role of the ego or conscious mind stressing the ego's function of integration and synthesis.

Erik H. Erikson made a startling new addition to Freud's work on dreams within the traditional psychoanalytic school.   He proposed a purposive perspective postulating that a dream may reveal more than a disguised wish fulfillment derived from infantile sources and can even be dreamed *in order to be analyzed* (Erikson, 1954).   Erikson draws attention to the importance of the manifest content of the dream and the way in which the patient reports it verbally.   He shows how the manner and content of the patient's verbalization highlights and makes evident the personal time-space of the dreamer and the nature of his defenses and accomplishments.   However, Green, Ullman and Tauber (1968, p. 148) indicate that "in spite of his attention to the verbal, sensory, spatial, temporal, somatic, interpersonal, and affective aspects of the manifest content, he never abandons the more narrow concept of latent dream material . . . . He goes beyond a concern with psychosexual issues and ego defenses to stress the importance of ego identity and a life plan, thus including much of the neo-Freudian contribution. In a more recent book, *Insight and Responsibility* (1964), Erikson adds a further dimension by assimilating the phenomenological emphasis on immediate subjective experience."   Medard Boss (1949), as an existentialist discusses the special quality or mode of existence that is exemplified in dreaming. "He points out that the person who dreams and recalls his dream is identical to the person who continues to function throughout the waking day. *Dreaming characterizes a separate and distinct form of existence for a person as the waking state or non-dreaming state of sleep characterizes another distinct form of human existence for the same identity"* (Green, Ullman and Tauber, 1968, p. 148). Here is the statement of the phenomenal nature of the dream as a form of existence in itself.

Gutheil (1951) utilized the contributions of Adler, Stekel, Jung, Freud, and particularly the *active* school of psychoanalysis and stressed the *past, present,* and *future* reference of the dream. His *Handbook* is perhaps the most practical exposition of dream interpretation.

Bonime (1962) in his handbook, *The Clinical Use of Dreams,* presents the use of dreams, clinically, in the tradition of Horney and Robbins. As Ullman (1962) states in his Foreword, "Like Horney, before him, he writes about analytic data within the context of the actual lives that people lead. In his own words he is interpreting the behavior of people who have dreams rather than engaging in dream interpretation. Horney saw dreams as attempts at solutions of conflicting needs in the organized personality structure. Horney herself, following in the tradition of Adler, saw in dreams a symbolic extension of the problems and adaptive maneuvers characteristic of the waking state.

Sullivan felt that the dream could never be accurately recalled in the waking state and that dreaming mostly takes place in the parataxic mode of experience. He made minimal use of dreams except to reflect back to the dreamer the significant statements to see if it provoked any particular thoughts in the mind of the patient (Sullivan, 1953). Fromm also de-emphasized the dream as a road to the unconscious but instead stressed how the dream illuminates the patient's struggle to avoid responsibility for himself. He also analyzes how the imagery of the dream illuminates "how the patient lives out life in false solutions, idolatrous pursuits, and evasions while it can, at the same time, reveal his hidden potentialities" (Green, Ullman, and Tauber, 1968, p. 150). Gutheil (1951) among others, stressed the problem solving properties of the dream and the proposed solutions inherent in the content.

EGO PSYCHOLOGY AND DEVELOPMENTAL PROCESSES

The development and functioning of the ego in all the stages of life is now considered, by most non-classical analysts and by the psychoanalytic ego psychologists, to be the most important focus in treatment. Perhaps the greatest impact upon psychoanalysis and psychoanalytic therapies has been made by the advances in ego psychology. Here, the results of the exploration of the family structure and its influence on the sexual and social development of the person must be considered. Significant advances have been made in the intensive study of the pre-genital experiences as the child grows and develops object relations.

In extending the range of applicability of psychoanalysis to children and adults suffering from psychopathology more severe than neurosis, the innovations of Melanie Klein must be cited. She developed methods for psychoanalytically treating many patients previously considered inaccessible to psychoanalysis.

Those analysts who have followed Kleinian techniques are more optimistic about psychoanalysis as a treatment method and may undertake patients suffering from severe character pathology, borderline and psychotic states, and regressed patients (Bychowski, 1952; Kernberg, 1967; Searles, 1965; Winnicott, 1963).

As an example of Bychowski's modification of psychoanalytic procedure for the treatment of borderline patients he stressed, "systematic elaboration of the manifest and latent negative transference without attempting to adhere to full genetic reconstructions on the basis of it, followed by 'deflection' of the manifest negative transference away from the therapeutic interaction through systematic examination of it in the patient's relations with others" and "utilization of environmental structuring conditions, such as hospital, day hospital, foster home, etc., if acting out outside the treatment hours threatens to produce a chronically stable situation of pathological instinctual gratification" and "utilization of the positive transference manifestations for maintenance of the therapeutic alliance, and only partial confrontation of the patient with those defenses that protect the positive transference, etc." (Bychowski, 1952, pp. 257-258).

Klein (1960) worked with the early material influences and the nursing situation as well as the pre-oedipal developmental process. The direct observation of infants (Spitz, 1965) and children and refined considerations of pre-genital phases and early narcissism resulted in new emphases in the treatment of regressed or severely disturbed adults. As these findings were applied to therapeutic techniques, new skills were developed to handle the levels of object relations and the early developmental processes.

With greater recognition of the complex intrafamilial influence and the recognition that the key to the treatment of the severely emotionally disturbed person is the understanding of the early maternal environment, it is a natural development to apply analytic principles to the treatment of the family as a group. Today, *analytic family therapy* is increasingly in use (Ackerman, 1958; Ferber, Mendolsohn and Napier, 1972).

Some of the culturist psychoanalysts who have focused on the ego processes have approached these from a combined existential and social interactive point of view. A representative view is that of Rollo May (1967) who speaks of modern man's loss of significance and the difficulties in maintaining personal identity in an "anonymous world." He relates his system to a phenomenological approach to psychotherapy and to existential therapy. Thus, he states, "I should like to make clear at the outset the relation of my views to what is called existential psychology and psychiatry. I am trained in psychoanalysis in the neo-Freudian, interpersonal school, but all my life I have been one to believe that the nature of man himself must be understood as a basis for our science and art of psychotherapy. The existential developments in our culture, whether in literature, art, philosophy or science, have precisely as their *raison d'être* the seeking of this understanding of man" (May, 1967, p. 87).

May's formulation with reference to the focus on consciousness is a clear statement of the current emphasis among the cultural and the existentialist analysts. He states, "I propose that unconscious experience can be understood *only* on the basis of our concept of consciousness. We must posit that the patient comes as a potential unit, no matter how clearly we can see that various neurotic symptoms have been blocked off and thereby have a compulsive effect on him" (May, 1967, p. 97). He goes on to indicate that "unconsciousness consists of the experiences that the person cannot permit himself to actualize. The questions in understanding unconscious phenomena, are, 'how does the individual reject or accept his possibilities for being conscious of himself and his world?' " May also points out the dangers in the relation of existentialism to psychotherapy and re-examines the ego and superego of *freedom* and *responsibility*.

The ego processes and the subject of ego identity and unity serve as the significant point of departure and development of modified technique in the treatment of psychosis, particularly schizophrenia. Most noteworthy in this regard is the work of R.D. Laing (1960) who regards the acute schizophrenic episode as a "metanoic process" in which the patient completely sheds the malfunctioning ego and, if not interfered with by repressive treatments, will grow a new and healthier ego. He likens the therapist to a midwife who presides at the birth of a new ego and whose role is to be with the patient, allay his terror and protect him from his own violence and fears while he is without a fully functioning ego. Laing speaks of the "embodied and unembodied self," the "inner self in the schizoid condition," the "false-self system" and "self-consciousness" (Laing, 1960).

The recapitulation of the developmental process and early relationship with the mother is illustrated in a most innovative approach which extends psycho-analytic treatment systematically to the treatment of *narcissistic personality disorders*. Kohut (1971) has made what may prove to be one of the great breakthroughs in ego psychology and psychoanalysis of the ego. He regards the narcissistic personality disturbance, which Freud felt was almost impossible to treat by psychoanalysis, as a defect in a person's inner cohesion and continuity — "An insufficient consolidation of the self" or ego. His systematic approach may open the door to the successful, rational treatment of one of today's most prevalent disorders.

"These patients establish a specific relationship to the psychoanalyst. They attempt to use him — as does a small child his mother — as a mirror in order to discover themselves and in order to be reflected in his admiration of them. Or they admire the analyst and attempt to experience themselves as part of him, feeling strong and good so long as this experience can be maintained." In the classical tradition such an approach to transference was looked upon as undesir-able and as impeding the growth toward realism and maturity. Kohut, however, feels that the therapeutic revival of these unfulfilled childhood needs, "allows the patients to obtain insight into the nature of their psychological imbalance and to gain mastery and control over it." He asserts that "the patients are thus enabled to make two crucial *developmental steps* which they had not been able to make in childhood: they convert their archaic grandiosity into healthy self-esteem, and they transmute external idealized omnipotent figures of their childhood into a set of internal guiding values and ideals."

Perhaps the most succinct summary statement of the contributions of the "ego analysts" such as Anna Freud (1946), Hartmann (1958), Kris (1951), Lowenstein (1955), and Erikson (1950) was made by Wolberg (1967, p. 203) as follows:

1. Behavior is determined by forces other than instinct in the form of response sequences encompassed under the classification of "ego."
2. The ego as an entity has an autonomy separate from both instinct and reality.
3. The ego supports drives for environmental mastery and adaptive learning which are divorced from sexual and aggressive instincts.
4. Female sexuality is an entity on a parity with, rather than inferior to male sexuality.
5. The classical topography does not explain the structure of the psychic apparatus.
6. The therapeutic encounter is more than a means of repeating and working through early traumatic experience; it is an experience in a relationship, containing positive growth potentials that can lead to greater self-actualization.
7. Activity and flexibility in the therapeutic approach are essential; this encourages eclecticism in method.
8. An optimistic, rather than a pessimistic viewpoint is justified regarding man's potentials as a creative, loving, and peaceful being.

THE IMPACT OF THE EXTERNAL ENVIRONMENT

When Horney wrote her first book, *The Neurotic Personality of Our Time,* she reflected on the effects of her immigration to the United States from Vienna, Austria, the birthplace of psychoanalysis. The change of cultural milieu revamped and changed her thinking and functioning as a psychoanalyst. She pioneered changes with the important aim of adapting psychoanalytic theory and practice to the American culture. Most of the non-Freudian analysts participated in the American "re-organization" of psychoanalysis. The modification included the following considerations: American emphasis on practical results through greater activity stimulated attempts to speed up and abbreviate psychoanalysis leading to less frequent sessions, shorter periods of treatment, and less time-consuming technical tools of psychotherapy. In all fairness, however, attempts to abbreviate psychoanalysis really started with original members of the Freudian inner circle who broke with the founder such as Ferenczi, Stekel, and Rank. Most of the non-Freudian schools moved in this direction. Psychoanalysis a la Freud was, of course, an original method of empirical clinical research, a theoretical system of personality, and a therapeutic system. It had to start as a time-consuming method.

It was the American influence that, on a massive scale, streamlined and developed variations and abbreviated forms of psychoanalysis and psychotherapy. One who bridged the gap by transferring his activity to the United States was Franz Alexander (Alexander and French, 1946). To what extent abbreviation and streamlining impaired the efficiency, the substance and depth of psychotherapy and analytic treatment is still being debated. Gutheil, who was at one time close to Stekel, pointed out that abbreviating psychotherapy could be compared to altering a father's suit to fit his son. You could not simply cut the length of the sleeves and pants, but you had to alter the whole suit.

Another American influence is definitely cultural. The frontier and open space psychology, the emphasis on personal freedom, ego identity and on activity brought about an amplification of trends toward activity, liveliness, and encounter in therapy. The use of the couch, for example, and the passive attitude of the analyst seems like an "undemocratic" procedure in the current scene. There is now a strong movement toward the extended family form of group analytic therapy, the therapeutic milieu type of treatment, and the growth of community mental health formats of treatment. Thus modified analytic techniques can be brought to bear on current problems of drug abuse, behavior disorders, and similar conditions. More active techniques now abound as do new active technical tools of psychotherapy. The action orientation fed by the American culture is reinforced further by the heavy American emphasis on social realities, equal opportunity, and relatively rapid social change.

The flowering of neo-Freudian and non-Freudian analytic procedures in the United States may certainly be related to strong indigenous social characteristics such as respect for the individual, the emphasis on personal differences and attention to human diversity. As Schwartz (1965) has stated, "The oversimplification and reductionistic systems of orthodoxy seem unacceptable to the American spirit. To treat all individuals and even all groups of individuals in exactly the same way, with the same techniques, is to deny the reality of individual differences and to create a new illusion rather than to cleave to reality. For some of the Freudian analysts, psychoanalytic concepts and principles do not allow modification in techniques."

The single greatest influence on the modification of Freudian psychoanalysis and the most relevant factor in the development of modified psychoanalytic therapies is the significance ascribed to the environment. The analysts of the non-Freudian schools generally place greater emphasis on environmental influences and outer reality than they do on inner processes. The pathogenic environment is given more weight than the instinctual drives, the psychosexual development, and intrapsychic processes as a basis for maladjustment or psychopathological behavior. Thus, the cultural analysts concentrate on the analysis of interpersonal relations and psychosocial factors in the context of societal influences.

A good example of a dynamic cultural approach in psychoanalysis is Erich Fromm's orientation toward treatment. Fromm stresses the value in therapy of uncovering what positive potentialities and healthy aspects of the self have been submerged or obliterated as a consequence of environmental restriction or condemnation. He distinguished between rational and irrational authority and the therapeutic task aims at helping the patient understand his passive compliance with irrational authority and to alter his character structure to relate more assertively and relevantly to the group in a healthy, productive way. Fromm made the task of distinguishing between rational and irrational authority through the patient's relationship with the therapist, the most essential aspect of the process of therapy. If this is correctly handled and achieved, the patient's unused potentialities for self-fulfillment through relationships with other people, can be released and developed.

An examination of most of the non-Freudian approaches shows an increasing emphasis on the analyst's values (Buhler, 1962). This involves such issues as the modeling behavior of the therapist, the question of the relative responsibility for the outcome of the therapy as between patient and therapist, the problem of cultural empathy and culture shock, as well as a host of other issues. Adler, Horney, Fromm, and May place great emphasis on the problems of alienation and the purposefulness of life. This addresses itself in the current scene to the increasing numbers of patients who are "hollow men and women" with symptoms of apathy, alienation from others, drug addiction, extreme passivity and social impotence, and dependency syndromes of one kind or another. College dropouts and executive "copouts" constitute a new group of patients who suffer from "emotional malnutrition." This is an age in which existing value systems are increasingly threatened. More non-Freudian therapies are addressing themselves to these "superego" deficiencies. A good example is Mowrer's *Integrity Therapy*. Many practitioners stress the responsibility of the analyst as well as that of the patient (Schwartz, 1956; Strupp, 1960).

CHOICE OF PSYCHOANALYTIC TREATMENT MODALITY

The variety of systems of psychoanalysis and the plethora of techniques, approaches, strategies, tactics, and analytically-oriented procedures and therapies, require some attempt to integrate them and to develop a rationale for choosing the strategy and approach best suited to the particular patient. For this purpose the author will utilize Federn's concept of ego boundaries as further developed by Gutheil (1958) and others, such as Zucker (1959), Ivey (1959), and Kutash (1963). We will also draw upon the view that each of the psychoanalytic schools was developed by its originators in response to the problems brought before them by patients who displayed the prevalent neuroses or psychopathological states *of their time and culture.*

We conceive of the ego as developing two major boundaries, one between itself and the outside world of reality and the other between itself and the inner world of the unconscious or id. As Kutash (1965, p. 952) has stated it, "In the psychologically well-functioning individual, these boundaries are optimally cathected and flexible so that the ego functions are properly exercised, including suitable repression and selective admittance into consciousness of primordial and instinctual drives from within and adequate reality testing and cognitive, perceptual experiencing of the external world. The major task of the ego is the successful integration of these pleasure drives and needs from within, with the reality considerations and requirements of the external world." We can thus define the mentally healthy state as even and satisfactory cathexes or homeostasis of the ego boundaries.

As previously stated, Freud developed the pioneering ideas and practices of classical psychoanalysis on a case load which consisted initially of cases of hysteria (Breuer and Freud (1955). In the hysterical personality structure the ego-id boundary is too rigid or over-cathected, reflecting massive repression of instinctual drive in varying degrees and the damming up of libido. This may have resulted from early specific trauma or a chronically traumatic or neurotic early childhood situation in which the major defense of repression was developed and much of the unpleasant, painful material was rendered unconscious. A good share of the libidinal or psychic energy became tied up in maintaining the repressions, leaving an inadequate cathexis of the ego-outer world boundary, which remains too permeable, resulting in such characteristic symptoms as extreme suggestiblity, histrionic acting out, problems of identity, tendencies toward dissociation reactions, emotional displays, and the usual kaleidoscopic array of hysterical symptoms which are acted out.

The rigidity of the inner boundary results in sexual naïvete , belle indifference, lack of drive, and in Freud's day the massive repression resulted also in conversion symptoms like hysterical paralysis, blindness, deafness, hyperesthesias and and anesthesias, etc. The various psychoneurotic reactions like the asthenic, hypochondriacal, conversion, dissociation, and phobic reactions may be thought of as varieties of hysterical personality structure developing under certain specific situations. Phobias may be regarded as symbolic representations of the repressed intrapsychic sources of the original anxiety, which are projected outward or displaced to less threatening objects in the outside world and perceived as external threats. This becomes possible only when the ego-outer world boundary is too fluid or permeable and the ego-id boundary is too rigid. For example, the repression of incestuous wishes and drives may be experienced in anxiety hysteria as a phobic reaction manifested by fear of enclosed places or of tunnels.

With this type of patient, the therapist in the outside world of reality easily makes contact with the patient's ego through the poorly cathected, loose outer boundary. An intense positive transference (described by Freud as "falling in love with the analyst") may be formed which is utilized by the analyst in the therapy to "help bring unconscious material into consciousness through release of repressions" (Kutash, 1965). "This is the classical type of neurosis prevalent in Freud's day as conversion, asthenic, dissociative, and hypochondriacal reactions in relation to which he developed his epoch-making theory and practice of classical psychoanalysis which was aimed at bringing the repressed unconscious material into consciousness, thus releasing libido cathexis from the inner ego boundary and making it available for more optimal cathexis of the outer ego boundary." For this purpose free association, dream interpretation, analysis of transference, the regression to, explanation, and reliving of childhood experiences and the classical techniques of Freudian analysis were useful and effective.

It is when Freud and his disciples and followers began to work with other types of patients such as the *obsessive-compulsive,* that modifications in analytic technique became necessary and began to be introduced. In the obsessive-compulsive personality structure it is the ego-outer world boundary that is too rigid, not permeable enough or overcathected. The individual has erected a barrier between himself and the outside world, bolstered by such character defenses as intellectualization, rationalization, isolation of affect, and compulsions. The inner boundary, by contrast, is too permeable and may be fractured, so that sexual thoughts, unacceptable ideas, and promptings from within continually enter consciousness in the form of obsessions. These are prevented from being acted out in the environment by the relatively impermeable outer boundary. This neurotic arrangement sets up the typical symptomatology of the obsessive-compulsive reaction in which "the anxiety is associated with the persistence of unwanted ideas and of repetitive impulses to perform acts which may be considered morbid by the patient" (American Psychiatric Association (1968). The individual is compelled by pushes from within to carry out his rituals.

A clear explanation of the situation of the obsessive-compulsive neurotic is given by Gutheil (1958, p. 351).

> Although the repressive effectiveness of their ego is reduced, they still must deal with their destructive anti-moral and anti-social tendencies. They are forced to use other means of defense to protect the integrity of the ego, means different from repression or sublimation. In the forefront of the new strategic approach stands magic. From the outset their situation seems desperate. The 'enemy forces' coming from the id, have overrun the weak barricades of repression and have penetrated into the center of the ego fortress. Unable to deal with the enemy at peripheral points, the ego is forced to invoke defenses it has used in its past, such as wishful thinking, feelings of omnipotence, magic formulas, symbolic gestures and compulsive rituals. It resorts to the mechanisms of denial and negation, to various oaths, clauses, and invocations, to ward off the danger of the id invasion.

The reality testing capacity of the obsessive-compulsive is preserved at the expense of rigid defenses around the ego-outer world boundary and its overcathexis. "Preoccupied as he is with warding off the instinctual forces, he is loath to deal with any influences from the outside world. He is rigid, incapable of absorbing much that impinges upon him from his environment. His views are extremely conservative since, above all, he is anxious to maintain the existing order" (*ibid*, p. 343).

The treatment of the obsessive-compulsive patient requires an analytic approach that aims at "de-cathecting" or softening the rigid defenses against and denial of external reality. There is a need, for example, for *character analysis* as developed by Wilhelm Reich (Reich, 1945) who worked with the negative transference and analyzed and dissolved the character defenses, rationalizations, denials, intellectualizations, and the compulsive mechanisms, thus releasing energy (libido) for use in sealing up the breaches and strengthening the inner ego boundary.

As stated by Kutash (1965)

> The obsessive-compulsive patient needs to undergo character analysis of the defenses and the rigid character structure since the symptoms are part of character structure and the defenses of rationalization, isolation of affect, etc., need to be penetrated and dissolved, relieving the rigidity of the outer boundary so that the inner boundary can be properly cathected. The obsessions would not be focused on nor would there be a heavy emphasis on bringing more unconscious material into consciousness since the inner boundary is already too vulnerable. The therapist faced by the rigid outer boundary may be confronted with a *negative transference,* hostility, and a host of defenses before he can get through to the patient's ego. The denial mechanisms and attempts at negation will be strong. Treatment not only would not necessarily involve an uncomplicated approach of bringing unconscious material into consciousness, but rather would be directed more toward analyzing the relationships with the outside world and people in it, as in Sullivanian interpersonal therapy (1958) and other neo-Freudian methods (Fromm-Reichmann, 1950: Fromm, 1947).

The Freudian psychoanalytic approach aims at releasing repressions, removing fixations, inhibitions and libidinal blockings. It *also* has the goal of increasing awareness and *insight* concerning inner processes and the unconscious, developing and enriching the ego through its greater awareness and improving its integrative function when its boundaries are in suitable homeostasis and flexibility. Some of the early variants from Freudian technique stressed different approaches to achieving these aims. The classical approach undoubtedly favored techniques for "bringing unconscious material into consciousness." Rank's Will Therapy (1945) aimed at mobilizing the will of the patient through greater awareness of his drives and inner promptings. He also stressed the emergence of these as a form of re-birth and tried to limit the therapy to nine months as a parallel to the gestation period in the birth process. The early abbreviators like Ferenczi, Stekel, and Rank, began the movements toward more streamlined analytic methods for increasing the ego's awareness of inner processes. Stekel (1950), for example, stressed inner conflicts as well as conflicts between anagogic and katagogic drives within the individual.

Freud originally felt that psychoanalysis of the obsessive-compulsive did not work well and encouraged the idea of modifications occasioned by the lack of the development of direct and clear-cut positive transference. Some of the newer schools "cut their teeth" on the character armored and obsessive-compulsive patients whose neurosis did not necessarily develop in the same way as the hysterical cases. According to this view hysteria developed from early traumatic events in the oedipal period or through fixations at various pre-oedipal stages, Such as the oral, urethral, and anal stages. Hysterical character structures showed "heavy loadings of oral, urethral, anal or oedipal influences; hence the emphasis on the past and the first six years of life."

The *obsessive-compulsive* may have weathered the early periods before the age of six without massive repression and become traumatized later by the impact of the outside world of reality. From a more secure, perhaps overpro-tected early life he developed difficulties in the school years through "traumatic" competitions with siblings and schoolmates. Adler's approach (1932) may be seen as focusing on this type of patient who represents an obsessive-compulsive in *statu nascendi.* The ego attempts to preserve even cathexis of the boundaries by constricting itself for the sake of economy in the distribution of cathexis. Adler thus aimed at overcoming the *inferiority complex* and developing social feeling and interest in the environment. Sibling rivalries were analyzed and ordinal position in the family is stressed as an important behavioral determinant.

With Reich the attention turned to more direct work with the ego-outside world boundary aiming at analyzing the defenses. It was almost inevitable that other therapies would evolve aiming at developing keener *outsight* (awareness of what is really happening in the outside world of people and events). The outward look in therapy leads to a better understanding of the type of lack of awareness referred to as *blind* spots or emotional scotomas (Stekel, 1950) and *selective inattention* (Sullivan, 1953). The inspection of and accurate perception of interpersonal processes and the patient's relationship to others became the major focus of the Sullivanian school and was included in most of the cultural schools. In choosing a therapeutic approach for the obsessive-compulsive patient who in the classical approach could conceivably obsess on the couch for many, many years and receive and verbalize tremendous intellectual insights with no remission of symptoms, but perhaps an increase in the obsessive thoughts that invade the ego, the neo-Freudians would advocate *not* bringing more inner material from the id into consciousness to increase the obsessions, but rather to discard the couch and concentrate on developing sharpness of perception of the outside world. What is really going on in his interpersonal relationships, in the transference, and are his interactions with people flexible and differentiated or based on rules and compulsions?

In the *ambulatory schizophrenic* or *pseudoneurotic schizophrenic* "both ego boundaries are damaged" or "fractured" and there is a danger of schizophrenic decompensation but there are islands of defense in terms of pseudoneurotic symptoms and rigidities in both boundaries, side by side with breaks in the boundaries" (Kutash, 1965). The treatment of the borderline patient has led to the development of a large variety of ego supportive and ego-building methods. Some innovators like Rosen (1953), Laing (1960), and all of the ego psychologists (Guntrip, 1973), have advocated acceptance of the patient in the *schizoid* position and the rebuilding of his ego in a nurturant fashion. Many therapists of the Kleinian school have also developed analytic techniques for repairing egos. Some of the family therapists and group analytic therapists have also made contributions along these lines. Essentially, the treatment of the ambulatory schizophrenic who has patches of rigid defenses and breaks in both ego boundaries requires a careful balance between supportive and uncovering techniques designed to release dammed up energy in the rigid islands of defense so that the cathexis can be available to "seal up the breaks."

In discussing the *depressive neuroses* Kutash (1965) states, "In the *neurotic depressive reaction* the attempt is made to preserve a homeostatic equilibrium in the boundaries by distributing the cathexis evenly through constricting the ego or contracting it. The depressive reaction in this sense may be understood as a defense against the development of actual defect in one of the ego boundaries and obviating the need for compensating in the other boundary in order to preserve equilibrium. In the depressive reaction the circumference of the two boundaries — particularly the outer boundary — become smaller through contraction of the ego, resulting in preservation of accuracy of perception, keen awareness of bodily processes, some hypochondriasis, and preserved and sharpened reality sense. Rather than allow the ego to become impaired, the depressive chooses to depreciate or squelch it until it can be expanded again when the stress or threat is lessened." The treatment of the depressed patient from the analytic point of view has stressed a bifocal approach — measures to expand the ego and its cathexis while lessening the outer or inner stresses by auxiliary measures. Some patients have mood swings and some schools of analysis and innovative techniques have concentrated on interpreting the bright spots when the patient has "black glasses on and everything looks dark" while pointing out the realities and less optimistic aspects when the "rose-colored glasses are on and everything looks rosy." The treatment of depressions have interested all the schools of analytic therapy and these patients have stimulated a large variety of "active" methods such as the *consciousness-raising* techniques and the encounter methods (Rogers, 1970).

The cathexis of the superego in relation to the ego and the ego-superego boundary is another major consideration in modified analytic therapies. Patients with punishing, over-developed superegos and conflicts between "moral" and "anti-moral" forces have been the focus of those of the approaches that have aimed at the clarification of the basic meaning of life, personal being in the world, and a variety of related considerations. Here we must include the *spiritual* emphasis of the Jungian school, the existential analysts and the schools that stress responsibility and committment. Values have become a major focus of the existential schools. Erich Fromm (Coleman, 1960, p. 522), for example, puts forth the thesis that "values are rooted in the very conditions of human existence; hence that our knowledge of these conditions, that is, if the 'human situation' leads us to establishing values which have objective validity; this validity exists, only with regard to the existence of man; outside of him there are no values." The current era presents us with a case load of patients who suffer from identity crises, who doubt the value of their existence, who have difficulty developing a usable system for themselves, and who become apathetic, withdrawn, and ineffectual. It is perhaps not a coincidence that these "new" breeds of neuroses occur in the atomic era when the existence of man as a species is in question since the means for his total self-destruction is available and is not under assured peaceful control. The external existential threat must indeed call forth new adaptive mechanisms to protect the ego and man's awareness.

An overview of the modified psychoanalytic therapies and the continuing new developments in ego psychology and psychoanalytic therapy of the ego raises the question of whether the analytcially oriented therapist can afford to adhere rigidly to a favorite system or school of psychoanalysis and fit the patient into his system or whether there is a need for a rebirth, already under way, of eclecticism in which the therapeutic approach is chosen to fit the particular patient. There is still need for much research and clinical experiences to aid in deciding which is the treatment of choice for whom.

REFERENCES

Ackerman, N. *The psychodynamics of family life.* New York: Basic Books, 1958.

Adler, A. *Individual psychology and its results in the practice and theory of individual psychology.* New York: Harcourt, Brace, 1932.

Adler, A. *The practice and theory of individual psychology.* Translated by P. Radin. New York: Harcourt, Brace, 1927.

Alexander, F. and French, T.M. *Psychoanalytic therapy: principles and application.* New York: Ronald, 1946.

American Psychiatric Association. *Diagnostic and statistical manual of mental disorders,* Third Edition, 1968.

Bach, G.R. *Intensive group psychotherapy.* New York: Ronald, 1954.

Bell, J.E. Recent advances in family group therapy. *J. Child Psycho. Psychiat.* 1-15 (1962).

Berne, E. *Transactional analysis in psychotherapy.* New York: Grove Press, 1961.

Berne, E. *Games people play.* New York: Grove Press, 1964.

Bonime, W. *The clinical use of dreams.* New York: Basic Books, 1962.

Boss, M. *Meaning and content of sexual perversions.* New York: Grune and Stratton, 1949.

Breuer, J. and Freud, S. (1895). Studies on hysteria. *Standard Edition,* vol. 2. London: Hogarth Press, 1955.

Buhler, C. *Values in psychotherapy.* New York: Free Press of Glencoe, 1962.

Bychowski, G. *Psychotherapy of psychosis.* New York: Grune & Stratton, 1952.

Coleman, J.C. *Personality dynamics and effective behavior.* Palo Alto: Scott, and Foresman and Co., 1960.

Erikson, E.H. Childhood and tradition in two American Indian tribes. *The Psychoanalytic Study of the Child,* I: 319–350. New York: International Universities Press, 1945.

Erikson, E.H. *Childhood and society.* New York: Norton, 1950.

Erikson, E.H. The dream specimen of psychoanalysis. *J. Amer. Psyc. Assoc.* 2: 5–56 (1954).

Erikson, E.H. Identity and the life cycle. *Psychol. Issues.* Mongr. No. 1, 1959.

Erikson, E.H. *Insight and responsibility.* New York: Norton, 1964.

Evans, Richard I. *Dialogue with Erik Erikson.* New York: Harper and Row, 1967.

Ferber, A., Mendelsohn, M. and Napier, A. *The book of family therapy.* New York: Science House, Inc., 1972.

Fine, R. *The healing of the mind.* New York: David McKay Co., 1971.

Fitzgerald, R.V. *Conjoint marital therapy.* New York: Jason Aronson, 1973.

Foulkes, S.H. and Anthony, E.J. *Group Psychology.* London: Penguin Books, 1957.

Freud, A. *The psychoanalytical treatment of children* (1926). New York: International Universities Press, 1946.

Fromm, E. *Man for himself.* New York: Rinehart, 1947.

Fromm, E. *The sane society.* New York: Holt, 1955.

Fromm-Reichmann, F. *Principles of intensive psychotherapy.* Chicago: University of Chicago Press, 1950.

Green, M.R., Ullman, M. and Tauber, E.S. Dreaming and modern dream theory. In: Marmor, J. (Ed.), *Modern psychoanalysis: New directions and perspectives.* New York: Basic Books, Inc., 1968.

Greene, B.L. *The psychotherapies of marital disharmony.* New York: The Free Press, 1965.

Guntrip, H. *Psychoanalytic theory, therapy, and the self.* New York: Basic Books, p. V, 1973.

Gutheil, E.A. *The handbook of dream analysis.* New York: Liveright, 1951.

Gutheil, E.A. Dreams as an aid in evaluating ego strength. *American J. Psychother.* 12: 338–355 (1958).

Harris, T.A. *I'm OK–You're OK.* New York: Avon, 1973.

Hartmann, H. (1939) *Ego psychology and the problem of adaptation.* New York: International Universities Press, 1958.

Hartmann, H. and Kris, E. *The genetic approach in psychoanalysis. The Psychoanalytic Study of the Child.* 1: 11–30. New York: International Universities Press, 1945.

Horney, K. *The neurotic personality of our time.* New York: Norton, 1937.

Horney, K. *New ways in psychoanalysis.* New York: Norton, 1939.

Ivey, E.P. Recent advances in diagnosis and treatment of phobias. *Amer. J. Psychother.* 13: 35–50 (1959).

Jung, C. *Collected papers on analytic psychology.* Translated by C.E. Long. London: Balliere, 1920.

Jung, C.G. *Modern man in search of a soul.* New York: Harcourt, Brace and World, 1933.

Kernberg, O. Borderline personality organization. *J. Amer. Psychoanal. Assoc.* **15**: 641–685 (1967).

Klein, M. *The psychoanalysis of children.* New York: Grove Press, 1960.

Klein, M. *Our adult world and other essays.* New York: Basic Books, 1963.

Kohut, H. *The analysis of the self.* New York: International Universities Press, 1971.

Kris, E. On preconscious mental processes. In: Rapaport, D. (Ed.), *Organization and Pathology of Thought,* pp. 474–493. New York: Columbia University Press, 1951.

Kutash, S.B. Treatment of symptoms, perceptual flexibility, and ego boundaries. Paper read at Eastern Psycholigcal Association, 1963.

Kutash, S.B. Psychoneuroses. In: Wolman, B.B. (Ed.), *Handbook of clinical psychology.* New York: McGraw-Hill, 1965.

Laing, R.I. *The divided self.* New York: Pantheon Books, 1960.

Langs, R.J. *The technique of psychoanalytic psychotherapy,* Vols. 1 and 2. New York: Jason Aronson, 1973, 1974.

Lewis, N.D.C. Historical roots of psychotherapy. In: Masserman, J.H. and Moreno, J.L. (Eds.), *Progress in psychotherapy,* Vol. III, pp. 20–26. New York: Grune & Stratton, 1958.

Lieberman, M.A.; Yolom, I.D. and Miles, M.B. *Encounter Groups: First Facts.* New York: Basic Books, In., 1973.

Lowenstein, R.M. Conflict and autonomous ego development during the phallic phase. *The psychoanalytic study of the child.* **5**: 47–52. New York: International Universities Press, 1950.

May, R. *Psychology and the human dilemma.* New York: Van Nostrand Reinhold, 1967.

May, R., Angel, E. and Ellenberger, H.F. *Existence, a new dimension in psychiatry and psychology.* New York: Basic Books, 1958.

Moreno, J.L. Psychodrama and group psychotherapy, *Sociometry.* **9**: 249–253 (1946).

Munroe, R.L. *Schools of Psychoanalytic Thought.* New York: Dryden Press, 1955.

Perls, F.; Hefferline, R.R. and Goodman, P. *Gestalt therapy.* New York: Julian Press, 1951.

Polster, F. and Polster, M. *Gestalt therapy integrated.* New York: Brunner/ Mazel, 1973.

Rank, Otto, *Will therapy; and truth and reality.* New York: Knopf, 1945.

Reich, W. *Character analysis.* New York: Orgone Institute Press, 1945.

Rogers, C. *Carl Rogers on encounter groups.* New York: Harper and Row, 1970.

Rosen, J.N. *Direct Analysis.* New York: Grune & Stratton, 1953.

Rosenbaum, M. and Berger, M. *Group psychotherapy and group functions: selected readings.* New York: Basic Books, 1963.

Schwartz, E.K. Non-Freudian analytic methods. In: Wolman, B.B. (Ed.), *Handbook of Clinical Psychology.* New York: McGraw-Hill, 1965.

Schwartz, E.R. Is there need for psychology in psychotherapy? In: Krout, M.L. (Ed.) *Psychology, psychiatry and the public interest,* pp. 113–134.   Minneapolis: University of Minnesota Press (1956).

Searles, H.F. Positive feelings in the relationships between the schizophrenic and his mother. *Int. J. Psycho-Anal.* **39**: 569 (1965).

Spitz, R.A. Hospitalism. *The psychoanalytic study of the child,* Vol. 1: 53–74. New York: International Universities Press, 1965.

Stekel, W. *Techniques of analytical psychotherapy.* New York: Liveright Publishing Corporation, 1950.

Strupp, H.H. *Psychotherapists in action.* New York: Grune & Stratton, 1960.

Sullivan, H.C. *The interpersonal theory of psychiatry.* New York: Norton, 1953.

Sullivan, H.S. *Conceptions of modern psychiatry,* (second edition.) New York: Norton, 1953.

Tarachow, S. *An introduction to psychotherapy.* New York: International Universities Press, 1963.

Thompson, C. *Psychoanalysis, evolution and development.* New York: Norton, 1950.

Ullman, M. Dreaming, life style and physiology: a comment on Adler's view of the dream. *J. of Individual Psychology.* **18**: 18–25 (1962).

Whitaker, C.A. and Malone, T.P. *The roots of psychotherapy.* New York: Blakiston, 1953.

Winnicott, D.W. *The maturational processes and the facilitating environment.* New York: International Universities Press, 1963.

Witenberg, E.G. Foreword. In: Guntrip, H., *Psychoanalytic theory, therapy, and the self.* New York: Basic Books, 1973.

Wolberg, L.R. *The technique of psychotherapy,* second edition, Parts I and II. New York: Grune & Stratton, 1967.

Wolf, A. and Schwartz, E.K. Irrational psychotherapy: an appear to unreason. *Amer. J. Psychother.* **12**: 300–314, 508–521, 744–759 (1958).

Wolf, A. and Schwartz, E.K. Irrational psychotherapy: an appeal to unreason. *Amer. J. Psychother.* **13**: 383–400 (1959).

Wolf, A. and Schwartz, E.K. *Psychoanalysis in groups.* New York: Grune & Stratton, 1962

Wolman, B.B. *Psychotherapy with latent schizophrenics.* **13**: 343–359 (1959).

Wolman, B.B. (Ed.) *Handbook of clinical psychology.* New York: McGraw-Hill, 1965.

Wolman, B.B. Quo vadis, psychoanalysis? *J. of Contemporary Psychotherapy.* **4**: 23–26 (1971).

Wyss, D. *Psychoanalytic schools.* New York: Jason Aronson, 1973.

Zucker, L.J. Ego weakness, ego defenses and ego strengthening. *Amer. J. Psychother.* **13**: 614–634 (1959).

6 Behavior Modification and Therapy

G. Terence Wilson and Arnold A. Lazarus

During the past two decades, an impressive technology of active treatment procedures derived from well-controlled clinical and experimental studies has been developing. *Behavior modification* and the roughly synonymous term *behavior therapy* are used to describe this applied experimental-clinical trend. In contrast with early stimulus-response formulations that attempted to reduce nearly all clinical complexities to phobic anxieties (e.g., Wolpe, 1958; Eysenck, 1960), the present-day behavior modifier draws on a wide range of social learning theories and techniques (Wilson and O'Leary, 1980).

Ebbinghaus's much quoted observation that "psychology has a long past but a short history" is particularly true of behavior modification. While the major historical roots of behavior modification are embedded in the animal laboratories of Pavlov, Bekhterev, Thorndike and early Skinner, current behavioral practices owe their impetus to work conducted no earlier than 1950. In England, Shapiro (1951) described the application of experimental psychology to the single case and contrasted it with the traditional approach in clinical psychology. Eysenck (1959) defined behavior therapy as the application of "modern learning theory" to emotional disorders, and together with his students and associates exercised a powerful influence on early developments.

In the United States, Lindsley and Skinner (1954) conducted laboratory studies to demonstrate that the behavior of severely disturbed persons followed the same learning principles as that of normal persons. Like Shapiro in England, Skinnerians also focused their attention upon the experimental study of the single case — although Skinner *et al.* worked mainly with psychotic patients. Their operant conditioning procedures were predicated upon the assumption that behavior is a function of its consequences. Whereas the English workers made use of hypothetical constructs to explain their findings, American behavior modifiers followed Skinner's eschewal of all mediating constructs.

The term "behavior therapy" first appeared in the literature when Lazarus (1958) used it to describe Wolpe's (1954) objective psychotherapy procedures. This work was carried out in South Africa, and was independent of the English and American efforts previously alluded to. Wolpe's (1958) book on "reciprocal inhibition" contained many of the points of emphasis that were first documented by Jones (1924), Dunlap (1932), Guthrie (1935), Herzberg (1941) and Salter (1949). Despite conceptual shortcomings, it was vigorously promoted by Eysenck (1960), who hailed its publication as "the coming of age of behavior therapy as an independent and practically applicable discipline" (Eysenck, 1960, p. xi). There was a widespread dissatisfaction among mental health workers with traditional approaches to psychodiagnosis and psychotherapy, and by the time Wolpe's (1958) book appeared, many were ready to examine alternative methods of treatment. Clinical psychologists were growing especially dissatisfied with their futile exercises in administering and scoring batteries of projective and other routine tests lacking in reliability and validity.

Since the 1960s behavior modification and therapy has gained and maintained an enormous momentum. There are several high-quality professional journals devoted to behavior modification or behavior therapy (during the 1960s two seminal journals were launched: *Behaviour Research and Therapy* was started in 1963, and the *Journal of Applied Behavior Analysis* first appeared in 1968), and in the past twenty years the number of books, monographs, chapters, articles and symposia has become quite overwhelming. In the early 1970s, a task force report on the field of behavior modification conducted under the auspices of the American Psychiatric Association concluded that "behavioral principles employed in the analysis of clinical phenomena have reached a stage of development where they now unquestionably have much to offer informed clinicians in the service of modern clinical and social psychiatry" (Birk *et al.*, 1973, p. 64). It has become increasingly evident that behavior modification and therapy is no passing fad but is an integral part of current psychological therapies, and may be viewed "as the single most significant development in the effective treatment of clinical disorders in recent times" (Rachman and Wilson, 1980, p. 194).

BEHAVIORAL ASSESSMENT AND DIAGNOSIS

Criticisms of conventional psychiatric diagnoses are by no means confined to behaviorally oriented clinicians; widespread dissatisfaction has been expressed about the nosological inadequacies, low reliability and limited prognostic value of traditional diagnostic labels. A valid and reliable diagnosis should lead to logical and specific forms of treatment. It has become clearly evident that terms like "schizophrenia," "neurosis," "psychosis," "character disorder" and similar labels usually suffer from internal inconsistency and imprecision, and lack the specificity for generating meaningful treatment interventions. A useful diagnosis should specify salient etiological antecedents (i.e., those that have current therapeutic relevance) and provide reasonable prognostic indications.

In behavior modification, the diagnostic process (usually referred to as the "functional analysis" or a procedure of "problem identification") endeavors to describe the patient's complaints in objective terms, while searching for antecedent and maintaining factors and the probable means by which each problem area can be resolved. Presenting complaints are usually divided into *behavioral excesses* (e.g., exhibitionism, compulsive checking, frequent rage reactions, overeating, etc.), and/or *behavioral deficits* (e.g., impotence, social withdrawal, timid and unassertive reaction patterns, etc.). In essence, the behavior modifier endeavors to increase or decrease the frequency of specific behaviors, depending upon their social context. A diligent search is conducted to uncover and clarify the variables in the patient's biological, psychological and sociological systems that maintain the current problem behaviors. Kanfer and Saslow (1969) provided one of the first comprehensive formats for achieving a detailed functional analysis of behavior. Their schema incorporates the patient's areas of adequate and optimal functioning into the analysis, and stresses that these assets are important for planning treatment strategies. The behavioral analysis is continually modified and refined as more information about the patient is gained. Wherever possible, an attempt is made to quantify the behavioral descriptions. Frequency distributions are compiled — how many aggressive outbursts, how many avoidance responses, how many negative self-statements, how many delusional remarks did the patient emit? Self-monitoring is also highly recommended, especially for well-motivated patients who can count their own positive and negative responses to a wide variety of stimuli.

In the practical details of his or her day-to-day work, the behavioral clinician, like any other well-trained therapist, attempts to understand his or her patients' personal constructs, their presenting complaints, the factors that gave rise to their difficulties, conflicts, perceptual distortions and idiosyncracies. Thus, history-taking, assessment and evaluation combine to yield an accurate portrait of the patient in a unique network of social interactions. But unlike general psychiatric anamnesis, no less attention is paid to overt behavior than to verbal reports of feelings, thoughts and fantasies. Second, as already mentioned, behavior modifiers do not regard the task of diagnosis as that of assigning the patient to a category and then applying the treatments that are considered to be best for members of that category. The behavior modifier seldom asks *why* questions. (Why do you become so anxious in crowded places? Why are you punishing yourself?) Questions starting with how, when, where, what and who are found to be more productive for eliciting the significant personal and situational variables that cause and maintain emotional disturbances. (How did you respond at the time? What were you doing? Who was with you? When did this happen? Where was your husband?) The upshot of a functional analysis is a detailed and specific range of hypersensitivities, shortcomings, avoidance behaviors and social inadequacies for each patient. *Specificity* is the hallmark of behavior therapy. Where a tradition-al therapist may speak of a patient as "an obsessive-compulsive personality with passive-aggressive tendencies," behavior therapists would say, "Mr. Smith washes his hands on an average of 96 times a day; he is inhibited with most authority fig-ures, although he is inclined to overassert his authority with subordinates; he avoids intimate contacts with women which he attributes to his premature ejaculation; he is hypersensitive to criticism, rejection and disapproval." Each of the foregoing problem areas would then be even more clearly articulated, with special emphasis being devoted to particular eliciting and maintaining conditions.

Lazarus (1973, 1976, 1981) has proposed a more detailed and systematic as-sessment process. During diagnostic interviews and throughout the course of ther-apy, his *multimodal orientation* examines seven interactive modalities: overt be-havior, affective responses, sensory reactions, emotive imagery, cognitive process-es, interpersonal relationships and a "biological modality" especially characterized by indications and contraindications for the use of drugs or medication. The ac-ronym BASIC ID (derived from *Behavior, Affect, Sensation, Imagery, Cognition, Interpersonal, and Drugs*) provides a useful mnemonic for remembering the sepa-rate yet interrelated modalities. Although *overt behavior* (e.g., compulsive rituals, tics, blushing, tremors, crying spells, stuttering, delusional speech, etc.) and *inter-personal responses* (e.g., arguments, discussions, affectionate gestures, etc.) are amenable to direct observation, the other modalities depend upon verbal reports. Affect, imagery, sensation and cognitive processes are hypothetical constructs — "off limits" to radical behaviorists, but clinically crucial to behaviorally oriented therapists. The application of various sensory exercises is clearly behavioral, how-ever (e.g., the prescribed use of tactile interchanges along a graded series of inti-mate encounters for overcoming sexual inhibitions). But the statement, "I have an image of my late mother's funeral" is, strictly speaking, verbal behavior. Yet within the multimodal framework, it is assumed that associated "verbal operants," involving interrelated "affective responses," "cognitions" and "subjective sensa-tions," can be elicited. "The image makes me feel sad and sorry for myself, as I keep thinking that I am to blame for her premature death, which, in turn, makes me feel tense all over." In terms of this framework, a multimodal behavior ther-apist would then pursue the following types of interventions:

Behavior: Increase the number of positive-reinforcing activities in which the patient participates.

Affect: Teach the patient to express anger in an assertive manner instead of lapsing into self-pity.

Sensation: Use deep muscle relaxation to overcome generalized tension.

Imagery: Show the patient how to dwell on pleasant memories instead of focusing on negative elements.

Cognition: Try to alter negative self-talk by disputing internalized guilt-inducing sentences.

Interpersonal: Be sure that friends and family members are not reinforcing the self-denigrating behaviors by inappropriately offering sympathy and warmth.

Drugs: If "sadness" or "depression" persists or becomes more intense, medication may be indicated.

While there is considerable overlap between Lazarus's multimodal orientation and the multifaceted and multidimensional procedures and practices of present-day behavior therapy, there are also significant points of departure (Lazarus, 1981). Kazdin and Wilson (1978) regard multimodal therapy as beyond the boundaries of behavior therapy and state that "although there is some historical connection and considerable overlap in terms of therapeutic techniques, multimodal therapy departs from behavior therapy on both conceptual and methodological grounds" (p. 21). Multimodal therapists examine each client's BASIC ID in detail and endeavor to assess specific problems (as well as assets) in each modality. They also pay considerable attention to the interactions of every modality with each of the six others. Multimodal therapists attempt to establish a specific "firing order" for each major problem. Thus, one client may appear to generate and maintain his or her problems by focusing on, say, sensory-imagery-cognitive-behavioral (SICB) sequences, whereas someone else with identical presenting complaints may reveal a CBIS (cognitive-behavioral-imagery-sensory) pattern. The selection of techniques is heavily guided by the individual "firing orders" that are obtained. These and many other aspects of multimodal therapy are described by Lazarus (1981), who contends that when behavior therapy gains additional sophistication, the multimodal orientation will no longer be considered outside its purview.

Special Clinical Considerations

The ardent behavioral clinician will from time to time encounter certain difficulties and therapeutic paradoxes. The systematic manipulation of environmental contingencies may alter people's responses to stimuli in remarkable ways, and yet in other instances zero progress will ensue. Echolalic children may learn coherent speech, backward schizophrenics may become more productive human beings, and chronically anxious, obsessive and depressive individuals may embrace a fulfilling and assertive *modus vivendi*. In more precise cases, such as the elimination of certain tics, temper tantrums, compulsive rituals, sexual deviations and withdrawal tendencies, the behavior modifier may even by able to employ ABA designs to demonstrate that his or her interventions were indeed the active ingredients of the observed changes. But the paradox to which we referred may enter suddenly when a seemingly simple encopretic child continues to soil himself despite ingenious modifications in various rewarding and punishing contingencies. Or perhaps a client consistently "forgets" to practice her relaxation exercises as a precursor to desensitization therapy.

The concept of "resistance" (behavioral nonresponsiveness) has become as important to behavior therapists as it has been for psychoanalysts, although their respective views on the subject differ markedly (Wachtel, 1982). Significant aspects of control and countercontrol should not be overlooked, as Lazarus and Fay (1982) emphasize, and from a behavioral perspective, the varieties of resistance may be attributed to four main factors:

1) Resistance as a function of the patient's individual characteristics.
2) Resistance as a product of the patient's interpersonal relationships (systems or family processes).
3) Resistance as a function of the therapist (or the relationship).
4) Resistance as a function of the state of the art (and science).

Lazarus and Fay (1982) elaborate on each of these areas and offer the caveat that a vague and general usage of "resistance" is more likely to obfuscate than illuminate the course of therapeutic endeavors. Some therapists tend to confuse resistance with rationalized failure!

It is easy to offer various post hoc explanations according to learning principles, but it is obviously useless to do so in terms of their predictive value. When examining therapeutic failures, to insist that target behaviors did not shift in a desired direction because the maintaining conditions and requisite reinforcements were inadequately manipulated, may be true in many instances, but this reasoning becomes tautological when consistently invoked as an explanatory principle. Social learning theory may be called upon to investigate and to add information regarding interpersonal expectancies that lead to various paradoxes in communication. The foregoing has been well documented from a different clinical perspective (e.g., Haley, 1973). To cite a specific case in point, it is often reported that by "prescribing the symptom" a rapid diminution of "symptomatic behavior" may ensue. Thus, certain impotent men may "defy" their therapists and become fully potent when instructed to refrain from sexual intercourse. Similarly, one of us found, in treating a seemingly refractory case of anorexia nervosa, that the woman gradually resumed normal eating patterns upon being told to try to lose another ten to fifteen pounds.

To point out that the behavior changed because the therapist altered the reinforcers that maintained her noneating behavior begs the question. It is difficult to account for the fact that other shifts in reinforcement failed to achieve the desired end (e.g., selective inattention, withdrawal of privileges and time-out procedures). It is also difficult to predict when a "paradoxical intervention" may exacerbate the situation. To prescribe a ten- to fifteen-pound weight loss is hardly a "cure" for anorexia nervosa! We are merely reemphasizing the fact that existing principles of learning cannot readily account for many of the phenomena that the practicing clinician encounters. The crucial question — as yet unanswered — is what combination of techniques will prove most effective with what types of problems, delivered by which therapists to what patients?

SIGNIFICANT BEHAVIOR THERAPY METHODS AND DIRECTIONS

Behavior therapy is characterized in part by a number of diverse techniques for treating a wide range of clinical disorders. Nevertheless, it would be a mistake to think of behavior therapy as a mere collection of techniques. Rather, it represents an approach in which the therapist flexibly draws upon the principles and procedures of behavior therapy in tailoring therapy to the individual client's specific problem(s). By and large, these principles and procedures are derived from, or at least are consistent with, the content of experimental psychology. For the sake of expositional convenience, we arbitrarily discuss individual treatment techniques in the remainder of this chapter. Yet we hasten to caution the reader that there is usually no substitute for a skilled therapist's assessment of the niceties of each case and the consequent use of a multidimensional treatment approach that features many forms of therapeutic intervention including both cognitive and behavioral methods. In addition to individual therapy, behavioral methods are often used with couples, with families and in groups. A good therapeutic relationship is a necessary but not sufficient basis for therapeutic success. Although the emphasis in what follows is on technical matters, this should not be misinterpreted to mean that the importance of the therapist-patient relationship is relegated to a secondary role. Discussions of the role of the therapeutic relationship in behavior therapy are provided by Lazarus (1981) and Wilson and Evans (1977).

Systematic Desensitization

The basic assumption behind desensitization procedures is that the fear evoked by subjectively threatening situations can be reduced by a graded and progressive exposure to a hierarchy of anxiety-generating situations. The client is taught to employ various "anti-anxiety" responses (e.g., deep muscle relaxation, pleasant imagery or rational self-assurance) and thereby systematically extinguish each level of anxiety. The most effective desensitization procedures appear to require actual exposure to real-life situations (Sherman, 1972) although imaginal desensitization (i.e., counterposing through relaxation the tensions and fears that arise while vividly picturing distressing events) has also proved effective in many instances (Paul, 1969, pp. 105-159).

Over the past decade, the range of experiments and case studies on the applications of systematic desensitization has been astoundingly widespread and numerous. As far as process mechanisms are concerned, data from both animal and human studies have discredited Wolpe's (1958) original reciprocal inhibition hypothesis, and have indicated that the necessary condition for the successful desensitization of fear/avoidance behavior is nonreinforced exposure to the fear-producing situation (Davison and Wilson, 1973; Wilson and Davison, 1971). In actual clinical practice, desensitization probably also involves important attitudinal and expectancy components, demand characteristics and cognitive labeling.

It is extremely laborious to construct intricate anxiety hierarchies, to present items over and over again to deeply relaxed clients and to proceed in this piece-meal fashion each session. Fortunately, when desensitization seems clearly indi-cated, most clients are capable of benefiting from the procedure as part of a self-management program (Goldfried, 1971). The client usually plays cassette record-ings of relaxation exercises at home at his or her own convenience, and then pic-tures a range of distressing scenes and/or systematically exposes herself or himself to actual life situations under conditions of relaxation. The therapist's role is to prompt, encourage and supervise the process by discussing various options for overcoming trouble spots, by facilitating the use of gradual rather than abrupt sequences of anxiety-provoking scenes and by offering support at each stage of the proceedings. In terms of increased cost-effectiveness and the hours saved for therapist time to be devoted to more crucial activities (e.g., behavior rehearsal, modeling, family intervention and cognitive restructuring), self-control and self-management procedures are of inestimable value.

Flooding and In Vivo Exposure Methods

Flooding involves therapist-controlled, prolonged exposure to high-intensity aver-sive stimulation with the soothing effects of relaxation training. Flooding should not be confused with *implosion therapy,* a technique developed by Thomas Stampfl (Stampfl and Levis, 1967). A major difference is that implosion therapy involves an emphasis on psychodynamic themes (e.g., aggressive and sexual impulses; oe-dipal conflict) that are assumed to play a role in the etiology and maintenance of neurotic disorders. The evidence shows that these psychodynamic themes are ir-relevant to the extinction of phobic reactions. This strengthens our conclusion that integrating psychodynamic and behavioral approaches is not only logically inadmissible, but without any scientifically acceptable evidence. Furthermore, whereas implosion therapy relies exclusively on the use of imagery, the current trend is to conduct flooding in vivo. In vivo exposure is similar to flooding except that it may be conducted on a graduated or hierarchical basis that is not designed to elicit very high levels of anxiety as in flooding. The rationale behind these methods is that repeated and systematic exposure to fear-producing cues will even-tually result in the habituation or extinction of the unrealistic fear response. In order to ensure full exposure to the stimuli that elicit anxiety, the client is en-couraged to refrain from avoiding or escaping from feared situations. Attempts to prevent clients' avoiding/escaping feared situations is known as *response pre-vention.* In the treatment of compulsive rituals, such as handwashing, the client is urged to refrain from engaging in the ritual (*avoidance behavior*) of washing his hands. In some instances of inpatient treatment, the client is literally prevented from engaging in rituals (see Foa and Tillmans, 1980).

Several well-controlled studies have demonstrated that flooding can be an extremely effective therapeutic technique in the treatment of different anxiety disorders. Some of these studies have involved comparisons between flooding and systematic desensitization. The overall pattern of results indicates that flooding appears to be the more widely applicable and more effective method, particularly with more severe, complex anxiety disorders such as agoraphobia and obsessive-compulsive disorders (Marks, 1978; Rachman and Hodgson, 1980; Wilson, in press). Available evidence leads to the following conclusions:

1) Flooding or exposure in vivo is more effective than exposure via imagery. 2) The longer the exposure to the feared situation, the more effective the treatment. 3) Gradual in vivo exposure seems to be as effective as rapid exposure to maximally anxiety-eliciting situations. 4) In vivo exposure can be conducted in a group setting, and client-controlled exposure may be as effective as therapist-controlled exposure, making this a cost-effective method. 5) Consistent with the foregoing conclusion, home-based treatment of agoraphobia, using a treatment manual, and with active spouse involvement, produces improvement comparable to that achieved with more intensive therapist-administered treatments in the clinic (Jannoun, Munby, Catalan and Gelder, 1980; Mathews, Teasdale, Munby, Johnston and Shaw, 1977). 6) Home-based, spouse-assisted treatment is not only cost-effective but might also result in superior maintenance of treatment-produced change (Munby and Johnston, 1980). 7) And finally, in vivo exposure carried out by nursing personnel under the supervision of a professional behavior therapist appears to be comparable to treatment carried out by clinical psychologists or psychiatrists.

Systematic evaluations of the long-term efficacy of treatment are relatively rare in research on the psychological therapies, including behavior therapy. Yet several studies of exposure treatment of agoraphobic and obsessional-compulsive disorders in Europe have included long-term (four or more years) evaluations of therapy outcome (Wilson, in press). For example, Munby and Johnston (1980), in England, have reported a follow-up of 66 agoraphobic patients treated with in vivo exposure methods in three separate studies. Ninety-five percent of these patients were compared with those obtained prior to treatment and six months after treatment ended. On most measures of agoraphobia the patients were much better at follow-up than they had been before treatment. The assessor's ratings suggested that there had been little change in the patients' agoraphobia since six months after treatment. Some of the patients' self-ratings showed evidence of a slight improvement over this period. No evidence of any symptom substitution was found. The patients who showed the greatest reduction in agoraphobia were, at follow-up, among the least anxious and depressed. Nevertheless, interpretation of these findings must be tempered by the report that a sizable number of these former patients had received additional treatment over the follow-up period. Excluding these subjects from the analysis of the results did not alter the outcome, however. It should be pointed out that several of these patients required psychotropic medication over the course of the follow-up period. In another informed evaluation of the effects of exposure methods with agoraphobia, Barlow (1980) has stated that in the studies reported, it appears that the drop-out rate alone . . . ranges between 8% and 40%, with a median of about 22%. Similarly, the improvement rate among those who complete treatment seems to average about 60% to 70% and this is without specifying the degree of improvement. Thus, the number who are unimproved or perhaps worse off as a result of (treatment) is as high as 40% of those who complete treatment. (p. 320)

Obsessive-compulsive disorders are among the most difficult of clinical disorders to treat effectively. As with other problems, the behavior therapy literature shows a progression toward the development of increasingly more effective methods. After methods like imaginal systematic desensitization proved to be largely ineffective, more effective alternative techniques, such as in vivo flooding and response prevention, were developed. Summarizing the current evidence, Rachman and Wilson (1980) stated that behavioral treatment

is capable of producing significant changes in obsessional problems, and fairly rapidly at that. Clinically valuable reductions in the frequency and intensity of compulsive behavior have been observed directly and indirectly. Significant reductions in distress and discomfort are usual. . . . The admittedly insufficent evidence on the durability of the induced changes is not discouraging; allowing for the provision of booster treatments as needed, the therapeutic improvements are stable. The successful modification of the main obsessional problems often is followed by improvements in social and vocational adjustment . . . the failure rate ranges between 10% and 30%. The reasons for such failures are not known but severe depression or the possession of over-valued ideas have been offered as possible villains. (p. 148)

Before concluding this section, we must emphasize a point that applies to all the techniques discussed here. The studies reviewed above evaluated the effects of a specific therapeutic technique (i.e., some form of exposure). The requirements of controlled research militated against individual assessment of each patient's problems as would be standard clinical practice. Such individual assessment, a cardinal feature of clinical behavior therapy, would in all likelihood have led to multifaceted interventions in many cases. In vivo exposure would have been supplemented with such diverse strategies as assertion training, behavior rehearsal, marital therapy and self-regulatory procedures, among others, where appropriate (see Lazarus, 1981). We must also add that the therapeutic relationship is often of vital importance in the treatment of these and other disorders, particularly in motivating patients to confront their fears and to desist from engaging in their compulsive rituals.

Behavior Rehearsal

Lazarus (1966) introduced the term "behavior rehearsal" into the literature and described it as "a specific procedure which aims to replace deficient or inadequate social or interpersonal responses by efficient and effective behavior patterns. The patient achieves this by practicing the desired forms of behavior under the direction and supervision of the therapist" (p. 209). *Role-playing* and *role-reversal* procedures are important components of behavior rehearsal. The therapist assumes the role of significant people in the client's life, and progressive series of important encounters are enacted. Feedback from videotapes or tape recordings is often useful in monitoring the client's mode of expression, verbal content, inflection, tone of voice and resonance, and for removing needless apologies, hesitations or querulous overtones. Nonverbal behavior, such as posture, facial expression, gait and eye contact, is also shaped. Behavior rehearsal, unlike other forms of role-playing such as "psychodrama" (Moreno, 1946), focuses primarily on modifying current maladaptive behavior patterns rather than "working through" symbolic conflicts.

The most frequent application of behavior rehearsal is within the context of assertion training, that is, for overcoming situations where clients complain that they are at a loss for words, exploited by others, timid and inhibited, or unable to express love, affection and other positive feelings. The use of instructions, modeling and behavior rehearsal is often referred to as "social skills training." Several studies have shown that individuals who received behavior rehearsal were subsequently rated as more socially adept and less anxious after treatment than at a pretreatment assessment, and more at ease interpersonally than comparable subjects in control groups (e.g., Bellack, Hersen and Turner, 1976; Goldsmith and McFall, 1975). An informative example of the value of this method can be seen in Chaney, O'Leary and Marlatt's (1978) use of social skills training to teach male alcoholics how to cope constructively with problematic interpersonal situations that typically had triggered abusive drinking. Compared to a control group that simply discussed the same issues without the structured role-playing component, the social skills training treatment resulted in significantly superior improvement at posttreatment. Moreover, a one-year follow-up indicated that the social skills training had decreased the duration and severity of relapses suffered by these alcoholics. To reiterate a basic point, while this study shows the efficacy of social skills training, Chaney *et al.* are quick to point out that an adequate treatment program for an alcoholic would necessarily include behavior rehearsal as one component of a multifaceted approach (see Lazarus, 1965).

Aversion Conditioning

In the early days of behavior therapy, *aversion conditioning* was commonly used to eliminate or control unwanted or undesirable behavior such as alcoholism, drug abuse and the sexual paraphilias. Typically, the undesirable response was repeatedly paired with an aversive event such as a painful electric shock or chemically induced nausea. Aversion conditioning has always been controversial, and erroneous beliefs about its effects abound. Thus, contrary to misleading fiction of the sort seen in the film *A Clockwork Orange,* it is very difficult to establish conditioned aversive reactions in people. Chemical aversion using Emetine is one of the most powerful forms of conditioning based on repeated pairings of alcohol with an intensely aversive physical reaction (nausea, hot flushes, sweating and vomiting). Yet even with this intensely aversive procedure, not all clients develop conditioned aversions to alcohol. Conditioned responses are most likely to be created with the client's deliberate, conscious cooperation. Considerations of efficacy combine with the ethical imperative that aversion conditioning be used only after the client's informed consent has been freely obtained. An intrusive procedure, aversion conditioning is also recommended only if more benign alternative methods have proved futile (see Wilson and O'Leary, 1980).

Aversion conditioning has often been used to try to eliminate homosexuality in clients (Feldman and MacCulloch, 1971). However, behavior therapists in general have urged the critical reconsideration of heterosexuality as the invariable therapeutic goal in the treatment of the homosexual client (Wilson and Davison, 1974). Instead, contrary to psychoanalytic theory, homosexuality is viewed as an alternative life-style that is not necessarily "pathological." Accordingly, behavioral methods (e.g., the Masters and Johnson procedures for treating sexual dysfunction) have been used to help homosexuals function more happily as homosexuals. Should an individual homosexual client genuinely seek a heterosexual orientation, most behavior therapists would try to develop heterosexual responsiveness directly, using positive procedures, as opposed to trying to suppress homosexual behavior.

Electrical aversion conditioning has proved effective in treating some of the sexual paraphilias such as transvestism and exhibitionism (Marks, 1978). Here again, this method must be part of a broader treatment approach that enables the client to cope with the psychosocial problems that frequently exacerbate these conditions.

Conditioned aversive reactions are not automatically established by simply pairing two external stimuli. The client's self-directed involvement in the learning process is probably crucial. As a result, symbolically generated aversive reactions are the preferred form of treatment. In this procedure the client is asked to imagine the aversive consequence. For example, an alcoholic might be asked to imagine experiencing nausea at the thought of a drink. This method is often referred to as "covert sensitization." Several advantages recommend such a method: it is more practical and can be implemented by the client in any setting without cumbersome apparatus; it focuses directly on the self-activation of a reaction that social learning theory regards as a crucial process in conditioning; and it is more humane, since it spares both the client and the therapist the unpleasant experience of electric shock or drug-induced nausea.

Both uncontrolled clinical reports and experimental analyses have indicated that covert sensitization is most useful in the treatment of sexual paraphilias. For example, Maletzky (1980), in a careful report of the treatment of some 186 exhibitionists with covert sensitization, found that close to 90% improved to the point where all overt acts of exposure were eliminated. Follow-ups were often as long as thirty months, and objective evidence of efficacy was obtained in several instances. Encouragingly, Maletzky also reports promising results along these lines with pedophiliacs. These findings do not prove that covert sensitization "works," and Maletzky notes that he employed "adjunctive" behavioral methods in some cases. Nonetheless, taken in conjunction with well-controlled studies demonstrating that covert sensitization can modify unwanted exhibitionism (Brownell, Hayes and Barlow, 1977), these data strongly recommend this approach to the practitioner.

Not without significance is the finding that covert sensitization is ineffective in the treatment of obese clients trying to control their overeating (Wilson, 1980). It does appear to be helpful in the treatment of excessive alcohol consumption, however. The probable reasons for this pattern of differential efficacy are beyond the scope of the present chapter. It should be noted, however, that differential efficacy across different disorders discounts the argument that the successes of covert sensitization can be explained away as due to some "nonspecific" factor such as placebo. It suggests specific causal relationships with certain problems.

Behavioral Self-Control

In contrast to the earlier stages of development of behavior therapy in which the sole emphasis was on the control of behavior by the external environment, the concern has turned to the role of *self-regulation* of behavior (Bandura, 1969). Behavioral conceptions of self-control range from the extreme operant position that maintains that self-control refers to certain forms of environmental control of behavior, to cognitive approaches in which self-regulatory mechanisms are said to mediate overt behavior (Thoresen and Mahoney, 1974). Kanfer and Karoly (1972) have defined self-control as those processes by which an individual maintains or alters a pattern of behavior in the absence of immediate external supports, and they have identified three component parts. Self-monitoring refers to the systematic observation of one's own behavior, e.g., the number of calories consumed on a daily basis. The person then self-evaluates his behavior, that is, judges the adequacy of his or her performance in terms of some standard or comparison criterion, e.g., a caloric intake in excess of 1,500 calories per day. Depending on whether the behavior matches the standard or not, the person then either applies self-reinforcement or self-punishment, covertly or in reality, e.g., watching a favorite T.V. show contingent on appropriate eating habits.

The way in which self-control is conceptualized in behavioral terms is less important to the practitioner than the application of specific self-control strategies to different problem disorders. The following are some examples of clinical self-control techniques. Self-instructional training is a procedure in which clients are explicitly trained to monitor irrational, self-defeating thoughts, realize how these thoughts or self-verbalizations are responsible for generating emotional turmoil and learn constructive self-statements that are incompatible with anxiety (Michenbaum,

1977). The assumption is that these covert processes obey the same psychological laws as do overt behaviors, and can be modified by the same techniques of modeling, reinforcement and aversive consequences. Controlled studies have indicated that self-instructional training is as effective as systematic desensitization in reducing irrational anxieties, and that it can even be used to significantly improve the attention span and abstract behavior of schizophrenics.

Among the best-known self-control methods for regulating problem behaviors are those that are used for treating obesity (Stuart, 1967), and which have since been extended to a variety of problems, including cigarette smoking, alcoholism and improving study habits. In the typical weight reduction program, for instance, the client is initially taught to keep detailed records of eating and exercise habits and the circumstances under which they occur. The client is instructed to narrow the number of stimuli associated with the act of eating (e.g., not eating while engaging in any other activity such as watching T.V. or reading). Procedures are then introduced to disrupt and control the actual act of eating (e.g., eating utensils have to be placed on the table between bites, all food has to be chewed slowly and completely swallowed before the next bite, etc.). Finally, explicit sources of reinforcement are arranged to support behavior that delays or controls eating. These may be provided by supportive family members or, even more practically, be self-administered. While behavior therapy is the recommended psychological approach for cases of mild to moderate obesity, the results that have been obtained are often inconsistent (see Wilson and Brownell, 1980, for a detailed evaluation of the long-term efficacy of behavioral treatment of obesity). Weight loss is maintained well at one-year follow-ups, although little further weight loss occurs after the end of formal treatment. Moreover, we are unable to predict who is likely to succeed in treatment programs.

Self-monitoring and self-evaluation strategies have been implicit in virtually all forms of behavior therapy, and are increasingly being investigated as important behavior change methods in and of themselves. The use of self-evaluation by disruptive children, for example, is discussed in the section on token reinforcement programs. In fact, most behavioral techniques are being viewed within the context of the self-management of behavior. Goldfried (1971) has characterized systematic desensitization as a self-control procedure, and Bandura (1969) has concluded that the aversion therapies such as covert sensitization are best construed as self-control methods in which the client cognitively re-creates the aversive consequences in order to control undesirable behavior.

Cognitive Restructuring

The 1970s witnessed the emergence of "cognitive behavior therapy" or "cognitive behavior modification" (Lazarus, 1971; Mahoney, 1974; Meichenbaum, 1977), a development that has received much attention both within and without the field of behavior therapy. Although some have heralded "cognitive behavior modification" as a major new advance, the truth is that cognitive strategies had already become part of the practice of clinical behavior therapy in the 1960s, just as cognitive conceptualizations of human behavior in general, and traditional behavioral procedures in particular, were refined in the late 1960s (e.g., Bandura, 1969). Nevertheless, the emphasis on the cognitive connection in behavior therapy over the past decade has introduced new techniques (e.g., self-instructional training), provided challenging and possibly superior theoretical frameworks for understanding therapeutic processes and procedures (e.g., the self-efficacy theory of Bandura, 1977) and helped to specify the so-called nonspecifics of behavior therapy (e.g., therapeutic expectancies, the therapeutic relationship, etc.).

The procedures that have received the most attention in the recent development of cognitive behavior therapy and that are the most important are those referred to as "cognitive restructuring." The therapies in this category are all based on the assumption that emotional disorders are the result of maladaptive thought patterns. The goal of therapy is to restructure these maladaptive cognitions. Included among these cognitive restructuring therapies are Ellis's (1977) well-known rational-emotive therapy (RET), Meichenbaum's (1977) self-instructional training and Beck's (1976) cognitive therapy. Contrary to Ellis's (1977) claim that the evidence on RET is "awesome," Rachman and Wilson (1980) concluded that the available studies "do not provide adequate information on which to reach firm conclusions about the efficacy of RET as a treatment method. Evidence on the long-term efficacy of RET is especially lacking." The second of these therapies, self-instructional training, has already been discussed.

Beck's approach is actually an explicit amalgam of behavioral and cognitive methods. The former include the prescription of an explicit activity schedule, graded tasks aimed at providing mastery and success experiences, and various homework assignments. The latter include several techniques, of which "distancing" and "decentering" are examples. Among the advantages of Beck's approach are the explicit manner in which he has spelled out his therapeutic methods, thereby allowing independent replication of studies; the fact that he capitalizes on the power of behavioral procedures to alter cognitive processes; and the preliminary findings on the efficacy of his treatment of depression (Rush, Beck, Kovacs and Hollon, 1978). Detailed evaluations of the use of cognitive procedures within behavior therapy are provided by Kendall and Hollon (1979) and Wilson and O'Leary (1980).

The expansion of behavior therapy to take explicit account of cognitive processes in the regulation of behavior has been greeted by strict behaviorists as a retrogressive slide into mentalism and by many nonbehavioral therapists as a welcome admission of the value of psychodynamic notions. Neither view is correct in our opinion. Contrary to the denunciations of the cognitive connection in behavior therapy by behaviorists (e.g., Wolpe, 1978), the analysis of cognitive processes is not only in the best tradition of current experimental psychology but can also be shown to be heuristic in refining existing clinical strategies and in generating innovative methods. Nor does an emphasis on cognitive processes necessarily reduce to any endorsement of psychodynamic notions, as Goldfried (1980) and others have alleged. Among the differences between cognitive behavior therapy and traditional psychodynamic therapies are the following:

a) cognitive methods in behavior therapy are concerned primarily with conscious thought processes, rather than unconscious, symbolic meanings; b) cognitive methods in behavior therapy emphasize the regulatory influence of current cognitions. It is unnecessary to determine the unconscious roots of inaccurate or irrational interpretations of reality. It is a general characteristic of behavior therapy that the therapist focuses on how the client distorts cognitively and what to do about it, rather than on why the distortion occurs; c) cognitive methods in behavior therapy are explicitly formulated and testable in contrast to the looser, more vaguely formulated concepts in psychodynamic approaches; d) initial studies show that some cognitive methods in behavior therapy appear to be more efficient and effective than psychoanalytically-oriented treatment. (Wilson and O'Leary, 1980, p. 280)

Overcoming Sexual Inadequacy

The direct use of sexual responses for eliminating anxiety-associated cues attached to sexual participation was described by Wolpe and Lazarus (1966). People suffering from sexual inadequacies (e.g., impotent men or nonorgasmic women) often display a performance-oriented anticipatory anxiety: "Am I going to obtain an erection?" "Will I have an orgasm?" "Will he consider me good in bed?" "How will I compare to her previous lover?" Fundamentally, discharges of the autonomic nervous system determine the character and quality of sexual performance. Anticipatory anxiety elicits predominantly sympathetic autonomic discharges that inhibit sexual arousal and/or performance. The basic strategy for overcoming sexual anxiety is for the client to approach his or her partner only as far as pleasurable feelings predominate. It is emphasized that one must never explicitly or implicitly press beyond the point at which sexual arousal remains in the ascendant over anxiety. A gradual and progressive in vivo sexual retraining occurs. The cooperation of a helpful and willing partner is often essential. The therapist briefs the partner beforehand concerning his or her role in the re-educative and desensitization process.

In many cases it helps simply to remove the onus of an expected level of performance by stressing that there are several ways of achieving orgasmic satisfaction and sexual fulfillment without penile-vaginal stimulation. The client is then instructed in the relevant oral, manual and digital manipulations. These activities generally provide powerful sources of sexual arousal, but they also distract attention from the sufferer's own problem through focusing on pleasures bestowed on the other person. The formal Masters and Johnson program insists upon certain elements that many behavior therapists have found to be unnecessary (e.g., the need for both a male and female therapist to treat a husband and wife unit) and omits certain procedures that we have found to be essential in certain cases. Systematic desensitization is often necessary for overcoming nonsexual fears that nevertheless inhibit sexual performance, such as irrational fears of blood, of assault, of control, and some claustrophobic reactions.

Another important imagery technique is *orgasmic reconditioning.* In applying this technique to a woman with vaginismus, the following sequence would be recommended. The woman would be instructed to masturbate in the privacy of her home, and immediately prior to achieving orgasm, she would vividly imagine penile insertion into her vagina. The image seldom interferes with arousal or orgasmic intensity. Thereafter, the client repeatedly imagines the intromission scene earlier in the masturbatory sequence, until the image of penile insertion can initiate sexual arousal. Upon completing the procedure in imagery, the next step is to repeat the process in actual behavior. Wilson (1973) described the successful use of orgasmic reconditioning in treating a severe case of vaginismus that had previously failed to respond to both graded sexual responses and systematic desensitization.

In cases of premature ejaculation, the use of Semans' (1956) method of controlled partner-induced manual stimulation has proved effective. "This consists of controlled acts of manual stimulation of the penis by the wife which lead to a progressive increase in the amount of tactile stimulation needed to bring about ejaculation. . . . When the husband feels a sensation which is, for him, premonitory to ejaculation, he informs his wife and removes her hand until the sensation disappears. Stimulation is begun again and interrupted by the husband when the premonitory sensation returns" (Wolpe and Lazarus, 1966, p. 106). Masters and Johnson (1970) recommend a "squeeze technique" in which the woman applies pressure to the penis before withdrawing contact.

In some instances, a breakdown of sexual responsiveness is often one clear-cut manifestation of a larger interpersonal problem involving anger, resentment and hostility. Hence, as with all behavior disorders, the need for adequate, multimodal assessment cannot be overemphasized. While many of the behavioral retraining procedures have a mechanistic overtone, the actual implementation of these procedures is within a context of affection, tender consideration, emotional warmth and mutual caring.

Behavior therapists often make use of "bibliotherapy" (prescribed readings) as part of their homework assignments. In treating women with orgasmic difficulties, we often recommend the book by Heiman, LoPiccolo and LoPiccolo (1976), and for male dysfunctions, Zilbergeld's (1978) book is extremely informative. For the professional therapist, two volumes are outstanding namely, LoPiccolo and LoPiccolo (1978) and Leiblum and Pervin (1980). These books contain highly informative chapters by experts in various areas of sexual deviation and dysfunction and cover a wide range of treatment methods on diverse conditions (e.g., desire discrepancies, dyspareunia, premature ejaculation, retarded ejaculation, anorgasmic women, erectile dysfunction, vaginismus, as well as special populations such as the elderly, people with coronary or renal disease, and pregnant women). The emphasis in behavioral sex therapy is on the comprehensive use of a variety of therapeutic procedures, with the ability to select appropriate methods of intervention that fit the special and often unique circumstances found in a given clinical situation.

Group Methods

Lazarus (1961) described the use of group desensitization and compared it to more traditional group methods in treating phobic disorders. Paul and Shannon (1966) conducted a rather elaborate study on "chronically anxious clients" and demonstrated the therapeutic value of employing group desensitization plus group discussion with re-educative goals. Lazarus (1968, 1971) described an additional range of group behavioral techniques (e.g., combined use of sexual responses and desensitization, as well as assertion training groups). More recently Lazarus (1975, 1981) has described the use of multimodal behavior therapy in groups.

A distinction needs to be made between behavior therapy in groups (where individuals receive therapy in a group, such as relaxing and picturing individual scenes for desensitization purposes) and group behavior therapy (in which the group process is employed to produce behavioral change, such as the use of social rewards for nondeviant responses). Kass, Silvers and Abroms (1972) described behavior therapy *through* the explicit use of a group by employing broad-spectrum group behavior therapy with a hysterical patient population. Lazarus emphasized that "the reason for practicing behavior therapy in groups is not merely that it provides a saving in therapists' time and effort, but because in many instances, learning, re-learning, and unlearning seem to be facilitated greatly in group settings" (Lazarus, 1968, p. 150). Behavioral groups facilitate the process of discrimination training by enabling clients to sample a range of experiences that highlight similarities and differences among people. Decrements in subjective feelings of isolation often seem to follow group participation. And a helpful "cooperative-competitive" atmosphere is fostered that enables the therapist to reach hitherto "unmotivated" group members.

There are several important differences between behavioral groups and traditional psychotherapy groups, T-groups, encounter groups and the various sensitivity-training procedures that abound. In the first place, the main objective of behavioral groups is to modify deviant and aberrant behaviors on a long-term basis. Whereas weekend marathon encounters often lead to short-lived joie de vivre, the purpose of group behavior therapy is to promote lifelong adaptive habits, to enhance social and interpersonal skills and to extinguish maladaptive responses, especially those that interfere with congenial and assertive person-to-person interactions.

In behavioral groups, relatively little time is spent on "process material" within the group. When friction between group members is an impediment to effective behavior change, process variables will be examined, and more facilitative responses will be modeled. But in general there is little evidence that group interactions inevitably capture the essence of each member's style of communication, or that the group becomes a microcosm of each client's significant personal interactions. Groups may frequently elicit situation-specific behaviors that are by no means prototypical of the individual's other intra- and interpersonal responses.

The main focus in behavioral groups is upon the clients' meaningful and significant encounters outside of the group. Each member brings to the group his or her own problems of adjustment outside of the group. The group medium then functions as a platform and springboard for training, rehearsing and equipping the participants to cope with life's problems in vivo. Special attention is taken to ensure that gains achieved within the group will transfer and generalize outside the protective confines of the group meetings. Thus, specific homework assignments figure prominently at the end of each behavioral group meeting.

Behavior therapy, with its strong emphasis on *social reinforcement and skill acquisition*, lends itself particularly well to group implementation. Upper and Ross (1979) have launched an annual review of behavioral group therapy to provide a coherent source of updated information on clinical and research findings, to stimulate scientific inquiry and to provide a forum for communication about behavioral group therapy. They have assembled several overviews as well as reports on specific target populations – behavioral group therapy in treating sexual dysfunction, smoking reduction, social skills training, adolescents, pain patients, alcoholics and overweight children.

Research in behavioral group therapy is concerned with factors such as the relationship between process variables and specific outcome measures; comparative factorial studies to assess the impact of various techniques across different sets of clients and treatment environments; parametric studies to operationalize the most efficient group procedures; and studies designed to develop valid and reliable assessment procedures.

OPERANT CONDITIONING PRINCIPLES AND PROCEDURES

The systematic use of operant conditioning methods in behavior therapy (often referred to as applied behavior analysis) derives directly from the animal laboratory research of Skinner and his students. Applied behavior analysis is the most theoretically consistent and the easiest to describe approach within the general compass of contemporary behavior therapy, but it is also the most restricted. Based on Skinnerian behaviorism, a model of human functioning is put forth in which overt behavior is regarded as the only acceptable subject of scientific investigation, and thoughts and feelings are relegated to the status of epiphenomena. The highly distinctive features of applied behavior analysis have been summarized by Krasner (1971) as follows: "the intensive study of individual subjects, the control of the experimental environment, the control of individual behavior, the emphasis on objective observation and recording of behavior, the importance of consequences of behavior, the empirical nature of the approach, and the intense involvement of most of its proponents." Of special importance has been the single-case methodology of the operant approach. The use of reversal (ABA), multiple-baseline, and multiple-schedule designs has added considerably to our knowledge of the behavior change processes and procedures (Hersen and Barlow, 1976).

Following the early laboratory studies of Skinner on psychotic behavior, operant procedures were progressively applied to a diverse array of psychiatric disorders. Indeed, Ullmann and Krasner (1975) have written a textbook on abnormal psychology that conceptualizes the development, maintenance and modification of all forms of abnormal behavior primarily in operant conditioning terms. Operant procedures have been extended to problems in clinical psychology and psychiatry, education, rehabilitation, community psychology and even medicine (Kazdin, 1978). In a chapter such as this, the massive literature explosion in this field calls for selectivity. We have chosen to focus on current developments in token economy programs and biofeedback procedures to illustrate the general developments within this burgeoning area.

Token Economy Programs

Perhaps the most impressive application of operant conditioning principles has been the modification of entire groups of individuals through the use of token economy programs. Since the pioneering introduction, by Ayllon and Azrin (1968), of a token economy program on a psychiatric hospital back ward for chronic psychotic patients, token reinforcement programs have multiplied to the point where Atthowe (1973) concluded that "most treatment, rehabilitative, correctional and educational settings use some form of contingent contracting." Token programs have been instituted with an extraordinarily wide range of different behaviors in diverse populations, including psychiatric inpatients and outpatients, retarded and autistic children, delinquent youths, normal and disturbed children in classroom settings and even low-income families in a community-improvement program (e.g., Kazdin, 1977).

Although the procedures and goals of the many procedures subsumed under the rubric of token economy programs may vary, they all share the following common defining characteristics. First, the specific behaviors that are to be modified or developed have to be identified and operationally defined. Typical target behaviors would include self-care behaviors in psychotic patients or improved academic performance in children. Second, the available reinforcers in the environment have to be determined. Reinforcers are the "good things in life" that people are willing to work for. In the case of the hospital patient these might range from such fundamental privileges as watching T.V. or securing a private room. For the child in the classroom a reinforcer might be candy, toys or extra recess time. Third, there are the tokens themselves. The token is a compound discriminative and secondary reinforcer that stands for the back-up reinforcers. The advantages of using tokens as reinforcers are that they bridge the gap between the target behavior and the back-up reinforcers, they permit the reinforcement of any response at any time, and they provide the same reward for patients who have different preferences in back-up reinforcers. The token itself might be a tangible item such as a poker chip or a plastic card, or else it might be a checkmark on a piece of paper. Finally, there are the exchange rules of the program, that is, how tokens may be earned and the cost of the back-up reinforcers. These exchange rules involve complex relationships that have been analyzed in terms of, and compared to, the economic principles governing real-life society outside of the immediate token economy environment (Winkler, 1972). Although token economy procedures have often been described in oversimplified reinforcement terms, Krasner (1971) has stressed that they incorporate many social influence processes including operant and classical conditioning, social reinforcement, modeling and expectancy of success. Within this general social influence context the specific token reinforcement contingencies play the decisive role in regulating behavior change.

Contrary to the frequently expressed criticism that token programs are simplistic, impersonal and mechanistic, their successful implementation demands a wide range of clinical skills, including flexibility, creativity, perseverance and "canny know-how" on the part of the behavior therapist. Perhaps the most formidable task involves staff training. The operation of the token program, and indeed all operant-based behavior modification procedures, can best be understood in terms of Tharp and Wetzel's (1969) triadic model of treatment intervention. According to this model, the therapist functions as a *consultant* who possesses the necessary knowledge of how to formulate and plan behavior change programs. These plans are then implemented by the *mediators,* those people who have the closest contact with the *target* — anyone who has a problem to be modified. Mediators may be parents, teachers, peers, nurses, attendants or employers — in fact, anyone who is in a position to control the important reinforcement contingencies in the target's environment.

Mediators have to be taught to systematically observe and reward behavior. Nurses and teachers, for example, have to be assured that this will facilitate their own job of managing patients or children rather than overburden them with additional responsibility. They have to feel that they are part of a worthwhile program, and their suggestions about how the program might be improved or revised should be encouraged. The personnel who dispense the reinforcers must themselves be rewarded for appropriate behavior. Controlled studies have shown that psychiatric aides and schoolteachers typically show low rates of positive reinforcement for appropriate patient or student behavior. Merely instructing aides about how to implement behavior modification procedures has scant effect on the targets. Providing personnel with regular feedback about the improvement of specific patients produces more appropriate behavior.

Outcome and Evaluation

In a major review of operant conditioning treatment approaches in institutional settings, Davision (1969) concluded that while they showed promise, they had not yet been proved to be effective in changing hospitalized patients to the point where they could function "normally" again in society. Based as they are on the application of social learning principles within an interpersonal context, the efficacy of behavioral treatment techniques cannot be evaluated in terms of medically-based concepts of "cure" and "spontaneous remission." Whereas the latter concepts are appropriate in describing the treatment of physical diseases, they are conceptually irrelevant to the assessment of the modification of abnormal behavior that is extensively controlled by social variables. As Bandura (1969) points out, it is important to distinguish between the induction of therapeutic change in a specific set of problem behaviors, the generalization of these changes to situations in the real world outside of the institution and the long-term maintenance of improvement. The induction, generalization and maintenance of therapeutic behavior change might be controlled by different factors, and might require different modification strategies. For example, the fact that token economy programs produce changes within the institutional setting where they are administered that do not, however, transfer to nontherapeutic situations is not necessarily a reflection of the inadequacy of token economies. The outcome of reinforcement methods depends both on the induction of treatment changes *and* on the nature of the posttreatment environment. If the environment is unchanged from the conditions that originally generated the patient's problems, then there is a very high probability that the problem behaviors will reappear. Deliberate steps have to be taken to ensure the generalization of therapeutic changes to the natural environment and to arrange for appropriate maintenance conditions.

The majority of token economy programs that have been reported have been concerned primarily with inducing behavior change within institutional settings. Initially the emphasis was simply on establishing that the group application of operant conditioning principles could produce behavior change. This demonstration was followed by studies showing that there is a causal relationship between the introduction of specific operant procedures and behavior change.

Alyllon and Azrin (1968) provided an excellent example of a token economy program that employed the within-subject ABAB or reversal design in demonstrating that the behaviors of chronic back ward schizophrenics could be systematically modified using operant conditioning principles. In this ABAB design, the target behavior is alternately reinforced, not reinforced and then reinforced again in consecutive phases of the study. The target behaviors chosen by Ayllon and Azrin were primarily work assignments both on and off the ward, and self-care behaviors. The back-up reinforcers were selected on the basis of the Premack principle, which states that any high-probability behavior can be used to strengthen any other behavior occurring at a lower probability. The importance of this principle is that it greatly extends the range of otherwise restricted reinforcers that can be used with chronic psychiatric patients who display little interest in their immediate environment. Ayllon and Azrin (1968) convincingly showed that increases in the target behaviors were a function of the response-reinforcement contingencies. Behavior increased only when contingently rewarded, and decreased markedly when the tokens were either withdrawn completely or distributed to the patients on a non-contingent basis. Withdrawing all tokens and making back-up reinforcers freely available to patients irrespective of how they behaved, resulted in their job performance deteriorating to less than one-fourth of its rate when contingently rewarded with tokens.

Other studies have shown that token economy programs produce significantly greater change than control groups receiving alternative forms of treatment. Fairweather (1964) found that rewarding small groups of hospitalized patients for improvements in problem-solving and self-management abilities resulted in significantly greater social interaction, decreased pathological behavior and enhanced communication, compared to a control group that received the conventional hospital therapeutic program. Maley, Feldman and Ruskin (1973) showed that chronic psychotic patients in a token economy were better oriented, were more cooperative and communicative, displayed greater social interaction and exhibited less psychotic behavior than closely matched subjects receiving a conventional treatment program.

The aim of these studies — to improve behavior within the hospital — was clearly accomplished. These changes are far from trivial. Operant procedures can successfully reverse the debilitating effects of institutionalization, which is often iatrogenic in nature. Token economies that result in greater self-management and social involvement mean a happier, more productive and more dignified life for patients — even if they remain hospitalized. The fact that the morale of the nurses and attendants on a successful token economy is greatly improved has obvious indirect benefits for the patients, who are then regarded as fellow human beings capable of improvement, rather than impersonal, faceless figures who are irreversibly "sick" and who have only to be kept clean and quiet (Rosenhan, 1973). Moreover, the very behaviors that have been shown to be so successfully modified by these token economy programs have often prolonged the psychotic patient's length of hospitalization, and the statistics indicate that the longer a patient remains in a psychiatric hospital the less likelihood there is of ever returning him or her to the community (Fairweather, Simon, Gebhard, Weingarten, Holland, Sanders, Stone and Reahl, 1960; Ullmann, 1967).

Given the limited yet important aims of these studies, it is not surprising that they have failed to accomplish the goal for which they were not designed, namely, returning patients to the community on a long-term basis. Although the Atthowe and Krasner (1968) program led to a doubling of the rate of discharge of patients, 11 of the 24 released patients returned to the hospital within nine months. Similarly, the recidivism rates for patients discharged from Fairweather's (1964) program were about equal, irrespective of the type of therapy they received. Fifty-five per-cent of all patients who had been hospitalized longer than two years had relapsed at a six-month follow-up.

A similar pattern of results has been duplicated with token economy programs in other settings, such as the classroom and in a community-based center for pre-delinquent boys (O'Leary and O'Leary, 1977; Phillips, Phillips, Fixsen, and Wolf, 1971). While token reinforcement procedures have resulted in substantial increase in academic performance and appropriate social behavior with normal and emo-tionally disturbed children and with delinquents, demonstrations of the long-range efficacy of these methods are lacking. Almost inevitably it has been found that treatment gains in social behaviors deteriorate once the reinforcement procedures are withdrawn. Nor have behavior modifiers been particularly successful in dem-onstrating generalization of the beneficial effects of token procedures to periods during which no token and back-up reinforcers are available to the children.

Extending the Token Economy into the Natural Environment

Even the most comprehensive token economy programs, such as Fairweather's (1964) which taught patients the socially relevant skills of decision making and problem solving, have failed to reverse the discouragingly high recidivism rate. This indicates that rehabilitation procedures have to be extended from the hospital set-ting to the natural environment to which the ex-patient returns so as to ensure the generalization and maintenance of improvement. In an extension of his previous treatment program, Fairweather transferred mental hospital patients to a semi-autonomous lodge located within the community as soon as they were functioning adequately on the hospital ward (Fairweather, Sanders, Maynard and Cressler, 1969). Under professional supervision, the patients took responsibility for oper-ating the lodge, organizing employment and earning money by running a janitorial service that they themselves managed. All income was distributed among the lodge members according to each person's contribution to the lodge's functioning. Peri-odically, some patients were readmitted to the hospital for brief periods of booster treatment sessions. The lodge became fully autonomous after thirty-three months, and a follow-up evaluation was made of the patients' status forty months after their discharge from hospital. Compared to a control group that received the tradi-tional assistance and outpatient therapy available to most hospital patients upon their discharge, patients who lived and worked together in the community fared significantly better in resuming a meaningful role in society. The median percent of time lodge members had spent in the community was 75% compared to 15% for the control group, while the figures for time of employment were 40% and only 1%, respectively.

Undoubtedly, the most impressive behavioral treatment program of institution-alized mental patients was conducted by Paul and Lentz (1977). The patients in this remarkable study were all diagnosed as schizophrenic, were of low socioeconomic status, had been confined to a mental hospital for an average of seventeen years and had been treated previously with drugs and other methods, without success. As Paul and Lentz state, they were "the most severely debilitated chronically institutionalized adults ever subjected to systematic study." Twenty-eight of these subjects were assigned to each of three treatment groups so that the groups were "identical on level and nature of functioning and on every characteristic of potential importance to treatment responsiveness." The three treatments were *social learning therapy*, *milieu therapy* and *routine hospital therapy*. The social learning therapy consisted of the direct application of the experimentally established principles of learning, including modeling, classical conditioning, reinforcement procedures, such as shaping and prompting, and the token economy. Patients who were released into the community were provided a special twenty-six-week intensive aftercare program designed to help them readjust to life outside the institution.

Two identical adjacent units were established at a mental health center to house the social learning and milieu therapy programs. Both were staffed by the same professional personnel at a level equal to that existing in a comparison state hospital where the routine hospital treatment was carried out. This unprecedented degree of experimental control allows us to draw clear-cut conclusions about the comparative efficacy of the three treatments.

The results are most illuminating. The social learning therapy was the most efficient and well as the most effective method, although both psychosocial programs produced significantly greater improvement than the routine hospital treatment. Compared to the milieu therapy and routine hospital programs, the social learning treatment produced significantly superior improvement in the residents' functioning while they were hospitalized, greater release rates and more successful adjustment in the community. Patients in the routine hospital treatment failed to reflect a significant change in functioning. These differences at posttreatment were essentially maintained during the one-and-a-half-year follow-up evaluation. In addition to being the most effective method in improving personal functioning, achieving the highest release rate from the hospital and maintaining subjects longer in the community, the social learning therapy program was the most cost-effective, costing roughly 30% less than the ineffective state hospital treatment program. As a whole, these are the best results ever reported in the treatment of the chronic institutionalized patient.

Biofeedback and Behavioral Medicine

Until the late 1960s, it was believed that the autonomic nervous system could be influenced only by classical conditioning procedures, and that operant conditioning was effective only in modifying skeletal responses. The dramatic demonstration that autonomic functioning could be brought under operant control has not only provided a model in terms of which the diversity and persistence of visceral functioning can be explained, but also suggests that psychosomatic problems might be eliminated directly by the therapeutic use of operant-feedback procedures.

The paradigmatic experiment that demonstrates the instrumental regulation of visceral responses in rats is one in which spontaneous fluctuations in a response such as heart rate are accurately measured and followed by reinforcing consequences if they are in the appropriate direction. The desired response is shaped by gradually requiring increasingly greater changes in heart rate for reinforcement to occur. The rat is curarized in these experiments and rewarded by means of direct electrical stimulation of rewarding centers in the brain. Consequently, the changes in heart rate that are obtained cannot be attributed to the indirect effects of skeletal activity or altered patterns of respiration. Using these procedures, rats have been trained to either increase or decrease their heart rate while other autonomic responses, e.g., intestinal contractions, remain unaltered. Conversely, intestinal contractions can be modified by operant-feedback procedures without producing any change in heart rate. The specificity of this control shows that it is the operant conditioning procedure that causes the change and not any other uncontrolled factor such as general autonomic arousal.

Similar findings have been obtained with human subjects, although the magnitude of the changes has generally been smaller, and it has been more difficult to rule out alternative explanations of the results in terms of indirect mediating influences caused by changes in respiration and other skeletal responses. Nonetheless, volunteer subjects have been trained to produce changes in an impressive range of physiological functions including heart rate changes, electrodermal activity, systolic and diastolic blood pressure, skin temperature, peripheral vasomotor responses, EEG rhythms and penile erection (Shapiro and Surwit, 1976). The question of interest to practitioners is how useful is biofeedback as a new form of therapy?

Bold and often innovative applications of biofeedback procedures to diverse clinical disorders have been made over the past decade. Two major conclusions can be drawn. First, although the results have often been encouraging, the clinical efficacy of biofeedback has yet to be conclusively established. Second, the claims for biofeedback are often exaggerated. The uncritical advocacy of biofeedback methods, especially by "biofeedback clinics" that specialize in this form of treatment, continues to be a problem. In contrast to the hard-sell tactics of biofeedback "believers" (see Brown, 1977, and Fuller, 1978, for examples), careful evaluations of the clinical outcome evidence by such experts as Blanchard, Katkin, Lang, Shapiro and others provide a more realistic picture of the state of the art. By way of illustration, Silver and Blanchard (1978), in a comprehensive paper, addressed the question of "Are the machines really necessary?" and reviewed the use of biofeedback and alternative forms of relaxation training in the treatment of a wide range of different psychophysiological disorders. Their conclusion is straightforward and in keeping with previous evaluations of the biofeedback literature:

> whenever direct comparisons have been made of biofeedback training and
> relaxation training, there is no consistent advantage for one form of treat-

ment over the other. This holds true for essential hypertension, migraine headaches, tension headaches, and asthma. Indirect comparisons of the two lead to similar conclusions for PVCs (premature ventricular contractions of the heart) and TMJ (temporomandibular joint) pain. Thus, on the most crucial issue in a comparison of treatment — efficacy, there is no advantage of one form of treatment over the other. (p. 230)

However, Silver and Blanchard also note that for disorders in which the approriate comparative studies have yet to be completed, such as Raynaud's disease, sinus tachycardia and fecal incontinence, "biofeedback seems to be a very promising treatment modality" (p. 217).

Kazdin and Wilson (1978) have argued that evaluation of treatment outcome must be done using broader criteria than have traditionally been used, including efficiency, durability, generality, convenience, cost-effectiveness, consumer satisfaction, disseminability and so on. In terms of efficiency, or speed of treatment, Silver and Blanchard found no difference between biofeedback and relaxation training. They suggest, however: "In terms of actual contact time with the treating agent, the meditative-passive relaxation form of treatment popularized by Benson (1975) may prove to be the most efficient" (p. 231).

There are few studies on the durability of biofeedback treatment effects, a problem that is shared by other treatment strategies. Similarly, little evidence is available to allow judgments about the relative convenience of biofeedback training versus alternative methods of relaxation training. Yet, there can be little doubt that alternative forms of relaxation training are more cost-effective than biofeedback. According to Silver and Blanchard, biofeedback is a relatively

high-technology form of treatment which requires equipment costing several hundred to several thousand dollars. Relaxation training, on the other hand, is a low-technology form of treatment requiring no special equipment, other than perhaps a cassette recorder for home practice. Thus at this point in time, on a cost-effectiveness basis, relaxation training would seem to be favored over biofeedback training in treating essential hypertension, migraine headaches, PVCs, tension headaches, TMJ pain, asthma, and primary dysmenorrhea. (p. 232)

It may well be, as Lang (1977) suggests, that the greatest contribution of biofeedback at the present time is its value as a powerful research tool that facilitates the detailed analysis of the functional role of physiological variables in behavior.

Biofeedback is part of what has come to be known as "behavioral medicine," which has been defined as the "interdisciplinary field concerned with the development and integration of behavioral and biomedical science knowledge and techniques relevant to health and illness and the application of this knowledge and these techniques to prevention, diagnosis, treatment, and rehabilitation" (Schwartz and Weiss, 1978, p. 250). In large part, it has been the application of behavioral principles and procedures, particularly operant conditioning methods, that has distinguished many of the therapeutic applications in this new field. Prominent examples include the successful treatment of *hypertension* with *progressive relaxation training* (e.g., Jacob, Kraemer and Agras, 1977), the study of compliance with doctors' instructions (e.g., Baile and Engel, 1978) and the prevention of cardiovascular disorders through community intervention programs (e.g., Maccoby, Farquhar, Wood, and Alexander, 1977). The development and the formal recognition of behavioral medicine as a new interdisciplinary field have evoked great enthusiasm and have been attended by much hoopla. The climate is in some ways reminiscent of the enormous surge of interest that greeted the emergence of biofeedback in the latter part of the 1960s. It is to be hoped that the exaggerated claims and premature optimism that biofeedback inspired in some quarters will be avoided in the development of behavioral medicine, under which rubric biofeedback now falls. And who better to underscore this caution than Neal Miller, a pioneer of biofeedback and now a prominent figure in the founding of the field of behavioral medicine:

> The increasing interest in Behavioral Medicine opens up significant opportunities for research and applications. But there is a danger that overoptimistic claims or widespread applications without an adequate scientific base and sufficient evaluation by pilot testing can lead to failure and disillusionment. Such disillusionment could block the promising developments in this new area for another generation. (1979, p. 5)

CONCLUDING COMMENTS

Considerations of space have prevented us from presenting anything more than brief and highly selective illustrations of current developments in behavior modification and therapy. The proliferation of ideas within the boundaries of behavior modification have been extremely vigorous. In the area of behavior modification with children, for instance, there is a vast literature on fears and phobias, autism and childhood schizophrenia, enuresis and encopresis, mental retardation, academic and social problems, and delinquency. Schaefer and Millman (1977) summarized a wide range of specific behavioral interventions for problem children (including the management of nightmares, obsessive-compulsive problems, hysterical behavior, depression, shy and withdrawn behavior, school phobias and other fears, nervous habits, eating difficulties, self-injurious behavior and many other conditions). A particularly good discussion of contemporary behavior therapy for childhood disorders can be found in Ross's (1981) comprehensive volume *Child Behavior Therapy*.

An important emerging behavioral area is the treatment and understanding of marital discord. Here again, even a summary of this area in terms of specific assessments and strategies is beyong the scope of the present chapter. The interested reader is referred to Jacobson and Margolin (1979), Paolino and McCrady (1978) and Stuart (1980), among the many influential publications appearing in this area.

In the relatively short span of some twenty years, behavior therapy has developed into one of the major psychological approaches in current practice. As already mentioned, it has evolved from a simplistic orientation to one that is not only complex but ever-changing. To remain truly dynamic, behavior modification must continue to struggle with the formidable task of combining scientific rigor — with its emphasis upon careful observation, data, testing of hypotheses and subsequent feedback — with an open-minded spirit of inquiry that holds nothing sacrosanct, has no disciples and is ever open to self-correction on the basis of empirically derived data.

REFERENCES

Atthowe, J.M. Behavior innovation and persistence. *American Psychologist.* **28**: 34-41 (1973).

Atthowe, J.M., Krasner, L. A preliminary report on the application of contingent reinforcement procedures (token economy) on a chronic psychiatric ward. *Journal of Abnormal Psychology*, **73**: 37–43 (1968).

Ayllon T. and Azrin, N.H. *The token economy.* New York: Appleton-Century-Crofts, 1968.

Baile, W.F. and Engel, B.T. A behavioral strategy for promoting treatment compliance following myocardial infarction. *Psychosomatic Medicine.* **40**: 413-419 (1978).

Bandura, A. *Principles of behavior modification.* New York: Holt, Rinehart and Winston, 1969.

Bandura, A. Self-efficacy: Toward a unifying theory of behavioral change. *Psychological Review.* **84**: 191-215 (a) (1977).

Barlow, D.H. Behavior therapy: The next decade. *Behavior Therapy.* **11**: 315-328 (1980).

Beck, A.T. *Cognitive therapy and the emotional disorders.* New York: International Universities Press, 1976.

Bellack, A.S., Hersen, M. and Turner, S.M. Generalization effects of social skills training in chronic schozophrenics: An experimental analysis. *Behaviour Research and Therapy.* **14**: 391-398 (1976).

Benson, H. *The relaxation response.* New York: William Morrow, 1975.

Birk, L., Stolz, S.B., Brady, J.P., Brady, J.V., Lazarus, A.A., Lynch, J.J., Rosenthal, A.J., Skelton, W.D., Stevens, J.B. and Thomas, E.J. *Behavior therapy in psychiatry.* Task Force Report, American Psychiatry Association, Washington, D.C., 1973.

Brown, B.B. *Stress and the art of biofeedback.* New York: Harper & Row, 1977.

Brownell, K.D., Hayes, S.C. and Barlow, D.H. Patterns of appropriate and deviant sexual arousal: The behavioral treatment of multiple sexual deviations. *Journal of Consulting and Clinical Psychology.* **45**: 1144-1155 (1977).

Chaney, E.F., O'Leary, M.R. and Marlatt, G.A. Skill training with alcoholics. *Journal of Consulting and Clinical Psychology.* **46**: 1092-1104 (1978).

Davison, G.C. Behavior modification techniques in institutional settings. In: Franks, C.M. (Ed.), *Behavior therapy: Appraisal and status.* New York: McGraw-Hill, 1969.

Davison, G.C. and Wilson, G.T. Processes of fear-reduction in systematic desensitization: Cognitive and social reinforcement factors in humans. *Behavior Therapy.* **4**: 1-21 (1973).
Dunlap, K. *Habits: Their making and unmaking.* New York: Liveright, 1932.
Ellis, A. Rejoinder: Elegant and inelegant RET. *The Counseling Psychologist.* **7**: 73-82 (1977).
Eysenck, H.J. Learning theory and behaviour therapy. *Journal of Mental Sciences.* **105**: 61-75 (1959).
Eysenck, H.J. *Behaviour therapy and the neuroses.* New York: Pergamon Press, 1960.
Fairweather, G.W. *Social psychology in treating mental illness: An experimental approach.* New York: Wiley, 1964.
Fairweather, G.W., Simon, R., Gebhard, M.E., Weingarten, E., Holland, J.I., Sanders, R., Stone, G.B. and Reahl, J.E. Relative effectiveness of psychotherapeutic programs: A multicriteria comparison of four programs for three different patient groups. *Psychological Monographs.* **74** (5, Whole No. 492) (1960).
Feldman, M.P. and MacCulloch, M.J. *Homosexual behavior: Therapy and assessment.* Oxford: Pergamon Press, 1971.
Foa, E. and Tillmanns, A. The treatment of obsessive-compulsive neurosis. In: Goldstein, A. and Foa, E. (Eds.), *Handbook of behavioral interventions.* New York: Wiley, 1980.
Fuller, G.D. Current status of biofeedback in clinical practice. *American Psychologist.* **33**: 39-48 (1978).
Goldfried, M.R. Systematic desensitization as training in self-control. *Journal of Consulting and Clinical Psychology.* **37**: 228-235 (1971).
Goldfried, M.R. Toward the delineation of therapeutic change principles. *American Psychologist.* **35**: 991-999 (1980).
Goldsmith, J.B. and McFall, R.M. Development and evaluation of an interpersonal skill-training program for psychiatric inpatients. *Journal of Abnormal Psychology.* **84**: 51-58 (1975).
Guthrie, E.R. *The psychology of learning.* New York: Harper & Row, 1935.
Haley, J. *Uncommon therapy: The psychiatric techniques of Milton H. Erickson, M.D.* New York: Norton, 1973.
Heiman, J., LoPiccolo, L. and LoPiccolo, J. *Becoming orgasmic: A sexual growth program for women.* Englewood Cliffs, N.J.: Prentice-Hall, 1976.
Hersen, M. and Barlow, D.H. *Single-case experimental designs: Strategies for studying behavior change.* New York: Pergamon Press, 1976.
Herzberg, A. *Active psychotherapy.* London: Research Books, 1941.
Jacob, R., Kraemer, H. and Agras, W.S. Relaxation therapy in the treatment of hypertension. *Archives of General Psychiatry.* **34**: 1417-1427 (1977).
Jacobson, N. and Margolin, G. *Marital therapy.* New York: Brunner/Mazel, 1979.
Jannoun, L., Munby, M., Catalan, J. and Gelder, M. A home-based treatment program for agoraphobia: Replication and controlled evaluation. *Behavior Therapy.* **11**: 295-305 (1980).
Jones, M.C. The elimination of children's fears. *Journal of Experimental Psychology.* **1**: 382-390 (1924).

Kanfer, F.H. and Karoly, P. Self-control: A behavioristic excursion into the lion's den. *Behavior Therapy.* **3**: 398-416 (1972).

Kanfer, F.H. and Saslow, G. Behavioral diagnosis. In: Franks, C.M. (Ed.), *Behavior therapy: Appraisal and status.* New York: McGraw-Hill, 1969.

Kass, D.J., Silvers, F.M. and Abroms, G.M. Behavioral group treatment of hysteria. *Archives of General Psychiatry.* **26**: 42-50 (1972).

Kazdin, A.E. *The token economy.* New York: Plenum, 1977.

Kazdin, A.E. The application of operant techniques in treatment, rehabilitation, and education. In: Garfield, S.L. and Bergin, A.E. (Eds.), *Handbook of psychotherapy and behavior change,* 2nd ed. New York: Wiley, 1978.

Kazdin, A.E. and Wilson, G.T. *Evaluation of Behavior therapy: Issues, evidence, and research strategies.* Cambridge, Mass.: Ballinger, 1978.

Kendall, P. and Hollon, S. (Eds.) *Cognitive-behavioral interventions: Theory, research, and procedures.* New York: Guilford Press, 1979.

Krasner, L. The operant approach in behavior therapy. In: Bergin, A.E. and Garfield, S.L. (Eds.), *Handbook of psychotherapy and behavior change,* pp. 612-652. New York: Wiley, 1971.

Lang, P.J. Biofeedback training. *European Journal of Behavioural Analysis and Modification.* **4**: 252-254 (1977).

Lazarus, A.A. New methods in psychotherapy: A case study. *South African Medical Journal.* **32**: 660-664 (1958).

Lazarus, A.A. Group therapy of phobic disorders by systematic desensitization. *Journal of Abnormal and Social Psychology.* **63**: 505-510 (1961).

Lazarus, A.A. Towards the understanding and effective treatment of alcoholism. *South African Medical Journal.* **39**: 736-741 (1965).

Lazarus, A.A. Behaviour rehearsal vs. non-directive therapy vs. advice in effecting behaviour change. *Behaviour Research and Therapy.* **4**: 209-212 (1966).

Lazarus, A.A. Behavior therapy in groups. In: Gazda, G.M. (Ed.), *Basic approaches to group psychotherapy and group counseling.* Springfield: Charles C. Thomas, 1968.

Lazarus, A.A. *Behavior therapy and beyond.* New York: McGraw-Hill, 1971.

Lazarus, A.A. Multimodal behavior therapy: Treating the "BASIC ID." *Journal of Nervous and Mental Disease.* **156**: 404-411 (1973).

Lazarus, A.A. Multimodal behavior therapy in groups. In: Gazda, G.M. (Ed.), *Basic approaches to group psychotherapy and group counseling,* rev. ed. Springfield, Ill.: Charles C. Thomas, 1975.

Lazarus, A.A. *Multimodal behavior therapy.* New York: Springer, 1976.

Lazarus, A.A. *The practice of multimodal therapy.* New York: McGraw-Hill, 1981.

Lazarus, A.A. and Fay, A. Resistance or rationalization? A cognitive-behavioral perspective. In: Wachtel, P.L. (Ed.) *Resistance: Psychodynamic and behavioral approaches.* New York: Plenum, 1982.

Leiblum, S.R. and Pervin, L.A. (Eds.), *Principles and practice of sex therapy.* New York: Guilford Press, 1980.

Lindsley, O.R. and Skinner, B.F. A method for the experimental analysis of the behavior of psychotic patients. *American Psychologist.* **9**: 419-420 (1954).

LoPiccolo, J. and LoPiccolo, L. (Eds.) *Handbook of sex therapy.* New York: Plenum Press, 1978.

Maccoby, N., Farquhar, J., Wood, P.D. and Alexander, J. Reducing the risk of cardiovascular disease: Effects of a community-based campaign in knowledge and behavior. *Journal of Community Health.* **3**: 100-114 (1977).

Mahoney, M.J. *Cognition and behavior modification.* Cambridge, Mass.: Ballinger, 1974.

Maletzky, B.M. Self-referred versus court-referred sexually deviant patients: Success with assisted covert sensitization. *Behavior Therapy.* **11**: 306-314 (1980).

Maley, R.F., Feldman, G.L. and Ruskin, R.S. Evaluation of patient improvement in a token economy treatment program. *Journal of Abnormal Psychology.* **82**: 141-144 (1973).

Marks, I. Behavioral psychotherapy of adult neurosis. In: Garfield, S.L. and Bergin, A.E. (Eds.), *Handbook of psychotherapy and behavior change,* 2nd ed. New York: Wiley, 1978.

Masters, W.H. and Johnson, V.E. *Human sexual inadequacy.* Boston: Little, Brown, 1970.

Mathews, A., Teasdale, J., Munby, M., Johnston, D and Shaw, P. A home-based treatment program for agoraphobia. *Behavior Therapy.* **8**: 915-924 (1977).

Meichenbaum, D. *Cognitive behavior modification.* New York: Plenum, 1977.

Miller, N. Behavioral medicine: New opportunities but serious dangers. *Behavioral Medicine Update.* **1**: 5-8 (1979).

Moreno, J.L. *Psychodrama.* New York: Beacon, 1946.

Munby, M. and Johnston, D.W. Agoraphobia: The long-term follow-up of behavioural treatment. *British Journal of Psychiatry.* **137**: 418-427 (1980).

O'Leary, K.D. and O'Leary, S.G. (Eds.) *Classroom management.* New York: Pergamon Press, 1977.

Paolino, T.J. and McCrady, B. *Marriage and marital therapy.* New York: Brunner/Mazel, 1978.

Paul, G.L. Outcome of systematic desensitization, II. In: Franks, C.M. (Ed.), *Behavior therapy: Appraisal and status,* pp. 105-159. New York: McGraw-Hill, 1969.

Paul, G.L. and Lentz, R.J. *Psychological treatment of chronic mental patients.* Cambridge, Mass.: Harvard University Press, 1977.

Paul, G.L. and Shannon, D. Treatment of anxiety through systematic desensitization in therapy groups. *Journal of Abnormal Psychology,* **71**: 124-135 (1966).

Phillips, E.L., Phillips, E.A., Fixsen, D.L. and Wolf, M.M. Achievement Place: Modification of the behaviors of predelinquent boys within a token economy. *Journal of Applied Behavior Analysis.* **4**: 45-59 (1971).

Rachman, S. and Wilson, G.T. *The effects of psychological therapy.* Oxford: Pergamon Press, 1980.

Rosenhan, D.L. On being sane in insane places. *Science.* **179**: 250-258 (1973).

Ross, A. *Child behavior therapy.* New York: Wiley, 1981.

Rush, A.J., Hollon, S.D., Beck, A.T. and Kovacs, M. Depression: Must pharmacotherapy fail for cognitive therapy to succeed? *Cognitive Therapy and Research.* **2**: 199-206 (1978).

Salter, A. *Conditioned reflex therapy.* New York: Farrar, Strauss, 1949.

Schaefer, C.E. and Millman, H.L. (Eds.) *Therapies for children.* San Francisco: Jossey-Bass, 1977.

Schwartz, G. E. and Weiss, S.M. Behavioral medicine revisited: An amended definition. *Journal of Behavioral Medicine.* **1**: 249-252 (1978).

Semans, J.H. Premature ejaculation: A new approach. *Southern Medical Journal.* **49**: 353-361 (1956).

Shapiro, D. and Surwit, R.S. Learned control of psychological function and disease. In: Leitenberg, H. (Ed.), *Handbook of behavior modification and behavior therapy.* Englewood Cliffs, N.J.: Prentice-Hall, 1976.

Shapiro, M.B. An experimental approach to diagnostic psychological testing. *Journal of Mental Science.* **97**: 748-764 (1951).

Sherman, A.R. Real-life exposure as a primary therapeutic factor in the desensization treatment of fear. *Journal of Abnormal Psychology.* **79**: 19-28 (1972).

Silver, B.V. and Blanchard, E.B. Biofeedback and relaxation training in the treatment of psychophysiological disorders: Or are the machines really necessary? *Journal of Behavioral Medicine.* **1**: 217-239 (1978).

Stampfl, T.G. and Levis, D.J. Essentials of implosive therapy: A learning-based psychodynamic behavioral therapy. *Journal of Abnormal Psychology.* **72**: 496-503 (1967).

Stuart, R.B. Behavioural control of over-eating. *Behaviour Research and Therapy.* **5**: 357-365 (1967).

Stuart, R.B. *Helping couples change.* New York: Guilford Press, 1980.

Tharp, R.G. and Wetzel, R.J. *Behavior modification in the natural environment.* New York: Academic Press, 1969.

Thoresen, C.E. and Mahoney, M.J. *Behavioral self-control.* New York: Holt, Rinehart & Winston, 1974.

Ullmann, L.P. *Institution and outcome.* New York: Pergamon Press, 1967.

Ullmann, L.P. and Krasner, L. *Case studies in behavior modification.* New York: Holt, Rinehart and Winston, 1965.

Ullmann, L.P., Krasner, L. *A psychological approach to abnormal behavior.* Englewood Cliffs, NJ: Prentice-Hall, 1975.

Upper, D. and Ross, S.M. (Eds.) *Behavioral group therapy, 1979.* Champaign, Ill.: Research Press, 1979.

Wachtel, P.L. (Ed.) *Resistance: Psychodynamic and behavioral approaches.* New York: Plenum, 1981.

Wilson, G.T. Innovations in the modification of phobic behaviors in two clinical cases. *Behavior Therapy.* **4**: 426-430 (1973).

Wilson, G.T. Behavior therapy and the treatment of obesity. In: Miller, W.R. (Ed.), *The addictive behaviors: Treatment of alcoholism, drug abuse, smoking and obesity.* New York: Pergamon Press, 1980.

Wilson, G.T. Behavior therapy for adults: Application and outcome. In: Wilson, G.T. and Franks, C.M. (Eds.), *Contemporary behavior therapy: Conceptual and empirical foundations.* New York: Guilford Press, in press.

Wilson, G.T. and Brownell, K. Behavior therapy for obesity: An evaluation of treatment outcome. *Advances in Behavior Research and Therapy.* **3**: 49-86 (1980).

Wilson, G.T. and Davision, G.C. Processes of fear reduction in systematic desensitization: Animal studies. *Psychological Bulletin.* **76**: 1-14 (1971).

Wilson, G.T. and Davison, G.C. Behavior therapy and homosexuality: A critical perspective. *Behavior Therapy.* **5**: 16–28 (1974).

Wilson, G.T. and Evans, I.M. The therapist–client relationship in behavior therapy. In: Gurman, R.S. and Razin, A.M. (Eds.), *The therapist's contribution to effective psychotherapy: An empirical approach.* New York: Pergamon Press, 1977.

Wilson, G.T. and O'Leary, K.D. *Principles of behavior therapy.* Englewood Cliffs, N.J.: Prentice-Hall, 1980.

Winkler, R.C. A theory of equilibrium in token economies. *Journal of Abnormal Psychology.* **79**: 169-173 (1972).

Wolpe, J. Reciprocal inhibition as the main basis of psychotherapeutic effects. *Archives of Neurology and Psychiatry.* **92**: 205-226 (1954).

Wolpe, J. *Psychotherapy by reciprocal inhibition.* Stanford: Stanford University Press, 1958.

Wolpe, J. Congnition and causation in human behavior and its therapy. *American Psychologist.* **33**: 437-446 (1978).

Wolpe, J. and Lazarus, A.A. *Behavior therapy techniques.* New York: Pergamon Press, 1966.

Zilbergeld, B. *Male sexuality.* New York: Bantam, 1978.

7 Hypnotherapy

Milton V. Kline

Since the review of the field of hypnotherapy originally published in the 1965 edition of the *Handbook of Clinical Psychology* (Kline, 1965), there has been a vast and significant expansion of research as well as clinical application in this field. The purpose of this chapter is not to review the tremendous amount of literature that has been reported in both experimental and clinical journals, but to emphasize specific clinical approaches, strategies and tactics that are representative of the contemporary utilization of hypnosis within a broad spectrum of psychological and psychiatric treatment.

For a very thorough review of the clinical and experimental literature the reader might consult *The Handbook of Hypnosis and Psychosomatic Medicine* by Burrows and Dennerstein (1980). Additional excellent reference works evealing the field of hypnotherapy including historical, experimental, therapeutic and research issues are the volumes by Roy Udolf (1981) and Chertok (1981).

It is now clear that hypnosis can be viewed neither as an instrument of suggestion by itself nor as a phenomenon of behavior that is set aside from the main stream of psychological theory and clinical concepts in relation to psychotherapy. Salient trends to be noted in the clinical utilization of hypnotherapy emphasize a significant distinction between the process of hypnotic induction and the hypnotic transference relationship. There is an increasing awareness that hypnosis is a dynamically patient-centered process, and the strategies and tactics of induction clearly show that patients may be hypnotized without conscious awareness of the process and with their implied rather than stated consent. There is also an increasing utilization of complex and specialized tactics in hypnotic techniques that emphasize reactive, ventilative and perceptual manifestations. It is clear that intervention on hypnotic levels in the therapeutic process emphasizes the

155

role that hypnosis plays in intervening with elements of memory, learning, perception and imagery.

With the wide range of strategies and tactics currently employed in the sophisticated utilization of clinical hypnosis in a variety of treatment situations, perhaps the most succinct and salient comment possible is that the contemporary phase of hypnotherapy points to hypnotic procedures and hypnotic processes being integrated within all forms of psychotherapy, ranging from behavioral and supportive approaches to intensive, dynamically oriented analytic therapies. Clinical problems treated on hypnotic levels include neurotic and psychotic illnesses, psychosomatic disorders, a variety of psychophysiological problems and a wide range of organic illnesses and pain syndromes. The hypnotic process can be integrated into a wide spectrum of treatment situations only after thorough patient evaluation, and such integration must be in keeping with therapeutic competence and patient need. Hypnosis does not by itself exclude potential problems, dangers and contraindications, all of which emphasize the need for required specialized training, supervision and experience before a therapist may be considered competent to utilize hypnosis as an integral and significant part of their therapeutic armamentarium.

The psychotherapist looking to hypnosis and planning to incorporate it into his or her treatment concepts and techniques can find significant application and substantiation for its incorporation in areas dealing with psychophysiological disorders with memory disturbances as well as with elements of resistance. Phobic disorders have proved particularly responsive to hypnotic therapies. In addition, hypnosis has a role in family medicine where outside of the area of formal psychotherapy its utilization has proved to be significant in dealing with aspects of terminal illness, hypertension, skin disease, smoking and obesity.

Patients on all age levels, from children to geriatric groups, are equally accessible to hypnotic therapies, and its incorporation in the comprehensive treatment of pain, psychosomatic disorders, psychosexual dysfunctions and major mental illnesses has been well substantiated (Burrows and Dennerstein, 1980).

CLINICAL HYPNOSIS WITH SPECIFIC RELATION TO BEHAVIOR THERAPY: THEORETICAL AND CLINICAL CONSIDERATIONS

Hypnosis as an intrapsychological and interpersonal experience can be used as an integrative and amplifying procedure in relation to biofeedback mechanisms and behavior therapy. The hypnotic capacity for linking cognitive to affective reactions within a feedback loop of sensory and motor imagery is a dynamic approach to behavior modification during psychotherapy.

The concept of behavior modification derived from experimental psychology is today the framework within which one can appropriately place all forms of behavioral therapy as well as biofeedback procedures. As learning theory and behavior modification have assumed increasing importance in the treatment of emotional and psychosomatic disorders, the need to integrate such techniques and concepts not only within the framework of learning theory but within the structure of a psychodynamic concept of human behavior and emotional disorder has increased.

Hypnosis, whether viewed as an ego state alteration in relation to consciousness, or an affective experience of a topologically regressive nature, plays an important role in an understanding of the underlying mechanisms by which patients respond to specific techniques and procedures involving alteration of voluntary and involuntary behavioral processes, and gain a sense of self-mastery through self-regulatory procedures. Thus a "cross-fertilization" between hypnosis, behavior modification and biofeedback procedures has become inevitable. Hypnosis as an altered state of perceptual receptivity and response formation makes available an interpersonal situation capable of dealing with the dynamics of intrapsychic experience and of regulating and integrating stimulus response and desensitization reactions within a treatment framework that may range from the meditative stress-reducing methods of simple behavioral therapy, to the desensitization and self-regulatory procedures more typically encountered in behavior therapy per se and biofeedback treatment. Thus an understanding of some of the fundamental mechanisms of hypnosis, as well as the manner in which both the hypnotic experience and the hypnotic relationship alter the level of ideational and affective behavior, is important in enabling the therapist to more effectively structure a behavioral modification approach and to add a dimension of psychodynamic intervention that frequently may not exist in more direct behavioral therapies.

Hypnosis can utilize the inborn feedback loop inherent in the psychobiologic apparatus of the human being, and thus adds another dimension to feedback as a process, and for the therapist permits a combination of controlling responses by both external reinsertion and internalized regulatory controls. Thus, all forms of behavior modification, whether one refers to behavior therapy as a desensitizing approach, as characterized by Wolpe (1969), or some of the more dynamic aspects of behavior therapy ranging from assertive training to biofeedback control of sensation, perception, pain and affective response, rests essentially upon the ability of the patient to detect signals of stress and tension, to learn how both to reduce the signal input and to bring about a state of reduction frequently described as relaxation, and to maintain that state on a relatively continuous basis.

Hypnosis as a behavioral process dealing with both cognitive and affective behavioral organization permits direct intervention into all levels of behavioral process. Ranging from stimulus perception to complex cognitive integration, it offers a basis for structuring a vital and dynamic interpersonal relationship. Hypnotic procedures may control the mechanisms involved in adaptive behavior and emerge as in integrated and effective clinical means of treating a wide range of psychological and physiological disorders.

In a study reported by Kline and Linder (1967) dealing with the experimental investigation of hypnotically induced emotions with particular reference to blood glucose measurements, it was found that acute emotional stress could be induced through hypnosis, but that the physiological correlates that would typically accompany that emotional stress could be minimized and become virtually nonexistent when the patient was in a deep hypnotic state. This was particularly true where abreactive techniques were used for the induction of stress.

Based on this and additional clinical work, it was found that relaxation from hypnosis lasting several hours can be maintained for long periods of time and easily reinforced through self-hypnosis. The use of hypnosis for prolonged stress reduction, the reinforcement of homeostasis and the alteration of sensory and perceptual mechanisms can, in selected patients, yield therapeutic results rapidly and can be linked effectively to both biofeedback and behavioral therapy approaches.

Of theoretical importance in connection with these results is the observation by O'Connell and Orne (1968) that some kind of "central relaxation" is involved and not simply muscular relaxation, since, in hypnosis, electrodermal activity is not muscular in origin but rather autonomic.

This observation is confirmed by work in our own laboratory utilizing polygraph techniques in which patients during prolonged hypnotic relaxation reveal a persistence and maintenance of relaxation and a reduction in sensory disturbances regardless of the type of stimulation provided.

In a related investigation, Black and Friedman (1968) found that hypnotic anesthesia produced a significant effect on the pituitary–adrenal access to pain. Black and Wigan (1961) also found that increased heart rate as a conditioned response could be abolished in hypnotic deafness. To Black and Walter (1965), these findings suggested the possible cerebral level where hypnotic blockage takes place, at least with regard to hearing, probably at some point below the frontal cortex but above heart-regulating centers in the medulla at the level of the hypothalamus.

In work with sensory hypnoanalysis, Kline patients undergo intense concentration on the sensory and motor components of their symptoms with complete absorption in them during a hypnotic state, afterward translating the sensory experience into verbal expression. With stress reduction under hypnosis, particularly that using biofeedback techniques, patients begin to verbalize different associations to the experiences, and as the tension levels are reduced, in terms of the monitoring of feedback from biofeedback instruments, the lexical expression takes on major modification. When the patients use the lexical changes in their expression as means for enhancing self-regulation, particularly within self-hypnosis, they learn rapidly and efficiently to control their own behavioral response and achieve symptomatic gains that appear to be meaningful and lasting. One particular approach, which the writer and colleagues have worked with during the past several years, involves the use of sensory hypnotherapy in conjunction with behavior therapy and biofeedback procedures. Sensory hypnotherapy was originally developed as an experimental form of psychotherapy for patients who were unresponsive in previous treatment situations, and it has been influenced by the primacy of sensory functioning in the hypnotic process and its relationship to the productive role of regression in dynamic psychotherapy. The importance of the sensory order has long been recognized as a vital element, not only in the hypnotic process but also in the reinforcement of stress or tension-produced symptoms in a wide range of emotional and behavioral disorders.

The utilization of hypnosis as a means for producing first emotional flooding (Kline, 1976), in order to intensify the components and parameters of the patient's stressful behavior, consists of the development of focal behavioral orientations and the intensification of sensory, motor and imagery responses based on the stimulation of the patient's perceptual apparatus. The resulting process brings about regression and frequently abreactive elements, some nonverbal in nature. These come later and only after the patient has learned what lexical expressions are connected with the high levels of stress converted into lexical expression during the homeostatic state achieved following protracted and eventually self-induced relaxation.

In its broader sense, emotional flooding with hypnosis produces abreactive behavior on a continuum from "silent" to "explosive" and from nonverbal imagery to spontaneous lexical expression. Hypnosis in this form of therapy involves the activation of strong transference phenomena as well as an alteration in psychophysiological functioning. Emotional flooding with hypnosis can be maintained for long periods of time and is very easily reinforced through self-hypnosis.

During the past two years, a large number of patients have been treated with a combined hypnobehavioral approach dependent upon sensory hypnotherapy, systematic desensitization and the use of biofeedback procedures. These patients included those suffering from chronic anxiety as well as somatization reactions involving migraine headaches, spastic colons, persistent lower back pain, disturbed sleep patterns, sexual dysfunction and some depressive reactions.

The procedure generally involves first inducing a relatively deep hypnotic trance state within which the patient is taught how to recognize emerging evidence of stress through sensory responses in various parts of the body, particularly those involved in symptomatic formation. Biofeedback instrumentation is used in order to show the patient the level of stress that can be produced spontaneously and then how the stress can be intensified through hypnotic procedures of sensory hypnotherapy, in which imagery and amplification of tension-related associations are presented repeatedly to the patient in the hypnotic state.

Abreactive behavior is encouraged on both a physiological and a verbal level. Patients also learn to recognize through the use of biofeedback the impact of their own abreaction, whether silent or expressive, on instrumentation and to recognize similar response formations in a waking interview situation when there is no deliberate attempt experimentally to intensify sensory or affective responses.

The patient is also given the opportunity during hypnosis to equate each marked sensory disturbance, each intensification of emotional stress with imagery, and to equate that imagery with his or her own spontaneous lexical expression.

Following this and the development of a hierarchy of images that reflect varying levels of stress response, measured not only by subjective feeling but also by
biofeedback means, the patient is taught how to maintain a degree of complete
relaxation through self-hypnosis and to observe the changes in images, the lexical
associations to the images and the changes in biofeedback measurements.

Thus, through the use of self-hypnosis the patient learns how to recognize his
own internal stress responses through his natural feedback loop which he has
now learned to associate with externalized biofeedback measurements. He has
also learned to identify levels and types of characteristic image reactions, sometimes even eidetic images, and to associate them with verbal equations. The patient has within himself, based on increasing experience with sensory stimulation,
established a biofeedback response and connection with imagery and lexical
reaction.

By repeated reinforcement and mastery of self-hypnotic procedures a state of
continuous ongoing homeostatic reduction of stress, related to presenting symptoms and problems, can be obtained.

In summary, it would appear that the use of hypnosis as an underlying treatment relationship, and as an aspect of hypnotic transference that permits alteration in ego functioning, is not only consistent with behavioral therapy and biofeedback in treatment procedures but actually permits an effective integration of
the underlying cognitive and affective components in behavior disorders. Thus,
the development of a hypnobehavioral approach within which carefully selected
patients can be treated on hypnotic levels, that includes the intensification of
those sensory and ideational elements involved in their disorder and at the same
time enhances self-regulatory mechanisms, provides a direct and integrated approach to behavior modification in a wide range of physiologic and psychologic
disorders. Such treatment, however, is dependent upon a careful assessment of
the patient's presenting problem and an understanding of the dynamics involved,
and of the ability to utilize the trance aspects of hypnotherapy within the treatment approach, using biofeedback and behavior therapy procedures.

TEMPORAL ALTERATION THROUGH HYPNOSIS

Time as a variable in the alteration of behavior has many characteristics as it
becomes a focal point in the practice of psychotherapy. Time may become
connected to related variables of age, attention and awareness. Time is perhaps
the most undefinable yet paradoxical of all things: The past is past, the future is
conjectural, and the present becomes the past almost spontaneously. We think
in reference to time; we feel in relation to time; we have awareness of the self
within a variety of constructs relating to age and place that are time-bound.
Temporal sequence is not absolute, since the human being is capable of projecting
himself backward in memory and forward in imagination. Historically, aspects
of hypnotic age regression and progression (Kline, 1960), while linked with

experiential and projected aspects of age, are nevertheless fundamentally connected with the issue of time. One sense of time arises from irreversible chemical reactions that serve as a biological clock. The linkage of subjective and objective time is thus understood through the participation of man's bodily processes. Time has been known to play a distinctive and vital role in daily cycles and hormonal activity, nutrient metabolism, body temperature, blood pressure, wakefulness and sleep (Cohen, 1967), all of which have direct lines with what we describe as aspects of awareness, and in one way or another are related to memory, attention and cognitive behavior.

There are many aspects of the psychopathology of time, which may embody temporal aberrations. Sometimes these are due to organic brain damage, and at other times are essentially psychodynamic, ranging from such phenomena as amnesia, deja vu sensation, dissociated states and experiences of revivification and age regression in trance. Time loses its objective reality in normal subjects with alterations in the rate of thought and feeling in emotional flooding, during dreams or in hypnosis, as well as, at times, as a direct result of drug input.

Thus, we see time as a multivariable element in both personality expression and behavior organization. The ability to deal with time, to control and alter behavioral concomitants of time, has long been an inherent goal of any psychotherapeutic system. It is with the additional contribution of hypnosis that we have been able to bring time and the perceptual mechanisms relating to experiential aspects of time under more direct control and influence, so that the hypnotic use of time has become a potent device in the practice of psychotherapy. The developmental implication of time in the structure of emerging personality was investigated and discussed by Piaget (1955), who observed that children pass through a stage in which they cannot differentiate between temporal and spatial order. A young child is not able to say how long an interval of time seems to last without being influenced by the correlative distance and speed. He has concluded that children younger than eight years have no clear notion of simultaneity. This has vast implications for the manner in which the evolving ego process and the impact of experiential involvement during the early years of life may quickly lead to time-bound behavior; and much of the neurotic structure of personality that we see in the adult may be the result of time-bound issues from childhood and their linkage to the present. Zimbardo, Marshall and Maslach (1972), in a provocative experimental investigation, were concerned with liberating behavior from time-bound control by expanding the present through hypnosis. Temporal perspective was experimentally manipulated by verbal instructions to expand the present while minimizing the significance of the past and future. The reactions of trained hypnotic subjects to this induction were compared with hypnotic simulators and nonsimulating controls. In a fourth group, time sense was made salient, but no suggestion was given to alter it. Across a variety of tasks, self-report measures and behavioral observations, this modification of the boundaries between past, present and future resulted in profound consequences among the hypnotic subjects.

Changes in affect, language, thought processes, sensory awareness and susceptibility to social-emotional contagion, resulted from an expanded present orientation. Nonreactive measures distinguished simulators from hypnotic subjects,
who apparently were better able to incorporate the induced time distortion and
perceive it as a viable alternative to their traditional time perspective. Some implications of time as a pervasive, nonobvious independent variable in the social
control of cognition and behavior were clear.

In addition to the use of hypnosis in order to reexperience the past through
hyperamnesia, to isolate the past through the intensification of attention, to
ventilate the past through the use of abreaction and revivification, to examine
the implications of the past in relation to the present through the use of imaginative age progression, the most significant work on hypnotic levels has dealt with
the issue of time distortion and time as a variable of age and experiential involvement. In relation to time as a dynamic variable in behavior, we have to differentiate between: experiential time, that is, the time of experience; world time,
which means essentially clock time; physical time or objective time; time awareness; and the personal reading of a time interval or event, that is, the distance
measured by time so that it becomes an experiential spacial concept. Seeming
duration of time (a person's answer to the question, "How long did it seem?")
is subject to much variation. This frequently leads to what might best be called
estimated personal time, a highly variable phenomenon influenced by the meaningfulness of the involvement, the degree of unconsciousness that may play a
role in the experience, the degree of association that takes place in the event and
the total state of awareness and attention that may be mobilized at that time.

Cooper and Erickson's (1954) experimental clinical work with hypnotic time
distortion has attempted to manipulate time awareness in much the manner
described by Huxley. The use of "special" time in which to execute certain tasks,
mental or motor, has been carefully observed and recorded in their experiments.
Generally, the most meaningful aspect of time distortion that Cooper has
recorded has to do with the subjective sensation of time and its effect upon
thinking, feeling, perception and particularly one's sense of awareness and bodily
orientation. Attempts to validate hypnotic time distortion against performance
increments usually of a motor or learning nature have, for the greater part,
yielded negative findings. Fischer (1967) notes, however, that such an attempt
at validation is an exceedingly limited one, since it is very possible to have "increased data content" with "no proportional increase in data processing and/or
data reduction." Zimbardo *et al.* (1972) have described an attempt to modify
one aspect of man's internal time machine, namely, his awareness of tempo or
rate of movement by time. The assumed changes in internal processes were
measured by analyzing the frequency, duration and degree of their interference
with a more easily measured process. In this connection, Zimbardo, Ebbesen
and Fraser (1971) have developed an apparatus and technique that uses the rate
of emission of a simple external response (key pressing) as an objective index of

subjective states. They demonstrated the validity of this approach in assessing preferences and attitudes as well as the impact of social and physical stimuli on behavior. They have extended in a situation where behavior is related to stimulus feedback as a function of a time-based rate of responding. Their results, which at present constitute some of the most provocative experimental investigations in this area, support the conclusion that the subjective experience of time awareness can be experimentally modified, and that this change has measurable consequence in behavior. The modification of subjective time sense would appear to require the concentration, imaginative involvement and suspension of usual modes of analytic thinking that can be achieved by the hypnotic experience. Only those subjects previously trained in hypnosis and in a state of hypnotic relaxation and concentration were able to translate the verbal suggestion of a syncronicity of clock time and personal time into a reality. In comparison with simulating subjects, Zimbardo's subjects given time distortion instructions under hypnosis were able to experience a change in time awareness. This change introduced an asynchrony between subjective time and task-relevant clock time that in turn exerted a controlling influence on their behavior. It would thus seem that the combination provided by the power of hypnotic intervention in experience and the objective precision of the operant conditioning methodology has been effective in demonstrating the validity of inducing changes in time awareness. The implication from this observation in addition to those clinical applications during the past number of years is that there is practical significance for the individual in extending these techniques to areas of problem solving, anxiety reduction and psychotherapy.

In a recent study, alteration in time awareness was also capable of producing significant changes in a number of individual reactions to the perception of the body in spatial orientation. Utilizing the rod and frame technique,[1] it was found that under hypnotic time distortion a number of subjects switched from field-dependent to independent status and consistently reverted back to their original field position when out of time distortion. Thus, in keeping with concepts of the developmental aspect of time and space in the logical thinking process that Piaget (1955) has attributed to children, it becomes clear that in hypnosis we can deal with highly integrated concepts of body image and affect aspects of self-awareness that are time-bound and experientially connected. By altering temporal factors, we frequently alter a whole range of cognitive and affective responses, thus bringing about significant changes in attitudes, feelings, and responses to the self as well as to the environment.

From the experimental literature (Cooper, 1954) dealing with hypnosis and time distortion, the following conclusions can be drawn: 1) Time distortion can

---

[1]Hypnotic Studies in Psychosomatic Disorders, The Institute for Research in Hypnosis and Psychotherapy.

be demonstrated in the majority of subjects in whom a moderately deep hypnotic trance can be produced. 2) In all likelihood, the subjects actually have the experience they allege, and if this be true, then time sense can be altered to a predetermined degree by hypnotic suggestion, and subjects can have an amount of experience under these conditions that is more nearly commensurate with the subjective time involved than with the world time. This activity, while seeming to proceed at a normal or natural rate as far as the subject is concerned, actually takes place with great rapidity. 3) Retrospective falsification or elaboration does not enter into the subject's reports when he is clearly in a hypnotic state. 4) Reported experiences during distorted time are continuous. 5) Thought under time distortion while proceeding at a normal rate in the subject's point of view can take place very rapidly relative to world time. Such thought may be superior in certain respects to waking thought. 6) There is some evidence that the recovery of material from the unconscious can be facilitated. 7) There is some evidence that creative thought can be facilitated. 8) There is little evidence that motor learning can be facilitated. 9) There are some findings that suggest that nonmotor learning can be enhanced. 10) As a result of time distortion, it would appear that experience per se can be isolated and treated in terms of countable events. In other words, the quantitation of experience becomes possible.

The concept of time distortion in relation to psychotherapy does not constitute in itself a definitive form of therapy, but rather offers a method by which access can be gained to the experiential life of the patient. Any therapy resulting derives from a separate process of reordering the significances and values of the patient's experiential subjective and objective realities. Some theoretical implications can be drawn from the concept of time and time distortion as it may well relate both to the development of human personality and, particularly, to psychotherapeutic attempts to bring about changes in behavior organization that are linked to personality dynamics.

The split between mechanistic and dynamic models of behavior is as invalid as the philosophical split between mind and body. For this reason, many therapeutic procedures in the area of behavior disorders involve more than meets the eye. If we are to objectively develop better methods of dealing with behavior disorders, we must continue to examine in greater detail the fullest meaning of those experiences that we may prematurely classify as technique.

Although there may in some quarters still exist a controversy as to the validity of hypnotic revivification, this controversy may in effect be a question as to what degree of hypnosis exists. With more exacting methods for measuring the nature and depth of hypnosis, the contradiction in reports of many validation studies of hypnotic phenomena may well be resolved.

At this point, both the clinical and experimental literature attests to the genuineness of hypnotically induced alterations in perception and particularly to its meaningfulness. That regressive behavior exists apart from hypnosis is clearly recognized. Its degree and dynamic balance often distinguish its appearance in normal functions of sleep, dissociation, dreaming and fantasizing from the psychopathological hallucination, stupor and delusional states.

Since this form of hypnotically induced behavior appears when fully developed to constitute a rather distinctive dissociation or ablation from temporal reality, it may be hypothesized that for the patient whose emotional disturbances are deeply rooted in the involuntary mechanisms of everyday living, such an approach might afford the possibility of disrupting patterns of behavior that are strongly reinforced and have been relatively untouched by previous therapy.

Clinical and Theoretical Considerations

The results point to the use of time and age lateration not as a technique in therapy but as an intense dynamic experience within which the patient's world of reality may for the first time since his own childhood be touched and influenced constructively and productively. Apart from its value as a component of psychotherapy, a major result of this investigation has been to focus our attention upon the nature of temporal alteration as phenomena of behavior; studied under the circumstances just described, the concept of time distortion has proved to those of us involved in this therapeutic approach to be provocative in connection with the very nature of hypnosis itself. We should now like to channel our attention in this direction and take the results of these experiences to the task of discussing the nature of hypnosis and hypnotic behavior.

In age regression the temporal appraisal that exists in the waking state is disrupted. Associative links with temporal, sensory and motor cues are either dissociated or so effectively blocked or masked as to permit the emergence of reality appraisal on a newly structured hypnotic basis that is relatively uninfluenced by the externalized perceptions of either the waking state or the chronological state within hypnosis. Subjects in time-altered states believe in the essential nature of the hypnotically induced reality not through suggestion but through the natural utilization of more primitive mechanisms of reality appraisal. These are essentially the regressive structures of cognition and the internalized process of perception that may be described under a variety of headings ranging from dissociation to subliminal.

The criterion for the appearance of time–age regression in hypnosis is the construction of invariants or concepts of the self through conservation. Conservation may be defined on a behavioral level as the activating element behind reality appraisal, structuring body image and awareness of self in relation to externalized symbols. In this respect, conservation is the process of logical organization even though it may deal with symbolic components. It may well be that much of what happens within the reconstructing-conservation process in hypnosis is very similar to what goes on in the condensation and reconstruction process in dreaming. The process of conservation must therefore be considered as the result of operational reversibility. Operational reversibility in this sense is based upon Piaget's (1954, 1957) genetic model of the development of logical structure in the mental development of children and relates to the capacity to manipulate observations through the logical associations of externalized connections as compared with the capacity to deal with observations through internalized associations. Response mechanisms relate to modality functions of tension, awareness and the gradations of consciousness as they may be viewed in terms of criticalness and vigilance. Operational reversibility in this sense is the structural process within which cognitive and perceptual mechanisms develop and emerge.

Hypnotic time-age regression and its various dimensions of behavior cannot be restricted to a criterion of "chronology" with respect to either validity or genuineness. Age, time, space and other externalized loci for the orientation of self can only be viewed as the initiating stimuli of operational structures within which reversibility and conservation compose the major mechanisms in the evolution of symbols and the development of expressive behavior.

Hypnosis and its phenomena can in this sense be best understood in relation to a classificatory system of cognition and perception that of necessity presupposes an existence and an understanding of the serial relations set off by operational reversibility. From this it follows that such emergent behavior will be greatly influenced by: 1) the degree of operational reversibility that is available (i.e., the depth of hypnosis, the degree of dissociation, the detachment from time appraisal, the plasticity of prelogical operations in the development of symbolic behavior) and 2) the nature of the construction of conservation (i.e., the elimination of invariants necessary for reality appraisal and their replacement by equally effective ones for the logical perception and reinforcement of the emergent operational reversibility). At this juncture, the process of hypnosis and its dissociative mechanism is greatly influenced by the dynamics of the hypnotic relationship both at its inception and during its management. The separation of the mechanistic from the dynamic components in hypnotically induced behavior must be considered; together they form the pathway through which the patient reconstructs his perceptual and cognitive functions.

The operational reversibility of time percepts and their replacement through symbolic conservation may constitute the major mechanism in the psychological development of hypnotic behavior. Simultaneous or serially synchronized functions of regression and the construction of a system of symbolic logical structures consistent with the regressed state, lead to the development of hypnotic behavior that is still structured as a whole, but with respect to waking reality levels is much more internalized and much less subject to external stimulation. In this respect, we believe that the process that leads to increasingly greater reliance upon the internalized process for reality appraisal and behavior-organizing operations in itself constitutes a gradient of perceptual masking or dissociation. The masking of external stimulation in itself would appear to constitute an archaic and regressive phenomenon that in varying degrees is to be found in all aspects of behavior, but assumes paramount importance in hypnosis.

PRELOGICAL THOUGHT IN THE HYPNOTIC PROCESS

During early childhood, prelogical modes of perception and thinking emerge, which include the construction of imagery. Thus the field of intelligence becomes enlarged in the normal development of mental functioning. Now, to actions occurring in the child's immediate externalized environment, are added actions that have occurred in the past. This involves the use of magical thinking and the need to utilize psychological operations as a solution for problems. Piaget writes (1954) that in this state there is the equating of percepts without recourse to critical judgment, which is only now beginning to emerge. For example, "a child during this phase of development may pour liquid from one glass jar into another of a vastly different shape and will believe that the actual quantity in the second bottle is increased or decreased in the process." When equal parts are taken away from two equal whole figures, the child refuses to believe that the remainders are equal if the perceptual configurations are different.

Thus the child at this level of psychological development has operationally moved past the level of sensory-motor adaptation and seeks conceptual solutions. Concept formation at this level is essentially prelogical — that which we might call magical in nature and restricted with respect to critical judgment. Internalized actions and experience are tied in with externalized perceptions to a very great extent. Behavioral responses weighted in part by externalized influences are the criteria of maturation in this stage of growth.

Most typical of regressed subjects in this connection is a lack of logical congruity with perceptual configuration. Illogical associations can be formed readily and accepted readily. This is true both for those induced hypnotically and those derived from spontaneous experience during hypnosis and particularly through time–age regression.

Study and observation of hypnotic time alteration over a long period of time, within psychotherapy and in experimental investigation, have continued to emphasize the meaningfulness of this aspect of behavior. The criterion of genuine age regression has little to do with chronological age but much to do with perception and time based on externalization as a cognitive-perceptual process, and the emergence of internalization as the major modality for experiential, perceptual and behavioral organization.

In view of the basically regressive characteristic of hypnosis, therapeutic results obtained through simple suggestion require an explanation apart from those of an oversimplified psychology of suggestion. The very meaning of suggestion and its nature mechanistically would seem to require reformulation psychologically. Awareness of the regressive components in hypnosis should be recognized by all who use it clinically, and increased attention to the interaction process rather than the behavioral responses alone may shed additional light on the essential nature of hypnosis and help in expanding its therapeutic application. The nature of psychological regression that characterizes hypnosis is significant from a psychopathological and neuropathological frame of reference, as well as from a general and developmental psychology of mental functioning. Within it are to be found the components of body image, self-concept and the structuring of perception. This is the interaction of pscyhology and physiology and the cornerstone of consciousness. Greater attention to the divergent processes within it are warranted and should prove rewarding in relation to psychotherapy.

SENSORY HYPNOTHERAPY IN THE MANAGEMENT OF CRISES AND EMERGENCIES DURING THE COURSE OF PSYCHOTHERAPY

The development of a therapeutic approach emphasizing the use of the sensory order within an analytic framework was described earlier as sensory hypnoanalysis (Kline, 1967). As an experimental treatment approach, it has been designed to expand sensory experience, at first with a restriction of verbal output, accompanied by the intensification of visual imagery as an intermediate experiential involvement between amplification of sensory response and verbalization.

To a considerable extent, the techniques described within the framework of sensory hypnoanalysis have been strongly influenced by recognition of the importance of the sensory order in relation to psychodynamics and the body language of communication in emotional disorders and psychosomatic disturbances. In addition, it has been recognized that within the hypnotic process the role of sensory-motor imagery activity assumes a level of accessibility that is frequently not encountered in therapeutic settings where hypnosis is not employed.

This was noticed in connection with the induction of hypnosis and the subjective reports that patients frequently made of the presence of sensory experience and its direct relationship to body image components, often with direct and meaningful linkage to pertinent aspects of the patient's memory, perceptual process, associative function and focal symptom development. Confirmation of the importance of the sensory order and the role of imagery in relation to hypnosis has been observed in connection with its utilization as an induction procedure, particularly in refractory subjects, and in the ability to utilize sensory and imagery components in both the amplification and the deeping of the hypnotic state. Particularly evident have been those neuropsychological reactions that, aroused by sensory experience, are reflected in alterations of time–space percepts. It is also evident that such changes often coincide with rapidly emerging transference phenomena that can become an integral part of the developing hypnotic process and can lend themselves not only to spontaneous experiential involvement, but also to the productive utilization of what has been described as rapid and spontaneous regression in the service of the ego.

Sensory-imagery techniques in hypnotherapy were originally reported in connection with the successful treatment of benign paroxysmal peritonitis, psoriasis and neurodermatitis. Since that time, modifications of this treatment procedure have been reported in connection with a wide range of neurotic, characterologic and psychophysiological disorders. Ament and Milgrom (1967) have reported on its incorporation in the successful treatment of pruritis with cutaneous lesions in chronic myelogenous leukemia.

The original introduction of hypnoplasty by Meares (1960), with its provocative relationship to the productively regressive development of the hypnotic process, was a further development in the intensification of sensations during hypnosis and of the fundamental changes in communication that were possible within the hypnotic relationship. Finally, the modifications and development by Raginsky (1962) of his therapeutic system and approach known as sensory hypnoplasty have served as a clinical conceptual basis for some of the approaches, techniques and mechanisms employed within psychotherapy structured as sensory hypnoanalysis. As described by Raginsky (1962), sensory hypnoplasty is a technique in which the hypnotized patient models plastic expression to repressed and suppressed material, which is then followed by verbalization of the conflicts. Thus, the investigative and therapeutic processes are initiated exceptionally quickly and intensified markedly. The conflicts are expressed first in plastic symbols, which in essence means sensory construction, and then, after a time gap, verbalized. Raginsky (1967) has also reported rapid regression to oral and anal levels through the use of sensory hypnoplasty.

This is consistent with the author's (Kline, 1981) observations of the rapidity with which a variety of regressive mechanisms are stimulated through the use of sensory procedures in hypnosis, and become expressed both through bodily reactions and behavioral output representative of various stages of ego development, particularly emphasizing oral, anal and phallic levels.

The function of the regressive process constitutes an area of exploration and discussion in and of itself. As Sullivan (1962) pointed out, the regressive process goes deeply into the mental structures, and the functions appearing in content and behavior become lower and lower in the scale of psychologic ontogenesis. He wrote:

It is here that we see the really dramatic demonstration of regression of the ultra-uterine mind, the prenatal attituide sometimes with makeshift sensory experience such as that of the tight wrapping blanket, darkness-wetness. Here we see the unmistakable evidence of prenatal experience. A certain experimental proof of ontogenic psychology is provided by the startling prompt recovery to accessibility and subsequent health which has been observed not infrequently upon a fortunately well timed regressive experience within an acceptable therapeutic context. It is, perhaps, imperative to know at this point that the regressive experience within the transference relationship in and of itself is frequently the healing process and that there may be vastly more harm than good to be accomplished by unstudied interpretation during this process. A fortunately well timed and carefully evaluated interpretation may be of value, but one would generally caution against it.

In this connection, the techniques described and utilized in the clinical situations reported here are based upon the fact that interpretations and other suggestions thrust upon the patient without close regard to the life situation from which his disturbance has resulted, and painstaking study of indices to the actual conflicts that necessitated the upheaval, in themselves represent a destructive approach that jeopardizes any success that might otherwise result from the crisis or psychotic episode that has emerged, and thus tend to determine an unfavorable outcome.

Sullivan (1962) also had pointed out that regression to genetically older thought processes and to infantile and prenatal mental functions, when successfully achieved, helps to reintegrate masses of life experience that had failed to form into a functional unity.

Just as the primitive thinking in more normal sleep solves many a problem, which we then feel able to deal with, so do these primitive processes in hypnotic regression, particularly with sensory and motor involvement, offer a field for direct therapeutic activity.

"The notion that regression is something rare, something highly morbid and so on, can be dismissed on the strength of one very simple observation. That in the course of the life of any child you can observe practically at twenty-four-hour intervals the collapse, when the child gets thoroughly tired, of patterns of behavior which are not very well stamped in." Sullivan's (1962) concept of regression, its history and its relationship to the management of severe emotional disorders and mental illness is consistent with what many therapists working with hypnosis in recent years have observed. In addition, Sullivan (1962) describes case material, and perhaps the only mention of the fact that Sullivan himself employed hypnosis selectively in the treatment of schizophrenia. As the regressive processes extend in their goal from the situation at hand to an imagined situation about to arise, the regressive processes suspend the imagined reference to the future goal situation and put in action references as if the present were actually the future. In hypnosis, this is most typical in that what is experienced can frequently be felt as if it actually were becoming part of the future.

All of this is a reflection of what has come to be the important formulation of positive anticipation in the recovery of patients in the group of serious emotional disorders so that in the total process of integrating past, present and the anticipation of the future, they can foresee the possibility of escape from the bind of their own dilemma and thus potential satisfactions and happiness.

In summary, it is important to note that with the use of sensory hypnotic procedures, there is frequently a rapid regression to a rather complete sensory and motor level of behavior with vivid intensification of imagery. Verbalization should not be encouraged until the patient reveals a decided wish to verbalize.

At times, the entire hypnotic experience may proceed on a completely nonverbal level and become incorporated into nocturnal dreaming and only later into verbal expression. In considering much of the material that comes forth during the period of sensory involvement and imagery associations, one is struck with its similarity to "inner speech" and "thought." This is, in fact, the articulation of feeling; the experience of thought that remains within the sensory order becomes much more available to the patient and frequently becomes revealed either through activity of an affective nature, or sensory response of physiological activity. When this continues for a sufficient time and the time element is of considerable importance, it will eventually be reflected in the cognitive activity and lexical expression. Observations to date, in both clinical and experimental situations utilizing this technique, suggest that what happens is a rapid intensification of speech impulses that then give rise, after a period of time, to mental operations that become articulated as speech, as well as the lexical or linguistic structure. We are dealing with a different kind of expression that can best be referred to as "inner speech," and its organization into spontaneous and, at times, clearly regressive aspects of cognitive expression.

It must be kept in mind that the concept of "inner speech" and the dynamics of "inner speech" cannot serve in a therapeutic sense as a direct means of communication, but is primarily a vehicle for the thought process. As such, it might best be described as talking to one's self for one's self.

This process of hypnotherapy helps teach the patient more effectively how to communicate with himself, to become more aware of his own inner speech and inner sensory articulation and to begin to develop comfortableness, ease and spontaneity in learning how to speak to himself for himself, with the therapist creating the context that makes this possible.

Conclusions

The contemporary utilization of hypnotherapy takes into account the now recognized facility with which hypnotic states may be elucidated through the management of transference phenomena, and the fact that within the hypnotic relationship direct as well as indirect intervention with basic response mechanisms in patient behavior is possible. The regressive nature of the hypnotic transference, when properly recognized, permits the incorporation of hypnosis into psychotherapy with a degree of directiveness and patient participation frequently characterized by increased feelings of self-mastery on the part of the patient as the ability to encounter heretofore difficult and dissonant aspects of the self now becomes manageable.

Hypnosis plays a significant role in the ability to intensify affect, reorganize ideational process and integrate both cognitive functioning and emotional responsiveness in a manner consistent with general therapeutic objectives and capable of integration within a variety of therapeutic approaches.

IMAGERY, AFFECT AND PERCEPTION IN HYPNOTHERAPY

Clinical studies[2] have attempted to evaluate both the meaningfulness and the genuineness of behavior induced through hypnotic techniques. Utilizing a polygraph, studies have been undertaken in connection with a variety of hypnotic phenomena including age regression, induction of hallucinations, hypnotic anesthesia and alterations in temporal and spatial orientation, as well as induced variation in body image awareness. The results have indicated that with increasing involvement in the hypnotic relationship, as evidenced by rapidity with which changes in sensory and motor behavior may be induced, there appears to be an increasing uncritical acceptance of the nature and the meaning of hypnotically induced behavior.

In this respect, we find that polygraphic evidence from patients reveals their essential belief in the reality of subjective experience and response in the same way that they would accept on a nonhypnotic level a sense of belief in other conscious experiences such as dreaming, thinking and perceptual recognition. The acceptance of hypnotically induced behavior would appear psychodynamically to be consistent with the implication that hypnosis involves a degree of self-exclusion and the capacity to accept subjective responses without the necessity for critical evaluation by the self, allowing for the structuring of hypnotic perception through the ego involvement with the hypnotist and the focusing of attention upon that process.

In recent studies[3] we have been primarily concerned with establishing some objective, descriptive characteristics of the emotional meaningfulness of hypnotic dreaming and of its relationship, in terms of affective responsiveness, to the characteristic behavioral patterns that surround hypnotic dreaming — *specifically, the prehypnotic state of the subject, the hypnotic state prior to the dreaming and the hypnotic state following the dreaming.*

We have not, in this preliminary investigation, been concerned to any great extent with an analysis of the content of dreams, although illustrations of this material will indicate the functional characteristic of the dream process. We have been more concerned with observing and recording the degree of emotional responsiveness as one index of meaningfulness in relation to the process of dreaming in hypnosis.

For this purpose, we have used a polygraph, to which the subject had been connected prior to induction. Polygraph monitoring started with the person awake and was maintained throughout the hypnotic induction, the early stages of hypnosis, the hypnotic-dream sequence, as well as the postdream sequence.

---

[2] The Morton Prince Center for Hypnotherapy, The Institute for Research in Hypnosis and Psychotherapy.

[3] From the Institute for Research in Hypnosis and Psychotherapy.

In this phase of the investigation, the polygraph was used for continuously recording two separate reactions: *upper-thoracic breathing and midthoracic breathing.*

Discussion

In considering the meaningfulness of hypnotically induced behavior, one has to be extremely critical of that which we term hypnotic and of the determinants of the hypnotic state. In hypnotic dreaming, much of the dream content, like other hypnotic behavior, reflects the transference relationship and the equated or symbolic meaning of the hypnotic experience. It is inconceivable that one can exclude the function of the encounter that takes place between the hypnotist and subject as an important determinant of the behavior that results.

It has frequently been noted that the hypnotic suggestion to dream, when broad and nonspecific enough, leads to spontaneous behavior such as age regression to specific earlier chronological periods, some of which may involve revivification. Frequently, subjects will have a number of dreams in response to a suggestion to have a single dream. Usually the suggestion to dream will be open enough so that the subject can interpret it as he wishes. It has also been found that the experience of dreaming under hypnosis leads to an increase in the frequency of nocturnal dreams during several nights and sometimes weeks following the hypnotic experience.

Therapeutic Constructs

Clinical observation and experience have indicated that the hypnotic activation of imagery and the spontaneous behavioral concomitants of this process are among the most productive aspects of the hypnotic experience. The extension of hypnotic imagery to hypnotic dreaming and finally to hypnotic hallucinations is part of a visual perceptual continuum that begins with simple scene visualization.

Polygraphic studies have revealed that as the patient progresses from scene visualization through hypnotic dreaming to hypnotic hallucination, there is a corresponding degree of increasing emotional responsiveness. Variations from what might be termed "base line" response patterns (in relation to respiratory reactions on the polygraph) are considerable, but internal consistence is clearly to be noted.

The greater the degree of exposure to hypnotic dreaming and hallucinosis, the greater the degree of spontaneous behavior related to the image content. Initial brief exposure of either hypnotic imagery or dreaming, as well as hallucinosis, may yield little evidence of emotional response. However, as the patient is permitted to prolong his experience, frequently beyond a thirty-minute period, respiratory evidence of affective response becomes most evident, particularly in relation as the resting base line of respiratory activity levels on the polygraph record. After a few such experiences, most patients can move rapidly into the imagery-dreaming sequence, with almost instantaneous spontaneity of emotional response.

In the utilization of imagery-dreaming procedures, it has been found that the spontaneous behavior that emerges may at times incorporate age regression material, at other times project experiences containing much symbolic implication and frequently reveal repressed fantasies, memories and impulse correlates.

Therapeutic value results from the cathartic release of the repressed material in a significant number of cases. The relating of the released affect and the ideational constructs to personality problems of current focus in the patient's life is both frequent and, at times, rapid. Insightful awareness with concomitant changes in behavior is not unusual and would appear to occur significantly more frequently than in nonhypnotic sessions of comparable time duration.

Compared to the nonhypnotic evocation of repressed psychological material and its utilization for both rapid symptomatic relief and the meaningful utilization of behavioral insights, the use of hypnotic imagery through dreaming and hallucinosis has proved more effective. Polygraphic monitoring of nonhypnotic sessions dealing with associative material and recalled nocturnal dream material has revealed far less evidence of emotional involvement than have comparable hypnotic sessions.

Over the past three years, more than two hundred patients have been treated with a major emphasis on the hypnotic evocation of imagery, the incorporation of this imagery into dreaming and, in approximately 50% of the cases, the extension of this material into induced emotional states utilizing some aspect of hallucinatory behavior. Most of these patients have been treated for not more than one hundred hours; thus this particular approach can be considered among the briefer psychotherapies.

Recent investigations of hypnotic dreaming and imagery with the polygraph have validated the evidence of emotional responsiveness and spontaneous ideational involvement. This, of course, had been observed in clinical behavior, but it had not been sharply delineated, as in the experimental studies. It would also appear to substantiate the impression that the intensification of hypnotic imagery-dreaming-hallucinosis leads to an increasing degree of hypnotic depth, within which primary process and regressive projections tend to dominate.

It is our understanding and position at the present time that the increase in primary process responses and the accessibility of impulse reactions at regressed levels of ego functioning constitute the core of the therapeutic mechanism directly related to this hypnotic process.

The experiential value of encountering both affective and cognitive levels of regressed ego functioning lies essentially in the fact that this process tends to disrupt or interrupt the more fixed or psychoeconomically stabilized patterns of symptomatic behavior and expression. In relation to contemporary ideas of learning theory and conditioning, it would seem that the alteration of repressive defenses, secondary process thinking and regressive impulses interrupts the learned symptoms of the patient's disturbed behavior. The hypnotic process permits this alteration to take place in an integrated manner, usually with minimal resistance and with the advantage of being able to integrate the evoked behavior with nonhypnotic levels of consciousness, such as nocturnal dreams, cognitive insights and the waking verbalization.

Thus there is no sharp demarcation between the emergence of the regressed ego material and the insightful management of cognitive reflections, since both take place within the framework of the same therapeutic transference, and there tends to be a natural gap between the hypnotic and nonhypnotic experiences in the treatment situation.

In considering the nature of these therapeutic results, it seems that the primary advantage of inducing regressive states is that it makes possible a transference relationship that assumes great importance to the patient and permits a degree of spontaneity and freedom most characteristic of the preadolescent period. In this respect, it is more open, since it lacks the criticalness typical of later psychological development. The lack of critical capacity is, of course, accompanied by a reduction of ego defenses and reality testing. When reinforced through the use of strong supportive and ego-recognizing devices, the breach in defenses of the individual does not pose any more of a problem than it would in the nonhypnotic therapeutic situation.

At this level, therapist and patient interact at a point where, with such uncritical ego functioning as exists in regression, it is possible to induce, strengthen and initiate drives, affects and complex reaction patterns. With intensification, such responses tend to assume greater validity and reality and, moving into the nonhypnotic state, become synthesized into workable and acceptable ideas, feelings, wishes and desires.

The results point to the use of induced states of regressiveness within which primary process and the metaphoric equivalents that take place constitute a fertile field for the development of direct and brief forms of hypnotherapy, which in a wide variety of problems can bring about lasting and effective treatment results.

REFERENCES

Ament, P. and Milgrom H. Effects of suggestion on pruritis with cutaneous lesions in chronic myelogenous leukemia. *N.Y. State J. Med.* **67**: 833 (1967).

Black, S. and Friedman, M. Effects of emotion and pain on adrenocortical function investigated by hypnosis. *Br. Med. J.* i: 477–481 (1968).

Black, S. and Walter, W.G. Effects on anterior brain responses of variation in the probability of association between stimuli. *J. Psychosom. Res.* **9**: 33–43 (1965).

Black, S. and Wigan, E.R. An investigation of selective deafness produced by direct suggestion under hypnosis. *Br. Med. J.* ii: 736–741 (1961).

Chertok, L. *Sense and Nonsense in Psychotherapy.* New York: Pergamon, 1981.

Cohen, J. *Psychological time in health and disease.* Springfield, Ill.: Charles C. Thomas, 1967.

Cooper, L.R. and Erickson, M. *Time distortion in hypnosis.* Baltimore: The Williams & Wilkins Co., 1954.

Graham, Burrows and Dennerstein, L. *Handbook of hypnosis and psychosomatic medicine.* New York: Elsevier/North-Holland Biomedical Press, 1980.

Kline, M.V. Sensory-imagery techniques in hypnotherapy: Psychosomatic considerations. *Top. Prob. Psychother.* 3: 161 (1960).

Kline, M.V. Hypnotherapy. In: Wolman, B. (Ed.), *The handbook of clinical psychology.* New York: McGraw-Hill, 1965.

Kline, M.V. and Linder, M. Psychodynamic factors in the experimental investigation of hypnotically induced emotions with particular reference to blood glucose measurements. *Acta Medica Psychosomatics.* (1967).

Kline, M.V. Emotional flooding. In: Olsen, T. *Emotional flooding. A technique in sensory hypnoanalysis.* New York: Human Sciences Press, 1976.

Meares, A. *Shapes of sanity: A study in the therapeutic use of modeling in the waking and hypnotic state.* Springfield, Ill., Charles C. Thomas, 1960.

O'Connell, D. and Orne, M.T. Endosomatic electrodermal correlates of hypnotic depth and susceptibility. *J. Psychiat. Res.* 6: 1–12 (1968).

Piaget, J. *The construction of reality in the child.* New York: Basic Books, 1954.

Piaget, J. The development of time concept in the child. In: Huch, P.H. and Zubin, J. (Eds.), *Psychopathology of childhood,* pp. 34–44. London: Grune & Stratton, 1955.

Piaget, J. *Logic and psychology.* New York: Basic Books, 1957.

Raginsky, B.B. Sensory hypnoplasty with case illustrations. *Intl. J. Clin. Exp. Hypnosis.* 10: 205 (1962).

Raginsky, B.B. Rapid regression to oral and anal levels through sensory hypnoplasty. In: Lassner, J. (Ed.), *Hypnosis and psychosomatic medicine: Proceedings of the International Congress for Hypnosis and Psychosomatic Medicine,* p. 257. New York: Springer-Verlag, 1967.

Sullivan, H.S. *Schizophrenia as a human process.* New York: W.W. Norton, 1962.

Udolf, Roy. *Handbook of hypnosis for professions.* New York: Van Nostrand Reinhold, 1981.

Wolpe, J. *The practice of behavior therapy.* New York: Pergamon Press, 1969.

Zimbardo, P.G., Ebbensen, E.G. and Fraser, S.C. The objective measurement of subjective states. *J. Personal. Soc. Psychol.* (1971).

Zimbardo, P., Maslach, C. and Marshall, G. Hypnosis and the psychology of cognitive and behavior control in hypnosis: Research development and perspective. In: Fromm, E. and Sho Shor, R.E. (Eds.), *Hypnosis: Research development and perspective.* Chicago and New York: Aldine-Atherton, 1971.

8 Interactional Psychotherapy

Benjamin B. Wolman

Treatment of mental disorders is an interactional process conducted within the framework of a certain *cultural system,* and the methods of treatment are greatly influenced by the prevailing ideas and beliefs. As long as disturbed behavior was believed to be masterminded by Satanic forces, exorcism performed by clergymen was the choice method, and witch-hunt was the generally accepted and almost universally practiced treatment method.

Although mental disorders are as old as humanity, their rational treatment started with Phillippe Pinel's history-making declaration: "These people are mentally sick, far from being guilty people deserving of punishment." These are "sick people whose miserable state deserves all the consideration that is due to suffering humanity" (quoted after Zilboorg and Henry, 1941, p. 323).

Pinel believed that mental disorder is an ailment of the nervous system. In his time scientists had no alternative. Pinel, Esquirol, Broca, Wernicke and Charcot studied the connection between the nervous system and disordered behavior. Mental disorders were called "nervous diseases," and neuroanatomical and neurophysiological studies were believed the only possible path of research.

However, this research was not successful. Despite the discoveries by Helmholtz, Hunghling-Jackson, Ludwig, Brücke and many others, there was no substantial progress in the treatment of mental disorders, and no one really knew how to treat mental patients.

The treatment of mental disorders consisted of unproven physico-chemical methods and common-sense suggestions that rarely if ever helped anyone. The doctors dealt with poorly described symptoms, with some not necessarily logical data and with the incomprehensible behavior of mental patients. Psychiatry reached an "impasse of therapeutic nihilism," Abraham wrote in 1911 (p. 156).

Then came Freud. In the best tradition of empiricism, Freud maintained that scientists must form fresh hypotheses when the old ones do not lead to the discovery and interpretation of empirical data. Scientists must introduce new hypothetical constructs that would enable them to view the mass of empirical data in a causal chain. "The psychological processes," Freud explained,

> are in themselves just as unknowable as those dealt with by other sciences by chemistry or physics, for example; but it is possible to establish the laws which those processes obey and follow over long and unbroken stretches their mutual relations and interdependences. . . . This cannot be effected without framing fresh hypotheses and creating fresh concepts. . . . We can claim for them the sense value as approximations as belongs to the corresponding intellectual scaffolding found in the other natural sciences, and we look forward to their being modified, corrected and more precisely determined as more experience is accumulated and sifted. So too it will be entirely in accordance with our expectations if the basic concepts and principles of the new science (instinct, nervous energy, etc.) remain for a considerable time no less indeterminate than those of the older sciences (force, mass attraction, etc.).

The application of the *causal principle* to psychopathology led to the discovery of symptom formation. Freud's strict determinism could not provide a causal continuum; Freud formed "fresh hypotheses" that explained pathogenesis of mental disorders in psychogenic terms. Viewed from the vantage point of the philosophy of science, this was the only possible solution (Wolman, 1980).

Freud adhered to the philosophical principles of monism. He was aware of "the mysterious leap from mind to body," and his early theory of anxiety postulated a transformation of the physical into the mental. Freud's explaination was both bold and cautious:

> We know two things concerning what we call our psyche or mental life; firstly, its bodily organ and scene of action, the brain (or nervous system), and secondly, our acts of consciousness, which are immediate data and cannot be more fully explained by any kind of description. Everything that lies between these two terminal points is unknown to us and, so far as we are aware, there is no direct relation between them. If it existed, it would at the most afford an exact localization of the processes of consciousness and could give us no help toward understanding them. We assume as the other natural science have taught us to expect, that in mental life some kind of energy is at work; but we have no data which enable us to come nearer to a knowledge of it by analogy with other forms of energy. (Freud, 1938)

THE RATIONALE OF TREATMENT

The above-mentioned of Freud's principles, of empiricism, determinism and monism, are fundamental rules of all sound therapeutic techniques.

Freud did not fight against symptoms; his main concern was the causes of mental disorders. Freud discovered that the causes are buried in the unconscious, and treatment cannot be successful until they are brought up to the surface and resolved. One cannot fight an invisible enemy; *insight* into and resolution of the unconscious conflicts has become the guiding principle of the psychoanalytic techniques.

Initially, Freud tried to force the unconscious to become conscious. He used hypnosis and later on suggestive pressure to overcome amnesia and resistance. Soon Freud discovered that whatever had been repressed tended to reappear on the surface. Unhealed wounds always call for help, and past traumas are never totally forgotten. The principle of *repetition compulsion* was a logical inference from Freud's strict determinism: a thwarted emotional energy calls for a discharge.

Two conclusions were drawn by Freud at this point. The first was the rejection of the cathartic method. The second was the introduction of the method of free associations.

Freud introduced the principle of *overdetermination* that included the hereditary factors in the id, the biologically determined developmental stages and the individual interaction with the environment. Freud's method covered phylogenetic and ontogenetic factors in interaction with environmental forces. Small wonder that both disciples and dissidents went further and stressed one or another aspect of Freud's theory and technique.

YESTERDAY'S SOCIOCULTURAL CLIMATE

We are witnessing a growing concern and increasing awareness of the need to improve the training methods of contemporary psychotherapy. While the works of Kraepelin, Freud, Jung and Adler continue to serve as pioneering guideposts, more voices are heard in favor of change in methods and content of treatment (Masserman, 1977).

There are four main reasons why the psychotherapeutic methods must be modified: 1) the changing society, 2) the changing patient, 3) the changing concepts in psychopathology and 4) the changing methods of treatment.

Yesterday's society was characterized by six fundamental traits:

In the first place, it was based on a more or less *stable class stratification.* Freud's life-span was almost equally divided between the nineteenth and the twentieth centuries (1856-1939). He was brought up when the declining Austro-Hungarian empire of the Habsburgs was still basking in the golden sun of past glories, and the conservative regime of the Emperor Franz Joseph (1849-1916) still enjoyed the good life in its Schonbrunn Palast. Freud's formative years and middle age passed before the World War I (1914-1918).

Second, Freud's contemporaries lived in accordance with *traditional* cultural values and within the well-established and generally accepted norms of the Viennese bourgeoisie. Freud believed that a psychoanalyst does not need to take a stand on moral issues because Freud, as well as his associates and adversaries, were all members of the same conservative middle class with its well-established morals and mores. The moral norms were self-evident, deeply rooted in the Judeo-Christian tradition and implicit in daily life.

Third, the respective *socio-sexual roles* of males and females were clearly delineated. Men worked; women took care of home and children. Men were busy in industry, commerce, politics and arts, while women were busy in the kitchens, nurseries and the salons (drawing rooms). Sigmund Freud was Herr Professor Doctor, and his wife, Martha Bernays, was Frau Professor by virtue of being married to the important Herr Professor Doctor. The clear-cut socio-sexual male and female roles left no room for misunderstanding who was what and what one's responsibilities were at home and in public.

Fourth, the organization of family life was determined by the Jewish and Christian traditions. The father was the undisputable head of the family, and there was one head only. The father was not necessarily a tyrant; he could be as good-natured and benevolent as any Christian ruler in the times of the "enlightened absolutism," or as the typical Jewish father in the "Haskala" period (Jewish emancipation and enlightenment). Grandparents, uncles and aunts were frequent and welcome participants in the family relationships.

Fifth, the educational system was based on obedience to parents and teachers. The cultural heritage of the adult society was transmitted in an authoritarian and unilateral way to the children. There was no mistake who was educating whom. The children were going to school not to find expression for their whims and wishes, but to listen, obey and learn. The teachers taught what the adult society believed they had to teach and *not* what the students would like to be taught. Children were not consulted in matters of their education. "The function of education therefore, is to inhibit, forbid, and suppress," wrote Freud (1933, p. 204).

Sixth, public opinion was definitely on the side of the inhibitions erected in the span of thousands of years. Sex and aggression were taboos. Certainly, neither sex nor aggression disappeared, and violations of law and of public mores did happen frequently even in the Victorian era, but they were neither publicized nor viewed permissively. Public opinion stood solidly behind the wall of bigotry, and sexual and aggressive acts were unanimously condemned.

When one views the psychoanalytic revolution in the perspective of the Viennese *Spiessbürger* environment and *Gemütlichkeit* (both terms are untranslatable), one cannot help but admire Freud's moral courage in unraveling the hidden sexual impulses of Eros, in pointing out the true belligerent, Thanatos nature of mankind, in scrutinizing the allegedly angelic emotional life of children, in unmasking love and hate and in going against the traditional beliefs despite the protests of many outraged Viennese *Bürgers,* including the physicians (cf. Jones, 1953).

PRESENT-DAY SOCIETY

Present-day society has precious little in common with yesteryear. First, there are *no stable social classes* in this country or elsewhere in the Western world. The two world wars and the technological and economic revolutions are responsible for horizontal and vertical mobility in the United States and throughout the world.

Second, our civilization of electronics, jets, Telstar, atom bombs, computers and space travel is *all but traditional*. The moral principles implicit in Freud's writings are no longer obvious and certainly not self-explanatory. Today, if a psychotherapist professes moral neutrality, he practices moral nihilism. Freud's implicit humanitarianism can no longer be taken for granted; apparently it is not a built-in mechanism in psychotherapeutic procedure. Today moral norms must be stated clearly and courageously (Wolman, 1982).

Third, the line dividing the respective *socio-sexual roles* is all but clear today. In this country most women work and take part in supporting their families. This process is rapidly spreading all over the world. In Freud's Vienna teachers and physicians were men. Today in the United States a teacher is "she," and in the Soviet Union the medical profession is usually the province of women. Street cleaners, taxi drivers, physicians, professors, engineers, party leaders and scientists are not exclusively males. What is going to happen in the future with sex identification, the oedipus complex, penis envy and so on remains to be seen.

Fourth, the *modern family* is moving away from the traditional pattern (Doherty and Jackson, 1982). The large family composed of three or more generations with uncles and cousins has seemed to shrink in our time to a fraction of what it used to be. Metropolis and suburbia, international trade and horizontal mobility have weakened the large-family ties, reducing them in most cases to the "nuclear" family structure that includes parents with one or two children.

Fifth, the present-day educational system, victim of the confusion of democracy as a goal of education with pseudo-democracy as a classroom practice, is all but authoritarian. The "blackboard jungle" would have been unthinkable in the Victorian era.

In view of these socio-cultural changes, Freud's once revolutionary ideas must undergo radical changes, for orthodox disciples of Freud could become ultraconservative followers of what was once a revolutionary movement.

THE CHANGING PATIENT

Freud and his associates worked with a small number of patients. Freud saw his patients daily, six days a week, for several years. These patients were mostly middle- and upper-class Viennese, and some middle- and upper-class foreigners. Although Freud occasionally worked with psychotic patients, he was much more successful with neurotics than with psychotics.

Present-day psychiatrists and clinical psychologists work in clinics and in hospitals with patients of all social classes and all types and levels of mental disorder. Freud's therapeutic technique evolved in his daily work in the privacy of a doctor's office. This is perhaps one of the reasons why classic psychoanalysis and some other psychotherapeutic techniques seem to fit best the middle- and upper-class mentality (see Hollingshead and Redlich, 1958). In fact, a great many concepts concerning the nature of mental health were geared to the mentality of educated classes. Consider some of Dr. Rennie's criteria of mental health (quoted from Srole *et al.*, 1962, p. 395): "Independence of action, thought and standards. . . . Concern for others, a respect for differing religions and ethics. . . . The establishment and maintenance of a home; etc." These middle-class ideals have been frequently imposed on the theory and practice of psychotherapy, although the connection between living up to those ideals and mental health has not been proved.

The lessening of sexual restraints has gone quite far in our times. Little children watch sexy television programs and see sexy advertisements in subways, buses, newspapers and magazines, and the adult population as a whole is less inhibited in sexual behavior.

The nature of the patient population is obviously changing. There seems to be, in general, an increase in the ratio of sociopathic and psychotic individuals at the expense of the hysterics and obsessive-compulsive neurotics (Spitzer, 1980).

Today, in a society full of horizontal and vertical mobility, with a high divorce rate, with economic and political instability, one cannot tell the patient, "No changes while under analysis," or "No swimming until you have learned to swim." Most contemporary patients are in difficult life situations here and now, and, unless saved, they may drown in the stormy waters of contemporary life. Thus, even when one intends to apply a psychoanalytic rationale to individual and group therapy, family therapy, therapeutic community, aftercare and so on, one must rethink and reformulate some of the principles and methods.

PSYCHOTHERAPY AS A PROCESS OF INTERACTION

From a sociological point of view, there are two partners, one who seeks help and the other who is supposed to offer that help. One partner feels that his life went wrong and needs some kind of adjustment, whereas the other believes that he can help, and the person who asks for help believes this too. Without that faith in psychotherapy, without the belief of the patient that he can be helped, he will never come for therapy, at least not willingly.

The process of psychotherapy is actually a split-level or two-level process. On the one hand, it is an interaction of two adults; one of them has an office, calls himself M.D. or Ph.D., has passed some examinations and got his license or certification and is approved by society for the job he is doing. The other can be a lawyer, a teacher, an accountant, a housewife or a garbage collector who feels disturbed. There is little chance of helping somebody unless he or she feels perplexed by being disturbed. On one level, psychotherapy is an *interaction* of two adults that resembles the type of interaction that occurs between an accountant, a lawyer, a dentist and a person who needs help. On a deeper level, it implies deep emotional involvement, called "transference." The interaction that takes place between a psychotherapist and his patient transcends the usual man-to-man relationship. We are not lawyers, dentists or surgeons; we deal with the emotional problems of people, and a particular phenomenon, transference, takes place.

Transference is not just a one-way street. Any kind of human relation (called by Freud "object relation") is a cathexis, or an investment of one's emotions in the other person. However, whereas Freud stressed the point of view of the person who cathects, I have developed an additional concept that takes into consideration the person who is at the receiving end of cathexis. Thus, instead of using the term "cathexis" as described in classic psychoanalysis, I deal with the concept of "interindividual cathexis," which represents the emotional load *directed* by one person toward another and *received* by the other person. In other words, if a mother loves a child, the mother is cathecting her sublimated or neutralized libido in the child, and the child is at the receiving end. The way the child feels about it, how he perceives the mother's love, is a highly important factor in his emotional balance and personality development.

The cathectic situation in any kind of psychotherapy is also a two-way process. The patient cathects his emotions in his therapist, and the therapist cannot be totally unaware of the fact that the patient did invest some of his emotions, positive or negative, in him. A psychotherapist need not assume that he has the right always to deal with these cathected processes in transference in the same way, no matter who the patient is. Alexander and French (1946) introduced the concept of *intentional* manipulation of transference by decreasing or increasing the number of sessions. I went further than Alexander and French; I maintain that whether the therapist is aware of it or not, his behavior influences the patient's transference, and thus I suggested making a more efficient use of transference.

I believe that the nature of transference cathexis depends on the nature of the disorder. The obsessive-compulsive and schizophrenic patients (the hypervectorial type) tend toward object-hypercathexis, which means overinvolvement with others. They suffer from self-hypocathexis, inadequate cathexis in themselves (Wolman, 1973). One may, therefore, expect a most profound and sometimes vehement positive transference phenomenon in psychotherapy with schizotype patients (obsessive-compulsives and schizophrenics).

Working with a great many hypervectorial patients, I noticed how easily they become overcathected and overinvolved in the transference. Some of them worry about the therapist the way they used to worry about their parents. They notice whether he looks pale or suntanned; they worry about his future; they would like to take care of him. On the other side, the sociopaths (hyperinstrumental narcissistic patients) do not worry at all about him. They worry about themselves only. Being narcissistic, they display strong paranoid tendencies and are unable to develop a positive transference. They usually develop a negative transference attitude, blaming the analyst for their misfortunes or lack of achievement (Krauss and Krauss, 1977).

There are no foolproof methods for dealing with transference, but I strongly object to a uniform way of dealing with transference with no consideration of the particular clinical type of the patient. I do believe that one of the main aspects of interactional psychotherapy is individualization in dealing with each case.

What is happening in therapy is a series of libido and destrudo cathexes in which both the patient and the psychoanalyst participate. The psychoanalyst cannot escape the fact that he likes or dislikes his patients, although he must control his countertransference phenomena — otherwise he violates the professional ethics. However, he must be aware of the fact that he does not react the same way to all people, and *being aware of his shortcomings as an individual may make him a better therapist.*

No human being can avoid being somewhat influenced by what is going on in relationship to other people. Some patients show love for the therapist, which is flattering; some patients show much hatred, which may be damaging to his ego. However, one of the main duties of the psychotherapist is always to be aware of what is going on and never to be carried away by his emotions.

A responsible psychotherapist *gets involved with the case of his patients,* for this is his moral obligation to the people who seek his help, but under no circumstances must the psychotherapist become involved with the person of the patient.

The task of psychotherapy is to help patients progress toward adulthood and counteract infantile regression. The regressive phenomenon that facilitates corrective experience and resolution of past emotional problems, transference, must not be allowed to go haywire. Manipulation of transference and prevention of its going too far and too deep contribute to a successful psychotherapy. Inadequate transference does not provide an adequate climate for recall and recollection of the past and healing of past wounds, but a too deep transference may make the therapeutic process interminable. Transference should be viewed as a partial and temporary step backward that enables the patient to move further ahead. A too deep transference might substitute one umbilical cord with another.

The goal of psychotherapy is to make itself superfluous.

Interactional psychotherapy proceeds in three phases. The first phase is *analytic;* its task is overcoming emotional obstacles and irrationalities in early childhood. It involves the removal of infantile inhibitions and the resolution of infantile conflicts that cripple the personality and prevent adults from acting in an adult and mature way. As soon as the past conflicts are resolved and the patient is liberated from past handicaps and able to put his intelligence and energy to productive use, the psychotherapy moves toward two phases that I have called *"Search for Identity"* and *"Becoming: Self-realization,"* respectively.

In order to define oneself and become a mature adult, one must go through the analytic phase in which one acquires a sense of reality, emotional balance and social adjustment. A *sense of reality* is a necessary prerequisite for any adjustment to life. People who distort reality, who have exaggerated notions of themselves and the world, or who underestimate themselves or overestimate the obstacles, can hardly if ever act in accordance with their abilities and opportunities.

Emotional balance includes four factors: First, the emotional reaction must be *appropriate;* one reacts with sorrow to defeat and with joy to success. Disturbed people react in a paradoxical way, enjoying their defeat and finding success unacceptable. Well-balanced emotionality is also *proportionate;* disturbed individuals overreact or underreact to success and failure. The third factor in emotional balance is *self-control.* Infants and disturbed people are unable to control their emotions; mature adults control their emotions and react in a way that helps them in attaining their goals. The fourth factor is *adjustability.* No matter how deep was the sorrow or how great was the joy, one cannot live in the past. Neurotics live in the past; well-adjusted adults never deny the past but go ahead in life with wisdom and courage.

The third achievement in the analytic phase should be *social adjustment.* People who have undergone the analytic phase of interactional psychotherapy are able to develop meaningful relationships with one or more individuals and form a rational give-and-take relationship that will not hurt them and will prevent them from being hurt. One can distinguish three attitudes toward other people: The first attitude is *instrumental,* that is, using people for the satisfaction of one's own needs. This narcissistic attitude is typical for an infant because he needs to be supported. As the child grows, he learns that one cannot get unless one gives, and gradually he develops a *mutual* attitude based on giving and receiving. This attitude is typical for friendship, sexual relations and marriage; each party tries to please the other and expects the same in return. The third type of attitude is giving without expecting anything in return. This *vectorial* attitude is typical for the parent-child relationship. This attitude can be directed toward one's social, religious and other ideals. To be a giver and a creator is the highest level of personality development.

A balanced individual should be able to function at all three levels. He is instrumental in bread-winning functions, mutual in friendship and in marriage, and vectorial in regard to his children and/or his ideals.

THE ANALYTIC PHASE

It is always easier to slide down than to climb up, and for many people it is both tempting and frightening to become mature adults who must make their own decisions and be responsible for their consequences — it is easier to go back to childhood patterns and expect parental care and protection. Regression is easy, and many people wish to go back to the bittersweet helplessness of infancy. Some people act in a constructive manner, but then, when faced with obstacles, undercut their own efforts themselves, as if wishing to win mother's love by failing. When they come for psychotherapy, they often offer staunch resistance against being cured. Obviously, the handling of resistances is of prime importance in psychotherapy.

In some cases the patient's complacency creates additional difficulties. People unaware of their problems are poorly motivated to cooperate with the therapist, whereas people painfully aware of their difficulties are more cooperative and therefore improve faster. The patient's desire to grow up and to assume adult responsibility greatly contributes to successful psychotherapy. The patient's *motivation* is a highly relevant factor, for it is exceedingly difficult to treat patients who do not wish to be helped. My policy in private practice is to refuse to work with patients who were forced by relatives to come to my office. Usually, at the first session I make explicit to the patient that both of us enter an alliance. My job is to apply all my knowledge, skill, experience and efforts for the well-being of the patient, but he/she must commit him/herself to full cooperation with my work. Psychotherapy, unlike other healing processes, requires the active cooperation of both the therapist and the patient.

One of the main aspects of interactional psychotherapy is to help patients to overcome past problems and prepare them for their present and future tasks. Emotionally disturbed people tend to regress to infantile modes of behavior. Their behavior resembles that of the man born in Alaska who migrated to Texas. On a cloudy day in Texas he puts on a fur coat despite the heat because in his childhood he was expected to wear a fur coat on cloudy days.

"Regression," Freud wrote in 1900, "plays a no less important part in the theory of the formation of neurotic symptoms than it does in that of dreams" (1900, p. 548). Every human being goes through developmental stages from birth toward adulthood; those who did not grow up or who went back are mentally disturbed.

The past does not die; it is merely buried in the unconscious. Chunks of the past could be revealed in dreams, in free associations and in hypnosis. Sometimes huge chunks of infantile wishes and emotions surface in crisis situations. It is not always necessary to dig out forgotten traumas; digging in a weak personality structure could cause a psychotic episode. The therapist must carefully weight 1) how much digging in the patient's past is necessary, and 2) how deep one should dig without jeopardizing the total personality structure. Certainly one need not use a bulldozer to remove a pimple.

The child in an adult person never dies but must not be allowed to take charge of adult life. Once in a while one may allow oneself to act in a childish manner. The consciously regressing person allows him/herself to behave, for a while, in a relaxed and carefree behavior, but his/her ego is in full control, able to stop the regression and restore adult behavior. In alcoholics and drug addicts such control is suspended or totally lost, and the regression to a carefree mood leads to irresponsible and self-destructive behavior.

S-D OR S-D

Newborn infants have no inhibitions. Their reactions are instant, impulsive and spontaneous. They are unable to exercize control over their impulses: they vacate their bladders and move their bowels instantly. Their mental apparatus, called id by Freud, operates on the principle of immediate reaction and total disinhibition, called by Freud *Lustprinzip* (erroneously translated as pleasure principle). Actually Freud's *Lustprinzip* means lust principle, that is, the impulse of urgent reaction and instant gratification.

In many instances (especially those observed by Freud many decades ago) parents imposed on children harmful taboos, restrictions and inhibitions. Quite naturally some of their infantile inhibitions should be removed in psychotherapy, and adult patients should develop their own rational inhibitions. Mature adults do not follow momentary impulses but exercise rational control over their behavior. Adults weigh their actions and try to anticipate their consequences. Their egos exercise control over their ids, and they apply the mature reality principle (see below) instead of the infantile pleasure principle.

The inability to control one's emotions and the impulsive acting-out of one's wishes, whims and desires are a clear indicator of a weak ego. Apparently, the weaker the ego, the more severe the mental disorder is. Neurotics may not be able to control their impulses in certain areas, and their lack of self-discipline (S-D) leads to self-defeating (S-D) behavior. Character neurotics tend to rationalize and to justify their neurotic behavior, and latent psychotics may not be able to control it. Manifest psychotics are usually unaware of their self-defeating actions, and at the lowest level of psychological deterioration one does not have any inhibitions whatsoever. Disinhibition does not lead to mental health but to psychosis, and therapists who advocate disinhibition play havoc with their patients' mental health.

The first, analytic phase of interactional psychotherapy aims at the removal of infantile inhibitions, and helps to develop self-imposed inhibitions of adulthood that enable one to act in a rational manner. When the inner conflicts are resolved, the patient becomes capable of using his or her energy productively. The id operates on the *lust principle,* meaning that as soon as tension arises in the system, the tension leads to immediate action and immediate gratification of the need. The ego operates on *reality principle.* The ego postpones the gratification through reconsideration and thought processes. Reality principle is not the opposite of the pleasure principle because both principles fall in line with Freud's hedonistic philosophy of seeking pleasure and avoiding displeasure. But, whereas the id operates on the principle of immediate discharge of energy without paying attention to the consequences, the ego calculates. The ego may postpone gratification in order to get better gratification later, and denounces gratification if it creates too much conflict.

Reality principle is the bedrock of a strong ego. A weak ego bypasses things. The egos of hysterics and depressive dysmutuals are sleepy, and they allow themselves to make mistakes. Mature people know what they are doing and are always in charge of their emotions. Their egos exercise full control over their behavior.

There are more aspects to *working through,* such as neutralization and/or control over antisocial or disturbing impulses. Consider sex. According to early ideas, any sex other than the union of the two sexual organs in the right way was believed to be abnormal. A whole generation of women were made to believe that there was something wrong with their sexuality if they didn't reach a vaginal orgasm. Oral sex, for instance, was believed to be perverse.

There are many problems on which there is no uniformity of opinion, but people can lead their lives in more than one way. To offer direct guidance in these matters would be tantamount to imposing the therapist's private opinions. The task of psychotherapy is not to transform apples into oranges, but to enable patients to live in accordance with *what they are* and to play *their* cards. All this leads to the second phase of psychotherapy: the *search for identity*. But before we start with this issue, a few words on reassurance and support in psychotherapy.

REASSURANCE AND SUPPORT

One of the main tasks of psychotherapy is to support the patient's ego and its functions. The ego battered and/or damaged by inner conflicts needs outside support that should be offered by the therapist. In hyperinstrumental sociopaths, the ego is, as it were, inflated by an abundant self-hypercathexis, and these persons are overconcerned with themselves. In hypervectorial neurotics (obsessionals) and psychotics (latent and manifest schizophrenics), the ego is impoverished by excessive object hypercathexes and inadequate self-cathexis; the hypervectorials are overinvolved with others and underconcerned with themselves. The dysmutual depressives (hysterics and manic-depressives) go from one extreme to another. In addition, the therapist must consider the five levels of damage caused to the ego's normal functioning, usually the neurotic, character neurotic, latent psychotic, manifest psychotic and total collapse of personality structure.

Interactional psychotherapy aims at strengthening the ego; thus the therapeutic strategy must be adjusted to the nature of the disorder. At this point it is necessary to reintroduce the concept of *interindividual cathexis*. A lot of nonverbal communication goes on in psychotherapy, and the *therapist's attitude* is usually more important than his or her words. The patients usually perceive and/or empathize the therapist's attitude, which is a most important source of interindividual cathexis that helps to restore the patients' intraindividual balance of cathexes. The therapist's friendly and reassuring attitude cathexes (charges) loads of neutralized libido. It conveys the therapist's sincere concern for the patients' well-being and the determination to get them well, for it resembles the vectorial attitude of parents who care for their children irrespective of the children's behavior.

The hyperinstrumental sociopaths tend to be suspicious of everyone including the therapist. In my treatment of sociopaths I noticed considerable *negative transference* elements in their accusations based on their past experience, but there was also a good deal of here-and-now testing of the therapist's attitude and intentions. It is possible for a therapist to feel hurt and angry, but such reactions are clearly antitherapeutic. The task of the therapist is to help, even when those who need help act in an irrational and unfriendly manner. The therapist vs. patient friendly attitude has a calming and disarming effect on sociopaths who expect to provoke an angry and rejecting reaction that would confirm their view of the world as a place full of enemies, and thus justify their own enmity.

Hypervectorials on the neurotic, character neurotic and latent psychotic levels doubt whether anyone is capable of helping them. They believe that it is their obligation to take care of others. Some of my obsessive-compulsive and schizoid character neurotics and latent schizophrenics expressed concern for my health and well-being as if it were their obligation to help me. Apparently, they did not care enough for themselves, and their self-hypocathexis and object hypercathexis caused them to be overconcerned for the therapist, who was supposed to help them.

Offering reassurance and support to dysmutual neurotics (hysterics) and psychotics (manic-depressives) involves certain risks, for no matter how friendly the therapist is, these persons expect and often demand more than is appropriate for therapeutic interaction. Their childhood experiences of usually being rejected and accepted only when their true or imaginary misery elicited parental love and compassion, are often reenacted in therapeutic situation. They usually exaggerate in describing their sufferings and quite often report nonexisting tragedies. Some of my depressive and hysterical patients start the therapy sessions with a tirade about their "excruciating pain," "unbelievable suffering" and "bottomless misery."

Woe to the therapist who allows him/herself to be caught in the web of their unsatiable demands for love and affection. It is absolutely necessary to state clearly the therapist's position when either male or female patients ask the trapping question: "You don't love me, do you?"

My answer has always been unequivocal. I say, "I care for you and your well-being. But I am not in love with you. My responsibility to you is to help you and not to please you."

It is even more difficult to handle depressive self-hating moods. Depression can be exogenous if it is caused by real misfortunes such as serious disease, loss of someone beloved, financial catastrophe and so on. Such a depression if related to one's own neglect or error presents quite a challenge in psychotherapy and requires a head-on, realistic appraisal of the situation and a rational search for remedies. Endogenous depression is not related to any real events, and requires a highly specialized therapeutic strategy that cannot be described within the framework of the present chapter.

THE SECOND PHASE: THE SEARCH FOR IDENTITY

The analytic phase enables the individual to think clearly and to act in a realistic way, but it does not solve the problem of direction in life. What the individual is going to do with himself, what life should mean to him, what his goal in life is — these are the problems dealt with in the second phase of interactional psychotherapy, called the search for identity.

The main issue to be dealt with at the second psychotherapeutic phase is the awareness that life is a gift. When patients ask, "Where am I going, what am I going to do with myself?" I reply with a question, "What would you like to do? Assume for a minute that you don't exist. Would it make a difference to you that today is Monday, Tuesday or Wednesday? Would traffic congestion bother you?" These questions usually bring one answer, "Of course not; if I am not here, who cares?"

And this is the crucial issue: the awareness that one is the center of one's own universe; that one's own existence is the prerequisite of joy and sorrow, success and failure; that there is nothing more in life than life itself; that human beings are poor because they have nothing else but life, and they are rich because life contains all possibilities.

Awareness of oneself is not necessarily acceptance of one's faults and errors and shortcomings. Awareness of oneself is the awareness of the fact that here are the cards that one received from heredity and experience. One must play his cards the best he can, and he may use some of his defenses. For instance, compensation can be turned into a useful tool in adjusting to life. Reaction formation may not necessarily be a neurotic symptom; if one is belligerent, he may use his belligerence for conquering disease or misery and not necessarily for fighting people. One may neutralize some of his energies; one may sublimate some of his energies; one may decide that this is what he is. One does not necessarily accept all the aspects of his personality, nor does he necessarily subscribe to all his possibilities. A person may make a choice between various ways in life and find fulfillment in what is the most important aspect of his or her life.

It is necessary at this point to make a distinction between the self-centered awareness of oneself and selfishness. Selfish people do not care for others. They are narcissistic sociopaths whose entire emotional energy is invested in themselves, with very little if anything left for other people. They tend to exploit others and take advantage of whomever they can. They are *takers* who want to take without giving. They treat others as instruments to be used, and that's why I call them "hyperinstrumentals."

Self-centered people, on the other hand, believe themselves to be of utmost importance to themselves. They are usually congenial and considerate people who use their energies toward helping themselves as well as others. All great creative men and women have been self-centered. They have used their energies for enriching their own mental, emotional and intellectual life. They have believed that they are the center of whatever is going on around them, and have believed that all people have the same rights. One could compare self-centeredness to the solar system, the sun being the center and everything else being planets and satellites. But the sun doesn't receive light; it gives light. The sun does not take away anything from anybody; being rich, it distributes its enormous energy and gives it to the whole universe around it.

Self-centered individuals take care of themselves, and they learn to swim before they try to save drowning people.

SELF-RESPECT

People identify themselves with their occupation and should be able to take pride in the competence and success qualities that are related to one of the most relevant issues of mental health, namely, *self-respect*. Although every human being wants to be successful in his or her endeavors, no one is promised an unbroken chain of success. It is highly important to retain self-respect even in defeat, however.

Those who don't try can never be happy; they do not have the excitement of challenge and the victory of attainment. Failure brings pain, but it need not affect one's self-esteem. When one can say, "I did what I could," one can be proud of oneself despite defeats.

Self-confidence and self-respect are initially acquired in childhood in child-parent interaction. Parental approval gives the child a feeling of security, and the child's own efforts respectfully acknowledged by the parents contribute to the child's self-confidence and self-respect. As the child grows older, peer approval becomes more important. Finally, mature men and women learn to depend mainly on themselves, and approval by others plays a less significant role.

At the second phase of psychotherapy, patients do not need the therapist's approval. Having resolved their transference, they become more capable of depending on themselves. They set realistic goals for themselves and begin to evaluate their wishes, thoughts and deeds objectively. They come to terms with themselves and perceive themselves in a realistic manner.

At the second phase of psychotherapy there comes a moment of serenity and awareness when the patient realizes *who he is and what he could and should do.* "This is what I am," a patient may say. "No use to pretend, to play silly games, and to try to be what I am not. These are the cards given to me by heredity and experience. I must play them the best I can. I don't know how long I will live, but I shall live the way that offers fulfillment and self-realization." During the second therapeutic phase the patients acquire *courage and wisdom* — courage to be aware of their potentialities, to face life, to determine how to live and to decide what they *should do.*

Then comes a careful checking against reality and determining what one *could do.* Courage is not enough; mature people also need the *wisdom* to make rational decisions. Rational decisions imply coping with hardships and taking advantage of opportunities.

Toward the end of the first phase many patients feel lonely. The umbilical cord is cut, and adult patients realize that they have no daddies and mommies to depend on. The past attachments and grievances are resolved, the infantile emotions neutralized, and the patients accept the adult responsibilities for their actions. At the second phase they realize that human relations are a give-and-take interactional process. They appreciate their friends and family but do not overdepend on them. Usually, they become more cordial and less demanding in their maritial relationships as well.

PERSONALITY INTEGRATION

Apparently, every human being is a "split personality," but some personalities are more split than others. Some are badly disorganized, and their feelings, thoughts and actions contradict each other and bring defeat and misery. The task of the analytic phase is to resolve the infantile conflicts that prevent personality growth and integration. The task of the second phase is the search for identity and personality integration.

Setting goals and establishing an order of their priority is of vital importance in personality integration. One cannot follow all one's whims, wishes and desires; people must choose what is important for them and pursue their selected objectives.

The integration of personality is attained through reconciliation of one's *shoulds* and *coulds*. The goals one sets for oneself reflect what an individual believes *should* be done, but some goals could be unattainable, and their pursuit produces unnecessary frustration. It is therefore advisable to carefully check the roads leading to the desired land and, if necessary, modify or even abandon one's goals. Quite often at the second phase the patient's energies, freed from inner conflict, infuse the patient with a feeling of unlimited powers. In such instances, testing reality becomes imperative, and such patients must be helped to correctly assess their own resources and the objective possibilities.

Perceiving things as they are is one of the main criteria of mental health, and the second phase of interactional psychotherapy reaffirms the need for avoiding too easy as well as too difficult tasks. The *level of aspiration* should correspond to the person's psychological resources and to what could be done at a given time in a given environment. The courage to be oneself (the shoulds) must be combined with the wisdom of acting in a rational manner (the coulds).

The task of human life is not an achievement, for no achievement can be final, and no achievement justifies resting on laurels. Life is a process of achieving and following the bumpy road toward new achievements and new peaks. Looking backward gives a sense of what one has achieved so far, and looking forward inspires fresh efforts toward new achievements.

The three main phases — the analytic phase, the search for identity and self-realization — should serve as guidelines for the psychotherapist who wants to help human beings to understand the limitations of human life and the possibilities of living a full life.

THE THIRD PHASE: BECOMING — SELF-REALIZATION

Two men brought a revolution in man's ideas concerning his place in the universe: Copernicus and Darwin. Copernicus dethroned man's earth and made it into a little speck circulating in space. Darwin destroyed the myth of creation, put man on the top of the evolutionary ladder and made him part and parcel of organic nature. The Darwinian principle of fight for survival is the universal law of nature and the arch-motive of human behavior.

The drive for power is the chief corollary of the universal struggle for survival. Power is the ability to satisfy needs, and survival is the arch-need, and prerequisite for everything else.

The need to feel powerful appears in many forms, shapes, disguises and degrees. It is often called self-esteem, self-respect, self-confidence and so on. It may lead to extensive efforts to accumulate wealth, to acquire property, to win a contest, to conduct a war, to gain fame and so on.

The need to feel powerful is always *goal-directed.* One feels strong when one sets a goal and attains it. The more difficult the task, the more power to the winner. Pleasure and displeasure are daily occurrences, but happiness is a winged creature that comes at moments of great victory and triumph.

Life without goals is meaningless drudgery. To have nothing to live for deepens the existential crisis of lack of identity and purpose. The intrinsic built-in goal of human life is to stay alive, but every human being has the right to choose how he or she wants to live.

The second phase of interactional psychotherapy helps people to become *aware* of themselves and their potentialities. At the third phase, the time comes to put all these factors together and set satisfactory and attainable goals.

Everyone's life brings ups and downs, successes and failures, victories and defeats. No human being is immune to illnesses and accidents, material gains and losses, approval and rejections, love and hate. The second phase of psychotherapy enables individuals to enjoy success and cope with hardships and defeats. The third phase enables them to *gain mastery over themselves and develop constructive plans.*

BEING – LASTING – BECOMING

Human beings have three choices: being, lasting or becoming. One can *be* by satisfying his immediate needs of food, sex, fun, prestige and violence. One may try to *last* by believing in the hereafter and building everlasting pyramids and monuments in the hope that he will last forever as a mummy or in a mystical way.

To *become* human implies accepting the inevitability of death without sinking into animalistic hedonism and violence, and without escaping into mystical superhuman beliefs. Human beings hang in midair between God and animal. They may go down into animalistic *being* or hallucinate godlike *lasting.*

Contemporary life provides plenty of neurotic ropes for people to hang themselves, with their animalistic or mystical hangups. There is, however, a third road, the road of becoming human. Becoming human means continuous change toward becoming more human than one was yesterday.

There are two fundamental differences between men and other animals: intelligence and morality. All animals including the human race fight for survival, and their lives are governed by biochemical laws. But humankind can satisfy its need without using claws and teeth, guns and nuclear weapons. Violence is the rule of the animal world, and the survival of the fittest is the law of jungle.

One can fight *against* others, but one cannot become human alone. To be human means to be human to other human beings. Other animals fight *against* one another; humans work *with* one another. Whatever was created by human beings –

including houses, bridges, ships, factories, schools, art galleries, symphonic orchestras and space travel — was created by people *working together.* Whatever was destroyed, was destroyed by animalistic regression to selfishness and violence.

To become human implies the use of human *intelligence and compassion* for helping other human beings. *To become human* means to be understanding and considerate of the needs and rights of other human beings. Human intelligence has created an enormous scientific and technological power. This power need not be dissipated in being or lasting.

In the third phase of interactional psychotherapy one must help patients to develop worthwhile goals. To be a fully developed individual, one cannot remain on an instrumental level; one should be capable of mutual relationships (marriage, sexual relations, friendship), but one must also be able to develop the ability and the desire to give. Getting is limited; giving is unlimited.

Consider two individuals, one who stretches out his hand to get something and the other to give; who is more happy? The one who gets is fully aware of his inadequacy, of his shortcomings, of his need to receive from others. He is weak and dependent. The one who gives has the glorious feeling of being able to give, of making other people happy. He is powerful and is aware of his power.

Not every human being can be a creative artist, but every human being can create joy and happiness for himself and for others; by giving happiness to others, he achieves the highest degree of joy and happiness for himself.

The third phase of interactional psychotherapy should enable people to decide in which direction they will utilize energy as well as intellectual and emotional resources. At this phase, patients find out the meaning of their lives. They discover that they can create something and add something to life. Giving is a sign of power.

REFERENCES

Abraham, K. (1911) *Selected papers on psychoanalysis.* London: Hogarth Press, 1927.

Alexander, F. and French, T. *Psychoanalytic therapy.* New York: Ronald Press, 1946.

Doherty, W. and Jackson, N. Marriage and the family. In: Wolman, B.B. (Ed.), *Handbook of developmental psychology.* Englewood Cliffs, N.J.: Prentice Hall, 1982.

Freud, S. (1900) The interpretation of dreams. *Standard edition,* vol. 4. London: Hogarth Press, 1962.

Freud, S. (1933) New introductory lectures on psychoanalysis. *Standard edition,* vol. 22. London: Hogarth Press, 1964.

Freud, S. (1938) *An outline of psychoanalysis.* New York: Norton, 1949.

Hollingshead, A.B. and Redlich, F.C. *Social class and mental illness.* New York: Wiley, 1958.

Jones, E. *The life and work of Sigmund Freud.* New York: Basic Books, 1953-57.

Krauss, B.J. and Krauss, H.H. Sociopaths. In: Wolman, B.B. (Ed.), *International encyclopedia of psychiatry, psychology, psychoanalysis, and neurology*. New York: Aesculapius Publishers, 1977.

Masserman, J. American psychiatry. In: Wolman, B.B. (Ed.), *International encyclopedia*. New York: Aesculapius Publishers, 1977.

Spitzer, R.L. (Ed.) *Diagnostic and statistical manual of mental disorders* (DSM III). Washington, D.C.: American Psychiatric Association, 1980.

Strole, L. *et al. Mental health in metropolis*. New York: McGraw-Hill, 1962.

Wolman, B.B. *Call no man normal*. New York: International Universities Press, 1973.

Wolman, B.B. *Contemporary theories and systems in psychology*, Rev. ed. New York: Plenum, 1980.

Wolman, B.B. Ethical problems in termination of psychotherapy. In: Rosenbaum, M. (Ed.), *Ethics and values in psychotherapy*. New York: Free Press, 1982.

Zilboorg, G. and Henry, G.W. *A history of medical psychology*. New York: Norton, 1941.

9 Brief Psychotherapies

John F. Clarkin and Allen Frances

We may well be entering (if we are not already in) an era in which the brief psychotherapies are the predominant form of psychiatric treatment. A number of factors have all been responsible for the flowering of the brief therapies: pressures for economy in the deployment of resources, the development of pre-paid health care plans, a cultural impatience with things that take a long time, a rediscovery of the roots of the psychotherapeutic process, which was originally brief and has gradually grown in length, and the desire to make mental health services available to all who need them. Indeed, whether this is planned in advance or not, most patients now treated with psychotherapy engage in it for only a short period of time. It has been reported that patients seeking out-patient psychotherapy in a clinic setting generally expect it to last no more than three months (Garfield, 1971), and a very high percentage of patients actually remain in treatment for fewer than twelve sessions (Butcher and Koss, 1978; Garfield, 1971). Treatments of this brief duration are characteristic not only for lower socioeconomic patients in clinics but also for the general practice of psychotherapy in private settings (Koss, 1979). As Gurman points out (1981), most therapy has probably always been brief — what is new is the notion of time-limited therapy by explicit design. Training programs in psychiatry have recognized these signs of the times, and most of them now offer supervised clinical experience in the brief therapies (Clarkin, Frances, Taintor and Warburg, 1980) as part of the core curriculum. Publications on brief treatment are in-creasing in number and quality and demonstrate clearly that this alternative is not just a practical necessity but is also inherently interesting from both a clinical and a research standpoint.

ESSENTIAL FEATURES OF THE BRIEF THERAPIES

The brief psychotherapies differ among themselves in goals, treatment techniques, strategies, format (group, family or individual), setting (inpatient, day hospital, outpatient) and selection criteria. In fact, the different models of brief therapy are at least as diversified as those applied in longer treatments. There are, however, certain essential features that generalize across the brief therapies and justify considering them together. In all the brief therapies, the therapeutic attention is focused more or less exclusively on one issue. Depending on the particular school of brief therapy, this focal issue may be a dynamic conflict, a crisis, a specific symptom that shows itself in a specific setting (e.g., phobia), a relationship problem, disturbed behavior and so on. Powerfully influenced by the purposeful limitation of therapeutic time, the therapist and patient must engage quickly, rapidly assess the range of problems, agree to focus on the problem of paramount importance and establish limited goals. The therapist maintains a relatively high degree to activity, and planning and decisions must often be made with incomplete data. In brief encounters, errors of omission may be more harmful than errors of commission.

The definition of what duration still constitutes a brief therapy varies from author to author and model to model. Malan (1963) considers brief focal therapy to have an upper limit of about forty sessions. Mann (1973) sets a limit of twelve sessions. Others have written about six-session brief therapy (Bellak and Small, 1978), and there is some evidence of therapeutic effect occurring after just one session (Malan, Heath, Bacal and Balfour, 1975). While there is no clear consensus and definitions are arbitrary, we will consider brief therapy to mean interventions of from one to forty sessions.

BRIEF VERSUS LONGER-TERM THERAPY

The first step in treatment planning is to decide whether to recommend a brief or a longer-term outpatient intervention. Some clinicians offer brief therapy as the initial treatment for all patients except those few who have already had an unsuccessful experience with it or those who present with clear motivation and indications for long-term treatment. Since it is difficult to predict from one or two interviews which patients require and can benefit from longer interventions, a trial of brief therapy is often useful as an extended evaluation and/or role induction.

The available research comparing the effectiveness of brief versus longer-term treatment has yet to demonstrate the possible advantages of the latter, but this probably reflects design and instrument limitations. Luborsky's box score (Luborsky, Singer and Luborsky, 1975) for brief versus longer therapies consisted of five ties, two studies in which brief was better, and one in which longer was better. Butcher and Koss (1978) reviewed essentially the same studies and agree with the conclusion of no difference. Smith, Glass and Miller (1980) found no simple relationship between duration and effect of therapy. Peak therapy effect occurred between the first and seventh sessions, but these results were achieved mostly in behavior therapies and may not generalize to other modalities. There are many limitations in the literature comparing brief and longer treatments: a) it's not always clear whether brevity is planned or reflects dropping out; b) severity of impairment is often uncontrolled; and c) briefer treatments are favored by the use of symptom relief outcome measures and by regression to the mean.

The indications for brief therapy, of whatever model, include the presence of a definite focus, precipitating event or target for intervention. The patient's overall motivation and goals may be limited, but are sufficient for cooperation with the brief treatment, and the patient is judged to be capable of separation from treatment. The patient's usual level of functioning is adequate and does not require long-term or maintenance treatment. Limited financial and/or time resources on the part of the patient or the delivery system may incline toward brief treatment. Brief may be chosen in preference to longer treatment to avoid secondary gain, negative therapeutic reactions, unmanageable transferences or other iatrogenic effects. The relative contraindications to brief therapy include special difficulties with separation and/or chronic or pervasive problems that demand more extended help (e.g., schizophrenia or other psychosis, severe anxiety and somatoform conditions, persistent and uncontrolled acting-out or self-destructiveness, severe personality disorders, terminal illness). Longer-term therapy (often maintenance or supportive) may be necessary for these conditions and is also indicated when the patient's problems are too numerous, complicated and/or unfocused for briefer intervention; when the goals of treatment include a more pervasive character change; or when a patient will be unable to tolerate a quick separation.

MODELS OF BRIEF THERAPY

Within their shared context of a time limit, the brief psychotherapies have gradually differentiated into several relatively distinct, but also overlapping models — each with somewhat different goals, techniques and selection criteria. A partial listing conveys the diversity of orientations that have been adapted to a time-limited format: psychodynamic (with or without genetic, resistance and transference interpretations), behavioral, cognitive, abreactive, task-oriented and problem-solving, interpersonal, strategic, crisis intervention, biofeedback, hypnosis, marital/family and sex therapy. The particular nature of the therapist-patient relationship and the content of the assessment, formulation and focus vary widely across these approaches. None of the suggested classifications of brief treatments is altogether satisfactory (Butcher and Koss, 1978; Sifneos, 1972). We have found it convenient to describe the rationale, goals, techniques and selection criteria for each of five categories — psychodymanic, problem-solving, behavioral, crisis intervention and family. This is an admittedly illogical collection — one treatment defined by urgency, another by inclusion of family members and three others by leading techniques. The categories are not mutually exclusive or jointly exhaustive. For example, cognitive therapy could be considered either a behavioral or a problem-solving approach, or be considered on its own separately. We have chosen these five categories for discussion because they seem more clinically useful than alternative possibilities.

Brief Psychodynamic Therapy

The history of the brief therapies is usually told from the perspective of the dynamic model. The more recent models have had a shorter and less compli-cated history.

As Malan (1963) has pointed out, Freud's early work involved active inter-vention on the part of the therapist concentrated within a brief period of time. But as psychoanalytic experience accumulated, treatments became longer, and therapists became increasingly passive, encouraged regressive transference and discovered the importance of progressively earlier memories, patient resistance, the overdetermination of symptoms and the necessity for working through. Psychoanalysis gradually developed a sense of relative timelessness. Ferenczi was one of the first to attempt to shorten the length of psychoanalysis by what he called "active therapy." He would, for example, prohibit patients from certain activities, and unfortunately then went so far as hugging, kissing and nonerotic fondling of his patients — risky activities for which he was roundly chastised by Freud. In 1925, Ferenczi and Rank published *The development of psychoanalysis,* in which they anticipated most of what has since been sug-gested about focal therapy. Influenced by Rank, Freud himself reported upon a case (the wolf man) in which he set a time limit. Rank's interest in birth trauma led naturally to his emphasis on the need to work through the patient's anxieties concerning separation from the therapist by setting a time limit.

Alexander and French (1946) were next in making strenuous efforts to develop briefer forms of psychoanalytic psychotherapy. They described many techniques to shorten and intensify the treatment, the most well-known and criticized of which is the control and manipulation of the transference rela-tionship to provide a corrective emotional experience. Following this lead were Balint, his student Malan and their colleagues at the Tavistock Clinic in London. In 1955, this research group began a series of investigations into brief psycho-analytic psychotherapy that have culminated in their major publications (Malan, 1963, 1976a,b). They have used sophisticated statistical methods to study naturalistically an eloquently executed and reported series of case studies in focal therapy. Malan has spelled out his selection criteria and has demonstrated that his central technique (transference interpretations linking the present transference distortions to the early experience of parental figures) is correlated with good outcome. His work is similar in most essentials to that recently done in the United States by Sifneos (1972) and Mann (1973) and in Canada by Davanloo (1978). Sifneos (1972) restricts the treatment to somewhat healthier patients with oedipal problems and may be more directive and cognitive in his approach. Mann (1973) emphasizes the ubiquity of separation/individuation conflicts in all patients and uses time-limited treatment as an especially apt paradigm to explore such problems. Davanloo (1978) and Malan (1976a) have recently been collaborating and offer the most flexible approach to technique and selection criteria.

Rationale, Goals and Techniques. The application of psychodynamic principles and techniques within a time-limited context has been well described (Alexander and French, 1946; Burke, White and Havens, 1979; Davanloo, 1978; Ferenczi and Rank, 1925; Horowtiz, 1976; Malan, 1963; Mann, 1973; Sifneos, 1972). The distinguishing technical device is the interpretation of unconscious wishes, fears and defenses in order to clarify, and hopefully resolve, a narrowly defined intrapsychic conflict. In addition to symptom relief, psychodynamic brief therapy attempts to promote character change, at least in the area of focal conflict.

Applicability. The two alternative approaches most often considered in differential therapeutic decisions are a longer-term psychodynamic therapy (including psychoanalysis) and one of the nondynamic brief therapies. The indications for brief dynamic therapy are wide, but the patient enabling factors are extremely demanding, and there are many contraindications. The patient must be especially ripe for this form of treatment. There are important differences in some of the particular recommendations offered by leading commentators. Sifneos selects patients with odeipal conflicts, Mann those with conflicts over separation; Malan and Davanloo do not insist upon any one specific conflict; Sifneos and Mann restrict the treatment to one focus; Malan and Davanloo sometimes deal with more than one focus. Most authors emphasize the importance of resistance, transference and genetic interpretations, but Horowitz describes a treatment for stress response syndromes with interpretations restricted to the conflicts aroused by the precipitating situation. Although disagreements among authors influence selection criteria, there remains enough similarity to distinguish the psychodynamic from other forms of brief treatment.

Indications

__The patient's presenting problem is best understood as a manifestation of a focal intrapsychic conflict. Conflicts may center around separation (Mann, 1973), oedipal issues (Sifneos, 1972), narcissistic injury (Goldberg, 1973) or stress response syndromes (Goldberg, 1973; Horowtiz, 1976).

__The goal of treatment is character change, at least in one circumscribed area of conflict.

Patient Enabling Factors

__Patient reports at least one significant interpersonal relationship in early childhood.

__Patient quickly and flexibly relates to the consultant and can freely express feelings.

__Patient and consultant can agree to work on a focal conflict whose nature then becomes increasingly clear as they explore it. The patient responds productively to interpretations dealing with the conflict. Ideally, the focal conflict underlies the patient's presenting problems, transference responses and infantile neurosis.

__Patient is motivated to change his behavior and to understand himself better, not merely to attain symptom relief. He is willing to make sacrifices in order to participate in the treatment, and is honest, curious and realistic about the outcome of therapy.

__Patient has psychological-mindedness and willingness to study his behaviors and feelings, including those that occur during the interview in regard to the therapist. He recognizes that his difficulties are psychological in origin.

__Patient has the ability to experience, tolerate and discuss painful affects.

__Patient has relatively high ego strength as evidenced by educational, work and sexual performance and the ability to accept responsibility.

__Patient is intelligent and able to communicate verbally his thoughts, feelings and fantasies.

Contraindications

__Psychosis
__Long-term hospitalization
__Drug addiction
__Serious suicide attempt
__Chronic alcoholism
__Incapacitating, chronic obsessional state
__Grossly destructive acting-out
__Severe character disorder
__Another treatment taking precedence
__More ambitious character change desired or necessary
__Problem too diffuse, or multiple foci of conflict

Case Illustration

A 30-year-old professional woman presents with panic attacks and work inhibition following a promotion. She is also afraid of pregnancy, although otherwise happily married. Mrs. A's associations during the evaluation clearly suggest that she feels guilty about outdoing her mother and sister and unconsciously expects punishment for her success and good fortune. When the consultant points this out, the patient cries and recalls a memory in which the women in the family had been extremely jealous of each other. Later she wonders whether she is doing as well as most new patients and is surprised, but interested, when the consultant suggests that this is a further example of her competitiveness. The patient is bright, is motivated to understand herself and to master her fears of success and has psychological-mindedness. She would be a suitable candidate for any dynamic therapy — brief, long-term or psychoanalysis — and also for many non-dynamic therapies. The presence of a clear focus, the early development of transference manifestations and her overall high suitability and good functioning suggest an initial trial of brief dynamic therapy. Alternatively, one could argue for the selection of behavior therapy and/or medications if the goal of treatment were quicker symptom relief and did not include character change. The patient forms a quick, positive attachment to her male therapist, regarding him as remarkably perceptive and understanding. She simultaneously describes numerous bad experiences with female bosses, both past and present, and makes clear that she prefers to work for and with a man. This transference manifestation is readily connected to her experience of her father as attractive and appreciative and her mother as competitive, jealous and critical. Mrs. A. believed that her mother disliked her special relationship with her father, and she did her best to hide it from her mother. She tried to appear a dull and unhappy child while simultaneously relishing what seemed to her to be a special place in her father's heart. Mrs. A. comes to realize that her current fears of success and pregnancy reflect a lingering sense that her progress usurps her mother's place and invites her scorn. She is able to use this insight to become more open in her competitiveness and desire to succeed and show off. After a while, she came to session in a bright yellow dress, the first article of clothing worn by her in years that was not a nondescript brown or green. On the follow-up she had continued professional success without panic attacks and was pregnant. Therapy had lasted seventeen sessions.

Brief Problem-Solving Therapy

It is difficult to write a coherent history of the problem-solving therapies because this grouping includes a heterogeneous collection of investigators and clinicians who, in the last twenty-five years, became discontented with the longer and more indirect approaches to solving patient problems. The term problem solving is admittedly a very broad one, referring to any therapeutic orientation that focuses very specifically on the patient's presenting problem(s), and sets out in a more or less directive fashion to help solve them. The term is, of course, broad enough to also include the behavior therapies, but we have chosen to discuss them in a separate section.

In 1949, the noted anthropologist Gregory Bateson began to analyze human and animal communication patterns with a team including Jay Haley and John Weakland. From this fresh approach to the study of human behavior, with its systems and cybernetic point of view, there arose a number of approaches to change problematic human behaviors. Influenced not only by Bateson but also by Milton Erikson, the psychiatrist and utilizer of hypnosis and many "uncommon" and directive modes of therapeutic intervention (Haley, 1973), Jay Haley (1976) developed a brief and focused problem-solving approach to human dilemmas, with a special emphasis on the therapist assisting a patient to solve specific problems with directive approaches geared to the individual and the family context. John Weakland, Bateson's other student, also developed a systems and directive approach, utilizing such techniques as reframing and paradoxical injunctions to change human logjams (Watzlawick, Weakland and Fisch, 1974). It is in this same tradition that Rabkin (1977) developed his strategic approach to solving specific patient problems in brief periods of therapeutic contact.

While the activist problem-solving tradition mentioned above emphasized the social context of the family, others have utilized problem-solving approaches with more focus on the individual, and influenced more by a prior psychoanalytic tradition. Barten (1969) and Bellak and Small (1978) have taken part in the community mental health movement and have responded to the diverse needs of patients presenting in these settings by advocating a flexible use of diverse problem-solving techniques.

Rationale, Goals and Techniques. This is the most variable, eclectic and versatile of brief approaches. There is no one characteristic feature except perhaps careful attention to defining and resolving a specific presenting problem. A variety of techniques are applied to meet the opportunities and constraints of the given moment. These include clarifying the situation, exploring implications of alternative possible decisions, advice, prescribing specific action, paradoxical injunction, role playing, abreaction, reassurance, environmental manipulation and mobilizing the social network. The goals are symptom relief, reintegration, healthier management of the current crisis, the development of new problem-solving skills and reversing demoralization (Bellak and Small, 1965; Weissman, Neu, Rounsaville, Dimascio, Prusoff and Klerman, in press; Wolberg, 1965). Although a dynamic understanding of the patient may inform treatment interventions, the interpretation of unconscious process is generally not made, and the goals of treatment do not particularly include insight or personality change.

Applicability. This model has the widest of indications and the fewest patient suitability requirements or contraindications of any form of psychiatric treatment. It should be recommended in preference to the dynamic model if the more demanding suitability requirements or ambitious goals of the latter are not present.

Indications

__Any patient sufficiently disturbed by a precipitating event to require a psychiatric intervention. In some instances, the patient's usual state of functioning is normal; in others, the problem is superimposed on a long-standing but stable disorder that will not be a major focus of the treatment.

Patient Enabling Factors

__Patient is willing to attend sessions as needed.
__Patient is able to cooperate with the therapist's suggestions and interventions.
__Patient is willing to make changes to meet his acute problem.
__Personality reconstruction is not a primary goal.
__A more urgent or more ambitious treatment is not indicated.

Contraindications

__Same as general contraindications for brief therapy.

Case Illustration

The patient is a 33-year-old unemployed guitarist whose wife left him with complaints about his passivity and inability to provide financial support. He is tearful, feels lost and alone. The patient is not psychological-minded and wants concrete help with his current problem, not a throughgoing analysis of it. The treatment plan includes abreaction and the mapping of strategies for finding work and winning back his wife. An argument could also be made for behavior therapy (especially assertiveness training) or marital therapy, or for some combination of these treatments. The patient's fears in looking for work and his passive expectation that musical agents will take the initiative in calling him are highlighted as reasons for his lack of advancement and poor financial position. He is given direct advice about job seeking and is supported in taking chances he had previously avoided. The therapist and patient together write a long letter to his wife explaining his new-found understanding of her concerns, desire to turn a new leaf and efforts taken in this direction. His wife writes back agreeing to return if he has steady work. Before long, both events indeed occur. Therapy lasted seven sessions.

Brief Behavior Therapy

Goldfried and Davidson (1976) have emphasized three trends in the historical development of clinical behavior therapy. First of all, in the 1950s, Joseph Wolpe and Arnold Lazarus, emphasizing Hulliam and Pavlovian theories, applied data about the acquisition and alleviation of fear derived from animal experiments to the human situation. Wolpe utilized deep muscle relaxation while at the same time having the individual imagine the feared stimulus. A second major trend was the development and utilization of the operant orientation of B.F. Skinner. Human maladaptive behavior was seen as instrumental in nature and therefore subject to the principles of operant conditioning, which have been applied particularly in psychiatric hospital settings. A third and more recent trend in the history of clinical behavior therapy is the growth of an orientation that emphasizes the role of cognitive activities in the acquisition and maintenance of both adaptive and maladaptive behaviors. Workers such as Rotter, Bandura, Mahoney and Meichenbaum have made important contributions, in addition to those of Beck and Ellis, which will be discussed in more detail below.

Since the behavioral therapist is oriented to specific behaviors and target symptoms, his therapy is by definition limited to specific foci and is often but not always limited to forty sessions, the somewhat arbitrary cutoff used in this review for the brief therapies. In fact, Wilson (1981) has reported that the average treatment duration at a large metropolitan behavior treatment center was fifty sessions, a surprisingly high number. Nevertheless, the nature of the behavioral orientation (specific target symptoms, specific treatment regiments, goal-directed, measurement-oriented) lends it to a brief-therapy style and orientation.

Rationale, Goals and Techniques. Recently a number of brief behavioral treatment packages have been developed for specific clinical problems (Lazarus, 1973; Lewinsohn, Biglan and Zeiss, 1976). The variety of behavior therapy techniques include: systematic desensitization (in vitro and in vivo), implosion, modeling, social skills, cognitive approaches and operant techniques.

An increasingly popular and extensively used offshoot of behavior therapy includes the various forms of cognitive therapy, perhaps best exemplified by two proponents, Albert Ellis and Aaron Beck. Ellis (1973) teaches his patients that the key to emotional upset and distress is incorrect perceptions and illogical beliefs, and that the patient can change his experience of anxiety and other unpleasant emotions by changing his irrational belief system. In similar fashion, Beck (Beck and Greenberg, 1979) maintains that cognitive interpretations mediate between an event and the emotions that follow from the meanings that are attributed to the event. Thus, individuals who suffer from depression, anxiety and phobias are really victims of a form of thought disorder or cognitive misperception, and Beck proceeds to treat such conditions with a cognitive therapy that directs the individual to observe and correct his "automatic thoughts." Beck describes his treatment as brief, problem-oriented and highly structured, and he makes use of homework, reading outside of sessions and role-playing. Applying his cognitive approach to the depression, Beck teaches the patient to correct the automatic negative thoughts that lead to the depressed mood, concomitant lack of motivation and low activity level. Homework assignments (e.g., instructing the patient to attend a pleasurable movie) are used to obtain information about the patient and his functioning, especially the cognitive processes that precede the depressive mood. In typical behavioral tradition, tasks graded in terms of difficulty are assigned to ensure some initial successes that reinforce the patient's further attempts. The patient is helped to perform tasks by cognitively rehearsing the various parts necessary to their accomplishment. Guided by the cognitive therapist, the patient repeatedly tracks the irrational cognitive beliefs that influence his interpretation of events and begins to recognize the pattern of interpretational biases that he attributes to common events in his life space.

Wilson (1981) has recently reviewed the application of behavior therapy as a brief treatment for assorted clinical symptoms and problems. Specific phobias can be treated by in vivo exposure in a brief period of time (Marks, 1978), and this is also true of more complex phobias such as agoraphobia (Marks, 1978; Rachman and Wilson, 1980). Specific sexual dysfunctions have been success-fully treated in a brief behavioral format by such approaches as that of Masters and Johnson (1970).

Applicability. We are assuming in the criteria listed below that virtually all of these disorders can be treated within a brief format. Our purpose is to dis-tinguish criteria that favor behavior therapy in comparison to the alternative brief models that have so far been discussed, not to discriminate among the specific behavioral techniques. Brief behavioral treatment might be done indi-vidually, in groups or in a marital/family setting.

Indications

__Anxiety disorders: agoraphobia with or without panic disorder (Gelder, Marks, Wolff and Clarke, 1967), panic disorder, generalized anxiety, hyperven-tilation, examination anxiety, interpersonal anxiety.

__Depression of mild to moderate intensity (Lewinsohn, Biglan and Zeiss, 1976; McLean and Hakstian, 1979; Rush, Beck, Kovacs and Hollon, 1977).

__Deficits in social skills (e.g., assertiveness, heterosexual behavior) (Argyle, Bryant and Trower, 1974; Meichenbaum and Turk, 1976; Percell, Berwick and Beigel, 1974).

__Sexual dysfunctions (Masters and Johnson, 1970).

__Compulsive rituals (Rachman, Hodgson and Marks, 1971).

Contraindications

Same as general contraindications for brief therapy.

Case Illustration

Mrs. C. is a 23-year old schoolteacher who enjoys her work and does well except when observed by her supervisor. She then has panic symptoms, becomes flustered, loses her train of thought, blushes and performs poorly. She has a long history of test anxiety and some shyness with strangers. Otherwise, she has no particular problems, enjoys many friendships and is happily married. Her motivation for treatment is clearly centered around the presenting symptom, and she is quite satisfied with the rest of her life. The patient is begun in a behavioral treatment consisting of a hierarchy of desensitization steps first in fantasy and then in vivo. The behavioral assessment was begun by putting the patient through an imagery procedure. In this exercise she was asked to, with her eyes closed, imagine the supervisor watching her work. She described him as a harsh, older-looking man with a scowl on his face who, in her imagination, was looking over her shoulder from behind as she taught her class of eighth grade math students. In her imagination, several students responded to her queries with the wrong answer, and her immediate thought was, "Oh, how stupid the supervisor must think I am. He must think any good teacher would insure that these students would have the right answer." Thus, a theme of anxiety was established concerning the fears of being disapproved of, looking foolish, losing control, fainting, becoming nauseous, feeling rejected, being ignored, all in the context of supposed critical thoughts by the supervisor. With the isolation of themes of anxiety, the next few sessions were used to construct a stimulus hierarchy, i.e., a graded series of events all related to the particular anxiety themes that gradually evoked increasing degrees of anxiety, starting with the situation that elicited just a small amount of anxiety and ranging up to those situations that provided her with an extremely high degree of anxiety. The following hierarchy was constructed:

1. One hour before the supervisor was to observe her performance in the classroom.
2. One half-hour before the supervisor was to observe her in the classroom.
3. Fifteen minutes before the supervisor was to observe her in the classroom.

4. Walking down the hallway toward her classroom, just before being observed by the supervisor.
5. Entering the classroom and greeting the class.
6. Explaining the supervisor's visit to the class with the supervisor present.
7. Teaching and examining the students with the supervisor present.
8. With the supervisor present, the elicitation of remarks by students that were incorrect answers to instructional material.

The formulation of hierarchies was combined with teaching the patient the procedure of deep muscle relaxation. Following the training in relaxation, desensitization was initiated. The imagined hierarchy items were paired with relaxation and with the imagination of coping responses, beginning of course with the scenes that provoked the least amount of anxiety. In the next ten sessions, the patient was able gradually to imagine herself in the presence of the supervisor while relaxed with lowered anxiety. With suggestions, she could imagine certain coping responses such as talking with the supervisor afterward about the responses of students, which, after all, could be expected given the range of intelligence and mastery of the students in the class. Introduction of such statements as "this student has not learned the proper math procedures yet, but will do so in the future and has actually progressed under my instruction," was also initiated. As the patient began to make progress in the desensitization procedures and in the imagination of coping responses, she was instructed to initiate coping responses in the actual situation by making a visit to the supervisor who would observe her later in the semester, and chatting with the supervisor about what he would be looking for. The combination of relaxation, desensitization in imagery and actual demystification of the conception of the supervisor by contact with him enabled the patient to successfully handle the next supervisory observation in her classroom.

Crisis Intervention

Lindemann (1944) and Caplan (1964) were the pioneers in the development of the theory of crisis intervention. Following the Coconut Grove fire in the 1940s, Lindemann studied and described the grief work of the survivors, noting that while some individuals resolved the crisis in a time-limited (roughly six weeks) period, others came to a maladaptive resolution. Caplan (1964) subsequently defined a crisis as having the following elements: an obstacle to ordinary and important life goals presents itself that is not solvable through ordinary coping patterns; a period of disorganization and crisis follows in which the individual tries many forms of coping; over a period of time a resolution is achieved that may be adaptive or nonadaptive.

Rationale, Goals and Techniques. Crisis intervention is, then, an intense, timely, brief (usually under one month) and goal-directed treatment intended to resolve a crisis of major and urgent proportions and recent onset. The treatment often requires frequent (perhaps daily) and prolonged sessions, twenty-four-hour staff availability, the use of psychotropic medications, the mobilization of family members and other community resources, environmental manipulations and a multidisciplinary team. The intervention is focused on the presenting problem, particularly an exploration of its precipitating events. The goal is the relief of the symptoms, avoidance of further decompensation and development of more adaptive coping skills for future crises (Ewing, 1978; Jacobson, 1974).

Applicability. For severely disturbed patients, the most frequent alternatives to crisis intervention are inpatient or day hospitalization. Toward the other end of the severity spectrum, patients experiencing distress that is not urgent may be managed in less intense formats, discussed later in this chapter.

Indications

__The patient's symptoms, distress and risk factors must be severe enough to warrant urgent and intense attention — perhaps to require inpatient hospitalization if a crisis intervention is not offered (Langsley, Flomenhaft and Machotka, 1969). This degree of urgency may result from: suicidal threats or acts, psychosis, severe depression, anxiety or panic disorders, grief, excited states or somatic symptoms.
__Often there is a major precipitating stress that provides a clear focus for the intervention. This may be:

1) Accidental — injury, illness, death, job loss, etc.
2) Interpersonal — an affair, a bitter argument, etc.
3) Developmental — child born or goes to school, marriage, etc. (Caplan, 1964).

__Onset of symptoms is an indication if relatively recent (Wolkon, 1972).
__Intervention may be especially appropriate for patients of lower socioeconomic status (Duckworth, 1967).

Patient Enabling Factors

__Patient is willing to participate, keep appointments, be available for home visits, take medication, etc.
__Social and family networks are adequate or can be mobilized.
__A crisis intervention comprises the total treatment when the patient is not motivated for more treatment and/or not chronically disturbed. Otherwise, crisis intervention may serve as an induction for brief or long-term individual, family or group treatment.

Case Illustration

Ms. C. is a 20-year-old college student who recently moved from her parents' home to her own apartment. She presents in the emergency room with her first suicide attempt, an impulsive ingestion of 100 aspirins after a lover's quarrel. The patient is not hospitalized for three reasons: a) the acute risk of another attempt appears small; b) she refuses hospitalization and does not meet commitment requirements; c) she is suggestible and might develop new symptoms if exposed to psychiatric inpatients. Although the patient is casual and uncooperative at the beginning of the emergency room consultation, she gradually forms a working relationship with the therapist, begins to recognize the seriousness of her act and agrees to daily sessions until the risk of another attempt is removed. During the first week, she is seen at times alone and at times with her parents or with her boyfriend in sessions that last between thirty and ninety minutes. These occur daily for four days, then three times a week for the next three weeks. It becomes clear that Ms. C. is very dependent; she is furious at her parents for letting her leave home at so young an age and resentful that her boyfriend did not take better care of her. She both wants to be on her own and feels completely incapable of managing for herself. The therapist recommends that the patient keep her apartment but that she spend three days a week at her parents' home in order to effect a more gradual and orderly transition. The patient's easy acceptance of suicide as a solution of life's problems is highlighted and made more ego-dystonic. She learns that separations are for her an especially severe stress that will require extra endurance, patience and preparation. She is also taught that when upset she loses perspective and needs to step back and take a longer view of her prospects. At the end of the crisis intervention, the patient is referred for more definitive therapy in a group consisting of young adults with problems more or less similar to hers.

Brief Marital/Family Therapy

Gurman (1981) has recently pointed out that one can call a treatment brief only in relative reference to a standard of greater length. Brief individual psychotherapy is judged against the standard of two-to-five-year treatment in long-term individual dynamically oriented psychotherapy. In the more recent developed behavioral, problem-solving and marital treatments, a standard of two-to-five-year treatment has *never* existed. Indeed, marital and family treatment has always been relatively brief in its duration. Judging from reviews of research in marital and family treatment and reports by practitioners (Framo, 1981), an average length from fifteen to twenty sessions seems to be the norm. Gurman suggests some interesting hypotheses as to why marital therapy seems to entail relatively short time periods. The therapist focuses on the problematic aspects of the current problem rather than relating to the historical antecedents involving dynamics of the problem. The patients who enter marital therapy have shown themselves capable of having at least one (more or less) meaningful relationship judged by the very fact of their being married, and thus these individuals are likely to constitute a selected good-prognosis population. In addition, the interpersonal and/or transferential aspects of the problems are not only talked about but also exhibited in the therapy sessions themselves, since both parties are present. Finally, the loss of the therapist at the termination of the treatment is not as threatening as the ending of an individual treatment because the partners leave with each other as company. These hypotheses must be balanced by the fact that marital and behavioral therapies have perhaps not had a long enough history in which to lengthen their therapeutic processes. Indeed, there is some indication that behavioral treatments are getting longer.

Rationale, Goals and Techniques. The basic premise of marital and family therapy is that symptom and problems can be viewed as interpersonal in etiology and/or current maintenance, and changed by altering the family system. Various technical orientations have been utilized in brief marital/family therapy.

Kinston and Bentovim (1981) have applied the psychoanalytic focal therapeutic approach of Balint and Malan to children and their families. The family is treated in six to ten sessions over a four-to-six-month period. These authors describe their work as psychoanalytic in its conceptualization, and eclectic and pragmatic in their selection and utilization of therapeutic techniques. Thus, focal hypotheses about malfunction are conceived in psychoanalytic terminology (e.g., the family has conflicts over assertiveness; the family has failed to integrate sexuality and aggression; the mother is overprotective and is paired with a passive father). A major technique in this form of brief family treatment is to bring the underlying meanings attributed to events by the various family members into their awareness by interpretation and reframing. The therapy is judged to be successful only if insight is achieved, and if there are actual changes in the behavioral repertoire of the family.

Kessler and Glick (1979) have described an approach to brief family therapy that is very much in the eclectic and problem-solving tradition. They include weekend growth groups, two-to-six-session crisis intervention treatments or sector treatment of specific aspects of family interaction in durations of up to several months. A variety of techniques are recommended, including setting a defined limit to the treatment time, exploring upsetting events that triggered the crisis, providing support for the resulting upset, directing the family to stick to the primary focus and goals at hand, eliciting and reinforcing the use of family strengths, active exploration of alternatives to action, assigning extra-session homework assignments with the intent of increasing communication and role-playing pro-social behaviors.

Weiss and Jacobson (1981) have described a brief behavioral marital therapy of eight to ten sessions' duration. The therapy begins with an assessment of the specific behavioral areas of importance to a marriage, communication skills, competencies such as the ability to objectify one's environment, the supportive functions of adult intimacy, problem solving and the ability to change behavior within a relationship. These skills and competencies are assessed in twelve defined content areas such as affectional communication and instrumental areas of interaction. Once specific areas of marital difficulties are targeted, various behavioral techniques are utilized to make interventions. For example, patients are taught that many marital conflicts are actually a patterned sequence of mutually reinforcing events, and are taught how to increase positive reward for one another in order to increase the likelihood of beneficial positive change. Couples may be asked to systematically track a set of their relationship behaviors through a chain of events over a period of time. Such tracking enables the partners to become cognitively aware of the sequence and thus able to avoid behaviors that precede conflictful events.

Gurman (1981) has recently advocated what he terms an integrative marital therapy approach that is brief because of its emphasis on a specific focus, and is integrative because it recognizes the psychodynamic, systems and social learning aspects of dyadic relationships. He points out that the goal of this brief marital treatment is not simply change in the marital interaction pattern, which is emphasized by systems theorists, but also change in each individual in the marriage. While the therapist is encouraged to address negative transference reactions toward the therapist that may limit the usefulness of or terminate the therapy, the emphasis is placed on the transference distortions that each partner has of the other. True to the term integrative, Gurman recommends the use of expansion of awareness and insight into the spouse's self-percept, the use of behavioral techniques such as anxiety management training and the teaching of coping skills and the use of systems thinking in understanding and changing marital interaction.

Applicability. The following criteria specify indications that favor a choice of the marital/family treatment format as opposed to the individual (Azrin, Naster and Jones, 1973; Haley, 1976; Jacobson, 1974; Rabkin, 1977; Weakland, Sisch, Watzlawick and Bodin, 1974; Weiss, Hops and Patterson, 1973). The criteria that influence selection of specific techniques (dynamic, problem-solving, behavioral) and duration have been outlined separately for individual therapy; they may be similarly applied to marital/family therapy, and are not repeated here.

Indications

__When there is focal marital or family conflict — examples include the need to separate from family of origin; to establish marital commitment; to resolve ambivalence over intimacy and dependency; to establish modes of conflict resolution, decision making and negotiation; to clarify role expectations; to develop channels for expression of positive and negative feelings.

__When there is evidence that family members are contributing collusively or openly to the identified patient's problems.

__When family cooperation must be mobilized as an induction to another mode of therapy.

__When the family situation is baffling, and brief therapy is chosen as an extended evaluation.

__When the couple needs immediate help to decide whether to separate (or divorce).

Patient Enabling Factors

__Family can meet together without uncontrollable fighting.

__Family and therapist are able to agree on a focal area of intervention.

__Significant family members are able to participate and motivated to change relationship patterns.

Contraindications

__Extreme schizoid or paranoid pathology.

__One or more family members' insight on privacy (e.g., valid secrets).

__When individuation of one or more family members would be compromised.

__Family breaking up with no desire for reconciliation or need for help in the separation.

__When problems are chronic, multiple or unfocused and require longer treatment.

Case Illustration

Mr. R. is a 40-year-old man who presents after a temper outburst in which he slapped his fiancee. Although he loves her a great deal, he also becomes extremely irritable and jealous with her and worries that this will ruin their marriage. On the next visit, the couple is interviewed together. It is clear that each of them is possessive of the other, but simultaneously unwilling to surrender any independence. They are able to discuss this and are motivated to jointly explore the issue further during the several months before their wedding. The couple's treatment reveals that he is especially suspicious of her friendship with a childhood woman friend and moreover worried that this relationship might have had, or still has, homosexual overtones. This "accusation" infuriates her, and she responds by becoming even more demonstrative with her friend and wondering whether she should call off her wedding. The therapist's intervention combined cognitive reframing with the imparting of insight. To the groom, he pointed out that friendships among women are very often close and very rarely sexual — did he, for instance, think his mother and aunt were lesbians because they had talked on the telephone every night for the past 30 years? The groom's excessive and unnecessary jealousy and fears of betrayal were interpreted as secondary to a sense that no woman would want to marry him and that something would inevitably go wrong. This was further connected to his own doubts about marriage which had kept him a bachelor so long — e.g., fear of involvement, sense of betraying his mother, with whom he had lived off and on, and a concern that he might hurt anyone he loved. The bride's own need to flaunt her independence and her fear of being submerged by the powerful personality of the groom were also explored. They were married on schedule and have done well. The treatment consisted of nine sessions.

Compairson of the Major Models of Brief Therapy

The five various models of brief psychotherapy presented here can be compared with long-term therapy and with one another in their relative effectiveness, indications, enabling factors and goals.

Relevant Outcome Research. In their review of research in brief psychotherapy, Butcher and Koss (1978) conclude that the brief therapies are beneficial, and that from 70 to 80% of the patients show improvement. Various reviewers such as Luborsky, Singer and Luborsky (1975) have concluded that the brief therapies are just as effective as the longer-term psychotherapies. However, one must handle this interpretation with caution, as the outcome measures, the therapy designs and treatments used tend to favor the initial impact of the brief treatments.

Most relevant to the current chapter is the question of which brief therapy format or model is the most effective for particular patients who are suited to a time-limited approach. Probably the best-designed psychotherapy outcome study contrasting two models of brief psychotherapy is that of Sloane, Staples, Cristol, Yorkston and Whipple (1975). These investigators contrasted brief behavioral treatment to brief psychoanalytic treatment as done by expert therapists with ambulatory nonpsychotic patients. The results indicate that both treatment approaches produce significant change as contrasted to no-treatment controls, and the two approaches were found to be about equal in their therapeutic effectiveness. The authors of the study concluded that behavior therapy produces change sooner and in a more focused fashion. Patterson, Levene and Breger (1971) compared brief behavior therapy with brief psychodynamically oriented psychotherapy. The patients were unselected ambulatory patients, and the therapists were in training. At the end of treatment, the patients in brief therapy rated themselves as more improved than did the patients treated in brief analytically oriented psychotherapy, and the ratings by therapists and independent judges showed insignificant differences in the same direction. The authors comment that brief behavioral techniques may be more easily taught and effectively learned by beginning therapists than are the techniques of brief psychoanalytic psychotherapy. Nichols and Reifler (1973) and Nichols (1974) compared insight-oriented psychoanalytic psychotherapy with brief cathartic therapy. Experienced therapists delivered both types of psychotherapy, but only the insight-oriented psychotherapy showed a significant reduction in psychopathology as measured by the MMPI.

There are a few other comparison studies that pit various forms of brief therapy against one another. However, the remaining studies typically do not use patient populations and therefore will be omitted here. Most reviewers would conclude from the sparse research to date that there are few data to support differential assignment of patients under specific conditions to different brief therapy formats. It seems to us that there are only tantalizing leads that the clinician must use with caution. For example, the impressive clinical experimental work of Malan (1963, 1976a,b) suggests that certain constellations of motivation and focusing ability are predictive of success in brief focal dynamic psychotherapy. In addition, the study of Sloane et al. (1975) suggests that individuals with acting-out behavior as opposed to those without such symptomatology may do better in a brief behavioral psychotherapy as opposed to insight-oriented psychotherapy.

Relevant Process Research. In their very useful and extensive review, Butcher and Koss (1978) summarize recent process research in the brief psychotherapies. They highlight relevant research findings on the impact of several major technical and situational aspects said to be particularly relevant to the brief therapies: the setting of time limits, relationship factors, the arousal of expectation and hope, influencing the patient when he is in an emotionally charged state and the activity level of the therapist.

The intensive clinical research by Malan and his group suggests that change in brief analytic psychotherapy is correlated with analyzing the transference relationship, especially as it relates to early parental relationships. The patient's expectation and hope of receiving help have been related to achievement of therapeutic change (Frank, 1974). And it may be that this heightened expectation of more or less immediate help and change may be more important in brief psychotherapy than in longer-term therapy. Studies of role-inducing patients into various forms of psychotherapy suggest that instruction about the treatment and arousal of expectation of change may indeed lead to more significant improvement. Patients in brief psychotherapy are likely to be in a heightened emotional state due to the crisis or upset that brought them to treatment, and there is some suggestion that individuals in such a heightened state are more susceptible to influence from others and thus hopefully from a therapist (Frank, 1974; Hoehn-Saric, Liberman, Imber, Stone, Pande and Frank, 1972).

Setting a time limit on the length of the treatment at the beginning is often hypothesized by brief therapists as having a therapeutic effect in and of itself, but Butcher and Koss (1978) conclude that there is little current research evidence to substantiate this claim. For example, Shlien, Mosak and Driekurs (1962) compared time-limited psychotherapy with unlimited psychotherapy and found similar results. In both groups improvement occurred early in the treatment and then leveled off. Likewise, many theoreticians of brief therapy emphasize the activity and directiveness of the therapist. In the Sloane *et al.* (1975) study mentioned earlier, it was found that the behavior therapists were more controlling of the content of the sessions than were the dynamically oriented psychotherapists. In addition, the behavior therapists initiated more new topics in the conversation and prescribed more courses of action. However, the more active behavior therapists did not achieve a better outcome than did the dynamic psychotherapists. It may be that the nature of the therapeutic relationship itself with its supportive and empathic aspects is more important to outcome than the concrete measures of directiveness or control.

Applicability. The range of applicability of the various brief psychotherapy models can be judged comparatively by inspecting their indications, contraindications, enabling factors and goals (Table 9-1). The brief psychoanalytic model is the most stringent in that it requires an identified focal dynamic conflict and also very stringent enabling factors such as motivation for insight, capacity for reflection, high frustration tolerance and so forth. The problem-solving model is probably the most versatile in that it has the fewest enabling factors and combines a vast array of techniques that can be applied in a flexible manner. The behavioral approaches seem most appropriate when a specific problem or symptom can be specified in clear behavioral terms, and a behavioral technique can be applied to the situation (i.e., specific phobias, specific anxieties, interpersonal skill deficits and possibly minor depressions). The brief marital and family therapy model is most applicable when the individual symptoms can be traced to interaction difficulties in either an etiologic or exacerbating sense, or when the family interaction problems themselves constitute the initial complaint. The differentiating indication for crisis intervention is urgency.

The most important factor in differentially determining assignment to a particular model of brief therapy is often the patient's goals, both mediating and ultimate. The goal of the crisis-intervention model is to avoid a negative reaction to crisis in an individual or family unit, to avoid hospitalization, to reverse any symptoms that have developed, to help the individual or family unit deal with the stress, to return the patient to premorbid levels of functioning and hopefully to instill new coping mechanisms that will be available in future similar crisis situations. The behavioral and the problem-solving models focus explicitly on the alleviation of symptoms and/or problems. The brief marital and family therapies have mediating goals that usually include better and more healthy communication patterns and interaction skills than existed

TABLE 9-1 COMPARISON OF BRIEF THERAPY MODELS.

	Techniques	Mediating goals	Ultimate goals	Selection criteria
Focal dynamic	•Transference and resistance interpretations •Genetic reconstruction	•Insight	•Character change •Symptom change	•Focal conflict •Stringent enabling factors
Problem solving	•Direct advice •Planning •Assignment of extra-session tasks •Paradoxical injunction	•Carrying out tasks	•New coping skills •Change in system	•Flexible
Behavioral	•Desensitization •Operant conditioning •Cognitive	•Successive approximation to new behaviors	•Problem resolution •Symptom disappearance •New skills	•Specific problem or deficit
Crisis intervention	•Support •Environmental manipulation	•Stabilization	•Decrease in stress •New coping skills •Prior adaptation achieved	•Crisis, stimulated by developmental or accidental events, urgency
Family/ Marital	•Any of above	•Changes in family interaction	•Changes in relationships •Changes in individuals	•Chief complaint is family interaction problem •Current family interaction is responsible for individual symptoms

in the marital/family unit before therapy. The behavioral therapies emphasize putting into actual behavior new skills and thoughts that are learned as the patient during the treatment is brought to closer and closer approximations of the kinds of behavior that are desired as the ultimate goal. The problem-solving approaches have as their mediating goals the imparting of the cognitive and emotional skills that are needed to plan, dissect a problem, plan alternate strategies and execute the most viable ones. The focal dynamic brief therapies are most distinguished by their hope to provide as an ultimate goal not only symptom relief but also characterological or intrapsychic structural change even if circumscribed.

There is, of course, major disagreement among the various schools of thought as to the viability of the distinction between symptom and character change.

Those of a more behavioristic and learning tradition question whether anything but symptom change is measurable, whereas Malan and the Menninger study have attempted to operationalize measures of character change. Currently available outcome measures are certainly more reliable and valid in measuring symptom than character changes.

CONCLUSIONS

The many limitations in the present body of psychotherapy research may account for its inability to specify which treatment works best for which problems. On the whole, there is evidence that brief planned treatments are significantly more beneficial than no treatment (Smith, Glass and Miller, 1980), although it is not yet clear for which patients they are the treatment of choice and whether the different models of brief therapy are differentially effective in particular situations.   There are shared characteristics of the brief therapies that distinguish them from the open-ended and longer-term therapies: they offer encouragement to action via setting a time limit; they engender a hopeful attitude by the unspoken notion that something (if not perfection) can be achieved within a limited amount of time; they convey the attitude that the patient has strengths, can function independently and is not terribly impaired; and they provide a constant reminder that life itself is limited in time, and one cannot put off what one wishes to accomplish.

REFERENCES

Alexander, F. and French, T. *Psychoanalytic therapy*. New York: Ronald Press, 1946.

Argyle, M., Bryant, B. and Trower, P. Social skills training and psychotherapy: A comparative study. *Psychological Medicine.* 4: 435–443 (1974).

Azrin, N.H., Naster, B.J. and Jones, R. Reciprocity counselling: A rapid learning based procedure for marital counselling. *Behavior Research and Therapy.* 11: 365–384 (1973).

Barten, H.H. The coming of age of the brief psychotherapies. In: Ballak, L. and Barten, H. (Eds.), *Progress in community mental health,* vol. 1. New York: Grune & Stratton, 1969.

Beck, A.T. and Greenberg, R.L. Brief cognitive therapies. In: Sloane, R.B. and Staples, F.R. (Eds.), *The psychiatric clinics of North America: Symposium on brief psychotherapy,* vol. 2, no. 1, April 1979. Philadelphia: Saunders, 1979.

Bellak, L. and Small, L. *Emergency psychotherapy and brief therapy.* New York: Grune & Stratton, 1965.

Bellak, L. and Small, L. *Emergency psychotherapy and brief psychotherapy,* 2nd ed. New York: Grune & Stratton, 1978.

Burke, J., White, H. and Havens, L. Which short-term therapy? *Archives of General Psychiatry.* 36: 177–186 (1979).

Butcher, J. and Koss, M. Research on brief and crisis-oriented psychotherapies. In: Garfield, S. and Bergin, A. (Eds.), *Handbook of psychotherapy and behavior change: An empirical analysis,* 2nd ed. New York: Wiley, 1978.

Caplan, G. *Principles of preventive psychiatry.* New York: Basic Books, 1964.

Clarkin, J.F., Frances, A., Taintor, Z. and Warburg, M. Training in brief therapy: A survey of psychiatric residency programs. *American Journal of Psychiatry.* **137**: 978–979 (1980).

Davanloo, H. *Basic principles and techniques in short-term dynamic psychotherapy.* New York: Spectrum Books, 1978.

Duckworth, G.L. A project in crisis intervention. *Social Casework,* **48**: 227–231 (1967).

Ellis, A. *Humanistic psychotherapy: The rationale-immotive approach.* New York: McGraw-Hill, 1973.

Ewing, C.P. *Crisis intervention as psychotherapy.* New York: Oxford, 1978.

Ferenczi, S. and Rank, O. *The development of psychoanalysis.* New York: Nervous & Mental Disease Publication Co., 1925.

Framo, J. Integration of marital therapy with sessions with family of origin. In: Gurman, A. and Kniskern, D. (Eds.), *Handbook of family therapy.* New York: Brunner/Mazel, 1981.

Frank, J.D. Therapeutic components of psychotherapy: A 25-year progress report of research. *Journal of Nervous and Mental Diseases.* **159**: 325–342 (1974).

Garfield, S.L. Research on client variables in psychotherapy. In: Bergin, A. and Garfield, S. (Eds.), *Handbook of psychotherapy and behavior change.* New York: Wiley, 1971.

Gelder, M.G., Marks, I., Wolff, H.H. and Clarke, M. Desensitization and psychotherapy in the treatment of phobic states: A controlled inquiry. *British Journal of Psychiatry.* **113**: 53–73 (1967).

Goldberg, A. Psychotherapy of narcissistic injuries. *Archives of General Psychiatry.* **28**: 722–726 (1973).

Goldfried, M.R. and Davidson, G.C. *Clinical behavior therapy.* New York: Holt, Rinehart & Winston, 1976.

Gurman, A.S. Integrative marital therapy: Toward the development of an interpersonal approach. In: Budman, S.H. (Ed.), *Forms of brief therapy.* New York: Guilford Press, 1981.

Haley, J. *Uncommon therapy.* New York: Ballantine Books, 1973.

Haley, J. *Problem-solving therapy.* New York: Harper, 1976.

Hoehn-Saric, R., Liberman, R., Imber, S.D., Stone, A., Pande, S.K. and Frank, J.D. Arousal and attitude change in neurotic patients. *Archives of General Psychiatry.* **26**: 51–56 (1972).

Horowitz, M. *Stress response syndromes.* New York: Jason Aronson, 1976.

Jacobson, N.S. Problem-solving and contingency contracting in the treatment of marital discord. *Journal of Consulting and Clinical Psychology.* **45**: 92–100 (1974).

Kessler, D.R. and Glick, I.D. Brief family therapy. In: Slaone, R.B. and Staples, F.R. (Eds.), *The psychiatric clinics of North America: Symposium on brief psychotherapy,* vol. 2, no. 1, April 1979. Philadelphia: Saunders, 1979.

Kingston, W. and Bentovim, A.   Creating a focus for brief marital or family therapy. In: Budman, S.H. (Ed.), *Forms of brief therapy*. New York: Guilford Press, 1981.

Koss, M.P.   Length of psychotherapy for clients seen in private practice. *Journal of Consulting and Clinical Psychology*. **47**: 210–212 (1979).

Langsley, D., Flomenhaft, K. and Machotka, P.   Follow-up evaluation of family crisis therapy. *American Journal of Orthopsychiatry*. **39**: 753–759 (1969).

Lazarus, A.A.   The results of behavior therapy in 126 cases of severe neurosis. *Behavior Research and Therapy*. **1**: 68–79 (1973).

Lewinsohn, P.M., Biglan, T. and Zeiss, A.   Behavioral treatment of depression. In: Davidson, P. (Ed.), *Behavior management of anxiety, depression and pain*. New York: Brunner/Mazel, 1976.

Lindemann, E.   Symptomatology and management of acute grief. *American Journal of Psychiatry*. **101**: 141–148 (1944).

Luborsky, L., Singer, B. and Luborsky, L.   Comparative studies of psychotherapy: Is it true that "Everyone has won and all must have prizes?" *Archives of General Psychiatry*. **32**: 995–1008 (1975).

Malan, D.H.   *A study of brief psychotherapy*. New York: Plenum, 1963.

Malan, D.H.   *The frontier of brief psychotherapy*. New York: Plenum, 1976a.

Malan, D.H.   *Toward the validation of dynamic psychotherapy*. New York: Plenum, 1976b.

Malan, D.H., Heath, E.S., Bacal, H.A. and Balfour, F.H.G.   Psychodynamic changes in untreated neurotic patients: II. Apparently genuine improvements. *Archives of General Psychiatry*. **32**: 110–126 (1975).

Mann, J.   *Time-limited psychotherapy*. Cambridge, Mass: Harvard University Press, 1973.

Marks, I.   Behavioral psychotherapy of adult neurosis. In: Garfield, S.L. and Bergin, A.E. (Eds.), *Handbook of psychotherapy and behavior change*, 2nd ed. New York: Wiley, 1978.

Masters, W. and Johnson, V.   *Human sexual inadequacy*. Boston: Little, Brown, 1970.

McLean, P. and Hakstian, A.   Clinical depression: Comparative efficacy of outpatient treatments. *Journal of Consulting and Clinical Psychology*. **47**: 818–836 (1979).

Meichenbaum, D. and Turk, D.   The cognitive-behavioral management of anxiety, anger and pain. In: Davidson, P.O. (Ed.), *The behavioral management of anxiety, depression and pain*. New York: Brunner/Mazel, 1976.

Nichols, M.P.   Outcome of brief cathartic psychotherapy. *Journal of Consulting and Clinical Psychology*. **42**: 403–410 (1974).

Nichols, M.P. and Reifler, C.B.   The study of brief psychotherapy in a college health setting. *Journal of the American College Health Association*. **22**: 128–133 (1973).

Patterson, V., Levene, H. and Breger, L.   Treatment and training outcomes with two time-limited therapies. *Archives of General Psychiatry*. **25**: 161–167 (1971).

Percell, L.P., Berwick, P.T. and Beigel, A.   The effects of assertive training on self-concept and anxiety. *Archives of General Psychiatry*. **31**: 502–504 (1974).

Rachman, S., Hodgson, R. and Marks, I.M. Treatment of chronic obsessive-compulsive neurosis. *Behavior Research and Therapy.* **9**: 237-247 (1971).

Rachman, S. and Wilson, G.T. *The effects of psychological therapy.* Oxford: Pergamon Press, 1980.

Rabkin, R. *Strategic psychotherapy.* New York: Basic Books, 1977.

Rush, A.J., Beck, A.T., Kovacs, M. and Hollon, S. Comparative efficacy of cognitive therapy and pharmacotherapy in the treatment of depressed outpatients. *Cognitive Therapy and Research.* **1**: 17-37 (1977).

Shlien, J.M., Mosak, H.H. and Dreikurs, R. Effects of time limits: A comparison of two psychotherapies. *Journal of Counselling Psychology.* **9**: 31-34 (1962).

Sifneos, P. *Short-term psychotherapy and emotional crisis.* Cambridge, Mass.: Harvard University Press, 1972.

Sloane, R., Staples, F., Cristol, A., Yorkston, N. and Whipple, K. *Psychotherapy versus behavior therapy.* Cambridge, Mass.: Harvard University Press, 1975.

Smith, M.L., Glass, G.V. and Miller, T.I. *The benefits of psychotherapy.* Baltimore: John Hopkins University Press, 1980.

Watzlawick, P., Weakland, J. and Fisch, R. *Change: Principles of problem formation and problem resolution.* New York: W.W. Norton, 1974.

Weakland, J., Sisch, R., Watzlawick, P. and Bodin, A. Brief therapy: Focused problem resolution. *Family Process.* **13**: 141-168 (1974).

Weiss, R.L., Hops, H. and Patterson, G.R. A framework for conceptualizing marital conflict, a technology for altering it, some data from evaluating it. In: Hamerlynck, L.A., Handy, L.C. and Mash, E.J. (Eds.), *Behavior change: Methodology, concepts and practice.* Champaign, Ill.: Research Press, 1973.

Weiss, R.L. and Jacobson, N.S. Behavioral marital therapy as brief therapy. In: Budman, S.H. (Ed.), *Forms of brief therapy.* New York: Guilford Press, 1981.

Weissman, M.M., Neu, C., Rounsaville, B.J., DiMascio, A., Prusoff, B.A. and Klerman, G.L. Short-term interpersonal psychotherapy (IPT) for depression: Description and efficacy. Anchin, J.C. and Kiesler, D. (Eds.), *New perspectives in interpersonal psychotherapy,* in press.

Wilson, G.T. Behavior therapy as a short-term therapeutic approach. In: Budman, S.H. (Ed.), *Forms of brief therapy.* New York: Guilford Press, 1981.

Wolberg, L.R. The technique of short-term psychotherapy. In: Wolberg, L.R. (Ed.), *Short-term psychotherapy.* New York: Grune and Stratton, 1965.

Wolkon, G.H. Crisis theory, the application for treatment, and dependency. *Comprehensive Psychiatry.* **13**: 459-464 (1972).

10 Group Psychotherapies

Max Rosenbaum

GROUP THERAPIES

The first edition of this chapter was written in 1974. This revised chapter is being written in 1981, and we are well embarked on the decade of the eighties. Since the time the original chapter was written, the clinical practice of group psychotherapy has continued to expand in many forms though the theory has continued to lag far behind.

Clinical practitioners may be overwhelmed by the proliferation of group techniques that are classified as group therapy. The field of group psychotherapy continues to grow, and this growth has been in the nature of a geometric progression, as shown by the number of articles published in the field. The overwhelming majority of the articles are clinical in their presentation. The theoretic contributions are rather barren, and the preponderance of material is testimonial in nature. As one observes the entire field of treatment, there is no evidence that any school that has followed and developed a particular approach to psychotherapy, has agreed to disband because the approach simply did not work. Each school of psychotherapy continues to exist, and the adherents to a particular approach continue to cling to the concepts and techniques that they believe effective. While their loyalty is to be applauded, systematic research is in short supply.

There is a plethora of techniques and maneuvers, all labeled as group psychotherapy. A conference held in 1972 put the following under the rubric of group psychotherapy: encounter, sensitivity training, Gestalt therapy, bioenergetics, family therapy, consciousness-raising, transactional analysis, interactional analysis, psychosynthesis, theatre of encounter, group games, movement in depth, fantasy imagery, alexander techniques, rolfing. In a conference held in 1980 additional terms such as conjoint therapy entered the group therapy vocabulary.

There are many misconceptions about group psychotherapy, and it is important to differentiate group psychotherapy from the many group endeavors that psychiatrists, psychologists, social workers, counselors, pastoral counselors, psychiatric nurses and some paraprofessionals are engaged in (Mullan and Rosenbaum, 1962, 1978). I have defined group psychotherapy in my text on group therapy (Mullan and Rosenbaum, 1962, 1978) and have described the continuum of group psychotherapy. This ranges from the reparative and supportive approaches that are directed to strengthening weak defenses to the reconstructive approach that aims for deep-seated personality change. Many people mistakenly assume that every gathering of three or more persons who meet at the same time and in the same place and talk about their problems is a form of group psychotherapy. This is a distortion. In the broadest sense, there is some kind of release at work and probably some kind of therapy, but it is generally unplanned and may be called group interaction of a nontherapeutic nature. The emphasis here is not on personality change but on minimal personality alteration (not as in the practice of intensive group psychotherapy). People have joined groups to advance causes or interest since the beginning of recorded time. There are some who claim that they can validate group interaction experiences as far back as the early Egyptian civilization. In the Western culture, the Old and New Testaments give us detailed pictures of people working together in groups to advance or promote a variety of causes. Certainly if people sit down and face one another's problems in open discussion, there is the real possibility of serious communication. Generally, many distortions about one another come to the surface, and there is a feeling of relief among the participants. There is more sharing of responsibility as the process of communication develops. Distortions are lessened as a result. Optimally this results in a change in the culture and climate of the industry, school or institution — or wherever the group meeting is taking place. These groups are *human relations groups,* described by some people as meetings where "rap sessions" take place. The members of such groups are able to set goals that are comfortable for group participants. Decisions can be made without resort to parliamentary rules of procedure and legalisms. It is at this point that the small nontherapeutic group comes to an end. Communication has been enhanced and promoted. The institution within which the group was organized can function as an integrated setting and serve its community and goals more realistically. But there is a difference between the small nontherapeutic group and group psychotherapy. I favor a psychoanalytic approach to group psychotherapy, although other approaches will be described and discussed in this chapter.

When I refer to group psychotherapy in this chapter, I refer to planned therapeutic intervention. For the group members, there is almost always some preliminary diagnosis of psychopathology, however labeled, which can be described as personality malfunctioning that is to some degree disabling.

The intensive psychotherapeutic group is generally made up of seven to ten patients. The group meets two or more times each week, although some psychotherapists prefer to meet with group members once or more individually and then see them in the group once a week. This is referred to as combined psychotherapy. The interaction in the group is verbal as opposed to reactional or other motor methods. Nonverbal communication, such as body posture, facial mannerisms, seating arrangements (where the group member sits; is he or she part of the circle of patients or sitting on the outside; does he or she always take the same seat, etc.) are all noted by the group leader. The group members rarely know one another before they meet in the group. In smaller communities, some patients are concerned about meeting someone they know in other settings before they are placed in the group. They are encouraged to explore this fear, or, if it is too uncomfortable, they are given the option of leaving the group. I prefer the consistent use of the group method when patients are placed in the group. Therefore, patients are encouraged to discuss all problems within the group and are not encouraged to meet with the psychotherapist individually. The individual therapy setting is often used by patients as an opportunity to avoid material that may be more profitably explored in the group. Very dependent personalities, ambulatory psychotics, patients who have had very deprived childhood experiences with little contact with a stable parent figure or a parent surrogate may need continued individual meetings with the therapist even after they have joined the group. While it is true that the group experience may be *diluted* by these individual meetings, it is also true that the experience of the group therapy may create enormous pressure upon such a patient — pressure that he or she is unable to bear without the support of additional individual therapy sessions.

The group therapy setting differs greatly from discussion groups or groups that discuss events of the day and that are largely supportive. Structure and an agenda are kept to a minimum by the group therapist, who has prepared and selected patients for the group experience. The therapist who works with a group fosters interaction and the deep expression of emotion. Patients are encouraged to engage in continuous and deep exploration of childhood experiences. The interpersonal and intrapsychic problems of the present and past are discussed. In a therapy group that is psychoanalytically oriented, relationships that are based on transference are fostered, explored by continuous contact and "worked through." Toward the end of intensive group psychotherapy, transferences are markedly reduced, and people are seen as they are. The therapist who leads a group should have training in individual psychotherapy, psychopathology and psychodynamics and therefore be able to recognize and interpret transference phenomena. Unless he is unusually gifted, an untrained group leader cannot do this job. Through the model of the group therapist, members of the group are sensitized and become aware of transference phenomena. These transference distortions are then worked through in group setting.

There has been some distortion of what the term *transference* means. Transference is a basic concept in intensive psychodynamic therapy. In its simplest form the patient seeks, mostly on an unconscious level, to relieve or relive in the relationship with the therapist, his gratifying but usually traumatic experiences with significant figures from his earlier years. As a result of this working through in therapy, the patient's self-awareness is enhanced. He begins to recognize the roots of his patterns of interacting with other people in the therapy group. He begins to recognize his patterns of interaction with the group leader. Some practitioners become confused and do not realize that other group techniques that foster socialization, interaction and a feeling of belonging are not group psychotherapy of an intensive nature. Basic to intensive psychoanalytic group psychotherapy is the recognition of transference and countertransference phenomena. *Countertransference,* a term that is often distorted, means that the therapist uses his own distorting and restrictive defenses against a clear perception of and response to the material that the patient brings up either in the group or in individual meetings. The therapist usually uses these defenses because he has learned them as a way of avoiding the experiencing of his own anxiety and guilt. It should be noted that a large group that has too many participants precludes member-to-member interaction, and the goal of deep-seated characterological change is blocked or thwarted.

When the student of group therapy is confronted with the variety of techniques that are professed to be group psychotherapy, it is valuable to have some guidelines or structure, or else the entire field appears to be in a state of chaos. I suggest that the reader constantly keep in mind as the reference point that group therapy should be conceived of as a continuum rather than a compartmentalizing of the "systems" of group treatment. The continuum ranges from the repressive-inspirational to the regressive-reconstructive, which reflect the two extremes in the goal of effecting personality change. Between these two extremes are the reparative and supportive types of therapy. The reparative approaches are directed toward the strengthening of weak defenses.

In earlier writings I have discussed in detail the history of group psychotherapy in the United States (Mullan and Rosenbaum, 1962, 1978; Rosenbaum and Snadowsky, 1976; Rosenbaum, 1965). The field has grown to the point where there are many competitors for the term "founder." As far as I can observe, Pratt, a Boston internist, introduced the use of group procedures in his work around the turn of the twentieth century. It is worth mentioning that group psychotherapy evolved in Boston, the heartland of American democracy. Indeed, it is a technique that stresses peer relationships and the "wellness" of the patient rather than the "illness." From its beginnings, many of group psychotherapy's origins were pragmatic, and practice usually ran far ahead of systematic theory. It is certainly true that group therapy can be practiced very authoritatively, but this is not recommended if one wants to make optimum use of the potentials lying dormant when a group of patients assembles to engage in group therapy.

Some writers have described Freud as a *basic figure* in group psychotherapy, but in my opinion it is inaccurate to attribute this type of importance to Freud. While Freud did outline a concept of group psychology in 1921 (Freud, 1957), his focus was on individual psychodynamics. Freud's bias was a biological orientation. In the history of psychoanalysis, instincts were pursued as the central theme. Only much later were object relations perceived as important (Diatkine, 1978). Freud spoke of a "group of two," but he did not incorporate the concepts of group dynamics or cultural anthropology other than the early writings of Le Bon, the French sociologist who described mob-behavior. Possibly Freud's interest in the group was "turned off" by his personal difficulties with Adler and Jung, both of whom appear to have been involved with the idea of group psychology. In this respect, Jung looked for a rather mystical or religious significance in his approach to the group. Adler, very interested in the political concepts of socialism, was always attracted to the idea of working with community groups as well as with working-class patients. Many of his students became involved in work with groups early in the history of group psychotherapy. None of what has been written should minimize Freud's contribution to social psychology and ego psychology. While many students have emphasized that Freud based his theories on instinct, Freud never ignored the relationships of people to one another. In my opinion he overemphasized psychoanalysis as a basis for social psychology. "The contrast between individual psychology and social or group psychology, which at first glance may seem to be full of significance, loses a great deal of its sharpness when it is examined more closely . . . . In the individual's mental life someone else is invariably involved, as a model, as an object, as a helper, as an opponent; and so from the very first individual psychology, in this extended but entirely justifiable sense of the words, is at the same time social psychology as well" (Freud, 1957, p. 69). Freud's major conclusion with regard to groups is as follows: In the group, the individual surrenders his own ego ideal and replaces it with the group ideal of the leader of the group. The process is unconscious. Freud's major points concern the significance of the superego in the behavior of the group: the importance of the group leader and the libidinal ties between group members that are at work in the formation of a group.

Many of the "new" techniques that proliferate almost daily can be traced back quite easily to early pioneers in the fields of individual psychotherapy and group therapy. Many of the "new pioneers" — if indeed one can call them pioneers — have not done their homework. A trip to the library will quickly indicate the history of the "newly discovered approach." For example, many contemporary psychotherapists feel that they have originated something truly innovative in using techniques of self-disclosure in which the therapist shares feelings or problems with the group members. Yet Paul Schilder, an early figure in the field of psychotherapy, who based his work on psychoanalytic concepts and who had a great genius for grasping psychological and physiological concepts, was carrying out experimental projects in group psychotherapy with low income patients at Bellevue Hospital in New York City as far back as the early 1930s. At that time he was quite forthright in expressing his value systems with the group he was working with. He was quite outspoken in defense of his value system and made no effort to obscure or conceal his feelings (Schilder, 1939, 1940). There is a tendency to overlook the fact that different practitioners often express their ethnic and cultural origins. Schilder, who stemmed from an Austro-Hungarian background, was very conscious of the community in which he existed. His personality was active and his attitude inquiring, and this reflected itself in his practice of group psychotherapy.

Those who treat people in groups stem from every school of individual psychotherapy; and every major school has attempted to apply its theoretic orientation to group psychotherapy with resultant confusion. On occasion there is a breakdown in communication because there is no common language. For example, in academia there is a group known as *social learning* theorists. In psychoanalysis, there is a group known as *object relations* theorists. There are some marked theory differences between the two groups, but there is a tremendous similarity. Both groups believe that behavior patterns can be radically modified by the effect of one person upon another. Both groups agree that the personality of the infant and the young child is especially vulnerable to behavior modification that is permanent in nature. This confusion in language and possibly theory puzzles the student of group psychotherapy, but one should remember that the relief of suffering is primary for the practitioner who cannot wait for theory to catch up to practice. The majority of practitioners who work with groups and who come from training that is psychoanalytic in nature or influenced by the concepts of psychoanalysis, attempt to explain group psychotherapy in terms of individual dynamics. Some have struggled beyond Freud's speculations, expressed in his book *Group psychology and the analysis of the ego* (1957). The International Congress of Group Psychotherapy held in Copenhagen in August 1980 showed evidence of the continuing interest and desire to move beyond Freud's ideas.

As noted above, Freud was highly influenced by the concepts of Le Bon, the French sociologist who described the group as a collective entity — a distinct being. From this, Freud deduced that the group is held together by common identification with a leader, and in his book Freud described what he called the *primary group.* Freud's speculations, which is what they actually were, have been adopted by many group psychotherapists as fact and as a theoretic rationale for their work in group psychotherapy. Freud stated: "The indestructible strength of the family as a natural group formation rests upon the fact that this necessary presupposition of the father's equal love can have a real application to the family." Therefore, to extend this concept, the therapist's love for the patient and the patient's positive feeling for the therapist sustains the individual patient in the move to the psychotherapy group.

The greatest strides in group treatment appear to have been made in the United States, but there was a great deal of activity going on in Great Britain at the same time. Most of this clinical work was stimulated during World War II, and is very active at this time.

During the 1930s patient groups were formed in and out of mental hospitals in the United States. The purpose of this repressive inspirational approach was to foster a sense of group identification. A.A. Low, a Chicago-based psychiatrist, organized a movement called Recovery, Incorporated (Low, 1950). His groups were generally large and self-directed, and he called his method "will training," since he rejected psychoanalysis as a therapeutic technique and philosophy. His first group began in 1937 and was composed of patients who had been in Illinois psychiatric hospitals and who had received shock treatments or physical therapies. The emphasis in Recovery, Incorporated groups is upon self-help with much attention paid to group camaraderie. It is questionable whether Low ever researched the literature when he began to work with his groups. Interestingly, Pratt (1953), the pioneer in group therapy in the United States, and a whole group of therapists after him, also made much use of group camaraderie. Although Pratt worked closely with clergy, at the outset of his work with groups of patients, *his* groups were not oriented to religion but to health care. All of these people with the exception of Pratt, without being aware of it, were following the precept of Dejerine, the French psychiatrist who at the turn of the twentieth century wrote: "Psychotherapy depends wholly and exclusively upon the beneficial influence of one person upon another" (Dejerine and Gauckler, 1913). Many therapists, as noted earlier, are quick to label their techniques as new discoveries, but these discoveries seem to vanish very quickly. In 1957 Corsini tried to identify and label more than twenty-five different methods of group psychotherapy by name. Many of the methods that he listed and labeled have disappeared from the literature, which supports the point made earlier — practice has been way ahead of theory.

The earliest group treatment techniques used in state mental hospitals consisted of groups of patients organized with a leader presenting the material that was to be used for guided discussion. This *directive-didactic* approach is still used in many mental hospitals. The stress is verbal-intellectual, and the technique is very applicable to regressed, psychotic patients in hospitals settings. With its emphasis on conditioning and pedagogy, the technique is also helpful in prisons, where group members evidence marked social distortion patterns. This technique is also used with paroled convicts or juvenile offenders in penal settings. The therapist serves as a leader in this approach. He may deliver talks or lectures, which must be well planned so that there is a maximum structure for group members. Often the materials are printed in a kind of book, and there is a logical and planned sequence. On occasion a group member will be encouraged to bring up a problem that is then used for general discussion. It is believed that the planned presentation of material both stimulates and controls the associations, as the group members gradually begin to participate in the lectures and group discussion. The technique is helpful in a hospital where there is a staff turnover. Since the program is carefully planned, another group leader may take over rather easily. The idea of the printed word is not too unlike that of a Bible-reading group, and the book format carries additional weight. The lecture and discussion approach discourages silence, which is not helpful when one works with psychotics, in contrast to a group leader's experience with a group of neurotics where silence in the group might indicate reflection or introspection about a particular issue. The *directive-didactic approach* does not pressure the group participant. The group leader may stop his presentation at any time or return to material that has been presented previously. Some hospitals, with the help of creative library staffs, have organized programs of bibliotherapy with assigned selected readings. Recently there has been an interest in poetry therapy where poetry is used as a bibliotherapy technique. The approach described has been effective in working with a variety of regressed patients. It makes maximum use of personnel, who are encouraged to follow the planned program (Klapman, 1950, 1952).

The work of behavior therapists (see Chapter 6) falls into the broad category of directive-didactic approaches, since specific symptoms are treated with an intellectual approach. In one study patients in a group who suffered from phobic disorders were exposed to group desensitization. The group leader constructed a hierarchy of anxiety stimuli, and patients were exposed to training in muscle relaxation. The group leader then introduced stronger anxiety stimuli while at the same time encouraging muscular relaxation. It should be noted that such techniques work with homogeneous groups – patients all suffering from comparable symptomatology. There have been very positive results presented with groups composed of people who feared airplane travel. The stress in the behavioral approach is upon relief of symptoms. It is believed that relief of symptoms will lead to relief of anxiety, which is the goal of treatment.

The idea of *desensitizing* patients in group structure was applied by Wynne (1979), who placed chronic psychotic patients in a "normalization procedure" that she described as "movable group therapy." The patients were transported in an unlabeled car from a state mental hospital to parks and restaurants in the community. Although the majority of studies of group therapy with chronic psychotics indicated that the technique was only minimally effective (Bednar and Lawlis, 1971; Parloff and Dies, 1977), Wynne decided to move the group of patients *out* of the hospital *into* the community. She moved the group out of the hospital onto the hospital lawn and from there into a small park with meetings held around a picnic table. Her results were very encouraging, since after one year twenty of the original patients in the group of forty had been discharged, and after three years only eight patients of the group of forty remained in the state hospital. Whether this result is due to the method employed or whether any techniques will work that disrupts the stagnation which occurs when patients become "fossilized" in the structured state hospital will be left to the reader to decide.

It is possible that an insight-oriented approach is harmful for the majority of acutely psychotic patients (although there is debate about this), and an insight-oriented group therapy approach may be too much to handle for the psychotic patient with weak ego structure, in whom "ego-disruptive" techniques may create too much anxiety. Leopold (1976), working with psychotic patients in a mental hospital, used a group approach that stressed principles of support and reality testing. The rationale behind this approach is related to the early work in group psychotherapy which stressed group comaraderie. In Leopold's approach, used with inpatient therapy groups composed of patients diagnosed as psychotic, the groups are run along a gradient that is based upon the patient's regressive levels of fixation. Patients are moved into "graded groups" as they show that they are able to tolerate more therapeutic intervention and independence. Maxmen (1978) appears to have expanded on this when he used an educative model. Here the emphasis is upon the patient's capacity to *think* clinically and note the consequences of the emotional disturbance. This goes beyond symptom relief.

In 1975, a long-term follow-up study was conducted in a British mental hospital. The patients were treated by didactic group psychotherapy and relaxation techniques (Bovill, 1977). The study came after an earlier follow-up study. The author of the study concluded that the group psychotherapy offered was beneficial to the neurotic patients who came to the hospital and "economical of doctors' time . . . ." While the researcher stressed the term neurotic in her report, she was clearly working with a population of more acutely disturbed patients.

Sotile, Kilmann and Follingstad (1977) formed a sexual enhancement workshop where group systematic desensitization was the technique used to alleviate sexual anxiety. The workshop consisted of a combination of very specific procedures presented to couples in both individual sessions and group settings. Some of the procedures included masturbation retraining and sexual fantasy exercises.

Lawrence and Walter (1978) used behavior modification with a therapy group. Each client joined a group to alleviate a *specific problem*. Their before and after therapy findings indicated that group behavioral treatment worked.

Since the beginning of the practice of group therapy in the United States, there have been many advocates of the *repressive-inspirational approach*. In this approach the emphasis is upon fostering a sense of group identification (Marsh, 1931; Kotkov, 1950). The group that is formed is strongly supportive, and a subculture of support is set up. The leader's enthusiasm or charisma plays a major part in the success or failure of such a group. Many group movements, such as the original Synanon (the drug addicts' treatment approach), [1] Alcoholics Anonymous, the Christian Science religious movement, Weight Watchers, are part of the repressive-inspirational approach. The members of the group realize that they are "all in the same boat," and this realization leads to a tremendous sense of relief for group participants and serves as a stimulus to move forward. For the practitioner of the *repressive-inspirational* approach, the following mechanisms are at work and may be utilized at any time: esprit de corps, communal feelings, an environment that is friendly, group status, group identification, socialization of the group, loss of isolation, ego support. The sharing of experiences and reassurance are of major importance, as are the testimony and example of others.

It is interesting to note that many practitioners of a repressive-inspirational approach appear to have little or no awareness of the history of the approach. Rogeness and Stewart (1978) describe "The Positive Group: A Therapeutic Group in the Treatment of Adolescents," where the technique consists of permitting only positive comments. The "chairman" of the group, patient or staff member, makes positive statements about himself or other in the group. It is believed that the adolescent members of the group, through role modeling, begin to make positive comments about themselves, recognize their own strengths and improve their self-esteem and self-image. While the group is supposed to provide models of a "different type of interpersonal interaction," it is clearly a group where the principle of positive reinforcement is at work. It also has the elements of a religious experience comparable to the "born again" Christian movement. In all fairness, this type of approach does not claim to make an enduring impact upon personality or personality difficulties, but it may serve as the opening wedge in group psychotherapy. This type of technique I label as "interventionist," and if used with discretion and minimal abrasiveness, it may prove helpful. Patients who are placed in a group during the first three weeks of their hospitalization appear to benefit and do not fall into the routine of chronic institutionalization (Kanas, Rogers, Kreth, Patterson and Campbell, 1980).

In a very novel use of the inspirational and supportive technique, Campbell, Brock, Van Gee and Greenfield (1980) used the model of a multiple-family group for a crisis intervention technique. The group members consisted of the families of burn patients who were hospitalized after a tank car exploded in a small town in Tennessee, a community with traditional Southern "rural values," where the people were skeptical if not outright distrustful of psychiatry. The group process was used for support, for catharsis and to demonstrate alternative ways of coping with the problems of the burn patients, who required enormous personal care. The group was able to utilize representatives of several disciplines — the hospital chaplain, medical social worker, psychiatric nurse consultant and

---

[1] Before Synanon became a totalitarian cult.

liaison psychiatrist, as well as medical personnel. It enabled the group members to focus upon and face post-hospital concerns as well as the present. A comparable type of intervention is used with families of people who are terminally ill, or currently with families of those who are taken as political hostages.

When patients face illnesses that appear totally disabling, panic often overwhelms them. In work with adult diabetics who were going blind, group therapy was found to be very effective as it counteracted the patients' fear of retinopathy and death. Oehler-Giarratana and Fitzgerald (1980) found that group therapy was an important first step in the rehabilitation of blind diabetics, and they were able to carry on this program in the office of a large private ophthalmology practice.

Patients suffering from other physical disorders that they belive to be totally disabling are clearly helped by the group therapy experience, as they find that they are not alone and that others have surmounted the same problems (Bilodeau and Hackett, 1971). In the group of blind diabetics, it was particularly reassuring for the patients to have a group leader who had been totally blind for six years and had outlived the five-year death statistic that they feared.

Cunningham, Strasberg and Roback (1978) have reported on the use of group psychotherapy for medical patients in nonpsychiatric settings. Among the types of medical patients who have been treated in groups and profited from such therapy are patients suffering from eczema, allergies, asthma, emphysema, gastric or duodenal ulcers, myocardial infarctions, Parkinson's disease, multiple sclerosis and cancer, as well as quadriplegics, chronic hemodialysis patients and patients with recurrent osteomyelitis. Groups have been organized in a wide variety of hospital and outpatient clinic medical settings. Amputees have been treated in groups (Rogers, MacBride, Whylie, and Freeman, 1977-78), as well as rheumatoid arthritics (Udelman and Udelman, 1978) and parents of children with leukemia (Gilder, Buschman, Sitarz and Wolf, 1978). In all of these groups, the sharing of experiences and group support were of major help.

There are three major forces at work in group psychotherapy: an approach that stresses *action;* an approach that stresses the *emotional;* an approach that stresses the *intellect.* The *action approach* and the *emotional approach* are embedded in the repressive-inspirational psychotherapy method.

PSYCHODRAMA

Jacob L. Moreno introduced psychodrama into the United States in 1925. Prior to this he had worked in Vienna with a theatre of spontaneity based on action methods. He claimed that he devised the terms group therapy and group psychotherapy to emphasize the importance of the group in the treatment of the individual. In his theatre of spontaneity he bagan to use play and role-playing techniques. His original Theatre of Spontaneity was located near the

Vienna Opera, which may have influenced his entire approach. Moreno, who died in 1974, was himself an outgoing, dynamic man — and like a performer in grand opera appeared to be larger than life. His techniques reflected his approach to human behavior. He was very charismatic, and his personality, which may have been abrasive to some psychiatrists, has obscured his outstanding contribution to the field of group psychotherapy.

After introducing psychodrama, Moreno developed modifications of the method such as sociodrama, role-playing, sociometry and axiodrama. He stated that five instruments are used in his method of psychodrama:

The First Instrument — The Stage. The stage is intended to be an extension of life and is beyond the reality of life. It provides the patient with a "space for living." The earliest American psychodrama theatre was built with three stage levels, with the top stage, the balcony, used for superego figures. A circular stage may be seen as the aspiration levels of the patient on stage, as he moves from one circle to another.

The Second Instrument — The Patient or Subject. The patient is requested to be himself on stage. He is encouraged to share his thoughts and feelings, and here the skill of the psychodrama director becomes very important. According to Moreno, the patient is *not* to perform but to respond as things come to his mind. This is related to the theory of spontaneity, and Moreno stated that spontaneity operates in the present. He distinguished between the creativity that is related to the act itself and spontaneity, which is related to the readiness for the act. Whether many of these definitions involve playing with language is debatable, but the reader should attempt to look further to see what Moreno was striving for   freedom of expression. Once the patient expresses himself, a process of enactment occurs in which the patient may present a current problem, discuss his concerns about a future problem or engage in role-playing to clarify his fears or anxieties. The stress is upon the *actional* and *emotional,* with the patient in psychodrama actively discouraged from performing but encouraged to be what he is. Terms have been invented to describe the techniques that are used: mirror techniques, reversal of roles, double ego, auxiliary ego and others too numerous to list. Some of the techniques that Moreno listed seem to obscure rather than clarify, but some terms have been incorporated into the language of everyday life. A very popular technique in psychodrama is role-reversal. A father and son who are constantly bickering or overtly hostile to one another are encouraged to reverse roles — the father taking the part of the son and the son the part of the father. They are encouraged to feel, think and experience the behavior of the person whom they are role-playing and role-reversing. Auxiliary egos represent absent people or ideals, delusions or hallucinations.

The Third Instrument — The Psychodrama Director. The director is a *psychotherapist;* he may attack, joke or laugh with the patient. He may decide to be passive or active, or may feel that it is wiser for the patient to dominate the psychodrama session.

The director, as a *producer,* keeps the action going. Through all this he maintains rapport with the audience, which is always an integral part of the psychodrama.

The director is also an *analyst;* he integrates into his interpretation of the psychodrama information that he has obtained from the patient's family, friends or neighbors. He also integrates and interprets the responses of members of the audience watching the psychodrama.

The Fourth Instrument – The Auxiliary Egos. The use of auxiliary egos (staff or therapeutic aids) helps the director, for this group of people serves as an extension of the director. The auxiliary egos are important, since they serve as therapeutic actors and represent ideals, delusions or absent people in the patient's world.

The Fifth Instrument – The Audience Watching the Psychodrama. The patient may help audience participants as he reenacts all of the combined problems of the members of the audience. The audience is very important because it serves as a sounding board for the patient. The audience is a mixed group, and this heterogeneity elicits spontaneous responses from both audience and patient. Moreno believed that an isolated patient who lives in a world of hallucinations and delusions will be helped by an understanding and accepting audience. To this writer's knowledge there is no record of a hostile audience that was destructive to the patient.

According to Moreno, Freud was either ignorant of or did not understand the valuable therapeutic implications of the Greek drama. He also stated that he rediscovered the Greek drama and brought it up to date. With his usual expansiveness he overlooked the fact that Freud was concerned with different approaches to human behavior. It is extremely unlikely that Freud was either ignorant of or unaware of the Greek drama and its value, particularly when one observes Freud's interest in antiquities.

In the psychodramatic approach to group therapy Moreno effected mental catharsis by concentrating on the initial phase rather than the end phase of the drama. He believed catharsis to be embodied in every form of human activity and said that his technique and theory were devoted to finding both the different forms of catharsis and what catharsis means. He declared spontaneity to be the principle behind catharsis, and claimed that he placed the psyche itself on the psychodramatic stage. According to his theory, the psyche originally came from the group, was transformed into a stage performance by an actor on the stage, and is returned to the group in the form of psychodrama.

Psychodrama as a treatment modality and theory has gone through many ups and downs. It has never really caught on as part of the mainstream of psychotherapeutic practice. Moreno constantly sturggled to spread his concepts in the field of psychiatry, psychology, social work and education. His books have been translated into many languages, and he informed me that his technique had been used in Russia and in Shanghai, China. The techniques he pioneered are embodied in many so-called avant-garde techniques. His approach has found its way into many industrial counseling settings, and possibly with the resurgence of interest in the use of paraprofessionals in psychiatric settings there may be a marked renewal of interest in psychodrama (Moreno, 1953, 1969). Since Moreno's death, his wife, Zerka Moreno, has carried on his work.

THERAPEUTIC SOCIAL CLUBS AND COMMUNITIES

Recovery, Incorporated was discussed earlier. In England there were also psychiatrists concerned about methods of reaching large groups of psychiatric patients. During the late 1940s there were professional papers presented indicating that many varieties of group psychotherapy were being practiced in England. One of the important techniques, promoted by the British psychiatrist Joshua Bierer (1948), is the *therapeutic social club.* This technique is particularly directed toward the promotion of social participation skills among patients who have just left a closed mental hospital setting. In these clubs the therapist plays a largely passive role and minimizes his presence. Bierer began his work in England in 1938, and the first club was formed at Runwell Mental Hospital. The patients were and still are encouraged to organize the social clubs along parliamentary lines and to follow rules of parliamentary procedure. It is clear that considerable social skill and awareness are required. In fact, what Bierer may have proposed without knowing it was a form of modeling behavior, since patients learn from others as they are encouraged to collect dues, arrange their own social activities and care for the premises where they hold their meetings. This group of experiences is an introduction to the stresses of the "world outside" the mental hospital, and the acquisition of a behavioral repertoire helps patients deal with "culture shock" as they leave the protected mental hospital. Even today, with the so-called open mental hospital, there remain many institutional settings where patients begin to lose the skill of social participation. The day hospital that gained favor in the 1950s is very much along the lines of Bierer's original orientation, although Bierer did not originate it. Another outgrowth of the therapeutic social club is the "halfway house," where patients often reside as they move from the mental hospital to the stresses of the community.

While Maxwell Jones (1953), the exponent of the therapeutic community concept, has not based his work upon Bierer's experiences, his entire effort to promote parity among professionals and patients and break down the caste structure and heiarchies that exist in mental hospitals is all part of a concept that encourages patients to stress their strengths rather than their pathology. There are probably mental hospital and outpatient clinics that do not encourage.

or promote equalitarian structures because of many unresolved status needs of the professional personnel. However, study of the early history of therapeutic social clubs indicates that long before World War II efforts were made to encourage mental patients to rely more upon their own resources.

ACTIVITY GROUP THERAPY AND GROUP PSYCHOTHERAPY WITH CHILDREN AND ADOLESCENTS

In the treatment of children the effort is made to support the child's ego growth. During this period the child learns to cope with his inner chaos, the emotions that almost, or on occasion do overwhelm him. This child finally achieves an adequate interaction with the world and the community he lives in. The group experience provides a family-like setting, which leads to corrective emotional experiences.   The group therapist guides by clarifying verbally, directs and restrains protectively.

In 1896 Witmer, an American psychologist, established the first psycho-educational clinic for emotionally disturbed children who manifested evidence of their confusion in the school setting. There was no substantive work done in a psychodynamic approach to treatment of children in groups until 1934, when Slavson began working with groups of children at the Jewish Board of Guardians in New York City. He described his concepts as stemming from group work, progressive education and psychoanalysis. It is interesting that Slavson's social philosophy was that of a Socialist, and he was very interested in reaching groups of people. He described his approach as therapy *by* the group rather than therapy *in* the group. By the time he reported his work at a conference in 1943, he had treated 800 children in sixty-three different groups. Describing his treatment as "interpersonal therapy," he treated children who ranged in age from eight to fifteen years. Because his emphasis was on *activity* rather than *interview*, his approach is called *activity group therapy*. Children were placed in a structured situation, and the group leader planned his actions according to a theory (Slavson, 1943). This approach is not to be confused with a variety of recreational approaches to children.[2]

In the controlled group the leader sets up a permissive environment for the children. He does not offer interpretations but permits the children to act out conflicts and emotions. He sets the ground rules, and there are specific limits. Slavson formulated his approach as he observed that children communicate largely through motor activity, and the use of play gives them an opportunity to work out fantasy life and tensions. This can easily be observed as one watches children at play. They do not need an automobile to create and fantasy the

---

[2]Forty-nine of Slavson's most significant papers have been collected in a volume, *Dynamics of group psychotherapy* (1979).

driving experience. His goal was and is the control and education of the emotions of the child.

Generally the setting for activity group therapy is work in arts and crafts. The activity group lasts for about an hour and a half — a time span that does not unduly fatigue either the child or the group leader. The group leader then provides a meal for the children, and they all work together in this task. The meal preparation, eating together, cleaning the utensils and dishes are all part of the sharing experience. The group leader gratifies the orality of the child and functions as a benign parent surrogate. There may be planned picnics or swim parties, but all of this is done within the theory of educating and controlling the child's emotions. The warm, accepting and giving group leader has set up a positive transference, and the therapy is situational in nature. It is believed that insight develops gradually as the child is accepted. The group leader studies the interaction of the children and obtains a comprehensive picture of the child's conflicts and behavior problems. An activity group is composed of eight children of the same age, and careful structuring is necessary to achieve a balance. For example, the group leader might place in the same group a motoric, aggressive child to counter the passive, withdrawn child.

Many of Slavson's ideas were quickly adopted in outpatient clinics, hospitals and social agencies. Modifications of his approach are used with children of pre-school age, in an extension of activity group therapy. The emphasis here is particularly on play. The very infantile and demanding child is able to express his enormous needs for mothering through the use of play materials. But unlike the situation of individual play therapy, the child has to share and cannot have the group leader to himself. When the age range moves up to adolescence, there is more emphasis on the *discussion* group, but attention is still paid to meal planning, feeding and so on, activities that would generally be discouraged in the adult therapy group (Godenne, 1964).

In low-income, ghetto-type community settings the patient population may stem from such disordered home settings that there is a great need for a stable parent surrogate who serves as a model and provides a benign and accepting climate. By means of this model, early adolescents learn to move from infantile impulse behavior to a more *real* appreciation of the *real* world's demands. In this case the group, based on activity group therapy, meets a specific need and is much more effective than the intellectual approach, which may work with adolescents who come from middle-class settings where there is a more stable family structure and more attention is paid to the resolution of emotional problems through verbal interaction.

There are arguments among practitioners of activity group therapy as to the wisdom or inadvisability of placing only adolescents of the same sex in the same group. There are reports of mixed groupings, but much of this work seems related to the therapist's own personality, the supply of patients and treatment goals. There has been work in groups with psychotic children and adolescents (Sobel and Geller, 1964; Speers and Lansing, 1964, 1968).

There are few follow-up studies of group therapy with children and adolescents, and the studies that have been carried out do not control for time and other factors. But one can fairly say that group therapy for children and adolescents helps them feel unconditionally accepted by group members and the group leader. This in turn helps trigger the child's or adolescent's own growth possibilities.

In a culture where basic values are constantly being challenged and reevaluated, where the very concept of the family as a social unit is being attacked, the need for a planned group therapy for children and adolescents would seem more than ever a critical need in psychotherapy — especially when the suicide rate for adolescents is increasing.

As an additional note of caution to the practitioner, Slavson (1964) has cautioned against the use of traditional psychoanalytic psychotherapy with adolescents. He states:

> The essentiality of groups in the treatment of the young lies more than it does with adults in corrective relationships in the living situation, and all that it implies, in addition to reweighing of psychic forces.

In the treatment of adolescents in groups there should be an emphasis on the functioning of the ego. Consequently, the approach will combine education, guidance and psychotherapy. The group should have a minimum of a didactic approach. The actuality of the here-and-now problem should be emphasized in the group meetings rather than unconscious material. The group leader should use every opportunity, without becoming pedantic, to encourage psychological awareness in group members. Slavson called this the stimulation of psychological literacy.

For some period of time, *activity group psychotherapy* was eagerly used by professionals; then it feel into a period of disuse. It is now being used again as the treatment modality for emotional problems of latency. It appears to be the best method for *primary behavior disorders,* and one paper (Beard, Goertzel and Pearce, 1958) even reported its use with regressed adult psychotics. The practitioner should remember that activity group therapy was the first method of group treatment of children with a theoretic design. It is basic to activity-interview group psychotherapy and therapeutic play groups in schools, as well as play group therapy. While interpretations of behavior are not advanced, the principles and practices of these therapy approaches are rooted in psychoanalytic concepts based upon Freud's writings. The practitioner should always remember that the basic concept in activity group therapy is that behavioral problems of children and personality problems that result are to be attributed to experience. Further, these experiences can be modified by corrective experiences in a conditioned environment. This is *not* behaviorism, since the approach is based upon psychoanalytic concepts. Rosenthal (1977) has set forth specific qualifications and tasks for the activity group therapist.

Williams, Lewis, Copeland, Tucker and Feagan (1978) used group therapy with latency-age children in a short-term inpatient setting. They used Slavson's model of the leader, permissive and accepting, but were more active. They incorporated Redl and Wineman's model, which combines clinician and educator. Finally, they incorporated Vintner's "rehabilitation" model, where the leader is active and the group is used to model socially accepted norms and values.

Ginsberg, Stuttman and Hummel (1978) trained parents to do client-centered play therapy with their own child. Training is done in groups, in an expanded version of the activity group approach.

The field of adolescent group psychotherapy is weak with respect to theoretic models. The emphasis is upon techniques that may be effective, such as confrontational techniques, encounter techniques, marathon groups, peer groups. Many of the models are borrowed from work with adults and add little to our understanding of the uniqueness of adolescence.

Psychoanalytic group therapy was discussed earlier in this chapter, and the more specific approaches have been detailed in other writings (Mullan and Rosenbaum, 1978; Yalom, 1978). There are other modifications of this basic approach. The "newer approaches" appear to be a reaction to the more rigid application of psychoanalytic concepts. They seem to reflect the disenchantment of some practitioners who had hoped for a much quicker solution to the emotional difficulties of patients. Berne, the founder of transactional analysis (Rosenbaum and Berger, 1975), looked forward to the time when patients would be "cured" after one meeting with a group therapist. It is a dream worth pursuing, but I remain skeptical as to whether it is feasible. Two approaches that are part of current therapy methods are the Gestalt therapy approach with groups and the transactional analysis approach to groups.

GESTALT THERAPY AND ITS USE IN GROUP THERAPY

Frederick S. Perls, known as Fritz Perls, was born in Germany and stated that he was trained in psychoanalysis with some of its outstanding teachers (Wilhelm Reich, Karen Horney). He moved to South Africa and there developed his concepts of Gestalt therapy. The term *gestalt* stems from the classic work of psychologists in Germany who used the word to describe the holistic quality of the human organism. It is extremely doubtful that they envisioned its use in the way Perls decided to employ the term. In fact, the leading exponent of Gestalt psychology states that it has nothing in common with Gestalt therapy (Henle, 1978). Gestalt therapy encompasses a highly flexible approach to intensive psychotherapy, and Perls believed it to be a theory of personality. Some of his students use the term to describe an entire approach to life. Perls moved to New York City, where with his then-wife he trained many therapists.

He moved to Miami, Florida; Cleveland, Ohio; Carmel, California (Esalen); and, just before his death, Vancouver, British Columbia. In each place he trained younger therapists, and they became his enthusiastic followers.

Perls was a brilliant and charismatic therapist. He was remarkably intuitive, but could become easily bored with a patient. He did not hesitate to express his boredom and simply dismiss a patient. He believed that individual therapy had outlived its usefulness. Although his students describe his work as group therapy, he actually conducted one-to-one therapy in a group setting: He would sit next to a chair called the "hot seat," where he would work with the patient, who was seated in that chair. He would vary in his approach. He placed great value on dreams, but he might respond to posture, voice patterns or a problem that the patient presented. For the most part, the entire responsibility for participation was placed upon the patient, who was part of the group. There was no encouragement to participate. Perhaps Perls felt that observation of others was therapeutic. He stressed the immediate, and many of his techniques were and are related to psychodrama although he never acknowledged this specifically. He attempted to evoke intense emotional responses by asking the patient to take on different roles; for example, he might encourage the patient to role-play the experience of being dominated as a child, although he would not use terms such as role-play. He was able to evoke very intense emotional responses and memories. In his approach to dreams he stated that each part of the dream, objects as well as human beings, represented a part of the shelf of the patient who presented the dream. This he called a part of the individual dreamer's gestalt. The patient was urged to express each of the dream symbols. Again, this is very closely related to psychodrama. The stress in the Gestalt therapy approach is upon catharsis, which is very dramatic and which Perls believed would lead to basic change in personality. Perls theorized about the neurosis as follows: There are five layers. The first is the layer of social behavior. This he believed to be meaningless, consisting of trite or stereotyped behavior. The second is role-playing, which is dependent upon which stereotyped piece of behavior is to be examined. Third is impasse — when the therapist refuses to accept this stereotyped behavior. The patient then experiences enormous fear and a sense of emptiness. Fourth is implosion. The opposing forces within the patient are in battle, and the patient may often describe this as terrifying. Perls felt that this was a fear of death. The fifth layer is an explosion, which may express itself in enormous joy, anger or grief. While there has been distortion of Perls's viewpoint, he was too aware a therapist to settle for abreaction per se. Toward the end of his life he was quite blunt in attacking the practitioners who espouse instant joy or instant cure. He called them "phoney therapists."

His techniques, while stimulating, appear to be primarily a reaction to group therapists who become too static and too intellectual in their approach. He discouraged free group interaction and was definitely in control of the group. Since he was a gifted therapist, he may have justified this type of control as necessary in order to achieve his goals. Perls treated any comments made by other group members as interference. Many participants in the groups that Perls conducted state that they were helped by a process of *empathic identification*. Perls stressed simple terms and used vernacular expressions. His approach has been modified by students of his who maintain a longer involvement with patients who come for treatment. Of course, there are others more fascinated by the "gimmickry" his approach may foster. It is reasonable to ask what happens to the resistant or rather detached patient who is exposed to Gestalt group therapy. In my opinion such a patient would get lost. Perls's work, like many contemporary approaches, may reflect a certain impatience with a more introspective approach and is probably very feasible with patients who desire much more interaction with the therapist. Also, being the center of attention, in the "hot seat," may be very important for some patients. (See Perls, 1969a, b; Perls, Hefferline and Goodman, 1961; Fagan and Shepherd, 1970; Polster and Polster, 1973.) A fundamental premise of the Gestalt approach is that the patient is an active agent capable of effecting change. Gestalt therapy does *not* uncover past trauma.

TRANSACTIONAL ANALYSIS AND ITS USE IN GROUP THERAPY

Eric Berne, a psychiatrist originally from Montreal, began training in psychoanalysis in New York City and finally moved to San Francisco. Although Berne stated that he was trained as a psychoanalyst, neither of the institutes he attended will attest that he was accredited by them. However, Berne began work on his ideas as early as 1949 when he published articles on intuition. He was concerned with the capacities of the ego and stated that the child ego state was the most valuable part of the personality. Transactional analysis, the technique that Berne developed, began to be used actively in about 1954. He organized a group of professionals in the San Francisco Bay area, who met with Berne from 1958 until his sudden death in 1970. Since then, his students have organized themselves into formal societies where they offer courses of training with accreditation.

Transactional analysis postulates three forms of ego function: the parent, the adult and the child. According to Berne, these are observable states, unlike the abstract superego, ego and id. The *child* ego state is indicated by the fact that a person behaves the way he did as a child. Since society frowns upon *child* behavior, there is not much of it to be observed except at parties or sports events where "highjinks" are accepted. People who are locked into the *child* ego state use *child* expressions such as "gee whiz" or "golly" or "jiminy," or they may walk like children or sit like children or act in a "wide-eyed" fashion. The *adult* ego state is rational but divorced from feelings. It is data-gathering and very arbitrary. The *parent* ego state is basic to civilization's survival. It is modeled after the parent figures or authority figures who served as parent surrogates. People are believed to live with ego states working at the same time but very quickly. Sometimes people successfully obscure ego states, acting like an *adult* while actually being the *child*. An individual may have learned to verbalize the arbitrary and capricious behavior of a *child* in reasonable adultlike language patterns. What has been presented is a very concise picture of the theory. In many ways Berne, without being aware of it, reformulated the role theory of many social psychologists. For example, can one be a father, husband, lover all at the same time, or what intervening processes are involved?

As far as group therapy and transactional analysis is concerned, a patient's behavior is understood in terms of ego states. The behavior that exists between two people should be examined in terms of a transaction. The transactional analysis at work is the transaction that occurs in the ego states (*child, adult, parent*) within one person rather than transactions among people. According to Berne, people's lives can be seen as a series of games that are endlessly repeated. He described these games in detail and stated that they are something more than what Freud called the repetition-compulsion. He said that while the repetition-compulsion is the reenactment of past life experiences that have never been resolved, his concept of games looks both forward and back. From this, Berne described his concept of a script in which games follow a predetermined way, based on decisions that the patient made in early childhood, when he was too young to make such serious decisions. People, then, make decisions in early childhood that become the blueprint for life, and, seeing life as a movie or stage script, they function according to the plan.

In clinical practice the transactional analyst observes the transaction, discovers the games of the patient and works out the script that the patient is following. The group of patients is very heterogeneous, and Berne did not believe in or encourage selection procedures. He did place restrictions on certain patients, however, such as those in the manic phase, hysterics, phobics and obsessionals. It is interesting to note that he recommended they be treated psychoanalytically. Today, many psychoanalysts recommend that *phobias* are best treated by *behavior therapists*. When one observes the patients he excluded, in spite of his declared position of "no selection," he seems to have settled for very verbal and very motivated patients. The goal in transactional analysis is "cure" – a most elusive term. It is stated by the transactional therapist that there is a contractual statement in which patients agree to meet in a group setting, and the patients often decide with the therapist what material is irrelevant or meaningless. It is questionable whether this goal is as simply achieved as Berne believed. A transactional approach to group therapy is very much leader-oriented; the leader is very much in control, and this is not too unlike Gestalt therapy. The leader works with each group member in turn. Therapy is conducted, according to Berne, *in* a group rather than *with* a group. The therapist exercises strong leadership, and he does not abdicate this role. Once he does, the treatment group becomes a "party." Transactional analysis is very pragmatic and yet is effective among patients who need a very structured setting and strong leadership (Berne, 1949, 1963, 1964, 1966).

The techniques of Gestalt therapy and transactional analysis have their antecedents in the work of Wilhelm Reich (1949), who has had a renaissance in contemporary psychotherapy with interest in "body language" and "body armor." Perls, a contemporary of Reich, was probably well aware of what he took from Reich's work. Berne may have been aware but never expressed his indebtedness. One thing is clear — many of the innovators have never really studied the history of psychotherapy. A trained psychoanalyst who has incorporated transactional approaches in his work is Abell (1978). He has also integrated Gestalt approaches, as has Denes-Radomisli (1978).

Recently, there has been an interest in the use of videotape techniques in work with groups. There is a great deal of interest in the use of confrontation and the immediate replay of behavior that has occurred in the group. Although there is much excitement about videotape approaches, it is too early to say whether the approaches will withstand the scrutinty of time (Rosenbaum, 1978).

Over the past decade there has been an interest in marathon group meetings, but the interest appears to have peaked. The marathon group is a time-extended group in which the group members agree to meet for a long time period — ranging from 12 to 48 hours. The group meets continuously, and food is served. Occasionally either group members or the group leader takes a short nap. According to its proponents the physical exhaustion induced by the prolonged time span as well as the intense psychological contact between group members who are "locked in" with one another leads to very accelerated group movement and interaction. The intensity is supposed to dissolve long-established defenses. In fact, the group quickly attacks such defense mechanisms and simply will not tolerate them. The proponents of such an approach feel that the honesty, intensity and confrontation more than justify the abrasiveness and wear and tear that occur. The question is whether patients need time intervals between therapy sessions to digest and assimilate the awareness and insights they have gained. Advocates of the marathon approach to group therapy deny the significance of such time periods.

Many of the techniques used in group therapy are an effort to treat a population of patients who have in the past been considered "untreatable" or so impulse-oriented that they made little effort to remain in psychotherapy. Borriello (1979) prefers group psychotherapy for these "acting out patients" who "characteristically handle life's problems through action" rather than reflection. Clinicians find that more and more of these patients are seen in practice. These patients are often diagnosed as antisocial personalities or impulse-ridden neurotics, but however they are labeled, they are patients who come to therapy only when they are in deep trouble. Much of Borriello's initial contact involves educating the patient to what psychotherapy is all about and the fact that the crisis that brought the patient to a therapist's office has occurred in the past and will occur again in the future. Because the patient is agitated, this is a time when some significant impact can be made. The therapeutic inquiry for these patients when they are placed in a heterogeneous group is analytic in nature, and the emphasis is upon the here and now. The patient is encouraged to touch upon his anxiety and loneliness and to build a higher tolerance level for anxiety so that there is no longer the need for "acting out."

The practitioner who approaches group therapy may often find what appears to be chaos but is not. What is at work is a field in ferment. The growth of the population, the demand for services in mental health (Kiesler, 1980), the exigencies of training and the all too eager adherence to a theoretical position by some group therapists, contribute to the sense of confusion. There are conflicting statements presented between those who espouse a psychoanalytic position and those who take a sociological stance. This conflict appears in approaches to marital therapy, family therapy and couples therapy. There are differences between those who stress a *group* approach to group therapy and those who focus on the *individual* in group therapy. The term group therapy covers a great range of activities, and many of these activities are aimed at different goals. The goal of each practitioner influences in profound ways the style and approach that is used. In addition, different approaches often reflect different personalities. A more motoric psychotherapist will often stress a different approach from that of a quieter and more reflective group therapist. There is no single approach and technique that is effective in the treatment of emotional problems.

There continues to be some degree of excitement about the use of encounter techniques in group psychotherapy. The entire encounter movement appears to have "crested" in both the United States and Western Europe, but some of the experimental and encounter approaches will probably persist in group psychotherapy. If encounter techniques are used selectively and at the appropriate time, they may stimulate a transient experience of regression that in turn permits a degree of affect to emerge. Of course, the trained leader knows what to do at this point. The untrained leader will simply promote abreaction. For those patients who are very intellectual in their defense mechanisms, the regressive experience that is promoted through encounter techniques may work effectively. For other patients, the techniques are merely experienced as brutal intervention and confrontation. The reports of destructive experiences that patients undergo with encounter techniques are beginning to accumulate. Perhaps this is more an expression of poorly trained group leaders than of the techniques. We shall have to await further research.

Because of the confusion surrounding different types of group practice, it is very important to point out the responsibilities of the group leader in the different types of groups. Rosenbaum (1982) has pointed out the ethical problems involved in group therapy, and Braaten (1979), a Norwegian psychologist who has studied in the United States, has listed the ethical dilemmas in conducting personal growth groups, as well as the guidelines that should be set up and the pressing need for more comprehensive research. Since Braaten is identified with the human potential movement, his comments have special relevance. In his work (1978) he also attempts to distinguish the different developmental phases at work in encounter groups as well as the types of inter-actional experiences within the group process.

It is critically important to be aware of the theoretical questions that underlie clinical practice. Cooper and Gustafson (1979; Gustafson and Cooper, 1979) have attempted to "organize group therapy theory" and integrate individual and group approaches. Their aim is to organize a framework for group therapy practice and theory.

There are definite indications that group therapy is often the therapy of choice and not a therapy used because of a shortage of personnel or an effort to "bail out" the waiting list in a clinic or hospital. The climate of a group that is led by a trained professional moves toward a peer relationship; an atmo-shpere is encouraged that taps the "best" in the patient. Individual therapy on the other hand, often encourages hanging on to pathology. When a democratic atmosphere is provided in the group, the person begins to experience different ethical systems and different social models. The therapist is finally seen more realistically and not as an idealized parent. The integration into a culture is promoted, and the patient begins to experience life as a person.

At this time, some group psychotherapists are attempting to utilize general systems theory in order to gain a broader perspective in work with groups (Bertalanffy, 1968). Some effort is being made to stress the use of positive feed-back in establishing change in group members. This work is in very early stages, and its advocates are struggling for answers. But all this bodes well, for it indicates that group psychotherapy is alive and well and growing.

Probably the most important sign of the vitality of group psychotherapy is given by the clinicians who work with groups and with patient populations that they never before would have treated in a group. Horwitz (1976) stated that group therapy was *not* indicated for suicidal or very depressed persons. Yet Asimos and Rosen (1978) are optimistic about work with overtly suicidal and depressed patients and feel that groups have a "valuable, supportive and crisis intervention function." They report: "The results and outcome of this group activity to date have been quite impressive and encouraging." In addition they find that open-ended therapy programs are an effective method of suicide prevention for both young and old depressed and suicidal patients. It is clear that if clinicians are trained and believe in the efficacy of group therapy, it is a modality with enormous possibilities.

There are increasingly imaginative ways of using the group. Menks, Sittler, Weaver and Yanow (1977) established a psychogeriatric activity group in a small rural community. The group helped maintain the aged patient in the community by promoting self-esteem, self-expression and new interests. As the American population grows and as people live longer, we face an increasing patient load of older people who exhibit emotional problems. Those who are ambulatory can make their own contacts with psychotherapists, and more and more of these patients do enter group therapy. Those aging people who enter long-term care facilities (nursing homes) often become depressed and lethargic and quite discouraged about life. Those groups that have been formed among the aged have been largely task-oriented. The emphasis has been upon educative group process experiences that are goal-directed, but there has been increasing use of discussion-oriented groups that are insight-oriented. Some of the major concerns expressed by the aged are fear of death and illness, and the group experience enables participants to develop a sense of perspective and to work against the sense of isolation and loneliness. This type of group needs a mature and secure group leader who is comfortable with problems such as fear of illness or fear of death. The group should not be used to foster dependence but to encourage the growth of group members, no matter how old they are (Maizler, Solomon and Ronch, 1979).

With the escalating divorce rate, group therapists have entered new areas. Gleason and Orescott (1977) used group counseling as a technique for premarital preparation and found it to be the best-suited technique for that purpose. Because of the current interest in teaching human sexuality in professional schools, it is pertinent to cite the use of group process where an atmosphere is set up in which students feel more at ease to comment, raise questions and ventilate their personal observations or anxieties. Whereas the group process experience begins as a course in human sexuality for mental health professionals, it very rapidly becomes a discussion group in which the students are sensitized to all aspects of sexual life and sexual difficulties (Hallowitz and Shore, 1978).

Over the past twenty-five years, more and more psychiatric patients have been treated in the group therapy setting, with many of the group therapy techniques of a supportive nature. The desire to use support approaches may be related to limited competency among group therapists. But until very recently there were no formal guidelines concerning training of group psychotherapists. Although some authors (Mullan and Rosenbaum, 1962, 1978) have outlined specific training programs, there has been little emphasis on the importance of formal training, so that competence levels have varied among therapists. Thus there is a paucity of systematic research, in addition to the various levels of demonstrable competence, when group psychotherapists compare their clinical experiences. Recently, professional organizations have begun to offer training programs in different parts of the United States, and the American Group Psychotherapy Association, which for some twenty-five years has offered a three-day training institute at its annual conference, finally set up specific requirements for standards and training of group psychotherapists. The danger exists that growth in the field without careful regulation will lead to a negative public image of group psychotherapy (Salvendy, 1980).

Finally, it may be concluded that the use of group therapy is only limited by the vision of the clinicians who use the modality.

REFERENCES

Abell, R.G.   Transactional analysis, Gestalt therapy and psychoanalysis in group psychotherapy: A synthesis. Chapter 14 in: Mullan, H. and Rosenbaum, M. (Eds.), *Group Psychotherapy*, rev. ed. New York: Free Press–Macmillan, 1978.

Asimos, C.T. and Rosen, D.H. Group treatment of suicidal and depressed persons. *Bulletin of the Menninger Clinic.* **42**: 515–518 (1978).

Beard, J.H., Goertzel, V. and Pearce, A.J. The effectiveness of activity group therapy with chronically regressed adult schizophrenics. *International Journal of Psychoanalysis.* **8**: 123–136 (1958).

Bednar, R.L. and Lawlis, B.F. Empirical research in group psychotherapy. In: Bergin, A.E. and Garfield, S.L. (Eds.), *Handbook of psychotherapy and behavior change: An empirical analysis,* pp. 812–833. New York: John Wiley, 1971.

Berne, E. The nature of intuition. *Psychiatric Quarterly.* **23**: 203–218 (1949).

Berne, E. *The structure and dynamics of organizations and groups.* Philadelphia: J.B. Lippincott, 1963.

Berne, E. *Games people play.* New York: Grove Press, 1964.

Berne, E. *Principles of group treatment.* New York: Oxford University Press, 1966.

Bertalanffy, L. von. *General systems theory – Foundations, development, applications.* New York: Braziller, 1968.

Bierer, J. (Ed.) *Therapeutic social clubs.* London: H.K. Lewis, 1948.

Bilodeau, C.B. and Hackett, T.P. Issues raised in a group setting by patients recovering from myocardial infarction. *American Journal of Psychiatry.* **128**: 105–110 (1971).

Borriello, J.F. Group psychotherapy with acting-out patients: Specific problems and techniques. *American Journal of Psychotherapy.* **33**: 521–530 (1979).

Bovill, D.   An outcome study of group psychotherapy. *British Journal of Psychiatry.* **131**: 95–98 (1977).

Braaten, L.J.   Developmental phases of encounter groups and related intensive groups. *Interpersonal Development.* **5**: 112–129 (1974–75).

Braaten, L.J.   Some ethical dilemmas in sensitivity training, encounter groups and related activities. *Scandanavian Journal of Psychology.* **20**: 81–91 (1979).

Campbell, T.W., Brock, G., Van Gee, S.J. and Greenfield, G. Use of a Family Group for Crisis Intervention. *General Hospital Psychiatry* **2**: 95–99 (1980).

Cooper, L. and Gustafson, J.P.   Toward a general theory of group therapy. *Human Relations* **32**: 967–981 (1979).

Corsini, R.J. *Methods of group psychotherapy.* New York: McGraw-Hill, 1957.

Cunningham, J., Strassberg, D., and Roback, H. Group psychotherapy for medical patients, *Comprehensive Psychiatry,* **19**: 135–140 (1978).

Dejerine, J. and Gauckler, E. *The psychoneuroses and their treatment.* Philadelphia: Lippincott, 1913.

Denes-Radomisli, M. Gestalt group psychotherapy. Chapter 15 in: Mullan, H. and Rosenbaum, M. (Eds.), *Group psychotherapy,* rev. ed. New York: Free Press–Macmillan, 1978.

248   MAX ROSENBAUM

Diatkine, R. The Development of object relationships and affects. *International Journal of Psychoanalysis.* **59**: 277–284 (1978).
Fagan, J. and Shepherd, I.L. (Eds.) *Gestalt therapy now: Theory, techniques, applications.* Palo Alto, Calif. Science and Behavior Books, 1970.
Freud, S. Group psychology and the analysis of the ego (1921). In: *Standard edition of the complete psychological works of Sigmund Freud,* vol. 18. London: Hogarth Press, 1957.
Gilder, R., Buschman, P.R., Sitarz, A.L. and Wolf, J.A. Group therapy with parents of children with leukemia. *American Journal of Psychotherapy.* **32**: 276–287 (1978).
Ginsberg, B.G., Stuttman, S.S. and Hummel, J. Group filial therapy. *Social Work.* **23**: 154–156 (1978).
Gleason, J. and Crescott, M.R. Group techniques for premarital preparation. *Family Coordinator.* **26**: 277–280 (1977).
Godenne, G.D. Outpatient adolescent group psychotherapy. I. Review of the literature of use of co-therapist, psychodrama and parent group therapy. *American Journal of Psychotherapy.* **18**: 584–593 (1964).
Gustafson, J.P. and Cooper, L. Unconscious planning in small groups. *Human Relations.* **32**: 1039–1064 (1979).
Hallowitz, E. and Shore, D.A. Small group process in teaching human sexuality. *Health and Social Work.* **3**: 132–151 (1978).
Henle, M. Gestalt psychology and Gestalt therapy. *Journal of History of the Behavioral Sciences.* **14**: 23–32 (1978).
Horwitz, L. Indications and contraindications for group psychotherapy. *Bulletin of the Menninger Clinic.* **40**: 505–507 (1976).
Jones, M. *The therapeutic community: A new treatment method in psychiatry.* New York: Basic Books, 1953.
Kanas, N., Rogers, M., Kreth, E., Patterson, L. and Campbell, R. The effectiveness of group psychotherapy during the first three weeks of hospitalization. *Journal of Nervous and Mental Disease.* **168**: 487–492 (1980).
Kiesler, C.A. Mental health policy as a field of inquiry for psychology. *American Phychologist.* **35**: 1066–1080 (1980).
Klapman, J.W. The case for didactic group psychotherapy. *Diseases of the Nervous System.* **11**:(2): 35–41 (1950).
Klapman, J.W. and Lundin, W.H. Objective appraisal of textbook mediated group psychotherapy with psychotics. *International Journal of Group Psychotherapy.* **3**: 116–126 (1952).
Kotkov, B. Bibliography of group therapy. *Journal of Clinical Psychology.* **6**: 77–91 (1950).
Lawrence, H. and Walter, C.L. Testing a behavioral approach with groups. *Social Work.* **23**: 127–133 (1978).
Leopold, H.S. Selective group approaches with psychotic patients in hospital settings. *American Journal of Psychotherapy.* **30**: 95–102 (1976).
Low, A.A. *Mental health through will-training.* Boston: Christopher, 1950.
Maizler, J.S., Solomon, J.R. and Ronch, J.L. Group therapy with nursing home residents: A survey. *Health and Social Work.* **4**: 211–218 (1979).

Marsh, L.C. Group therapy of the psychoses by the psychological equivalent of the revival. *Mental Hygiene.* **15**: 328–349 (1931).

Maxmen, J.S. An educative model for inpatient group therapy. *International Journal of Group Psychotherapy.* **28**: 321–338 (1978).

Menks, F., Sittler, S., Weaver, D. and Yanow, B. A psychogeriatric activity group in a rural community. *American Journal of Occupational Therapy.* **31**: 381–384 (1977).

Moreno, J.L. *Who shall survive?* New York: Beacon House, 1953.

Moreno, J.L. The Viennese origins of the encounter movement, paving the way for existentialism, group psychotherapy and psychodrama. *Group Psychotherapy.* **22**:(1–2): 7–16 (1969).

Mullan, H. and Rosenbaum, M. *Group psychotherapy: Theory and practice,* rev. ed. New York: Free Press–Macmillan, 1978.

Oehler-Giarratana, J. and Fitzgerald, J. Group therapy with blind diabetics. *Archives of General Psychiatry.* **37**: 463–767 (1980).

Parloff, M.B. and Dies, R.R. Group psychotherapy outcome research 1966–1975. *International Journal of Group Psychotherapy.* **27**: 281–289 (1977).

Perls, F.S. *In and out of the garbage pail.* Lafayette, Calif.: Real People Press, 1969a.

Perls, F.S. *Gestalt therapy verbatim.* Lafayette, Calif.: Real People Press, 1969b.

Perls, F.S., Hefferline, R.F. and Goodman, P. *Gestalt therapy.* New York: Julian Press, 1961.

Polster, E. and Polster, M. *Gestalt therapy integrated: Contours of theory and practice.* New York: Brunner/Mazel, 1973.

Pratt, J.H. The use of Dejerine's methods in the treatment of the common neuroses by group psychotherapy. *Bulletin New England Medical Center.* **15**: 1–9 (1953).

Reich, W. *Character analysis.* New York: Orgone Institute Press, 1949.

Rogeness, G.A. and Stewart, J.T. The positive group: a therapeutic technique in the hospital treatment of adolescents. *Hospital and Community Psychiatry.* **29**: 520–522 (1978).

Rogers, J., MacBride, A., Whylie, B. and Freeman, S.J.J. The use of groups in the rehabilitation of amputees. *International Journal of Psychiatry in Medicine.* **8**: 243–244 (1977–78).

Rosenbaum, M. Group psychotherapy and psychodrama. In: Wolman, B. (Ed.), *Handbook of clinical psychology.* New York: McGraw-Hill, 1965. pp. 1254–1274.

Rosenbaum, M. The issue of privacy and privileged communication. Chapter 26 in: Berger, M.M. (Ed.), *Viedotape techniques in psychiatric training and treatment,* rev. ed., pp. 315–325. New York: Brunner/Mazel, 1978.

Rosenbaum, M. (Ed.) *Ethical problems in the practice of psychotherapy.* New York: Free Press, 1981.

Rosenbaum, M. and Berger, M.M. *Group psychotherapy and group function,* rev. ed. New York: Basic Books, 1975.

Rosenbaum, M. and Snadowsky, A. *The intensive group experience.* New York: Free Press, 1976.

Rosenthal, L. Qualifications and tasks of the therapist in group therapy with children. *Clinical Social Work Journal.* **5**: 191–199 (1977).

Salvendy, J.T. Group psychotherapy training: A quest for standards. *Candian Journal of Psychiatry.* **25**: 394–4203 (1980).

Schilder, P. Results and problems of group psychotherapy in severe neurosis. *Mental Hygiene.* **23**: 87–98 (1939).

Schilder, P. The current of criminals and the prevention of crime. *Journal of Criminal Psychopathology.* 149–161 (1940).

Slavson, S.R. *An introduction to group therapy.* New York: Commonwealth Fund, 1943.

Slavson, S.R. Para-analytic group psychotherapy. In: *Pathways in child guidance,* vol. 6, no. 1, 1964.

Slavson, S.R. *Dynamics of group psychotherapy.* Edited in consultation with M. Schiffer. New York: Jason Aranson, 1979.

Sobel, D. and Geller, J.J. A type of group psychotherapy in the children's unit of a mental hospital. *Psychiatric Quarterly.* **38**: 262–270 (1964).

Sotile, W.M., Kilmann, P. and Follingstad, D.R. A sexual enhancement workshop: Beyond group systematics desensitization for women's sexual anxiety. *Journal of Sex and Marital Therapy.* **3**: 249–255 (1977).

Speers, R.W. and Lansing, C. Group psychotherapy with preschool psychotic children and collateral group therapy of their parents: A preliminary report of the first two years. *American Journal of Orthopsychiatry.* **34**: 659–666 (1964).

Speers, R.W. and Lansing, C. Some genetic dynamic considerations of childhood symbiotic psychosis. *Journal of the American Academy of Child Psychiatry.* **7**: 329–349 (1968).

Udelman, H.D. and Udelman, D.L. Group therapy with rheumatiod arthritic patients. *American Journal of Psychotherapy.* **32**: 288–299 (1978).

Williams, J., Lewis, C., Copeland, F., Tucker, L. and Feagan, L. A model for short-term group therapy on a children's inpatient unit. *Clinical Social Work Journal.* **6**: 21–32 (1978).

Wynne, A.R. Movable group therapy for institutionalized patients. *Hospital and Community Psychiatry.* **29**: 516–519 (1978).

Yalom, I.D. *The theory and practice of group psychotherapy,* rev. ed. New York: Basic Books, 1978.

11 Hospital Care

Arthur H. Schwartz, Barry B. Perlman and Marshall Swartzburg

THE SCOPE OF THE PROBLEM

Large numbers of patients require hospital care for the treatment of mental illness each year, reflecting the importance of this problem for the health of the nation. In 1971, there were 1,336,312 admissions to inpatient services in the United States (Utilization of mental health facilities, NIMH, 1971). By 1977 this number had increased to 1,558,964 (unpublished data, Information Division of Biometry and Epidemiology, NIMH). Inpatient care episodes accounted for 27% of all admissions to psychiatric services in 1977 as compared with 43% in 1971 and 77% in 1955, reflecting a shift to ambulatory care for the mentally ill. Patients residing in mental hospitals at the end of a year fell from 633,500 in 1955 to 391,000 in 1970. However, more than 1.8 million people were hospitalized for mental illness at some point during 1977 (Trends in patient care episodes in mental health facilities, 1955-1977, NIMH, 1980), whereas in 1955 only 1.3 million people were treated in mental hospitals.

Currently, the inpatient care episode rate is approximately 842 individuals per 100,000 population. Males have a higher admission rate to mental hospitals than females, with the ratio being essentially 7 to 5. Of the patients admitted, schizophrenics account for 27%, depressives for $22\frac{1}{2}$%, alcoholics and drug abusers for 21% and organic brain syndromes for 6%.

By 1978 there were 2,433 inpatient services and 1,581 day treatment services in the United States. More than one-third of these inpatient services are located in general hospitals, one-fourth in purely psychiatric hospitals, almost one-fifth in residential treatment centers for emotionally disturbed children and almost one-sixth in community mental health centers. Although state and county mental hospitals account for only 12% of the total number of inpatient facilities in the nation, they receive 26% of the admissions and house 62% of all the patients in mental hospitals at any one time.

INDICATIONS FOR PSYCHIATRIC HOSPITALIZATION

Broadly speaking, patients are admitted to psychiatric hospitals for the same purposes for which they are admitted to general medical services. Hospitalization may be considered 1) in the face of difficult diagnostic questions, 2) when it is necessary to give specialized treatment and 3) when it is necessary to protect the patient and society from the effects of the illness.

A patient may be hospitalized for diagnostic purposes when extended and close observation of his behavior and mode of relating to others or special diagnostic procedures are indicated.

Certain therapeutic interventions, particularly those that carry a substantial risk of morbidity, often should be undertaken in a setting where response and reaction to treatment can be conveniently monitored. For example, such procedures as electroconvulsive therapy, withdrawal of drug-dependent individuals and the use of psychopharmacological agents at therapeutic dose levels in patients whose physical condition is compromised usually require an inpatient setting. Psychiatric hospitals also provide a structured setting within which psychotherapeutic interventions are possible for disturbed patients whose illness precludes their use on an ambulatory basis.

The supports provided by a multidisciplinary professional staff on a 24-hour basis make it possible for anxiety-laden material to be dealt with more rapidly and effectively than could ever be possible if the patient were not hospitalized. In addition, the psychiatric hospital can be established to provide a complete milieu within which the patient's interactions with others and with authority figures can be directed and utilized, so as to become the major focus of treatment. In a sense, the total life pattern of the patient can be examined and treated within the "small society" created in the psychiatric hospital.

Hospitalization also provides an opportunity to interrupt the deleterious psychosocial interactions that patients may have been experiencing in their family, work or social environment. Such an interregnum enables the patient to reassess his position and his relationships, so that pathological interactions may be changed. Hopefully, new adaptive patterns are then developed so that vital relationships may be preserved and situational crises mastered.

Some patients' adaptive skills are so poor that only long-term residential treatment centers can provide a setting within which these skills may be developed and vital maturational tasks such as education may be accomplished. Such centers also provide viable living situations for individuals whose home environments are so pathological that no amount of outpatient treatment could hope to ensure normal growth and development.

Finally, it may be necessary to hospitalize patients, even against their will, to protect them and society from suicidal, homicidal or assaultive behavior. Extremely regressive behavior, during which the patient essentially becomes incapable of functioning on an independent basis, may also force hospitalization. In fact, it is such an inability to function effectively in any nonstructured setting that accounts for most of the patients who are hospitalized for prolonged periods of time, often on a custodial basis after having received either inadequate or unsuccessful treatment.

The Group for the Advancement of Psychiatry (GAP Report, 1969), in discussing the use of the psychiatric hospital, stressed the fact that "there are positive reasons for hospital care." In their view, hospitalization was not to be undertaken as a last resort, but rather as a positive step toward health when that health could be best achieved within a hospital setting.

To accomodate changing concepts of care and to take into account advances in treatment techniques, hospitals have been evolving slowly for almost two hundred years, with rapid change occurring in the last two decades.

THE DEVELOPMENT OF THE MODERN INPATIENT UNIT

In 1793, Philippe Pinel removed the chains confining patients at the Bicêtre, a hospital for the mentally ill in Paris, and began a new era in the treatment of the mentally ill. Anton Muller, in Germany, Vincenzo Chiarugi, in Italy, and William Tuke, in England, were pioneers in their countries in the development of the "moral treatment" of the mentally ill. In the United States, Dorothea Dix successfully crusaded for the development of new psychiatric hospitals. However, the ideals of Pinel and Dix were lost in the rapid population growth and urban industrialization that characterized the first decades of the twentieth century.

By the 1930's, the typical mental hospital was a large public institution, isolated in a rural setting, away from the patient's family and home. Instead of a pleasant, restful setting, where warm and kind attention could be paid to the patient, the institution had become an overcrowded prison-like environment where custodial care alone was available. The less disturbed patients could work in housekeeping and ground-tending activities, but for a large number of patients, not even labor was available to break the monotony of confinement in barren wards. Staffing was usually inadequate. With the exception of a few "interesting" patients seen in psychotherapy, an atmosphere of therapeutic nihilism pervaded the hospitals. The introduction of insulin coma and electroconvulsive therapy in the late 1930's generated some therapeutic enthusiasm but did not change the basic atmosphere. Change began to appear only when theoretical principles elucidated by the growing disciplines of social psychology and anthropology and reinforced by practical experiences from World War II led to a rethinking of the basic concepts of hospital care.

The necessity of administering large numbers of men during World War II and the need to maintain effective leadership and good morale led to an increased awareness of the importance of social factors in human life and institutions. When these principles were applied to mental hospitals, it was gradually realized that the way a mental hospital was organized had something to do with the behavior of the patients within it and the outcome of their illness (Rowland, 1938; Bateman and Dunham, 1948; Dunham and Weinberg, 1960). Goffman (1961) vividly described the devastating effects of the mental hospital as an organized institution upon the patients. Bellnap (1956) documented how the culture of a mental hospital was carried on by its infrastructure of nurses, aides and long-term patients and was impervious to reform from the top. That a different approach to patient care was possible was demonstrated during and immediately after the war when the necessity to treat large numbers of psychiatric disorders led to the use of rapid and intensive treatment and manpower-saving devices such as group therapy and patients assisting each other.

Perhaps the greatest jolt to the status quo came from the study of Stanton and Schwartz (1954) in which they described a hospital as a total culture in which staff and patients interact within a single social system where events in one area affect all others. They described how covert conflicts between two staff members could have an adverse effect on patients and pointed out that when such disagreements were brought out into the open and resolved, not only the patients' behavior, but also the mental health of the staff would improve. Caudill (1958) described, in detail, the processes that characterized hospital life. To understand life within a hospital it was necessary to take into account not only the individual attributes of a group of patients and staff members, but also their relative positions in the status and role structure of the hospital.

At the same time that social scientists were documenting the structure and processes of the mental hospital, an effort was being made by mental health professionals to develop new models of patient care. If the social structure was capable of exerting a profound antitherapeutic effect upon patients, then by utilizing the principles developed by the social scientists a social structure could be created that would have a therapeutic effect upon patients. This structure came to be known as a therapeutic milieu or community.

Maxwell Jones (1962), a pioneer in the field, described the therapeutic community as an attempt to utilize the institution's total resources, especially the nurses, aides and other patients, in an attempt to help the sick individual. To accomplish this it was deemed necessary to establish open communications and to eliminate the hierarchical system of authority so that patients and staff could examine what they were doing and how it affected them and others. These principles proved to be successful in a variety of settings including state, military and general hospitals (Greenblatt, York and Brown, 1955; Artiss, 1962; Kaufman, 1965). The role of the psychiatric administrator on both the hospital and single ward level became increasingly important (Wessen, 1964; Clark, 1964).

It should be noted, however, that during the decade from 1955 to 1965 great advances were made in the field of psychopharmacology, with the development of the phenothiazines and the antidepressants. These drugs made it possible to manage disturbed patients in an open setting and by reducing agitation enabled the patient to participate in the milieu. By making fundamental changes in the course of a patient's illness, they allowed for fundamental changes in the hospital setting.

Developments in ego psychology provided a further theoretical base for milieu therapy (Cumming and Cumming, 1962). Cumming and Cumming conceived of patients as individuals with impaired ego function and postulated that ego growth occurs through crisis resolution. Milieu therapy was seen as offering a patient a structured and protected environment in which the individual could solve a series of graded problems in adaptation. The patient could thus master the role behavior necessary to be a participating member of society. Traditional psychotherapeutic techniques could be interwoven with milieu therapy, making both more meaningful and effective (Edelson, 1964).

The importance of the individual's being returned to the community as a functioning member of society was emphasized in *Action for mental health,* a report published by the Joint Commission on Mental Illness and Health in 1961. This report noted that the innovative developments in hospital care in the previous decade had made such a goal possible and recommended that mental health services be provided on a local community level. The Community Mental Health Center Act of 1963, passed to implement this concept, mandated inpatient units as one of the five essential services of a community mental health center. The need to develop new inpatient units in centers whose needs and facilities varied greatly has led to further innovations in models of hospital care that use the principles of milieu therapy as the prime therapeutic modality or as an adjunct to other forms of treatment.

MILIEU THERAPY AND THE THERAPEUTIC COMMUNITY

Programs emphasizing milieu therapy with a therapeutic community model as their core have been developed throughout the country. Although these programs have been established in diverse settings including state hospitals, veterans hospitals, military hospitals, general hospitals, mental health centers and private psychiatric centers, they share many features in common.

Ideally, the ward should avoid an institutional appearance and should be so designed that small group interactions and a sense of community are fostered (Osmond, 1957; Lebensohn, 1965). An open door policy is usually considered to be an important element of a therapeutic community (Stern, 1957; Rubin and Goldberg, 1963; Schwartz, Mako and Smith, 1972). Its purpose is to foster a sense of self-reliance in the patient and to discourage tendencies toward regression. The message to the patient is that he must assume at least a partial responsibility for his behavior and functioning even in the face of very real psychopathology. It should be stressed that the feasibility of having an open door on wards treating acutely disturbed patients could not have been considered prior to the advent of psychotropic medications and other somatic therapies. Before the development of chemotherapy, locked wards and seclusion rooms were the rule whenever acutely disturbed individuals were hospitalized. Hopefully, the appeal to the so-called healthy part of the patient's ego enhances dignity and promotes trust and a sense of collaboration between patients and staff.

In a well-functioning milieu program, patients are introduced to the expectations of the ward culture by both staff and other patients at the time they enter. The patient is quickly taught that open communication is valued. Secrets between patients and other patients or staff members are discouraged so that decisions may be made in an open forum with the full participation of the entire community.

Patients are urged to assume responsibility not only for themselves but also for their fellow patients, and may be asked to aid in the care of more disorganized individuals. Such an emphasis leads to group interaction and a tendency for peer assessment. Patients are encourage to comment on each others' behavior, pathology and life difficulties, even though the assumption of such familiarity would be somewhat inappropriate in the world at large. Such activity further enhances the sense of community. All events and interactions that take place on the ward are discussable and become grist for the treatment process. The usual arenas for such discussions are the so-called patient-staff or community meetings and patient government meetings (Kaufman, 1970; Williams, 1970; Gerhardt, 1968).

In theory, the closer the actual functioning of a particular milieu approaches to its stated value system, the more effectively these values can be used in treating patients. These values usually include free and open communication, analysis of all events in terms of individual and interpersonal dynamics, examination of each individual's role and how it affects others and a flattening of hierarchical layers of authority so that power and responsibility may be shared.

Some inpatient units attempt to achieve these values by creating a therapeutic milieu program consisting of group-centered activities such as group therapy programs, psychodrama and an active ward activity and recreational program. Others go further and attempt to build therapeutic communities with an emphasis on patient government. The stumbling blocks to an actualization of any ideal model are difficulties concerning the sharing of power between staff and patients and problems relating to role definitions among the staff (Rubenstein and Lasswell, 1966; Greenley, 1973). Sharing of power varies from systems in which patients make virtually all of the decisions affecting their lives, including which patients may be discharged or placed in seclusion (Schwartz and Farmer, 1968), to systems in which patients have an advisory function but no real authority. The more disturbed the patient body, the more critical the decisions, and the more rapid the patient turnover, the less possible it is for the staff to share authority and control with patients. However, as Maxwell Jones (1962) has pointed out, there is no one model of a therapeutic community.

Certain attempts have been made to study the atmosphere actually achieved in therapeutic communities and to elucidate the processes by which values are transmitted to patients and staff (Moos and Houts, 1968; Jackson, 1969; Marohn, 1970; Pierce, Truckett and Moos, 1972). Findings suggest that factors such as a pleasant ward atmosphere, adequate physical facilities and a high degree of patient motility and freedom to leave the ward unattended reflect humanistic concerns but are not crucial to therapeutic effectiveness. Small hospital size, high ratios of nurses and attendants, frequent staff-patient interaction and a high degree of patient involvement in treatment programs appear to be the important determinants of hospital effectiveness (Linn, 1970). Increasing the size of the ward or decreasing the staff ratios tends to lead to a more rigid structure with greater staff control and decreased patient responsibility. Interactions between staff and patients become not only less frequent but also less spontaneous, supporting and understanding. Even with adequate staffing there is a tendency toward less well-developed treatment programs and greater cultural disorganization on large wards (Moos, 1972). The division of staff and patients into separate teams has been one approach to solving this problem on such wards.

The process by which a ward culture is achieved and maintained has also been studied (Almond, Keniston and Boltax, 1968, 1969a,b). It has been shown that the therapeutic ideology of the staff is transmitted to the patients only through the social structure of the ward. Regardless of how frequently staff values are articulated, they will have minimal impact unless the ward culture integrates these expectations with the patients' role in the particular setting. In order to maintain a stable ward ethos, constant reinforcement by the senior leadership of the values felt to be essential to the milieu must be carried out within the staff as well as with the patients. New additions to the staff, as well as new patients, must be carefully initiated into the predominant value system.

Almond and his co-workers, studying a typical acute psychiatric ward organized as a therapeutic community, found that while patient acceptance of the prevalent value system within the ward setting correlated with staff assessments of patient inprovement, these assessments had no critical relationship in actual fact to how a patient fared behaviorally during or after hospitalization. They found that the maintainance of the ward value system was really of importance not to the health of any particular patient but rather to the health of the milieu itself. The milieu in turn provided the social controls necessary for an acutely disturbed patient to be maintained in an active treatment program. However, they questioned whether some patients, depending upon their age, severity of illness or expectations for care, might not fare just as well or better in alternate settings.

In addition to their proponents, therapeutic communities have generated a fair amount of criticism. They have been criticized for holding to a unitary concept of the treatment of the patient, regardless of the clinical problem, with a resulting loss in the diversity and flexibility needed for a varied patient population (Fisher and Weinstein, 1971). Problems of role blurring and role confusion have been noted (Herz, Wilensky and Earle, 1966). The ability of disorganized acute schizophrenics to participate meaningfully in group interaction has been questioned (Spadoni and Smith, 1969; Herz, 1972). It has also been suggested that many patients might prefer a more traditional hospital setting (Levinson and Gallagher, 1964; Linn, 1969). Advocates of traditional psychotherapeutic approaches complain about the increasing shift in the treatment focus within the therapeutic community from intrapsychic factors to the interpersonal and socially disruptive aspects of a patient's illness. On the opposite side of the philosophic spectrum, therapeutic communities have been criticized for encouraging prolonged hospitalization for patients who could have been treated just as adequately in crisis intervention or brief treatment wards. Other criticism has focused on such issues as permissiveness, lack of lockable doors, avoidance of ECT and the practice of consensus medicine. In fact, however, these criticisms are unrelated to the presence or absence of a therapeutic milieu and focus on issues that might arise in any hospital setting.

MILIEU ON INTERMEDIATE AND ACUTE TREATMENT SERVICES

With the advent of psychotropic medication, halfway houses and rehabilitation programs in recent years, there has been a sharp trend toward a shorter period of hospitalization for each index episode. The trend toward shorter periods of inpatient care has been accelerated by the limited benefits provided by insurance companies, the increased cost of a hospital stay and the community mental health center movement which has committed limited resources to the care of large numbers of potential patients. There has, therefore, been a shift from the reconstruction of the individual patient while he is still hospitalized to the suppression of acute symptomatology and the development of outpatient aftercare programs which are available to the patient upon discharge.

As a result of the above-mentioned trends and policy shifts, the percentage of acutely upset patients in psychiatric hospitals has increased. Patients now tend to enter hospitals when upset for the first time or when they suffer exacerbation of an ongoing illness. This population shift has made it necessary for hospital wards to seek a way to establish an orderly and systematic treatment approach in the face of potential chaos.

From the moment a disturbed patient arrives on the ward, he is told that aberrant behavior is not permissible and will not be tolerated. At first glance such a statement appears bizarre. After all, has the patient not already received such admonitions from friends, family and society at large prior to his entrance into the hospital? Was it not because of his inability to adhere to ordinary patterns of behavior that he was admitted? The reasons for the success of such an approach in the hospital, despite earlier failures, are complex. In the first instance, somatic therapies are available. In the second instance, the ward setting makes it possible for the patient to receive assistance in what becomes a joint endeavor. Before hospitalization, the patient was asked by angry contacts to cease and desist. In the hospital people genuinely interested in his well-being and, usually, without rancor offer their assistance and help the patient modify his behavior. This is most effective when other patients participate in the process. A disturbed patient can be taught, for example, that an alternative to assaultive behavior when upset is to ask for medication. A patient who becomes agitated after a visit with relatives can be taught that talking to other members of the community often affords an alternative to intensification of a psychotic process. Perlman and Hogben have shown that prn (as needed) medication can be minimized if standing doses are properly timed (1977). For example, knowing that visiting hours are often stressful, it would be worth considering giving one of the standing doses at the conclusion of visiting. Most important, skilled personnel help the patient recognize the apparent reasons and situations that trigger bizarre behavior. The establishment of a working alliance between the patient and other patients and staff contributes significantly to the amelioration of disturbed patterns of interaction. Psychotropic medication helps the psychotic patient control his behavior, while at the same time community supports help him reflect upon and modify it.

The skilled staff is able to break into the upsetting behavior patterns by sifting out, contacting and utilizing those aspects of the patient's ego that have remained intact. Crucial to the functioning of an acute unit is the confidence that staff and patients have that upsetting behavior can be controlled and, in fact, often has been controlled in the past with substantial benefit to other patients. Patients who have lived through such interactions themselves are invaluable in ensuring the success of a milieu approach. Without this sense of cohesiveness and common purpose, acute wards disintegrate into either chaos or a collection of overmedicated and somnolent individuals.

Regardless of how effective such a setting may be, there are times when the social structure begins to fall apart. Sudden, rapid turnover of patients or staff, a particularly disturbed group of patients or evidence of malfunctioning within the system, such as a suicide on the service, may all lead to a crisis of confidence in the system.

At such times it is essential for the staff to rebuild the sense of community. This can be accomplished in many ways. One approach follows the principles elucidated by Almond et al. (1968, 1969 a,b). Maintenance of the ward milieu assumes paramount importance. All other activities are subordinated to this overriding need. The door, if open, may be shut. Patients may be prohibited from going on pass, regardless of their individual state of progress. Individual psychotherapy, if present, ceases and is replaced by group meetings. The purpose of these activities is to focus the attention of staff and patients onto the community itself, and the focus does not shift until the milieu is reestablished.

The shortening of the hospitalization period has made it necessary for psychiatrists to continually keep one eye, if not both, firmly fixed on the factors that will make it possible for the patient to survive as soon as possible in the community at large. This necessitates an active involvement of the patient's family in the treatment process, as well as possible intervention in the patient's work situation. Work with the families of patients is necessary not only to alter maladaptive patterns, but to make the family more accommodating to the patient and his symptomatology. Schwartz, Myers and Astrachan (1975) have shown that families are much more satisfied with the results of the patient's treatment, and thus more receptive toward maintaining him at home, if they have been actively involved in the treatment process. Depending upon the resources at a particular institution's disposal, family involvement can be quite intense and include individual work with various members of the family, as well as a focus on the whole family, or it may be limited to so-called family nights when families of patients come into the hospital and meet with the patients and staff. The purpose of the latter procedure is to at least ensure a feeling of involvement and avoid the development of a feeling of isolation on the part of the patient.

The treatment approaches subsumed under the therapeutic community concept have had their greatest impact on patients for whom a six-week to six-month hospitalization is both indicated and possible. While all diagnostic categories have been treated in such settings, they have proved particularly useful for the treatment of acute schizophrenics, patients suffering from affective disorders and patients with an acting-out proclivity triggered by marital or familial conflict. During the first two to four weeks of the hospitalization, the acute symptoms that prevent the patient from fully participating in the life of the community as a responsible member are actively treated with medication and community support. The effectiveness of such an approach is enhanced by the fact that the patient is removed from most of his external stresses. In this regard, where indicated, family should be asked to refrain from visiting during the initial period of a patient's stay. Stresses will not be reintroduced until such time as it is felt the patient can begin to cope with them without decompensation. After the acute symptomatology (e.g., delusions, hallucinations, confusion, extreme agitation, psychomotor retardation, etc.) has abated, the focus of treatment shifts to the stressors that impinged upon the patient prior to hospitalization. The importance of the role that psychosocial stressors play in the onset of illness in a given patient is recognized in the new Diagnostic Nomenclature of the American Psychiatric Association (APA) (*Diagnostic and statistical manual of mental disorders,* 1980). Axis four of the *Diagnostic and statistical manual* (DSM-III) of the APA codes the extent to which the clinician feels stress played a role in the onset of the illness. It is at this point that marital conflicts, difficulties between parents and adolescents and other adaptational difficulties that patients have had are dealt with. The chronic pattern of maladaptive behavior, no longer hidden by the gross presenting symptomatology, becomes the focus of work within the ward setting.

Nonpsychotic patients, who present with acting-out behavior that could not be tolerated within their social setting, often spend the first few weeks testing the limits of how much disruption the ward will tolerate. Like psychotic behavior, this often provocative behavior must be dealt with as it presents, in order to allow these patients to begin to deal in a reflective way with the causes of their difficulties in the outside world. Some of these patients have what might be termed an initial "honeymoon" with the hospital staff, during which none of their maladaptive behavior patterns is manifested. This period of quiescence usually passes within a few weeks as the intense relationships developed within a therapeutic community setting effectively mirror difficulties that these patients have had in other close relationships. During the latter phases of their hospitalization, patients become models for more recent admissions and are able to help the staff care for disturbed patients. The ability to function in a responsible manner enhances patients' dignity and self-esteem. It is questionable whether this group of character-disordered patients can be successfully treated in the short-stay units that have become the national norm.

The process of discharge involves a step-by-step assumption by the patient of the responsibilities that he will be expected to assume in the outside world. Passes to home, work or school and social activities are approved and monitored by the entire community of patients and staff. There are times when the community must prod a reluctant or regressed patient into moving forward, and times when the community must rein in overeager but underprepared members. Wherever possible, arrangements for outpatient therapy should be made before discharge, and preliminary contacts should have taken place. Stabilization of the patient on his maintenance medication dose, which usually involves a reduction from the levels required initially, should be accomplished well before discharge. It is not advisable to reduce medication just as the patient is being discharged. Ideally, the principle is followed that only one major change at a time is allowed.

Supportive care and warmth engendered by the hospital setting as well as the intense involvement that patients have with one another and the staff in a therapeutic community are very difficult for the patient to relinquish. The outside world is usually not so solicitous as the hospital, but it is often possible to ease the discharge process by gradually extending the period of time that a patient is outside of the hospital prior to total discharge. However, it has become more difficult to utilize therapeutic passes during a bridge period between hospital stay and discharge because of the pressures exerted by utilization review and Professional Standards Review Organizations. As politics rather than clinical knowledge exerts an increasing influence on decision making about patient care, the natural history of a disorder is less often taken into account in formulating clinical treatment plans. Meetings in the hospital that recently-discharged patients routinely attend serve the dual purpose of providing supportive contact to the discharged patient and, through discussion of the problems of reentry into the community, preparing other patients for their discharge.

Intense involvement within a ward means that successes and failures are deeply felt. Patients who do not respond to treatment, who leave against medical advice, who commit suicide or who have to be transferred to other hospitals for prolonged care have a major impact upon the community. This is best handled by frank discussion between staff and patients. Without such discussions, morale may be expected to fall, and it will be hard to maintain a sense of community.

There are, of course, some patients who have the need to grow in a structured and protected environment over a prolonged period of time. Finances are usually a determining factor in whether or not such a treatment approach can be initiated. Currently, such well-known long-term residential intensive treatment facilities as Austin Riggs and the Yale Psychiatric Institute charge in the neighborhood of $45,000/year. Should such funds be available, this treatment is of particular value for disturbed adolescents whose families are in chaos, when a resolution of this chaos is not possible. It is also of great value in the treatment of patients whose pathology is such that community facilities (e.g., schools) or the home environment cannot tolerate the particular individual when it is felt that the particular difficulties are not yet so established that they cannot be altered by intensive treatment.

THE THREE- TO SIX-WEEK SERVICE

Increasingly, general hospitals are opening wards devoted to the care of psychologically disturbed patients. These wards, as a result of insurance policies and hospital costs, as well as the need to serve large numbers of disturbed patients seeking help, have tended to focus their attention on patients who can benefit from a three- to six-week period of hospitalization. Such wards have also tended to become the standard in the burgeoning community mental health centers, and those general hospitals that formerly took patients for longer periods of time are tending to follow this emerging pattern of care as well. This shortening of the period during which patients are hospitalized for acute illness necessitates the structuring of a unit in a somewhat different fashion from that described for wards in which patients stay for longer periods of time. Differential goal setting is also mandated.

In addition, a new conceptual framework may be needed. For example, a unit group might adapt the time-centered frame of reference that James Mann has applied in his approach to brief psychotherapy (1973). In such a model it would be important for staff to help patients identify with feelings about separation at a projected midpoint in their stay. This might come soon after the abatement of florid symptomatology. What seems most important is not which model is selected but, rather, that a model exists that everyone acknowledges.

Psychotic patients hospitalized on three- to six-week services spend a larger proportion of their hospital time in severely disturbed states than they do in longer-term settings, and they are not able to serve as models for incoming patients. Thus such wards tend to have a high ratio of acutely disturbed patients receiving care at any one time. Either the ward has a high staff-patient ratio, or it must limit the number of psychotic patients who can be admitted at any particular time. Biological and physical methods of dealing with disturbed behavior must take precedence over social interventions if large numbers of acutely disturbed patients are to be treated. The staff must become actively involved in the details of the patient's problem, since there is little time or opportunity for intense community relationships to emerge. Without such interpersonal and social controls it becomes considerably more difficult to maintain the so-called open door policy on short-term wards.

It has been pointed out that maintaining an open door does not constitute good patient care per se; and in short-term settings an insistence upon holding to an open door at all costs may limit the type of patient who can be treated or may actually compromise patient care (Abroms, 1973). Open doors have been said to limit regressive proclivities and to focus the patient's attention on the world to which he must return. However, regressive pulls are weaker in settings in which patients know that they must receive a very time-limited treatment, and in which patients are discharged almost as soon as their acute symptomatology has begun to abate.

The open door cannot, therefore, be made a goal in and of itself. A balance must be struck among the physical, biological and social controls that can be achieved in such settings. The dangers of rigidly insisting that an open door be maintained are that patients may be refused admission if they are considered disruptive, be overmedicated to the point of somnolence if admitted or be placed in seclusion rooms keeping them isolated from social experiences for a longer period of time than might be considered desirable.

An example of how such a balance can be achieved follows: An agitated psychotic patient is admitted to such a service. Initially he requires medication at high levels and may be kept in a quiet room, if such a room exists, for a period of two to three days. At the end of that time, if it is possible to keep the door to the ward closed, he can join the other patients on the ward, and when his judgment has improved even further, the door may be opened. Such considerations play a role on longer-term services, but because of a higher rate of turnover on shorter-term services, decisions as to the "state of the door" come up more frequently and require constant assessment of the ward atmosphere as well as the clinical functioning of the patients currently being housed.

Short periods of stay influence the type and frequency of treatment that may be given to patients. ECT, for example, may be used for the treatment of severe depression, as opposed to medications that take longer to act. These choices are often dictated by external realities such as the amount of insurance and regulatory decisions about length of stay. The guiding principle is the suppression of acute symptomatology as rapidly as possible. The brief period of time available between the accomplishment of this task and discharge must be used to focus on reentry into the community. As opposed to longer-term settings, patients are often discharged on high doses of medication, with reduction to maintenance levels becoming possible only after the patient is reintegrated into the community.

There is little opportunity to use the therapeutic milieu to enhance the dignity and self-esteem of patients by encouraging them to assume responsibility within the hospital setting. Assumption of responsibility must occur outside the hospital, and in some cases must be deferred until after discharge. Step-by-step assumption of life responsibilities from within the hospital is not possible, and patients who require such a procedure do not fare well in such brief settings. Patients who can return to a reasonably functioning state following a brief hospitalization, or those who can return home and use outpatient therapy to accomplish this task, indeed are benefited.

In a setting where milieu therapy is emphasized, the patient is given the message that he is in the hospital to work on his problems, without much relief. On some three- to six-week units the concept of an interregnum is applicable. The medical model in which patients are quickly treated and allowed to recuperate is more closely approximated. Such settings place a premium on there being effective outpatient follow-up resources available within the community. In fact, this is a cornerstone principle of the community mental health center movement. Without such follow-up resources, short-term wards are doomed to failure in the treatment of many patients, especially schizophrenics, and tend to become revolving-door facilities with patients periodically entering hospitals and then decompensating upon their return to the community.

The concept of a patient as a member of a group within the hospital setting is muted on a short-term ward. There is substantially less role blurring and a tendency for staff-patient distinction to be maintained. After all, patients are less involved with each other and it is left to the staff to structure the social milieu.

Occupational and recreational therapy as a mode of rehabilitation and as a means of helping patients to deal with inner conflicts becomes less meaningful as hospital stay diminishes. If such professionals are part of the hospital staff, they must become expert in job finding and occupational testing, and they must shift many of these functions to the outpatient follow-up sphere. Following hospitalization they can effectively aid in the rehabilitation and resocializing of the patient.

It is very difficult during a three- to six-week hospitalization to intervene in a patient's chronic maladaptive patterns and long-standing intra-psychic conflicts. Therapeutic interventions focus on the "here and now," and attempts are made to restructure parts of the environment. Contacts between staff and patients tend to be supportive in nature, and there is usually little, if any, attempt to engage in explorative psychotherapy unless it is anticipated that such intervention will be continued upon discharge.

CRISIS INTERVENTION UNITS

One of the more recent innovations in inpatient care has been the development of crisis-oriented brief treatment units, spurred by the practical needs of community mental health centers mandated to provide comprehensive care to a given population and by the growing popularity of crisis intervention as a treatment technique. Crisis theory as originally postulated by Lindemann (1944) and elaborated and popularized by Caplan (1964) states that rapid and appropriate intervention in a time of a hazardous life situation can prevent the development of maladaptive coping mechanisms that may lead to regression into illness. By preventing the effects of adaptational failure and the resulting disability, crisis intervention is supposed to avoid the need for more extensive treatment at a later time. In addition, it is postulated that resolution of the crisis can promote psychological growth and healthier adaptive patterns in the future. Ideally, crisis intervention should be done on an outpatient basis, but since seriously disturbed or suicidal patients require hospitalization, it became necessary to develop a new model of inpatient treatment that could utilize the principles of crisis intervention.

While the exact format varies from unit to unit, most crisis oriented brief treatment wards share the same treatment principles. Every effort is made to prevent the patient from adopting the identity of a hospitalized psychiatric patient. The length of hospitalization is made as brief as possible, varying from twenty-four hours to a week. The patient is urged from the first day to begin to plan for discharge and often is told that he will not be allowed to stay on the unit beyond a fixed period of time. Treatment is intensive, and psychiatric symptoms are suppressed with medication as rapidly as possible. Family, friends and appropriate social agencies are immediately involved in the patient's care to reestablish the supports necessary for the patient to be discharged. Treatment goals are formulated as soon as possible and are limited in their scope. Therapy is focused on the "immediate precipitating issue." Every effort is made to correct those factors that made it impossible for the patient to function in his usual role and thus necessitated hospitalization.

Brief treatment units are characterized by a high degree of flexibility. Scheduled ward activities are usually held to a minimum. A daily patient and staff meeting to plan the day's activities and to review progress is often the only ward meeting in crisis units. Work passes, home visits and day or night hospitalization programs are tailored to fit the needs of the individual patient. The patient is continually encouraged to assume as much of his usual role in society as possible.

Discharge takes place when the acute symptomatology improves and a social network in which the patient will be able to survive is established. Patients who are unable to be discharged are referred for further hospitalization. Outpatient follow-up is often provided by the staff of the crisis unit for a period of time to provide continuity of care during the critical period immediately following discharge from the hospital. The patient is later referred to other outpatient facilities or discharged from treatment. The more risks a unit is willing to run in its discharge policy, the more crucial close follow-up becomes, since significant numbers of patients will be unable to tolerate discharge and will have to be readmitted.

Patient care on brief treatment units is by its very nature intensive, demanding and stressful work requiring rapid assessment and decision making. For this reason the team format is often used so that the stresses and anxieties may be shared among team members who can mutually support each other. One team member may be working with the patient, a second with the patient's family and a third with social agencies. Because of the short duration of the patient's stay, many clinical activities must take place in the evening hours and during weekends, and thus more staff members become involved in the patient's treatment. This further magnifies the need for careful coordination and good working relationships among team members.

In one setting that utilized a three- to five-day hospitalization format, 63% of all patients admitted were able to be discharged without further hospitalization during a follow-up period of one year. Of those patients with a schizophrenic diagnosis, 50% were able to be discharged without the need for further hospitalization (Weisman, Feirstein and Thomas, 1969). Similar results have been reported by other units (Rhine and Mayerson, 1971).

Brief treatment units are ineffective in treating illnesses where no amount of social intervention can significantly shorten the course of the illness. Patients with severe psychotic depressions, full-blown manic attacks, severe schizophrenic reactions and certain organic states rarely can recover sufficiently to be discharged within one week. However, brief treatment units are often very successful in treating chronic schizophrenics who have adjusted their lives to the limitations imposed by their illness, but who have had a mild to moderate exacerbation of their symptoms because of some life stress. Patients with mild hypomanic episodes often can be started on medication and safely discharged within a week. The protective setting of a hospital and the facilities for rapid intervention in the social field make brief treatment units especially useful in the treatment of patients with neurotic depressions, those with suicidal ideation or those who have made a suicide gesture.

Crisis intervention units have been criticized on both theoretical and practical grounds. Crisis reactions are varied and unclassified. In a strict sense a "crisis" refers to a life event or circumstance that brings about a disruption of adaptation in which the usual modes of coping no longer work. Used in its loosest sense, crisis becomes almost synonymous with the concept of precipitating event, and almost any patient can then be designated a "crisis patient."

It has been questioned whether crisis theory in its strictest sense is in fact applicable to many of the patients admitted to crisis intervention wards. Schizophrenic patients have been shown to decompensate in life situations that are not particularly hazardous, and schizophrenia as an illness does not fit the crisis model of rapid resolution (Beck and Worthen, 1972). There is also a growing awareness that many other patients who appear to be in an acute crisis have long-standing characterological problems and ego weaknesses that make the psychological growth and long-term therapeutic gain that theoretically should follow crisis resolution highly unlikely. In general, it can be said that the ability of crisis intervention techniques to promote growth and to facilitate more effective coping in the future is far from proven (Langsley, 1972).

Brief treatment units have also been criticized for taking too many risks with disturbed and suicidal patients, for forcing patients to make important life decisions before the implications are fully understood by either staff or patients and for giving patients the sense that they are being hurried out of the hospital. At times there is a tendency to overconcentrate on the life events that precipitated the patient's entrance into the hospital and to pay inadequate attention to the psychopathology of the underlying illness. When prevention of hospitalization to avoid regression is seen as an end in and of itself, clinicians may become reluctant to refer the patient for further hospitalization despite the clinical indications for such a referral.

Although brief treatment units have many theoretical shortcomings and practical problems, the popularity of these units continues to grow. Large numbers of patients are presenting themselves for treatment at the emergency rooms of hospitals or at the walk-in clinics of mental health centers, and many require inpatient treatment. The advantage of brief treatment units is that they enable hospitals to treat large numbers of patients and provide at least symptomatic relief. Brief treatment units are a relatively new development and are still in a period of evolution. Although crisis theory provided the initial rationale for these units, the theory is not crucial to their functioning, especially as they become integrated into systems of services and facilities that can provide comprehensive mental health care. Pragmatic and empirical considerations and observations must take precedence. Brief treatment should be applied where it can work, and crisis intervention is only one brief treatment model.

In addition to offering brief treatment, these units can serve as highly sophisticated admission units where skilled evaluation can be done and appropriate dispositions, either to further inpatient care or to outpatient treatment, can be made. In a system of mental health care that is becoming more varied and complex, this task has assumed increasing importance.

THE STATE HOSPITAL AND PROBLEMS OF CHRONICITY

It was initially believed by some mental health administrators that new techniques of treatment combined with the increasing availability of community mental health facilities would allow state hospitals to be gradually phased out (Stewart, LaFare, Grunberg and Herjanic, 1968; Hecker, 1970). This hope was given some credence by a steadily falling census, since new medications, expanded ward treatment programs and increased community facilities allowed patients to be discharged from state hospitals to their families or to convalescent homes, halfway houses and boarding houses (Lamb, 1968). However, not all patients could be discharged, and many who were, returned to the state hospital after short periods of residence in the community. It has become apparent that while the typical state hospital may be changing, reports of its imminent demise were premature.

Among the new developments at state hospitals, as well as Veterans Administration hospitals, has been the use of behavior modification techniques. Behavior therapy has been used to treat patients with severe regression manifested by such symptoms as mutism, eating disorders or deviant behavior (Ayllon and Michael, 1959; Ayllon, 1963; Ayllon and Azrin, 1964). Verbal conditioning has been used to convert irrational and delusional speech into more appropriate communications (Rickard, Dignam and Horner, 1960; Ullmann, Krasner, Collins, 1961; Meichenbaum 1966a,b). The theoretical basis of these techniques has been questioned as well as the amount of generalization that occurred, i.e., the extension of improvement to other areas of the patient's behavior (Greenspoon, 1962; Davidson, 1969). While it has yet to be shown that patients can improve sufficiently to be discharged with the use of these techniques alone, they may be used to ease problems of ward management and allow the patient to participate in other treatment approaches.

Behavior modification techniques have also been used to organize wards as token economies. In a token economy, patients are given tokens for desired behavior. The rewarded behavior can be anything from a simple activity such as self-care in the case of a regressed patient, to more difficult accomplishments such as satisfactory job performance in the case of a patient approaching discharge. The tokens, in turn, can be exchanged for simple privileges such as watching T.V. or more significant rewards such as obtaining a more desirable job within the hospital. In state and V.A. hospitals, where a shortage of personnel often exists, these programs are especially useful in dealing with chronic patients whose discharge is prevented, not by acute psychiatric symptomatology, but rather by decreased social skills and motivation. This is especially true in V.A. hospitals where patients with service-connected disabilities are literally paid for remaining sick and hospitalized. How effective token economies are in producing an increased discharge rate is still uncertain. In one study, following the establishment of a token economy, twice as many men were discharged from the hospital compared with the previous year. However, half of the discharged patients returned in nine months (Atthowe and Crasner, 1968).

Despite the recent advances in the treatment of chronic patients, it has become apparent that there is a hard core of patients who are refractory to treatment and cannot be discharged (Lamb and Goertzel, 1972). One group of hard-core patients consists of those who cannot manage outside a hospital setting. Such patients include assaultive patients, extremely regressed patients, patients with severe organic pathology and patients with antisocial proclivities such as fire setting or deviant sexual behavior. Another group consists of those patients who are determined to lead an institutional existence and who will defeat any attempt to maintain them outside of a hospital setting.

It is also being recognized that the placement of patients in the community does not guarantee an existence preferable to a hospital (Lamb and Goertzel, 1971). An individual can lead an institutionalized existence in a boarding house as well as in a state hospital, and in many instances a hospital environment may be more humane (Aviram and Segal, 1973).

In addition to long-term patients, the state hospital must serve new patients who continue to enter. Despite the expansion of the community mental health center system, many communities have inadequate or no facilities. In other cases, efforts on the part of community hospitals to achieve open wards result in the referral of severely agitated patients to state hospitals. Difficult-to-treat patients such as alcoholics, drug addicts and patients with organic pathology are often selectively referred to state hospitals. Modern treatment techniques have resulted in a progressively shorter length of stay in the hospital, but inadequate follow-up often results in the revolving-door phenomenon in which patients are discharged only to return again and again to the hospital. Significantly more patients released without referral are rehospitalized compared to those referred for outpatient care (Zolik, Lantz and Sommers, 1968). Even when adequate referral resources are available, the referral process may be subverted. Hostile and belligerent demands for release on the part of the patient or his family may lead to inadequate discharge planning. In other instances the staff may feel that the patient will not follow through, and hence they make only a half-hearted effort to arrange a proper disposition. For example, it is very common to see schizophrenics stop their medication as soon as the supply issued to them at discharge by the hospital runs out, and reenter the hospital with a recurrence of psychotic symptoms. Furthermore, if the lag time between discharge and the first outpatient visit exceeds two weeks, an inordinately high rehospitalization rate results (Zolik, et al., 1968). The scarcity of resources for patients unable to obtain private treatment may make it difficult for such individuals to be engaged in appropriate treatment within this critical time period and thus may also contribute to the revolving door phenomenon. Although Medicaid has extended the possibility that the poor and medically indigent may receive care in the private sector, the system is structured such that a majority of practitioners will not wish to participate (Schwartz, Perlman, Paris and Thornton, 1981).

In an effort to provide continuity of care, many state hospitals have adopted a program of regionalization in which a given unit of the state hospital serves a particular geographic catchment area (Greenblatt, Sharaf and Stone, 1971). Follow-up services may also be provided by this unit and close linkages can be developed between a catchmented unit and community resources in this area.

It has been suggested that the policy of early discharge may not be the wisest course for many patients. Kris, Schiff and McLaughlin (1971) have noted that many chronic patients do not begin their chronic hospitalization with their first hospitalization but are discharged only to return and then become chronic hospital patients. This is especially true of adolescents, who may require a more substantial in-hospital effort to master developmental tasks prior to discharge if rehospitalization and chronicity are to be avoided.

While many state hospital systems have made marked progress in improving the quality of care offered to mentally ill patients, recent court decisions applying the concept of "right to treatment" have tended to prod laggard systems into modernizing and upgrading their programs. Courts have held that patients who are involuntarily hospitalized have a right to treatment, and that merely offering custodial care does not satisfy this right (Bazelon, 1969). In some cases, the courts have gone so far as to decree the number and qualifications of mental health professionals required to provide adequate care for a given patient population (Robitscher, 1972). These mandates, however, ignore the hard reality that there are some patients and conditions that, given the present state of the art, often do not respond to even the most intensive treatment approaches (Twerski, 1971). The resolution of this conflict may lie in the development of objective standards of patient care that would allow the care offered by any institution to be evaluated and compared with other facilities.

DEINSTITUTIONALIZATION

The result of shortened hospital stays within both the state and private sectors is that hospitals that previously warehoused the mentally ill are now increasingly discharging chronically ill patients when exacerbations have been controlled (Deinstitutionalization, 1979; Deinstitutionalization: NIMH, 1979). The state system model increasingly parallels the acute care units of general hospitals. The social consequences of deinstitutionalization, which saw large numbers of patients without resources or the skills to obtain them left to fend for themselves in urban areas, created a demand for better discharge planning and aftercare. Federal and state governments began to legislate requirements for comprehensive discharge planning, and limited monies were made available to fund community support systems agencies (CSS). Discharge planning now must begin at the onset of hospitalization and cannot be relegated to a later dispositional phase. Indeed, this planning approach extends the hospital's responsibility beyond the time of discharge (Lamb, 1971; Barten, 1973).

The kind of activities that the staff will be involved with include financial planning, living arrangements, employment counseling and vocational rehabilitation. To ensure that these activities are carried out and that regulatory requirements are met, the Joint Commission on Accreditation of Hospitals (JCAH) mandates that such activities be charted. Failure to comply may jeopardize accreditation. The frustration involved in discharge planning stems from the fact that most communities have negligible resources allocated for these purposes. Making the need for good discharge planning more compelling were studies that questioned the need for long-term hospitalization for most psychiatric patients (Mattes, Rosen and Klein, 1977).

PARTIAL HOSPITALIZATION

The first modern psychiatric day hospital was begun by Dzhagarov in Moscow in 1933. However, it was not until after World War II that such hospitals were established in the Western world (Cameron, 1947; Bierer, 1951). Between 1958 and 1963 the number of day and night treatment centers increased from 8 to 141.

(*APA Proceedings,* 1958; Conwell, Rosen, Hench and Bahn, 1964). Partial hospitalization peaked in popularity during the 1960s with the development of community mental health centers, since it was one of the five mandated services qualifying a center for public support (Kramer, 1962).

In recent years the popularity of day hospitals has declined as it has become possible to specify more clearly the various tasks performed by day hospitals and to compare the efficacy and efficiency of the day hospital and other treatment settings with respect to these functions (Astrachan, Flynn, Geller and Harvey, 1970).

Day hospitals can perform three basic functions. They can function as an alternative to full-time hospitalization, as a stepping stone from full hospitalization to outpatient treatment and as a setting for the rehabilitation of the chronically ill.

Day hospitals, as an alternative to inpatient wards, can be organized as free-standing units not attached to an inpatient service. The purpose of such an arrangement is to keep the patient involved, at least partially, with his family and his community. Treatment techniques that have been found useful on inpatient wards (e.g., milieu) are applied in similar fashion in these settings. Whereas day hospitals can be organized in many different ways, they lend themselves particularly well to a team structure. In such settings a particular group of staff members become expert in the problems of a specific group of patients. Since patients leave the hospital each day, interteam difficulties are minimized.

Therapeutic activities in the day setting have included group, individual and family therapy, occupational and recreational therapy, psychodrama and, where indicated, somatic therapies including electroshock therapy. A typical feature in most day settings is a "wrap-up" meeting at the end of each day to assess each patient's progress and to evaluate whether or not each individual may return to the community for the night. The more disturbed the patient population, the more vital such a wrap-up becomes.

A variety of clinical conditions can be treated in a day hospital setting. Such conditions include schizophrenia, depression and character disorders. In general, schizophrenics treated in day hospital settings are less confused, show fewer cognitive disturbances and have a greater degree of social competence than those treated in inpatient settings, whereas depressed patients in day hospitals tend to be more similar to those found on inpatient wards (Hogarty, Dennis, Guy and Gross, 1968). Unless no other treatment facilities are available, acutely suicidal, homicidal or confused patients are not ordinarily accepted into day hospitals.

With the development of comprehensive mental health services, the range of patients referred to day hospitals as an alternative to inpatient hospitalization has narrowed. Severely disturbed patients are sent to inpatient units; acute patients, with a potential for rapid recompensation, are referred to crisis intervention units. Patients without gross disturbance are, increasingly, being treated on an outpatient basis, which has been increasingly made possible by advances in psychopharmacology. As a result there is a tendency for day hospitals, established as alternatives to inpatient units, to concentrate their efforts on patients who tend to be more chronic, and who see active treatment as a threat to long-standing regressive needs and patterns of dependency. Such patients tend to stay in day hospitals for prolonged periods of time, exceeding in average stay the amount of time more acute patients have to spend on inpatient units.

While the popularity of the free-standing day hospital has, for the above reasons, declined in recent years, it has left an impact on the care of hospitalized patients. It is now recognized that the use of day status is a valuable tool in facilitating a patient's reentry to his home, community or work after a period of hospitalization. Day hospitals fulfilling this transition function are best associated with an inpatient service so that continuity of care may be preserved, a consideration that has further tended to limit the utilization of free-standing day hospitals for the care of patients. Day hospitals associated with inpatient services function best if patients are first admitted to the inpatient service. This allows each patient to become a part of the total program. If patients are directly admitted to day status, they may view themselves as "better," more privileged and less sick than the inpatients. Alternatively, they may feel deprived, less cared for and barred from "real" treatment.

While not as common as day hospitalization, night hospitalization offers specific advantages, especially for the male patient, over traditional hospitalization (Beigel and Feder, 1970a). A patient may continue to work and at the same time be protected from stresses in his home environment. Concentrated hospital treatment is possible without jeopardizing the patient's job. Its main use is as a transition from inpatient care when it is important to determine if patients who work can function on the job.

At present, day settings can play a major role in the rehabilitation, reeducation and resocialization of the chronically ill, particularly those patients with reduced social skills who cannot be expected to achieve a consistently high level of functioning. In such settings, therapy would ideally be more supportive and conducted over a longer period of time than on acute services or in free-standing day hospitals. Social and vocational rehabilitation, geared to the specific potential of each patient, becomes more important than therapies focusing on intrapsychic conflicts. The service may be geared to psychotic patients, neurotic patients or both (Freeman, 1962; Jones, Cormack and Bow, 1963).

It has been suggested that chronic patients who cannot tolerate the total push of acute services and who drop out of such services will do better in a less stressful day care setting (Beigel and Feder, 1970b). These day care centers, as opposed to the earlier day hospital models, may have treatment programs conducted primarily by social workers, occupational and recreational therapists and community mental health workers. They may be located outside of hospital settings and within the community they are supposed to serve. In this way, they can become a part of the total rehabilitative programs operant in a particular region, including sheltered workshops and halfway houses. They can also operate on a flexible schedule providing a range of care for those who need to be seen weekly or less for socialization and/or medication and those patients who require daily care.

Day care centers may serve an especially useful function for schizophrenic patients who come from families that have been described by Brown, Birley and Wing (1972) and Vaughn and Leff (1976) as having a high level of expressed emotionality. Removal of the patients from the family setting enhances their chance of remaining out of the hospital.

EVOLVING PATTERNS OF HOSPITAL STAFFING

The rapid expansion of facilities for the care and treatment of the mentally ill that occurred during the past decade highlighted the necessity for adopting a multi-professional approach to treatment. With limited personnel, it was necessary to expand the role of psychiatric nurses, aides and social workers, to encompass tasks that had formerly been reserved for psychiatrists and psychologists. Simultaneously with the breakdown of a system that rigidly defined professional role, psychiatrists and hospital administrators became increasingly cognizant of the important tasks that had been performed by aides and nurses and the tremendous influence that such interventions had on patients. Once this influence became apparent, upgrading of skills and in-service education programs became imperative and commonplace. The increasing value placed upon paraprofessionals is reflected in the evolution of terms that have been used to designate them. Orderlies became psychiatric aides, who then became mental health workers. Career ladders have been established within the civil service system to allow for career progression within this latter category.

The assumption of increased responsibility by mental health workers created an increased sense of professionalism that led to enhanced morale, a feeling of professional self-worth and an insistence that an egalitarian social system be established on hospital wards. The psychiatrist has abandoned his earlier position of total command and authority and has become, instead, the leader of a team composed of nurses, social workers and aides (Bauer, 1970). While usually the best educated and informed member of the team, the psychiatrist has learned to share decision-making power with his colleagues and to function as a "coach, consultant and teacher." The team is ideally able to bring differential expertise to bear on individual patients or particular problems. In addition, it provides a vehicle for coordinating the efforts of all staff involved in particular cases and for providing vital exchanges of information about each case. Team members need not each have identical skills or similar needs to know everything about each patient. Every contribution made by each member is not necessarily valid or acceptable.

Teams get into difficulty because of problems that arise within each team as well as those that result when various teams function in a single setting. Patients live in a ward or hospital setting, and they interact with other patients and many staff members, irrespective of team boundaries. Should interactions between patients on different teams take place, the team member involved may neglect to look at the total picture, focusing only on the patient who is the team's responsibility. Disruptive behavior may be inadequately handled or ignored if another "team's patient" is involved. On the other hand, interventions on the part of one team's staff with another team's patients may be viewed with disfavor by the patient's team. To avoid such chaos, it is essential that teams interact with one another and the unity of the total setting be preserved. Such problems are markedly diminished in day hospital settings because patients can more easily be separated according to team assignment, which accounts for the popularity of the team approach in such settings (Astrachan *et al.*, 1970).

Regardless of the setting, intrateam difficulties may arise. The structure of the team may lead to diffusion of responsibility. The concept that everyone is responsible can lead in practice to no one's being responsible. Attempts to practice democracy can lead to decisions being made by consensus, with expertise having to yield to less qualified opinion. Individual team members are often loathe to act independently when necessary for a patient's benefit, choosing the safer course of waiting for team meetings to thoroughly consider each issue. The close working relationships between staff members engendered by the team setting may lead to a tendency for team members to protect each other and team cohesiveness at the expense of patient care. Team members may be reluctant to challenge a staff member's work with patients, rather than risk the ire of the criticized person. The team may label patients as difficult to work with rather than acknowledge that certain team members have difficulty working with certain patients. Such difficulties are not unique to teams, but the degree of cooperation demanded in team settings fosters such behavior unless the teams are acutely aware of this tendency.

In hospitals that depend on the admission of private patients by psychiatrists who will follow the cases, it is important that a psychiatrist be attached to the unit on at least a halftime basis. Without such an individual to serve as a coordinator, a team approach is not possible.

Nurses and aides have, increasingly, been called upon to assume new responsibilities and duties (e.g., history taking, mental status examination, group leadership and team coordination). They have also, in various settings (Cline and Rouzer, 1971; Stern, Beck and Mack, 1972), become the primary therapist for patients, assuming responsibility for the patient's psychotherapy. As a result of these new role definitions, aspects of patient care formerly associated with the nursing role have tended to become devalued, and the newer roles, felt to have more prestige, are the only ones seen as capable of giving work satisfaction. What was formerly perceived as excellent nursing care may now be viewed as pill pushing and mere drudgery, left over from an antiquated medical model. The once highly prized ability to provide intimate and constant contact with very disturbed patients, still a clinical necessity, is viewed as custodial care. Battles between hospital administrators and nurses over whether street clothes or traditional uniforms will be worn are the tip of the iceberg in nursing's push for recognition, prestige and work satisfaction (Klein, Pillsbury, Bushey and Snell, 1972). While uniforms may not be the issue, there is a real need in mental hospitals for traditional nursing care.

THE NEW FRONTIER: THE INTEGRATION OF TECHNOLOGY

In the field of biological psychiatry a multiplicity of clinically useful approaches to more precise diagnosis and treatment are becoming available. They are derived from research conducted over the past decade in areas of neurochemistry, psychopharmacology and neurophysiology. Several have already been integrated into the current state of the art, while others, which have shown substantial potential, are still under investigation. These tools can be expected to appear and be useful in any of the settings previously discussed.

By way of illustration and without attempting to be exhaustive, several of the promising approaches will be presented. The dexamethasone suppression test as pioneered by Carroll, Curtis and Mendels (1976) helps identify patients who are depressed and may be useful in predicting the response of individual patients to antidepressants and perhaps to ECT. Positive responders to this test, called non-suppressors, do not show the suppression of cortisol secretion that characteristically follows the administration of dexamethasone. The dexamethasone suppression test extended basic research findings in the area of neuroendocrine concomitants of affective disorders. Several research groups had noted cortisol hypersecretion during major depressive disorders that resolved at the time of clinical recovery without being influenced by psychological stress (Gibbons and McHugh, 1962; Carroll and Mendels, 1976; Sachar, Roffwarg, Gruen et al., 1976).

Another substance that has been investigated and may represent a prototype of biological markers of use in clinical situations is urinary 3-methoxy-4-hydroxyphenylglycol (MHPG), 80% of which is derived from the metabolism of brain norepinephrine. It has been found that depressed patients who best respond to imipramine have low pretreatment levels of MHPG. Those with high pretreatment MHPG levels are less likely to respond to imipramine (Fawcett, Maas and Dekirmenjian, 1972; Maas, Fawcett and Dekirmenjian, 1972; Maas, 1975).

The quantification of urinary MHPG and the dexamethasone suppression test are two examples of clinically applied neurochemistry. Pharmacologic research has presented the clinician with the ability to monitor serum levels of antidepressants and thus may help in gauging optimal dosage. For example, the work of Asberg, Cronholm, Sjoquist et al. (1971) and Kragh-Sorensen, Asberg and Eggert-Hansen (1973) with nortriptyline and Whyte MacDonald, Naylor et al. (1976) with protriptyline has demonstrated a "window effect" for the therapeutic efficacy of these medications. In effect, their findings imply that the drugs do not work optimally outside of a circumscribed therapeutic range. These findings may not necessarily be extended to all tricyclic antidepressants (Glassman, Perel, Shostak et al. 1977).

Physiologic research offers the clinician another approach to the verification of depressive disorders through the EEG monitoring of sleep patterns. Kupfer has reported that the existence of reduced REM latency is evidence of primary rather than secondary depression (Kupfer and Foster, 1972; Kupfer, Foster, Reich *et al.*, 1976).

Other examples of new biologic information having the potential for influencing clinical understanding and practice include the following:

1) Computed axial tomography (CAT Scan) as an aid in decision making with respect to the long-term use of neuroleptics in schizophrenia.
2) The use of cortical evoked potentials to help in the differential diagnosis of hysterical disorders.
3) The use of amphetamine as a biologic probe in order to ascertain whether a patient is likely to respond well to imipramine.

The burgeoning discipline of neuropsychology is adding precision to the clinician's ability to elaborate an individualized treatment and rehabilitative plan. For example, when making a referral of a patient to a vocational rehabilitation program it is useful to be able to go beyond merely providing a diagnosis and state which tasks a patient is best or least equipped to perform.

CONCLUSION

Until recent years psychiatric hospitals were considered to be the most traditional and stable setting for the care of the mentally ill. Today the field of hospital care is in ferment. Basic issues (e.g., what is psychiatric illness, who is sick, who needs hospitalization, what is good hospital care, who is capable of treating mentally ill patients, what is recovery, when should a patient be discharged) have become hotly debated and remain unresolved. The continuum of opinion ranges from those people who feel that hospitalization should be avoided whenever not absolutely necessary (Decker and Stubblebine, 1972) to those who feel that prolonged hospitalization offers a patient the best possibility for restructuring his personality and recovering from his illness. Scarce resources, time limits dictated by third-party payments and the need to provide care for large numbers of patients have required innovative solutions and procedures. Hospital treatment today includes crisis intervention units, intensive milieu units with emphasis on group interaction, behavior modification wards, day hospitals and long-term settings with emphasis on individual psychotherapy. Newly available are a host of biologic diagnostic and therapeutic interventions that in the decade to come may be expected to add precision to the care of the psychiatric patient. Within each setting, hospitals vary according to who treats patients, with what modality of treatment and according to which theoretical framework. In some settings only psychiatrists do traditional psychotherapy, whereas in others members of other disciplines or generic mental health workers are the therapist of record. In large cities, mental health workers with little formal training but with knowledge of the patients' cultural origins and familiarity with the patients' language, are often called upon to take major treatment responsibilities. Such trends are upsetting to some professionals, welcomed by others and a matter of indifference to a third group who believe that medication and removal of the patient from his conflictual environment are all that can be accomplished in a hospitalization, especially a brief one.

While pioneer studies in evaluation research (Schwartz, Myers and Astrachan, 1973; Riedel, Brauer, Goldblatt, Schwartz, Myers and Klerman, 1968, 1971) and nascent studies in utilization review may eventually help us determine the answer to some of the preceding questions, as well as establish good and accepted standards of care, at the present time decisions as to what kind of hospital is appropriate for which patient, with which syndrome, rest in the hands of the referring clinician.

REFERENCES

Abroms, G.M. The open-door policy: A rational use of controls. *Hospital and Community Psychiatry*. **24**: 81-84 (February 1973).

Almond, R., Keniston, K. and Boltax, S. The value system of a milieu therapy unit. *Archives of General Psychiatry*. **19**: 545-561 (November 1968).

Almond, R., Keniston, K. and Boltax, S. Value change in milieu therapy. *Archives of General Psychiatry*. **20**: 339-351 (March 1969a).

Almond, R., Keniston, K. and Boltax, S. Milieu therapeutic process. *Archieves of General Psychiatry*. **21**: 431-442 (October 1969b).

American Psychiatric Association Proceedings, 1958. Day Hospital Conference, Washington, D.C., 1958.

Artiss, K.L. *Milieu therapy in schizophrenia*. New York: Grune & Stratton, 1962.

Asberg, M., Cronholm, B., Sjoquist, F. *et al*. Relationship between plasma level and therapeutic effect of nortriptyline. *British Medical Journal*. **3**: 331 (1971).

Astrachan, B.M., Flynn, H.R., Geller, J.D. and Harvey, H.H. Systems approach to day hospitalization. *Archives of General Psychiatry*. **22**: 550-559 (1970).

Atthowe, J.M., Jr. and Crasner, L. A preliminary report on the application of contingent reinforcement procedures (token economy) on a "chronic" psychiatric ward. *Journal of Abnormal Psychology*. **73**: 37-43 (1968).

Aviram, U. and Segal, S.P. Exclusion of the mentally ill. *Archives of General Psychiatry*. **29**: 126-133 (July 1973).

Ayllon, T. Intensive treatment of psychotic behavior by stimulus satiation and food reinforcement. *Behavior Research and Therapy*. **1**: 53-61 (May 1963).

Ayllon, T. and Azrin, N.H. Reinforcement and instructions with mental patients. *Journal of Experimental Analysis Behavior*. **7**: 327-331 (July 1964).

Ayllon, T. and Michael, J. The psychiatric nurse as a behavioral engineer. *Journal of Experimental Analysis Behavior*. **2**: 323-334 (October 1959).

Barten, H.H. Developing a multiphasic rehabilitation program for psychotic patients in a community mental health clinic. *Psychiatric Quarterly*. **47**: 159 (1973).

Bateman, J. and Dunham, H.W. The state mental hospital as a specialized community experience. *American Journal of Psychiatry*. **105**: 445-448 (1948).

Bauer, W. Recent developments in mental health manpower. *Hospital and Community Psychiatry.* **21**: 11-17 (January 1970).

Bazelon, D. The right to treatment: The courts role. *Hospital and Community Psychiatry.* **20**: 129-135 (May 1969).

Beck, J.C. and Worthen, K. Precipitating stress, crisis theory, and hospitalization in schizophrenia and depression. *Archives of General Psychiatry.* **26**: 123-129 (1972).

Beigel, A. and Feder, S.L. A night hospital program. *Hospital and Community Psychiatry.* **21**: 26-29 (1970a).

Beigel, A. and Feder, S.L. Patterns of utilization in partial hospitalization. *American Journal of Psychiatry.* **126**: 101-108 (1970b).

Bellnap, I. *Human problems of a state mental hospital.* New York: McGraw-Hill, 1956.

Bierer, J. *The day hospital: An experiment in social psychiatry and syntoanalytic psychotherapy.* London: Lewis, 1951.

Brown, G.W., Birley, L.T. and Wing, J.K. Influence of family life in the course of schizophrenic disorders: A replication. *British Journal of Psychiatry.* **121**: 241-258 (1972).

Cameron, D.E. The day hospital. *Modern Hospital.* **69**: 60-62 (1947).

Caplan, G. *Principles of preventive psychiatry.* New York: Basic Books, 1964.

Carroll, B.J., Curtis, G.C. and Mendels, J. Neuroendocrine regulation in depression: II. Discrimination of depressed from nondepressed patients. *Archives of General Psychiatry.* **33**: 1051-1058 (September 1976).

Carroll, B.J. and Mendels, J. Neuroendocrine regulation in affective disorders. In: Sachar, E.J. (Ed.), *Hormones, behavior and psychotherapy,* p. 193. New York: Raven Press, 1976.

Caudill, W. *The psychiatric hospital as a small society.* Cambridge, Mass.: Harvard University Press, 1958.

Clark, D.H. *Administrative therapy.* London: Tavistock Publications, 1964.

Cline, D.W. and Rouzer, D.L. The physician as primary therapist in hospital psychiatry. *American Journal of Psychiatry.* **128**: 407-411 (October 1971).

Conwell, M., Rosen, B., Hench, C. and Bahn, A.K. The first national survey of psychiatric day-night services. In: Epps, R.L. and Hanes, L.D. (Eds.), *Day Care of Psychiatric Patients,* pp. 91-105. Springfield, Ill.: Charles C. Thomas, 1964.

Cumming, J. and Cumming, E. *Ego and milieu: Theory and practice of environmental therapy.* New York: Atherton Press, 1962.

Davidson, G.C. Appraisal of behavior modification techniques with adults in institutional settings. In: Franks, C.M. (Ed.), *Behavior therapy,* pp. 220-278. New York: McGraw-Hill, 1969.

Decker, J.B. and Stubblebine, J.M. Crisis intervention and prevention of psychiatric disability. *American Journal of Psychiatry.* **129**: 725-729 (1972).

Deinstitutionalization: The evolution and evaluation of health care policy in the United States and Great Britain. *Milbank Memorial Fund Quarterly/Health and Society.* Vol. 57, no. 4 (1979).

Diagnostic and statistical manual of mental disorders, 3rd ed. Washington, D.C.: American Psychiatric Association, 1980.

Dunham, H.W. and Weinberg, S.K. *The culture of the state mental hospital.* Detroit: Wayne State University Press, 1960.

Edelson, M. *Ego psychology, group dynamics and the therapeutic community.* New York: Grune & Stratton, 1964.

Fawcett, J.A., Maas, J.W. and Dekirmenjian, H. Depression and MHPG Excretion. *Archives of General Psychiatry.* **26**: (1972).

Fisher, A. and Weinstein, M.R. Mental hospitals, prestige, and the image of enlightenment. *Archives of General Psychiatry.* **25**: 41-48 (July 1971).

Freeman, P. Treatment of chronic schizophrenia in a day center. *Archives of General Psychiatry.* **7**: 259-265 (1962).

Gerhardt, S. The evaluation of a patient government. *Hospital and Community Psychiatry.* **19**: 329-330 (1968).

Gibbons, J.L. and McHugh, P.R. Plasma cortisol in depressive illness. *Journal of Psychiatric Research.* **1**: 162 (1962).

Glassman, A.H., Perel, J.M., Shostak, M. *et al.* Clinical implications of imipramine plasma levels for depressive illness. *Archives of General Psychiatry.* **34**: 197 (1977).

Goffman, E. *Asylums.* New York: Doubleday, 1961.

Greenblatt, M. Sharaf, M. and Stone, E. *Dynamics of institutional change.* Pittsburgh: University of Pittsburgh Press, 1971.

Greenblatt, M., York, R. and Brown, E.L. *From custodial to therapeutic care in a mental hospital.* New York: Russell Sage Foundation, 1955.

Greenley, J.R. Power processes and patient behaviors. *Archives of General Psychiatry.* **28**: 683-688 (May 1973).

Greenspoon, J. Verbal conditioning and clinical psychology. In: *Experimental foundations of clinical psychology,* pp. 510-553. New York: Basic Books, 1962.

Group for the Advancement of Psychiatry. *Crisis in psychiatric hospitalizations.* Report #72, 1969.

Hecker, A.O. The demise of large state hospitals. *Hospital and Community Psychiatry.* **21**: 261-263 (1970).

Herz, M.I. The therapeutic community: A critique. *Hospital and Community Psychiatry.* **23**: 69-71 (March 1972).

Herz, M.I., Wilensky, H. and Earle, A. Problems of role dysfunction in the therapeutic community. *Archives of General Psychiatry.* **14**: 270-276 (March 1966).

Hogarty, G.E., Dennis, H., Guy, W. and Gross, G.M. "Who goes there?" – A critical evaluation of admissions to a psychiatric day hospital. *American Journal of Psychiatry.* **124**: 934-944 (1968).

Jackson, J. Factors of the treatment environment. *Archives of General Psychiatry.* **21**: 39-45 (1969).

Joint Commission on Mental Illness and Health. *Action for mental health.* New York: Basic Books, 1961.

Jones, A.L., Cormack, G. and Bow, L. Within the day hospital. *American Journal of Psychiatry.* **119**: 973-977 (1963).

Jones, M. *The therapeutic community.* New York: Basic Books, 1962.

Kaufman, A. The role of the staff advisor in patient government. *Hospital and Community Psychiatry.* **21**: 298-300 (1970).

Kaufman, M.R. *The psychiatric unit in a general hospital.* New York: International Universities Press, 1965.

Klein, R.H., Pillsbury, J., Bushey, M. and Snell, S. Psychiatric staff: Uniforms or street clothes. *Archives of General Psychiatry.* **26**: 19-22 (January 1972).

Kragh-Sorensen, P., Asberg, M. and Eggert-Hansen, C. Plasma nortriptyline levels in endogenous depression. *Lancet* **1**: 113 (1973).

Kramer, B.M. *Day hospital.* New York: Grune & Stratton, 1962.

Kris, A., Schiff, L. and McLaughlin, R. Susceptibility to chronic hospitalization relative to age at first admission. *Archives of General Psychiatry.* **24**: 346-352 (April 1971).

Kupfer, D.J. and Foster, F.G. Interval between onset of sleep and rapid eye movement sleep as an indicator of depression. *Lancet* **2**: 684 (1972).

Kupfer, D.J., Foster, F.G., Reich, L. *et al.* EEG sleep changes as predictors in depression. *American Journal of Psychiatry.* **113**: 622 (1976).

Lamb, H.R. Release of chronic psychiatric patients into the community. *Archives of General Psychiatry.* **19**: 38-44 (July 1968).

Lamb, H.R. Coordination: The key to rehabilitation. *Hospital and Community Psychiatry.* **22**: 46 (1971).

Lamb, H.R. and Goertzel, V. Discharged mental patients – Are they really in the community? *Archives of General Psychiatry.* **24**: 29-34 (January 1971).

Lamb, H.R. and Goertzel, V. The demise of the state hospital – A premature obituary. *Archives of General Psychiatry.* **26**: 489-495 (June 1972).

Langsley, D.G. Crisis intervention. *American Journal of Psychiatry.* **129**: 734-736 (1972).

Lebensohn, Z.M. Facilities and organization. In: Kaufman, M.R. (Ed.), *The psychiatric unit in a general Hospital,* New York: International Universities Press., 1965.

Levinson, D.J. and Gallagher, E.B. *Patienthood in the mental hospital.* Boston: Houghton Mifflin Company, 1964.

Lindemann, E. Symptomatology and management of acute grief. *American Journal of Psychiatry.* **101**: 141-148 (1944).

Linn, L.S. Social characteristics and patient expectations toward mental hospitalization. *Archives of General Psychiatry.* **20**: 457-469 (April 1969).

Linn, L.S. State hospital environment and rates of patient discharge. *Archives of General Psychiatry.* **23**: 346-351 (October 1970).

Maas, J.W. Biogenic amines and depression. *Archives of General Psychiatry.* **32**: 1357 (1975).

Maas, J.W., Fawcett, J.A. and Dekirmenjian, H. Catecholamine metabolism, depressive illness, and drug response. *Archives of General Psychiatry.* **26**: 252 (1972).

Mann, J. *Time-limited psychotherapy.* Cambridge, Mass.: Harvard University Press, 1973.

Marohn, R.C. The therapeutic milieu as an open system. *Archives of General Psychiatry.* **22**: 360-364 (1970).

Mattes, J.A., Rosen, B. and Klein, D.F. Comparison of the clinical effectiveness of "short" versus "long" stay hospitalization. II. Results of a 3-year post-hospitalization follow-up. *Journal of Nervous and Mental Disease.* **165**: 387 (1977).

May, P.R.A. *The treatment of schizophrenia,* New York: Science House, 1968.

Meichenbaum, D.H. The effects of social reinforcement on the level of abstraction in schizophrenics. *Journal of Abnormal Psychology.* **71**: 354-362 (1966a).

Meichenbaum, D.H. The effects of instructions and reinforcement on thinking and language behaviors of schizophrenics. Unpublished doctoral dissertation, University of Illinois, 1966b.

Moos, R. Size, staffing, and psychiatric ward treatment environments. *Archives of General Psychiatry.* **26**: 414-418 (May 1972).

Moos, R. and Houts, P. Assessment of the social atmosphere of psychiatric wards. *Journal of Abnormal Psychology.* **73**: 595-604 (1968).

National Institute of Mental Health. Series D, No. 4, Deinstitutionalization: An analytical review and sociological perspective, DHEW Publication No. (ADM) 79-351. Superintendent of Documents, U.S. Government Printing Office, Washington, D.C. 20402, 1979.

National Institute of Mental Health. Trends in patient care episodes in mental health facilities, 1955-1977. Mental Health Statistical Note Number 154, September 1980.

National Institute of Mental Health. Utilization of mental health facilities, 1971, DHEW Publication No. NIH-74-657. Superintendent of Documents, U.S. Government Printing Office, Washington, D.C. 20402, 1973.

Osmond, H. Function as the basis of psychiatric ward design. *Mental Hospitals.* **8**: 23-30 (1957).

Perlman, B.B. and Hogben, G. Effects of changes in standing medication distribution times on prn drug use. *Diseases of the Nervous System.* **38**: 181-185 (1977).

Pierce, W.D., Truckett, E.J. and Moos, R.H. Changing ward atmosphere through staff discussion of the perceived ward environment. *Archives of General Psychiatry.* **26**: 35-41 (1972).

Rhine, M.W. and Mayerson, P. Crisis hospitalization within a psychiatric emergency service. *American Journal of Psychiatry.* **127**: 1386-1391 (1971).

Rickard, H.C., Dignam, P.J. and Horner, R.F. Verbal manipulation in a psychotherapeutic relationship. *Journal of Clinical Psychology.* **16**: 93 (1960).

Riedel, D.C., Brauer, L., Brenner, M.H., Goldblatt, P., Schwartz, C., Myers, J.K. and Klerman, G. Developing a system for utilization review and evaluation in community mental health centers. *Hospital and Community Psychiatry.* **22**: 229-232 (1971).

Robitscher, J. Courts, state hospitals, and the right to treatment. *American Journal of Psychiatry.* **129**: 298-303 (September 1972).

Rowland, H. Interaction processes in the state mental hospital. *Psychiatry.* **1**: 323-328 (1938).

Rubenstein, R. and Lasswell, H.D. *The sharing of power in a psychiatric hospital.* New Haven: Yale University Press. 1966.

Rubin, B. and Goldberg, A. An investigation of openness in the psychiatric hospital. *Archives of General Psychiatry.* **8**: 264-276 (March 1963).

Sachar, E.J., Roffwarg, H.P., Gruen, P.H. *et al.* Neuroendocrine studies of depressive illness. *Pharmako Psychiatrie.* **9**: 11 (1976).

Schwartz, A.H. and Farmer, R.G. Providing milieu treatment in a military setting. *Hospital and Community Psychiatry.* **19**: 271-276 (1968).

Schwartz, A.H., Perlman, B.B., Paris, M. and Thornton, J.C. Private psychiatric participation in Medicaid: Practitioner ebb and flow. *New York State Journal of Medicine.* **81**: 42-44 (1981).

Schwartz, C., Myers, J.K. and Astrachan, B.M. The outcome study in psychiatric evaluation research. *Archives of General Psychiatry.* **29**: 98-102 (1973).

Schwartz, C., Myers, J.K. and Astrachan, B.M. Concordance of multiple assessments of the outcome of schizophrenia: On defining the dependent variable in outcome studies. *Archives of General Psychiatry.* **32**: 1221-1227 (1975).

Schwartz, R.A., Mako, A.E. and Smith, Q. Patient management in a 100% open hospital. *Hospital and Community Psychiatry.* **23**: 85-87 (March 1972).

Spadoni, A.J. and Smith, J.A. Milieu therapy in schizophrenia. *Archives of General Psychiatry.* **20**: 547-551 (May 1969).

Stanton, A. and Schwartz, M. *The mental hospital.* New York: Basic Books, 1954.

Stern, E.S. Operation Sesame. *Lancet.* **1**: 577-578 (March 1957).

Stern, M.J., Beck J.C. and Mack, J.E. Training nurses to be therapist on a psychiatric inpatient service. *Hospital and Community Psychiatry.* **23**: 218-221 (July 1972).

Stewart, A., LaFare, H.G., Grunberg, F. and Herjanic, M. Problems in phasing out a large public psychiatric hospital. *American Journal of Psychiatry.* **125**: 82-88 (July 1968).

Twerski, A.D. Treating the untreatable. *Hospital and Community Psychiatry.* **22**: 261-264 (September 1971).

Ullmann, L.P., Krasner, L. and Collins, B.J. Modification of behavior through verbal conditioning: Effects in group therapy. *Journal of Abnormal and Social Psychology.* **62**: 128-132 (1961).

Unpublished data. Information Division of Biometry and Epidemiology, National Institute of Mental Health.

Vaughn, C.E. and Leff, J.P. The influence of family and social factors on the course of psychiatric illness: A comparison of schizophrenic and depressed neurotic patients. *British Journal of Psychiatry.* **129**: 125-137 (1976).

Weisman, G., Feirstein, A. and Thomas, C. Three day hospitalization – A model for intensive intervention. *Archives of General Psychiatry.* **21**: 620-629 (1969).

Wessen, A.F. *The psychiatric hospital as a social system.* Springfield, Ill.: Charles C. Thomas, 1964.

Whyte, S.F., MacDonald, A.J., Naylor, G.J. *et al.* Plasma concentrations of protriptyline and clinical effects in depressed women. *British Journal of Psychiatry.* **128**: 384 (1976).

Williams, E.W. Advanced levels of patient government. *Hospital and Community Psychiatry.* **21**: 300-301 (1970).

Zolik, E.S., Lantz, E.M. and Sommers, R. Hospital return rates and prerelease referrals. *Archives of General Psychiatry.* **18**: 712-717 (June 1968).

12 Aftercare

Daniel N. Hertz

INTRODUCTION

Aftercare, which had been the stepchild of mental health services, has become the focus of world attention since 1955, when the tremendous increase in mental hospital discharge rates forced the spotlight onto this previously neglected area. With the advent of tranquilizing drugs and antidepressants, more active and innovative treatment modalities, and an optimistic treatment climate, hospitalizations are now shorter and chronic patients remarkably fewer, despite the increasing admission rates. A great many long-hospitalized patients have been released to the community. Yet along with this trend has been an alarmingly high readmission rate, a "revolving door" syndrome of discharge and readmission. In New York State, statistics show that 28% of patients discharged from state mental hospitals in recent years have been readmitted within six months of their release, and up to 50% are expected to be readmitted eventually (Wren, 1973). Clearly, something is wrong.

The pendulum of concern for the rights of mental patients has shifted along with the trend to ready discharge. Dr. Robert Reich, Director of Psychiatry for the New York City Department of Social Services, eloquently expressed his concern (1973, pp. 911-912):

Newspapers and psychiatric journals have in recent months featured stories about the great strides in the treatment of severe chronic mental illness . . . . But what has happened to these chronically ill patients . . . . Few have families of their own and many are too mentally dysfunctional to live within a normal family setting. Confused and delusional, they turn to welfare departments to look after them . . . In New York City the Department of Social Services attempts to place these patients in whatever settings are available. The aged are referred to nursing homes, where they receive little psychiatric care and no real therapy . . . (C)hronically mentally ill persons (occupy proprietary home beds) . . . There are no day programs, little recreation, and nobody to check into the physical well being of the occupants. There people, many of whom have been in state institutions for fifteen years or more, rarely leave the building. They sit and stare into space, and regress as if in the back wards of state hospitals . . . . Most of the mentally ill are referred to cheap single-room occupancy hotels and rooming houses . . . They share this space with prostitutes, discharged prisoners and drug addicts.

Alarmed, Dr. Reich (p. 912) concludes that "our policy of discharging helpless human beings to a hostile community is immoral and inhuman." The development of satisfactory aftercare facilities is a moral imperative.

The demand for better aftercare facilities is echoed by relatives of discharged patients. A group of relatives of patients at Manhatten State Hospital accused the New York State Department of Mental Hygiene of "callous indifference" to the plight of released patients. The group demanded that the authorities rescind directives designed to empty state mental hospitals until there were decent facilities in the community for those released. "To assert the noble principle of 'community treatment' without making adequate provision for proper housing, follow-up care and treatment, rehabilitation and job training . . . is an immoral and malicious mockery of these helpless and ill people" (Wren, 1973).

As the concerns of officials and relatives alike have shown, there are many basic unanswered questions concerning aftercare. What happens to those discharged patients for whom no special treatment provisions are made? How many stay out of the hospital, and for how long? If they remain out, how well do they function, and what is the course of their illness? For those who decompensate, are there any high risk periods? Why do they decompensate? Does aftercare influence the course of the illness or the chance of readmission? If so, are there any aftercare programs that are particularly effective? Which are not? Unless there are answers to these and other questions, post-hospital treatment will remain a morass of well-meaning guesswork. This chapter will examine the evidence currently available, attempting to form a more coherent picture from the great mass of scattered data. Specific programs for children, drug addicts, alcoholics and offenders will not be covered.

A clarification about the use of the studies covered by this chapter is in order. "Aftercare" is used in the psychiatric literature to describe the *total* treatment program for the psychiatric patient after his discharge from the hospital. It encompasses all patients and all programs; it includes predischarge readiness and planning, post-hospital residential arrangements, resocialization techniques, vocational rehabilitation and professional care for all patients released from a psychiatric hospital, regardless of diagnosis. Statistics quickly reveal the wide variety of patients loosely lumped together as "discharged mental patients" for whom aftercare is sought. In New York State, excluding facilities for narcotics addicts, there were 41,531 patients discharged from state mental hospitals in the year ending March 31, 1971. Diagnostic categories were (Weinstein, DiPasquale and Winsor, 1973):

	%
Schizophrenia	40.6
Alcohol-related conditions	17
Other and undiagnosed	14
Psychosis of old-age	5.6
Affective disorders	4
Personality and behavior disorders	3.8
Organic brain syndrome	2.9
Drug-related conditions	2.4
Other psychoses	2
Mental retardation	1.3

All these categories are included in the patient population lumped together in most studies of "aftercare." It must be kept in mind that this breadth creates built-in limitations for such studies. Because of them, general studies of aftercare are limited to espousing broad treatment principles; yet treatment programs, to be effective, must be tailored to the needs of the individual patient.

In an excellent detailed study of those patients discharged from New York State mental hospitals from 1966-1971, (Weinstein, DiPasquale and Winsor, 1973), it was found that of those admitted during 1971, 35.3% left the hospital alive within 1 month, 55.9% within 2 months, and 85.1% within 9 months. Their median stay was 1.5 months; for those admitted in 1954, it had been 8 months. In terms of readmission of those released during 1971, 11.0% returned within 1 month, 15.8% within 2 months, 28% within 6 months and 32.8% within 9 months of their release. Readmission rates of those patients discharged in the earlier years of the study follow a similar curve, and gradually rise to about 50% in 4 years. The highest rates of return within 6 months (re-entry) were found among the mentally retarded (35.2%), those with alcohol-related conditions (31.5%) and those with schizophrenia (30.9%). The lowest re-entry rates were among those diagnosed with other psychoses (19.1%) and psychoneuroses (21.6%). There was a strong relationship between the number of previous admissions and the length of time out of the hospital: For those with no previous admissions, only 16.3% returned within 6 months; for those with one previous admission, the comparable rate was 26.3%, and the rate increased with each additional previous stay, reaching 69.7% for those with eight or more. There was very little association between the length of hospitalization and the re-entry rate. The six-year trend in the exit rate (discharge rate per time period) showed a pronounced upward movement, from 34.0% in 1966 to 55.9% in 1971. The re-entry rate also increased during the six-year period, from 20.4% in 1966, to 28.5% in 1970, and dropped slightly to 27.7% in 1971.

The Illinois Department of Mental Health reports similar hospital trends (Levy, 1971). They believe that the high readmission rate reflects the need for further work in the development of community resources to maintain patients in the community after discharge.

In a study of 229 male patients discharged from mental hospitals in the London area, all of whom had been in the hospital for two or more years, 68% remained out of the hospital for at least one year (Brown, Carstairs and Topping, 1958). Of those who relapsed during the six years of the study, 74% of the schizophrenic patients did so in the first year, compared to only 58% of the non-schizophrenics.

Prediction of post-hospital success or failure is extremely difficult. With the multitude of illnesses and symptoms represented by the mental hospital population, specific personality or symptom criteria do not statistically hold up. Yet with the schizophrenic patients, premorbid factors rather than age at hospitalization are crucial in determining post-hospital adjustment (Pollack, Levenstein and Klein, 1968). Premorbid asocial schizophrenics have a poorer chance for a favorable outcome (Gittelman-Klein and Klein, 1969), with withdrawal being the most important single measure in predicting success-failure when all variables are considered collectively (Sherman, Moseley, Ging and Bookbinder, 1964).

In an interesting ten-year follow-up study of female ex-mental patients and matched "normal" neighbors, interviews with the women and their husbands elicited data on domestic performance, social participation, expectations of performance, psychological functioning, and marital and family adjustment. It was found that 45% of the ex-patients were treated for psychiatric problems in the ten-year period, compared to 11% of the controls. The Langner Psychiatric Screening Scale indicated poorer functioning for patients and their husbands than for controls and their husbands. Controls were much better adjusted and happier in their marriages than the ex-patient couples. The children of ex-patients tended to be more poorly adjusted in school, at home and in the community than the children of the controls. Ex-patients centered more of their social activities around home and family, whereas controls were more likely to hold jobs (Molholm and Dinitz, 1972).

BACKGROUND

Aftercare has been with us for hundreds of years in many forms. The family placement programs in Geel, Belgium, for instance, date back to the seventeenth century. Yet it has only been since 1955, with hundreds of thousands of patients being discharged to their home communities, that there occurred a worldwide shift in treatment emphasis from hospital to community (Ryan, 1969). Prior to that, with long-term hospitalization the rule, patients were not uncommonly hospitalized to the end of their lives. Understandably, community facilities for released patients were rare.

From a historical overview the shift in treatment emphasis seems also a shift from private to public concern, voluntary to legislative, remedial to preventive. In England, the Mental Health Act of 1959 stressed the need for preventive and aftercare facilities and sheltered workshops in the community (Sharpe, 1972). The Federal Community Mental Health Centers Act of 1963 in the U.S. stressed the return of treatment responsibility to the local communities (McGarry and Kaplan, 1973).

The need for community aftercare facilities is now recognized worldwide. In England, Sharpe (1972) noted advances in treatment methods necessitated by the change from custodial to progressive patient care. Therapeutic communities, preventive therapy and resocialization techniques are being actively pursued in Italy (Scarzella, 1970). There are aftercare programs in Poland (Tretor, 1972) and in Russia (Babayan, 1969). All "Developed" countries have some aftercare services, and many "developing" countries have experimental programs (Lin, 1968).

Yet, despite the need, aftercare facilities have developed slowly. In 1961, the Final Report of the Joint Commission on Mental Illness and Health reported that "(a)ftercare services for the mentally ill are in a primitive state of development almost everywhere." In the U.S., the report noted, there were at that time only nine halfway houses, less than two dozen day hospitals, eight rehabilitation centers, seventy ex-patient clubs, and foster-home services for discharged patients in less than one-quarter of all the states. We will survey what has happened since then.

PRE-DISCHARGE PLANNING

The hospitalized patient commonly develops a dependence on the hospital and his doctor, and a sense of security associated with the hospital setting. Thus he feels ambivalent about leaving. Unless his conflict is resolved, chances for successful rehabilitation are diminished. Helping the patient develop an expectation of rehabilitation and a positive attitude toward it is therefore an important step toward achieving that goal. Ideally, such planning should begin as soon as the patient enters the hospital.

The programs developed to meet this challenge have been varied. Establishing small groups of patients to discuss problems of daily living while increasing their personal responsibility in order to simulate normal life as closely as possible is one method which has been used to ease the transition (Ritchey, 1971). Where possible, involving family in the treatment program and post-discharge planning seems advisable. The V.A. hospital at Perry Point, Maryland prepares chronically ill psychiatric patients for discharge through use of social group techniques, early and continued involvement with the patient's family, and direct contact with the community through the use of the services of selected, supervised volunteers. The program has worked well as a means of breaking through the patient's fears of new situations and leaving the security of the hospital (McGriff, 1965). To help the patient adjust to the post-hospital social situations he'll encounter and make use of the community facilities and programs available, Rosenberg and Colthoff (1967) took a group of patients and had *them* "volunteer" to serve as helpers or assistant group leaders in program areas at local community centers. Each volunteer contributed four hours of service each week and attended all volunteer conferences. This introduction to community facilities through active rather than passive participation seems to have been of significant and lasting value. Follow-up studies indicated that almost all of the patients continued to use the community centers in various ways after their discharge from the hospital.

The chronic patient who has spent much time in a hospital setting presents a special challenge in pre-discharge planning. He has been rewarded repeatedly in the hospital environment for being compliant, passive and uninterested in changing his behavior. Now he must be taught new habits and given new directions: improving his appearance, working at a job, social interaction. Liberman (1971) adapted behavior modification techniques to these goals at the Laboratory of Human Behavior at St. Elizabeth's Hospital in Washington, D.C. He attempted to structure the hospital setting in such a way as to make it more like the world outside the hospital, theorizing that if the patient is to learn behaviors which will enable him to adjust to the community, he must have the opportunity to practice these behaviors prior to release.

A coordinated transition between hospital and aftercare is extremely important to the successful adjustment of the patient once out of the hospital. If the same therapist can continue treatment, the continuity can be an important bridge. Unfortunately, particularly when hospital training programs are involved, I have noted from my own experience that artificial criteria are often established separating the staffs treating inpatient and outpatient groups. Both patient and therapist suffer under this arrangement.

The transition from hospital to community is the key point in successful aftercare. Yet it is currently the weakest link in the aftercare chain. Without active and imaginative programs to familiarize patients with community treatment facilities, discharged patients are largely lost to aftercare. Pre-discharge planning is a vital first step in assuring patients the benefits of available aftercare programs. Personal contact is vital; simply instructing a patient that after discharge he must contact his local outpatient department is largely ineffectual. Without help, only the well-motivated and better-functioning patient is likely to reach the aftercare facilities so much needed by the very patient who is unable or unwilling to seek them on his own. Without appropriate pre-discharge planning and aggressive follow-up techniques, aftercare becomes a public relations word rather than an effective post-hospital program, and the stage is set for the cycle of rehospitalization.

Statistical studies demonstrate the value of specific pre-discharge planning. One such study analyzed the correlation between readmissions and types of discharge referrals. Some 4,376 discharged patients, representing the entire patient population discharged from four Virginia state hospitals between 1963 and 1964, and 2,122 readmitted patients were studied. Significantly, the largest percentage of readmissions was in the patient group which had no specific referral to an aftercare facility at the time of discharge. Of these patients, 56.4% were readmitted. Of those referred to mental health services, only 32.8% were readmitted; the rates dropped further with those referred to supportive agencies (26.9% readmitted) and to family care or nursing homes (17.8% readmitted) (Zolik, Sommers and Lantz, 1967).

Studies of readmission rates of patients not in specific aftercare programs generally show 1- to 5-year readmission rates of 35-50% (Charalampous, 1963; Gaviria and Lund, 1967; Kris, 1965; Pollack, Levenstein and Klein, 1968; Sherman, Moseley, Ging and Bookbinder, 1964; Silverman, 1971; Zolik, 1967). High as they are, these figures may reflect a significant underestimation of psychiatric hospital readmissions. Other studies show rates which soar as high as 90% (Burvill and Mittelman, 1971; *Lifeline: Aftercare*, 1962; *Medical World News*, 1969). By defining readmission so as to exclude prior hospitalization at other institutions, inadequate search to uncover prior inpatient experience elsewhere, breakdown of communications between the office doing the statistical reporting and the staff members eliciting this information, and premature submission of statistics, reported rates may underemphasize the "revolving door syndrome." One study of 1,137 admissions to the Cleveland Psychiatric Institute showed that two out of five readmissions had been misclassified as first admissions (Friedman, Lundstedt, Von Mering and Hinko, 1964).

Effective aftercare programs can and do significantly affect the functioning and readmission rates of discharged patients. In a seven-year follow-up study, Kris has shown that the ratio of rehospitalization can be reduced to 10% or less with a thorough and aggressive follow-up program. In this program, patients were started in a special research aftercare clinic on the day immediately following their release from the hospital, and were seen weekly during the first two or three months and, when necessary, more often. In cases of recurrence of severely disturbed behavior and reappearence of overt psychotic symptoms, control of the relapse was brought about by treating such patients in a day hospital established in conjunction with the clinic. This aftercare research unit maintained close contact with the patient's family and friends, and used aggressive follow-up techniques if the patients failed to keep an appointment. Within 24 hours there would be a phone call, followed by a letter. If a second appointment was broken there would be a home visit. Maintenance pharmocotherapy was required with most patients, especially chronic schizophrenics. Drug therapy was considered safe; there were minimal complications. Families were indoctrinated and educated to appreciate the patient's need for prolonged medication, like a diabetic's need for insulin. Thirty-five percent found jobs on their own, and only 10% needed vocational rehabilitation. Outstanding factors causing failure to readjust in the community were friction in the family, isolation and inadequacy of pharmacotherapy.

In Georgia, a special aftercare clinic, emphasizing group therapy, reduced the one year rehospitalization rate to 11.4% with a patient group of 25% alcoholics (Fleurant, Hicks, Norris, Gouge and McKay, 1972). From Houston, Charalampous reports that 35-50% of the patients generally are readmitted within a year. He feels that poor results at rehabilitation facilities are possibly caused by their emphasis on milieu therapy and psychotherapy, which he feels are of limited usefulness for patients with chronic functional psychoses. Many chronic mental patients can be maintained in the community if properly kept on ataractic drugs. An aftercare clinic was set up in the Houston State Psychiatric Institute where patients with chronic functional psychoses are followed and maintained on drugs after discharge. The author reports that the attrition rate is less than 10%, and fewer than 5% of the patients have to return to inpatient care (Charalampous, 1963).

In another study (Caffey, Jones, Diamond, Burton and Bowen, 1969), patients were divided into three groups. Group A received normal hospital care with discharge at the physician's discretion and normal aftercare for a year. Group B received brief intensive treatment aimed at discharge in three weeks with a special schedule of aftercare visits and outpatient treatment. Group C received normal hospital care with discharge at the physician's discretion and a special schedule of aftercare visits and outpatient treatment. Group C produced the lowest number of readmissions; Group B was next. The authors' conclusion was that an intensive aftercare program seems to play an important role in reducing or preventing readmissions.

Many other studies, using a variety of techniques and approaches, give support to the value of aftercare programs (Brooks, 1961; David, 1971; Ellsworth, 1968; Myers and Bean, 1968; Nol and Fuller, 1972; Rutman and Loeb, 1970). Dissenting findings are few and far between.

Lamb and Goertzel (1972) randomly assigned long-term ex-state hospital patients to high or low expectation community programs. The high expectation group had pre-release group sessions at the state hospital. Focus was on problems the patients might encounter in the community and their ambivalence about ending hospital dependency. They were taken to visit family and friends, halfway houses and day treatment centers. Group methods and resocialization were emphasized, and vocational rehabilitation was available. The low expectation group had little pre-discharge assistance; they were released primarily to family care or boarding homes, where little was required of them. The results of Lamb and Goertzel's study showed that the high expectation program was superior not so much in keeping patients out of the hospital longer as in increasing their level of social and vocational functioning. There was no significant difference in how long the patients remained in the community either in the early months or after two years.

The other recent major study with negative results (Lagey, 1972) states that a ten-year follow-up survey of former mental hospital patients in an experimental program showed no significant differences among four treatment groups in hospital recidivism five and ten years after the termination of the project. The four groups were treated as follows: the first group received the routine services both in the hospital and in the community following discharge from the hospital; the second group received at least 30 days of intense pre-discharge planning and preparation for discharge in the hospital, and the routine services in the community. The third group received the routine hospital services and special professional and community help. The fourth group received the special treatments both in the hospital and in the community. All four groups spent about three of the ten years since the termination of the original project in accumulated hospital recidivism.

Despite these two largely negative studies, the preponderance of evidence supports the hypothesis that most aftercare programs do help patients function well and remain well. Clinical experiences would also indicate that, with most patients still partially symptomatic at the time of discharge and affected by residuals of their illness, access to total professional care, good living arrangements, socialization and vocational help can only improve the situation. Though some illnesses have an etiology and pathogenesis not yet understood, which may be tied into physiological, anatomical and/or genetic pathology, their liability is lessened when the patient functions in a healthier environment. While there may be some patients with a progressive intractable illness that present treatment methods do not effectively reach, the great majority of patients do respond to the psychological, social and biochemical resources that we have available to offer.

Let us, therefore, attempt to determine what we have to offer in aftercare programs that *can* make a difference.

RESIDENTIAL ARRANGEMENTS

The right living climate can be a major factor in creating an environment for successful rehabilitation. An appropriate residential setting can provide the ex-patient with not only a healthy climate and an atmosphere conducive to growth, but also with an opportunity for developing skill in social interaction and and the ability to care for himself and move out into the world. The availability of appropriate residential facilities is often a major determinant in the decision to discharge the psychiatric patient. In a 1968 study of chronic schizophrenic patients, Hogarty concluded that discharge was more a function of hospital and community resources than of patient condition. Pokorny and Frazier (1968) concluded that 25% of the entire patient population at seven Texas mental hospitals could be discharged immediately if suitable living facilities were available.

The family unit has been the traditional focus of discharge planning, and still remains the first resource which should be considered. However, the family setting is not always a satisfactory answer to the problem of a healthy living climate even when the patient has family available with whom he could live;

often, pathological interactions make return to the family setting inadvisable. Further, an increasing number of patients have no family unit to return to. Must they be released to the isolation of a lonely room?

If the ex-patient has family willing and able to have him return, a decision as to the advisability of such placement is required. The only specific data available for guidance concerns schizophrenics. In an article entitled "Some Data Concerning readmission of Discharged Schizophrenic Patients," Cropley and Gazan (1969) report a two-year follow-up study of chronic schizophrenic patients to determine whether living with one's own family after discharge is a significant variable affecting retention of released schizophrenics in the community. The subjects were classified as members of either an immediate family group, a foster home group or a living alone group. Tabulating the number of readmissions to the hospital and total length of rehospitalizations, results failed to show a significant difference among groups. However, when the two sexes were considered separately, there was a tendency for foster home females to do better than the other two groups of females.

Although there are many comments in the literature about negative effects of schizophrenics' returning to live with their families, this conclusion is not supported by exacting studies. Possibly there is no valid generalization. In each specific case, the clinician must exercise his judgment as to what role the family pathology is playing in the individual's illness.

HALFWAY HOUSES

One creative solution to the problem of providing a healthful living environment for released patients has been the establishment of supervised residences, the so-called psychiatric halfway houses. Dr. Richard Budson (1973), in a thorough review, states:

> The entire delivery of care to troubled and needy people is in a period of rapid change. Throughout the fabric of a variety of care-delivery systems, one constant pattern emerges — diminishing importance of the large institution and strong augmentation of small community-based residential facilities commonly known as half-way houses or community residences. These facilities are being established in great numbers, not only for the emotionally troubled, but also for the mentally retarded, the drug dependent and alcoholic, youths from broken homes, and youthful and adult offenders and other handicapped people (p. 64).

Their numbers have grown rapidly — from 7 in 1961, to 40 in 1964, to 148 in 1969. Now they number in the thousands. Budson believes that the rationale for this new movement was four basic deficiencies of the traditional institution. First, its large size and limited staff lead to a social breakdown syndrome, an "iatrogenically induced withdrawal from interpersonal exchange." Second, the patient was considered sick 24 hours a day, the passive recipient of care, which reinforced his image as defective and helplessly dependent on the hospital staff. Third, the closed society of the hospital, with its harsh rules and codes of punishment, induced compliance to the power system and reduced patient initiatives toward health. Fourth, the patient was isolated from the community.

The halfway house provides an antidote for many of the deficiencies of the traditional institution. The typical community residence is small, usually limited to 10 to 25 residents in a family-like atmosphere. Ideally, the occupants are considered residents, not patients. The house is in an open setting, part of a neighborhood, responsive to general social codes and mores, and integrated within the community. Supervision is provided by houseparents, managers and/or social workers.

The goals and philosophy of the supervising body and the make-up and degree of disability of the resident group influence the structure and model of the many halfway houses. Some require the residents to be admitted directly from a psychiatric hospital; others require only that the resident suffer from an emotional illness and anticipate benefit from the residence. Many have a maximum period of residence, commonly in the six-month to one-year range. Those that don't are finding their places increasingly occupied by those residents who can function in a halfway house but can't make the transition beyond. Some halfway houses require their residents to work or attend school with a short time of arrival; others require all residents to be in psychotherapy. Most, but not all, have live-in staff, commonly referred to as houseparents. Some have daytime staffing; some none at all. Consultant social workers, psychologists and psychiatrists are available to most. Cooking, shopping and housecleaning may be done by staff or residents, or by some combination. Generally at this time most programs want house managers who have personal stability, integrity, common sense, warmth, and a commitment to helping people, instead of formal training.

Community residences are still in the early stages of development and much experimentation is in process. Wilder, Kessel and Caulfield (1968) reported their experience after one year with the Overing Apartments, a "high expectation" halfway house supervised by the Albert Einstein College of Medicine. Overing Apartments was designed to provide a temporary, sheltered, homelike environment for ex-patients who either had no home or whose home was not conducive to recovery. Clinically, the residents had severe psychiatric disorders, with 77% diagnosed as schizophrenic reaction. To emphasize healthy aspects of their personalities, the rent was lowered if the tenant worked or studied. Tenants could come and go as they wished, and had full responsibility for their own personal care, meals and maintenance of apartments. Originally there was a six-month time limit on residence; it was later changed to nine months. Tenants were rated during residence and for six months afterward in clinical, social, and vocational areas. At their six-month follow-up, 41% of the females and 50% of the males were living on their own. The study concluded that the older, better motivated, more employable tenant did best in this setting, while the adolescents required a separate, more structured, nurturing program.

The high expectation approach is also reported from England, with some variations. Darley and Kenny (1971), analyzing the low success rates of traditional day treatment centers for psychiatric patients, found that former patients were generally not accepted by the community as recovered, but assigned a new and damaging role as citizens-on-probation. They called this expectation of failure the "Queequeg Syndrome." To counteract the progressive deterioration in self-respect and confidence they felt was caused by this systematic undervaluing of the ex-patient's ability, they designed a rehabilitation program aimed at relearning the ability to cope with normality in all its forms and limitations, and regaining the ability to accept unpleasant emotions as normal. The new program set up a therapeutic community in which all responsibility was shared by the staff and members equally. Darley and Kenny concluded that this experience of self-direction in a group setting eliminated the feeling of chronic disability.

Other creative efforts to solve the problem of a healthful environment for ex-patients have varied the halfway house approach. Undergraduates of Harvard and Radcliffe established a cooperative halfway house in which the eager and intense students live together with ex-"chronic patients" Additional schools in the Boston area have joined the program, with encouraging results (Greenblatt and Kantor, 1962). In Fort Worth a study project used the YMCA as a transitional facility for rehabilitating chronic psychiatric patients. It was found to be an excellent alternative to the conventional halfway house, producing excellent results at less cost (Baganz, Smith, Goldstein and Pou, 1971). Cooperative apartments are another variation. One such program in Brookline, Massachusetts was set up by the MHA with a social worker as apartment coordinator. Residents paid a weekly fee and were responsible for general maintenance, shopping and cooking (Stein and Sorenson, 1972).

The halfway house has also been used as a pre-discharge program. Brooklyn State Hospital established its own halfway house on the grounds of the hospital. Harmony House is used for patients who no longer require intensive psychiatric care, to eliminate their hospital dependency and prepare them for self-sufficiency in the community (Klein, 1972). Three major programs are provided: a pre-vocational evaluation and exploration program to develop work potential and work habits; a personal adjustment training program for learning socially acceptable behavior and attitudes; and a homemaking program to develop independent community living and self-sufficiency. These adjustments are thus included as a part of the institutional treatment, before discharge into the community and the possibility of loss of the patients to aftercare.

To meet the problem of the resident who is unable to move from the halfway house into totally independent living, the El Camino House in California has developed a satellite housing program. Residents who are able to care for themselves but need some continued supervision are discharged to live in scattered apartments, usually with one or more roommates who are discharged at the same time. The apartment occupants must agree to attend a meeting of apartment residents at least twice a month and to remain in treatment. Follow-up services include a social club. The satellite program has reduced the length of stay at El Camino House; it is hoped it will reduce rehospitalization (Richmond, 1970).

It is difficult to make valid comparisons between programs of different halfway houses. Because of their small size, their samples are small and statistically unreliable. Furthermore, some programs take only carefully selected patients with predictably better prognosis. Others serve primarily schizophrenic patients who probably present a high risk of hospital readmission, the most common criteria used in rating program "success." General evaulation of the trend of development of such facilities is more feasible. Glasscote, Gudeman and Elpers published a comprehensive review of the programs of eleven halfway houses in 1971. Their conclusions, and the tone that pervades the literature, indicate that halfway houses represent a major step forward in rehabilitation.

FAMILY CARE PLACEMENT

Another residential alternative is family care placement. By moving patients into the homes of relatively healthy families in the community, the family setting can be utilized as a positive therapeutic milieu. The ex-patient can thus spend most of his time in the context of normal family life rather than in an institutional environment, while avoiding returning to the setting which originally fostered his illness.

The oldest family care program is the famous one in Geel, Belgium. The Geel program and two others, in Beilen, the Netherlands, and Lierneux, Belgium, are described by Kernodle (1972). Surveying the legendary and historical origins of the Geel program, Kernodle concludes that in Geel the "practice of adopting the mentally ill and retarded into their homes and providing them with love and understanding is an ancient tradition." In 1952, the colony became a state institution, and the families that "adopt" patients are now paid by the government.

Currently there are 1,600 patients in foster care in Geel, of whom 65% are mentally retarded. About one-eighth of the households in the village have patients in foster care, with a maximum of two patients allowed in one family. The family placement program is an adjunct of the colony hospital, which has a yearly admission rate of 500 selected patients, 100 of whom are sent to foster care. Placement procedures are often informal, as the staff reside in the community and know many of the families personally. After family placement, the hospital is used mainly as a back-up resource, and the staff continue to provide any professional services necessary. However, psychotherapy tends to be minimal after placement. Many patients remain as permanent family members after their release from the program. The programs at Lierneux and Beilen are similar.

The most important factor in the success of the family placement programs seems to be the prestige bestowed on the family who adopts patients. However, the program is presently threatened by encroaching urbanization.

In *The Case for Family Care of the Mentally Ill,* Morrissey (1967) has reviewed the history of family care. He notes that research findings vary considerably and are at times contradictory. Perceptions of family care vary from extensions of the custodial hospital to dynamic selective treatment resources. According to Morrissey, the most important factor in family care treatment and rehabilitation is its acceptance as a valuable therapeutic resource, which he strongly feels it is. His study shows that considerably fewer patients are rehospitalized with family care placements than with regular home visits to their families. However, this may be due to more careful selection of patients placed in family care or to a more contrived environment and more careful supervision. Morrissey believes that schizophrenia, in particular, can be treated more effectively in a family care home than in a hospital.

Family care programs have been met with resistance in the U.S., possibly due to ignorance concerning mental illness. One study in New Haven, Missouri strove to overcome this resistance by establishing the positive involvement of the townspeople in the development of a program to integrate released psychiatric patients back into the community, with some success (Keskiner, Ruppert and Ulett, 1970). It seems clear that the underutilization of family care placement as a resource for placement of ex-patients will be reversed only by further education of both professionals and the community.

OTHER LIVING ARRANGEMENTS

Many patients are not discharged to supervised residences or well-meaning families, but go to some form of licensed community boarding home. This is largely a stop-gap measure used when other more desirable placements are unavailable. A major problem with such placements is keeping the residents active enough to prevent apathy and regression. Few boarding home operators have enough training or experience to conduct activity programs. Many have no inclination to do so, and feel they lack the time. In an attempt to overcome the problem, Simon (1972) describes one-day workshops for boarding home operators where instruction is given in simple activities. Professional participants included the total range of hospital personnel, with the chaplain not forgotten.

A more successful integration of non-professionals in providing alternative living arrangements for ex-patients was achieved in a Boston Hospital program of landlord-supervised cooperative apartments, described by Chien and Cole (1973). From the program's inception in December, 1967, 35 apartments have been established in the area around Boston State Hospital. The landlords, who were not initially a part of the mental heatlh team or trained for mental health work, are screened by the hospital staff. They serve as paid houseparents, doing more at first and less as time goes on. The program is closely supervised by a hospital team. Results have been encouraging; the readmission rate has been a low 18% and the program is enthusiastically endorsed by most patients. Chien and Cole quote an annual cost of $2,183 per patient per year and believe that this program is financially and logistically superior to other residences.

The problem of patients who need long-term, possibly permanent care but can function away from the hospital under drug therapy was solved at Graylongwell Hospital in England by the establishment of a group home away from the hospital for these patients. Capstick and Kirby (1970) found this a successful alternative to long-term hospital stay.

DAY AND NIGHT HOSPITALS

Partial hospitalization has become an important alternative to full-time hospital care and an essential element in the new community mental health centers. As defined by NIMH, "a psychiatric day-night service is one having an organized staff whose primary purpose is to provide a planned program of milieu therapy and other treatment modalities. The service is designed for patients with mental or emotional disorders who spend only a part of a 24-hour period in the program."

The first day care facility in the U.S. dates back to 1935, when Dr. J.M. Woodall admitted day patients to Adams House Sanitarium in Boston. The first organized day hospital in the western hemisphere was reported in 1946 at Allan Memorial Institute of Psychiatry in Montreal, Canada. Yale Psychiatric Clinic began one in 1948, the Menninger Clinic, one in 1949. By the early 1970s they were numerous, some affiliated with psychiatric hospitals, others with a clinic or general hospital.

A typical day care program runs from 9 A.M. to 5 P.M. and offers individual and/or group psychotherapy, patient-staff meetings, recreational, social and vocational activities. The programs tend to be flexible, and geared to the needs of the individual. Those that offer children's programs allow for family participation; the child is not totally separated from his family, the parents have a respite during the day and special teaching or training can be provided.

Night hospitals typically run from evening until work or school in the morning, and benefit those patients who can handle their job during the day but are unable to deal with their family or other home situation at night.

Kalmans (1970) describes a day treatment center at the Arlington Mental Health Center which offers individualized treatment plans for three categories: people in crisis who might otherwise be hospitalized; former patients who need a bridge to the outside world; and outpatients whose problems cannot be dealt with in once-a-week therapy. The majority of the patients are schizophrenics, often with overt psychotic symptoms. Many of the patients would have to be hospitalized if the center did not exist. Four-fifths of the patients are women; to facilitate their attendance, a nursery class and playroom for their preschool children is provided. Family members are encouraged to keep in touch with the staff for assistance with both personal and practical problems concerning the patient. The program offers individual, group and family psychotherapy, work therapy, psychodrama, art and dance therapy, community meetings and adult

education.   Kalmans concludes that the program has successfully encouraged
patients to accept responsibility for their own destiny.

The Fort Logan Mental Health Center in Denver has a large day hospital
program, described by Bonn (1972). The day center is only one part of a coordinated mental health center which also includes inpatient services, crisis intervention, outpatient follow-up care, and various types of sheltered residential
facilities and vocational rehabilitation. The Fort Logan day hospital program is
able to service a large number of patients. Three reasons are cited by Bonn. First,
satellite day centers were established, eliminating problems of transportation and
serving patients in preferred familiar community surroundings. Second, day care
is used for a wide spectrum of patients. The clinical criteria used for admission
is the patient's need for ego-supportive activities for a fairly extended time. The
presence of suicidal or homicidal tendencies or confusion does not automatically
contraindicate day care. Third, the administrative structure facilitates the use of
day care. All treatment modalities are available within each unit; thus patients
are easily moved into different intensities of treatment. The day program offers
large and small group therapy, psychodrama, family therapy, marital counseling,
crisis intervention, activity therapies, medication follow-up, and training to
improve self-care, social skills and interpersonal relationships. Some centers also
offer vocational rehabilitation. Bonn concludes that all diagnostic categories
benefited from the program.

Table 10-1 shows the use of day care in fiscal 1970-1971 by all divisions of
Fort Logan:

TABLE 10-1.

	Total Patients	No. Patients Using Day Care	No. Days in Day Care	No. Patients Using Only Day Care
Adult psychiatry	1,902	624	48,042	103
Alcoholism	1,251	251	3,214	22
Geriatrics	251	10	947	1
Crisis	391	22	1,205	2
Child psychiatry	170	30	3,027	7
Adolescent psychiatry	125	25	681	5
Total	4,090	962	57,116	140

(Bonn, 1972, p. 159.)

As professionals are gaining more experience with the part-time hospital, its
use has been extended beyond its original role as a purely transitional facility. It
is being found to be an effective primary treatment method for many types of
patients, regardless of diagnosis or socioeconomic background. Nevertheless, it is
still underutilized for this purpose. Feder (1971), in "The Indications and
Techniques of Partial Hospitalization," states that the sustained underutilization
of the part-time hospital may be due to an incomplete understanding of the

concept by patients, families, and the professional community. When partial hospitalization is seen not as a reduction of inpatient care but rather as an extension of outpatient care, it may then become the logical portal of entry to treatment for any patient for whom hospitalization is being considered.

There are many day care results published (Carney, Ferguson and Sheffield, 1970; Kris, 1962; Shammas, 1971; and Thomson, 1968 are examples) including one from the USSR (Kutin, 1971). They are uniformly enthusiastic and optimistic about day care programs. Results show shorter hospitalizations, less likelihood of readmission, better employment records of ex-patients, and better results generally. The overall success of the programs seems logically to militate a future trend toward greater expanded part-time hospital facilities.

The one major problem encountered to date has nothing to do with the clinical efficacy of the programs. Although the cost is much less than that of full hospitalization, to date most private insurance plans do not cover partial hospitalization. Thus, for economic reasons, part-time hospitalization is only available to the rich or indigent. Until this nonsensical situation is remedied, partial hospitalization will remain underutilized.

PROFESSIONAL CARE

Professional post-hospital treatment of the psychiatric patient, like other phases of aftercare, is an area in which the choice of treatment is dependent both on the individual patient and on the disorder from which he is suffering. There are, however, numerous studies indicating that psychotherapeutic contact in aftercare does lower readmission rates (Prince, Ackerman and Barksdale, 1973; Donlon, Rada and Knight, 1973; Fleurant, Hicks, Norris, Gouge and McKay, 1972; Lamb and Goertzel, 1972; Langsley and Kaplan, 1970; Lurie and Ron, 1971; Pittman, Flomenhaft and Langley, 1971; Racklin, 1972; Safirstein, 1969). Most of the studies cover the total population of ex-hospital patients; the statistics reported present an impressive indication of the value of psychotherapy as part of the total treatment program in aftercare.

Prince, Ackerman and Barksdale (1973) collected data for patients diagnosed as functional psychotics who were released from the South Carolina State Hospital from February, 1970 through January, 1972 (see Table 10-2). Before release, patients from the 22 counties served by the project took part in a pre-release group and were given specific appointments for follow-up group treatment in the clinic nearest their home. Patients who came from the other 24 counties generally received the more traditional individual follow-up treatment, with the majority seen once monthly by a psychiatrist for a brief medication check and supportive psychotherapy. All patients were allowed the choice of a mental health clinic or a private physician (not necessarily a psychiatrist). The form of treatment group varied with the clinic. The most common approach was a monthly group meeting lasting 60 to 90 minutes in which between 10 and 20 patients were seen jointly by a psychiatrist and a nonmedical staff member. Problems were discussed and ideas shared for most of the session, after which medications were reviewed.

TABLE 10-2 FOLLOW-UP DATA ON 1,182 DISCHARGED CHRONIC PSYCHOTIC PATIENTS.

Method of Treatment	No. of Patients	Returned During Year	In Hospital at End of Year
Referred to mental health center but never reported	328	49%	43%
Referred to mental health center and treated (all methods)	690	37%	23%
Referred to private physician but never reported	91	46%	41%
Referred to private physician and treated	73	26%	22%

(Prince, Ackerman and Barksdale, 1973, p. 931.)

In analyzing those cases treated at the mental health center clinics, interesting statistics emerged (see Table 10-3).

TABLE 10-3 BREAKDOWN OF MENTAL HEALTH CLINIC TREATMENT CASES.

Method of Treatment	No. of Patients	Returned During Year	In Hospital at End of Year
Group follow-up with medication (special group)	216	25%	14%
Individual medical checks	258	44%	30%
Other: intensive psychotherapy, family therapy, or combination	216	40%	24%
Total	690		

(Prince, Ackerman and Barksdale, 1973, p. 932)

Thus only 14% of the patients seen in groups were in the hospital on the anniversary of their release, compared with 30% and 24% treated in other ways. Their conclusion is that group methods are quite practical for the treatment of large numbers of chronic psychotic patients, and may well be the preferred treatment.

The group of schizophrenias is the largest diagnostic category among aftercare patients. The value of psychotherapy in treating schizophrenia remains an open question. In the excellent article *"The Psychotherapy of Schizophrenia: Does it Work?"* Dyrud and Holzman (1973) state: "Empirical studies of the treatment of schizophrenia show the unequivocal ameliorative effects of psychoactive drugs. No comparable effects have been claimed for psychotherapy. As a result, psychotherapy has tended to be negated as a viable therapeutic factor in the treatment of schizophrenia." Dyrud and Holzman suggest, however, that the conclusion is invalid, and has been based on inadequate and misleading data. Among the criticisms which they aim at the studies are charges of serious methodological errors, inappropriate outcome criteria, inadequate assessment procedures to measure change, unsound selection of therapists, and unclear diagnostic appraisals. They point out that the heterogenous nature of psychotherapeutic intervention clouds the issue further; there is no "dose" of psychotherapy, and the term itself covers a vast range of methods, techniques and goals.

Schizophrenia itself encompases a heterogeneity of conditions, including "the clear-cut process schizophrenias, insidious in their onset in early adolescence and proceeding ever more malignantly into dementia; the oscillating, phasic schizophrenic conditions; the rigid, litigious paranoid schizophrenic processes that appear in the third and fourth decades of life; and the acute schizophreniform psychotic episodes, from which some patients apparently recover completely . . . . There are nonpsychotic conditions, too, that we label schizophrenic: the so-called latent schizophrenias, incipient schizophrenia, ambulatory schizophrenias and even remitted schizophrenias" (Dyrud and Holzman, 1973, p. 671). The authors emphasize that a crucial diagnostic task is the assessment of the relative contributions of familial, genetic, conflict, biochemical, psychological and sociocultural factors in order to be able to aim a treatment program at its proper target. Many therapeutic methods could be used. Evaluation of the benefits of psychotherapy should include a measurement of the patient's level of functioning and other more sophisticated criteria, not just discharge or readmission rates.

Presently our research armamentarium lacks sensitive instruments to detect the myriad intrapersonal changes that occur with and without psychotherapeutic intervention. Many acutely schizophrenic patients improve dramatically regardless of what we do; some remain psychotic in spite of what we do, but there is the large group of patients for whom it can matter very much what we do. The proper function of psychotherapeutic intervention in "what we do" is clearly not settled; the question remains open as to what treatment is appropriate and adequate for which patients.

A major factor in the success of aftercare programs depends on keeping patients on enough medication for a long enough time. The literature is filled with emphasis on the importance of medication in the treatment of previously psychotic patients. Kris (1962, 1963, 1965) documents this thoroughly in her detailed aftercare studies. Other U.S. studies agree (Capstick, 1970; Chalalampous, 1963; Cole and Davis, 1968; Ehrhardt, 1967; Lamb and Goertzel, 1972; Varsamis, 1970); foreign studies echo this conclusion (Heinrich and Baer, 1969 in Germany; Kruglova, 1970 in the USSR; Roder, 1970 in Denmark).

The large majority of hospitalized patients have had psychotic illnesses. The aforementioned studies clearly show the importance of drug treatment in their aftercare. Phenothiazines are most commonly used with schizophrenic patients; there is a newer trend toward using long-acting intramuscular phenothiazines for those patients who are undependable medication takers. The treatment of manic-depressive disorders now emphasizes pharmacotherapy, with the use of lithium being a major breakthrough. The involutional disorders are usually treated with pharmacotherapy and/or ECT in addition to psychotherapy. No effective drug treatment is available for the organic psychoses associated with the aging process, but research with RNA and hyperbaric oxygen is in its early stage.

Lamb and Goertzel (1972) found that patients often do not understand the goals of treatment, and that educating them is important. It must be brought home to the patients that their illness does not stop the day they leave the hospital, and that, for some, medication will be necessary indefinitely. The patient must be helped to overcome the common tendency to equate the need for medication with the concept that he is "still sick."

A small percentage of ex-hospital patients are diagnosed as neurotic or as having character disorders. For these patients the prevalent treatment is psychotherapy, with anti-anxiety drugs used when indicated. There is growing use of behavior therapies for some of these disorders.

The studies in the literature present overwhelming evidence that patients who remain in aftercare treatment programs do much better than those who do not. Yet there are many patients who never get started in aftercare treatment, some because of the failure of pre-discharge planning. More drop out after starting. Raskin and Dyson (1968) conducted a study to delineate the reasons for the failure of the aftercare facilities to prevent rehospitalizations. They found that the majority of readmitted patients are not in treatment at the time of their rehospitalization, and postulated three reasons for this finding: first, patients with an impulsive and stormy life-style persistently fail to keep their aftercare appointments; second, occasionally patients are discharged from aftercare because the chronicity of their illness is not recognized; third, patients drop out of aftercare because of increasing hopelessness about the chronic difficulties of their lives. This last problem was largely prevented during follow-up by the therapists' activity in keeping the patient in treatment and by the use of family therapy and vocational rehabilitation to lessen the patient's hopelessness.

Readmissions of patients who remain in treatment were found by Raskin and Dyson to occur for two main reasons: first, there are patients who require hospitalization whenever they experience a change of therapists; and second, there are patients who are so lonely within the community that they cannot be maintained there despite aftercare.

Huessy (1963) emphasizes the benefits of involving the family physician, who often is the only treatment modality in rural areas. From Japan, Hiraoka (1969) points out that patients often live far from aftercare facilities, and do not attend because of transportation difficulties.

Aftercare programs utilize a wide range of professional and paraprofessional personnel. Psychiatric nurses can play a valuable role (Nickerson, 1972).

SOCIAL CLUBS

Social clubs for ex-patients have sprung out of a recognition that a frequent contributing cause of hospital readmission is a recurrence of withdrawal from society and a breakdown in the area of communication with other people. Since 1938 when the first social club was founded in Great Britain by Dr. Joshua Bierer, they have grown in number, membership and variety. The social club movement in the U.S. began in California in the 1950s.

In "Psychiatric Social Clubs Come of Age," Grob (1970) lists the common elements of social clubs: they are community-based, noninstitutional, intrinsically social, democratic in emphasis, exhibit a preference for horizontal ordering of staff, use volunteers, and concentrate on group activity. A typical social club program includes such unstructured activities as games, picnics, movies, exhibits and coffee klatches, and such structured activities as discussion groups, hobby groups, classes and sports.

For many, social clubs have become an important part of their rehabilitation program, the main weapon in learning social techniques. A conference on social clubs reported in *Social Clubs, Yes* (1963), stated the purpose of the social club:

> to help its members achieve and maintain positive social and vocational adjustments in the community by providing opportunities, situations, and experiences calculated to help prevent both social isolation and further social disability. Under qualified leadership, the social club can achieve its purpose by providing activities in the community which combine social interaction, recreation, personal development, and ego support.

This conference felt that patients should be professionally referred, and concluded that the director is the key figure in success, with volunteers essential. It seemed vital to the conferees that the social club develop and maintain good relationships with physicians, hospitals and clinics, day and night hospitals, government agencies (DVR, state employment agencies, welfare departments) and private and volunteer agencies (family service, MHA's community and volunteer services).

There is a diversity of opinion whether ex-patients should remain members of a social club indefinitely. Regardless, the social club should certainly be used as a stepping-stone toward regular community resources and services.

A controlled, experimental study to evaluate the effects of a social rehabilitative program showed that patients involved in such programs were rehospitalized less and functioned better in the community (Wolkon, Karmen, and Tanaka, 1971). Hillside Hospital (Lurie and Ron, 1972) developed a socialization program for younger patients using multiple family group therapy, activity group therapy, task-centered groups, individual and family counseling, and vocational counseling. Alumni Group Therapy, a program developed for the aftercare of chronic schizophrenics at the Chicago State Hospital, may have been responsible for a drop from 55% to 37.5% rehospitalization during the first year after discharge (Craig, 1971).

Winston, Papernik, Breslin and Trembath (1972) report about an ex-patient club from Kings County Hospital in Brooklyn, N.Y.   They found that earlier ex-patient clubs had run into six principal problems:

1) There was a lack of professional involvement.
2) The clubs were often a long distance from the member's homes.
3) The more socially adequate patients joined, and those patients most in need were not members.
4) The more competent members left the club.
5) The hard core of sick persons remaining repelled others from joining.
6) Some were reluctant to have anything to do with reminders of their having been psychiatric patients.

The new Kings County club was designed to provide a structure for the continuation of relationships formed in the inpatient therapeutic community. It was necessary because "(t)hose patients with severe ego deficits in the area of object relations tended to return to withdrawal and isolation after discharge, despite the fact that while in the hospital they were able to interact with other patients and gain gratification from these relationships." It was expected that club membership be transitory rather than an ongoing experience. The authors believe the club was a success primarily because it was an extension of common inpatient experiences for all members, and the staff members' involvement provided organizational benefits as well as a link with therapeutic facilities.

In 1937, Dr. Abraham A. Low, a psychiatrist, founded the group called Recovery, Inc., in Chicago. It is now a nationwide organization, with many members. Its purpose is to prevent chronicity in new patients and relapses in former mental patients. The organization is managed and controlled by former patients.

The recovery method consists of reading the writings of Dr. Low, attending meetings, and putting the method to work in daily life. The Recovery meetings have five steps. First, members gather around a table and introduce each other by first names. Following this, they read aloud from Dr. Low's writings. Examples from daily life are then followed by a question and answer period, and mutual aid. Recovery members discover that their suffering is not unique and that life consists mainly of trivialities. There is mutual support and encouragement.

Lee (1971) used Recovery meetings at the Camarillo State Hospital in California to help bridge the gap between hospital and community. Self-help was an active concept in Lee's program. He felt Recovery was a useful aid and, used flexibly, supported other therapeutic efforts.

VOCATIONAL REHABILITATION

Vocational rehabilitation is based on the premise that work is good for mental health. For many patients who have been family breadwinners, economic necessity militates that they return to a level of functioning where they can again work. For many who have never learned a vocational skill, the feeling of competence and productivity resulting from the mastery of a trade produces positive psychological reinforcement. It can enhance self-respect, increase feelings of maturity and responsibility, lead to a feeling of independence, and increase the patient's standard of living.

Aftercare vocational rehabilitation was an outgrowth of the "industrial therapy" initiated in British psychiatric hospitals in the 1920s — simple contract assembly work for patients to perform. In the U.S., the nation's first paid work program for the mentally ill was inaugerated at the Northampton (Massachusetts) V.A. Hospital in 1947. Vocational rehabilitation then evolved into a program outside the hospital and began to include vocational testing, counseling, vocational training, sheltered job learning situations, sheltered work programs, and job placement. It was only in 1954 that psychiatric patients were included in the Federal Vocational Rehabilitation Act. Formal "industrial therapy" organizations developed as a result, such as the Altro Workshops and the V.A.'s CHIRP program (Black and Benney, 1969).

In an article "Spinning Straw into Gold," Durie, Gardner and Matthews (1972) describe the program of Forward House in Montreal where that social rehabilitation center set up a vocational rehabilitation program. Over a three-year period 266 patients were referred. Approximately half of this group, those whom the staff felt they could relate to and work with, were accepted. At first, four programs were set up: small business; domestic; transitional employment placement; and remotivation sessions. Later a Forward House store was added which served as an outlet for Forward House handicrafts and took consignments from other communities and hospitals. The authors concluded that: patients are best referred during a period of active treatment; there should be a close liaison between the hospital and the rehabilitation center; diagnostic categories have little predictive value of success or failure; group leaders should be autonomous, and the staff flexible; individually tailored programs are desirable; and follow-up of successful placements in the community is desirable. They felt the program was of definite benefit to many patients.

A novel program was instituted at the Westboro State Hospital in Massachusetts (Grimberg, 1970). Patients were diverted from a noncompetitive system, where everything is given free, to a competitive situation where everything is earned. A monetary system was set up and patients were paid 1.5 tokens per hour for working in hospital industrial placement or in a voluntary work program. From wages earned, patients were expected to pay for room, board, medication and therapy. A hierarchy of dining areas and sleeping quarters meant that a patient had to acquire a "better paying" job if he wished better facilities.

Eighteen months was the maximum time allowed in the program. During the final months the work program varied between a sheltered workshop placement and actual job placement in the community. Employed by community industry, the patient leaves the hospital and enters a halfway house where follow up and therapy are provided. Grimberg feels that an inhospital competitive society has proven more effective than the institution regulated society in preparing patients for jobs in the community and complete discharge from the hospital.

The literature abounds with the assumption that work is therapeutic, with little attempt to validate this hypothesis. Many studies used work rehabilitation as an index of "treatment success" or "recovery," so that work and successful treatment of mental illness become synonymous and a self-fulfilling prophesy. Micek and Miles (1969) attempted to evaluate the rehabilitative and therapeutic value of work for psychiatric patients. The subjects were assigned to groups where work therapy was either compulsory or forbidden. Follow-up information was obtained at 3- and 12-month intervals after discharge or transfer to low intensity treatment. At the time of transfer, the staff gave clinical ratings of response to treatment, and at the follow-up the patients were asked to rate individual therapy methods as most or least helpful. The staff ratings showed no significant differences between subjects in work therapy and those in other therapies. When the patients subjectively rated helpfulness of the various therapies, however, work therapy was frequently listed as "most helpful" and seldom as "least helpful."

Else Kris (1962), in her extensive experience at the Research Unit of the New York State Department of Mental Hygiene Aftercare Clinic, found that about 35% of the patients referred to the clinic were able to find gainful employment on their own, and only about 10% needed some form of vocational rehabilitation, either to learn new skills, to brush up on old skills, or to develop work tolerance.

Ryan (1969) conducted a survey for the National Association for Mental Health which adds a wry note. Studying the problems facing patients leaving mental hospitals in their search for work, he reports tentative indications that their return to the labor force is not as much of a problem as might have been expected. Ironically, they are finding difficulty not so much with prospective employers as with those statutory agencies which are specifically designed to help them.

SUMMARY

Aftercare, a previously neglected area of psychiatric treatment, is now getting major emphasis. It encompasses pre-discharge planning, professional care, residential arrangements, socialization techniques and vocational rehabilitation. It is effective in improving patient functioning out of the hospital and decreasing readmission rates. Dynamic programs are necessary to keep patients in aftercare programs. Continuing psychotherapy and maintaining long-term pharmacotherapy are essential. We must provide these necessary treatments. "Freedom to be sick, helpless, and isolated is not freedom" (Reich, 1973, p. 912).

REFERENCES

Action for Mental Health. Final Report of the Joint Commission on Mental Illness and Health. New York: Basic Books, 1961.

Aged long-term hospital patients show "restorative potential." *Frontiers of Hospital Psychiatry.* 5: 1, 2, 11 (1968).

Angrist, S., Dinitz, S., Lefton, M. and Pasamanick, B. Rehospitalization of female mental patients. Social and psychological factors. *Archives of General Psychiatry.* 4: 363-370 (1961).

Arthur, G., Ellsworth, R.B. and Kroeker, D. Readmission of released mental patients: a research study. *Social Work.* 13: 78-84 (1968).

Babyan, E.A. Zakondatel'stvo SSSR i nekotorykh zarubezhnykh stran po psikhiatrii. *Zhurnal Nevropatologii I Psikhatrii Imeni S.S. Korsakova.* 69: 1617-1623 (1969).

Baganz, P.C., Smith, A.E., Goldstein, R. and Pou, N.K. The YMCA as a halfway facility. *Hospital and Community Psychiatry.* 22: 156-159 (1971).

Bass, R. *A method for measuring continuity of care in a community mental health center.* Mental Health Statistics, Series C., No. 4. Rockville, MD: NIMH, 1972.

Bentinck, C. Opinions about mental illness held by patients and relatives. *Family Process.* 6: 193-207 (1967).

Bey, D.R., Chapman, R.E. and Tornquist, J. A lithium clinic. *American Journal of Psychiatry.* 129: 468-470 (1972).

Black, B.J. Industrial therapy in the United States. In: Black, B. *Principles of industrial therapy for the mentally ill,* pp. 60-120. New York: Grune & Stratton, 1970.

Black, B.J. and Benney, C. Rehabilitation. In: Bellak, L. (Ed.), *The Schizophrenic syndrome,* pp. 735-756. New York: Grune & Stratton, 1969.

Bok, M. and Bourestom, N. Age, patients: desires, residential facility and community tenure among chronic elderly mental patients. *Gerontologist.* 8: 35 (1968).

Bonn, E.M. Day care: a vital link in services. *Hospital and Community Psychiatry.* 23: 157-159 (1972).

Boriskov, V.P. Vliyaniye podderzhivayushchey terapii neyroleptikami na prisposoblyaemost k trudu bolnykh shizofreniyey. In: Vosstanov. *Terapiya I sots-trudov readapt bol'nykh ner-psikh zabolevanyami,* pp. 66-70. Leningrad: Nauch-issled psikhonevrolog inst vm bekhtereva, 1965.

Brooks, G.W. Effective use of ancillary personnel in rehabilitating the mentally ill. *Texas State Journal of Medicine.* 57: 341-347 (1961).

Brooks, G.W., Deane, W.N. and Ansbacker, H.L. Rehabilitation of chronic schizophrenic patients for social living. *Journal of Individual Psychology.* 16: 189-196 (1960).

Brown, B.S. Pathways and detours to and from the mental hospital. *Missouri Medicine.* 60: 253-256 (1963).

Brown, G.W., Carstairs, G.M. and Topping, G. Post-hospital adjustment of chronic mental patients. *Lancet,* pp. 685-689. September 27, 1958.

Brown, J.K. Mental patients work back into society. *Manpower.* **2**: 23–25 (1970).

Bryant, J. and Sandford, F. Psychiatric nursing in the community. *Nursing Mirror and Midwives Journal.* **134**: 37-39 (1972).

Budson, R.D. The psychiatric halfway house. *Psychiatric Annals.* **4**: 64-83 (1973).

Burvill, P.W. and Mittelman, M. A follow-up study of chronic mental hospital patients, 1959-1969. *Social Psychiatry.* **6**: 167-171 (1971).

Caffey, E.M., Jr., Galbrecht, C.R. and Klett, C.J. Brief Hospitalization and aftercare in the treatment of schizophrenia. *Cooperative Studies in Psychiatry.* **78**: 1-17 (1969).

Caffey, E.M., Jones, R.D., Diamond, L.S., Burton, E. and Bowen, W.T. Brief hospital treatment of schizophrenia: Early results of multiple-hospital study. *Psychiatry Digest.* **30**: 62 (1969).

Capstick, N. Long-acting drug treatment in overall psychiatric management. *Diseases of the Nervous System.* Supplement **31**: 15-17 (1970).

Capstick, N. and Kirby, J. A group home project. *Lancet,* pp. 516-518. September 5, 1970.

Carney, M.W.P., Ferguson, R.S. and Sheffield, B.F. Psychiatric day hospital and community. *Lancet.* **7658**: 1218-1220 (1970).

Charalampous, K.D. The long-term care of the chronic mentally ill patient, a medical approach. *Medical Record and Annals.* **56**: 257-258 (1963).

Cheadle, J. The psychiatric nurse as a social worker. *Nursing Times.* **66**: 1520-1522 (1970).

Cheney, T.M. and Kish, G.B. Job development in a veterans administration hospital. *Vocational Guidance Quarterly.* **19**: 61-65 (1970).

Ch'en, C.C. An examination of social resources in the rehabilitation of the mentally ill. *Mental Health Bulletin.* **14**: 11–12 (1969).

Chien, C. and Cole, J.O. Landlord-supervised cooperative apartments: a new modality for community-based treatment. *American Journal of Psychiatry.* **130**: 156-159 (1973).

Clark, M.C. Alpine House. *Provo Papers.* **7**: 68-70 (1963).

Cohen, E.S. and Kraft, A.C. The restorative potential of elderly long-term residents of mental hospitals. *Gerontologist.* **8**: 264-268 (1968).

Cohen, P.H. Sheltered industry in psychiatric rehabilitation. *Medical Journal of Australia.* **2**: 200-203 (1967).

Cohen, S., Leonard, C.V., Farberow, N.L. and Shneidman, E.S. Tranquilizers and suicide in the schizophrenic patient. *Archives of General Psychiatry.* **11**: 312-321 (1964).

Cole, J.O. and Davis, J.M. Clinical efficacy of the phenothiazines as antipsychotic drugs. In: Efron, D.(Ed.), *Psychopharmacology: A review of progress 1957-1967* #1836, pp. 1057-1063. Washington, D.C.: USPHS 1968.

Coleman, J.V. and Arafeh, M.K. The Connecticut cooperative care project. *Current Psychiatric Therapies.* **9**: 234-240 (1969).

Coohan, J.P. A lot more of the usual — community mental health in Manitoba. *SK & F Psychiatric Reporter.* **35**: 13-16 (1967).

Craig, R.J. Alumni group therapy for chronic schizophrenic outpatients. Hospital and Community Psychiatry. **22**: 204-205 (1971).

Cropley, A.J. and Gazan, A. Some data concerning readmission of discharged schizophrenic patients. *British Journal of Social and Clinical Psychology.* **8**: 286-289 (1969).

Crow, N. The multifaceted role of the community mental health nurse. *Journal of Psychiatric Nursing and Mental Health Services.* **9**: 28-31 (1971).

Daniel, G.R. and Freeman, H.L. *The treatment of mental disorders in the community.* Baltimore: Williams & Wilkins, 1968.

Darley, P.J. and Kenny, W.T. Community care and the "Queequeg syndrome": A phenomenological evaluation of methods of rehabilitation for psychotic patients. *American Journal of Psychiatry.* **127**: 1333-1338 (1971).

David, A.C. Effective low cost aftercare. *Mental Hygiene.* **55**: 351-357 (1971).

Denber, H.C.B. and Rajotte, P. Problems and theoretical considerations of work therapy for psychiatric patients. *Canadian Psychiatric Association Journal.* **7**: 25-33 (1962).

Dignity sounds the keynote. *Medical World News.* **10**: 34L-34M (1969).

Donlon, P.T., Rada, R.T. and Knight, S.W. A therapeutic aftercare setting for "Refractory" chronic schizophrenic patients. *American Journal of Psychiatry.* **130**: 682-684 (1973).

Driemen, P.M. and Minard, C.C. Pre-leave planning: effect upon rehospitalization. *California Mental Health Research Digest.* **8**: 196-197 (1970).

Durie, M., Gardner, R.V. and Matthews, C.J. Spinning straw into gold. *Mental Hygiene.* **56**: 39-42 (1972).

Dyrud, J.E. and Holzman, P.S. The psychotherapy of schizophrenia: Does it work? *American Journal of Psychiatry.* **130**: 670-673 (1973).

Ehrhardt, H. Medikamentose Voraussetzungen einer erfolgreichen rehabilitation bei endogen psychosen. *Psychotherapy and Psychosomatics.* **15**: 17 (1967).

Elder, M.E. and Weinberger, P.E. A family centered project in a state mental hospital. *California Mental Health Research Digest.* **8**: 189-190 (1970).

Ellsworth, R.B. Community measures of treatment effectiveness of released patients. In: *Nonprofessionals in psychiatric rehabilitation,* pp. 129-165. New York: Appleton-Century-Crofts, 1968.

Elosuo, R., Hagglund, V. Paakkinen, E. and Alanen, Y.O. Development of outpatient services in psychiatric departments: a study of the activities of an after-care clinic. *Social Psychiatry.* **4**: 82-84 (1969).

Evans, A.S. and Bullard, D.M., Jr. The family as a potential resource in the rehabilitation of the chronic schizophrenic patient. *Mental Hygiene.* **44**: 64-73 (1960).

Evje, M.C., Bellander, I., Gibby, M. and Palmer, I.S. Evaluating protected hospital employment of chronic psychiatric patients. *Hospital and Community Psychiatry.* **23**: 204-208 (1972).

Feder, S.L. The indications and techniques of partial hospitalization. In: Masserman, J. (Ed.), *Current Psychiatric Therapies,* pp. 167-174. New York: Grune & Stratton, 1971.

Fleurant, L., Hicks, E., Norris, M., Gouge, R. and McKay, A. A twelve-month review of the aftercare clinic activities in Barrow and Walton counties. *Journal of the Medical Association of Georgia.* **61**: 352-354 (1972).

Flomenhaft, K. and Langsley, D.G.   After the crisis.   *Mental Hygiene.*   **55**: 473-477 (1971).

Flynn, J.P.   The team approach: A possible control for the single service schism, an exploratory study.   *Gerontologist.*   **10**:   119-124 (1970).

Freeman, H.E. and Simmons, B.G.   *The mental patient comes home.*   New York: John Wiley & Sons, 1963.

Friedman, I., Lundstedt, S., Von Mering, O. and Hinko, E.N.   Systematic underestimation in reported mental hospital readmission rates.   *American Journal of Psychiatry.*   **121**:   148-152 (1964).

Furst, W. Daycare: Comprehensive management of the mentally ill patient in the community.   *Sandoz Panorama.*   **8**: 26-28 (1970).

Gardner, R.A. Community work therapy in a mental hospital setting.   *American Archives of Rehabilitation Therapy.*   **17**: 29-34 (1969).

Gaviria, B. and Lund, R.D.   Fort Logan patients two years later: A pilot study.   *Journal of the Fort Logan Mental Health Center.*   **4**:   163-176 (1967).

Gittelman-Klein, R. and Klein, D.F.   Premorbid asocial adjustment and prognosis in schizophrenia.   *Journal of Psychiatric Research.*   **7**:   35-53 (1969).

Glasscote, R.M., Gudeman, J.E. and Elpers, R.   *Halfway houses for the mentally ill: A study of programs and problems.*   Washington: The Joint Information Service, 1971.

Gottesman, L.E.   Extended care of the aged: Psychosocial aspects.   *Journal of Geriatric Psychiatry.*   **2**:   220–249 (1969).

Greenblatt, M.   *The prevention of hospitalization: treatment without admission for psychiatric patients.*   New York: Grune & Stratton, 1963.

Greenblatt, M. and Kantor, D.   Student volunteer movement and the manpower shortage.   *American Journal of Psychiatry.*   **118**:   809-814 (1962).

Grimberg, M.   The surrogate society: A new approach to rehabilitation.   *Journal of Rehabilitation.*   **36**:   34-35 (1970).

Grinspoon, L., Ewalt, J.R. and Shader, R.   Psychotherapy and pharmacotherapy.   **125**:   124 (1968).

Grob, S.   Psychiatric social clubs come of age.   *Mental Hygiene.*   **54**:   129-136 (1970).

Harms, E.   Aftercare of the psychiatric patient: an 1847 view.   *American Journal of Psychiatry.*   **125**:   694-695 (1968).

Harrison, E.   Mental aftercare.   *Assignment for the 60's.*   New York: Public Affairs Pamphlets, 1961.

Heinrich, K. and Baer, R.   Zur depot-neuroleptischen therapie schizophrener in der klinischen ambulanz.   In: Heinrich, K. (Ed.), *Neurolept, Dauer-Und Depottherapie in der Psychiatrie,* pp. 77-83.   Constance, Germany: Schnetztor, 1969.

Herz, M.I.   Crisis unresolved.   *International Journal of Psychiatry.*   **9**:   586-591 (1970).

Hiraoka, E.   The health center's view of a community issue — previously institutionalized schizophrenics.   *Community Psychiatry.*   **4**:   37-40 (1969).

Hogarty, G.E.   Hospital differences in the release of discharge ready chronic schizophrenics.   *Archives of General Psychiatry.*   **18**:   367-372 (1968).

Hogarty, G.E. and Goldberg, S.   Drug and sociotherapy in the post-hospital maintenance of schizophrenia.   *Archives of General Psychiatry.*   **24**:   54-64 (1973).

Howard, B.F.   An optimistic report on total rehabilitative potential of chronic schizophrenics. *Archives of General Psychiatry.* **3**: 345-356 (1960).

Huessy, H.R.   Increased use of the family physician in the aftercare of state hospital patients. *American Journal of Public Health.* **53**: 603-608 (1963).

Jansen, E.   The role of the halfway house in community mental health programs in the United Kingdom and America. *American Journal of Psychiatry.* **126**: 1498-1504 (1970).

Jones, M.   *The therapeutic community: A new treatment method in psychiatry.* New York: Basic Books, 1953.

Kalmans, E.T.   Low-cost individualized treatment in a day center. *Hospital and Community Psychiatry.* **21**: 394-397 (1970).

Kelley, F.E. and Walker, R.   A follow-up evaluation of a paid hospital activity program. *Newsletter for Research in Psychology.* **11**:   32-33 (1969).

Kernodle, R.W.   Three family placement programs in Belgium and the Netherlands. *Hospital and Community Psychiatry.* **23**: 339-345 (1972).

Keskiner, A., Ruppert, E. and Ulett, G.A.   The New Haven project. Development of a foster community for mental patients. *Attitude.* **1**:   14-17 (1970).

Kiev, A.   Community psychiatry: Observations of recent English developments. *Comprehensive Psychiatry.* **4**: 291-298 (1963).

Kiev, A.   Some background factors in recent English psychiatric progress. *American Journal of Psychiatry.* pp. 851-856 (1963).

Kinross-Wright, J. and Charalampous, K.D.   A recent development in the chemotherapy of schizophrenia. *Medical Records and Annals.* **56**: 224-225 (1963).

Kirby, J.H.   The discharged mentally ill patient: Aftercare and maintenance in the community. *Medical Times.* **97**: 127-132 (1969).

Klein, L.E.   The hospital halfway house. *Mental Hygiene.* **56**: 30-33 (1972).

Kobrynski, B. and Miller, A.D.   The role of the state hospital in the care of the elderly. *Journal of the American Geriatrics Society.* **18**: 210-219 (1970).

Kramer, B.M.   *Day hospital – A study of partial hospitalization in psychiatry.* New York: Grune & Stratton, 1962.

Kramer, M.   Problems in psychiatric epidemiology. *Proceedings of the Royal Society of Medicine.* **63**: 553-562 (1970).

Kris, E.B.   Effects of pharmacotherapy on work and learning ability – a five year follow-up study. *Recent Advances in Biological Psychiatry.* **3**: 30-34 (1961).

Kris, E.B.   Five-year community follow-up of patients discharged from a mental hospital. *Current Therapeutic Research.* **5**: 451-462 (1963).

Kris, E.B.   Five years' experience with the use of drugs and psychotherapy in a community aftercare clinic. *American Journal of Public Health.* **52**: (Part 2) 9-12 (1962).

Kris, E.B.   Post-hospital care of patients in their community. *Current Therapeutic Research.* **4**: (Supp.): 200-205 (1962).

Kris, E.B.   The role of the day hospital in the rehabilitation of mental patients. In: *Proceedings of the Institute on Rehabilitation of the Mentally Ill,* pp. 33-36. New York: Altro Health and Rehabilitation Services, 1962.

Kris, E.B.   The value of a psychiatric aftercare clinic. *Physician's Panorama,* pp. 19-23. November, 1965.

Kruglova, L.I. Dinamika sotsial 'no-trudovogo prisposobliniia bol'nykh shizofreniei v sviazi s shirokim primeniniem psikhotropnykh sredstv. In: Efimovich, N. (Klin.), *Patogenez I Lechenie Nervno-psikh. zabolevanii*, pp. 223-228. Moscow: Soviet Ministrov RSFSR, 1970.

Kutin, V.P. Rezhim Dnevnogo Statsionara I Problema Readaptatsii v psikhiatricheskikh bol'nitsakh. *Zhurnal Nevropatologii I Psikhiatrii Imeni S.S. Korsakova.* **71**: 1249-1250 (1971).

Lagey, J.C. *The Minnesota follow-up study ten years later.* New York: New York University, 1972.

Lamb, H.R. and Goertzel, V. Discharged mental patients – Are they really in the community? *Archives of General Psychiatry.* **24**: 29-34 (1971).

Lamb, H.R. and Goertzel, V. Evaluating aftercare for former day treatment center patients. *International Journal of Social Psychiatry.* **18**: 67-77 (1972).

Lamb, H.R. and Goertzel, V. High expectations of long-term ex-state hospital patients. *American Journal of Psychiatry.* **129**: 471-475 (1972).

Langsley, D.G. and Kaplan, D.M. Project summary: The family concept in comprehensive psychiatric care. *Final Report, NIMH Grants,* 1970.

Lear, T.E., Bhattacharyya, A., Corrigan, G., Elliott, J., Gordon, J. and Pitt-Aitkens, T. Sharing the care of the elderly between community and hospital. *Lancet.* **7634**: 1349-1353 (1969).

Ledvinka, J. and Denner, B. The limits of success. *Mental Hygiene.* **56**: 30-35 (1972).

Lee, D.T. Recovery, Inc.: Aid in the transition from hospital to community. *Mental Hygiene.* **55**: 194-198 (1971).

Leopoldt, H. Industrial therapy in psychiatric hospitals. *Nursing Mirror and Midwives Journal.* **128**: 16-18 (1969).

Levy, L. An evaluation of a mental health program by use of selected operating statistics. *American Journal of Public Health.* **61**: 2038-2045 (1971).

Liberman, R.P. Behavior modification with chronic mental patients. *Journal of Chronic Diseases.* **23**: 803-812 (1971).

Lifeline: Aftercare. Philadelphia: Smith Kline & French Laboratories, 1962.

Lin, T. Community mental health services: a world view. In: *Com. mental health, an international perspective,* pp. 3-17. San Francisco: Jossey-Bass Inc., 1968.

Ludwig, A.M. Responsibility and chronicity: new treatment models for the chronic schizophrenic. In: Abroms, G. *The New Hospital Psychiatry.* pp. 237-260. New York: Academic Press, 1971.

Lurie, A. and Ron, H. Socialization program as part of aftercare planning. *Canadian Psychiatric Association Journal.* **17** (Special Supp. 2): 157-162 (1972).

Lurie, A. and Ron, H. Multiple family group counseling of discharged schizophrenic young adults and their parents. *Social Psychiatry.* **6**: 88-92 (1971).

Lyashko, G.A. K Voprosu O Povtornykh Postupleniyakh V Psikhonevrologicheskiye Bol'nitsy Leningrada. *Voprosy Psikhiatrii I Nevropatologii.* **7**: 403-408 (1961).

Maeda, E. and Rothwell, N. *Discussion, listing and bibliography of psychiatric halfway houses in the U.S.* American Psychiatric Association. Psychiatric Studies and Projects, No. 9, 1963.

Manizade, A. The county mental health center and its role in community psychiatry. *Maryland State Medical Journal.* **16**: 49-51 (1967).

May, P.R.A. *Treatment of schizophrenia: A comparative study of five treatment methods.* New York: Science House, 1968.

McGarry, L. and Kaplan, H. Overview: Current trends in mental health law. *American Journal of Psychiatry,* pp. 621-630. **130**: 6 (June 1973).

McGriff, D. A co-ordinated approach to discharge planning. *Social Work.* **10**: 45-50 (1965).

Medical World News, 1969.

Mental Health Authority. Residential Services: Reports (Psychiatric and Informal Hospitals). In: *Report of the Mental Health Authority,* 1970, pp. 33-50. Melbourne: Government Printer, 1971.

Mental health hostels. *British Medical Journal.* **5709**: 552-553 (1970).

Micek, L.A. and Miles, D.G. Perspectives on work therapy. *Current Psychiatric Therapies.* **9**: 202-208 (1969).

Miller, A. The Lobotomy patient — a decade later: A follow-up study of a research project started in 1948. *Canadian Medical Association Journal.* **96**: 1095-1103 (1967).

Molholm, L.H. and Dinitz, S. Female mental patients and their normal controls: A restudy ten years later. *Archives of General Psychiatry.* **27**: 606-610 (1972).

Morrissey, J.R. *The case for family care of the mentally ill.* New York: Behavioral Publications, 1967

Myers, J.K. and Bean, L.L. Final considerations. In: *A decade later: A follow-up of social class and mental illness,* pp. 201-222. New York: John Wiley, 1968.

Myers, J.K. and Bean, L.L. Social class and the treatment process. In: *A decade later: A follow-up of social class and mental illness,* pp. 80-111. New York: John Wiley, 1968.

Nickerson, A. Psychiatric community nurses in Edinburgh. *Nursing Times.* **68**: 289-291 (1972).

Nol, E.A. and Fuller, W. Perspectives on psychiatric aftercare in the community. *Michigan Medicine.* **71**: 1009-1013 (1972).

Odegard, O. The pattern of discharge and readmission in Norwegian mental hospitals, 1936-63. *American Journal of Psychiatry.* **125**: 333-340 (1968).

Olshansky, S. The vocational rehabilitation of ex-psychiatric patients. *Mental Hygiene.* **52**: 556-561 (1968).

Oltman, J. and Friedman, S. Results at a "half-way house." *Diseases of the Nervous System,* pp. 317-318 (1964).

Over 65. *Medical World News.* **11**: 300 (1970).

Palmer, M. *The Social Club.* New York: National Association for Mental Health, 1966.

Partial hospitalization. U.S.P.H.S. Publication #1449. Bethesda, Md.: National Institute of Mental Health, 1966.

Pattison, E.M. Group psychotherapy and group methods in community mental health programs. *International Journal of Group Psychotherapy.* **20**: 516-539 (1970).

Payne, J. New Scope for industrial therapy. *Mental Health.* Winter 42-43 (1969).

Perkins, M.E. and Bluestone, H. Hospital and community psychiatric approaches. In: Bellak, L. (Ed.), *The schizophrenic syndrome,* pp. 667-713. New York: Grune & Stratton, 1969.

Pittman, F.S., III, Langsley, D.G., Flomenhaft, K., DeYoung, C.D., Machotka, P. and Kaplan, D.M. Therapy techniques of the family treatment unit. In: Haley, J. (Ed.), *Changing families: A family therapy reader,* pp. 259-271. NewYork: Grune & Stratton, 1971.

Pokorny, A.D. and Frazier, S.H. Local care would benefit many state psychiatric patients. *Texas Medicine.* **63**: 37-38 (1967).

Pokorny, A.D. and Frazier, S.H. Texas surveys its mental hospital population. *Hospital and Community Psychiatry.* **19**: 88-89 (1968).

Pollack, M. Levenstein, S. and Klein, D.F. A three-year post-hospital follow-up of adolescent and adult schizophrenics. *American Journal of Orthopsychiatry.* **38**: 94-109 (1968).

Prince, R.M., Jr., Ackerman, R.E. and Barksdale, B.S. Collaborative provision of aftercare services. *American Journal of Psychiatry.* **130**: 930-932 (1973).

Psychiatrisches Rehabilitationszentrum in Zurich. *Praktische Psychiatrie.* **49**: 78-80 (1970).

Racklin, S. Adolescent psychiatry in a foster care residence: Future directions. *Mt. Sinai Journal of Medicine.* **39**: 586-591 (1972).

Raskin, M. and Dyson, W.L. Treatment problems leading to readmissions of schizophrenic patients. *Archives of General Psychiatry.* **19**: 356-360 (1968).

Raush, Harold L. and Raush, C.L. *The halfway house movement: A search for sanity.* New York: Appleton-Century-Crofts, 1968.

Rawls, J.R. Toward the identification of readmissions and non-readmissions to mental hospitals. *Social Psychiatry.* **6**: 58-61 (1971).

Recovery, Inc., Chicago, Illinois: National Headquarters, Recovery, Inc., 1967.

Reich, R. Care of the chronically mentally ill — a national disgrace. *American Journal of Psychiatry.* **130**: 911-12 (1973).

Rene, A.D., Rice, R.G. and Ghertner, S. Assessing patient needs for counseling and rehabilitation services in hospital setting. *Newsletter for Research in Psychology.* **14**: 33-35 (1972).

Richmond, C. Expanding the concepts of the halfway house: A satellite housing program. *International Journal of Social Psychiatry.* **16**: 96-102 (1970).

Ritchey, R.E. Activity Groups help long-term patients solve everyday problems. *Hospital and Community Psychiatry.* **22**: 335-336 (1971).

Roder, E. A prognostic investigation of female schizophrenic patients discharged from Sct Hans Hospital, Department D, during the decade 1951-1960. *Acta Psychiatrica Scandinavica.* **46**: 50-63 (1970).

Romme, M.A.J. Organisatie gezondheidszorg en langerdurende psychiatrische opneming. *Tijdschrift Voor Sociale Geneeskunde.* **48**: 402-406 (1970).

Rosenberg, G. and Colthoff, P. A community participation program for the hospitalized mental patient. *Journal of Jewish Communal Service.* **43**: 253-259 (1967).

Roth, J.A. and Eddy, E.M. Where do they go from Rahab? In: Roth, J. (Ed.), *Rehabilitation for the unwanted,* pp. 144-167 New York: Atherton Press, 1967.

Rutman, I.D. and Loeb, A. *Comprehensive, Community-based rehabilitation services for the psychiatrically disabled.* Springfield, Virginia, NTIS, 1970.

Ryan, G. Back on the market. *Mental Health.* Winter, 8-9 (1969).

Ryan, W. *Community care in historical perspective.* Canada's Mental Health Supplement #60. Ottawa, Canada: Department of National Health and Welfare, 1969.

Safirstein, S.L. A system of secondary prevention in a psychiatric aftercare clinic of a general hospital. *Diseases of the Nervous System.* **30**: (supplement) 122-125 (1969).

Safirstein, S.L. Psychiatric aftercare including home visits. *New York State Journal of Medicine.* **71**: 2441-2445 (1971).

Salvesen, C. Treatment of suicidal patients in outpatient/aftercare department. *Tidsskrift for den Norske Laegeforening.* **92**: 1193-1194 (1972).

Scarzella, R. Attivita clinico-scientifica nell'ospedale civile di Ivrea.-II. Proposte per la realizzazione del servizo psichiatrico extraospedaliero nel settore psichiatrico del canavese. *Minerva Media.* **61**: 2731-2736 (1970).

Schuerman, J.R. Marital interaction and posthospital adjustment. *Social Casework.* **53**: 163-172 (1972).

Schwartzberg, A.Z. The older psychiatric patient and the community. *Geriatrics.* **22**: 182-186 (1967).

Scoles, P. The chronic mental patient: Aftercare and rehabilitation. In: Berlatsky, E. (Ed.), *Social work practice,* 1969. New York: Columbia University Press, 1969. pp. 61–75.

Searle, D.J. The psychogeriatric services. *Nursing Mirror and Midwives Journal.* **131**: 10-11 (1970).

Shammas, E. Day care centers in Rhode Island state hospitals. *Rhode Island Medical Journal.* **54**: 541-545 (1971).

Sharpe, D. Things have changed. *Nursing Mirror and Midwives Journal.* **134**: 21-23 (1972).

Sherman, L.J., Moseley, E.C., Ging, R. and Bookbinder, L.J. Prognosis in schizophrenia. A follow-up study of 588 patients. *Archives of General Psychiatry.* **10**: 123-130 (1964).

Shot in the Arm for psychotherapy. *Medical World News.* **9**: 62-63 (1968).

Siegle, A. Pioneer at work. SK & F *Psychiatric Reporter.* **37**: 16-17 (1968).

Silverman, M. Comprehensive department of psychological medicine: Three-year review of inpatients referred for aftercare visits. *British Medical Journal.* **3**: 99-101 (1971).

Silverstein, M. *Psychiatric aftercare: Planning for community mental health services.* Philadelphia: University of Pennsylvania Press, 1968.

Simon, C.S. Boarding Home Operators Participate in workshop. *Hospital and Community Psychiatry.* **23**: 1972.

Smith, C.M. Experiment in psychiatric home care. *Canada's Mental Health.* **13**: 8-13 (1965).

Social Clubs . . . Yes. Report of a Consultation on Social Clubs. New York: National Association for Mental Health, 1963.

Solomon, N. and Gorwitz, K. *Mental Hygiene Statistics Newsletter-x-12.* Maryland Department of Health and Mental Hygiene, December 10, 1969.

Spilken, A.Z. *The relationship of patient personality to dropout from psychotherapy.* Ann Arbor, Michigan: Univ. M-Films, No. 71-26488.

Stein, E. and Sorensen, K.D. A cooperative apartment for transitional patients. *Mental Hygiene.* **56**: 68-74 (1972).

Steiner, J. and Kaplan, S.R. Outpatient Group "Work-For-Pay" activity for chronic schizophrenic patients. *American Journal of Psychotherapy.* **23**: 452-462 (1969).

Taylor, I. The third life: Rehabilitation of a long-stay patient. *Nursing Times.* **66**: 956 (1970).

Thompson, P. *Bound for Broadmoor.* London: Hodder & Stoughton, Ltd., 1972.

Thomson, C.P. Developing a day program at the Royal Edinburgh Hospital. *Hospital and Community Psychiatry.* **19**: 14-17 (1968).

Tiffany, D.W., Cowan, J., Eddy, W., Glad, D. and Woll, S. Introduction. In: *Work inhibition and rehabilitation, Part I,* pp. 1-8. Kansas City, Missouri: Institute for Community Studies, 1967.

Treter, A. Z Zagadnien rehabilititacji psychiatrycznej. *Psychiatria Polska.* **6**: 203-207 (1972).

U.S. National Institute of Mental Health, Office of Program Planning and Evaluation. Bringing mental health services to the community. In: NIMH. *Mental health of urban America,* pp. 73-95. Washington: U.S. Government Printing Office, 1969.

University of Indiana Audiovisual Center. *Fountain House.* Bloomington, Indiana: (16MM Film), 1969.

Varsamis, J. Antipsychotic drugs: an essential tool of community psychiatry. *Canadian Journal of Public Health.* **61**: 432-435 (1970).

Wallis, R.R. and Katf, N.Y. The 50-mile bridge: consultation between state hospital and community mental health center staffs. *Hospital and Community Psychiatry.* **23**: 21-24 (1972).

Watt, N.F. Five-year follow-up of geriatric chronically ill mental patients in foster home care. *Journal of the American Geriatrics Society.* **18**: 310-316 (1970).

Wechsler, H. Halfway houses for mental patients: A survey. *Journal of Social Issues.* **16**: 21-22 (1960).

Weinstein, A.S., Di Pasquale, D. and Winsor, F. Relationships between length of stay in and out of the New York State mental hospitals. *American Journal of Psychiatry.* **130**: 904-909 (1973).

Weinstein, G.G. Pilot programs in day care. *Mental Hospitals.* **11**: 9-11 (1960).

Weiss, J. and Schaie, K.W. Factors in patients' failure to return to a psychiatric clinic. *Diseases of the Nervous System.* **19**: 429-430 (1958).

Whitehorn, J.C. and Betz, B.J. A study of psychotherapeutic relationships between physicians and schizophrenic patients. *American Journal of Psychiatry.* **111**: 321-331 (1954).

Widdowson, R.K. and Griffiths, K.A. A voluntary work program for outpatients. *Hospital and Community Psychiatry.* **22**: 151-153 (1971).

Wierig, G.J., Jr. and Robertson, R.J. Social connectedness and community adjustment. *Journal of Clinical Psychology.* **28**: 30–31 (1972).

Wiesel, B. Flexibility: Key to planning of hospital psychiatric services and facilities. *Journal of the American Hospital Association.* **41**: 65-68 (1967).

Wijffels, A.J.A.M. A psychiatric center in the Netherlands. *Hospital and Community Psychiatry.* **23**: 186-188 (1972).

Wilder, J.F., Kessel, M. and Caulfield, S.C. Follow-up of a "high expectations" halfway house. *American Journal of Psychiatry.* **124**: 1085-1091 (1968).

Wilder, J.F., Levin, G. and Zwerling, I. A two-year follow-up evaluation of acute psychotic patients treated in a day hospital. *American Journal of Psychiatry.* **122**: 1095-1101 (1966).

Williams, M.A. Social Worker and counsellor in vocational rehabilitation. *Canada's Mental Health.* **19**: 20-24 (1971).

Winick, W. An automated system for reviewing patient care. *Hospital and Community Psychiatry.* **23**: 27-29 (1972).

Winkler, W.T. Das Moderne Psychiatrische Krankenhaus. *Hippokrates.* **40**: 107-114 (1969).

Winkler, W.T., Kruger, H., Zumpe, V. and Veltin, A. Ergebnisse soziodiagnosticher und soziotherapeutischer massnahmen bei langjahrig hospitalisierten schizophrenen. *Psychotherapy and Psychosomatics.* **17**: 1-9 (1969).

Winston, A., Papernik, D., Breslin, L. and Trembath, P. Therapeutic club for formerly hospitalized psychiatric patients. *New York State Journal of Medicine.* **72**: 3027-3029 (1972).

Witkin, H., Lewis, H.B. and Weil, E. Affective reactions and patient-therapist interactions among more differentiated and less differentiated patients early in therapy. *Journal of Nervous and Mental Disorders.* **146**: 193-208 (1968).

Wolkon, G.H., Karmen, M. and Tanaka, H.T. Evaluation of a social rehabilitation program for recently released psychiatric patients. *Community Mental Health Journal.* **7**: 312-322 (1971).

Wolkon, G.G. and Tanaka, H.T. Professional's views on the need for psychiatric aftercare services. *Community Mental Health Journal.* **1**: 262-270 (1965).

Woodruff, C.R. Pastoral care of the discharged psychiatric patient. *Pastoral Psychology.* **21**: 21-26, 28-29 (1970).

Wren, C.S. 28% of state's mental patients return within 6 months after being released. *The New York Times,* p. 43, July 12, 1973.

Yolles, S.F. and Kramer, M. Vital statistics. In: Bellak, L. (Ed.), *The schizophrenic syndrome,* pp. 66-113. New York: Grune & Stratton, 1969.

Zolik, E.S., Sommers, R. and Lantz, E.M. Hospital return rates and prerelease referrals. *Virginia Medical Monthly.* **94**: 549-552 (1967).

13 Preventive Methods and Mental Health Programs

Jack R. Ewalt and Patricia L. Ewalt

"A strategy for health improvement should include personal health care, environmental control measures and measures of influencing health related behavior." (Breslow, 1973)

Preventive Methods

This section will present primary and secondary preventive methods only, since tertiary prevention is a public health term for the treatment and rehabilitation of illness which will be covered by other authors.

PRIMARY PREVENTION

Primary preventive methods will be discussed under two headings: (a) those methods which alter the individual through some biologic or metabolic manipulation within the body; (b) those methods which alter the environment. To be effective, a primary method must reasonably insure that the condition to be prevented will not occur when the person (or population) is exposed to the causal element.

The prevention of psychological or social behavior that is unacceptable to the individual or others requires an understanding of the complexity of the determinants of human behavior. Ewalt and Farnsworth (1963) discuss this as do Lindsley and Reisen (1968, p. 273):

Behavior is the end point in a series of consequences and interactions which begin with the genetic history of an organism, be it microbe or man. Growth, maturation, and development of an organism are embodied not only in the form and function with which it is endowed, but also in the modifications of these imposed by environmental influences. The chemical composition of its genes, as well as its subsequent soma, are important in the determination of the form and function of the organism, but perhaps no less so than intra- and extra-cellular exchange, intra- and extra-organismic relations, or physical, mental, and social interactions among organisms.

Manipulation of Immune or Metabolic Factors in the Body

Among the most successful methods of primary prevention under this category is the vaccination which prevents the development of smallpox due to an alteration in the body's immune capacities.

A rare but devastating form of mental retardation is prevented by routine examination of the urine of newborn infants to detect abnormalities in phenylalanine metabolism. Failure to detect these in the newborn state results in disastrous problems in growth and development. Detection of these abnormalities in phenylalanine metabolism and the maintenance of infants on a diet free of phenylalanine, enables them to develop normally. At about age six they may then go on a normal diet, free of the pathology which would have resulted in severe impairment in mental growth and development had they been given an ordinary infant diet.

Beri-beri, once a common mental disorder accompanied by severe physical illness and death, is known to be due to dietary deficiencies, particularly the inadequacy of the "B" vitamin factors. An adequate diet maintains the body's nutrition and the illness does not develop.

In the long view, hope for the primary prevention of schizophrenia and the manic depressive disorders, is in genetic, biochemical, and social and psychological investigations. Most people now believe that genetic predisposition is a necessary but not sufficient cause of schizophrenia. Just how this predisposition is manifested in the organism is unknown and we therefore cannot at this time pretest patients for susceptibility to schizophrenia as we can, for example, in the phenylalanine cases.

Investigation of the enzymatic and transmittor substances in the brain, particularly the catecholamine metabolism studies, lend hope that eventually the metabolic disorder of whatever origin may be discovered and perhaps corrective products or diets may effectively prevent the development of the symptomatology. Unfortunately, at the moment these are only hopes which should spur further research but should not lead to false claims of known preventive methods or specific therapies, even though such are offered from time to time. Genetic counseling which may offer opportunities for primary prevention must await more specific understanding of the genetic predisposition. At the moment some studies indicate that the predisposition may not be for schizophrenia *per se* but for more general psychopathology — the socioenvironmental and developmental factors determining which form of psychopathology becomes manifest. In the manic depressive disorders, genetic studies are fewer but perhaps a bit more specific than in the schizophrenic disorders. This may be so in part because the symptomatology of the manic depressive illness is a bit more specific and does not present the differential diagnostic problems sometimes seen in schizophrenias. Substantial progress has been made by Schildkraut (1973) and others to demonstrate with at least reasonable certainty a definite biochemical abnormality in catecholamine metabolism, probably genetically determined, in patients suffering from depressions. Unfortunately to date no biochemical or other test for an imminent attack of depression or mania has been developed although prodromal symtomatology has been fairly well established. Some patients live their whole lives in a mildly hypomanic state or in a mildly depressive state without showing either social or mental decompensation.

Patients with recurring manic attacks placed on lithium maintenance therapy are in most instances protected against further attacks. In a sense this is primary prevention, but some might call it follow-up therapy and rehabilitation. There is evidence that lithium therapy in bipolar manic-depressive patients prevents the depressive swings; and there is still other evidence, although less impressive, that unipolar recurring depressions of the depressive psychotic type may be prevented by lithium. While it is definitely known that the lithium replaces sodium ions, just how this acts to prevent the recurrence of manic attacks and how it acts to control manic symptoms is unknown at this time.

Environmental Manipulation

As examples of primary prevention owing to environmental manipulation, it is well known that malaria can be prevented by mosquito control in the environment and that typhus can be prevented by rat and lice control.

In the mental health field it is known that lead poisoning can cause certain forms of mental retardation and other pathology in infants and children. Lead poisoning can be prevented by environmental control such as insisting on the use of lead-free paint, cleaning up old premises with peeling lead-content paint, and checking air pollution for lead additives.

At the moment there is hope that environmental manipulation, particularly the improvement of family relationships and socio-economic conditions, will prevent at least the more serious manifestations of schizophrenia and manic depressive psychosis in persons congenitally predisposed to these disorders, and perhaps will cut down on the incidence of neuroses, character disorders, and other behavior decompensations thought to be principally due to psychological stresses.

From a historical perspective, however, one tends to be cautious in expecting an elimination of mental disorder through environmental manipulation. A premise of the "mental hygiene movement" — a precursor of "community mental health" at the beginning of this century — was that correction of the environment would contribute to the prevention of mental disorders. This hope accounts for the naming of the movement and of one of its products, the child guidance or "habit" clinics. Mental health consultation with courts, schools and employers was described at that time. Exposure of medical students to mental illness and its treatment with the purpose of increasing their ability to detect and refer "incipient cases" was begun. Classroom techniques devised by Ryan (1938), Prescott (1938) and others, have influenced teaching in regular classrooms and special classes for the emotionally disturbed. Although many of these techniques have been more systematically formulated, or at least differently formulated recently, none of them are new. Their influence over the years may be judged by the reader.

Even though the prevention of serious antisocial behavior and psychopathology has not occurred as was hoped, pessimism seems unwarranted in that the theory and the interventions were frequently too limited reasonably to expect success. It seems unlikely that any single genetic, chemical, psychologic, or social factor could cause diverse and serious problems in growth and development or that correction of any one could prevent illness. The view of Kahn (1970) seems a better approach to research on primary prevention:

> the conditions of life experienced by people of lower social class position tend to impair their ability to deal resourcefully with the problematic and the stressful. Such impairment would be unfortunate for all who suffer it, but would not in itself result in schizophrenia. In conjunction with a genetic vulnerability to schizophrenia and the experience of great stress, however, such impairment could be disabling.

A number of methods are now thought to aid in normal growth and development in the mental health aspects of behavior and are believed by some actually to prevent the development of serious pathology. A number of studies seem to show that emotional deprivation in infancy and early childhood can have serious long-term effects on the mental health and behavior of children. Anna Freud and Dorothy Burlingham (1943, 1944), and Spitz (1959) observed that infants deprived of adequate mothering failed to thrive either mentally or physically. These observations sparked a series of investigations on early development of children that continue to the present, but only the more recent studies will be mentioned (see La Veek, 1968 for a good review of recent work and Soddy for a presentation circa 1956).

In a ten-year follow-up study of several hundred consecutive births, Werner *et al.* reported in 1968 that "More than 10 times as many children were affected by deprived environment than by perinatal stress, indicating the need to refocus emphasis about diagnosis and remediation from 'reproductive casualties' to 'environmental casualties.' "

In a long-term study, Skeels (1966) demonstrated that children removed from an institutional environment to adoptive homes, when examined in adult life, had made significant gains in health and achievement as compared to a similar group who stayed in the institution.

As we have previously mentioned, it is likely that the course of schizophrenia is greatly affected by qualities of the environment, even though the condition is most probably genetically based. Similarly, it is likely that many other conditions, including those more common and benign than schizophrenia, are multiply influenced. For example, the studies of Bell (1968) and of Graham, Rutter and George (1973) suggest a cyclical interaction of genetic and environmental factors — the child's innate characteristics evoking certain behavior in parent figures, and they in turn evoking certain behavior, favorable or unfavorable, in the child.

Owing to observations of this nature, some recent preventive programs have attempted a broad impact on the very young child's environment. Since previous efforts may have failed through treating one aspect and ignoring others, several aspects of the preschool child's life situation have been taken into account. For example, Pavenstedt (1967) and associates described a program of multiple therapeutic and educational inputs for preschool children and their families.

On a national scale, Head Start programs also attempted to coordinate multiple services, both to remedy and to enhance physical, social, and educational capacities of preschool children. Head Start exemplifies the difficulty of demonstrating that primary or even secondary prevention has occurred. The program explicitly attempted to counteract multiple environmental influences previously shown to hinder learning and social adjustment of school-age children — factors such as lack of verbal and visual stimulation, poor health care, lack of social skills customary in classrooms, or alienation of parents from the educational system if not the social system as a whole. Yet despite a coordinated effort to deal with previously identified deficits and thus to prevent disability, substantiation of accomplishments achieved by the program has been strongly questioned. The Skeels study provides the most supportive evidence known to us that alteration of environment may be expected to alter individual functioning over time.

In summary, owing to the current difficulty, if not impossibility, of specifying either the incidence, the causes, or the results of most mental conditions in most individuals, it seems wise to be very cautious in use of the term primary prevention of mental illness. Continued support of research to identify causes and preventive methodologies is highly desirable precisely because so little is yet known. Diversion of mental health resources, as such, predominantly into environmental manipulation is not yet justified by scientific findings. However, even though improvement of the social and physical environment does not prevent mental disorder, it may not be necessary so to justify improvement of the quality of human experience.

SECONDARY PREVENTION

Secondary prevention is usually defined as early detection, early intervention, or early treatment.

There is abundant evidence to indicate that early detection and treatment of schizophrenia yields better results than similar efforts expended on patients allowed to become chronic. Patients with schizophrenia who start treatment within the first twelve months of their illness have a much better prognosis than those who are ill two or more years. There is also evidence that detection and treatment of problem drinking before it reaches a state of compulsive alcoholism is more effective than the treatment of the full-blown problem which tends to become a chronic recurring illness.

Aside from these relatively specific conditions, however, the *for whom, when,* and *how* of early detection and early treatment become unclear.

There is a grey zone of definition between those with mild forms or the beginning phases of mental illness and those who are anxious, angry, or depressed over real life situations. For example, to say that people from a ghetto are mentally ill because they are worried, depressed, or somewhat paranoid is not sound. Yet these people may need and want mental health services for such problems even though they are not mentally ill. Secondly, there are people who, owing to either environmental or personal deficits, are incapable of taking a customary amount of responsibility for themselves and their families. Many of these people would object to being considered mentally ill and yet others in the same circumstances may seek to obtain, and professional persons may seek to provide, the extra assistance that becomes available if their problems *are* considered mental illness. Examples from daily practice are numerous: the dependent, anxious, or improvident person who cannot work becomes defined as ill and eligible for disability payments if a physician gives him some diagnosis.

Shuval, Atonovsky, and Davis (1973) have shown that "Helping people cope with failure is a stable function of medical authorities and is likely to persist in the face of possible changes in the structure of professional roles." The physician thus has granting authority to make incapacity legitimate by naming it illness. Shuval, *et al.* think it unlikely that an equally attractive alternative will develop. Similarly, the alcoholic is ill by legislative act in some states, and in others the recidivist criminal and delinquent are defined as medical problems. Society has not really decided how to handle the so-called "sociopath" and other persons with antisocial characteristics. There is an increasing tendency to regard them as "sick" (Shuval *et al.,* 1973) and to refer them to various mental health agencies. Unfortunately many mental health agencies are not equipped in either staff or clinic and bed space to cope successfully with them. Not all of the tendency to define these people as mentally ill comes from within the mental health professions. The inability of the correctional system to rehabilitate any substantial number of offenders causes people, more in desperation than in firm belief in the "sick" theory, to look elsewhere. This rather confusing picture can be reduced to one simple fact. No matter how we categorize the extremely incapable or sociopathic persons, they are coming to mental health agencies, and it behooves us, as I (J.R. Ewalt) said in my APA Presidential Address in 1964, to learn how to cope with them.

Most secondary prevention will be done at the point of first contact with the caring professions, with family physicians, clergymen, school counselors, industrial health services, family service agencies, visiting nurses, and others who have contact with people who are under stress, troubled, or perhaps having mild somatic disturbances. A survey of the non-institutionalized U.S. population (Gurin, Veroff and Feld, 1960) revealed that one in four had been so troubled they feared a "nervous breakdown," and one in seven had sought help from a clergyman, family physician, or a psychiatrist, in that order of frequency of use. The education of family physicians in primary detection and intervention in early disorder, and the staffing of industrial and school programs, and pediatric, general medical, and surgical clinics with mental health consulting personnel, are well-established for the purpose of secondary prevention and need no documentation. When psychiatric services, as well as other medical services are made available in multi-service centers within neighborhoods, a number of people come forward for treatment who had apparently not been seen in the more formally established hospital clinics and private practitioners' offices. That satellite services reach an additional group of patients can be illustrated in almost any neighborhood health center. Where multi-services are available, patients seem to come earlier, and some patients who would have avoided going to a formal mental health clinic will in some instances come to a multi-service center. A preliminary survey in Massachusetts, as well as surveys in other states, shows that catchment areas with well-staffed mental health centers refer very few patients to state mental hospitals. As of 1972, there were within the United States, 295 community mental health centers, and an even larger number of psychiatric clinics and general hospital psychiatric units in addition to private, municipal, county, state, federal mental hospitals.

There is evidence, although not very substantial, that intervention at the court clinic level, can be of assistance to some types of offenders. The experience of the Legal Medicine Department in Massachusetts has also shown that incarcerated offenders treated in individual or group therapy during their sentence and after parole or discharge, have a lower recidivism rate than those who were not so treated. Unfortunately, one cannot generalize from the encouraging statistics to all prisoners because the prisoners involved are a self-selected group who have volunteered for therapy and may therefore represent those with a better prognosis.

Experience with "client-operated" drop-in centers has shown that young people on drugs or with general health problems such as venereal disease and malnutrition, come because these centers are thought to be non-establishment centers. In such settings properly oriented physicians and social service personnel may offer care and attention which otherwise would not have been sought.

In Boston, schools for children with special educational problems are better patronized by the people in the community if they are operated outside of hospital settings (Casey, unpublished).

Confrontation groups for treatment of drug abuse operated by non-professional people, frequently recovered addicts, are found in all parts of the country. They vary in style and technique: some have contact with a physician or hospital for withdrawal from the drug, others do not. The Joint Information

Service study on the effectiveness of these groups was somewhat discouraging (Glasscote, Sussex, Jaffe, Ball, Brill, 1972), but the validity of their data has been challenged by some. At the time of this writing, there seems to be some decrease in heroin use, and increase in cocaine and "downers," but it is a bit early to discover what effect, if any, this change in drug preference will have on the confrontation group movement. Some of the early groups (e.g., Synanon) have moved away from drug dependent cases and have now become communal living arrangements. Despite the discouraging results from the Joint Information study (Glasscote, Sussex, Jaffe, Ball, Brill, 1972) it seems reasonable to continue support and study the effectiveness of the confrontation method because of the undoubted success of Alcoholics Anonymous in treating severe alcohol addiction.

Owing to the variety of settings now accepted as providing early detection and intervention, it may be worthwhile to re-emphasize the importance of early and thorough evaluation of the nature of the problems encountered. A careful history and mental examination with an investigation of the milieu from which the patient comes are essential. Depending on the nature of the information obtained in the preliminary history-taking and examination process, psychological tests may or may not be helpful as well as a detailed neurological examination, EEG's and other lab tests. One's attitude toward the patient should be investigative as well as supportive during the early phases of management, and a flexible attitude as to the possible ultimate diagnosis should be maintained. By such procedures, one will avoid declaring an autistic child retarded, or considering a patient who is responding with hysterical symptoms to somatic disease either neurotic without giving attention to his somatic disease, or physically ill without attention to the neurotic aspects. The therapist at the secondary intervention level should take responsibility to select the modality of treatment most needed by the patient, not allowing dispositions to be confined to those with which he himself is most comfortable.

Community Mental Health

Since the chronological development of the community mental health legislation and implementation has so frequently been described, it will not be discussed here. Instead, some implications of the concept *community mental health* will be mentioned including emphases and problems which have evolved from the concept.

ENLARGEMENT OF THE COMMUNITY OF CONCERN

Following World War II a number of developments caused civilian problems with mental illness and mental retardation to become a national concern rather than solely the problem of the separate states and private agencies. A century before, Dorothea Dix had exposed the abuses of mental patients to state legislatures in order to make mental illness a responsibility of the states rather than cities, towns, or families. Similarly, during the late forties, journalists, especially Gorman and Deutch, described the extent of the problem of public neglect of mental illness. In addition, during World War II many became familiar with public mental hospitals as attendants during their alternative to military service, and those who did serve in the military had observed the rather common occurrence of emotional breakdown in previously "normal" persons under extreme stress. All of these occurrences, plus the very large number of draftees who had to be turned away owing to emotional disability, impressed a large number of previously uninformed persons with the extent of mental illness, the inadequacy or absence of treatment, and the enormous human waste involved.

AVAILABILITY OF SERVICES TO THE TOTAL COMMUNITY

During the same period of increase in public concern with mental problems, there was increasing scrutiny within the mental health professions of the distribution of services. Even though there has been criticism of some of its aspects, *Social Class and Mental Illness* by Hollingshead and Redlich (1958) raised questions that have had enormous influence on subsequent practice and research. These studies sought to describe subgroups of the population to be served and to question in what ways services rendered might differ for one subgroup or another. Specifically, they questioned whether wealthier, better educated people were likely to obtain what was thought to be better service than poorer, less well educated people.

Related to these were the earlier studies of Faris and Dunham (1939) on the greater occurrence of serious mental illness in the central areas of the cities. This resulted in a series of studies espousing the "drift" hypothesis versus the "causal" effect of ghetto life. These have been reviewed with new insights by Kahn (1973). (Perhaps it is worthy to note that no study has demonstrated any advantage to being born in the ghetto, although there is evidence that such areas offer a haven for decompensating alcoholics and other derelicts.) Taken as a whole, such studies imply that characteristics of the clients and the care-givers may, but should not be permitted, to interfere with the provision of service to segments of the community. Experience suggests that preoccupation with ethnic, racial, and socioeconomic differences is useful up to a point, and then may become destructive to the implementation of a spectrum of services. That is, too often a superficial interpretation of sociological data leads to categorization of types of service supposedly needed or not needed by types of people, ignoring the range of individual variations within groups. For example, statements are heard to the effect that poor people should have short-term treatment because they are incapable of awaiting delayed gratification or that mothers on welfare want money and not casework. A small but verbal minority may, by use of such statements limit or eliminate treatment facilities for an entire neighborhood.

When one considers the concept of mental health services for the total community, goals become ever more complex. What services in particular shall be considered *mental health?* One of the purposes of Dorothea Dix's campaign for state responsibility for mental patients in the mid-nineteenth century was to eliminate confusion of disturbed persons with offenders and paupers in prisons and poorhouses where their physical and mental problems were ignored. Similarly, a goal in the establishment of the psychopathic hospitals early in the twentieth century was more appropriate treatment of mentally ill persons who were often jailed. The proper place for treating or incarcerating an intoxicated person was an extremely lively issue in professional journals and the press then as it is now. Thus from the very establishment of public care-giving institutions in this country, there has been a consistent confusion in conceptualizing those who are to be considered poor, sick, criminal and/or mentally ill. There has also been a consistent tendency increasingly to classify all of these categories as problems of mental health (see also Shuval *et al.,* 1973). Therefore, in espousing the concept of an obligation to provide mental health services to all segments of the community, one is concerned not only with the quality of service to people with diverse socioeconomic conditions but to people with an ever-increasing diversity of what once had been considered social and legal problems.

Moreover, not only have the number of conditions considered appropriate for mental health services greatly increased, but the concept of what constitutes *services* has itself become enlarged. The conditions entitled to treatment are also considered causes or aggravators of further mental health problems. That is, criminal behavior in a certain individual may be considered to require direct treatment of that person. If, in addition, the prevalence of criminal behavior in a neighborhood is high, many feel that the causes of this criminality should be sought out and treated, and that this is also, or even predominantly, a mental health task. Hence, the concept of mental health service to total communities has produced a complexity and diversity of activity at least partly related to enlarged notions of what constitutes mental health's domain and of what constitutes service to this domain. As we have suggested in the earlier discussion of prevention, the all-inclusiveness of such goals contributes to the difficulty of evaluating the effectiveness of mental health services. The broadening of goals to such an extent, however desirable, may suggest the curability of conditions which we are far from precisely describing, let alone treating.

UTILIZING STRENGTHS OF THE COMMUNITY

Community mental health has included the idea that diverse elements of the community may be helpful as well as harmful to health maintenance and restoration. This idea, though it sounds self-evident, had not been emphasized nearly as much during the pre-World War II period. The formal responsibility for psychiatric treatment rested with highly specialized personnel treating people in institutions, often at a physical distance from the community. Even when outpatient treatment was used, the therapist-patient relationship was considered the curing agent with far less emphasis placed on the patient's family, social, and vocational circumstances than is currently common. One of the major assets of the mental health volunteer movement of the 1950s was thought to be their "bridging the gap" between the community and the mental hospitals, including both the patients and the professional persons therein. In those days, development of transitional settings such as halfway houses, sheltered workshops, foster home care for adult patients, then day and night hospitals, was considered a considerable advance in re-introducing patients to the community. Many thought, however, that it would be far better never to remove patients from the community, or if so, very briefly and not far. At the present time, some feel that a problem of an opposite nature has been created: whereas formerly there was a reluctance to retain any mentally ill persons or criminal offenders in the community, there is now a reluctance to exclude any of these individuals from it. Although such a view has high regard for the rights of the individual who might have been excluded, serious problems may occur for the spouses and children of these persons and for other community members. Neither is independent residence in the community necessarily the provision of choice for the disturbed individuals themselves. They may and sometimes do become isolated from sources of treatment and from other people altogether, re-introducing the situation prevailing when Dorothea Dix urged assumption of state and national responsibility for treatment of mentally ill persons. Alternative forms of residence may be necessary considering the rights and needs of both disturbed persons and others. Unfortunately no well-organized research information is currently available to suggest what alternatives would be more effective in improving the quality of life for the chronic patient.

COMMUNITY PARTICIPATION IN MENTAL HEALTH PLANNING

In addition to the expectation that citizens will tolerate and assist disturbed persons within the community, it is expected that community representatives will participate in selecting and planning the services to be offered. Citizen influence on the provision of psychiatric services has been prominent since the beginning of the mental hygiene movement, and while citizen influence has continued in the separate structure of national, state, and local mental health associations, it has been institutionalized in a second hierarchical structure representing area, regional, state, and national levels. These structures are too well-known to require further explanation. However, their involvement, despite the intra-professional and professional-citizen tensions thus created, seems essential in some form for at least two reasons: (1) it was observed from the beginning of the child guidance movement that community-based mental health services tended to die out unless local citizens provided both financial and advisory support; (2) the enormous diversity of activities under the rubric "mental health," whose influence we have emphasized throughout, again has its effects — it is necessary to select among all the possible objectives those which each community finds most urgent and is most willing to support. For several years the individualizing tendencies of local communities have been balanced by the stand-ard-setting influence of the federal government through the grant-giving power of the Institutes of Health and Mental Health and eligibility standards for Medicare and Medicaid payments. Even though some felt that federal standards were too arbitrary, with the withdrawal of categorical federal money, neglect of certain segments of communities is again a danger.

MANPOWER ADAPTATIONS

Once the range of disorders which is now called mental illness is considered, together with the range of preventive and/or therapeutic measures which is thought capable of affecting these disorders, it should be no surprise that the numbers and kinds of persons considered to be "mental health workers" have grown immensely. Not only have the numbers increased but the nature of train-ing for the traditional professions has changed. There has been more emphasis on work with allied professions, and individuals and groups without professional training have been added to the "mental health team."

If one considers mental health practitioners to be charged with the study and treatment (prevention and/or therapy) of individuals, groups, and communities, then all of these activities have grown in recent years. In all the major mental health professions, despite the addition of many other possible emphases, the practice of individual psychotherapy has continued to increase.   In both psychiatry and social work in which the treatment of individuals was a major emphasis even before World War II, the absolute number of persons primarily practicing psychotherapy or casework has grown although relative to the total number in these two disciplines the proportion of persons in this form of prac-tice has diminished somewhat. The training of clinical psychologists since World War II has increasingly emphasized psychotherapy.   The training of nurse therapists at the master and doctoral level has developed even more recently, and in occupational therapy, emphasis on psychodynamics and treatment of individ-uals has also increased in some programs.

In addition to individual practice, however, there has been vastly renewed interest in both the biological and social aspects of mental illness. Since the definition of mental problems is so vague and the influences upon these problems very poorly understood, the boundaries of professional responsibility for study and treatment of social problems have become very obscure. As a result, a great many persons who believe that the alteration of communities in some way or other is necessary for prevention of mental illness are occupied in ways that a great many other people consider having little to do with emotional problems. Such arguments are entirely unresolved at this time, and are unlikely to be resolved until the complexities of social influences on individuals are better understood and conceptualized (Kahn, 1973).

The question of where resources should be placed in practice is reflected in questions about emphases in training. While the majority in the various professions have felt that curricula should reflect the broader approach to mental health, the extent to which various areas should be incorporated into the curriculum is unsettled.   Various approaches have been used to resolve the dilemma: specialization by group to be servied, e.g., geriatrics, children; specialization by modality, e.g., behavior modification; generalization, e.g., a little of the biological, sociological, psychological, political, legal, etc. Although there have been many adaptations, there is little agreement with respect to core curriculum needs.   Several newer disciplines have also been added to the mental health professions in recent years, defining areas of specialization within older professions.   These include pastoral counselors, special class teachers, tutors of emotionally disturbed children, and child care counselors.

In addition to the traditional and newer mental health disciplines, individuals and groups without professional education have come to be considered mental health resources. While citizens have long been represented in policy-making and service-giving as volunteers, here we speak of persons or groups who are paid by individuals or communities for services thought to aid in mental health. These include sensitivity groups, drug rehabilitation centers, and indigenous non-professional workers. This development is a logical extension of the concept that "the community" is a major ally in the prevention, care, and rehabilitation of those with emotional problems. If it is, many think, let the community be organized and represented formally on the treatment team or resource referral list.   Some think that untrained persons from the poverty areas are capable of better understanding poor patients and of being better accepted by them. This movement has partly been fostered by lay persons who believe professional persons do not understand, or worse, are hostile or harmful. It nas also been promoted by professional persons who believe that additional forms of help could thus be provided; that a bridge could be formed between estranged groups and "establishment" resources; and the indigenous, non-professional helpers might themselves be helped by becoming active in others' behalf. It is interesting that the bridge-building which was formerly thought needed between the severely ill and the rest of the community is now thought needed between one segment of the community and another, irrespective of the extent of illness. Unfortunately, as time has gone on the claim by professionals that untrained persons could be helpful in mental health activities came to be interpreted by politicians, among others, as meaning that untrained people could do everything as well as trained people. Some professionals seem to think this as well. There is an even more delicate issue among professional persons as to whether the various trained disciplines are interchangeable. These personnel issues may well become clearer when the objectives for each person to be served and for the mental health field more generally become clearer. When it is obscure whether a person's mental health is to be treated by giving him money, cleaning his neighborhood, prescribing him medicine, improving his marital relations, or straightening out his head, then it is no wonder that there is confusion over who can best help him.

Finally, there is a combining of trained and untrained mental health personnel, with professions who serve the emotionally disturbed but whose primary function is defined otherwise. The most significant example of this collaboration has been the growth of psychiatric units in general hospitals. More community mental health center programs are organized using general hospitals than mental hospitals as their resource for hospitalization. For the past several years, there have been more admissions for mental disturbance to general hospitals than to mental hospitals. In addition to the advantage of providing hospitalization in a setting usually more acceptable to patients and families than mental hospitals, the inclusion of psychiatric units in general hospitals promotes interaction between psychiatric and general medical personnel. Other forms of collaboration between psychiatric facilities and schools, social agencies, health resources, and so on, are no longer "pilot programs" but in most places common.

Such collaboration is becoming formalized in consortia of the various health, education, and welfare services at the local level and administrative hierarchies organized so as to foster integration of services. Often called multi-service centers, family life centers, or some even more euphemistic name, they offer a place where a troubled person or a person in trouble, can come with an expectation of immediate help. If more extended or definitive help or treatment is needed, the agent of the multiple-service center can function as the patient's ombudsman in the hospital, welfare office, rehabilitation center, school department, or probation office, to list only a few.

There are many organizational, administrative, and financial problems to be solved as these agencies expand the number and kind of people they serve. The curtailment of federal funds for those in low income sections has slowed the growth of such services, but that neighborhood response to this problem is aiding in finding solutions is substantial evidence of the usefulness of the neighborhood family life center concept. These consortia seem to represent the current structural response to the vast proliferation of concerns which have come to be considered community mental health.

REFERENCES

Bell, R. A reinterpretation of the direction of effects in studies of socialization. *Psychological Review.* **75**: 81-95 (1968).

Breslow, L. Research in a strategy for health improvement. *International Journal of Health Services.* Vol. 3, No. 1, p. 7 (1973).

Casey, A. Unpublished data — special education. Division of Massachusetts Department of Education.

Ewalt, J.R. Presidential Address, A.P.A., *Journal of the American Psychiatric Association,* Vol. 121, June, 1964.

Ewalt, J.R. and Farnsworth, D.L. *Text book of psychiatry,* p. 14. McGraw-Hill, New York, 1963.

Faris, E.E. and Dunham, H.W. *Mental disorders in urban areas.* University of Chicago Press, Chicago, 1939.

Freud, A. and Burlingham, D. *War and children*. International Universities Press, New York, 1943.

Freud, A. and Burlingham, D. *Infants without families*. International Universities Press, New York, 1944.

Glasscote, R., Sussex, J.N., Jaffe, J.A., Ball, J. and Brill, L. *The treatment of drug abuse*. Joint Information Service. American Psychiatric Association and National Association for Mental Health. Washington, D.C., 1972.

Graham, P., Rutter, M. and George, S. Temperamental characteristics as predictors of behavior disorders in children. *American Journal of Orthopyschiatry.* **43**, No. 3: 328-339 (April, 1973).

Gurin, G., Veroff, J. and Feld, E. *Americans view their mental health*. Basic Books, New York. (A Joint Comm. Mono.), 1960.

Hollingshead, A.B. and Redlich, F.C. *Social class and mental illness*. John Wiley & Sons, New York, 1958.

Kahn, M.L. Social class and schizophrenia: A critical review and a reformulation. *Schizophrenia Bulletin,* p. 60. N.I.M.H. Issue #7, Winter, 1973.

LaVeek, G.D. (Ed.) *Perspectives on human deprivation: biological, psychological and sociological.* National Institute of Child Health and Human Development, U.S.P.H.S. - U.S. Dept. H.E.W., Washington, D.C., 1968.

Lindsley, D. and Reisen, A. *Biological substrates of development and behavior — in perspectives on human deprivation.* H.E.W., National Institute of Child Health and Human Development, Washington, D.C., 1968.

Pavenstedt, E. (Ed.) *The drifters: children of disorganized lower-class families.* Little, Brown & Co., Boston, 1967.

Prescott, D.A. *Emotion and the educative process.* American Council on Education, Washington, D.C., 1938.

Ryan, W.C. *Mental health through education.* Commonwealth Fund, New York, 1938.

Schildkraut, J. Norepinephrine metabolites as biochemical criteria for classifying depressive disorders and predicting responses to treatment. Preliminary findings. *American Journal of Psychiatry.* **130** (6): 695 (June 1973).

Shuval, J.T., Atonovsky, A. and Davis, A.M. Illness, a mechanism for coping with failure. *Social Science and Medicine.* **7**: 259 (1973).

Skeels, H.M. Adult status of children with contrasting early life experiences. Monograph Society for Research in Child Development. **31**: Serial #105 (1966).

Soddy, K. (Ed.) *Mental health and infant development,* 2 vols. Basic Books, New York, 1956.

Spitz, R.A. *A genetic field theory of ego formation*. International Universities Press, New York, 1959.

Werner, E., Bierman, V.M., French, F.E., Simonian, K., Connor, A, Smith, R.S. and Campbell, M. Reproductive and environmental casualties: A report on the 1-year follow-up of the children of the Kauai Pregnancy Study. *Pediatrics.* Vol. 42, No. 1, p. 123 (July, 1968).

Part Two
Specialized Techniques

14 Phenomenological Approaches to the Treatment of "Organic" Psychiatric Syndromes

Marshall F. Folstein and Paul R. McHugh

INTRODUCTION

Discussions of the treatment of so-called organic brain syndromes often reveal an Achilles heel in psychiatric thinking: confusion in relating the principles of empirical diagnosis and those of empathic understanding to the treatment of an individual patient. This confusion probably derives from the continuing internecine ware of psychiatrists who have tended to divide into one camp called "dynamic," marching under an empathic banner, and another "biological," flying the flag of empiricism.

We believe that methods espoused by both camps contribute to the care of patients and certainly of patients with brain disease, but their principles can be applied only after any patient's condition has been defined and his individual mental disposition appreciated. Diagnosis in this dual sense brings out the skills available for the two aspects of treatment: 1) The empirically discovered remedies for the particular class of disorder and 2) the empathical management of the difficulties emerging for this particular patient from his disabilities in his particular life situation and his individual nature.

In this chapter it will be demonstrated that the classical tradition of psychiatric phenomenology (Jaspers, 1963) that emphasizes an assessment of the forms of mental symptoms as much as their content in deriving a treatment of dementia and delirium is effective and comprehensive while avoiding the distraction of theroetical divisions. We will review briefly the definition of the particular syndrome being discussed, describe its actual clinical presentation with pertinent phenomenology and thus demonstrate that knowledge of these characteristics is required for a treatment plan that considers both the issues of the category of illness and the individual patient's human responses.

DELIRIUM

Definition.   By delirium we mean that mental disorder characterized by a disturbance of varying severity in consciousness: that aspect of mental function defined as a continuum from fully awake to coma. With it there is disruption of cognitive functions recognizable in disturbances of thinking and perception. The syndrome of delirium is the common outcome of any number of pathological physical conditions disrupting cerebral function without destroying cerebral tissue such as toxicity from chemicals and vital organ failure (Curran and Wolff, 1935). This definition can encompass the categories listed in several previous classifications (Kraepelin, 1968; Bleuler, 1924; D.S.M. II, 1968).   For the historical development of the definition of delirium, see Lipowski (1967).

Presentation.   A delirious patient can present in a variety of ways that can bewilder the observer.   He may be restless or drowsy, anxious or aggressive, fearful or unpredictable.   His behavior may fluctuate during the day; the patient may be alert at times or stuporous and groggy at other times.

The doctors are often faced with a puzzling amount of information and misinformation.   The patient is complaining of uncertainty and insecurity.   His family notices him change and they may report symptoms of hallucinations and delusions. Nurses reporting patients' inconsistencies may suggest he is exaggerating his problems or is purposely uncooperative. Diagnoses suggested by these features could include schizophrenia, hysteria, anxiety state or mania. Patient "E" appeared completely dressed in the middle of the night in December saying that she had heard it was time to go swimming. She was inattentive and over-talkative, pacing up and down.   Her mental state improved after antibiotic treatment and drainage of an abscess of the foot. Patient "H" became drowsy and assaultive when nurses tried to undress her.   On examination she was disoriented with poor concentration and felt she was being poisoned. Her mental state improved when her polymyalgia was treated with Prednisone.

Phenomenology.   These patients are usually comprehended only if a doctor conducts a methodical examination.   Then he will be impressed first by the difficulty in gaining the patient's attention and holding it focused in the interview.   The patient seems distractible, vague, falling back to sleep; and the doctor must repeat himself, sometimes shaking the patient to gain an answer and holding him in order to accomplish the simplest task of communicating. For all this, the patient may be easily distracted by extraneous events and become angry as the doctors try to force him to attend. It is apparent that the patients have great difficulty in sustaining the thinking process and in fact report that it is an effort. Usually though, the examination reveals that he is disoriented, sometimes simply in time and place but perhaps to a degree that he does not appreciate whether he is standing or lying, dressed or undressed, indoors or outdoors. He may have some insight into his difficulties and may react with emotional feelings. The talk of some patients is jumbled and confused as is their thought with one idea poorly linked to another. This may prompt some to think of a schizophrenic thought disorder. Patients experience hallucinations, usually of a vivid, visual kind but changing and multiple. Similarly delusions that are constantly changing and developing in response to environmental stimuli are common.

It is though, the recognition that the patient is beclouded in consciousness and can focus attention only with great difficulty that best explains his emotional distress and the confused variety of responses that he displays.

In addition to these mental experiences certain performances of the delirious patient are noteworthy. Complex motor functions such as writing a sentence or drawing an abstract design are frequently impaired. Disturbances of posture and coordination manifested by asterixis, ataxia and nystagmus are sometimes present as is an increase in undirected motor activity manifested by senseless picking at bed clothes or by the restlessness and agitation best seen in delirium tremens. The disturbance in cerebral physiology can be documented by a slowing of the EEG frequencies in most cases of delirium — an extremely useful diagnostic sign in some patients (Engel and Romano, 1944). Once the recognition of the syndrome of delirium is established on the basis of morbid mental phenomena, disturbed behavior and EEG changes, the search for its cause can begin.

Delirium is usually the result of a toxic or metabolic disturbance caused by either pathology of body organs or ingested poisons including drugs. The reversibility of the delirium will depend on the reversibility of the metabolic disturbance and its irreversible pathological cause, i.e., toxic chemicals that are eliminated in a few days or kidney failure will produce similar mental disturbances but different prognoses. The onset of a delirium, sudden or insidious as well as the duration, days to months, will also rest with the nature of the pathological lesion. Thus, delirium can be reversible or irreversible, acute or chronic, depending on its cause. For a classification of the causes of delirium see Posner (1971).

Rational treatment will be directed aganist the causal process — removal of the poison. However, while the search for etiology and hence rational treatment is in progess, empirical psychiatric treatments and empathetic management techniques are helpful. These general principles will be described later.

DEMENTIA SYNDROME

Definition. By dementia we mean that psychopathological syndrome characterized by a deterioration of intellectual capacity occurring in clear consciousness. The deterioration of intellect is manifest by a change of personality, amnesia, disorientation and the failure in performance of tasks involving language, calculation and construction. This global disturbance should be distinguished from the selective disturbances in either memory or language as found in Korsakov's and aphasic syndromes, respectively. It is further to be distinguished from mental retardation or mental defect which is a condition of limited intellect present from birth.

Presentation. Patients suffering from dementia syndromes present with a variety of experiences which are often of more concern to the family and friends than to the patient. Presenting symptoms are varied and will depend as much on the social situation and previous personality of the patient as on the extent of the neuropathology.

Patient "A" was brought to the attention of the physician when on a trip to Israel with his wife he left the tour party in a remote desert area and returned to his hotel without informing them. A minor manhunt was begun by his wife. Several years later he developed amnesia and disorientation and progressively, dementia. Patient "B" a conscientious, corporate attorney was reading and writing a complex contract in his law firm when a friend noticed his stained tie and wrinkled suit, a state which he would not have tolerated previously. Months later, while his law firm was still seeking his legal advice concerning matters familiar to him for over thirty years, he first came to the attention of physicians when, after an episode of incontinence following an overdose of laxatives, he became agitated and incoherent and was found on examination to have a clear dementia syndrome. Patient "C" presented after calling the police on numerous occasions complaining that she had been robbed and heard people talking about her outside her apartment door. She was found to have a dementia syndrome with vivid auditory hallucinations. Patient "D" presented because of delusions of jealousy which resulted in a physical attack on his wife. He had otherwise been apathetic, sitting at home watching television until this episode brought his dementia syndrome to the attention of physicians. Patient "E" was brought to the hospital when he signed away numerous stocks and bonds without recalling the transactions. This was the first sign of trouble. Symptoms of these patients could suggest a number of possible diagnoses including schizophrenia.

Phenomenology. In contrast to the delirious patient, the patient with dementia syndrome is fully alert. Although he characteristically will be unable to grasp fully the nature of his total situation, he will not be drowsy or even inattentive. Thus, he can be responsive to interested and friendly conversation and can be angered by neglect and restraint. The retention of the social graces can mask the extent of the patient's intellectual deterioration as seen in patient "L" who was a polite and dapper, elderly man who asked a visitor to let him out of his hospital ward and to direct him to the front door. On arriving at the front door, he politely, with hat in hand, asked at the information desk whether he could check out of his hotel.

The tools of thinking are affected. These patients cannot quickly perceive (Bleuler, 1924) and remember. They are unable to sustain a performance i.e., they cannot concentrate. Speech and writing are frequently affected. In some patients language is sparse and unproductive but words are correctly used. In others, speech is fluent but words are incorrectly formed and used. Reasoning and judging are also impaired and often thinking is experienced as difficult by these patients. In addition to these fundamental cognitive problems, patients with a dementia syndrome suffer from other experiences which further interfere with their remaining capacity.

Disturbances of mood frequently impair thinking. Short-lived recurrent disturbances related to task failure called catastrophic reactions, (Goldstein, 1952) are distressing and illustrated by patient "G." Patient "G" was a man who never liked or trusted physicians. He cooperated for several questions being asked him as part of a mental status examination, but when he was asked to perform a three stage command, his face flushed, he quickly rose from his chair and ran from the room shouting that he did not have to answer these questions and that he wanted to leave. Thereafter he pulled the doorknobs on successive doors trying to find his way out of the building. On a later trial he was able to follow a one stage command with no such reaction. More sustained moods of melancholy or elation can occur often with accompanying changes in self-attitude and with "somatic" signs of anorexia, insomnia and motor disturbances of agitation and retardation. Patient "L" frequently awoke in the morning in great distress, crying that he had lost all of his money and could not pay his bills. By afternoon, however, he was pleasant and cheerful. Delusions and hallucinations are common as noted in the Presentation. Perseveration, as fully described by Allison, of thought, speech and movement, often resembling a catatonic motor perseveration is common. On the other hand, true obsessions and compulsions are found only occasionally in these patients. Patients' cognitive remnants are further impaired by the change in interest and energy they experience, often considered a change in personality. Patients will sit for hours staring at the wall. Others need to be encouraged to listen to music, previously a life long passion. Some patients experience the feeling that there is no reason to remember since nothing is important.

The patient's insight or lack of it is puzzling and unpredictable. Certain patients with dementia syndrome usually mild, are acutely aware of their cognitive difficulty and will suffer from this knowledge. Others experience their thinking as being perfectly normal when in fact they are totally unable to make use of past experiences in order to modify their current behavior.

Accompanying these morbid experiences and faculty performances may be pathological somatic signs such as diffuse or focal abnormalities of reflexes, pathological reflexes such as sucking and grasping, or an abnormal electroencephalogram. These abnormalities will depend on the location of the pathological change.

The etiology and pathology of the dementia syndrome is sought first in the history and development of symptoms, and second by examination of the patient for the physical and laboratory signs that may accompany the syndrome. The history of sudden appearance of signs with subsequent improvement over days would suggest a vascular or demyelinative pathology. A progressive course of deterioration of weeks and months frequently with hemiparesis is suggestive of a brain tumor, abscess or subdural hematoma. Gradual appearance of jargon aphasia with apraxia and agnosia suggest a loss of cortical neurons perhaps associated with Alzheimer's plaques and neurofibrillary tangles. However, a progressive course may also be associated with signs of apathy, akinesia and postural defects which would suggest a subcortical pathology as is found in hydrocephalus or Parkinsonism or in some cases of affective disorder in the elderly (McHugh, 1964). A worsening syndrome can also be accompanied by the somatic and neurological signs of pellagra, pernicious anemia, hypothyroidism and syphilis. Thus, the course of the dementia syndrome can be seen to reveal the etiology and pathology. It can be sudden, insidious, acute or chronic. The reversibility of the dementia syndrome will also depend on the causal agent. In some cases the fundamental symptoms of disorientation and failure to recall can be completely reversed as in the case of hydrocephalus after shunting. However, even in those cases in which the cognitive defect is irreversible, many of the interfering symptoms can be reversible. Since reversibility does not distinguish dementia from delirium, this feature should not be used as a defining characteristic of the syndrome.

TREATMENT

We concur with Goldstein (1952) that the treatment of patients with psychiatric syndromes associated with brain changes is the same in principle as the treatment of any other psychiatric patient. Three methods of treatment must be considered in each case: 1) The applicability of rational treatment based on the knowledge of etiology; 2) the application of empirical treatments i.e., the application of remedies demonstrated by experience and experiment to be efficacious for particular classes of patients regardless of etiology; and 3) Empathic treatment or the application of techniques of management derived from an empathetic understanding of the individual and his reaction to his circumstances.

The recognition of the major classes of dementia syndrome or delirium allows the physician to be alert for rational treatment modalities based on etiology. For the delirious group he tries to remove the toxic and metabolic causal agent. This will entail a careful study of the cardio-respiratory, hepatogastro-intestinal, renal and endocrine systems. For the dementia syndrome he will study the nervous system for pathological processes leading to neuronal loss, demyelination or structural displacement by tumors or spinal fluid. Furthermore, he can rationally treat complicating conditions caused by infection particularly pneumonia, as well as symptoms of heart failure, anemia and nutritional deficiencies such as niacin, vitamin B-12, and thiamine. Even minor disturbances produced by these conditions can seriously affect the mental state of patients with some other central nervous system disease. This was recognized by Kraepelin who considered nutritional support to be a prime factor in the treatment of delirium and dementia.

Many patients with delirium and dementia can be helped by the application of those empirically discovered remedies available to the modern psychiatrist. Recognition of the class of patient determined by a clustering of the morbid experiences present is necessary for the application of the appropriate empirical treatment. Thus patients with mood disorders which are constant and accompanied by a change in attitude and somatic signs can be relieved by antidepressant medication, tricyclics or monoamine oxidase inhibitors or electroconvulsive therapy, if depressed, or by lithium or Haldol if elated. Prolonged moods of agitation or excitement without accompanying changes in attitude or somatic signs can be relieved by phenothiazines. Likewise, delusional and hallucinatory states accompanying dementia or delirium can be relieved by phenothiazines. All drugs should be used in small dosages in these patients and the mental state should be carefully monitored for signs of increasing drowsiness and intellectual impairment, since these treatments are themselves capable of inducing a delirious state.

Since the foundation of the principles of empathic treatment are derived from an understanding of a particular individual in a particular place, the application of those principles will be to an extent limited to a particular patient. However, principles derived from empathic understanding which were found to be helpful on our wards at the Westchester Division of the New York Hospital, in large part were also found to be helpful by Dr. Post in London. For this reason we feel that they might also be helpful for other physicians treating these patients.

Since patients with delirium or dementia suffer from a variety of bewildering experiences in the best circumstances, it seemed plausible that a strange impersonal and ever changing environment would make them even more upset. Furthermore, it seemed that a friendly, homelike, regular and routine environment would make him more comfortable and hence easier to manage. For these reasons inferred from an empathic understanding of the way these patients feel, a particular milieu was designed. Patients are housed in private bedrooms with as many of their personal belongings as possible. Floors are carpeted and hall furniture is provided with comfortable chairs, sofas and adequate lighting. The patients eat in a small dining room, sitting at the same table with the same fellow patients each meal. A regular daily schedule is followed which provides activity between meals. Patients are continually informed of the schedule as well as to the day, date and place. An empathic understanding of the particular patient and his family is also helpful. Appreciating the content of the patient's symptoms such as his financial or particular family concerns can lead to planning and reassurance which bring comfort. The appreciation of the burden of illness on family members can aid social workers in aftercare planning for these patients. A great strength of the empathic method is in promoting interest and a helping attitude on the part of the staff, and cooperation on the part of the patient. Treatment of patients in this way will require the same number of staff, including doctors, nurses and social workers as required for the general psychiatric population.

In summary, diagnosis and hence treatment based on the form of the mental experiences allows one to group patients into classes of disorder from which rational treatment based on etiology can be applied as well as empirically discovered treatments found to help particular clusters of symptoms. Psychological appreciation derived from a study of the patient's particular experience leads to a program of individual treatment for the specific patient and his family.

This approach to treatment which recognizes the patient's conscious mental experience first and then applies the appropriate modes of treatment has enabled us to encourage nurses, social workers and psychiatric residents to care for these patients who have been previously unsuccessfully treated in the usual general hospital setting before coming to our unit.

REFERENCES

Allison, R.S. *Senile Brain*, Arnold Ltd., 1962.

Bleuler, E. *Textbook of psychiatry*, authorized English edition, New York: MacMillan Co., 1924.

Curran, D. and Wolff, H. Nature of delirium and allied states. *Archives Neurology and Psychiatry*. **33**: 1175 (1935).

DSM II, APA, 1968.

Engel, C. and Romano, J. Delirium I EEG data. *Archives Neurology and Psychiatry*. **51**: 356 (1944).

Goldstein, K. The effect of brain damage on the personality in psychiatry, p. 245, Vol. 15, 1952.

Jaspers, K. *General psychopathology*. Chicago: University of Chicago Press, 1963.

Kraepelin, E. *Lectures on clinical psychiatry*. New Jersey: Hafner Publishing Co., 1968.

Lipowski, Z. Delirium, clouding of consciousness and confusion. *Journal of Nervous and Mental Disease*. **145**: 227 (1967).

McHugh, P.R. Occult hydrocephalus. *Quarterly Journal of Medicine*. **33**: 277 (1964).

Posner, J.B. Delirium and exogenous metabolic brain disease. In: Beeson, P.B. and McDermott, W. (Eds.), *Cecil-Loeb Textbook of Medicine*, 13th Edition, p. 88, Philadelphia: W.B. Sanders Co., 1971.

Post, F. *The clinical psychiatry of late life*. New York: Pergamon Press, 1965.

15 Geriatrics

David B. Larson, Alan D. Whanger and Ewald W. Busse

Definition of Terms

The science of aging called *gerontology* includes the study of aging and all of its aspects — biological, psychological and sociological. *Gero* is derived from the Greek and means "old man" or "pertaining to old age." *Geriatrics* means "old plus cure" and applies to the biomedical aspects of gerontology. *Psychiatry* is a combination of Greek derivation and means "mind-healing." Consequently, the term *geriatric psychiatry* is in some ways redundant. For this reason there are those who prefer the term *geropsychiatry,* which translated means "mind healing of those in old age."

Geropsychiatry is concerned with mental disorders occurring in late adult life, particularly those that are predominant after age 65. In addition, geropsychiatry is concerned with the mental problems of late life including alterations of memory, decision making, perceiving environmental events and interpreting feelings and behavior. In geriatrics, the term *senescence* is often utilized to identify those declines in efficiency of function accompanying passage of time; that is, the inevitable changes occurring during the aging processes. *Senility* or *senile changes* refer to pathological changes that are acquired secondary to infection, trauma, disease or degenerative deterioration.

Population Trends in Geriatrics

In 1978, there were some 22 million Americans older than age 65. This was approximately 11% of the total population. In 1870, there were 1.2 million

Americans over age 65, and that was 2.9% of the total population. Thus, in a period of almost 110 years, the actual number of elderly Americans has increased almost 19 million. Present projections for the number of elderly living in the year 2030 are some 50 million, which will account for 17-20% of the total population (Brotman, 1973; Wells, 1980).

In order to plan for the mental health needs of the elderly population one must consider what happens after age 65. The usual retirement age is 65, but some 38% of males continue some employment after 65, and 14% of females continue after 65 (Palmore, 1965). The age of 75 seems to be one at which the individual's health starts to worsen, and there is an increase in frequency of hospitalization, death, living alone and isolation and a special decrease in employment and income (Shanas *et al.*, 1968; Neugarten, 1974). Those 75 years and over are restricted in their activities because of illness about twelve days more per year than those aged 65-74. Of those 75 and over, 24% are unable to carry on major activities as opposed to 10% of those between the ages of 65 and 74 (Busse, 1969).

Extent of Psychiatric Disorders in the Elderly

It is difficult to determine the frequency of various psychiatric disorders in the older population because of both the peculiarities of the group studies and the diagnostic criteria used. Traditionally, most of the care for psychiatric disorders in the elderly was carried out in state mental hospitals. This represented a very skewed population. One percent of all those over age 65 are in some type of mental hospital (Kramer, Taube and Starr, 1968). An additional 1-2% have significant psychiatric disturbances and reside in other settings such as nursing homes, chronic disease hospitals and homes for the aged (Redick, Kramer and Taube, 1973).

A series of community surveys indicated that some 4-8% of the elderly living outside of institutions has psychosis or other severe psychiatric disturbances (Riley and Foner, 1968). In a study of over 200 community-living elderly volunteers in the first longitudinal study at the Duke University Center for the Study of Aging and Development, some 40% were considered psychiatrically normal, whereas 25% were psychoneurotic, almost half of them with severe neurotic reactions; 10% demonstrated relatively mild nonpsychotic organic changes; 20% had combined nonpsychotic, psychotic organic changes and neurotic symptoms; and 6% presented evidence of psychosis (Busse, Dovenmuehle and Brown, 1960). A study of state hospitals in North Carolina indicated that of those admitted for the first time after age sixty-five, 70% had a diagnosis of acute or chronic organic brain syndrome, 9% had functional psychoses, 8% had various personality disorders, and 7% had neuroses (Whanger, 1971). Of those initially admitted to private psychiatric facilities, the incidence of functional disorders is much higher. Redick *et al.* (1973) show that the elderly in this group demonstrate an incidence of about 16% schizophrenia, 19% other functional psychoses, 13% neurotic disorders and about 42% organic brain syndromes. Older people with a problem of alcoholism make up approximately 5-10% of admissions of those 65 and over. In summary, initial admissions to state hospitals show a far greater frequency of acute or chronic organic brain syndromes than do private psychiatric facilities, which show a greater frequency of psychotic as well as neurotic and affective problems. Turning from initial admissions to prevalence rates in hospital settings, figures vary, but among aged patients already in public psychiatric hospitals, approximately 50% have been diagnosed as having some type of organic brain syndrome, 42% have some functional psychoses, and 8% have other diagnoses (Whanger, 1971; Redick *et al.*, 1973). Among the aged in psychiatric wards of general hospitals and private psychiatric hospitals, about 46% have organic brain syndromes, 18% have functional psychoses, and 26% have neurotic disorders (Whanger, 1980). Thus, for those already present in public hospitals, we find high rates of organic brain disease and functional psychoses. There are high rates of organic brain disease alone in general and private settings.

Concerning outpatient therapy, people over 65 comprise some 2-4% of those receiving outpatient treatment for psychiatric illnesses (Eisdorfer and Stotsky, 1977), yet the elderly comprise some 10% of the population. The situation has been described by the committee on aging of the Group for the Advancement of Psychiatry as a situation in which the elderly suffered disproportionately from our "non-system of non-care." The situation is characterized by insufficient financing for both maintaining health and treating sickness and by fragmented delivery of services (Group for the Advancement of Psychiatry, 1970). Lazarus and Weinberg (1980) do not take a simplistic approach as to why the elderly have utilized psychiatric outpatient services at such a low rate. Rather, they feel that the low utilization of psychiatric outpatient services needs to be understood by considering attitudes about the elderly or about psychiatry from four different perspectives: 1) the attitudes of the patient, 2) the attitudes of the family, 3) the attitudes of the primary physician and 4) the attitudes of the psychiatrist. It is noteworthy to repeat the findings of one study to which they referred (Arnhoff and Kumbar, 1970). In this study, 56% of psychiatrists surveyed spent no time with patients over 65. In addition, 86% of the psychiatrists spent less than 10% of their working time with the elderly. Although it may be difficult for us as psychiatrists to change the attitudes of the patient, the family or the referring physician, it may be far easier for us to change our own "gerontophobia." This term, coined by Comfort (1967), points to a therapist's pessimistic outlook toward achieving any successful therapeutic gains in working with people over 65.

PROBLEMS AND FACTORS AFFECTING TREATMENT METHODS IN THE ELDERLY

Concurrent Physical and Mental Illness

The assessment of psychopathology in older persons is complicated by the frequent concurrent presence of physical diseases, multiple psychiatric disorders, socioeconomic factors and the all too common tendency to ascribe any problem in an older person to "hardening of the arteries." As Lazarus and Weinberg (1980) have stated, "mandatory retirement along with America's preoccupation with youth and emphasis on economic productivity tend to reinforce a view of the elderly as no real benefit to the generation past their 60's." They go on to further state that physicians "are not immune to these myths and misconceptions." Thus, the medical physician may inadvertently, consciously or unconsciously, miss or fail to examine complaints that have a true physical origin.

In addition, the elderly may not have a valid physical complaint evaluated. Osfelt (1968) found that although 50% of the elderly who were evaluated were in need of medical care, only 25% saw their need to be medically evaluated.

Concerning the frequency of physical disorders, 79% of those over 65 have at least one chronic physical disorder, with only 2% bedfast (Busse, 1972). An additional 11% are not bedfast but are basically restricted to their home environment. Kahn, Goldfarb, Pollack and Gerber (1960) point out the risks that this restricted 13% have, related to decreases in their social contacts contributing to their decline in mental capacities. One should be especially aware of neurological problems that particularly target the elderly. One study (Broe, 1976) surveyed over 800 elderly subjects living in their own homes and found 20% with either a completed stroke or a history of a transient ischemic attack, and another 10% with various neurologic disorders.

Another problem is the admission of an older person to an inappropriate hospital service. This problem was initially studied in England by Kidd (1962a,b), who rated patients on their ranges of psychiatric and medical disabilities and needs. He showed that some 69% of those admitted on the geriatric medical service had mental illness, whereas 43% of those admitted to mental hospitals had significant physical illness. He felt that 34% of those admitted to the medical service should have been admitted instead to a psychiatric service. On the other hand, 24% of those admitted to psychiatric facilities should have been on a medical service. Other studies have revealed a high incidence of mixed medical and psychiatric illnesses as well. Langley and Simpson (1970) found that 63% of geriatric medical patients had mental illness, and 65% of the patients on a psychiatric service had physical illness.

Unnecessarily prolonged hospital admissions can be a further problem. What seems to be especially important is first to keep the elderly out of an institutional setting until it is necessary, and then once they are in the institutional setting to get them back into their home environment as soon as possible. Butler and Lewis (1977) discussed "institutional neuroses" as a deterioration in the individual's basic personality structure with excessive dependence and loss of interest in the outside world. Whanger (1980) also emphasizes that in the traditional custodial ward situation, the elderly individual has a very low chance of leaving physically or psychiatrically "whole," but in an active milieu program well over half of the new admissions can be eventually discharged. He goes on to state that those discharged early in the admission have a much better chance of successful return to the community than those who are hospitalized longer. A similar study (Neiditch and White, 1976) also found that those discharged within the first few weeks after admission seemed to have the greatest therapeutic response, and those having to stay in a hospital for longer periods of time tended either to stabilize at a much lower level of functioning or to deteriorate.

Another therapeutic model that seems especially helpful for the concurrence of medical and psychiatric problems is a health care delivery system that would offer inpatient, outpatient and home care services as parts of the elderly's community. Hopefully, both physical and psychiatric services would be available (Poe and Rice, 1976). Such an effort would diffuse the splintered care efforts in which psychiatric patients end up on medical services and medical patients end up on psychiatric services. Here, all would be treated in the same place, and the patients treated very close to their homes. The British recommended the establishment of "psychogeriatric assessment units" and recommended that these units be jointly staffed by psychiatrists and geriatricians (Arie, 1971; Department of Health and Social Security, 1970). The United States followed their lead and is now establishing such facilities in some parts of the country (Poe and Rice, 1976; Levenson and Felkins, 1979).

Mental Illness Predisposing to Medical Illnesses

Several groups are at risk for medical problems within the elderly population, three of the most important being those with depression, those with anxiety and those with alcoholism. Garretz (1976) has made the point that a dangerous cycle of depression and faulty nutrition is common among the elderly. As a result, the elderly can become either overweight or especially underweight with resulting cardiovascular or endocrine disorders that increase mortality among the aged. Another study (Wigdon and Morris, 1977) found that in a comparison of medical histories covering a 20–24-year period for groups of paranoid and depressed males, the depressed group suffered a significantly greater number of medical disorders per individual. The medical disorders found were those especially associated with the aging process (cardiovascular disorders, diabetes and arthritis). Concerning anxiety, McCrae, Bartone and Costa (1976) found that anxious elderly males were far less concerned about their health than normal subjects. Thus, the clinician should look for and evaluate anxiety and depression in the elderly, and when these problems are found, appropriate psychotherapeutic or pharmacologic modes should be used in responding to them.

Alcoholism is seen with at least moderate frequency in the elderly. Simon, Epstein and Reynolds (1968) noted a 28% incidence of serious drinking problems among the elderly in a San Francisco psychiatric screening project; Gaitz and Baer (1971) noted a 44% incidence in patients over age 60 who came into their screening ward. Thus, the incidence of drinking problems in the elderly is not a small one. Nutritional deficiencies are often present, and naturally need to be treated with appropriate supplements. More important, as with the depressed patient, these nutritional problems can lead to worsening physical problems. Concomitant physical problems should always be looked for in the geriatric alcoholic, especially liver and cardiac disorders, pneumonia and subdural hematomas. Thus, the presence of anxiety, depression and alcoholism in the elderly should remind the clinician that medical illness might be present.

Altered Physiological Responses

As age increases, responses to drugs within the individuals change. The changes may be due to: alterations in metabolism, decreased capacity of the liver to detoxify, reduced renal capacity to excrete, decreased cerebral blood flow and cerebral metabolism and decreased overall body metabolism (Friedel, 1978; Beattie and Sellers, 1979). In addition, it is very important to remember that the body's capacity to maintain biochemical homeostasis is reduced. With the addition to drugs to the body's system, the probability of side-effects is increased. Once side-effects occur, it is even more difficult to return to physiological balance. The homeostatic mechanisms that usually re-create balance may be impaired as a result of alterations in: intestinal motility, cardiac output, tone of peripheral blood vasculature, mass of peripheral and central nervous tissue, renal excretion and sympathetic-parasympathetic autonomic balance (Salzman, Shader and Pearlman, 1970).

Absorption is often diminished as a result of multiple factors, including decreased abdominal blood flow, a reduction in size of absorbing gastrointestinal surfaces and the impairment of enzyme systems responsible for the transport across gastrointestinal membranes (Bender, 1971). Drug distribution is partially dependent upon the extent to which the drug is protein-bound within the plasma, and also upon the distribution patterns of the blood flow. Since plasma albumen decreases with advancing age, the amount of bound drug will also decrease, consequently altering drug distribution (Rafsky, Brill, Stern and Corey, 1952). As to blood flow, a lowered cardiac output in older people results in a redistribution of the blood flow to the cerebrum and heart with a consequent decrease in blood flow to the gastrointestinal tract (especially the liver) and kidney (Goldman, 1974). The kidney is the primary route for elimination, and the liver is the main metabolizer of drugs. As the person ages, both the kidney and the liver experience a decrease in their efficacy in excreting and metabolizing. Consequently, there may be an increase in the drug levels if "standard" amounts of drugs are used.

Greenblatt, Allen and Shader (1977), when evaluating responses to benzodiazepines, found that the larger the amount of drug and the older the person is past 60, the greater the chance for side-effects. Nies, Robinson and Friedman (1977) similarly found that the elderly on tricyclics develop higher steady-state plasma levels and thus are more susceptible to the side-effects of such antidepressants. Fann, Wheless and Richman (1976) make the point that the elderly certainly do experience altered metabolism, absorption and excretion processes, and that all create a potential of increasing toxicity for the elderly. Careful evaluation of the effects the drugs have on the elderly might keep toxicity to a minimum and allow an effective therapeutic response.

Polypharmacology: Iatrogenic

As if the elderly didn't have enough difficulties with drugs with their altered physiological responses, the problems are knowingly or unknowingly compounded by doctors who prescribe multiple drugs. These drugs end up affecting multiple biochemical systems. Furthermore, the elderly may take additional medicines on their own. One study of physicians' prescribing habits revealed an average of ten prescription medications per each Medicare patient (Fann, 1973). A study of the elderly in twelve Veterans Administration hospitals (Prien, Klett and Caffey, 1976) revealed multiple drug use in 24–41% of the elderly. Hale, Marks and Stewart (1979) looked at a large cohort of over 1700 elderly patients visiting a hypertension screening program over a three-year period and found a consistent increase in the mean number of drug categories with increased age. Their data revealed that some 77% of the sample were using at least one regular drug preparation, and that the number of drug categories increased from a mean of 1.6 in patients under 70 to a mean of 2.6 in patients over 84 years old.

Learoyd (1972) found that in Australia 16% of a group of psychogeriatric admissions were directly due to the ill effects of psychotropic drugs. In Scotland, a community survey of geriatric patients showed a mean of three prescription drugs each, with almost one-third receiving barbiturates. The investigators (Gibson and O'Hare, 1968) felt that three seemed to be the maximum number of drugs for an elderly person to stay reasonably alert and to manage and to cope successfully. Others (Salzman and Shader, 1978) emphasized that polypharmacy in the elderly may not only lead to depression but may also lead to other psychiatric symptoms such as confusion, delirium and psychosis, as a result of the interaction between the drugs or between the drug and the present medical status of the person. Few doctors would prescribe even to the non-elderly multiple hypnotics and sedatives, but Prentice (1979) documents a disproportionately high use of tranquilizers, sedatives, hypnotics and antidepressants in the elderly, with an especially high use of hypnotics and sedatives. Lamy and Kitler (1971) emphasized that care should be exercised in the elderly so that the most important disease is given primary consideration in terms of drug use. Thus, when possible, the clinician should treat the primary problem first and evaluate the potential use of other drugs in reference to whether the treatment of the secondary problems will make the primary problem worse or better.

Polypharmacy: Non-Iatrogenic

There is some drug use that the clinician can modify by just not prescribing. On the other hand, many elderly treat the discomforts of their minds and/or bodies by consuming a variety of medications on their own. Two common problems for the clinician to be aware of are: 1) the medicine cabinet, where there may be an increasingly large collection of old prescriptions that might be taken indiscriminately; and 2) visits to two or more doctors, each unaware of what the other is prescribing, who thus add to an increasing number of medications.

Many of the elderly want to maintain a sense of mastery in their later life. Thus, they might self-medicate in ways that could potentially harm them. Gibson and O'Hare (1968) felt that about one-third of the elderly administered their own drugs incorrectly. They may do so either because they can't read the label, and, wanting to deny the decline of their vision, they take medications as they see fit. Or, individuals may take medicine only when they think it is necessary, not taking it according to the prescription. A separate factor might be economics. Many of the elderly wouldn't want others to know of a worsening economic status, and may cut financial corners in terms of their medication. Thus, they do not purchase prescribed and needed medications (Lamy and Kitler, 1971), and may use borrowed, outdated or over-the-counter preparations instead.

Diet and Nutrition

Suboptimal nutrition is a very common problem among the elderly, especially those in the lower socioeconomic groups. Coursin completed a national nutrition survey in 1970 that showed 40% of the elderly poor were consuming diets with low levels of vitamins A and C, thiamine and riboflavin. Another study (Leevy, Cardi, Frank, Gellene and Baker, 1965) evaluated nutritional status in various institutional settings for the elderly and found that almost 90% of the subjects had a reduction in the blood levels in one or more of the vitamins, and that in 10% there was a decrease in the levels of at least five vitamins. A survey by one of the authors found that elderly patients in state psychiatric hospitals probably had inadequate diets in over 70% of those studied (Whanger and Wang, 1974). A large study completed by the U.S. Center for Disease Control (DHEW, 1972) found that persons 60 years and older consumed far less food than needed to meet the nutrient standard for their age, sex and weight. The most frequently reported deficiencies were those of protein, iron and vitamin A. Todhunter (1976) looked at how the life-styles of the elderly affected their nutrient intake. His findings included: 1) better education was correlated with an improved diet; 2) economic factors strongly influenced dietary adequacy; 3) neither health problems nor lack of teeth had much effect on food practices; 4) one-half of the group did not meet the RDA for protein; 5) less than half of the women studied had satisfactory iron levels; 6) less than half of the group were satisfactory for vitamin A, thiamine and riboflavin.

In summary, the elderly seem to be a group at risk for nutritional deficiencies. And if one deficiency exists, others are frequently present. Although the direct effect of various nutritional deficiencies is still not well understood, it seems safe to say that they worsen the medical status and decrease physical strength. Although nutritional status is not often a commonly considered part of the clinician's therapeutic regimen, it is very important to assist the elderly in evaluating their nutritional status and make recommendations when appropriate.

TYPES OF TREATMENT IN GERIATRIC MENTAL DISORDERS

In this section, we will deal with the treatment of functional psychiatric disorders. We refer the reader to other sections of this volume regarding organic brain syndromes. There may be some overlap, but we hope such overlap will reinforce basic therapeutic issues in dealing with the elderly. In this section, drugs will be referred to by their generic name, usually followed by their most commonly used American brand name for easier identification. This implies no endorsement of a particular product.

Most of the psychiatric disorders seen in younger persons can be found in the elderly. There tends to be a narrower spectrum of disorders that predominate in the elderly age group, including: 1) the organic brain syndrome, 2) acute affective disorders, 3) chronic affective disorders, 4) hypochondriasis, 5) anxiety states, 6) paranoid reactions and 7) alcoholism (Butler and Lewis, 1973; Busse and Pheiffer, 1973; Post, 1965; Stotsky, 1968). Our procedure in discussing most of these will be first to review the drug treatment of these diagnostic entities, and then to discuss other types of therapeutic modalities that may be helpful.

General Principles of Drug Use in the Elderly

Several factors should be kept in mind when using drugs in the elderly, the classic early reference for these principles being the text by Freeman (1963). Adequate diagnostic assessment is crucial for optimal drug usage. Hollister (1969, 1973) points out that much of drug therapy is toward symptomatic relief. However, there are enormous variations in the responsiveness of the elderly to medications. The safest course generally is to start with low doses and build up gradually. As previously mentioned in this chapter, variations in the physio-chemical mechanisms in the elderly cause side-effects to be frequent and severe. Our recommendations are that it is wise to use as few drugs as possible and also to become acquainted with how the elderly respond to these few drugs when they are taking them.

Some general guidelines are in order. First, establish a drug-free baseline by discontinuing other psychotropic medications that are not essential. Second, evaluate the patient's medical status and assure one's self that the drugs the person is taking for the medical problems are necessary. Third, decide if the psychotropic drug is really necessary for the disturbed behavior. In other words, be able to formulate some explicit psychodynamic notions as to why certain behaviors are going on. By making such causal decisions, one can keep such problems as overmedication, undermedication and the "shotgun" approach to a minimum (Kenny, 1979). Fourth, utilize the elderly patient's family members to make sure that the older person is taking the amount of medication prescribed. Fifth, forewarn the older person about possible side-effects of the drug, and caution him or her regarding potential drug–drug interactions (Bressler, 1981). If the latter occur, make yourself available for patients to call you as soon as possible and decide what to do from there. Sixth, regularly review both how the patient is responding to the medications and if any side-effects are occurring. Seventh, as the patient is improving or stabilizing, gradually taper back on the medication and watch the status while tapering back. As all psychotropic drugs (except lithium) are fat-soluble, a storage of the drug will occur, and a lessening daily oral intake may be needed. For further reference and discussion of the general guidelines, please refer to the chapter on psychopharmacology in Verwoerdt (1981).

Depression

There are many different clinical manifestations of depression in the elderly, determining to some extent the type of drugs or approach to take to a particular patient. Some of these variations are pointed out by Lippincott (1968), Post (1966), Verwoerdt (1981) and Zung (1980). The differences between depression in the elderly and depression in younger age groups are that depressions in the elderly might often be "masked," and that the usual psychological affective component is little in evidence. Additionally, there may be very few other psychological complaints or biological concomitants (such as sleep disturbance or energy). Depressions may cause the elderly to become so perplexed or withdrawn that they appear to have an organic brain syndrome. This organic brain syndrome has been referred to as pseudo-dementia. Madden, Luhan, Kaplan and Manfredi (1952) were among the first to describe the pseudo-dementia complex, and later Wells (1979) took up the description of the entity. Wells sees pseudo-dementia as a "caricature" of dementia with some of the important features being: 1) a more recent onset that can be dated; 2) rapid progression of symptoms after onset; 3) the patients' recognizing and emphasizing their disability; 4) affective change often pervasive; 5) the patients' giving "don't know" answers to mental status questions quite frequently.

Symptoms of depression increase in quantity and severity after age 40 (Lipton, 1976; Brink, 1977). Problems resulting from such depression are: pessimism, withdrawal from interpersonal relationships and decreased self-esteem. Physical debility, chronic illness, death of loved ones and movement toward retirement are factors that may precipitate or potentiate depression. Indeed the extent of the depression is not limited to mild-to-moderate psychiatric problems only, for suicide rates continue to increase for both males and females into their sixties and seventies. Grauer (1977) and Goldstein (1979) emphasize that depression in the aged is different from depression in younger age groups. Grauer feels that it is important for the depression to be understood utilizing a multidisciplinary approach. This includes the biological, psychodynamic, genetic and socio-cultural concepts. Gaitz (1977) has theorized that the depressive "complaints" in the aged may not be depression so much as they might be symptoms of the normal aging process. In a community survey he made of 1500 residents of Houston, the elderly were found to report more frequent symptoms and complaints characteristic of depression compared with the norm of the younger age groups. However, they reported fewer positive and negative experiences. Gaitz suggests caution in diagnosing depression in the aged. Another survey (Schwab, 1978) in a Southeastern county documents, as Gaitz does, a high frequency of depressive symptomatology, but also documents biological problems such as sleep and appetite problems in a cohort of aged with low socioeconomic status. Schwab emphasizes that the elderly living in adverse social conditions are at high risk for depression. Another author sums up the problems quite well (Jarvik, 1976) in stating that the subject of aging and depression poses many unanswered questions. She points out that the lack of precise definitions and inadequate nosology among the aged complicate the issues. In addition, she states that little is known regarding the differentiation of depressive illness from what she calls the "melancholic" response to the stress of the aging process. She feels that the answers to these questions may come from the interplay of the psychological abilities of the individual, his social environment and his various life stresses.

Psychopharmacology: Antidepressant Drugs

MAO Inhibitors. These drugs inhibit the breakdown of catecholamines and indoleamines, resulting in increased amounts of the neurotransmitters dopamine, serotonin and norepinephrine at the central receptor sites in the brain. There are a number of drugs with MAO inhibitor activity available in England, but few of them are available for psychiatric use in the United States. Those available are of one of two chemical groups: the hydrazides, with phenelzine (Nardil) as an example, and the nonhydrazides, with the example of tranylcypromine sulfate

(Parnate) (Quitkin, Rifkin and Klein, 1979; Goldfarb, 1967). MAO inhibitors should be used infrequently in the elderly (Epstein, 1978). In essence, they should be used when there has been a past history of responding well to MAO inhibitors or a poor response to other antidepressants (Hollister, 1979). These drugs run the risk of hypertensive crisis, which on occasion may be fatal, hallucinations and hyperreflexia. These side-effects are caused by the ingestion of foods that contain tyramine or of various medications containing presser amines such as cold remedies.

Tricyclic Anti-depressants. The tricyclic's mode of action seems to be to increase the amounts of biogenic amines at central receptor sites. The general effects of these drugs are adrenergic or anticholinergic, and they have side-effects within various other systems including the cardiovascular, gastrointestinal, hematogenic, endocrine and central nervous systems. These drugs have been classified especially according to their anticholinergic properties, with amitriptyline (Elavil) considered one of the most anticholinergic of the drugs and desipramine (Norpramin, Pertofran) considered the least anticholinergic. Snyder and Yamamura (1977) are noteworthy for their work in classifying the various anticholinergic levels of tricyclics; they say that desipramine might be the drug indicated for depressions in the elderly because of its low level of action in potentiating such side-effects as prostatic hypertrophy, glaucoma and cardiovascular problems. Other newer tricyclics and the tetracyclic antidepressants have also been found to have lower anticholinergic properties (Ayd, 1979, 1980). These drugs might be useful for depression in the elderly; clinical testing will be needed to document both the drug efficacy and the severity of the side-effects in these patients. Robinson and Nies (1977) found that patients over 65 years old had tricyclic levels that were twice those of younger patients. The half-lives of the tricyclics tested were also much longer for those over 65.

Considering the dosage of the tricyclics, they are similar in their potency of action except for nortriptyline (Aventyl, Pamelor) and protriptyline (Vivactil), which are both more potent. The dosage level for outpatient maintenance is often one-half to two-thirds of that administered in the hospital setting. It must be remembered that dosage levels for the elderly are generally lower than for the classic 160-pound adult. For the elderly, one should start with an initial smaller dose and increase the tricyclic at a slower rate, watching carefully for drug side-effects (Fann, 1976). The starting dose should be about 30 mg per day, increasing in small amounts at about three-day intervals as needed. Using this approach, the ceiling for an elderly individual will eventually be established. At times, it takes up to three weeks to find this ceiling. The total dosage for the elderly individual is frequently about one-third that of the younger person.

Physical side-effects are usually related to the anticholinergic action. These include: dry mouth, urinary retention, constipation, orthostatic hypotension, glaucoma, lowered threshold for toxic confusion and cardiovascular problems (Janowsky, El-Yowsef and Davis, 1974). One should be especially aware of anticholinergic side-effects, some of which can be especially serious. At times, extrapyramidal symptoms can occur while utilizing a tricyclic antidepressant. It would not be advisable to add an anti-Parkinson drug because of the increased potential for confusion. Rather, it would be preferable to lower the level of the tricyclic or change the tricyclic drug to another.

Agitated Depression

Agitated depression is somewhat common in the elderly and is a depression in which restlessness and anxiety are prominent. Roth (1964) noted that amitriptyline (Elavil) had a greater tranquilizing effect and was less likely to aggravate tension. Prange (1973) finds that amitriptyline (Elavil) and doxepin (Sinequan) are both more sedating. Thus, one might initially try amitriptyline or doxepin in a patient who has a depression of a biological type with agitation. It will be crucial, though, for the therapist to titrate the drugs very gradually as a result of their potent anticholinergic activity, which can affect the elderly especially severely. Again, it might be wise to start on a 10–30-mg daily dose and increment it every three days until the patient starts to experience sedation or is experiencing other stressful side-effects (Feigenbaum, 1973). Butler and Lewis (1973) state that most patients who are going to respond, do so in the first two weeks. Consequently, it would be advisable to keep the patient on this medication for a three-week period before trying another medication. We attempt one medication for agitated depression. If that medication is not effective, then because of the stress that is often felt both by the patient and the family, we proceed to ECT unless there are strong contraindications or the patient refuses. If the antidepressant is working well, it is continued for at least three months beyond the point of good clinical improvement to reduce the likelihood of a relapse. Occasionally, an elderly person may have a frequently recurring depression that may best be treated by staying on the antidepressant for a long period.

If the tricyclic antidepressant was ineffective, it probably would be advisable to try a low-dose anti-psychotic or an anti-anxiety drug as the regimen. Thioridazine (Mellaril) has been recognized as affording treatment in some agitated and/or hostile depressions (Fann, 1976). One should start at low doses and go to high doses gradually when using this drug. Anti-anxiety drugs may be beneficial in that they reduce some of the anxiety and agitation that is associated with the depression. Schatzberg and Cole (1978) noted that some patients with depression improved on benzodiazepines, but they felt the reduction of the depressive symptoms was related to the lessening of the anxiety, rather than the drug having an antidepressant effect. Again, with the elderly, whatever drug or combination of drugs one is using, one must keep an eye on the side-effects of the drugs.

We would encourage the use of a tricyclic antidepressant for an agitated depression first. One can then monitor the individual's response to the tricyclic

and establish a base line about other drugs. From there, the clinician should discuss with the patient and his family members how the individual is handling the
depression on the tricyclic. If the symptoms are getting worse and one is still
within the 10–14-day response period, one may want to try an anti-anxiety drug,
if there are no psychotic ideations, or Mellaril, or another anti-psychotic, if there
are psychotic thought processes. We would not recommend combining Elavil
and Mellaril because of their high anticholinergic properties. We have tended to
use one tricyclic with an agitated depression and, if unsuccessful, to proceed with
ECT. Others have gone on to try a second tricyclic if the first was unsuccessful.
When delusions or hallucinations are part of the clinical picture of the depression,
the addition of a major tranquilizer, in small doses, to the antidepressant may be
of help. Major indications for ECT would be: 1) an unsuccessful attempt with
tricyclics; 2) the side-effects due to the tricyclic and/or other drug combination
being dangerous to the welfare to the elderly person; 3) the elderly person being
suicidal.

There are other types of depression found in the elderly. For example, there
is the chronic depressive disorder which certainly continues into later life. In
addition, the elderly have grief reactions that may require treatment. Third,
there are depressive equivalents such as pain and irritability that occur with aging
in both male and female individuals (Salzman and Shader, 1978). Last, there are
mild depressions of recent onset. All these entities might require some drug
therapy, but often they require psychotherapy or a therapy involving the whole
family. For further reference and treatment on how to proceed with these diagnostic types, we recommend Verwoerdt (1981) and Busse and Blazer (1980) for
further reading.

Another rather common syndrome seen with the aged is a mixture of depression and paranoid ideation (Post, 1966b; Whanger, 1973). This entity seems to
be basically an affective disorder. The symptoms may respond either to an anti-
psychotic or to an antidepressant agent alone, but we agree with Stotsky (1973)
that the simultaneous administration of two agents usually gives better results.
We tend to avoid an anti-psychotic antidepressant mixture, but if such is needed,
we prefer the greater flexibility of deciding on our own what combination might
be optimal, based on whether a low or high anticholinergic anti-psychotic might
be most appropriate at the time. In treating the mixed depressive-paranoid syndromes, the authors frequently use a tricyclic antidepressant in the appropriate
amount plus a low-dose combination of trifluoperazine (Stelazine) or haloperidol
(Haldol) daily. A variety of such drugs in clinical combinations were used by
Fracchia, Sheppard and Merlis (1973).

Manic-Depressive Disorders

When the patient's activity is self-destructive, manic grandiosity and hyperactivity
require treatment. ECT may be considered when psychotropic drugs fail to

produce clinical improvement, especially considering the demands placed on the older person's physiology when manic, and the potential rapid response to ECT. Most of the discussion in this section will not center on ECT but rather will emphasize the utilization of lithium.

Classical manic-depressive disorders continue into late life, but as Stotsky (1973) emphasizes, these disorders become more of the depressed type with retardation, fears and sometimes delusion. Usually what looks like a manic reaction occurring for the first time in late life may be an indicator of an organic brain syndrome.

Lithium is effective in the treatment and prevention of bipolar affective disorders. However, it seems to be most effective in bipolar affective problems with mania and less beneficial in unipolar affective disorders with depression (Coppen, Noguera *et al.,* 1971). Lithium seems to reduce the amount of norepinephrine at the receptor sites in the brain. It also has an effect on sodium and potassium metabolism. As a result of the complications of the drug, lithium therapy for the elderly generally should begin in a hospital. Lithium is limited by its increased toxicity in the elderly (Van der Veld, 1971) because of: 1) frequent electrolyte imbalance, 2) decreased renal function and 3) marked sensitivity to side-effects. The toxic reactions include nausea, tremor, ataxia, confusion, muscular weakness and twitching. One should be especially cautious about lowered sodium levels and dehydration occurring in the elderly which highly increase the potential for lithium toxicity. These authors prefer to start lithium in older patients in the hospital, and agree with Butler and Lewis (1973) that the dose should be low. Our procedure is to start at a 300-mg daily dose and increase it at 300-mg increments every third day. Often, a marked reduction in the manic excitement occurs by the third or fourth day, although the serum lithium levels still may be no higher than 0.7 mEq/L. We have found it advisable to hold the serum lithium level (the morning fasting specimen) no higher than 1.0 to 1.4 mEq/L. Once stabilized, the lithium level should be checked monthly on an outpatient basis, and maintained as low as possible if the individual is remaining emotionally stable.

In establishing a dosage schedule for elderly patients who would use lithium, several differences between the elderly and younger patients should be kept in mind. First, the half-life of lithium is 24 hours in young patients, but in elderly it is prolonged to 36–48 hours. Second, since elderly patients excrete lithium more slowly, they can build up the desired blood levels with lower doses. Thus, the average daily dose for a younger patient might be 1500 mg, but for an elderly patient, it might be 600–900 mg (Davis, Fann, El-Yowsef and Janowsky, 1973). Third, the average lithium dose for a younger person is approximately 1.0 mEq/L, whereas for an older person, the range is between 0.7 and 0.9 mEq/L. Fourth, because of the elderly's sensitivity to drug reactions and their lowered ability to metabolize and excrete drugs, it is wise to check lithium levels more frequently than one might in a younger patient.

It may be especially helpful to use anti-psychotics in two different instances when treating the elderly with manic episodes. The first instance occurs when the person is experiencing manic excitement, and there is little or no lithium yet in his serum. It may here be helpful to add an anti-psychotic to deal with the psychotic processes. Another time when anti-psychotics may be helpful is when lithium cannot be used because of some type of metabolic problem. We have found chlorpromazine (Thorazine) or haloperidol (Haldol) especially helpful in these situations. If the anti-psychotic drugs are not able to effectively treat the mania, then ECT may be used.

Psychoses

In the elderly a variety of functional psychoses are somewhat common. They either occur as a result of a carryover from early life, such as in schizophrenia, or else they may arise for the first time in the later years, as with paranoia. In addition, different psychotic symptoms may accompany a mild or moderate organic disorder. With the entrance of the group of drugs called the major tranquilizers into the therapist's regimen, the outlook for treating the elderly with such disorders vastly improved.

Major Tranquilizers

One group of anti-psychotics are the phenothiazine drugs, which are divided into three classes according to the various side chains on their molecules. Each class has different dosages and clinical effects in the elderly, as described by Hollister (1973) and Stotsky (1968). The aliphatic type of phenothiazines is represented by chlorpromazine (Thorazine), noted for its sedative and hypotensive properties and low incidence of extrapyramidal effects. In older patients, chlorpromazine is used primarily with schizophrenics or where sedation seems important. It is not used in situations in which there might be cardiovascular problems, because of its potential for hypotension. If the patient is highly agitated, the therapist might want to give an intramuscular dose, watching for hypotensive responses, especially on the first dosage.

The piperidine group is represented by thioridazine (Mellaril), which has several features that are of benefit to the elderly. First, it is less sedative; second, it seems to have some antidepressant properties; and third, the incidence of extrapyramidal disorders is fairly low. Tsuang and his group (Tsuang, Lu, Stotsky, and Cole, 1971) found few side-effects from the drug's use, but we have found that the drug can produce a frequent incidence of hypotension, especially in the debilitated and institutionalized elderly. Thioridazine also has anticholinergic side-effects, and Branchey et al. (1978) found EKG changes and decreased blood pressure in elderly schizophrenic patients treated with the drug. Thioridazine can also cause more frequent inhibition of ejaculation than other drugs with alpha-adrenergic blocking properties (Baldesaarini, 1977).

Because of the potential for problematic side-effects, we start with Mellaril at a very low dose, 10 mg daily or 10 mg b.i.d., and increase it slowly at the same three-day intervals mentioned previously in the chapter. It is important to check the supine and standing blood pressures regularly as the dosage is increased. We do not usually go over 75 mg per day, giving the larger or total dose at night. Some have used up to 300 mg daily, however.

The third and final class of the phenothiazines is the piperazine group, represented by trifluoperazine (Stelazine), perphenazine (Trilafon) and fluphenazine (Prolixin). These drugs are potent at low dosage, and rarely cause any problems with hypotension. The problem with these drugs is that their use is limited in the elderly because of the high incidence of extrapyramidal symptoms, to which the elderly can be especially sensitive. Brain-damaged females are particularly sensitive (Fann, 1973). One piperazine reported to be beneficial in the elderly and having few extrapyramidal side effects is acetophenazine maleate (Tindal) (Dimascio and Goldberg, 1976).

A second group of major tranquilizers are the thioxanthenes. One of these, thiothixene (Navane), can be of benefit in withdrawn and apathetic schizophrenics, as well as in other psychotic states. Chlorprothixene (Taractan) is somewhat similar in its structure to chlorpromazine, but seems to have less hypotensive and sedative effects than the latter. We consider it primarily as an alternative drug in geriatric therapy.

The butyrophenones are the last group of the anti-psychotic agents, of which haloperidol (Haldol) is the main representative available in America. Tsuang *et al.* (1971) felt that haloperidol was quite similar to thioridazine in both efficacy and side effects. We find this drug beneficial because of its potent antipsychotic and calming properties, and convenient dosage forms, including injection and liquid forms. Also, there is little effect on the cardiovascular system. We especially use it in acute agitated psychotic states where an intramuscular dose might be needed, and in the presence of medical and surgical problems where a highly anticholinergic drug could cause cardiovascular, confusional or other physical problems. The main problem with haloperidol is the initial high incidence of extrapyramidal complications if it is used on a regular basis. A second, more serious problem with haloperidol, especially in older patients using this or other anti-psychotic drugs, is that of tardive dyskinesia, a syndrome that includes mouth and tongue movements along with grimacing and choreo-athetoid movements of the distal extremities (Dimascio and Goldberg, 1976). Its occurrence is greatest among older patients, especially women. In one study, Greenblatt, Dominick, Stotsky and DiMascio (1968) found a tardive dyskinesia incidence of more than 60% in geriatric patients treated with phenothiazines in nursing homes. This entity is very difficult to treat. The principal treatment is a preventive one, using a small dose (or no dose) of an anti-psychotic. When the syndrome is diagnosed, it may take several months to years to gradually taper the patient off the drug in combination with a gradual decrease in the motor movements. Jeste and Wyatt (1981) documented that the prevalence of tardive dyskinesia among psychiatric inpatients has been rising, reaching 25% in the past five years. They rate the prevalence of persistent tardive dyskinesia at about 13%. They discourage the routine and long-term administration of anti-psychotics to elderly nonschizophrenic patients, and suggest prescribing it only with caution.

Schizophrenia

Schizophrenia is a disease entity that can continue in a person's later life. Several studies have found that schizophrenia, when it continues into the older age groups, tends to maintain a rather long-term stable condition with certain personality abnormalities, but an increased level of social adaptation (Sukhovskiy, 1976; Dvorin, 1977). Bridge (1977) hypothesized that changes in the levels of certain neuro-transmitters during one's life may account for the gradual remission of some of the symptoms among older schizophrenics.

Kay (1972) believes that the prodromal signs of schizophrenia in the elderly usually occur with a period of seclusion that may continue for months to years before the family or concerned others contact a clinician. Along with this, a mild-to-moderate suspiciousness or irritability might occur. Because of the slowness of the development, the clinician might miss the problem. Another complicating factor in diagnosing schizophrenia in the elderly is that they may not have a well-defined symptomatology. Post (1973) believes that older patients with schizophrenia may show few of the Schneiderian first-rank symptoms. Thus, schizophrenia in the elderly may reveal some improvement in the signs of schizophrenia. In addition, it may be harder to pick up the "acute" stage because of the more quiet seclusion and/or withdrawal that may occur, as well as the lack of Schneiderian symptoms that the elderly schizophrenic may demonstrate.

Therapy of elderly schizophrenic patients varies little from that of younger adults with the same disease. The authors recommend starting with one of the less sedative or less hypotensive drugs such as haloperidol (Haldol) or thiothixene (Navane) (Branchey et al., 1978). If extrapyramidal signs develop using haloperidol, one can reduce the dose or make a change to thioridazine (Mellaril) or chlorpromazine (Thorazine). The goal is to avoid extrapyramidal symptoms, since the latter would require an additional drug (an anti-Parkinson agent). As we have stated before, our desire is to keep the elderly on as few drugs as possible (Janowsky et al., 1974). Most of the anti-psychotic drugs are equally effective, but individual patients respond differently to each anti-psychotic drug. Along with Hollister (1972), we recommend mastering the use of one of each of the three types of phenothiazines, one of the two thioxanthenes and a butyrophenone.

Concerning dosage, the same recommendation given previously holds again for treating elderly schizophrenics with drugs: One needs less drug for the elderly as compared to younger adult patients. This is based on lower metabolism, excretion rates and so on. Low dosage is particularly important for the elderly in order to reduce the risk of long-term toxicity or tardive dyskinesia (Hollister, 1979; Jeste, 1981). In addition, by keeping the level of particularly the less potent anti-psychotics such as thioridazine or chlorpromazine at a minimum, other side-effects such as postural hypotension (which may cause strokes, heart attacks and fractures from falls) may be prevented. Fann and Lake (1972) recommend limiting the frequency of tardive dyskinesia through the use of drug-free intervals, reducing anti-psychotic dosages and withdrawing drugs when they are no longer needed.

Anti-psychotics, in liquid preparations, may be especially useful for the elderly who cannot or will not swallow the tablet form. Several of the anti-psychotics are also available for intramuscular administration. The clinician must remember that the intramuscular form is often several times more potent than the oral form and may increase the potential for side-effects; in particular, one must watch for hypotensive reactions. One drug, fluphenazine (Prolixin) is available in a long-acting intramuscular form that may occasionally be helpful.

Paranoid Syndromes

Paranoid symptoms, delusions and states are quite common in the elderly (Davidson, 1964; Post, 1966b; Whanger, 1973). These symptoms can be especially distressing, since they often involve the family and neighbors of the elderly patient. An increased incidence is found in those who have difficulty hearing (Houston and Royse, 1954; Cooper, Kay, Curry, Garside and Roth, 1974). Cooper et al. imply that the paranoid thinking in these cases is mostly due to social hearing loss, with the individual aware of the unsatisfactory communication but projecting the problem onto the other person. Busse and Pfeiffer (1973) state that the best treatment for paranoid problems include reducing the threatening environment (often by hospitalization), appropriate psychotherapeutic intervention and anti-psychotic drugs.

Eisdorfer (1980) emphasizes the need of therapeutically intervening so that the elderly individual again feels a sense of mastery or control of the environment. First, he points out that a restoration of what is lost or a prevention of further loss is important with suspicious paranoid patients. Second, he encourages programs of exercise or alternative hobbies. Third, he emphasizes the need to observe the patient, especially when he moves to a new home. At this time paranoid beliefs may occur. Fourth, Eisdorfer states that mildly suspicious patients may need little (or few) psychotropic treatment(s). Anti-anxiety agents may be all that is necessary for the moderate to even, at times, severely paranoid patient. Naturally, the anti-psychotic agent will be appropriate for the psychotically paranoid individual, but frequently that person will also need hospitalization. It is important to remember when one is treating paranoid individuals that one not make the problem worse through sedating the elderly person even more — whatever drug might be used. Additionally, when a paranoid individual is admitted to a hospital setting, the clinician must be aware of the loss of control that hospitalization brings. Consequently, one should allow easy access to the patient's family, permitting walks on the grounds if at all possible, allowing objects from home in the patient's room, and so on, to increase the sense of mastery or control. In conclusion, whenever medications are utilized for paranoid symptoms or problems, the medications should be used on a temporary basis of weeks to months, and gradually decreased with observation until there is no longer a need for the medications. Both hospitalization and drugs should be used so as not to increase the already existing paranoia.

Anxiety

Anxiety in the elderly has been found by some to be associated with a denial of one's physical problems (McCrae et al., 1976). Others (Sathananthan, Gershon and Ferris, 1976) have documented that anxiety in the elderly is due to the worsening of premorbid personality characteristics that occur with aging. Verwoerdt (1980) discusses various types of anxiety experienced by the elderly. His list includes: 1) acute traumatic anxiety, 2) chronic neurotic anxiety, 3) helplessness anxiety, 4) anxiety-depression, 5) phobic disorders and 6) anxiety associated with psychosis.

Anti-Anxiety Agents

The anti-anxiety drugs include the benzodiazepines, propanediols and diphenylmethanes. Other drugs that have been used in the past for anxiety include barbiturates, alcohol and anti-psychotic drugs. Anti-anxiety drugs, if effective, will decrease both psychological anxiety and muscle tension, but do not alter psychotic symptomatology (Gershon, 1973; Piland, 1979; Prien and Cole, 1978).

The benzodiazepines include many drugs such as diazepam (Valium), chlordiazepoxide (Librium), oxazepam (Serax) and lorazepam (Ativan). Chlordiazepoxide, diazepam and the oxazepam are very similar in their muscle-relaxant, sedative and anti-convulsant aspects. There is a difference, however, in the dosage level needed and the duration of action. Oxazepam has a shorter half-life and requires larger doses than the others (Hollister, 1972). The half-life of diazepam is increased some three times in the elderly, making its use potentially hazardous. Chlordiazepoxide is effective with anxiety in the elderly, and doses need to be (approximately 5 mg b.i.d.) lower than for younger adults. It is moderately sedative and also produces a reaction that causes many patients to specifically ask for it and become habituated to it. Diazepam causes less sedation and does have skeletal muscle-relaxant properties, but because of the prolonged half-life in the elderly, using it even over several weeks may lead to problems. Thus, we recommend using oxazepam or lorazepam as benzodiazepines, because of their lowered half-life as compared to the other benzodiazepines mentioned.

Propanediol derivatives include such drugs as meprobamate (Miltown, Equanil) and tybamate (Tybatran). In studies of predictors of drug responses in geriatric patients, Lehmann (Lehmann and Ban, 1968; Lehmann, 1972) found that meprobamate caused drowsiness and reduced levels of spontaneous activity. There are a few elderly to whom it may give sufficient relief for the anxiety. The use of these drugs should be discouraged in the elderly because of the ease of overuse and the potential of somewhat serious withdrawal problems if addiction occurs (Kapnick, 1978).

The diphenylmethane derivatives include diphenhydramine (Benadryl) and hydroxyzine (Atarax, Vistaril). We recommend using these drugs when the elderly person has not responded well to the benzodiazepines. It should also be pointed out that both of these drugs may be sedatives, and the clinician should take this into account. In using these drugs, a general procedure that we follow is to start the elderly on a dose of about one-third of the usual adult dose and then to increase it slowly as needed. It is advisable to use these drugs for a several-month maximum and not to continue a patient on them indefinitely.

Other drugs that might be tried if there is anxiety that did not respond to either the benzodiazepines or the diphenylmethane derivatives, are barbiturates, ethyl alcohol and the anti-psychotic drugs. Barbiturates are infrequently used in the elderly because of their: 1) interaction with various enzyme systems, 2) potential for physical addiction and 3) depression of cortical function. One notable study (Stotsky and Borozne, 1972) revealed that low doses of butabarbital (Butisol) can be effective in the elderly. Ethyl alcohol is probably the oldest of anti-anxiety drugs in the elderly. Indeed, if the person is not reluctant to take alcohol for moral or religious reasons, it might be advisable to first recommend trying two or three ounces of wine or a glass of beer late in the afternoon. Several studies have revealed that such an "intervention" has improved the elderly persons' communication, sleep, anxiety and self-esteem (Chien, 1971; Kastenbaum and Slater, 1964). One must remember, however, that the elderly do have a decreased tolerance for alcohol. Also, if the elderly person is on other drugs, the alcohol may potentiate or alter the various side-effects of the other psychoactive drugs. Concerning anti-psychotic drugs, thioridazine (Mellaril) in doses of 10 mg b.i.d., or trifluoperazine (Stelazine) in doses of approximately 2 mg (q-day or b.i.d.), may be effective for anxiety, especially when there is psychotic ideation, or when neither the alcohol nor the benzodiazepines nor the diphenylmethane derivatives have been effective. One must be especially cautious because of the potency of the anti-psychotics and their potential for causing hypertension or tardive dyskinesia, both mentioned earlier.

Sleep Problems

One problem among the elderly with psychiatric disorders is sleep disturbance. The sleeplessness may often quickly exhaust the elderly person along with his family and support systems. The aged, in comparison to younger adults, often take longer to go to sleep. In addition, there are frequent awakenings, and the stage of deep sleep almost disappears (Kahn and Fisher, 1969). Also, old people tend to spend less time sleeping than younger adults (Goldfarb, 1967). Although sleep disturbances may not be considered unusual, it is still important for the clinician to assess both the older person's psychological and physical conditions before prescribing hypnotics. Indeed, the central cause of fitful sleep may be problems of: a physical nature, such as congestive heart failure, pain; metabolic abnormalities; psychological problems, such as depression or anxiety; or drug problems, such as habituation to drugs or too much coffee in the evening. To proceed with a hypnotic drug may worsen either the physical problems or the drug problems causing the anxiety. For further reference on sleep problems and the elderly, see Spiegel (1981).

Hypnotics

As to the frequency of hypnotics, one study revealed that 7–10% of people over the age of 60 living in the community were using hypnotics regularly (Busse, Barnes, Silverman, Thaler and Frost, 1955). An unpublished survey at Duke revealed that 25% of those mildly to moderately psychiatrically impaired and living in the community were taking sleeping pills at the time of the survey. Several reminders are in order before discussing the drugs themselves. First, it is true that restoration to a normal aging sleep pattern will greatly facilitate care of the patient. But, one should remember that a number of the hypnotics can cause habituation in two to three weeks.

The ideal drug for sleep would be one that would increase the onset of sleep without changing the phases of sleep. In addition, it would ensure a full night's sleep without creating a daytime hangover. There should be no risks of habituation, tolerance or suicide if the drug is taken as an overdose. The currently available hypnotics meet some of the above criteria individually, but none of them completely. Thus in treating the elderly and again recalling their difficulty with metabolizing and excreting drugs, the clinician should prescribe hypnotics for the treatment of simple insomnia, not the insomnia associated with depression, anxiety or physical problems.

Considering the available hypnotics, the best present hypnotic for the elderly is chloral hydrate (Noctec). This drug does not suppress REM sleep patterns, leaves little hangover or ataxia and has a low risk of habituation. It is given in 0.5- or 1.0-gram doses at bedtime. Its main drawback is occasional gastrointestinal irritation. The next most useful hypnotic is flurazepam (Dalmane). Again, this drug has little effect on REM sleep patterns and has a low risk of habituation. This drug does have a long half-life in the elderly, and accumulation can lead to hangover or central nervous system depressant activity (Piland, 1979). If the drug is used, it should be tried on 15-mg doses (as opposed to most adults who start on 30 mg), and taken not more than two or three times per week for sleep. Most hypnotics, such as secobarbital (Seconal), pentobarbital (Nembutol), methyprylon (Noludar), ethchlorvynol (Placidyl), methaqualone (Quaalude) and glutethimide (Doriden), are habit-forming in the aged, and potentially toxic. Thus, these drugs should be avoided in the elderly (Pattison and Allen, 1972). Mention should also be made of bromides that are available as over-the-counter hypnotics. Elderly patients may use them because they don't have to make "a doctor's appointment," but an increasing abuse of bromides may result in a subacute or acute organic brain syndrome. When such abuse is suspected, serum bromide levels should be tested. Treatment involves stopping the bromides and adding a chloride salt so that the chloride displaces the bromide, and the bromide is excreted.

In closing this portion of the chapter, we will discuss insomnia in combination with: 1) pain, 2) anxiety and 3) depression. When the elderly person is experiencing pain, especially due to arthritis, it may be especially beneficial to prescribe first an analgesic such as acetaminophen (Tylenol) or enteric coated aspirin at bedtime. The sleep pattern may improve from the treatment of the pain, and a hypnotic may be unnecessary. If there is anxiety along with the insomnia, it may be helpful not to try a pure hypnotic drug, but instead to try either a benzodiazepine such as oxazepam or an antihistamine such as diphenhydramine at night. Finally, if there is a biological depression, it may be indicated to give the patient medications for sleep during the first ten to fourteen days of treatment with the antidepressant. The hypnotic should be gradually reduced and then stopped, and the antidepressant should be utilized to assist with sleep by giving all or most of it in the bedtime dosage.

Anti-Parkinson Agents

The elderly are especially prone to develop Parkinsonism either as a primary disease or secondarily to psychotropic drugs, and, in particular, to the antipsychotic drugs. The more potent anti-psychotics are the most effective blockers of dopamine, and these are the ones that the clinician needs to follow most when treating the elderly. Holloway (1974) feels that patients between 40 and 50 are more prone to developing akathisias (motor restlessness syndromes), while those above 50 have a greater tendency toward Parkinson-like syndromes. He also estimates that some 50% of patients on anti-psychotics between the ages of 60 and 80 develop extrapyramidal symptoms; he highlights the importance of watching the patient during the first two months of therapy, for 90% of the symptoms occur during that time period.

Davis *et al.* (1973) recommend not using anticholinergic drugs prophylactically in the elderly, for the anticholinergic side effects of constipation, dry mouth and urinary retention are troublesome. Additionally, acute brain syndrome of an atropinic type or cardiovascular effects resulting from the use of the anticholinergic drug may occur. We recommend reducing the dosage of the anti-psychotic drug if extrapyramidal signs appear. If such is not possible, then diphenhydramine (Benadryl) is often a drug of first choice in the elderly (*AMA Drug Evaluations,* 1971). Initial doses should be some 25 mg at bedtime, and later up to 50 or even 75 mg if necessary. If the diphenhydramine is not working satisfactorily, then it may be wise to add one other drug. This drug would be trihexyphenidyl (Artane), starting with 1 mg in the morning, increasing it at 1-mg daily increments at three-day intervals. It should be recognized that the anticholinergic side-effects of the trihexyphenidyl may cause insomnia at night. Other agents that can be used as anticholinergic drugs in the elderly are noted here, with their starting dose for people in the elderly range: biperiden (Akineton) (at 1.0 mg b.i.d.) or benztropine mesylate (Cogentin) (at 1.0 mg daily). Again, as a reminder, there are several reasons why anti-Parkinson medications should be given only when extrapyramidal symptoms occur: 1) There is a possibility that anti-Parkinson drugs decrease the effectiveness of anti-psychotic drugs by increasing dopaminergic activities; 2) anti-Parkinson drugs may decrease the absorption of anti-psychotics; 3) anti-Parkinson drugs may exacerbate tardive dyskinesia; 4) the anti-Parkinson drugs may produce an acute brain syndrome and other anti-cholinergic side-effects that may make it more difficult for the elderly person to achieve and accomplish daily activities (Walker and Brodie, 1980). Orlov, Kasparian, Dimascio and Cole (1971) recommend that the anti-Parkinson drug be utilized for a one-month period and then gradually reduced to see if the symptoms recur.

In summary, anti-Parkinson drugs can be beneficial when there is a need. When they are not indicated, they should not be used in the elderly because of potentially harmful side-effects. When they are being used, they should be used as a result of existing extrapyramidal side-effects, and they should be used in low dose and tapered off as soon as possible.

Hormone Therapy in the Aged

Several different types of endocrine treatments can be considered in managing the elderly. These treatments include: 1) the gonadal steroids, 2) thyroid medications, 3) diabetic medications and 4) corticosteroid hormones.

Although we are unsure what role the gonadal steroids, or the sex hormones, play in the aging process, we are aware of the changes in physical appearance and function, and some of the effects on emotions, that may go along with a decrease in sex hormones. There is controversy about hormone use, but Greenblatt, Nexhat, Roesel and Natrajan (1979) feel that androgens are helpful for the climacteric male, and that androgen replacement therapy often lessens fatigue, depression and headaches, and may improve sexual drive. On the other hand, in the aging female, Greenblatt *et al.* feel that estrogens may improve headaches, post-menopausal depression and nervousness. There has been concern about estrogens increasing the incidence of endometrial carcinoma in post-menopausal women, but Greenblatt and his group feel that this should not be a concern, especially if regular cyclic courses of oral progestogen are added to the regimen. The frequency of older women experiencing depression, irritability or deficits in their general well-being have been noted to be up to 50% of patients (Kaufman, 1967; Tramont, 1966). It should be remembered, however, that estrogens cause depression in some women. The methods of administration for the estrogens are varied, but the common ones used are conjugated estrogens (Premarin) in 1.25-mg amounts daily for three weeks out of four, cyclically.

The use of oral or topical estrogens may be of help to women in maintaining functional genital capacity by preserving the tone of the vaginal structures.

Returning to testosterone or androgen, this hormone may be useful in improving appetite and weight for the male patient who seems to be experiencing a climacteric depression. Lehmann (1972) found that a significant number of elderly patients with a variety of psychiatric problems were helped by combining the androgen (Halotestin), 10 mg orally and daily for 12 weeks, with either nicotinic acid or thioridizine (Mellaril). The combination of the androgen with another drug gave better results than any single drug or the three together. For impotence in the older male, one might use medication (Jacobovits, 1970) or utilize some of the sex interventions as applied by Kaplan (1974).

Hypothyroidism is a diagnosis that should not be forgotten in old age. On occasion, it may resemble senile dementia, and if untreated, it can lead to dire consequences for the aged individual. Lloyd (1967) found that hypothyroidism occurred in almost 2% of all admissions to a geriatric unit. Hypothyroidism often shows up in the elderly as psychiatric problems; Whybrow, Prange and Treadway (1969) noted depression and anxiety as well as cognitive disturbances in the elderly with hypothyroidism. It is thus wise to routinely check the T3 and T4 levels in the elderly with recent organic brain changes, depression or marked anxiety. Thyroid preparations in the elderly should not be used without just cause (normal laboratory tests), for the elderly are quite sensitive to thyroid preparations, and can especially develop cardiac arrhythmias. Hyperthyroidism should also be mentioned briefly. This entity can at times cause a thyrotoxic psychosis, but in the younger age groups more usually manifests itself with anxiety and agitation. In the elderly though, this entity may first appear with apathy and depression. This condition has been named "apathetic hyperthyroidism" (Libow, 1973).

In diabetes, the problems that will appear in the elderly may be secondary to poor control or to diabetic drugs being used. A problem is the non-ketotic hyperosmolarity syndrome (hyperglycemia and confusion without ketosis). This syndrome and low insulin levels may be induced by drugs such as diphenylhydantoin (Dilantin). On the other hand, hypoglycemia may occur during treatment with either insulin or the sulfonylureas (Tolbutamide, Chlorpropamide). Factors that can increase a potential for such are: decreased caloric intake, decreased hepatic or renal function and physical or mental illness (Libow, 1973).

Electric Convulsive Therapy

The indications for general management of electric shock are similar in the aged to those in younger adults. Prout, Allen and Hamilton (1956) reviewed the early reluctance to use ECT in the aged. This reluctance has since been overcome. As Kalinowsky and Hippius (1969) demonstrate, depression in the elderly responds well to ECT. They have treated patients with ECT into their eighth and ninth decades of life. Goldstein (1979), some ten years later, still concurred with those findings and recorded a very low degree of mortality or problems secondary to ECT in the elderly. On some occasions when there was an uncertainty as to whether the person had a pseudo-dementia or a true organic or chronic organic brain process, we have used two or three ECTs as a diagnostic test. The pseudo-dementia (depression) responds with improvement, whereas the person with organic brain syndrome will often deteriorate with ECT. One important indication for ECT in the elderly occurs when the elderly person is suicidal. Kopell (1977) points out that the incidence of suicide among those over 65 is nearly twice the national average. He emphasizes that when the elderly person is suicidal, it may be very inadvisable to proceed with a two- to four-week trial on tricyclics, and, instead, one should start ECT as soon as possible. Elderly patients who respond extremely well to ECT are those with an endogenous depression with psychological and physical changes that are concomitant with the onset of the depression (Kral, 1976).

The older person should have a thorough physical exam and work-up prior to ECT. One should especially make sure that there are no space-occupying lesions in the brain or other problems that might cause increased intracranial pressure with ECT. In addition, one should rule out signs of recent coronary thrombosis or decompensated heart failure (Kral, 1976). With adequate muscle relaxation and oxygenation, the risk to the elderly is only mildly increased over a younger adult individual. On occasion, we have not used a barbiturate anesthetic in a geropsychiatry patient, feeling that it would increase the apnea rate somewhat. It is true that the person may then have some awareness for the procedure, but we feel it is safer, especially if there are less than optimal facilities for resuscitation, or the person is at risk due to respiratory problems. The elderly depressed individual may show marked improvement within two or three ECTs. We do not recommend a routine number of treatments, such as others suggest (Feigenbaum, 1973), but rather use the formula of ECT to good improvement plus two more for consolidation of gains. On the average, this comes out to five to seven ECTs. Some patients might relapse quickly and need two or three more.

Other useful suggestions would include those of Lowenbach (1973), who states that the convulsive threshold of the aged brain is higher, and thus an initial application of 150 volts is used to assure a full seizure. Additionally, he encourages the use of 60 mg of succinylcholine (Anectine) when osteoporosis is present. Finally, cyanosis should be avoided by allowing no longer than 45 seconds of apnea to persist without respirating the patient. To avoid or decrease post-ECT confusion, two recommendations might be utilized. The first is that the treatments could be spaced some three or four days (instead of the usual two) apart. Second, unilateral ECT given to the nondominant hemisphere may also reduce acute memory losses and confusion (Squire, 1977; Weiner, 1979). Thus, since the older individual might have more difficult problems with memory losses already, it might be wise to consider both unilateral ECT and the spacing of treatments further apart.

MODES OF PSYCHOTHERAPY

Individual Psychotherapy

The development of interest in, and techniques for individual psychotherapy for older persons has been somewhat slow. Part of this has been due to the influence of Freud, who felt that psychoanalysis would not be successful in treating the elderly because 1) much time would be required, with 2) the end of the cure being reached at a period of life in which "much importance is no longer attached to nervous health" (Freud, 1959a, p. 245), and 3) "older people are no longer educable" (Freud, 1959b, p. 258). A survey of thirty psychoanalytically oriented psychiatrists in private practice in 1968 showed that this view continued to hold, as none of them were treating any patients over 60 (Weintraub and Aronson, 1968). As previously cited in this chapter, one study found that the elderly make up 2-3% of all the patients seen in various types of outpatient clinics, and yet they make up over 10% of the population. Meerlo (1961) and other analysts (Gitelson, 1948; Berezin, 1972) have demonstrated that there are indeed psychodynamic aspects that are resolvable within the time period in which the aged continue to experience life.

Jung seemed more willing to deal with older persons than Freud, and realized the importance of reassessment of values and introspection in his studies, *The life cycle* (Jung, 1933, pp. 95-114). Erikson felt that old age had its own particular task, and that the task among the aged was the development and maintenance of a sense of "ego integrity" (Erikson, 1959). The existential problems have been studied by some, among them Turnier (1972) and Yalom (1980). Common phenomena among the elderly are remembering and reviewing their lives. Lewis and Butler (1974) present the use of reminiscence in therapies with older people. They point out that the emotions that accompany these experiences vary. In essence, one brings up past memories in order to review one's life (and put one's life in order). These authors emphasize that it is important for the therapist to start with where the patient is "and proceed with sensitivity and respect." Rechtschaffen (1959) wrote an early review article summarizing some of the modifications needed in therapy with the elderly. These modifications basically included: 1) the therapist should be more active; 2) environmental manipulation is needed, possibly with the therapist's assistance; 3) educational techniques may be utilized; 4) resistance and transference are handled gently; 5) the therapy is tapered but rarely terminated. Lazarus and Weinberg (1980) made more recent recommendations concerning the therapist's stance in the therapy with the elderly. First, they emphasized therapeutic flexibility in working with the elderly. They pointed out that sometimes the therapist needs to work individually with the elderly, and other times, the therapist may need to be called in to function as a family therapist, social planner or pharmacotherapist. Second, they emphasized that the psychotherapist needs to demonstrate genuine acceptance and regard. At times the therapist may need to demonstrate this by way of nonverbal communication, such as gesture and touch. Blazer (1978) emphasizes that the therapist should be able to communicate verbally and nonverbally with his or her elderly patients. He describes techniques that may improve such communications. Third, Lazarus and Weinberg encourage the therapist to recognize his or her role as "one member of a multidisciplinary team of health professionals." Often with younger patients, therapists can work by themselves, but with the elderly, the psychiatrist may need to interact efficiently with the family and religious networks, the primary physician, a community nurse, etc.

An excellent summary on direction for individual psychotherapy in the elderly (Blank, 1974) makes several suggestions. First, a major problem that seems to bring the elderly into therapy is that of depression, due to a sense of loneliness, helplessness or inadequacy. The therapy should be directed toward decreasing the sense of depression within the elderly. Many psychotherapies for younger adults encourage increasing one's independence. For the elderly, such a procedure might make their depression worse. Rather, in Blank's terms, the therapist needs to set up a satisfactory dependence between the elderly and their family or support system, one that both units seem to be satisfied with. Second, the therapist may need to be more active, in order to ask and find out what problems really brought the individual into therapy. The intent is to determine what the elderly person's need is, and not necessarily what the long-term historical conflict is. The therapy then should proceed so that the older person's needs are dealt with whether they are of an emotional, social or financial basis. Last, a supportive style should be utilized in the therapy. Again, as mentioned previously, the elderly seem to be very sensitive to warmth and caring coming from the therapist. Wolff (1970) found the self-esteem of many elderly to be low, and ego-supportive individual therapy seemed to be very beneficial.

Group Therapies

In the last thirty years, there has been a gradual increase in the use of various group therapies with psychogeriatric patients. The first reported use was by Silver (1950), working with senile psychotics. Linden (1953) soon followed with far more sophisticated programs. Goldfarb (1971), in a review of group therapy with the aged, differentiated at least two different types of group therapy settings. He classified the inpatient setting as one in which the goal of the group therapy is to increase the discharge rate and decrease the recidivism rate and management problems. For outpatient group therapy for the aged, the primary goals are to decrease depression, increase social interaction and improve interpersonal relationships. Oberleder (1970) illustrated a successful inpatient group in which the goal of therapy was to reduce panic. Not only was the panic reduced, but within a reasonably short period of time most of the patients participating in the group were discharged. Wolff (1970) observed that within three months, results from group therapy with institutionalized elderly included better ward adjustment and orientation, increased communication and activity, more favorable group identification and reduced anxiety and feelings of isolation. Two other studies (Liederman and Liederman, 1967; Schwartz and Papas, 1968) demonstrated the use of groups with elderly patients who had multiple physical complaints or problems, and were simultaneously having many difficulties coping with their lives. Both studies found that within the group the elderly patients were able to reduce their anxiety as they found a therapeutically supportive environment there. Identification with others who seem to have a similar problem seemed important to both group settings to decrease the depression and alienation that the patients were experiencing. This therapeutic aspect of group process has been recognized by Yalom (1975).

As in individual psychotherapy, the type of group therapy involved should be geared to the problems, needs and goals of the particular patients participating. Some generalizations about groups for the elderly are that: 1) they should be sexually mixed; 2) they should have some homogeneity regarding the mental capacities, needs and problems of the patients; and 3) the therapist should be warm, positive and fairly active.

The following are some types of group therapy that we and others have found helpful with elderly patients:

1. For organically impaired and confused patients — *reality orientation.* This is a technique developed by Folsom (1968) in which the instructor has a group of about six with whom he meets daily for some thirty minutes. The instructor will repeatedly go over current information and personal information with each individual. Such information would include the place, the date, the weather, the menu and events. More complex information, such as time telling, reading and object manipulation are added as the person improves. Correct responses are immediately rewarded verbally and nonverbally by recognition, praise and warmth.

2. For very regressed and apathetic patients — *remotivation groups.* This program was developed by the American Psychiatric Association (1965) to provide a structured framework for reaching these types of patients. The therapist will utilize nonthreatening material — such as history,

poetry or nature study in small groups. The goal is to reach healthy and intact areas of the patients' memory in hopes of interesting and involving them in the present real world.

3. For older hospital patients with lowered self-esteem — *grooming and homemaker groups*. These groups are usually mainly for women, and for women whose skills in these areas have often deteriorated.

4. *Inspiration and religious groups.* It is difficult to set a limit as to who might benefit from these groups, for it is often left to the voluntary interest of the elderly patient to participate in them. These groups can provide additional support, opportunity for participation and enhancement of life values. When elderly persons can participate enthusiastically (not necessarily based on the enthusiasm of the rest of the group), a sense of inspiration and increase in hope might occur for some.

5. For elderly within an institutional setting — *patient government.* In this, the elderly are involved in discussions and decisions regarding their own care. Such an involvement can give positive value in increasing the self-esteem and responsibility within an institutional setting, and can make institutions far more humane.

6. For elderly patients in a hospital setting — *pre-discharge groups.* In particular, this is helpful for elderly who have been hospitalized and are almost ready to return to the community setting. Many of them came into the hospital because of social problems and a sense of alienation, and the pre-discharge group gives an opportunity to talk over what it will be like for them as they are discharged and what they need to prepare for in order not to return to the hospital. The pre-discharge group also is a transition to start making an adjustment to a more normal existence, as indicated by Nevruz and Hrushka (1969).

7. *Discussion and socialization groups.* These groups are primarily created to talk over matters of interest, and to create a bond of friendship. Hopefully, groups of this nature will provide a sense of support with those taking part, and might extend to greater friendships outside of the group setting. These groups can be utilized both in and outside of institutions. Butler and Lewis (1973) describe some age-integrated "life crisis" groups that deal with the ups and downs of the life cycle, again providing support to the elderly. For further discussion of working with the elderly in institutional settings, see Weiner, Brok and Snadowsky (1978).

Behavior Modifications with the Elderly

Behavior modification techniques presume that behaviors are learned response patterns. Thus, maladaptive behaviors that are learned response patterns can be altered by manipulating stimulus variables or reinforcements. Lindsley (1964) has suggested the development of behavioral "prosthetic environments" for geriatric patients. He has recommended applying operant conditioning techniques to give the maximal support to the appropriate behavior of aged persons, and compensate for behavioral deficits in a sense comparable to the use of physical prostheses. Ankus and Quarrington (1972) report that behavior of the elderly is modifiable by reinforcement appropriate to the individual, such as money. Another study (Birjandi and Sclafani, 1973) described the use of positive reinforcement techniques in small groups of aged patients to increase more adaptive behavior.

Clinical experience with behavior modification techniques in geropsychiatry is limited, but still growing. It seems to have a potential, for even in cases of moderate-to-severe organic brain syndrome, the patient's behavior can be modified as long as the reinforcement is especially suited to the individual patient (Mueller and Atlas, 1972; Ankus and Quarrington, 1972). Thus far though, it has been found that older people are harder to condition, and extinguish what they have learned more quickly than younger adults (Botwinick, 1973). For a more thorough review of behavior modification in the elderly, one can refer to the works by Botwinick (1973) and Cautella and Mansfield (1977).

Involving the Family in Therapy

Verwoerdt (1981) lists some of the major problems that can occur with the elderly and the effects that they have within the family environment. Problems that he includes are: 1) reversal of roles between the elderly person and one (or several) of their children; 2) the loss of a spouse; 3) the loss of the home. Certainly, the problems related to aging itself can be stressful to the older person and the family, and depression, which has been previously stated to be a frequent problem in the elderly, can also be a problem that echoes within the whole family. An interesting study has been one undertaken by Reiffler and Eisdorfer (1980), who found a very low dropout and broken-appointment rate for Alzheimer's patients when the families were involved. They also found that a very high percentage of the family members: 1) would call if they needed further help; 2) would recommend the clinic to others; 3) were generally satisfied with the overall evaluation and treatment. These are very interesting findings, for the diagnostic entity involved (Alzheimer's disease) is one in which the clinician might expect a frequent dropout, broken-appointment rate, and breakdown of the family. With these therapists, though, involving the family, just the reverse occurred. Lazarus and Weinberg (1980) list several difficulties that the older person's children have with the aging parent, including problems accepting physical and mental deterioration in the parent, and difficulties coping with documentable psychological or physical problems experienced by the aged. The authors quote a study (Sanford, 1975) that demonstrated that 12% of all hospital admissions for the elderly were a result of relatives no longer being able to cope with the elderly at home. Over 90% identified problems that had to be dealt with before they could allow the elderly individual to return home.

It isn't easy for a family when they have coped well together through the years to be faced with problems of normal deterioration in an older relative and find themselves unable to continue to cope as a family. One of our group has previously written that many elderly families experience what he calls a "family adjustment reaction" (Larson, Larson and Blazer, 1981), and that study recommends that the therapist intervene in such a way as to restore the equilibrium experienced in the family earlier in its life. A case illustration is presented in which only several sessions were needed to bring the family back to its dynamic equilibrium. It is suggested that one first intervene educationally in the family in order to answer questions that they might have about aging or particular problems that the aging relative is experiencing. If that tact is unsuccessful, then organizational or reorganizational intervention should be attempted. Examples of the latter might be several family members taking care of their elderly relative instead of the previous one who has become very frustrated. Another organization (or environmental manipulation) might be to support the elderly person's getting out more to community activities instead of just visiting and/or being with the family throughout the day. The third level would involve conflict resolution. If a family has been coping well through the years, there might be a limited need for a conflict-resolving type of approach. Blazer (1978a) has written a short article on working with the elderly patient's family, in which he supports an open and communicative style that encourages the therapist to deal with the specific problem the family has with their aging relative and to offer the family education, training and recognition of their own feelings when needed. A recent book on the subject by Herr and Weakland (1979) emphasizes that realistic goals for helping the elderly are "revising the situation, instead of reforming the person." They point out that the situation is often an acute one that creates anxiety for all family members involved, and they make some very practical recommendations about what to pursue and what to avoid in dealing with families of the elderly.

Family or marital therapy has been written about as a complex therapeutic style, the use of which requires much experience, supervision and training. We would differ somewhat with such a supposition in working with the elderly, and recommend that many clinicians can help a family at least educationally, and probably organizationally, by manipulating the aging individual's environment. We would see that many elderly families are stressed with the normal deterioration of aging, or problems that have occurred because of aging. In helping the family, the therapist needs to help them accept the fact that these problems are indeed present, and help them to make a shift to cope better with the skills that they already have and have developed through years of living together.

Recreation Therapy

Recreation for the aged psychiatric patient should consist of more than television and bingo. It should provide for the restoration or preservation of creative functions of the person in addition to having fun. Physical activities such as walking, bowling, dancing and rhythmical exercises are important, as are sedentary activities such as games, reading and parties. Merrill (1967) and Davis (1967) give suggestions for such programs.

Music Therapy

Music is an enjoyable therapeutic activity for many older patients, providing socialization, renewal of happy memories and some exercises in coordination (if a rhythm section is added). Even among very demented patients, hymns and religious songs can be quite meaningful. Boxberger and Cotter (1968) reported that music therapy in psychogeriatric patients results in a decrease in the level of undesirable patient noise, a reduction in aggressiveness or inappropriate behavior, and less reaction to hallucinations.

Occupational Therapy

The various rehabilitation therapies may be handled in different ways in institutions caring for the mentally impaired. The occupational therapist is able to provide assessment of functional physical activities, and provide appropriate instructive activities to enhance capabilities in self-esteem, as Fish (1971) and Finkelstein, Rosenberg and Grauer (1971) detail.

Milieu Therapy

Following the development of the idea of the therapeutic community (Jones, 1953), the concept spread that the social milieu can be utilized as a treatment modality (Abroms, 1969; Gunderson, 1978). One of the first to apply this type of treatment to the elderly psychiatric patient was Gottesman (1967), who observed that the traditional mental hospital tended to make people worse by letting their ego skills deteriorate, in that no demands were made on them, and no new skills were taught. This theory was that treatment should offer a structured series of meaningful demands, and that the patient should be helped to learn to function in the various roles of normal society that he or she would meet outside of the hospital. Others, such as Eisdorfer (1970), Goldstein (1971) and Grauer (1971), have applied the techniques of milieu therapy often with good results, but with some difficulties. Bok (1971) analyzed some of the main problems of milieu treatment of the older mental patient, noting that some of them are: a lack of potential for patient change; difficulty with the staff; problems in the mental hospital itself in shortages of personnel, funds and flexibility; and, finally, deficiencies in the community that make staying in the hospital more desirable than getting out. Along the lines of Gunderson (1978), several milieu issues that might be of benefit to the elderly would include: 1) support — helping the elderly recognize their competence; 2) structure — helping the elderly to be more organized or ordered; 3) involvement — helping the elderly to recognize their abilities to be responsible; and 4) validation — helping the elderly recognize their strengths and their weaknesses.

Hospitalizations

Many elderly will require hospitalization for their psychiatric problems. Appropriate placement and care will greatly enhance the therapeutic effects. In this section, partial hospitalization and "optimal" hospitalization will be discussed.

Partial hospitalization has provided a helpful transition from the state hospital to the community for many mental patients. For elderly patients, this usually means treatment at the center during the day and returning home at night. This serves to support a person in the community by giving part-time relief to the family, and continuing care for the patient, as described by Bosin (1965). There are still, unfortunately, few such geropsychiatric centers, but Berger and Berger (1971) have described the establishment of such a private partial hospitalization unit.

Turning from partial hospitalization, we will now discuss two factors that might create a "more optimal" setting for geropsychiatry patients, namely: 1) length of time in the hospital and 2) multidisciplinary treatment within the hospital. Concerning length of time in the hospital, Whanger (1980) discusses how placing an older person in the hospital increases the risk of regression, and the breakdown of social relationships. Goldstein (1979) emphasizes the crucial importance of not letting the elderly patient, especially the depressed elderly patient, regress. He states that the clinician must "constantly reinforce" what the elderly can still do. He feels it is important to deal with the feelings of helplessness and hopelessness that the elderly experience. In one study (Neiditch and White, 1976), elderly patients who were admitted to a hospital and were discharged within six weeks of their admission seemed to show the most improvement in their clinical and cognitive conditions. On the other hand, those elderly who stayed in the hospital longer than two months seemed to stabilize at best at a level of functioning similar to the one they had on the day of admission, or else they gradually deteriorated during the hospitalization. Levenson and Felkins (1979) surveyed the literature and also state that a four- to six-week hospital admission seems to be the optimal one for geriatric patients. In addition, these authors highlight the importance of a multidisciplinary unit for geriatric patients. They document that during their first year of operation, they had a readmission rate of 4%. This was considerably lower than the 38% rate that they referred to as a more standard one. In their article, they emphasize: 1) restoring physiological homeostasis; 2) allowing treatment to result in remission of the psychological condition; 3) evaluating and treating the patient both physically and psychologically; 4) utilizing multidisciplinary team processes in affecting treatment; and 5) considering individual variability in the aged individual in deciding on treatment procedures. Others who support a multidisciplinary approach to the assessment and treatment of the elderly are Robinson (1975), Whanger and Busse (1975) and Poliquin and Straker (1977).

In summary, two factors that seem important in the optimal use of hospitalization for the elderly are: 1) utilizing a multidisciplinary team approach that assesses and treats both the physical and psychological aspects of the aging individual; and 2) proceeding actively in the hospital setting so that the aged individual does not regress, does not lose contact with his or her social involvements and yet achieves at least some remission of the clinical problems.

CONCLUSION

Until the last quarter of a century, the elderly, as a group, received comparatively poor care, in part because those of us within the therapeutic community had biases and fears about any potential success for treatment of those within this age group. Over the last twenty-five years, many changes have occurred, and they still are occurring in creating the most satisfactory contexts to treat the elderly individual. In many ways, the psychiatric treatment of the elderly individual differs from the treatment of younger adults. For example, one needs not only to assess psychiatric problems but also potential physical problems. In addition, there is a change in the physiological condition of the elderly so that one must be very careful in utilizing drugs, and following the person's physio-chemical responses to them. Throughout this chapter, we have documented how the elderly need less drugs than the younger individual. On the other hand, the elderly need far more social involvement in maintaining their already established social milieu. The diagnostic entities that are more prevalent among this group are also different from those in the younger age groups, and it is crucial to keep that in mind when treating and assessing the elderly.

We have come a long way in the last twenty-five years, but there are still areas where we need to grow. First, we must develop a more reliable (and hopefully valid) set of diagnoses that will fit those elderly persons with mental illness. Second, we need to learn more about how to use the elderly's social networks more successfully — whether family, church, neighbors or friends. Third, we must continue to improve our knowledge of when and when not to use drugs among the elderly. Indeed, it may be important to develop criteria for when not to use drugs in this age group. Our clinical learning emphasizes indications for use among the younger age groups. Among the elderly, it may be important to begin to emphasize the many contraindications of overutilizing drugs.

We close with a quotation from the Old Testament (Proverbs 16:31): "A hoary head is a crown of glory; it is gained in a righteous life." As clinicians, we must do what we can to assist our aged patients in maintaining the best possible cognitive skills and life satisfaction. To do so, we must minimize the overuse of drugs, maximize the use of social supports and optimize our therapeutic efforts by individualizing the treatment through active involvement of the elderly person.

REFERENCES

Abroms, G.M. Defining milieu therapy. *Archives of General Psychiatry*. **21**: 553–560 (1969).

AMA Drug Evaluations, American Medical Association Council on Drugs, pp. 247–265. Chicago: American Medical Association, 1971.

Ankus, M. and Quarrington, B. Operant behavior in the memory-disordered. *Journal of Gerontology*. **27**: 500–510 (1972).

Arie, J. Morale and the planning of psychogeriatric services. *British Medical Journal*. **3**: 166–170 (1971).

Arnhoff, F. and Kumbar, A. *The nation's psychiatrists – 1970 survey*. Washington, D.C.: American Psychiatric Association, 1970.

Ayd, F.J. Trazedone: A unique broad spectrum antidepressant. *International Drug Therapy Newsletter*. **14**: 33–40 (1979).

Ayd, F.J. Amoxapine: A new tricyclic anti-depressant. *International Drug Therapy Newsletter*. **15**: 33–40 (1980).

Baldesaarini, R. *Chemotherapy in psychiatry*. Cambridge, Mass.: Harvard University Press, 1977.

Beattie, B.L. and Sellers, E.M. Psychoactive drug use in the elderly. *Psychosomatics*. **20**: 474–479 (1979).

Bender, A.D. Drug therapy in the aged. Clinical aspects of aging. In: Chinn, A.B. (Ed.), *Working with older people,* pp. 308–318. Washington, D.C.: U.S. Department of Health, Education and Welfare, Public Health Service Publication No. 1459, 1971.

Berenzin, M.A. Psycho dynamic considerations of aging and the aged. *American Journal of Psychiatry*. **128**: 33–41 (1972).

Berger, M.D. and Berger, L., Jr. An innovative program for a private psychogeriatric day center. *Journal of American Geriatrics Society*. **19**: 332–336 (1971).

Birjandi, P.F. and Sclafani, M.J. An interdisciplinary team approach to geriatric patient care. *Hospital and community psychiatry*. **24** (11): 777–778 (1973).

Blank, M.L. Raising the age barrier to psychotherapy. *Geriatrics*. **29**: 141–148 (1974).

Blazer, D.G. Techniques for communicating with your elderly patient. *Geriatrics*. **33**: 79–84 (1978).

Blazer, D.G. Working with the elderly patient's family. *Geriatrics*. **33**: 117–123 (1978a).

Bok, M. Some problems in milieu treatment of the chronic older mental patient. *Gerontologist*. **11**: 141–147 (1971).

Botwinick, J. *Aging and behavior.* New York: Springer Publishing Co., 1973.

Boxberger, R. and Cotter, V.W. Music therapy for geriatric patients. In: Gaston, E.T. (Ed.), *Music in therapy,* pp. 269–290. New York: Macmillan, 1968.

Branchey, M.H. *et al.* High and low potency neuroleptics in elderly psychiatric patients. *Journal of the American Medical Association.* **239**: 1860–1862 (1978).

Bressler, R. Drug interactions in the elderly. *Drug therapy.* **11**: 119–130 (1981).

Bressler, R. and Palmer, J. Drug interactions in the aged. In: Fann, W.E. and Maddox, G.L. (Eds.), *Drug issues in geropsychiatry,* pp. 49–59. Baltimore: Williams & Wilkins Co., 1972.

Bridge, T.P. The dopamine hypothesis: Schizophrenia and aging. *Gerontologist* **17**: 43 (1977).

Brink, T.L. Depression in the aged: Dynamics and treatment. *Journal of the National Medical Association* **69**: 891–893 (1977).

Broe, G.A. Neurological disorders in the elderly at home. *Journal of Neurology, Neurosurgery and Psychiatry* **39**: 362–366 (1976).

Brotman, H.B. Who are the aging? In: Busse, E.W. and Pfeiffer, E. (Eds.), *Mental illness in late life,* pp. 21–39. Washington, D.C.: American Psychiatric Association, 1973.

Busse, E.W. The modern challenge of threescore and ten. *Journal of American Geriatrics Society.* **17**: 887–893 (1969).

Busse, E.W. The geriatric patient and the nursing home. *North Carolina Medical Journal.* **33**: 218–222 (1972).

Busse, E.W., Barnes, R.H., Silverman, A.J., Thaler, M. and Frost, L.L. Studies of the processes of aging, and the strengths and weaknesses of psychic functioning in the aged. *American Journal of Psychiatry.* **111** (12): 896–901 (1955).

Busse, E.W. and Blazer, D.G. *Handbook of geriatric psychiatry.* New York: Van Nostrand Reinhold Co., 1980.

Busse, E.W., Dovenmuehle, R.H. and Brown, R.G. Psychoneurotic reactions of the aged. *Geriatrics.* **15**: 97–105 (1960).

Busse, E.W. and Pfeiffer, E. (Eds.). *Mental illness in later life.* Washington, D.C.: American Psychiatric Association, 1973.

Butler, R.N. and Lewis, M.I. *Aging and Mental Health: Positive Psychosocial Approaches,* 1st ed. St. Louis: C.V. Mosby Co., 1973.

Butler, R.N. and Lewis, M.I. *Aging and Mental Health,* 2nd ed. St. Louis: C.V. Mosby Co., 1977.

Cautella, J.R. and Mansfield, L.A. Behavioral approach to geriatrics. In: Gentry, W.D. (Ed.), *Geropsychology: A model of training and clinical service,* pp. 21–42. Cambridge, Mass.: Ballinger Press, 1977.

Chien, C.P. Psychiatric treatment for geriatric patients: Pub or drug? *American Journal of Psychiatry.* **127**: 1070–1074 (1971).

Comfort, A. On gerontophobia. *Medical Opinion Review,* pp. 30–37 (September 1967).

Cooper, A.F., Kay, D.W.K., Curry, A.R., Garside, R.F. and Roth, M. Hearing loss in paranoid and affective psychoses of the elderly. *The Lancet* (October 12, 1974).

Coppen, A., Noguera, R. *et al.* Prophylactic lithium in affective disorders. *The Lancet.* **2**: 275 (1971).

Cosin, L. The role of the geriatric day hospital. Paper of British Council for Rehabilitation of the Disabled. International seminar, 1965.

Coursin, D.B. The national nutrition survey in the United States. *International Journal Vitamin Research.* **40**: 541–544 (1970).

Davidson, R. Paranoid symptoms in organic disease. *Gerontologia Clinica.* **6**: 93–100 (1964).

Davis, J.M., Fann, W.E., El-Yowsef, M.K. and Janowsky, D.S. Clinical problems in treating the aged with psychotropic drugs. In: Eisdorfer, C. and Fann, W.E. (Eds.), *Psychopharmacology and aging,* pp. 111–125. New York: Plenum Press, 1973.

Davis, R.W. Activity therapy in a geriatric setting. *Journal of American Geriatrics Society.* **15**: (5): 1144–1152 (1967).

Department of Health and Social Security. *Psychogeriatric assessment units.* Circular HM (70) 11. London: H.M.S.O., 1970.

DiMascio, A. and Goldberg, H. Pharmacotherapy in geriatrics. In: *Emotional disorders: An outline to diagnosis and pharmacological treatment.* 1976.

Dvorim, D.V. Progressive paranoid schizophrenia in the elderly. *Zhurnal Nevropatologii i Psikhiatrii imeni S.S. Korsakova* 77: 881–886 (1977).

Eisdorfer, C. Paranoia and schizophrenic disorders in later life. In: Busse, E.W. and Blazer, D.G. (Eds.), *Handbook of Geriatric Psychiatry,* pp. 329–337. New York: Van Nostrand Reinhold Co., 1980.

Eisdorfer, C. and Stotsky, B.A. Intervention, treatment and rehabilitation of psychiatric disorders. In: Birren, J.E. and Schaie, K.W. (Eds.), *The handbooks of the psychology of aging,* pp. 724–748. New York: Van Nostrand Reinhold Co., 1977.

Epstein, L.J. Anxiolitics, anti-depressants and neuroleptics in the treatment of geriatric patients. In: Lipton, M.A., DiMascio, A. and Killiam, K.F. (Eds.), *Psychopharmacology: A generation of progress.* New York: Raven Press, 1978.

Erikson, E.H. Identity and the life cycle. *Psychological Issues.* **1**: 101–164 (1959).

Fann, W.E. Interactions of psychotropic drugs in the elderly. *Postgraduate Medicine.* **53**: (3): 182–186 (1973).

Fann, W.E. Pharmacotherapy in older depressed patients. *Journal of Gerontology.* **31**: 304–310 (1976).

Fann, W.E., Davis, J.M., Wilson, I.C. and Lake, C.R. Attempts at pharmacologic management of tardive dyskinesia. In: Eisdorfer, C. and Fann, W.E. (Eds.), *Psychopharmacology and aging,* pp. 89–96. New York: Plenum Press, 1973.

Fann, W.E. and Lake, C.R. Drug induced movement disorders in the elderly: An appraisal of the treatment. In: Fann, W.E. and Maddox, G.L. (Eds.), *Drug issues in geropsychiatry,* pp. 41–48. Baltimore: Williams & Wilkins Co., 1972.

Fann, W.E., Wheless, J.C. and Richman, B.W. Treating the aged with psychotropic drugs. *Gerontologist.* **16**: 322–328 (1976).

Feigenbaum, E.M. Ambulatory treatment of the elderly. In: Busse, E.W. and Pfeiffer, E. (Eds.), *Mental illness in late life,* pp. 153–166. Washington, D.C.: American Psychiatric Association, 1973.

Finkelstein, M., Rosenberg, G. and Grauer, H. Therapeutic value of arts and crafts in a geriatric hospital. *Journal of American Geriatrics Society.* **19** (4): 341–350 (1971).

Fish, H.U. *Activities program for senior citizens.* West Nyack, N.Y.: Parker Publishing Co., 1971.

Folson, J.C. Reality orientation for the elderly mental patient. *Journal of Geriatric Psychiatry.* **1**: 291–307 (1968).

Fracchia, J., Sheppard, C. and Merlis, S. Treatment patterns in psychiatry: Relationships to symptom features and aging. *Journal of American Geriatrics Society.* **21** (3): 234–138 (1973).

Freeman, J.T. *Clinical principles and drugs in the aging.* Springfield, Ill.: Charles C. Thomas, 1963.

Freud, S. Sexuality in the aetiology of the neuroses. In: *Collected papers,* vol. I, pp. 220–248. New York: Basic Books, 1959a.

Freud, S. On psychotherapy. In: *Collected papers,* vol. I., pp. 249–263. New York: Basic Books, 1959b.

Friedel, R.O. Pharmacokinetics in the geropsychiatric patient. In: Lipton, M.A., DiMascio, A. and Killiam, K.F. (Eds.), *Psychopharmacology: A generation of progress,* pp. 1499–1505. New York: Raven Press, 1978.

Gaitz, C.M. Depression in the elderly. In: Fann, W.E. (Ed.), *Phenomenology and the treatment of depression,* pp. 447–449. New York: Spectrum Publishers, 1977.

Gaitz, C.M. and Baer, P.E. Characteristics of elderly patients with alcoholism. *Archives of General Psychiatry.* **24**: 272–278 (1971).

Garretz, F.K. Breaking the dangerous cycle of depression and faulty nutrition. *Geriatrics.* **31**: 73–75 (1976).

Gershon, S. Anti-anxiety agents. In: Eisdorfer, C. and Fann, W.E. (Eds.), *Advances in behavioral biology: Psychopharmacology and aging,* vol. 6, pp. 183–187. New York: Plenum Press, 1973.

Gibson, I.I.J.M. and O'Hare, M.M. Prescription of drugs for old people at home. *Gerontologia Clinica.* **10**: 271–280 (1968).

Gitelson, M. The emotional problems of the elderly. *Geriatrics.* **8**: (1948).

Goldfarb, A.I. Geriatric psychiatry. In: Freeman, A.M. and Kaplan, H.I. (Eds.), *Comprehensive textbook of psychiatry,* pp. 1564–1587. Baltimore: Williams & Wilkins Co., 1967.

Goldfarb, A.I. Group therapy with the old and the aged. In: Kaplan, H.I. and Sadock, B.J. (Eds.). *Comprehensive group psychotherapy,* pp. 623–624. Baltimore: Williams & Wilkins Co., 1971.

Godlman, R. Speculations on vascular changes with age. *Journal of American Geriatrics Society.* **22**: 296–303 (1974).

Goldstein, S. A critical appraisal of milieu therapy in a geriatric day hospital. *Journal of American Geriatrics Society.* **19** (8): 693–699 (1971).

Goldstein, S.E. Depression in the elderly. *Journal of American Geriatrics Society.* **27**: 38–42 (1979).

Gottesman, L.E. The response of long-hospitalized aged psychiatric patients to milieu treatment. *Gerontologist.* 7: 47–48 (1967).

Grauer, H. Institutions for the aged – therapeutic communities? *Journal of American Geriatrics Society.* 19 (8): 687–692 (1971).

Grauer, H. Depression in the aged: Theoretical concepts. *Journal of American Geriatrics Society.* 25: 447–449 (1977).

Greenblatt, D.J., Allen, M.D. and Shader, R.I. Toxicity of high dose flurazepam in the elderly. *Clinical Pharmacology and Therapeutics.* 21: 355–361 (1977).

Greenblatt, D.L., Dominick, J.R., Stotsky, B.A. and DiMascio, A. Phenothiazine induced dyskinesia in nursing home patients. *Journal of American Geriatrics Society.* 16: 27 (1968).

Greenblatt, B., Nexhat, C., Roesel, R.A. and Natrajan, P.K. Update of the male and female climacteric. *Journal of American Geriatrics Society.* 27: 481–490 (1979).

Group for the Advancement of Psychiatry. *Toward a public policy on mental health care of the elderly,* Report No. 79. New York, 1970.

Gunderson, J.G. Defining the therapeutic process in psychiatric milieus. *Psychiatry.* 41: 327–335 (1978).

Hale, W.E., Marks, R.G. and Stewart, R.B. Drug use in a geriatric population. *Journal of American Geriatrics Society.* 27: 374–377 (1979).

Hollister, L.E. Clinical use of psychotherapeutic drugs: Current status. *Clinical Pharmacology and Therapeutics.* 10 (2): 170–198 (1969).

Hollister, L.E. Psychiatric and neurologic disorders. In: Melmon, K.L. and Morrelli, J.F. (Eds.), *Clinical pharmacology.* New York: Macmillan Co., 1972.

Hollister, L.E. *Clinical use of psychotherapeutic drugs.* Springfield, Ill.: Charles C. Thomas, 1973.

Hollister, L.E. Neuropsychiatric side effects of drugs in the elderly. In: Levenson, A.J. (Ed.), *Psychotropic drugs.* New York: Raven Press, 1979.

Holloway, D. Drug problems in the geriatric patient. *Drug Intelligence and Clinical Pharmacy.* 8: 632–642 (1974).

Houston, R. and Royse, A.B. Relationship between deafness and psychotic illness. *Journal of Mental Science.* 100: 990–993 (1954).

Jakobovits, T. The treatment of impotence with methyltestosterone thyroid. *Fertility and Sterility.* 21 (1): 32–35 (1970).

Janowsky, D., El-Yowsef, M.D. and Davis, J.M. Side effects associated with psychotropic drugs. In: Fann, W.E. and Maddox, G.L. (Eds.), *Drug issues in geropsychiatry,* pp. 19–28. Baltimore: Williams & Wilkins Co., 1974.

Jarvik, L. Aging and depression: Some unanswered questions. *Journal of Gerontology.* 31: 324–326 (1976).

Jeste, D.V. and Wyatt, R.J. Changing epidemiology of tardive dyskinesia. *American Journal of Psychiatry.* 138: 297 (1981).

Jones, M. *The therapeutic community.* New York: Basic Books, 1953.

Jung, C.G. *Modern man in search of a soul.* New York: Harcourt, Brace and World, 1933.

Kahn, E. and Fisher, C. The sleep characteristics of the normal aged male. *Journal of Nervous and Mental Disease.* 148: 477–494 (1969).

Kahn, R.L., Goldfarb, A.L., Pollack, M. and Gerber, I.E. The relationship of mental and physical status in institutionalized aged persons. *American Journal of Psychiatry.* **11**: 120–124 (1960).

Kalinowsky, L.B. and Hippius, H. *Pharmacological, convulsive and other somatic treatments in psychiatry.* New York: Grune & Stratton, 1969.

Kaplan, H.D. Erectile dysfunction. In: *The new sex therapy,* pp. 255–288. New York: Brunner/Mazel, 1974.

Kapnick, P.L. Organic treatment of the elderly. In: Storandt, M., Siegler, I.C. and Elians, M.F. (Eds.). *The clinical psychology of aging,* pp. 225–251. New York: Plenum Press, 1978.

Kastenbaum, R. and Slater, P.E. Effects of wine on the interpersonal behavior of geriatric patients: An exploratory study. In: Kastenbaum, R. (Ed.), *New thoughts on old age,* pp. 191–204. New York: Springer Publishing Co., 1964.

Kaufman, S.A. Limited relationship of maturation index to estrogen therapy for menopausal symptoms. *Obsterics and Gynecology.* **30**: 399–407 (1967).

Kay, D.W.K. Schizophrenia and schizophrenialike states in the elderly. *British Journal of Hospital Medicine.* 369–372 (1972).

Kenny, A.D. Designing therapy for the elderly. *Drug Therapy.* **9**: 49–64 (1979).

Kidd, C.B. Criteria for admission of the elderly to geriatric and psychiatric units. *Journal of Mental Science.* **108**: 68–74 (1962a).

Kidd, C.B. Misplacement of the elderly in hospital. *British Medical Journal.* **2**: 1491–1495 (1962b).

Kral, Vojtech. Somatic therapies in older depressed patients. *Journal of Gerontology.* **31**: 311–313 (1976).

Kramer, M., Taube, C. and Starr, S. Patterns of use of psychiatric facilities by the aged: Current status, trends, and implications. In: Simon, A. and Epstein, L. (Eds.), *Aging in modern society.* Washington, D.C.: American Psychiatric Association, 1968.

Kopell, B.S. Treating the suicide patient. *Geriatrics.* **32**: 65–67 (1977).

Lamy, P.P. and Kitler, M.E. Drugs and the geriatric patient. *Journal of American Geriatrics Society.* **19** (1): 23–33 (1971).

Langley, G.E. and Simpson, J.H. Misplacement of the elderly in geriatric and psychiatric hospitals. *Gerontologia Clinica.* **12**: 149–163 (1970).

Larson, D.B., Larson, S.S. and Blazer, D.G. Family therapy with the elderly. In: Siegler, I.C. and Blazer, D.G. (Eds.), *Working with the family of older adults.* Reading, Mass.: Addison-Wesley, 1981.

Lazarus, L.W. and Weinberg, J. Treatment in the ambulatory care setting. In: Busse, E.W. and Blazer, D.G. (Eds.), *Handbook of geriatric psychiatry,* pp. 427–452. New York: Van Nostrand Reinhold Co., 1980.

Learoyd, B.M. Psychotropic drugs and the elderly patient. *Medical Journal of Australia.* **1**: 1131–1133 (1972).

Leevy, C.M., Cardi, L., Frank, O., Gellene, R. and Baker, H. Incidence and significance of hypovitaminemia in a randomly selected municipal hospital population. *American Journal of Clinical Nutrition.* **17**: 259–271 (1965).

Lehmann, H.E. Psychopharmacological aspects of geriatric medicine. In: Gaitz, C.M. (Ed.), *Aging and the brain,* pp. 193–208. New York: Plenum Press, 1972.

Lehmann, H.E. and Ban, T.A. Pharmacological load tests as predictors of pharmacotherapeutic response in geriatric patients. In: Wittenborn, J.R., Solomon, C. and May, P.R.A. (Eds.), *Psychopharmacology and the individual patient*, pp. 32–54. New York: Raven Press, 1968.

Levenson, A.J. and Felkins, B.J. Prevention of psychiatric recidivism: A model service. *Journal of American Geriatrics Society.* **27**: 536–540 (1979).

Lewis, M.I. and Butler, R.N. Life-review therapy: Putting memories to work in individual and group psychotherapy. *Geriatrics.* **29**:   (1974).

Libow, L.S. Pseudo-senility: Acute and reversible organic brain syndromes. *Journal of American Geriatrics Society.* **21**: 112–120 (1973).

Liederman, P.C. and Liederman, V.R. Group therapy: An approach to problems of geriatric outpatients. *Curr. Psychiatr. Ther.* **7**: 179 (1967).

Linden, M.E. Group psychotherapy with institutionalized senile women. II. Study in gerontologic human relations. *International Journal of Group Psychotherapy.* **3**: 150–170 (1953).

Lindsley, O.R. Geriatric behavior prosthetics. In: Kastenbaum, R. (Ed.), *New thoughts on old age,* pp. 41–60. New York: Springer Publishing Co., 1964.

Lippincott, R.C. Depressive illness: Identification and treatment in the elderly. *Geriatrics.* **23** (2): 149–152 (1968).

Lipton, M. Differentiation in depression: Biochemical aspects. *Journal of Gerontology.* **31**: 293–299 (1976).

Lloyd, W.H. Some clinical features of hyper- and hypo-thyroidism in the elderly. *Gerontologia Clinica.* **9**: 337–346 (1967).

Lowenbach, H. How well does electroshock treatment work in depression in the elderly? How safe is it, and how can it be given? In: Busse, E.W. and Pfeiffer, E. (Eds), *Mental illness in late life,* pp. 246–248. Washington, D.C.: American Psychiatric Association, 1973.

Madden, J., Luhan, J., Kaplan, L. and Manfredi, H. Nondementing psychosis in older persons. *Journal of the American Medical Association.* **150**: 1567–1572 (1952).

McCrae, R.R., Bartone, P.T. and Costa, P.T. Age, anxiety and self-reported health *International Journal of Aging and Human Development.* **7**: 49–58 (1976).

Meerlo, J.A.M. Modes of psychotherapy in the aged. *Journal of American Geriatrics Society.* **9**: 225–234 (1961).

Merrill, T. *Activities for the aged and infirm.* Springfield, Ill.: Charles C. Thomas, 1967.

Mueller, D.J. and Atlas, L. Resocialization of regressed elderly patients: A behavioral management approach. *Journal of Gerontology.* **27**: 390–392 (1972).

Neiditch, J.A. and White, L. Prediction of short-term outcome in newly admitted psychogeriatric patients. *Journal of American Geriatrics Society.* **24**: 72–78 (1976).

Neugarten, B. Age groups in American society and the rise of the young-old. *Tha Annals* (September 1974).

Nevruz, N. and Hrushka, M. The influence of unstructured and structured group psychotherapy with geriatric patients on their decision to leave the hospital. *International Journal of Group Psychotherapy.* **19**: 72–78 (1969).

Nies, A., Robinson, D.S. and Friedman, M.J. Relationship between age and tricyclic anti-depressant plasma levels. *American Journal of Psychiatry.* **134**: 790–793 (1977).

Oberleder, M. Crisis therapy in the mental breakdown of aging. *Gerontologist.* **10**: 111 (1970).

Orlov, P., Kasparian, G., DiMascio, A. and Cole, J.O. Withdrawal of anti-Parkinson drugs. *Archives of General Psychiatry.* **25**: 410–412 (1971).

Osfelt, A. Frequency and nature of retired persons. In: Corp, F.M. (Ed.), *Retirement Process.* Washington, D.C.: U.S. Public Health Service, No. 1778, 1968.

Palmore, E. Differences in the retirement patterns of men and women. *Gerontologist.* **5**: 4 (1965).

Pattison, J.H. and Allen, R.P. Comparison of the hypnotic effectiveness of secobarbital, pentobarbital, methyprylon, and ethchlorvynol. *Journal of American Geriatrics Society.* **20** (8): 398–402 (1972).

Piland, B. The aging process and psychoactive drug use in clinical treatment. In: Service Research Monograph Series, No. 79–813, DHEW, *The aging process and psychoactive drug use,* pp. 1–16. Washington, D.C., 1979.

Poe, W.D. and Rice, H.L. Friendship manor: A community geriatrics model. *Journal of American Geriatrics Society.* **24**: 283–284 (1976).

Poliquin, N. and Straker, M. A clinical psychogeriatric hospital organization and function. *Journal of American Geriatrics Society.* **25**: (1977).

Post, F. *The clinical psychiatry of late life.* London: Pergamon Press, 1965.

Post, F. Somatic and psychic factors in the treatment of elderly psychiatric patients. *Journal of Psychosomatic Research.* **10**: 13–19 (1966a).

Post, F. *Persistent persecutory states of the elderly.* Oxford: Pergamon Press, 1966b.

Post, F. Paranoid disorders in the elderly. *Postgraduate Medicine.* **53**: 52 (1973).

Prange, A.J. The use of anti-depressant drugs in the elderly patient. In: Eisdorfer, C. and Fann, W.E. (Eds.), *Advances in behavioral biology,* vol. 6, pp. 225–237. New York: Plenum Press, 1973.

Prentice, R. Patterns of psychoactive drug use – Among the elderly. In: Services Research Monograph Series, No. 79–813, DHEW, *The aging process and psychoactive drug use,* pp. 17–41. Washington, D.C., 1979.

Prien, R.F. and Cole, J.O. The use of psychopharmacological drugs in the aged. In: Clark, W.G. and del Guidice (Eds.), *Principles of psychopharmacology,* 2nd ed., pp. 593–605. New York: Academic Press, 1978.

Prien, R.F., Klett, C.J. and Caffey, E.M. Polypharmacy in the psychiatric treatment of elderly hospitalized patients. *Journal of Diseases of the Nervous System.* **37**: 333–336 (1976).

Prout, C.T., Allen, E.B. and Hamilton, D.M. The use of electric shock therapy in older patients. In: Kaplan, O.J. (Ed.), *Mental disorders in later life,* 2nd ed., pp. 446–459. Stanford: Stanford University Press, 1956.

Quitkin, F., Rifkin, A. and Klein, D.F. Monoamine oxidase inhibitors. *Archives of General Psychiatry.* **36**: 749–760 (1979).

Rafsky, H.S., Brill, A.A., Stern, K.G. and Corey, H. Electophoretic studies on the serum of "normal" aged individuals. *Am. J. Med. Sci.* **224**: 522 (1952).

Redick, R.W., Kramer, M. and Taube, C.A. Epidemiology of mental illness and utilization of psychiatric facilities among older persons. In: Busse, E.W. and Pfeiffer, E. (Eds.), *Mental illness in later life,* pp. 199–231. Washington, D.C.: American Psychiatric Association, 1973.

Reifler, B.V. and Eisdorfer, C. A clinic for the impaired elderly and their families. *American Journal of Psychiatry.* **137**: 1399–1403 (1980).

Riley, M. and Foner, A. *Aging and society.* New York: Russell Sage Foundation, 1968.

Robinson, D.S. and Nies, A. Increased steady-state plasma levels of tricyclic anti-depressants in the elderly. *Clinical Pharmacology and Therapeutics.* **21**: 116 (1977).

Robinson, R.A. The assessment center. In: Howells, J. (Ed.), *Modern perspectives in the psychiatry of old age,* pp. 375–396. New York: Brunner/Mazel, 1975.

Roth, M.J. Prophylaxis and early diagnosis and treatment of mental illness in late life. In: Anderson, W.F. and Isaacs, B. (Eds.), *Current achievements in geriatrics,* pp. 155–170. London: Cassell, 1964.

Salzman, C. and Shader, R.I. Depression in the elderly: II Possible drug etiologies. *Journal of American Geriatrics Society.* **26**: 303–308 (1978).

Salzman, C., Shader, R.I. and Pearlman, M. Psychopharmacology and the elderly. In: Shader, R.I. and DiMascio, A. (Eds.), *Psychotropic drug side effects,* pp. 261–279. Baltimore: Williams & Wilkins Co., 1970.

Sanford, J.R. Tolerance of debility in elderly dependents by supporters at home: Its significance for hospital practice. *British Medical Journal.* **3**: 471–473 (1975).

Sathananthan, G.L., Gershon, S. and Ferris, S.H. Psychological aspects of aging (unpublished manuscript). Rockville, Md.: NIMH, 1976.

Schatzberg, A.F. and Cole, J.O. Benzodiazepines in depressive disorders. *Archives of General Psychiatry.* **35**: 1359–1365 (1978).

Schwab, J.J. Depression among the aged. *Southern Medical Journal.* **69**: 1039–1041 (1976).

Schwartz, W. and Papas, T. Verbal communication in therapy. *Psychosomatics.* **9**: 71 (1968).

Shanas, E. *et al. Old people in three industrial societies.* New York: Atherton Press, 1968.

Silver, A. Group psychotherapy with senile psychiatric patients. *Geriatrics.* **5**: 147–150 (1950).

Simon, A., Epstein, L.J. and Reynolds, L. Alcoholism in the geriatric mentally ill. *Geriatrics.* **23** (2): 125–131 (1968).

Snyder, S.H. and Yamamura, H.I. Antidepressants and the muscarinic acetyleholine receptor. *Archives of General Psychiatry.* **34**: 236–239 (1977).

Spiegel, R. *Sleep and sleeplessness in advanced age.* Jamaica, N.Y.: Spectrum Publications, 1981.

Squire, L.R. E.C.T. and Memory Loss. *American Journal of Psychiatry,* **134**: 997–1001 (1977).

Stotsky, B.A. *The elderly patient.* New York: Grune & Stratton, 1968.

Stotsky, B.A.   Psychoses in the elderly. In: Eisdorfer, C. and Fann, W.E. (Eds.), *Psychopharmacology and aging,* pp. 193–203, New York: Plenum Press, 1973.

Stotsky, B.A. and Borozne, J.   Butisol sodium vs. librium among geriatric patients, younger outpatients and nursing home patients. *Diseases of the Nervous System.* **33**: 254–267 (1972).

Stotsky, B.A., Cole, J.O., Tang, Y.T. and Gahm, I.G. Sodium butabarbital (butisol sodium) as an hypnotic agent for aged psychiatric patients with sleep disorders. *Journal of American Geriatrics Society.* **19** (10): 860–870 (1971).

Sukhovskiy, A.A.   Clinical picture and dynamics of long-term remissions as an outcome of shift-like schizophrenia. *Zhurnal Nevropatologii i Psikhiatrii imeni S.S. Korsakova* **76**: 563–568 (1976).

Todhunter, E.N.   Lifestyle and nutrient intake in the elderly. In: Winick, M. (Ed.), *Nutrition and aging,* New York: John Wiley and Sons, 1976.

Tournier, P.   *Learn to grow old.* New York: Harper & Row, 1972.

Tramont, C.B.   Cyclic hormone therapy. *Geriatrics.* **21** (2): 212–215 (1966).

Tsuang, M.M., Lu, L.M., Stotsky, B.A. and Cole, J.O.   Haloperidol versus thioridazine for hospitalized psychogeriatric patients: Double-blind study. *Journal of American Geriatrics Society.* **19** (7): 593–600 (1971).

U.S. Center for Disease Control. *Ten state nutrition survey,* DHEW Publication No. (HSM) 72-8130. Washington, D.C., 1972.

Van der Velde, C.D.   Toxicity of lithium carbonate in elderly patients. *American Journal of Psychiatry.* **127** (2): 1075–1077 (1971).

Verwoerdt, A.   Anxiety, dissociative and personality disorders in the elderly. In: Busse, E.W. and Blazer, D.G. (Eds.), *Handbook of geriatric psychiatry,* pp. 368–380. New York: Van Nostrand Reinhold Co., 1980.

Verwoerdt, A. *Clinical geropsychiatry,* 2nd ed. Baltimore: Williams & Wilkins Co., 1981.

Walker, J.I. and Brodie, H.K.H.   Neuropharmacology of aging. In: Busse, E.W. and Blazer, D.G. (Eds.), *Handbook of geriatric psychiatry,* pp. 102-124. New York: Van Nostrand Reinhold Co., 1980.

Weiner, M.B., Brok, A.J. and Snadowsky, A.M. *Working with the aged.* Englewood Cliffs, N.J.: Prentice-Hall, 1978.

Weiner, R.D.   The psychiatric use of electrically induced seizures. *American Journal of Psychiatry.* **136**: 1507–1517 (1979).

Weintraub, W. and Aronson, H. A survey of patients in classical psychoanalysis: some vital statistics. *Journal of Nervous and Mental Diseases.* **146**: 98–102 (1968).

Wells, C.E.   Pseudodementia. *American Journal of Psychiatry.* **136**: 895–900 (1979).

Wells, C.E.   Presentation at Southern Medical Association Meeting, San Antonio, Texas, 1980.

Whanger, A.D. Geriatric mental health in North Carolina. *North Carolina Journal of Mental Health.* **5**: 43–49 (1971).

Whanger, A.D. Paranoid syndromes of the senium. In: Eisdorfer, C. and Fann, W.E. (Eds.), *Psychopharmacology and aging,* pp. 203–211. New York: Plenum Publishing Corporation, 1973.

Whanger, A.D. Treatment within the institution. In: Busse, E.W. and Blazer, D.G. (Eds.), *Handbook of geriatric psychiatry*, pp. 453–472. New York: Van Nostrand Reinhold Co., 1980.

Whanger, A.D. and Busse, E.W. Care in the hospital. In: Howells, J. (Ed.), *Modern perspectives in the psychiatry of old age*, pp. 450–485. New York: Brunner/Mazel, 1975.

Whanger, A.D. and Wang, H.S. Vitamin B_{12} deficiency in normal aged and elderly psychiatric patients. In: Palmore, E. (Ed.), *Normal aging, II*. Durham, N.C.: Duke University Press, 1974.

Whybrow, P.C., Prange, A.J., Jr. and Treadway, C.R. Mental changes accompanying thyroid gland dysfunction. *Archives of General Psychiatry*. **20**: 48–63 (1969).

Wigdon, B.T. and Morris, G. A comparison of twenty year histories of individuals with depressive and paranoid states. *Journal of Gerontology*. **32**: 160–163 (1977).

Wolff, K. *The emotional rehabilitation of the geriatric patient*. Springfield, Ill.: Charles C. Thomas, 1970.

Yalom, I.D. *The theory and practice of group psychotherapy*, 2nd ed. New York: Basic Books, 1975.

Yalom, I.D. *Existential psychotherapy*. New York: Basic Books, 1980.

Zung, W.W.K. Affective disorders. In: Busse, E.W. and Blazer, D.G. (Eds.), *Handbook of geriatric psychiatry*, pp. 338–367. New York: Van Nostrand Reinhold Co., 1980.

16 The Treatment of Schizophrenia

Benjamin B. Wolman

THEORETICAL CONSIDERATIONS

The choice of treatment method is largely determined by the therapist's view of the nature of the disease or disorder. As long as physicians believed that hysteria was caused by a uterus (hysteros) wandering inside a female body, surgery was the chosen therapeutic method. In 1882, Dr. Pean surgically removed an ovary in order to cure hysteria. According to Charcot, "it is to the ovary and to the ovary alone that one has to look for the source of the fixed iliac pain of hysteric" (1887-1888, vol 1, p. 339).

There are, probably, more theories of schizophrenia than of any other mental disorder. Accordingly, practitioners, whether they are psychiatrists or clinical psychologists, have a variety of methods to choose from. Usually, the practitioners who believe that schizophrenia is an organic mental disorder prefer to use physicochemical methods, while those who believe in a psychogenic origin of schizophrenia prefer psychotherapy.

But the controversy does not end at the crossroads between the somatic and nonsomatic factors. Students of schizophrenia represent a rainbow of theoretical colors, with all the possible combinations thereof. Those who believe in a genetic etiology of schizophrenia greatly differ from those who trace schizophrenia to a variety of biochemical determinants. Moreover, those who believe in a psychosocial etiology of schizophrenia do not necessarily exclude the possibility of a combination of genetic and environmental factors, or an interplay of biochemical predisposing causes with precipitating experiential factors.

This chapter does not intend to do justice to all the various theories and their offshoots. Nor do I plan to describe all the diversities of treatment methods. My intention is to describe briefly some of the theoretical approaches and treatment techniques, and to describe in detail my own interpretation and treatment technique.

Statistical Indicators

According to *Mental Health Statistics,* published by the National Institute of Mental Health (1971), there were 1,269,000 admissions to inpatient services in the U.S. in one year, and 27% of these were schizophrenics, as compared to 22.5% depressives, 21% drug and alcohol addicts, and 6% with brain damage, tumors, etc.   However, schizophrenics make up about 50% of all inpatients in mental hospitals at any given time (Rosenthal, 1970), which indicates a lower rate of discharge and, probably, a lower level of therapeutic success.

Etiological Studies: Genetics

One may try various methods to fight the symptoms of a physical disease or a mental (behavioral) disorder, but there is a great advantage in knowing the causes of the problem and developing a rational therapeutic strategy directly aimed at counteracting the noxious causes.   Scores of research workers have spent their lifetime trying to unravel the enigma of schizophrenia without, so far, being able to arrive at a generally accepted etiological theory.

A great many workers believe that schizophrenia is an inherited disorder. According to Kallmann's findings (1946, 1948, 1953), children with one schizophrenic parent have a 16.4% probability of developing schizophrenia, while children with two schizophrenic parents have a 68.1% probability.   More impressive are the data obtained by comparison of fraternal and identical twins. Where one fraternal twin has developed schizophrenia, there is a 16.4% probability that the other will develop it also; in identical twins the chances are 86.2%. In Kallmann's study of 691 twins, dizygotic twins have shown concordance with schizophrenia in 14.7% of the cases, as compared to 77.6 to 81.5% in monozygotic twins.   The higher of the latter percentages applies to twins who have been together for five years prior to breakdown.   Thus, according to Kallmann, "inheritance of schizophrenia follows a biological genetic pattern" (1946, p. 318).

Moreover, Kallmann believed the outcome of schizophrenia to be "the result of intricate interaction of varying genetic and environmental influences."

A summary of Kallmann's studies of expectancy of schizophrenia is represented below (Kallmann, 1962):

	%
One-egg twins	86.20
Two-egg twins	14.50
Siblings	14.20
Half siblings	7.10
General population	0.85

Altshuler (1957) confirmed Kallmann's findings and stressed the fact that expectancy rates for relatives of schizophrenics are much higher than for the general population.   Vorster (1960) found 17% incidence of schizophrenia in two-egg twins, as compared with 70% incidence of schizophrenia in one-egg twins.

The idea of recessive heredity was strongly criticized by Böök (1960) and Slater (1953, 1958).   Since the corrected risk figures of schizophrenia "do not differ to a significant degree between parents, siblings, and children with one or no affected parent" (Böök, 1960, p. 29), the hypothesis of a recessive heredity becomes untenable.   Also Gregory (1960) noticed that the incidence of schizophrenia in various classes of relatives does not follow a simple dominant or simple recessive pattern.

Böök hypothesized that schizophrenia could be caused by gene differences expressed in homozygotes in a recessive and, occasionally, in heterozygotes in a dominant manner.   This hypothesis is based on the concept of "reduced penetrance," i.e., on the assumption that the presence of a genetic factor may not affect the person carrying it.   Garrone (1962) applied the penetrance hypothesis to a study of the Geneva population and maintained that schizophrenia was inherited in a simple recessive mode with 67% of homozygous penetrance.

Loretta Bender (1956) believes schizophrenia to be a process of dysmaturation and arrest of development on the embryonic level, determined by genetic factors. Resultingly, the child is born with a sort of primitive *plasticity*.   The entire neurological system bears witness to the organic lag of development.   The infant's sleep, respiration, blood circulation, muscular tone, and metabolic processes are disturbed.   The trauma of birth activates certain defense mechanisms which develop in the well-known behavioral patterns of schizophrenia.   Thus schizophrenia is a sort of *encephalopathy*.

Fish (1959) reported that a child diagnosed at the age of five and one-half years as schizophrenic had shown neurological and physiological disturbances as early as one month of age.   However, Goldfarb (1961) found no significant differences in physical appearance between normal and schizophrenic children. Also Eisenberg (1957) questioned the anatomical evidence of Bender's theory of encephalopathy.   On the other hand, Bergman and Escalona (1949) reported unusual sensitivity in infants later diagnosed as psychotic.

Roth (1957) remarked that "no simple genetic hypothesis accords with all the facts."   Rosenthal (1960), while in favor of a genetic interpretation of schizophrenia, stated that the question of what is actually inherited would remain unclear "until the specific metabolic error can be located or the specific patterns of influence defined or established."

Jackson (1960) has critically examined the literature pertaining to genetics in schizophrenia.   Schizophrenia apparently does not follow the rules of dominant heredity; were schizophrenia a product of recessive heredity, as Kallmann maintains, the rate of expectancy for monozygotic twins should be 100%; it would also be 100% for children of two schizophrenic parents. Since Kallmann's rates are substantially lower, the hypothesis of recessive heredity is also excluded (Jackson, 1960, p. 46).

The research concerning morbidity risk for schizophrenia in children of two schizophrenic parents is an important contribution to the study of genetic factors. Rosenthal (1970), after analysis of six relevant studies, concluded:

> Since an unqualified theory of recessiveness or dominance predicts an incidence of 100 or 75 percent, respectively, the risk figure obtained, like all others in this section, falls below expectancy for either theory . . . . we had noted that the morbidity-risk estimate for the children of one schizophrenic parent was 9.7 percent. Thus, the risk when both parents are schizophrenic increases about fourfold. An increase is predicted by genetic theory, but not one of this particular magnitude. An increase would also be predicted by environmentalist theories that stress the contribution to schizophrenia made by rearing in a psychosis-ridden or turbulent home (pp. 116–117).

Apparently, at the present time it is rather difficult to assess the role of genetic factors in schizophrenia.

Biochemical Determinants

Several research workers, among them Hoagland (1952) and Reiss (1954), maintain that hormonal disbalance is the cause of schizophrenia. There has been a wide range of disagreement among the workers as to whether it was thyroid or adrenaline or some other endocrine disorder that served as a cause. M. Bleuler (1954), H. Freeman (1958), and others stated, however, that at that time no connection had been established between schizophrenia and endocrine factors.

According to Hendrickson (1952, p. 10), schizophrenia is "an organic abnormality of the nervous system, really a complex and subtle type of neurological disorder." However, most detailed research in brain activity (Davidson, 1960; Hyden, 1961) has not reached the point where one could safely say schizophrenic behavior *is* caused by a smaller amount of RNA in the ganglion cells, as compared with normal.

Kety (1960) expressed serious doubts as to whether "a generalized defect in energy metabolism . . . could be responsible for the highly specialized features of schizophrenia." Also Böök (1960, p. 32) found the toxicity data rather controversial. Richter (1957), in a review of his own studies as well as of research conducted by others, concluded that no evidence was found of free aminos or any specific toxic compounds or abnormal metabolites in the blood of schizophrenics.

Heath and associates reported on several occasions that a psychosis-inducing gamma globulin fraction in the sera of schizophrenic patients, designated *taraxein*, was demonstrable by passive transfer in volunteer non-psychotic recipients and in rhesus monkeys. In a paper published in 1968, Heath and Krupp stated that "the presence of taraxein in the sera of schizophrenic patients is specifically related to acute psychotic episodes and that serum fractions of patients with psychotic diseases other than schizophrenia produced negative results."

However, Heath's experimental results could not be consistently replicated in other laboratories. His theoretical conclusions based on his own observations are therefore open to doubt.

Kety (1960) reported that injection of taraxein caused symptoms resembling schizophrenia, but that there is no evidence that taraxein causes schizophrenia. Furthermore, there is no evidence supporting the amino acid metabolism hypothesis. "The chromatographic search for supportive evidence is interesting and valuable," wrote Kety, but "the preliminary indications of differences that are characteristic of even a segment of the disease rather than artifactual or incidental has not yet been obtained" (1960, p. 127). For instance, the presence of phenolic acids in the urine of schizophrenics has been, according to the study of T.D. Mann and E.H. Lambrosse, "better correlated with the ingestion of this beverage (coffee) than with schizophrenia" (Kety, 1960). Kline (1958) pointed out that the alleged link between biochemical aberrations and psychosis is often a product of the peculiar food intake of institutionalized patients.

Several research workers experimented with injecting schizophrenic serum into animals and human subjects. Walaszek (1960) injected schizophrenic serum into rabbits. The hypothalamic adrenaline level rose to three to five times the normal level in a period of four to eight days. Bishop (1963) found that the injection of schizophrenic serum into rats considerably affected learning and retention processes. German (1963) found significant differences in the reaction of rats to the injection of human normal and schizophrenic serum. However, a comparative study of blood serum of schizophrenic and non-schizophrenic children failed to discover significant differences concerning optical density and slope and lag time (Aprison and Drew, 1958).

Woolley's hypothesis (1958) with regard to the role played by the serotonin enzyme has been tested in the so-called "model psychosis." Yet Kety (1960) and others report failure to find significant differences between normal controls and schizophrenics.

Somato-psychic or Psychosomatic?

Human behavior, normal as well as abnormal, has traditionally been related to two distinct factors, namely mind and body. Some contemporary students of human life try to bypass this division or simply ignore it. The fact remains, however, that brain waves are not human thoughts and an act of artistic creativity is not a biochemical reaction.

These two aspects of human life remain as far apart today as they have been for millennia, and no pseudo-sophistication could do away with the complexity of the mind-body problem.

Yet there is a good deal of interaction between the two. A decision to take a walk puts one's muscles and joints into action, and an upset stomach influences one's thoughts and feelings. Apparently, nature frequently crosses this mind-body bridge, but science lags behind in interpreting this *causal* psycho-soma or soma-psyche relationship.

Practicing therapists are fully aware of the fact that some mental (or, one may call them, behavioral) disorders start with damage to the physicochemical functions of the human organism, while other disorders start with damage to one's self-esteem or other psychological determinants. The fact that chemotherapy and psychotherapy can both favorably affect the course of a mental disorder could serve as a proof that human behavior is susceptible to attack from either angle, soma or psyche.

There is, however, clearly a greater chance of making the treatment effective if it is directed toward the causes of a disorder rather than toward their effects. Thus, should schizophrenia be proven to be primarily of an organic origin, the therapists should give priority to physicochemical treatment methods. Should, however, schizophrenia be a sociogenic or sociopsychogenic disorder and its physical symptoms be of a psychosomatic nature, the therapists should prefer the use of psychotherapeutic methods. In either case, there is no reason for exclusion of alternative routes, for apparently schizophrenia can be alleviated, if not cured, by more than one treatment method.

Arieti (1955), Shattock (1950), Doust (1952), and others observed several pathological phenomena in schizophrenics, including cyanosis or bluing of the feet and hands caused by venous stasis, and other defects of the vasomotor system, such as a decrease in systemic blood pressure, decrease in the volume of flow of blood, and a tendency to vasoconstriction. Yet Kety and his associates (1948) could not find significant differences between the oxygen consumption and the flow of blood in the brains of schizophrenics and those of normal controls. There was no evidence for a cerebral anoxemia; yet the disturbances in the circulatory system of schizophrenics are well-established facts.

According to Arieti, vasoconstriction in schizophrenics is a compensatory mechanism that prevents dissipation of bodily heat. The bizarre postures of catatonics activate antigravity vasoconstrictor mechanisms. "Without these mechanisms, edema due to blood stasis would be very frequent" (Arieti, 1955, p. 395).

Several physiological peculiarities have been observed in schizophrenics, such as little reactivity to stimuli; reduced sensitivity to pain, combined with an increased fear of anticipated pain; strong inclination to skin diseases; frequent colds and an increased sensitivity to colds; sharpening of olfactory sensitivity; lowered body temperature, etc. (Arieti, 1955; Bleuler, 1950; Buck, *et al.,* 1950; Wolman, 1957, 1964; and others).

However, the research that points to the etiologic organicity of schizophrenia has been conducted on chronic schizophrenics, most of them in their middle or old age. For instance Brambilla *et al.* (1967) in a study of 72 chronic schizophrenics aged 14-53 found that endocrine glands are impaired, and that the severity of the glandular impairment corresponds to the severity and the age of onset of the disorder. Most striking pathology was found in hebephrenics with onset at puberty. The results obtained with schizophrenics whose manifest disorder was recent were rather negative. Especially striking are the negative results obtained by Aprison and Drew (1958) and Fourbye et al. (1966) in regard to children. These results indicate that *biochemical symptoms follow psychological* (behavioral) symptoms, suggesting that in schizophrenia the psychological changes are the *cause* and not the results of somatic changes.

For instance, a study by Becket and associates of carbohydrate metabolism in schizophrenia offers further support to the sociopsychosomatic theory. Becket *et al.* (1963) found that premorbid social isolation and diminished heterosexual drive were related to biochemical abnormalities. Specifically the mother of the schizophrenic patient was a "shielding, protecting person who did not allow her son to experience the ordinary stimulation and challenges of childhood . . . . A hypothesis is presented suggesting that a certain amount of stimulation in early life is necessary for the proper maturation of the energy-producing metabolic system."

Practically all empirical findings speak in favor of such a causal chain. There is no doubt that many (but not all) adult schizophrenics and some children with severe cases of schizophrenia develop somatic symptoms. There is little evidence that schizophrenic behavior is a result of these biochemical afflictions, for many individuals with metabolic troubles ascribed to schizophrenia never become schizophrenic. There is, however, substantial, though by no means conclusive, evidence that *schizophrenia can produce all these biochemical disorders.*

There is no doubt that emotional stress may cause biochemical changes, especially in the adrenocortical and thyroid systems, as well as in the production of epinephrine and norepinephrine. These changes are not a cause but an *effect* of emotional stress.

The hypothesis of somatic symptoms resulting from hypocathexis of bodily organs completes the *sociopsychosomatic* theory. My observations have led me to believe that noxious *environmental* (social) factors cause an imbalance in *interindividual cathexes*. This imbalance produces a severe disbalance in the *intraindividual* cathexes of libido and destrudo; this, in turn, introduces a disorder in the personality structure (psychological factors). The personality disorder causes somatic changes, either through a transformation of deficiency in mental energy into organic deficiencies or through the process of conditioning (Wolman, 1966, 1967).

Research in conditioning reported by Buck *et al.* (1950), Bykov (1957), Gantt (1958), Ivanov-Smolensky (1954), Lynn (1963), Malis (1961), and others distinctly points to such a possibility. Psychologically induced changes in heartbeat, rate of metabolism, circulation of blood, or respiration are not limited to Charcot's hysterics. They are common to all human beings, including schizophrenics, and can be produced by conditioning or cathexis or both. In schizophrenia these processes follow the direction of a "downward adjustment."

The magnitude of the general metabolism can be changed through conditioning by word signals. The sound of a metronome and the command, "Get ready for the experiment," caused in experimental subjects a marked increase in oxygen consumption and pulmonary ventilation. In one experiment, "a man who remained quietly lying on a couch showed an increase in metabolism when suggested that he had just completed some very hard muscular work" (Bykov, 1957, p. 179). In another experiment the rate of metabolism went up in a subject who imagined that he was working.

In terms of the sociopsychosomatic theory, schizophrenia is an impoverishment of one's own resources and a struggle for survival, caused by a morbid hypervectorialism. This state of mind may correspond to cerebrospinal hypertension, for *sociopsychological stimuli cause somatic changes.*

Analgesias are another example of the same issue. E. Bleuler wrote in 1911: "Even in well oriented patients one may often observe the presence of a complete *analgesia* which includes the deeper parts of the body as well as the skin. The patients intentionally or unintentionally incur quite serious injuries, pluck out an eye, sit down on a hot stove and receive severe gluteal burns," etc. (Bleuler, 1950, p. 57).

Analgesias can be produced by conditioning (Bykov, 1957, p. 342) and/or by a low self-cathexis. The decline in self-cathexis makes the schizophrenic less capable of loving and protecting himself, but in face of real danger, schizophrenics may display a self-defensive reaction. Severely deteriorated cases, however, with their lowest sensitivity to pain, may fall victim to any danger.

Severely deteriorated schizophrenics appear insensitive when the flame of a candle is passed rapidly over the skin. They may sit near the radiator, and, if they are not moved, they may continue to stay there even when, as a result of close contact, they are burned. They "seem to have lost the sensation of taste. When they are given bitter radishes or teaspoons of sugar, salt, pepper, or quinine, they do not show any pleasant or unpleasant reaction" (Arieti, 1955, pp. 373–374).

This is the *schizophrenic paradox:* real life is sacrificed for a pseudo protection of life. The schizophrenic feels he has to give away his life to protect those upon whom his survival depends. His lavish hypercathexis of his "protectors" leads to his own impoverishment and eventual death (Wolman, 1966).

A radical decline in pain sensation, whether interpreted as conditioning or lack of self-cathexis, destroys the individual's ability to protect his own life.

Arieti (1955, p. 392) believes that the following four changes usually take place in the cardiovascular system of schizpohrenics: (1) a decrease in the size of the heart, (2) a decrease in the volume of blood flow, (3) a decrease in systematic blood pressure, and (4) an exaggerated tendency to vasoconstriction and a resulting diminished blood supply. Arieti believes that all these are psychosomatic products of schizophrenia.

Theories of Schizophrenia

Initially Freud related schizophrenia to an early repression of libido. However, in 1907 he shifted the emphasis from sexual traumata to more general concepts of libido development.

In 1908, Abraham hypothesized that schizophrenia was caused by a regression of libido from object relationship into the autoerotic stage. According to the Freud-Abraham timetable, mental disorders are a product of fixation and/or regression. More severe disorders are a product of earlier fixations.

"The psychosexual characteristics of dementia praecox is the return of the patient to autoeroticism, and the symptoms of this illness are a form of autoerotic activity," wrote Abraham in 1908. "The autoeroticism is the source not only of delusions of persecution but of megalomania" (Abraham, 1955, pp. 74–75. "The psychosexual constitution of dementia praecox is based, therefore, on an inhibition in development." It is "an abnormal fixation to an erotogenic zone − a typical autoerotic phenomenon" (ibid., p. 77). In dementia praecox "a person who has never passed out of the primary stage of his psychosexual development is thrown back more and more into the autoerotic stage as the disease progresses" (ibid., p. 78).

Freud (in 1911 and 1912) accepted Abraham's ideas regarding the pathogenesis of schizophrenia and saw in schizophrenia a struggle between the regression of libido and its withdrawal from object relations and its efforts to recapture or restore the object relations.

According to Freud, the way people go through developmental phases depends upon interactional patterns. Whether a child will pass safely through an oral or anal stage or remain fixated or regress eventually depends on the amount and quality of satisfaction and frustration received by the child in the *interaction* with his close environment. According to Freud, "owing to the general tendency to variation in biological processes it must necessarily happen that not all these preparatory phases will be passed through and completely outgrown with the same degree of success; some parts of the function will be permanently arrested." The development can be "disturbed and altered by current impressions from without" (Freud, 1949, pp. 297 ff.).

These "impressions from without" have been studied by H.S. Sullivan. Sullivan pointed to peculiarities in the personalities of parents of schizophrenics and related the origins of schizophrenia to a state of panic disastrous to the patient's self-esteem. Parent-child relationships that prevent the establishment of the "self-esteem," and especially panic states producing dissociation (the not-me feeling), have been perceived by Sullivan as causes of schizophrenia (Sullivan, 1947, 1953).

Several workers began to study the peculiar parent-child relationship. Whether these relationships caused schizophrenia as interpreted by a Freudian withdrawal of libido or Sullivanian dissociation or any other theory, the nature of these relationships became a major topic in research in schizophrenia.

Research workers failed to find any definite pathology in the parents of schizophrenics. One worker (Alanen, 1958) found 10% of the parents of schizophrenics to be disturbed and slightly over 5% of them schizophrenic. I have found (Wolman, 1957, 1961, 1964) about 40% of fathers and 50% of mothers of schizophrenics displaying a great variety of pathological conditions, but it was impossible to state that schizophrenia in offspring is caused by any particular mental type of parents.

Lidz and his associates (1957, 1968, 1960; Lidz, 1963, 1973) found a lack of mutual understanding and cooperation between the parents of schizophrenics.

> We realized soon, that the intrapsychic disturbances of the mothers were not nearly as relevant to what happened to one or more children in the family (especially to the child who became schizophrenic) as was the fact that these women were paired with husbands who would either acquiesce to the many irrational and bizarre notions of how the family should be run or who would constantly battle with and undermine an already anxious and insecure mother (Fleck, 1960, p. 335).

Similar findings have been reported by Wolman (1957, 1961), Lu (1961, 1962), and many others.

The reported data differ in detail, but they show an almost uniform pattern of interaction. Thus, a sociopsychological theory has been proposed that links all the data into one coherent system (Wolman, 1966, 1970, 1973).

Three types of social relationship, depending upon the objectives of the participants, have been distinguished. Whenever an individual enters a relationship with the objective of receiving, it is an *instrumental* type, for the partner or partners are used for the satisfaction of the individual's needs. The infant-mother relationship is the prototype of instrumentalism. The infant is weak, the mother is strong; the infant must receive, yet cannot give. Whenever an individual enters a relationship with the objective of satisfying his own needs and also the needs of others, it is *mutual* relationship. Friendship and marriage represent mutualism. Sexual intercourse is probably the prototype of mutualism. Whenever an individual's objective is to satisfy the needs of others, it is a *vectorial* relationship. Parenthood is the prototype of vectorialism; parents are strong, infants are weak; parents give love and support and protect their children.

Normal adults are capable of interacting in all three ways. In business they are instrumental; in friendship and marriage, mutual; and in parenthood and in their ideals, vectorial.

In normal families, parents are perceived by their children as strong and friendly adults who relate to each other in a *mutual*, give and get manner and have a *vectorial* attitude toward the child, irrespective of what the child may be or do. Parental love is unconditional; the smaller and weaker the child, the more vectorial the parental attitude.

The intrafamilial relationship that produces schizophrenia does not fall into the usual descriptive categories of rejection, overprotection, overindulgence, etc.

The schizogenic family relationship represents a *reversal of social positions* and, resultingly, causes in the mind of the child who will become schizophrenic a *confusion in social roles of age, sex, family position, etc.*

Mother confuses the child by presenting herself as a martyr. She appears to be strong, for she controls the entire family and imposes her will on all in the household. She does it in a protective-hostile manner with the child: she tells the child that he is weak, sick, stupid, or ugly and that she must protect him and do things for him. Yet she presents herself as a self-sacrificing, suffering, almost dying person.

She cannot tolerate any independence, any growth of the child, any success not brought about by mother. These mothers are possessive, control their children's lives, and demand from the child an unlimited love, gratitude, and self-sacrifice for the self-sacrificing tyrant-martyr mother (see Davis, 1961; Foudraine, 1961; Lu, 1961, 1962; Weakland, 1960; Wolman, 1961, 1965; and many others).

The future schizophrenic starts his life in the same way as any other child. He is helpless and depends upon aid from outside. His attitude is instrumental, as he depends upon "narcissistic supplies." Soon he cannot fail to realize that there is something wrong with his parents. The child lives under the threat of loss of his martyr-type mother and nonparticipant baby-father. All schizophrenics, as Sullivan amply observed (1953), are panic-stricken. The child begins to worry about his parents and takes on a premature and much too costly protective hypervectorial attitude toward them. In order to survive, he must protect his protectors. *Vectoriasis praecox* (the new name for schizophrenia) sometimes comes very early and uses up the child's mental resources (Wolman, 1957, 1958, 1959b, 1961, 1962, 1965).

Certainly no woman could destroy her child without the active or tacit approval of her husband, and all fathers of schizophrenics participate in the development of schizophrenia in offspring. The father-mother relationship causes the woman to demand from the child what she failed to get from her husband. When the "mutual" interparental relationship fails, chances are that mother will develop an instrumental, exploitative attitude toward the child.

The fathers trigger the tragic involvement. They expect the child to give them what they failed to get from their wives. Most of these fathers are seductive to children of both sexes, spreading confusion with regard to age and sex identification. Some of them fight against their own wives and children. Many schizophrenic families live under father's tyranny in terror.

Schizophrenia has been thus interpreted as an *escape for survival.* It is a process of downward adjustment in an irrational struggle to stay alive. The schizophrenic withdraws from social contacts, avoids emotional involvement, and regresses into a lower level of intellectual functioning, as if acting on in unconscious belief that this is the only way to survive.

Symptomatological Issues

E. Bleuler's initial distinction between deteriorating and recovering cases gave rise to a division of schizophrenia into process and reactive types. Kant (1948) believed the malignant *process schizophrenia* to be characterized by a gradual decline in activity, dullness, autism, ideas of reference, and thought disturbances. Oscillation between excitement and stuporous depression, and periods of almost normal functioning alternating with states of confusion are characteristics of the benign *reactive schizophrenia.*

Chase and Silverman (1943) studied recovery rates in Metrazol and insulin shock therapy. Pyknic body type, acute onset, short duration of severe symptoms, premorbid good adjustment, and extrovert personality type have been related to a good prognosis. Asthenic body type, apathy, introversion, insidious onset of severe symptoms, dissociation, and awareness of personality disintegration, have been related to poor prognosis. The Metrazol and insulin shock therapies have produced satisfactory results in the good-prognostic cases only. Apparently all these cases belong to the reactive type.

Kantor, Wallner, and Winder (1953) mention that reactive schizophrenics have good premorbid adjustment, good physical health, adequate adjustment at home and in school, extroversion, no somatic delusions, etc. The process schizophrenics have a prolonged history of maladjustment, poor physical health, difficulties at home and in school, abnormal family relationships, insidious onset of psychosis, somatic delusions, etc. However, Rorschach tests administered to patients diagnosed as process and reactive schizophrenics failed to prove psychosis in most of the process schizophrenics. Thus, serious doubts have been voiced as to whether the so-called process schizophrenics are schizophrenics (Herron, 1962) and, if so, whether the distinction of two types is justified. King (1954) found, according to the above-mentioned Kantor *et al.,* that reactive schizophrenics reacted to mecholyl with a substantially greater drop in blood pressure than the process schizophrenics. Research conducted by Zuckerman and Gross (1959) contradicted King's findings.

Brackbill and Fine (1956) and many others hypothesized that the process schizophrenia is related to organic factors. No definite evidence has been adduced. Arieti (1955), Wolman (1957), and other workers did not find clear indications for a reactive versus process distinction. On the other hand, Herron (1962) has stated that it is possible to demonstrate differences between these two groups. Phillips (1953), Garmezy and Rodnick (1959), and others believed that such a distinction had some prognostic value; however, the premorbid history of each patient is determined to a great extent by his environment, and eventually Garmezy (1965) and Offord and Cross (1969) arrived at the conclusion that the process and reactive types represent two gradual levels rather than two distinct clinical types.

Division of symptoms related to ego strength has been proposed (Wolman, 1958, 1964). The *ego-protective* symptoms indicate the struggle of the ego to retain the control over the unconscious impulses. All "defense mechanisms" and varieties of neurotic symptoms belong to this category. The preschizophrenic has been called pseudoneurotic by Hoch and Polatin (1949); most probably he is a schizo-type neurotic before he becomes a schizophrenic psychotic. The main ego-protective symptom of this hypervectorial or preschizophrenic neurotic is the overmobilization of the ego, reflected in his constricted, introverted, high-strung, tense personality. The preschizophrenic neurotic is overconscientious, moralistic, and dogmatic. He often develops phobias, obsessive-compulsive behavior, and partial withdrawal from social contacts. All these *ego-protective* symptoms may postpone and even prevent psychotic breakdown.

Therefore, one can present schizophrenia and related disorders in a continuum using sociopsychological determinants as the uniting factor. According to the aforementioned sociopsychomatic theory, schizophrenia, in a broad sense of the word, starts with the peculiar disbalance of libido cathexes. Precocious object hypercathexis and resulting self-hypocathexis, or, in terms of overt social behavior, a precocious hypervectorialism, is the core of the group of schizothymic or hypervectorial disorders.

One may distinguish five *levels* of mental disorders; namely, neurosis, character neurosis, latent psychosis, manifest psychosis, and dementive stage. In hypervectorial or schizo-type disorders the neurotic step includes phobic, neurasthenic, and obsessive-compulsive patterns. The schizoid character neurosis corresponds to what is usually called the schizoid personality. The next step in schizophrenic deterioration is latent schizophrenia. Next comes manifest schizophrenia, called *vectoriasis praecox*. The manifest psychotic level may come in four syndromes; namely, the paranoid, catatonic, hebephrenic, and simple deterioration. The last, dementive level is the end of decline and a complete collapse of personality structure. All five levels represent an ever-growing disbalance of cathexes of sexual and hostile impulses. The decline of the controlling force of the ego is the most significant determinant of each level. As long as the ego exercises control, it is neurosis. When the ego comes to terms with the symptoms, it is character neurosis. When the ego is on the verge of collapse, it is latent psychosis. When the ego fails, it is manifest psychosis, or the full-blown schizophrenia in one of its four syndromes.

The first syndrome roughly corresponds to what has usually been described as *paranoid schizophrenia* and is characterized by the ego losing contact with reality and leaving it to the superego. In the second syndrome, the *catatonic*, the superego takes over control also of the motor apparatus. In the *hebephrenic* syndrome the ego yields to the id; the superego is defeated and the id takes over. In the *simple deterioration* syndrome there is a process of losing life itself.

PHYSICOCHEMICAL TREATMENT TECHNIQUES*

The treatment of schizophrenia is no less enigmatic than the disorder itself. The same technique may produce favorable results in one case and fail lamentably in another. Even well trained and experienced practitioners cannot tell for sure whether they will be successful with a new schizophrenic patient, and every therapist can tell about unpredictable successes and failures. Sometimes poorly trained and inexperienced beginners can produce miracles, and in some instances schizophrenics considerably improve without being exposed to systematic treatment. Moreover, different techniques based on diametrically opposed theories may produce satisfactory results. Apparently, any therapeutic process is an interactional process, that is, a *psychosocial field,* and the prognosis seems to be considerably influenced by who interacts with whom and how.

ECT AND ICT

Experts throughout the world seem to concur that the older methods of physical treatment (ECT and ICT) still have value in treating severely disturbed patients. Remy, in his article in the *Biological Treatment of Mental Illness* (1966), emphasizes ICT's long-lasting effects. Dramatic reversal in patients' behavior was also demonstrated with ICT by Dunlop (1966), particularly in patients who had made little progress with the psychotropic drugs.

The most important addition to ICT technique has been the introduction of Glucagon by Braun and Parker (1959), which was further developed by Dussik *et al.* (1961, 1966), and Ramirez *et al.* (1966), and others. Glucagon serves two functions: (1) it facilitates insulin-induced hypoglycemia, and (2) it is the most effective and simplest way to terminate a coma (this, however, is used only in rare cases).

Alexander (1953) emphasized that success with ICT depends upon adequate depth and duration of treatment. He believed that a full course of insulin therapy should include sixty deep comas and that the effect of ICT is enhanced by the periodic use of ECT.

ECT and ICT have taken a back seat to the antipsychotic drugs in the research literature, as the dearth of studies soon will show. Smith *et al.* (1967) compared the effects of ECT and chlorpromazine with chlorpromazine alone and discovered that the combination of the two treatments was more effective than the drug alone. Markowe *et al.* (1967) studied the effect of insulin shock and chlorpromazine on 100 previously untreated schizophrenics. A ten-year follow-up study revealed no difference between those treated with insulin shock and those given chlorpromazine: 25% of both groups remained psychotic, while 45% showed no or few symptoms. ICT was used on 24 male and 18 female schizophrenics over a five-year period (Felipa-Rejas *et al.,* 1968). The findings encourage early application of ICT to hebephrenics and catatonics. Psychotherapy and ergo-

---

*In the preparation of this part of the chapter, I was assisted by Ms. Linda Pasternak, Doctoral Candidate in Clinical Psychology, Long Island University.

therapy were also considered helpful. Two Belgian psychiatrists (Luyssaert and Pierloot, 1969) have reviewed the history of insulin therapy. These doctors believe that one of the most active principles in insulin shock treatment is regression, which enables the patient to be more open to psychotherapy. Weinstein and Fischer (1971), like Smith *et al.,* maintain that the real benefit of ECT is its dual synergism with antipsychotic drugs, particularly in lifting cases off plateaus and in consolidating the patient's gains and avoiding relapses.

Psychosurgery

Despite the fact that lobotomy is an unpredictable method that causes irreversible results, psychosurgery seems to have returned to favor, and it is still occasionally in use. Vaernet and Madsen (1970) treated 12 persons who either had personality disorders or who were schizophrenic by bilateral stereotaxic electrocoagulation of the amygdala. In 11 of the subjects the surgery resulted in either the disappearance of or marked reduction in aggression. In 2 subjects with a history of self-mutilation, symptoms disappeared after an additional basofrontal tractotomy. Kelly *et al.* (1972) reported that varieties of psychosurgery produced improvement in 70% of 78 patients. The best short-term prognosis was with depression and anxiety, while 50% improvement was obtained with obsessional neurosis, schizophrenia, and personality disorders.

Chemotherapy

Most antipsychotic drugs are shown to be more effective than placebos. Several studies have compared reserpine with chlorpromazine (Davis, 1965). Twelve of these studies showed chlorpromazine to be more effective than reserpine; the other 14 found the two drugs to be about equivalent in effect. No studies demonstrated reserpine to be more effective than chlorpromazine. In fact, in the carefully controlled V.A. study comparing reserpine to the widely used phenothiazines (Lasky, 1962), reserpine was shown to be less effective than the phenothiazines in reducing excitement withdrawal and agitated depression. The evidence indicates that the antipsychotic drugs produce improvement, but it is not clear whether the improvement is significant and lasting.

The NIMH Pharmacology Research Branch (1967, 1968) reported that two-thirds of phenothiazine-treated patients showed much improvement, while only one-fourth of placebo-treated patients were comparably improved. Half of the placebo patients were unchanged or worse, whereas only one-tenth of the phenothiazine patients had such poor results. The best effects are obtained when the drugs are taken consistently for a long enough period to allow them to achieve maximum effect. Data from the NIMH Collaborative Study II (1968) indicate that patients make gains from the beginning of treatment to 26 weeks.

Several studies show that when phenothiazines are withdrawn, psychotic symptomatology re-emerges (Freeman, 1962; Clark *et al.*, 1967; Majerrison *et al,* 1964; and others). In addition, such symptoms as nausea, vomiting, increased sebaceous secretion, tension, restlessness, and physical complaints occur

(Simpson *et al.*, 1965). Simpson *et al.* have suggested that some of the side effects may also be attributed to withdrawal from anti-Parkinsonian medication which is often given in conjunction with phenothiazines.

One issue which clinicians are debating is whether a combination of drugs is better than a single psychotropic drug. Michaux, Kurland, and Agallianos (1966) compared various drug combinations and found that no combination of drugs showed superiority to chlorpromazine alone. Chlorpromazine seems most effective in dealing with the core symptoms of schizophrenia, especially in the reduction of schizophrenic disorganization.

Trifluoperazine and chlorpromazine were found to be equal to insulin coma therapy. Chlorpromazine was found to be equal to or more effective than ECT. Experience suggests that combining ECT with antipsychotic drugs can be useful. Also sociopsychological therapies in combination with drug treatment seem to be highly effective in facilitating return to the community for chronic patients (Greenblatt, 1965).

The NIMH Collaborative Studies I and II (1967, 1968) found that certain phenothiazines were better predictors of successful treatment of specific disorders than others. Bellak and Loeb (1969) maintain that the difference between a specific phenothiazine and a nonspecific one is as great as the difference between phenothiazine therapy and a placebo.

Some psychiatrists believe that the phenothiazines are merely sedatives and that they dull the patients' sensibilities.

The antipsychotic drugs probably have a beneficial effect on schizophrenic thought. The NIMH Psychopharmacological Study (1968) showed that there was marked improvement (with a high I.Q. group) in the patients' ability to abstract with a concomitant decrease in the amount of concrete thinking, and that the patients did not evidence as much bizarre, circumstantial, and inappropriate responses as before treatment. There is evidence that phenothiazines reduce schizophrenic thought disorders.

Comparing phenothiazines with barbiturates, Irwin (1966) found that the phenothiazines decrease motor activity, exploratory behavior, and responses to environmental stimuli; barbiturates tend to increase motor activity, exploratory behavior, and responses to environmental stimuli, and to act as disinhibiting agents.

Stupenchenko (1969) compared the effect of psychotropic drugs on schizophrenics with hereditary involvement and those whose condition was more easily attributable to exogenous factors. He discovered that the psychotropic drugs are more effective with those schizophrenics in whom heredity plays a part and least effective with catatonics.

Prien *et al.* (1971) tried to identify which sub-groups of schizophrenics had a sufficiently low probability of relapse to warrant discontinuation of medication. Relapse was found to be linked to the dosage of medication the patient received before being put on placebo (the higher the dosage the higher the probability of relapse). Results suggest that the large majority of schizophrenics who have been hospitalized for more than 15 years and are receiving low dosages can remain off drugs for six months without serious side effects.

Polak and Laycob (1972) described the treatment of acute schizophrenics in which patients were rapidly tranquilized by titrating dosages until they reached a tranquilized end point within six hours. The dosage was adjusted daily and chemotherapy was integrated with intensive social systems intervention centered on the patient's real life setting.

The NIMH Study (1968) compared high dosage and low dosage treatments using chlorpromazine. The study indicated that high dosage produced significantly more side effects and was significantly more effecitve with patients under 40 who had been hospitalized for less than 10 years. Chlorpromazine has been shown to raise serum cholesterol levels consistently and significantly. Prior to therapy with chlorpromazine, cholesterol seemed inversely related to symptoms of pathology. Following therapy, however, there appeared to be no relationship between cholesterol level and behavior. Goldberg et al. (1970) evaluated prolixin and found that prolixin enanthate is significantly superior to oral phenothiazine in drug reluctant patients, particularly in paranoid cases and those living at home who would otherwise require hospitalization. Trifluoperazine and trifluperidol were compared by Schiele et al. (1969). The comparison indicated that subjects treated with trifluoperazine showed greater improvement and fewer side effects than those treated with trifluperidol.

Two psychotropic drugs have received more attention than others, namely haloperidol and fluphenazine, from which prolixin is derived. Towler and Wick (1967) treated 59 patients with haloperidol. Of this number 45 improved but 26 required further treatment. Chronic schizophrenics with paranoid reactions showed the most significant response. Side effects occurred in one-third of the patients, but they were easily controlled. Lucky and Schiele (1967) compared the effects of haloperidol and trifluoperazine using 26 schizophrenic patients, 13 of whom took both drugs. Of the 13, only 9 completed the three-month trial. According to the authors, only 2 of the patients improved with haloperidol. There was a high incidence of extrapyramidal reactions, development of weakness, drowsiness, and depression which necessitated withdrawing haloperidol from three subjects. It was posited that the drug may be useful for chronic paranoids.

Studies dealing with fluphenazine seem to agree that the drug is most effective for chronic schizophrenic patients. Lowther (1969) concluded that fluphenazine is quite effective for maintenance therapy with chronic patients. DeAlarcon and Carney (1969) found that with slow-release intramuscular fluphenazine injections, 16 patients suffered severe depressive episodes. In five cases, the drug was thought to be responsible for suicide. The authors recommended that patients on fluphenazine be carefully supervised. The research of Itil et al., (1971) on the effect of fluphenazine on the full-night sleep process of 11 chronic schizophrenics suggests that the length of REM periods and the number of REM cycles increased significantly during fluphenazine treatment. When subjects were divided into therapy resistant and therapy responsive groups, responsive patients were found to have an augmentation of awakening states which may imply that the improvement obtained with fluphenazine may be related to its "stimulatory" effect.

Some new phenothiazine derivatives as well as other antipsychotic drugs have come to the fore. Butaperazine (NIMH, 1967), corphenazine (Havenson, 1967), metronidazole (Holden *et al.*, 1968), thiothixene (Sterlin *et al.*, 1970), and mepiprazol (Goncalves, 1972) seem to produce significant changes in patients, particularly chronic ones. Other recent drugs such as oxypertine and lyogen are in more experimental stages and have stirred some controversy. SKF 16336 seems comparable to chlorpromazine in eradicating schizophrenic thought disorder, but it is less potent (DeVito *et al.*, 1969). It is considered to be more effective in combating the depressive mood disorders of schizo-affective schizophrenics. Chanoit *et al.* (1969) treated 102 schizophrenics with thioproperazine and have indicated that it is highly effective with hebephrenics and young patients with short hospitalizations. Seventy percent of the chronic patients were judged improved. Ezhkov (1968) used triperidol in the treatment of 84 schizophrenic patients. He noted that in small doses triperidol was a stimulant, in higher doses a sedative. Ezhkov recommended it for (1) nuclear schizophrenics with polymorphic symptomatology, (2) simple and nuclear paranoid schizophrenics, (3) the termination of manic states, and (4) the treatment of periodic schizophrenia.

It should be mentioned that the antipsychotic drugs often produce adverse side effects. These side effects are relatively mild, however, and frequently "adapt out" with continued drug treatment. There seems to be some controversy as to which drug produces the most severe side effects (V.A. Cooperative Study, 1960; Adelson and Epstein, 1962; Lasky *et al.*, 1962), but no conclusive evidence has turned up to prove any significant differences.

PSYCHOTHERAPY

The aim of any psychotherapy is to cure the patient. I have suggested four criteria for considering a case cured: (1) reasonably realistic perception of oneself and others (cognitive functions), (2) emotional responses appropriate to the stimuli (emotional balance), (3) ability to relate to other people, and (4) achievements commensurate with one's innate abilities and external opportunities.

Classic psychoanalysis is not the choice treatment of schizophrenia. The reclining position and the psychoanalyst's spare comments are likely to increase anxiety in the patient and facilitate regression. Even Freudians, such as Bychowski (1952), Brody and Redlich (1952), Eissler (1947, 1952), Federn (1952), Knight (1953), Rosen (1947, 1953), and Wolman (1959a) deviate from Freud's techniques when they treat schizophrenics. Thus the gulf between Freudians and non-Freudians like Sullivan (1947, 1962), Fromm-Reichmann (1950, 1952, 1959), and Arieti (1955) has been reduced. Today, both groups emphasize face-to-face relations as essential for a successful treatment.

Melanie Klein and her school interpret unconscious processes in treating schizophrenia (Pichon-Riviere, 1952; Rosenfeld, 1953; Winnicot, 1955). But Eissler (1952, p. 143), in discussing Rosen's direct interpretation, says that "another set of interpretations might have achieved a similar result." An evaluation of Rosen's methods did not prove that his interpretations were specifically helpful (English, 1961).

The fact that poorly trained and even untrained individuals have been successful in treating schizophrenia while some prominent psychotherapists, among them psychoanalysts have failed, sheds bright light on the problem. An orthodox psychoanalyst may give the impression of being impersonal and not interested, and his silence may be regarded by the schizophrenic as a sign of hostility.

But when a kind, friendly person shows interest in a schizophrenic and displays a profound desire to help him, this is a giving, vectorial attitude that helps the patient improve the balance of libido cathexes. A visit by an old friend who comes to the hospital and shows consideration and affection may do miracles and cause remission (cf. Bleuler, 1919). The fact that Freudian, Adlerian, Jungian, Sullivanian, and Horneyan psychotherapists can be successful in the treatment of schizophrenia indicates that differences between their theories are *insignificant* for the treatment. What is significant is common to all successful therapists, whatever their theoretical differences and irrespective of the method of their interpretations. Federn relied mostly on environmental help, Rosen applied "direct" interpretation of the unconscious, Fromm-Reichmann avoided interpretation, and Schwing mothered the patients. Yet, despite the highly diverse theoretical assumptions and notwithstanding the differences in the techniques and personalities of the therapists, the *interaction was basically the same in all known cases of successful treatment of schizophrenia.* In all these cases the therapist was perceived as a *strong* and *friendly* person, and his attitude was one of a *genuine vectorialism.*

A few excerpts from the writings of successful psychotherapists will illustrate this point. One may agree or disagree, for instance, with Schwing's interpretations of what was going on in the minds of her patients. But it is an undeniable fact that she has been a devoted, giving person. One cannot read her book without being moved by the humanitarian approach to her patients, as described below:

I went to the patient. She was lying there with a burning face, swollen eyes, and parched lips . . . . The nurse interrupted me and warned: "You must not open the lattice, or in five minutes you and the rest of us will be killed!" . . . I felt unsure of myself. Could I influence a patient who should only rage or turn completely away from the world? . . . "I am sad," I said gently, "but nevertheless I will try to be very near you." . . . I obtained a chair and placed it close to the bed. I inquired sympathetically if the strait-jacket made her hot and uncomfortable and if she were not miserable lying that way. I suggested that perhaps she would like something to drink . . . . "There is much sadness in you!" I continued, "I would like to be able to help you, may I try?" Two big tears indicated that her armor of negativism had been pierced . . . (Schwing, 1954, pp. 34–35).

A kind, giving, vectorial attitude also permeated K.R. Eissler's work with schizophrenics (Eissler, 1952). To Eissler the patient's disorder was a challenge that the therapist had to master. The patient must feel how important he is to the omnipotent and benevolent therapist.

A similar approach was applied by Arieti. Arieti wrote, "At the very beginning of treatment, when the patient's suspiciousness and distrust are very pronounced, he should leave the session with the feeling that he has been given something, not with the feeling that something, even diagnostic information, has been taken from him. The patient must feel that a benevolent, sincere effort is being made to reach him with no demand being made on him" (Arieti, 1955, p. 439).

It is easier to be the all-giving parent for a short while than to continue giving. The psychotherapist, being human himself, can only keep giving up to the point at which his own emotional resources begin to dwindle. While the therapist's personality will be discussed later, it is worthwhile to mention here that psychotherapy with schizophrenics is a serious drain on the psychotherapist's emotional resources. Hill noticed the danger of regression in the psychotherapist himself. "It is not likely that the regression will go so far as to suggest schizophrenia, but it is most likely that it will frequently extend to the level at which the physician finds himself acting in a childish fashion, indulging in wish-fulfillment and in efforts to dominate. He finds himself resenting helplessness, responding with anger and guilt and with all sorts of defenses against these unpleasant states" (Hill, 1955, p. 193). The therapist is likely to try to escape these feelings "by a resort to the defense of omnipotent fantasy."

In a review of psychotherapeutic techniques, Redlich (Brody and Redlich, 1952, p. 30) stated that there was a very broad similarity between the new psychoanalytic techniques as developed by Eissler (1947), Federn (1952), Ferenczi (1926), Fromm-Reichmann (1950), Knight (1946), and Schwing (1954) and "the eternal common-sense methods of love and patience. However, no generally accepted theory accounts for the vast differences of approach in the psychotherapeutic process with schizophrenics, varying from rather different, ego-supporting approaches to the direct id interpretations, from rigorous manipulation of the patient to marked passivity of the therapist."

Such a general theory is here proposed. My theoretical frame of reference is a modified Freudian model. Sullivan's emphasis on interpersonal relations has been invaluable, and the need to include interindividual relations dictated some modifications in Freud's theory. A new theoretical construct, "interindividual cathexis," revises Freud's pleasure and pain theory, and a new interpretation of the role of hate and destructive impulses in mental disorders is offered.

Interaction patterns are divided into instrumental (take), mutual (give and take), and vectorial (give) types of interaction. In normal families, the relationship of parent-to-parent is mutual, parent-to-child vectorial, and child-to-parent instrumental.

In families with schizophrenic offspring, the parent-parent relationship is hostile-instrumental; the mother's attitude toward the child is pseudo-vectorial, but actually exploitative-instrumental; and the father-child relationship is frankly instrumental, in a seductive or competitive fashion. The preschizophrenic child is forced to hypercathect his libido in his parents instead of having his parents worry about him. The reversal of social roles turns the child into a "protector of his protectors."

These abnormal interactional patterns represent a dysbalance in interindividual cathexes. A child, normally a "taker" (instrumental), is forced into precocious giving (hypervectorial). Hence, *vectoriasis praecox* is the proposed name for schizophrenia.

The normal reaction of a child to this emotional extortion should be hatred. But the avenues of hate are blocked. Mother convinces the child that she protects him, and the child begins to hate himself for having hostile feelings toward his self-sacrificing mother.

Schizophrenia develops as a paradoxical reaction of an organism that abandons its own protection to protect those who should protect it. The dysbalance of interindividual cathexes leads to a severe dysbalance in intraindividual cathexes of libido and destrudo.

These psychological changes affect the nervous system, endocrine, and other organic processes. Somatic symptoms of schizophrenia are psychosomatic (Arieti, 1955).

The main aim of the interactional psychotherapy process is the reversal of libido cathexes with a resultant reorganization of personality structure. Many psychotherapists who otherwise differ from each other have *a vectorial, unconditionally giving attitude. It is a helping, giving attitude irrespective of the friendly or hostile reactions of the one who receives (just as good parents love good and bad children alike).*

This is more than "common-sense love and patience." A successful psychotherapy is a distinct interactional pattern aiming at the restoration of an intraindividual balance of cathexes and a realistic perception of life. A detailed description of the interactional rules follows.

Rules of Therapeutic Interaction

1. The first rule is *unconditional support,* protecting the patient's self-esteem by siding with him, by accepting him as an individual, by treating him in a dignified and respectful manner. A genuinely friendly attitude and atmosphere are a *conditio sine qua non.* The therapist must encourage adult (never regressive) pleasure procuring activities. An unreserved yet rational support is necessary to counteract the process of regression and downward adjustment.

2. The second rule is *ego-therapy*. The main aim of interactional psychotherapy is to strengthen the patient's ego. In neurosis the ego is struggling against undue pressures from within; the *ego-protective*, neurotic symptoms bear witness to the struggle. In psychosis the ego has lost the battle and psychotic, *ego-deficiency* symptoms develop, such as loss of reality testing (delusions and hallucinations), loss of control over unconscious impulses, deterioration of motor coordination, etc.

Ego-therapy means the strengthening and reestablishment of the defeated ego. Thus, the therapist must never become part of the irrational transactions of the psychotic mind, be they delusions, hallucinations, or anything else. He must never offer support to erroneous perceptions of reality, and he must not interpret unconscious motivation processes if this interpretation may weaken the patient's ego.

Control of instinctual impulses is one of the most severe issues in schizophrenia. A catatonic patient in remission described this inner struggle: "I want to be strong to be able to control myself and here I am again doing terrible things."

A gifted latent schizophrenic woman said once: "I can't do what I want to do. I feel like expressing my feelings with quick motions of the brush over the canvas, but something holds me back and I paint silly little houses that I detest. I would like to let myself go in non-objective art, but something tells me it must be a composition, a plan. Maybe I am afraid to let myself go, for I may do something wrong. So I sit for hours, as if paralyzed, afraid to move . . . "

Inability to make decisions and restraint of motor freedom are typical for the schizophrenic. This conflict between the desire to "let go" and the fear of one's own impulses may, in some cases, lead to catatonic mutism and stupor. One could not therefore encourage the young painter to follow her need for a free expression, for it would have inevitably led to a panic state and perhaps even to a catatonic episode. Nor would it be wise to encourage self-restraint that would produce an unbearable tension. Thus, the best method was to foster self-esteem; with her increasing self-confidence the painter was less afraid to express her feelings on canvas. She began to believe in herself, despite her past experiences.

3. *"One step up"* is the third rule. It implies support of less dangerous symptoms against more dangerous ones, never forgetting that the ultimate goal is to strengthen the patient's ego. When the patient seems to be giving up life, even simple pleasures should be used a a lure.

Schizophrenia is a regression for survival. The psychotherapeutic vectorial interaction makes it unnecessary to lose mind in order to survive. It calls the patient back to life, to growth, to joy, to normal self-protection and self-esteem.

4. The fourth rule is *pragmatic flexibility of interaction.* When the failing ego is unable to control outbursts of unconscious impulses, the patient's moralistic superego must be supported instead. In hebephrenia, the ego has lost the battle to the id; thus, it may be advisable to strengthen the super-ego in order to prevent further deterioration. The therapist may, therefore, take a stern and demanding attitude and support whatever moral or religious convictions the patient has. When the failing ego cannot control incestuous or homosexual or destructive

impulses, the therapist may decide that he must, so to speak, "take over" and check the flood. It is, however, a temporary device for the supremacy of the ego and not of the superego is the therapeutic objective.

5. The fifth rule is *individualization.* I have supervised psychotherapists for many years, and quite often a young therapist has asked me:

"And what would *you* have done in this case?" My answer is always the same: "Psychotherapy is an interaction and depends upon the two interacting individuals. There are rules, but each therapist applies them differently depending upon who is the *therapist* and who is the *patient.* Your job is to understand *your* patient. He is not the same, even if he seems to be, as any of the 'cases' described by the masters. In fact, he is not a 'case' at all. He is a definite individual, an unhappy and disturbed human being. Try to understand him, and at the same time try to understand yourself. Your patient is a withdrawn, or an irritable, or hallucinating, or a hostile individual. Can you take that? Can you face that much of an emotional demand? Please don't try to be what you are not. You cannot treat him the way Sullivan, or Fromm-Reichmann, or Schwing, or Rosen did. But if you understand your patient, and are aware of *your* limitations and resources, and are genuinely interested in the patient, the chances are that you will be a successful psychiatrist."

6. The sixth rule is *reality testing.* The problem of interpretation and insight cannot be answered by a flat "yes" or "no."

For example, a 30-year-old paranoid patient told me once that his beloved girlfriend, who lived 1000 miles away, had disguised herself and came to a restaurant as a waitress. He blamed himself for not chasing her; he felt she must be angry with him for he had deserted her. But in the evening she had returned to the restaurant; this time her hair was dyed so that he would not recognize her. The patient wanted to approach her, but she disappeared.

The patient said he expected me to "side with him" or he would be "through" with treatment. It was obvious that disagreement would have been perceived by the patient as rejection and would have caused further deterioration and possibly an outburst of violence. Yet an acceptance of the patient's delusion could have served no therapeutic purpose.

I started to test reality with the help of the patient. I asked him about his girlfriend. He told me that she had married two years before and was living in the south, about 1000 miles away from New York. His sister had written him that the young lady had recently had a baby. Gradually the patient himself began to doubt whether the two waitresses were one person. The patient remarked, "How could she work in a restaurant if she has a baby? But it was a striking similarity, wasn't it, doc?" At this point I felt that there was a good opportunity to strengthen his reality testing. I admitted that some people strikingly resemble others and all of us may err. My comment was welcome and the patient smiled with obvious relief. He said, "So, after all, I am not completely crazy. This girl looked exactly like my girlfriend. It was just a little mistake."

In the past the patient had had visual and auditory hallucinations. He was often ridiculed, ostracized, and insulted. His parents had never missed an opportunity to call him crazy or a lunatic. An overt disapproval of his delusions and hallucinations, and even efforts to undermine them by rational reasoning were doomed to failure. A too early interpretation might have caused, in this case, deeper regression and withdrawal.

A realistic attitude on the part of the therapist helps the patient to keep contact with reality. One patient I had, insisted on his "right" to call my home whenever he pleased, at any time of the day or night, whenever he felt upset. I told him that if he did that, I would discontinue my work with him. He accused me of being selfish and inconsiderate. I calmly replied that I needed rest and sleep; otherwise I would not be able to help anyone. If someone asks more than I can do, I must refuse.

7. The seventh rule is *parsimony of interpretation.* The question is not whether to interpret but *when, how,* and *how much.* I give priority to certain types of unconscious material, namely to those that threaten to disrupt the functioning of the ego. A profound guilt feeling is often the most urgent issue and must be interpreted. If such an interpretation alleviates guilt feelings and reduces suicidal tendencies, it is a sound therapeutic step.

I have, as a rule, avoided interpretations unless firmly convinced of their therapeutic usefulness at a given moment. In some cases the last phase of psychotherapy was conducted on more or less psychoanalytic lines, bringing deep insights through interpretation of unconscious phenomena. In most cases interpretations were given by the patients themselves.

8. The eighth rule is *realistic management of transference.* In his deep transference the schizophrenic expects love, forgiveness, and care from the therapist. Many schizophrenic patients wish to be fed, dressed, supported, and taken care of by the therapist, who represents the dream-parent. Some patients develop an infantile, symbiotic attachment and call the therapist at any time of day or night, just as a baby would call its mother. Most patients develop powerful hetero- or homosexual desires toward their therapists, reflecting incestuous involvement with their parents, and try to act on them here and now. To accept the patient on his terms means to share his psychosis, but to reject him may cause further aggravation and regression.

The maintaining of a *vectorial professional attitude* is a *conditio sine qua non* for a successful treatment. The eventual emotional maturity of the patient will make future protection and guidance superfluous. Psychotherapy is an interaction that aims at being terminated. Once a satisfactory level of cure is attained, the doctor-patient relationship must be dissolved.

A thorough cure is impossible without a resolution of the oedipal entanglements, but this must be postponed until the patient's ego has gained adequate strength. In some cases, this ideal solution may be unattainable, and it may be advisable not to analyze the incestuous impulses but rather to repress them. In many cases it may not be advisable to analyze transference at all. The strength of the patient's ego is the chief determinant of how far one may go in interpretation.

9. The ninth rule requires a firm *control of counter-transference.* Any transgression of the vectorial attitude on the part of the therapist is a violation of professional ethics. The therapist must like the patient, but this libido cathexis must be vectorial and aim-inhibited. The therapist's love for the patient must be de-sexualized, and he must never ask anything of the patient except the agreed-upon fee.

Any intimacy between doctor and patient is a severe violation of professional ethics and of the psychotherapeutic interaction. It may confuse the patient and bring back memories of inecestuous parents who, instead of caring for the child, demanded the child's love.

10. The tenth rule calls for *rational handling of hostility.* A patient's acting-out of hostile impulses may be catastrophic to his environment, as well as damaging to his weak ego. Thus, violence must be banned, repressed, and kept under iron control. When patients describe their fights, I do not condemn them, for this would increase their guilt feelings and weaken their egos. But permissiveness on my part would be even more harmful. Whenever the superego has lost control, permissiveness would mean an invitation to license, freedom to the id, and further deterioration of the ego.

The Concept of Cure

The therapist's ideas concerning cure may adversely affect his therapeutic judgment and his work. Ideally, one should bring one's patients to a state of balanced behavior as described in the first chapter of this handbook. Specifically, this implies adequate cognitive functioning, emotional balance, social adjustment, and achievements commensurate to one's abilities and environmental possibilities.

Such an ideal solution is rarely possible. No human being lives in a vacuum, and a "cured" schizophrenic has to cope with more hardships than a person who never was a schizophrenic. In cases of hospitalization, the return to open society may be traumatic; but even an ambulatory schizophrenic faces a social environment which may harbor prejudice against him and is quite often alienated by his former bizarre behavior. Moreover, the emotional scars may heal reasonably well, but they can rarely, if ever, completely disappear.

Over-ambitious therapists may expect the impossible. I have had an opportunity to see patients discharged from hospitals and/or from private practice who pretended to be more healthy than they really were, just in order not to disappoint their doctors. Some of them continued for a while to function in open society, until overwhelming anxieties caused a second or third psychotic breakdown. Relapses occur not only in post-shock cases but also after prolonged psychotherapeutic treatment, and certainly it is most frequent following chemotherapy.

My policy has been one of cautious empiricism according to the previously described principle of "one step up." When I deal with a catatonic schizophrenic or any other form of manifest schizophrenia, I am often satisfied if I can bring the patient to the state of a schizoid character neurosis. Quite often, any further work would be detrimental to the patient's health. An effort to reconstruct a poorly built house may end up in a total collapse, and on several occasions I have treated patients who were thrown into abysmal psychotic states by too-ambitious colleagues.

I once had a case of an hallucinating, suicidal, paranoid schizophrenic who intented to murder her boyfriend, her sister, and everyone else. It took a great deal of work to bring her to a state of schizoid character neurosis. In this state her hostility was channeled into bigotry (she is an ardent church-goer); she hates Protestants, Jews, and almost everyone else, but she holds a good job and gets along reasonably well in her home environment.

Whenever I discharge a post-schizophrenic patient, I use the following figure of speech. "Suppose you had a broken leg. We fixed it, and now you can walk around and do whatever you please. I would not advise, however, that you take part in the Olympics — in other words, avoid too much emotional challenge. On rainy and stormy days you may feel some pain; please call me and come in for a check-up. I believe you will never need a second surgery — that is, prolonged psychotherapy — but an occasional check-up is advisable. Even though things go well for you, please call me once in a while.

REFERENCES

Abraham, K. *Selected papers on psychoanalysis.* New York: Basic Books, 1955.

Alanen, Y.O. The mothers of schizophrenic patients. *Acta Psychiatrica et Neurologica Scandinavia.* **33**, Supp. 724, (1958).

Alexander, L. *Treatment of mental disorder.* Philadelphia: Saunders, 1953.

Altshuler, K.Z. Genetic elements in schizophrenia. *Eugenics Quarterly.* **4**: 92–98 (1957).

Aprison, M.H. and Drew, A.L. N, N-Dimethyl phenylenediamine oxidation by serum from schizophrenic children. *Science.* **127**: 57–58 (1958).

Arieti, S. *Interpretation of schizophrenia.* New York: Brunner, 1955.

Becket, P.G.S., Senf, R., Frohman, C.E. and Gottlieb, S. Energy production and premorbid history in schizophrenia. *Archives of General Psychiatry.* **8** (2): 155–162 (1963).

Bellak, L. and Loeb, L. *The schizophrenic syndrome.* New York: Grune & Stratton, 1969.

Bender, L. Schizophrenia in childhood: Its recognition, description, and treatment. *American Journal of Orthopsychiatry.* **26**: 499–506 (1956).

Bergman, P. and Escalona, S.K. Unusual sensitivities in very young children. *The Psychoanalytic Study of the Child.* 3-4: 333-352 (1949).

Bishop, M.P. Effects of plasma from schizophrenic subjects upon learning and retention in the rat. In: Heath, R.G. (Ed.), *Serological fractions in schizophrenia.* New York: Harper & Row, 1963.

Bleuler, E. *Das autistisch-undisziplinierte Denken in der Medizin und seine Uberwindung.* Berlin: Springer, 1919.

Bleuler, E. *Dementia praecox or the group of schizophrenias.* New York: International Universities Press, 1950.

Bleuler, M. *Endokrinologische Psychiatrie.* Stuttgart: Thieme, 1954.

Böök, J.A. Genetical aspects of schizophrenic psychoses. In: Jackson, D.D. (Ed.), *The etiology of schizophrenia.* New York: Basic Books, 1960.

Brackbill, G. and Fine, H. Schizophrenia and central nervous system pathology. *Journal of Abnormal and Social Psychology.* 52: 310-313 (1956).

Brambilla, F., *et al.* Endocrinology in chronic schizophrenia. *Diseases of the Nervous System.* 28 (11): 745-748 (1967).

Braun, M. and Parker, M. The use of Glucagon in the termination of therapeutic insulin coma. *American Journal of Psychiatry.* 115: 814-820 (1959).

Brody, E.B. and Redlich, F.C. (Eds.) *Psychotherapy with schizophrenics: A symposium.* New York: International Universities Press, 1952.

Buck, C.W., *et al.* Temperature regulation in schizophrenia. *American Medical Association Archives in Neurology and Psychiatry.* 64: 828-842 (1950).

Rychowski, G. *Psychotherapy of psychosis.* New York: Grune & Stratton, 1952.

Bykov, K. *The cerebral cortex and the inner organs.* New York: Chemical Publishing, 1957.

Chanoit, P., *et al.* L'utilisation de la thiopropérazine dans la schizophrenie. Encephale. 58 (2): 112-157 (1969).

Charcot, J.M. *Leçons sur les maladies sur le système nerveux,* 2 vols. Paris: 1887-1888.

Chase, L.S. and Silverman, S. Prognosis in schizophrenia. *Journal of Nervous and Mental Diseases.* 98: 464-473 (1943).

Clark, M.L., *et al.* Chlorpromazine in women with chronic schizophrenia: The effect on cholesterol levels and cholesterol on behavior. *Psychosomatic Medicine.* 29 (6): 634-642 (1967).

Davidson, J.N. *The biochemistry of the nucleic acids.* New York. Wiley, 1960.

Davis, D.R. The family triangle in schizophrenia. *British Journal of Medical Psychology.* 34: 53-63 (1965).

De Vito, R.A., *et al.* SKF16336 versus schizophrenia. *Diseases of the Nervous System.* 30: (6): 405-406 (1969).

Doust, J.W.I. Spectroscopic and photoelectric oximetry in schizophrenia and other psychiatric states. *Journal of Mental Science.* 98: 143-160 (1952).

Dunlop, E. Concomitant use of insulin therapy and pharmacology. In: Rinkel, M. (Ed.), *Biological treatment of mental illness,* pp. 800-807. New York: Farrar, Straus & Giroux, 1966.

Dussik, K.T., *et al.* Increased control of insulin coma by prior administration of Glucagon: A preliminary communication. *American Journal of Psychiatry.* 118: (July): 66-69 (1961).

Dussik, K.T., *et al.*   Serial Glucagon tests in schizophrenics. In: Rinkel, M. (Ed.), *Biological treatment of mental illness,* pp. 837–847. New York: Farrar, Strauss & Giroux, 1966.

Eisenberg, L.   The fathers of autistic children. *American Journal of Orthopsychiatry.* **27**: 715–724 (1957).

Eissler, K.R.   Dementia praecox therapy — psychiatric ward management of the acute schizophrenic patient. *Journal of Nervous and Mental Diseases.* **105**: 397–402 (1947).

Eissler, K.R.   Remarks on the psychoanalysis of schizophrenia. In: Brody, E.B. and Redlich, F.C. (Eds.), *Psychotherapy with schizophrenics.* New York: International Universities Press, 1952.

English, O.S., *et al.*   *Direct analysis and schizophrenia.* New York: Grune & Stratton, 1961.

Ezhkov, A.A.   The treatment of schizophrenia with Triperidol. *Zhurnal Neuropatologii i Psikhiatrii.* **68** (9): 1394–1400 (1968).

Federn, P.   *Ego psychology and the psychoses.* New York: Basic Books, 1952.

Felipa-Rejas, E., *et al.*   La cure d'insuline: Evaluation d'une technique psychotherapique. *Annales Medico-Psychologiques.* **2** (5):   647–663 (1968).

Ferenczi, S.   *Further contributions to the theory and technique of psychoanalysis.* London: Hogarth Press, 1926.

Fish, B.   Longitudinal observations of biological deviations in the schizophrenic infant. *American Journal of Psychiatry.* **116**: 25–31 (1959).

Fleck, S.   Family dynamics and origin of schizophrenia. *Psychosomatic Medicine.* **22**: 333–344 (1960).

Foudraine, J.   Schizophrenia and the family: A survey of the literature 1956-1960 on the etiology of schizophrenia. *Acta Psychotherapeutica et Psychosomatica.* **9**: 82–110 (1961).

Fourbye, A., *et al.*   Failure to detect 3, 4-dimethoxyphenylethylamine in the urine of psychotic children. *Acta Psychiatrica Scandinavia.* **42**, Supp. 191. (1966).

Freeman, H.   Physiological studies.   In: Bellak, L. (Ed.), *Schizophrenia: A review of the syndrome.* New York: Logos, 1958.

Freeman, P.   Treatment of chronic schizophrenia in a day center. *Archives of General Psychiatry.* **7**: 259–265 (1962).

Freud, S.   *An outline of psychoanalysis.* New York: Norton, 1949.

Fromm-Reichmann, F.   *Principles of intensive psychotherapy.*   Chicago: University of Chicago Press, 1950.

Fromm-Reichmann, F.   Some aspects of psychoanalytic psychotherapy with schizophrenics. In: Brody, E.B. and Redlich, F.C. (Eds.), *Psychotherapy with schizophrenics.* New York: International Universities Press, 1952.

Fromm-Reichmann, F.   *Psychoanalysis and psychotherapy.* Chicago: University of Chicago Press, 1959.

Gantt, W.H.   *Physiological basis of psychiatry.* Springfield, Illinois: Charles C. Thomas, 1958.

Garmezy, N.   Process and reactive schizophrenia: Some conceptions and issues. In: Katz, M.M. *et al.* (Eds.), *Classifications in psychiatry and psychopathology.* Washington, D.C.: U.S. Government Printing Office, 1965.

Garmezy, N., and Rodnick, E.H. Premorbid adjustment and performance in schizophrenia. *Journal of Nervous and Mental Diseases.* **129**: 450–466 (1959).

Garrone, G. Statistical genetic study of schizophrenia in the Geneva population between 1901–1950. *Journal of Genetic Psychology.* 89–219 (1962).

German, G.A. Effects of serum from schizophrenics on evoked cortical potential in the rat. *British Journal of Psychiatry.* **109**: 616–623 (1963).

Goldberg, S.C., *et al.* A clinical evaluation of prolixin enanthate. *Psychosomatics.* **11** (3): 173–177 (1970).

Goldfarb, W. *Childhood schizophrenia.* Cambridge, Mass.: Harvard University Press, 1961.

Goncalves, N. Clinical effects of mepiprazol on hospitalized chronic schizophrenics. *Psychopharmacologia.* **25** (3): 281–290 (1972).

Greenblatt, M. (Ed.) *Drug and social therapy in chronic schizophrenia.* Springfield, Illinois: Charles C. Thomas, 1965.

Gregory, I. Genetic factors in schizophrenia. *American Journal of Psychiatry.* **116**: 961–972 (1960).

Havenson, I. Corphenazine in the intensive care of chronically ill psychotics. *International Journal of Neuropsychiatry.* **3** (4): 332–336 (1967).

Heath, R.G. and Krupp, I.M. Schizophrenia as a specific biologic disease. *American Journal of Psychiatry.* **124**: 1019–1027 (1968).

Hendrickson, W.J. Etiology in childhood schizophrenia: An evaluation of current views. *Nervous Child.* **10**: 9–18 (1952).

Herron, W.G. The process-reactive classification of schizophrenia. *Psychological Bulletin.* **59**: 329 (1962).

Hill, L.B. *Psychotherapeutic intervention in schizophrenia.* Chicago: University Chicago Press, 1955.

Hoagland, H. Metabolic and physiologic disturbances in the psychoses. In: Cobb, S.S. (Ed.), *The biology of mental health and disease.* New York: Hoeber, 1952.

Hoch, P.H. and Polatin, P. Pseudoneurotic forms of schizophrenia. *Psychiatric Quarterly.* **23**: 248 (1949).

Holden, I., *et al.* The effects of metronidazole on schizophrenic psychopathology. *Journal of Clinical Pharmacology and Journal of New Drugs.* **8** (5): 333–341 (1968).

Hyden, H. Satellite cells in the nervous system. *Scientific American.* **205** (6): 62–70 (1961).

Itil, T., *et al.* Effects of fluphenazine hydrochloride on digital computer sleep prints of schizophrenic patients. *Diseases of the Nervous System.* **32** (11): 751–758 (1971).

Ivanov-Smolensky, A.G. *Essays on the patho-physiology of higher nervous activity.* Moscow: Foreign Language Publishers, 1954.

Jackson, D.D. (Ed.) *The etiology of schizophrenia.* New York: Basic Books, 1960.

Kallmann, F.J. Genetic theory of schizophrenia: Analysis of 691 twin index families. *American Journal of Psychiatry.* **103**: 309–322 (1946).

Kallmann, F.J. Genetics in relation to mental disorders. *Journal of Mental Science.* **94**: 250 (1948).

Kallmann, F.J. *Heredity in health and mental disorders.* New York: Norton, 1953.

Kallmann, F.J. (Ed.) *Expanding goals of genetics in psychiatry.* New York: Grune & Stratton, 1962.

Kant, O. Clinical investigation of simple schizophrenia. *Psychiatric Quarterly.* **22**: 141 (1948).

Kantor, R., *et al.* Process and reactive schizophrenia. *Journal of Consulting Psychology.* **17**: 157–162 (1953).

Kety, S.S. Recent biochemical theories of schizophrenia. In: Jackson, D.D. (Ed.), *The etiology of schizophrenia.* New York: Basic Books, 1960.

Kety, S.S., *et al.* Cerebral blood flow and metabolism in schizophrenia: Effects of barbiturate seminarcosis, insulin coma. *American Journal of Psychiatry.* **104**: 765–770 (1948).

King, H.E. *Psychomotor aspects of mental disease.* Cambridge, Massachusetts: Harvard University Press, 1954.

Kline, N.S. Non-chemical factors and chemical theories of mental disease. In: Rinkel, M. and Denber, H.C.B. (Eds.), *Chemical concepts of psychosis.* New York: McDowell, 1958.

Knight, R.P. Psychotherapy of an adolescent catatonic schizophrenic with mutism. *Psychiatry.* **9**: 323 (1946).

Knight, R.P. Management and psychotherapy of the borderline schizophrenic patient. *Bulletin of the Menninger Clinic.* **17**: 139 (1953).

Lidz, T. *The family and human adaptation.* New York: International Universities Press, 1963.

Lidz, T. *The origin and treatment of schizophrenic disorders.* New York: Basic Books, 1973.

Lidz, T., *et al.* The intrafamilial environment of schizophrenic patients: II. Marital schism and marital skew. *American Journal of Psychiatry.* **114**: 241–248 (1957).

Lidz, T., *et al.* The intrafamilial environment of the schizophrenic patient: IV. Parental personalities and family interaction. *American Journal of Orthopsychiatry.* **28**: 764–776 (1958).

Lidz, T. and Fleck, S. Schizophrenia, human interaction and the role of the family. In: Jackson, D.D. (Ed.), *The etiology of schizophrenia.* New York: Basic Books, 1960.

Lowther, J. The effect of fluphenazine enanthate on chronic and relapsing schizophrenia. *British Journal of Psychiatry.* **115** (523): 691–692 (1969).

Lu, Y.C. Mother-child role relations in schizophrenia. *Psychiatry.* **24**: 133–142 (1961).

Lu, Y.C. Contradictory parental expectations in schizophrenia. *Archives of General Psychiatry.* **6**: 219–234 (1962).

Lucky, W.T. and Schiele, B. A comparison of haloperidol and trifluoperazine in a double blind controlled study on chronic schizophrenic patients. *Diseases of the Nervous System.* **28** (3): 181–186 (1967).

Luyssaert, W. and Pierloot, R. Insulinotherapie et schizophrenie. *Acta Neurologica et Psychiatrica Belgica.* **69** (5): 315–335 (1969).

Lynn, R. Russian theory and research in schizophrenia. *Psychological Bulletin.* **60**: 486–498 (1963).

Malis, G.A. *Research on the etiology of schizophrenia.* New York: Consultants Bureau, 1961.

Markowe, M., *et al.* Insulin and chlorpromazine in schizophrenia: A ten year comparative survey. *British Journal of Psychiatry.* 113 (503): 1101–1106 (1967).

National Institute of Mental Health Psychopharmacology Research Branch. Differences in the clinical effects of three phenothiazines in "acute" schizophrenia. *Diseases of the Nervous System.* 28 (6): 369–383 (1967).

National Institute of Mental Health. High dose chlorpromazine therapy in schizophrenia: Report of the National Institute of Mental Health Psychopharmacology Research Branch Collaborative Study Group. *Archives of General Psychiatry.* 18 (4): 482–495 (1968).

National Institute of Mental Health. *Mental health statistics.* Washington, D.C.: U.S. Government Printing Office, 1971.

Offord, D.R. and Cross, L.A. Behavior antecedents of schizophrenia: A review. *Archives of General Psychiatry.* 21: 267–283 (1969).

Phillips, L. Case history data and progress in schizophrenia. *Journal of Nervous and Mental Diseases.* 117: 515-535 (1953).

Pichon-Riviere, de E. Quelques observations sur le transfere de patients psychotiques. *Review Française de Psychanalyse.* 16: 254–262 (1952).

Polak, P. and Laycob, L. Rapid tranquilization. *American Journal of Psychiatry.* 128 (5): 640–643 (1972).

Prien, R.F., *et al.* Discontinuation of chemotherapy for chronic schizophrenics. *Hospital and Community Psychiatry.* 22 (1): 4–7 (1971).

Ramirez, E., *et al.* Glucagon in terminating insulin coma: Clinical and biochemical aspects. In: Rinkel, M. (Ed.), *Biological treatment of mental illness,* pp. 694–714. New York: Farrar, Straus & Giroux, 1966.

Reiss, M. Correlations between changes in mental states and thyroid activity after different forms of treatment. *Journal of Mental Science.* 100: 687–703 (1954).

Remy, M. Lasting value of insulin shock treatment. In: Rinkel, M. (Ed.), *Biological treatment of mental illness,* pp. 793–799. New York: Farrar, Straus & Giroux, 1966.

Richter, D. (Ed.) *Schizophrenia: Somatic aspects.* New York: Macmillan, 1957.

Rosen, J.N. The treatment of schizophrenic psychosis by direct analytic therapy. *Psychiatric Quarterly.* 21: 117–119 (1947).

Rosen, J.N. *Direct analysis.* New York: Grune & Stratton, 1953.

Rosenfeld, H. Considerations regarding the psychoanalytic approach to acute and chronic schizophrenia. *International Journal of Psychoanalysis.* 35: 153 (1953).

Rosenthal, D. Confusion of identity and the frequency of schizophrenia in twins. *Archives of General Psychiatry.* 3: 297–304 (1960).

Rosenthal, D. *Genetic theory and abnormal behavior.* New York: McGraw-Hill, 1970.

Roth, M. Interaction of genetic and environmental factors in the causation of schizophrenia. In: Richter, D. (Ed.), *Schizophrenia: Somatic aspects.* New York: Macmillan, 1957.

Schiele, B.C., et al. A double-bind comparison of trifluperidol and trifluoperazine in acute schizophrenic patients. *Comprehensive Psychiatry.* **10** (5): 355–360 (1969).

Schwing, G. *A way to the soul of the mentally ill.* New York: International Universities Press, 1954.

Shattock, M.F. The somatic manifestations of schizophrenia: A clinical study of their significance. *Journal of Mental Science.* **96**: 32 (1950).

Slater, E. Psychotic and neurotic illnesses in twins. In: Medical Research Council, *Special report no. 278.* London: H.M. Stationery Office, 1953.

Slater, E. The monogenic theory of schizophrenia. *Acta Genetica.* **8**: 50–56 (1958).

Smith, K., et al. ECT and chlorpromazine compared in the treatment of schizophrenia. *Journal of Nervous and Mental Diseases.* **144** (4): 284–290 (1967).

Sterlin, C., et al. The place of thiothixene in treatment of schizophrenic patients. *Canadian Psychiatric Association Journal.* **15** (1): 3–14 (1970).

Stupenchenko, M.V. Clinico-statistical analysis of the results of treating with psychotropic agents schizophrenics whose psychosis follows a continuous progradient course. *Zhurnal Neuropatologii i Psikhiatrii.* **69** (3): 428–431 (1969).

Sullivan, H.S. *Conceptions of modern psychiatry.* Washington, D.C.: W.A. White, 1947.

Sullivan, H.S. *The interpersonal theory of psychiatry.* New York: Norton, 1953.

Sullivan, H.S. *Schizophrenia as a human process.* New York: Norton, 1962.

Towler, M.L. and Wick, P.H. Treatment of acute exacerbations in chronic schizophrenic patients. *International Journal of Neuropsychiatry.* **3**: 61–67 (1967).

Vaernet, K. and Madsen, A. Stereotaxic amygdalotomy and basofrontal tractotomy in psychotics with aggressive behavior. *Journal of Neurology, Neurosurgery and Psychiatry.* **33** (6): 858–863 (1970).

Vorster, D. An investigation into the part played by organic factors in childhood schizophrenia. *Journal of Mental Science.* **106**: 494–522 (1960).

Walaszek, E.J. Brain neurohormones and cortical epinephrine pressor responses as affected by schizophrenic serum. *International Review of Neurobiology.* **2**: 137 (1960).

Weakland, J.H. The double-bind hypothesis of schizophrenia and three party interaction. In: Jackson, D.D. (Ed.), *The etiology of schizophrenia.* New York: Basic Books, 1960.

Weinstein, M. and Fischer, A. Combined treatment with ECT and antipsychotic drugs in schizophrenia. *Diseases of the Nervous System.* **32** (12): 801–808 (1971).

Winnicot, D.W. Regression et repli. *Revue Française de Psychanalyse.* **19**: 323–330 (1955).

Wolman, B.B. Explorations in latent schizophrenia. *American Journal of Psychotherapy.* **11**: 560–588 (1957).

Wolman, B.B. The deterioration of the ego in schizophrenia. Paper presented at Eastern Psychological Association, 1958.

Wolman, B.B. Psychotherapy with latent schizophrenics. *American Journal of Psychotherapy.* **13**: 343–359 (1959a).

Wolman, B.B. Continuum hypothesis in neurosis and psychosis and the classification of the mental disorder.   Paper presented at Eastern Psychological Association, 1959b.

Wolman, B.B. The fathers of schizophrenic patients. *Acta Psychotherapeutica et Psychosomatica.* **9**: 193–210 (1961).

Wolman, B.B. Research in etiology of schizophrenia. Paper presented at Eastern Psychological Association, 1962.

Wolman, B.B. Non-participant observation on a closed ward. *Acta Psychotherapeutica et Psychosomatica.* **12**: 61–71 (1964).

Wolman, B.B. Family dynamics and schizophrenia. *Journal of Health and Human Behavior,* 1965.

Wolman, B.B. *Vectoriasis praecox or the group of schizophrenias.* Springfield, Illinois: Charles C. Thomas, 1966.

Wolman, B.B. The socio-psycho-somatic theory of schizophrenia. *Psychotherapy and Psychosomatics.* **15**: 373–387 (1967).

Wolman, B.B. *Children without childhood.* New York: Grune & Stratton, 1970.

Wolman, B.B. *Call no man normal.* New York: International Universities Press, 1973.

Woolley, D.W.   Serotonin in mental disorders. *Research Publications of the Association for Nervous and Mental Disease.* **36**: 381–400 (1958).

17 The Treatment of Depression

Stephen DeBerry and Itamar Salamon

> *for this particular disease, him that shall take upon him to cure it . . . will have to be a magician, a chemist, a philosopher, an astrologer.*
> *(Robert Burton, The anatomy of melancholia, 1621)*

As a mood, depression is ubiquitous. Nearly every person, at least once in his lifetime, will experience feelings of depression. Historically, every major thinker has commented on this most normal of human experiences. Plato and Hippocrates referred to depression as a disturbance of body juices; the term melancholia most likely originated in their postulation of a preponderance of black bile in those afflicted with the illness (Zilboorg and Henry, 1941). Yet, in terms of clinical treatment, depression is more than a mood; it is a symptom, a syndrome and an existential reality. It is incumbent, therefore, that the clinician not only distinguish depression from "normal" sadness, but likewise make a thorough differential diagnosis within the depressive spectrum itself (Klerman, 1980).

In an evolutionary sense, depression has been thought to have adaptational value, in that depressive behavior may serve as a signal designed to elicit nurturing from the environment (Bowlby, 1969; Harlow, 1959). In certain situations such as mourning or bereavement, depression can be an effective behavioral response (Salzman, 1975). The key element in distinguishing normal depression, grief, discouragement, sadness and disappointment from clinical depression is the extended period in which clinical depression is manifested, as well as the exaggerated nature of the symptoms.

The variety of ways in which depressive symptoms appear, differ according to environment and culture. According to Kiev (1977), depression presents itself in markedly different forms in various areas of the non-Western world. In parts of Africa, the element of guilt, a most prominent symptom in Western society, is singularly lacking (Escobar and Tuason, 1980). In place of guilt, overt symptoms tend to manifest themselves through the projection and externalization of feelings. In Western societies, it seems that internalization (i.e., a repression of angry feelings) is more likely to occur so that the core symptoms of depression center around guilt, mental anguish, suicide, irritability and agitation. The clinician should be aware of the mode of expression available within the culture or subculture being examined. In order to be clinically depressed, one does not necessarily have to say he feels depressed. In fact, more often than not affective disorders initially present with other problems (e.g., sleep difficulties, lack of concentration or somatic complaints).

Depression is best described as a mood disturbance of prolonged duration and intensity. As a mood disturbance depression is subsumed under the more general category of affective disorders, unipolar and bipolar. Therefore, we must bear in mind that depression's sister, mania, must likewise be considered. Patients with affective disorders are considered unipolar if they manifest depressions only, and bipolar if they experience depressions with hypomania or mania. Manic and depressive disturbances have clinically been linked together as far back as the time of the Greek writer Aretaeus (A.D. 150–200), who suggested that melancholia may be followed by mania. Recent discoveries in the biochemistry of brain neurotransmitters, as well as advances in clinical, familial and pharmacological studies, have somewhat established the validity of the unipolar and bipolar continuum (Klerman and Barrett, 1975; Klerman, 1980; Winokur, Clayton and Reich, 1969).

In order to initiate treatment, the clinician must first identify the entity being treated. An understanding of the nosology and classification of depressive disorders is obviously necessary. This chapter will focus on the classification of depressive disorders as outlined in the third edition of the *American Psychiatric Association's diagnostic and statistical manual of mental disorders – DSM III (1980)*. Because of the extensive literature concerning depression, the emphasis of this chapter will be on diagnosis and treatment. Readers interested in a more involved description of etiology and dynamics should consult *The comprehensive textbook of psychiatry* (Kaplan, Freedman, and Sadock, 1980), *Personality development and psychopathology* (Cameron, 1963), *Handbook of studies on depression* (Burrows, 1977) and a review article by Akisal and McKinney (1975).

Affective syndromes represent a range of phenomena that have been difficult to classify accurately. This, in fact, is a testimony to the complexity of the phenomena as well as a reflection of a long-standing nosological dilemma (Kendel, 1977). Although the descriptive approach of the DSM III is a step in the right direction, confusion still exists for those weaned on earlier analytic writings and DSM II classifications. Blinder (1969) summarized the situation as follows:

Perhaps the greatest problem is that the phenomena lumped together under the term depression are a mixed bag containing some essentially physiological disturbances, and some unconscious, habitual patterns of behavior that may bring the patient repeatedly to grief. Any schema of classification attempting to assimilate such an odd assortment is apt to be unsatisfactory as a guide to either diagnosis or treatment. (p. 9)

Historically, confusion over the nature and treatment of depression began with Freud (1917) and his study of mourning and melancholia. As Mendelson (1975) points out, many therapists have tended to apply Freud's formulations on melancholia to all depressions, while failing to realize that Freud was unknowingly discussing what we now know to be a major depressive episode with psychotic features.

Subsequently, confusion arose over the endogenous and nonendogenous criteria, the former being associated with autonomous and psychotic illness, while the latter was associated with reactive, psychogenic, exogenous and neurotic illness. Hence, the distinction between endogenous and neurotic (exogenous) depressions. Endogenous depressions were then thought to be lacking an external precipitant. The terms psychotic and endogenomorphic depression were also used to refer to this entity (Nelson and Charney, 1981). Symptomatically, endogenous depressions were characterized by classic vegetative (i.e., autonomic) signs such as psychomotor retardation/agitation, anxiety, loss of appetite, dryness of mouth, constipation and sleep disturbance. Exogenous depressions were characterized by the absence of vegetative signs, the presence of a precipitating event coupled with a tendency to blame the environment, and a family history of psychiatric illness. It is now understood that etiology, especially as applies to external precipitants, has little to do with the presence of classical endogenous symptoms. Research indicates that a significant proportion of depressed patients with endogenous symptoms report definite external precipitants, and that the endogenous/exogenous dichotomy represents a continuum rather than a clear-cut distinction (Katz and Hirschfeld 1978; Kendell, 1968).

Diagnostic confusion was further compounded by differences between American and European nomenclature as well as the development of various subsystems. These lesser-known schematas were designed to provide research diagnostic criteria (RDC) for analyzing the affective disorders, and for that reason should be applauded. Among these research-oriented subsystems are Paykel's typology (Paykel, 1971), the St. Louis system (Robins and Guze, 1972), Klein's system (Klein, 1974) and the Schildkrout (1973) system. The DSM III is a product of these early attempts to classify affective and other mental disorders in terms of reliable and valid research diagnostic criteria.

One important subsystem for categorizing affective disorders, not used in the DSM III, is the primary/secondary dichotomy (Feighner, Robins and Guze 1972).

Primary affective disorders are seen in patients who have a good premorbid history, or whose only previous episodes of psychiatric disease were mania or depression. Secondary affective disorders occur in patients manifesting other psychiatric problems (e.g., schizophrenia), organic syndromes or systemic medical diseases. Distinguishing primary from secondary affective disorders is obviously crucial in determining a treatment plan. The focus of this chapter will be on primary affective illness not secondary to other psychiatric or medical problems.

The DSM III attempts to clarify the nosological dilemma without sacrificing the psychobiological tradition of American psychiatry. The essential feature of affective disorders in the DSM III is, as stated, a mood disturbance of either prolonged depression or elation, or both. The major divisions are as follows:

Major Depressive Disorders

Bipolar disorder: mixed
                    manic
                    depressed

Major depression: single episode
                    recurrent

Other Specific Affective Disorders

Cyclothymic disorder
Dysthymic disorder (depressive neurosis)

Atypical Affective Disorder

Atypical bipolar disorder
Atypical depression

If a depressive reaction is clearly identified as a specific response to an identifiable psychosocial stressor, and if it is assumed that the disturbance will eventually remit or change when the stressor ends or is altered, then a diagnosis of adjustment disorder with depressed mood may be considered.

The DSM III employs a multi-axial diagnostic coding system that allows the clinician to evaluate several related, yet distinct phenomena simultaneously. The advantage of the multi-axial evaluation in the DSM III is that it lends itself most suitably to holistic diagnoses. Affective disorders are an example par excellence of the interplay of genetic, psychodynamic, biological and environmental factors (Gordon, 1981). Thus, Axis II — personality disorders, Axis III — physical disorders and conditions, Axis IV — severity of psychosocial stressors and Axis V — highest level of adaptive functioning in the past year, are of invaluable assistance to the clinician in designing an accurate diagnosis, a realistic prognosis and an effective treatment plan.

The DSM III likewise allows for fifth-digit coding so that, for example, a major depressive episode with depressive features (296.50) can be coded as follows: 6 = in remission; 4 = with psychotic features (the ICD 9-CM fifth-digit number 7 may be used in place of the number 4 if the psychotic features are mood-incongruent); 3 = with melancholia; 2 = without melancholia; and 0 = unspecified.   Fifth-digit coding in combination with a multi-axial evaluation provides the clinician with a most thorough diagnostic profile.

CLINICAL SIGNS OF THE AFFECTIVE DISORDERS

Bipolar Disorders: Manic Symptoms

The bipolar disorders may present with elation, depression or a combination of both. The essential features of mania are distinct periods in which the person's mood is elevated, expansive, labile and at times irritated. Hyperactivity is often present and is usually accompanied by a decreased need for sleep. Speech is usually pressured, and the patient may manifest a flight of ideas. Self-esteem is inflated, yet may easily be punctured, leading to disappointment and irritability. Excessive involvement with people and activities is characteristic, but the attention span may be short and distractability high. When characteristic symptoms are less severe, the syndrome is described as hypomania. Criteria for this diagnosis have been summarized by Feighner, Robins and Guze (1972) and are described in the DMS III as:

1. A change in mood, i.e., elation or irritability, which may alternate or intermingle with depression, lasting at least one to two weeks. In addition, at least three (four if mood is only irritable) of the following must be present.
   a. increase in activity or physical restlessness
   b. increase in speech which may be pressured
   c. flight of ideas or feelings that thoughts are coming too fast
   d. grandiosity
   e. decreased need for sleep
   f. distractability
   g. excessive involvement in activities that may be foolish or have painful consequences, e.g., promiscuity, recklessness, spending sprees

Major Depressive Episode: Depressive Symptoms

Essentially this entity is characterized by dysphoria (unpleasant mood) and a loss of interest in usually pleasurable activities. A decreased energy level is invariably present, along with a concomitant loss of self-esteem. Feelings of exaggerated worthlessness are common, as well as feelings of guilt over past or current events. The sense of worthlessness, self-blame, pity, hopelessness and helplessness may reach delusional proportions.   Difficulties in attention and concentration are usually present.   Suicide is always a threat, and care must be taken to evaluate its potential carefully.   It is estimated that about 15% of persons suffering from a major depressive episode commit suicide, and that at least 50% of all successful suicides are the end result of a major depression (Guze and Robins, 1970; Silverman, 1968).

In Western societies guilt is a prominent symptom.   Patients may constantly criticize themselves for not functioning up to previous capacity.   Depressive emotions may be recognized from a tense or sad facial expression, crying or sobbing.   The person may manifest agitated signs such as pacing, restlessness or tension, or retarded signs such as reduced motility, diminished activity and low or slowed speech.   Delusions, if present, are usually of a hypocondriacal or nihilistic and self-depreciatory nature.   The elderly frequently present with somatic complaints that may mask an underlying depression (Birren, 1964). In children or adolescents there may be marked apathy, withdrawal from activity and academic or behavioral problems.   A major depressive episode may begin at any age and manifest a variable course.   Episodic variation is common, with some patients showing long periods of normal functioning between symptomatic periods, while others manifest short clusterlike periods of cyclic variation.

In most major depressive illnesses there is some improvement toward evening (Wolpert, 1979).   A variety of autonomic features are usually present.   These so-called vegetative signs are summarized by Mendels and Cochrane (1968) as follows:

a. psychomotor retardation or agitation
b. distinct quality of dysphoria
c. lack of reactivity to environment
d. loss of interest in usual activities
e. decreased sex drive
f. poor appetite
g. weight loss
h. early morning awakening

Diagnostic laboratory tests are becoming useful confirmatory techniques for identifying depressed patients with vegetative signs.   The dexamethasone suppression test (Carroll, Curtis and Mendels, 1976; Nuller and Ostroumova, 1980) is a fairly reliable biologic marker for distinguishing subgroups of unipolar major depressive episodes with endogenous features.   The release of 11-hydroxycorticosteroids in normal subjects is suppressed for a period of time following the administration of dexamethasone.   Patients with endogenous symptoms of unipolar depression, however, fail to manifest this suppression phenomenon. While a dexamethasone suppression test may identify only 50% of patients manifesting unipolar endogenous type depressions, false positive findings are exceedingly rare.   Therefore, a positive outcome (i.e., lack of 11-hydroxycorticosteroid suppression following dexamethasone administration) is a reliable diagnostic indicator (Gold, Pottash, Extein and Sweeney, 1981).

Dysthymic Disorders

The term dysthymic disorder is now employed in place of depressive neurosis as a means of avoiding the etiological pitfalls inherent in the term "neurosis." In part, dysthymia represents a lesser version of a major depressive episode. Although similar clinical features are present, there are no psychotic manifestations. Vegetative signs are less common, as are signs of clear-cut diurnal variation. For a diagnosis of dysthymic disorder a depressed mood, either persistent or inter-mittent, must be present for at least two years. Impairment of functioning is of a lesser degree than in a major depression, and there is a lack of vegetative signs, although some disturbance in sleep and appetite may be present. Mood, energy and self-esteem are low, but not as low as in a major depression where the poten-tial for psychosis is much greater. Dysthymic disorders usually begin early in adult life, have no clear onset and maintain a chronic course. In the authors' opinion a majority of outpatient psychotherapy cases present with some sympto-matic variation of dysthymia. The patient will typically complain of low energy, lack of interest, decreased academic or professional productivity and social with-drawal. Obsessive brooding, pessimism and a tendency to interpret events in a negative manner are common presenting complaints. If asked about the onset of these problems, the patient's response indicates that the complaints have been long-standing. Common responses are: "I've always been this way"; or, "no one has ever liked me; I've never had any enjoyment; I'm always suffering." A distinct quality of anhedonia is usually present, and the clinician may notice tendencies of a martyrlike or self-pitying nature. Despite the chronicity and potentially disabling consequences of dysthymic symptoms, patients are usually able to lead fairly "normal" lives. That is, ego functions remain intact, though obviously limited. As Cameron (1963) points out:

> Neurotic depressions (dysthymia) are not merely mild forms of psychotic depression; they involve a qualitative difference in object relationships. The regression in neurotic depressive patients is to deep oral dependent levels but it is only a partial regression. Object relations remain fairly in-tact; the defensive organization is well preserved and genuine communi-cation can be maintained with other persons at more or less realistic levels. (p. 441)

This is a key point in terms of determining a treatment plan and prognosis, for, as we shall see, dysthymia is amenable to psychotherapy whereas major de-pressions are less responsive to nonpharmacological interventions.

It must be emphasized that both unipolar and bipolar major affective disorders represent severe psychiatric problems. The potential for psychotic regression and suicidal behavior is always a threat. The differential between major affective disorders and milder forms of dysthymia or hypomania is obviously crucial in determining a treatment plan. The clinician is more likely to consider the use of hospitalization, antidepressant medication and/or electroconvulsive therapy when treating a major affective disorder. Furthermore, care must be taken to differentiate affective disorders from schizophrenic disorders and organic mental disorders. It is always possible that affective symptoms may be superimposed on schizophrenic or organic pathology, thus masking the underlying disease process. For a more thorough exposition the reader is referred to the chapters on schizophrenia and geriatrics.

Cyclothymic Disorders

The essential feature of cyclothymia is a chronic mood disturbance of at least two years, but not of sufficient duration or intensity to warrant a diagnosis of bipolar disorder. Like dysthymia, the disorder usually begins without a clear on-set, and it likewise maintains a chronic course. The patient typically will present with complaints of experiencing "highs and lows." Depressive and hypomanic periods may be separated by periods of normal mood, or may alternate con-currently. The unpredictable nature of these mood swings is a source of dis-tress, for the patient will often report no apparent external precipitant. Hypo-manic periods are often reported as pleasurable periods during which the patient may experience increased energy, euthymia and a heightened sense of well-being. While enjoyable, the hypomanic stage is usually followed by a downward mood swing, anhedonia, low self-esteem and decreased energy levels. According to Akiskal (1981), depressive and hypomanic periods are of roughly equal frequency, with the most common subtype consisting of depressed cyclothymics.

The remaining categories, atypical bipolar disorder and atypical depression, are simply variations on the same theme, having features not easily classified. In atypical depressions, the patient may present with depression for the first time or, as is often the case, present a history of cyclic variation. Symptoms usually do not follow typical patterns. It should always be remembered that major depressions and manic episodes as well are usually time-limited and episodic. If the depression is chronic and noncyclic, characterological factors should be explored. Certain personality disorders such as masochistic characters or schizoid personalities may present with depressive symptoms; usually, how-ever, they are not very severe and are notably lacking in autonomic involvement (Cameron, 1963; Freedman, Kaplan and Sadock, 1980). The differential in these patients is more likely to involve dysthymic, cyclothymic and Axis II (personality disorder) differentiation. A careful history is mandatory, as some patients may not be aware of their own cyclic variation.

Atypical affective disorders as well as dysthymia and cyclothymia are usually intricately intermeshed with personality structure. Recent research suggests a strong link between borderline personality disorders and affective and subaffective (i.e., atypical, dysthymic or cyclothymic) disorders. In a study examining 100 consecutive patients diagnosed as borderline personalities according to DSM III criteria, nearly 50% (N = 45) also had concurrent diagnosis of affective disorder, 39 of whom were diagnosed as having atypical or subaffective disorders (Akiskal, 1981).

TREATMENT OF AFFECTIVE DISORDERS

Ideally, the optimal treatment for depression, or, for that matter, any mental illness, would be its prevention. It would be most helful if tendencies toward developing affective illness could be identified before a full-blown clinical picture developed. Such an approach, termed primary prevention, involves identifying predisposing factors in high-risk populations (e.g., children of parents diagnosed as being clinically depressed). However, screening of subpopulations is difficult, poses many problems and is not yet a reliable indicator of who will become clinically depressed (Meyers and Weissman, 1980). Most intervention is still of a secondary and tertiary nature (i.e., diagnosis and treatment). While programs of primary prevention are still in the beginning stages, the clinician can still improve on secondary and tertiary skills.

The psychiatric treatment of depression and mania has made rapid advances. Yet, in a sense, Burton's admonishment, which begins this chapter, still stands. The clinician, whether practicing psychotherapy alone or in combination with medication, will most likely find his clinical skills sorely put to test by the depressed patient. Major depressive disorders with psychotic features often manifest severely regressed behavior with suicidal potential. The patient's pathology may reveal itself through deep and insatiable oral needs. Clinging, dependency and primitive behaviors designed to elicit nurturance and sympathy are common. The more neurotic depressive (dysthymic) may cleverly manipulate the clinician into satisfying certain nontherapeutic demands, possibly eliciting countertransference feelings of guilt, impotence and frustration. The depressed patient's repressed anger and hostility may effect the clinician in such a way that he unconsciously hurts or rejects the patient. The pervasive sense of hopelessness and futility found in depressed patients may likewise produce similar feelings of despair in the clinician. Patients with bipolar illness in a manic phase may act out so extensively as to put their life in danger as well as jeopardize the most careful treatment plan. Countertransference and transference problems abound in this most fertile of pathological entities.

The development of antidepressant medications such as the tricyclics, the MAO inhibitors and the more recent tetracyclics, while of tremendous clinical importance, has proved to be no panacea. For one, many of the affective substypes, especially the dysthymics (Gonzalez, 1980; Klerman, 1980; Luborsky, Singer and Luborsky, 1975; Rush, Beck, Kovacs and Hollon, 1977). Monoamine oxidase (MAO) inhibitors, while indicated in atypical unipolar, bipolar or mixed disorders, are often not tolerated well, have potentially dangerous side-effects and interact negatively with other drugs or food stuffs (Marks and Pare, 1965; West and Dally, 1959). More important is the consideration that one of the primary goals in treating affective illness is the prevention of relapse. Quitken, Rifken and Klein (1976) reviewed trials involving 400 to 500 unipolar depressed patients and reported that maintenance therapy with tricyclics reduced the relapse rate by approximately 20 to 50%. While pharmacotherapy is a step in the right direction, it remains clear that more than medication might be indicated. Furthermore, many patients may receive antidepressants unnecessarily, the problem being that it is not yet possible to predict who will benefit from continued medication (Paykel, DiMascio, Haskell and Prusoff, 1975). The clinician, then, in addition to being aware of medication issues, must likewise sharpen his therapeutic skills.

One additional caveat before proceeding into treatment. Quite recently, clinical psychiatry has made tremendous advances, largely as a result of rapid progress in biological research. Discoveries in the chemistry and action of the biogenic amines (the catecholamines; norepenephine, dopamine, indoleamine and serotonin) have increased our understanding of the biological mechanisms underlying depressive disorders. Some clinicians would go as far as to say that depression is a biological disorder mandating a biological cure. Yet, as others point out, such a viewpoint is not only reductionistic, but simplistic (Depue, 1970; Isenberg and Schatzberg, 1976).

Psychiatric treatment takes place within the context of a relationship. One need not practice psychoanalysis to be aware of the interpersonal dilemmas inherent in patient treatment (Balint, 1957; West, 1975). It is an all too common frustration for the psychiatrist to make the correct diagnosis, prescribe the indicated medication and see treatment fail. If the holistic nature of the problem is ignored, the likelihood of treatment failure increases (Gorden, 1981). Because etiological and sustaining factors are so complex in affective disorders, the clinician must take care to view the patient in a total sense, initiating treatment in an atmosphere of therapeutic support and understanding. Such an approach is not only the best theoretical way to treat depression, but the best practical way as well.

Once a thorough evaluation, leading to an accurate diagnosis, has been completed, a course of therapy can be chosen. In those patients with a major affective disorder in whom psychotic symptoms, serious suicidal risks, severe nutritional deficiencies or considerable excitement or agitation are present, hospitalization is usually indicated. Treatment within a hospital setting may include pharmacotherapy, electroconvulsive therapy, milieu therapy and individual and/or group supportive psychotherapy (see Chapters 2 and 11).

Patients with less severe manifestations of a major affective disorder may be treated in an outpatient setting. Pharmacotherapy is an essential element in the

MAJOR DEPRESSIVE DISORDERS	DYSTHYMIC, CYCLOTHYMIC DISORDERS
Unipolar and Bipolar	Atypical and Adjustment Disorders
Hospitalization: Inpatient	Outpatient

a. ECT	a. Pharmacotherapy
b. Pharmacotherapy	1. Tricyclics, tetracyclics
1. Tricyclics, tetracyclics	2. MAO inhibitors
2. MAO inhibitors	b. Psychotherapy
c. Milieu Therapy	1. Supportive
d. Psychotherapy	2. Pscyhoanalytically oriented
1. Individual	3. Behavioral
2. Group	4. Cognitive
	5. Group*

*Note: With the exception of restrictions related to the combination of MAO inhibitors with tricyclics and tetracyclics, all other modalities may be intermixed.

Fig. 17-1. Treatment strategies in the affective disorders as related to diagnoses.

therapeutic regimen for any patient with a major affective disorder regardless of the setting in which it occurs. A thorough understanding of the uses and risks of neuroleptics, antidepressants and lithium is necessary in order to treat these patients adequately. In addition, there is good evidence that a combination of psychotherapy and pharmacotherapy will achieve better therapeutic results than either treatment alone, and will result in far fewer treatment dropouts (DiMascio, Weissman, Prusoff, Carlos, Zwilling and Klerman, 1979). Figure 17-1 provides an outline of treatment modalities as related to diagnosis.

The initial approach to the patient needs to be reassuring and educative. In the authors' experience, it is useful to explain that there are biochemical factors involved in the etiology of the major affective disorders, and that medication is necessary to restore the "chemical imbalance" to normal. An outline of the patient's symptoms and how they fit into the general category of affective disorders is helpful. The purpose of this approach is to enable the patient to assume some objectivity toward his symptomatology, to make it ego-alien, and then to reassure him that his condition is well known and treatable, and that recovery is likely. This attitude on the part of the clinician is likely to induce hope, remove shame, lessen anxiety and ensure compliance with treatment. At the same time, it can be pointed out that psychological factors may have an important role in precipitating an episode of an affective disorder, and that careful exploration and understanding of these factors may help reduce the likelihood of future episodes.

The early stages of treatment, during which frequent contact with the patient is necessary, are usually occupied with explanations of medication side-effects, reassurance about the length of time necessary to achieve a remission (usually up to two to three months for complete disappearance of all symptomatology) and general supportive measures. At the same time, a more extensive history can be obtained (a process that enhances the therapeutic relationship), involving a joint decision by patient and therapist as to the usefulness of continued psychotherapy. If such an approach is believed to be indicated, the therapeutic focus can gradually be altered as the patient's symptoms clear up. It is the experience of the authors that intensive psychotherapy, with a full range of transference and countertransference issues, can be entered into without compromise, even with the therapist handling the prescription and regulation of medication.

Psychotherapy of Affective States

In a general sense the treatment of depression should include the following goals:

1) Amelioration of debilitating symptoms (i.e., vegetative signs, suicidal potential, regressed behavior)
2) An improvement in object relations
3) An improvement in self-esteem
4) Reinstatement at a more adaptive level of functioning in terms of work, social and family relationships
5) Increased awareness of the circumstances involving the depression with the provision of effective coping skills
6) A reduction in guilt-proneness, self-doubt and self-recrimination

In short, the therapy should improve ego functions (Bellack and Hurvich, 1977), soften the superego and buffer the id.

Although psychotherapy grew out of psychoanalytic tradition, recent advances in the behavioral sciences have done much to increase our therapeutic armamentarium. Behavior therapy (Lewinshon, 1975), cognitive therapy (Beck, 1976) and interpersonal therapy (Klerman, 1981; Weissman, 1979) have added greatly to our treatment of the affective disorders. Although seemingly different, the therapeutic approaches have several common factors, differences being more a matter of polemics than reality. It must be remembered that arguments on a theoretical or academic level, at times, have little to do with clinical practice. Clinicians from different schools often do the same thing yet use different language to explain the process.

Lazarus (1973, 1980) provides an excellent framework for all therapies within what he calls the multimodal model. He employs the acronym BASIC ID to describe various aspects of the patient's problem that must be explored:

B — Behavior
A — Affect
S — Sensations
I — Imagery
C — Cognitions
I — Interpersonal behaviors
D — Drugs

All psychotherapeutic approaches, some more systematically than others, are going to involve these factors. In a similar vein, Marmor (1964) provides the mnemonic device C-Crip to describe mechanisms that occur in psychotherapy regardless of orientation. These are:

C — Catharsis
C — Cognition
R — Relearning
I — Identification
P — Practice

Whether one has a behavioral, cognitive, psychoanalytic or pharmacological approach, these five factors will in all likelihood be in operation.

Psychoanalytic Psychotherapy

The psychotherapeutic management of the depressed patient places rather special demands on the clinician. Traditionally, Abraham (1911) set the tone by stating that psychoanalysis was the only rational cure for the manic-depressive illnesses. Yet, even within the psychoanalytic school much pessimism exists (Cohen, Baker, Cohen, Fromm-Reichmann and Weigert, 1954; Jacobsen, 1971; Mendelson, 1980). Many seasoned clinicians remain highly equivocal concerning the effectiveness of insight-oriented psychotherapy. Wolberg (1954) believes that patients manifesting major depressive episodes are impervious to insight psychotherapy, while Diethelm (1953) states that patients recovering from a bipolar illness are unable to undergo penetrating analysis. The nature of the depressive patient's interpersonal relationships are a prime contributing factor. Fenichel (1945) summarizes the depressive as follows:

> Depression is based on the same predisposition as addiction and pathological impulses. A person who is fixated on the state where his self-esteem is regulated by external supplies or a person whose guilt feelings motivate him to regress to this state vitally needs these supplies. He goes through the world in a condition of perpetual greediness. (p. 357)

Likewise, Wolberg (1954) has commented on the difficult nature of the depressive:

Psychotherapy is also very difficult in depressed patients because their demands for help and love are insatiable. No matter how painstaking the therapist may be in supplying their demands, they will respond with rage and aggression . . . . (p. 628)

The manic patient also presents serious problems. It is generally agreed that during a manic phase the patient is not amenable to psychotherapy. The treatment choice would be between lithium, hospitalization or a combination of both (see chapter on pharmacotherapy). After the mania has subsided and the patient is more stable, psychotherapy can be a useful adjunct in terms of increasing insight. Manic episodes are often prefaced by hypomania or a sense of inflated well-being, which the patient can be taught to identify and control. Hypomania is an extremely seductive state, and often people will not want to lose it, even if it means experiencing disruptive manic and depressive episodes. Psychotherapy should be geared toward helping the patient accept a more stable mood and energy level.

The clinician attempting insight-oriented work with any of the affective syndromes must be aware of these problems. A thorough understanding of dynamics and therapeutic principles is necessary. Chapters 1 and 3 of this volume summarize many of these essential points. Some special considerations more specific to affective disorders will be outlined. It should be understood that in considering outpatient psychotherapy we are, in most cases, talking about the dysthymic, cyclothymic or atypical patient. Those patients with more severe unipolar and bipolar disorders, whose object relations are severely impaired, are immediate candidates for hospitalization, electroconvulsive therapy and/or chemotherapy.

The initial phase of treatment with the depressed patient is often characterized by an immediate positive transference and intense rapport with the therapist (Jacobsen, 1971; Wolberg, 1954). The clinician must be wary of being seduced by the patient's immediate improvement. Pitfalls include satisfying nontherapeutic goals and mutual acting-out (e.g., becoming friendly, overextending oneself or being overly solicitous and identifying with the idealized projections of the patient). This is a crucial phase of therapy, for if a firm therapeutic alliance is established, the clinician can then utilize the patient's dependency to foster growth. The healthier ego of the therapist becomes the guide within the therapeutic relationship. The clinician must be careful to realistically point out the patient's idealizations and misconceptions while maintaining a feeling of empathy and understanding (Arieti and Bemporad, 1980). It is quite important to set a tone of affective resonance so that the patient knows his feelings are understood even if his perceptions are misplaced.

The initial phase is very frequently followed by an extended period of growing frustration as the idealized image of the therapist and magic wish for a cure begin to fade (Mendelson, 1980). Feelings of hopelessness, ambivalence toward treatment and self-doubt begin to appear. At this point, patients are at their most provocative in attempting to induce guilt in the therapist for the failure in treatment. This phase can be followed by a deepening of the depression and a withdrawal from object relations. Both Jacobsen (1971) and Mendelson (1980) emphasize that the danger of termination is quite high during this subphase. During these periods the therapist must be strong and reassuring yet warm and empathic. The therapeutic stance is one of acceptance and understanding with an emphasis on working through and improvement of the patient's situation.

During periods of marked retardation or narcissistic withdrawal, the therapist must become more active and show interest in whatever the patient is able to produce. Jacobsen (1971) cautions against the overuse of analytic detachment, stating that analysts who by nature are detached are going to experience diffi-culty in treating depressed patients. Long and empty silences are usually not helpful. The therapist should always be "empathically present," balancing his interventions between giving too much or too little. West (1975), for example, outlines four general elements crucial to the psychotherapy of depression: 1) rapport, 2) reassurance, 3) revelation and 4) reorganization. That is, in some way the therapist, after establishing an empathic relationship, must attempt to change the depressive patterns. This is what the more contemporary behavioral and cognitive approaches attempt to do more directly.

Behavior Therapy

In general the behavioral approach to the affective disorders reflects the be-havioristic philosophy that pathology is rooted in specific symptoms or behaviors (Kanfer and Phillips, 1970; Lewinshon, 1975). Whitehead (1979) describes the main objectives of the behavioral approach as follows:

1) Depressive behavior per se constitutes the disorder and can be modified by manipulation of reinforcers.
2) There exists a decrement of positive reinforcement that can be manipu-lated and increased.
3) The decreased sense of control over one's life as well as the person's sense of helplessness can be extinguished through selective positive and negative reinforcement.
4) Negative viewpoints should be replaced with positive viewpoints.

This is clearly a phenomenological approach emphasizing the here and now. The attempt is to build a new system of reinforcers and responses in place of a deteriorating and maladaptive set of responses. Lewinshon (1975) states that a major focus in the behavioral treatment of depressive disorders should involve interruption of the vicious cycle of decreased positive reinforcers, leading to decreased activity, leading to decreased positive reinforces and so on (see chapter on behavioral treatment).

Further impetus to the behavioral approach has come from Seligman's work (Seligman, Klein and Miller, 1976) on the phenomena of learned helplessness in animals and people. According to this model, depression is partially a result of a decrease in one's sense of self-control over external and internal events. Behavioral approaches are designed to reduce helplessness and increase one's sense of mastery. Recent studies using clinical populations support the efficacy of decreasing helplessness as a means of improving depressive symptoms (Rapps, Reinhard and Seligman, 1980).

Cognitive Therapy

Beck (1967, 1973), has developed an approach called cognitive psychotherapy. The focus on thought processes or cognitions, while present in all psychotherapeutic approaches, is the main emphasis of Beck's system. Treatment is predicated on the theory that overwhelming stress, either specific or nonspecific, in combination with idiosyncratic thought patterns precedes depressive states. Therapy attempts to alter these maladaptive cognitions. For example, a person with depression-prone cognitions is more likely to conclude that an insensitive friend is rejecting him rather than to assume the friend might be having a bad day (Kovacs, 1980). The approach is mainly an insight-oriented one that attempts to identify the faulty cognitions and precipitating stressors that lead to depression (Mendelson, 1980). One of the advantages of cognitive therapy (as well as behavior therapy) is the amount of controlled clinical research it has produced. When cognitive treatment was being developed, one of its limitations was that most outcome studies involved nonclinical populations. It was unclear whether the treatment was effective in true clinical depression (i.e., chronic dysthymia or major depressive episodes), or whether it was limited to subclinical states of depression or sadness. Even Beck (1967) acknowledged that the cognitive approach was most effective in treating the less severe depressions without endogenous components.   However, evidence is beginning to accumulate that the cognitive approach may be of greater clinical use (Kovacs, 1980).   In a twelve-week study, Rush et al. (1977) compared the effectiveness of imipramine and cognitive therapy for treating primary dysthymia on an outpatient basis. The psychotherapy subjects received up to twenty, 50-minute sessions while the medication group met once a week for 20 minutes. At the end of twelve weeks, results indicated significant symptom differences between groups on the Beck Depression Inventory (BDI), Hamilton Rating Scale (HRS) and Raskin Depression Scale (RDS). Furthermore, the authors report significantly more dropouts in the medication group.   Differences in improvement were maintained for three months but unfortunately become insignificant at a six-month follow-up. Furthermore, the study could be solidly criticized on methodological grounds (e.g., twelve weeks of twelve to twenty psychotherapy sessions as compared with twelve weeks of 20-minute medication sessions).

Interpersonal Psychotherapy

The premise of the interpersonal approach is that depression is the result of faulty communication, misperceptions and misunderstanding, occurring within the context of a relationship. The therapy, which originated from the work of the *New Haven–Boston Collaborative Depression Project*, emphasized the identification and correction of faulty relationship patterns (Klerman, Rounsaville and Chevron, 1981). Resolution of personal difficulties takes place within the context of a short-term, brief-psychotherapy approach, usually of twelve to sixteen weeks' duration. Technique is active, with emphasis on exploration of the relationship pattern, combined with "directive" techniques. Klerman and his associates advocate taking an interpersonal inventory of four problem areas leading to depression. These areas are: 1) abnormal grief, 2) interpersonal disputes, 3) role transition and 4) interpersonal deficits. The focus of the therapy is then concentrated on one of these areas.

The astute clinician will undoubtedly sense that the psychoanalytic, behavioral, cognitive and interpersonal approaches overlap, dovetailing nicely on common premises. Basically, the therapeutic stance is one of active empathy, so that although the clinician is sensitive enough to accept the patients "feelings," he is likewise transmitting the message that life does not have to be this way. The treatment of depression is an area that seems to represent a pragmatic meeting ground for the analytic and behavioral schools. As Glass (1981) points out:

> One intriguing possibility in this regard is that psychodynamic therapists who are successful with depressed patients make use of some of the empirically validated cognitive, behavioral and interpersonal techniques without explicitly recognizing them as such. (p. 14)

Pharmacological and Electroconvulsive Treatment

Pharmacology and electroconvulsive therapy were extensively covered in Chapter 2 and will be only briefly mentioned here. The main groups of antidepressant drugs can be generally classified as follows:

1) Tricyclics and tetracyclics
2) Monoamine oxidase inhibitors (MAOI's)
3) Lithium salts
4) Amphetamines

It is widely agreed that in most major depressive disorders or any depression with an endogenous component, tricyclics are the drug of choice (Klerman, 1980; Kline, 1976; Pare, 1977). For bipolar disorders and manic states, lithium carbonate is considered the medication of choice. The monoamine oxidase inhibitors are thought to be indicated in the atypical depressions where ECT is often not helpful and tranquilizers, while relieving the patient's tension, do not ameliorate the depression (Prange, 1975; Sack and Goodwin, 1974). The MAOI's are considered by many to be relatively dangerous drugs because of their potentiation of sympathomimetic substances such as amphetamines, dopamine, norepine-phrine, tryptophan and tyramine. The last two substances pose a special problem because of their natural occurrence in foods such as certain cheeses, beers, wine, chicken livers and other foods. Certain authors such as Lessee (1978) claim that with minimal precautions the MAOI's are very safe and are the drug of choice in any depression with severe agitation. Traditionally, clinicians have been cautioned not to use MAOI's in combination with tricyclics and if necessary to wait at least ten days after discontinuing the tricyclic. Although care must always be exercised with MAOI's, more studies are indicating that they are safer than was once thought. A recent study compared amitriptyline (a tricyclic), tranylcypromine (an MAOI) and the two drugs in combination, and found all three medications equally effective for treating minor and major depressive disorders (White, Pistole and Boyd, 1980). Amphetamines are rarely used because of their tendency to produce dependence as well as the worsening of depression that tends to follow the mood elevation they produce. The reader is referred to Chapter 2 for a complete description of pharmacologic and electroconvulsive treatment including dosages, indications, treatment strategies and side-effects.

Comparison of Pharmacotherapy and Psychotherapy

In general, the literature is beginning to support the effectiveness of combination treatment in the management of affective disorders (Glass, 1981). DiMascio et al. (1979) compared amitriptyline and short-term interpersonal psychotherapy in a sixteen-week randomized controlled study. Results indicate that the treatments were additive in terms of effect. Psychotherapy affected mood, suicidal tendencies, ideation, work and interests, whereas the amitriptyline had its effect mainly on the vegetative symptoms such as sleep and appetite. Wolpert (1979) believes that psychotherapy is a useful supplement in the major affective disorders and a necessity in the dysthymic or atypical affective disorders. Paykel et al. (1975) likewise concludes that medication is necessary to improve symptom discomfort, while psychotherapy helps to improve social effectiveness. In most studies, psychotherapy has been shown to be more effective than a no-treatment group. Several experiments suggest that combinations of medication and psychotherapy are equivocal, whereas most research supports the notion of combining treatments for different reasons (Cristol, 1972; Luborsky et al., 1975; Rush et al., 1977). Most clinicians would agree that affective disorders have a psychological component amenable to psychotherapy and a biological component that might indicate pharmacotherapy (Whitehead, 1979). There is no evidence for a negative interaction effect between psychotherapy and pharmacotherapy (Glass, 1981).

Conclusions drawn from outcome research in psychotherapy present many problems (see Chapter 23). According to Weissman (1979), the lack of operational definitions as well as the heterogeneity of diagnoses and patients makes generalities difficult to maintain. In a recent review of the literature, Lieberman (1975) claims that at least 200 articles on the psychotherapy of depression failed to reach even minimal clinical and methodological competence. The clinician is best-off avoiding dogmatism. An orientation that utilizes the best possible combination of treatment modalities chosen by clinical experience, validated research and patient needs, is, in all likelihood, the most effective approach.

REFERENCES

Abraham, K. Notes on the psychoanalytic investigation and treatment of manic-depressive insanity and allied conditions. *Selected papers on psychoanalysis.* London: Hogarth Press, 1911.

Akiskal, H.S., and McKinney, W.T. Overview of recent research in depression. *Archives of General Psychiatry,* **32**: 285–305 (1975). 25–46 (1981).

Akiskal, H.S., and McKinney, W.T. Overview of recent research in depression. *Archives of General Psychiatry,* **32**: 285–305 (1975).

→ Arieti, S. and Bemporad, J.R. The psychological organization of depression. *American Journal of Psychiatry.* **137**: 1360–1365 (1980).

Balint, M. *The doctor, his patient and the illness.* New York: International University Press, 1957.

Ban, T.A. New antidepressants. *Psychopharmacology Bulletin.* **15**: 22–25 (1979).

→ Beck, A.T. *Cognitive therapy and the emotional disorders.* New York: International Universities Press, 1976.

Beck, A.T. *Depression: clinical, experimental and theoretical aspects.* New York: Harper & Row, 1967.

→ Beck, A.T. *The diagnosis and management of depression.* Philadelphia: University of Pennsylvania Press, 1973.

Bellack, L and Hurvich, M. Ego functions and their components. *Psychiatric Annals.* **7**: 562–581 (1977).

Birren, J.E. *The psychology of aging.* Englewood Cliffs, N.J.: Prentice-Hall, 1964.

Blinder, M.G. Classification and treatment of depression. *International Psychiatry Clinics.* **6**: 3–26 (1969).

Bowlby, J. *Attachment.* New York: Basic Books, 1969.

Burrows, G.D. (Ed.) *Handbook of studies on depression.* New York: Elsevier, 1977.

Burton, R. *The anatomy of melancholia.* New York: Dutton, 1961.

Cameron, N.A. *Personality development and psychopathology.* Boston: Houghten Mifflin, 1963.

Carroll, B.J., Curtis, G.C., and Mendels, J. Neuroendocrine regulation in depression. *Archives of General Psychiatry,* **33**: 1039–1044 (1976).

Cohen, M.B., Baker, G., Cohen, R.A., Fromm-Reichmann, F. and Weigert, E. An intensive study of twelve cases of manic-depressive psychosis. *Psychiatry.* **17**: 103–137 (1954).

Cristol, A.H. Studies of outcome psychotherapy. *Comparative Psychiatry.* **3**: 189–200 (1972).

Depue, R.A. (Ed.) *The psychobiology of depressive disorders: Implications for the effects of stress.* New York: Academic Press, 1979.

Diethelm, O. The fallacy of the concept: Psychosis. In: Hoch, D.H. and Zubin, J. (Eds.), *Current problems in psychiatric diagnosis.* New York: Grune and Stratton, 1953.

DiMascio, A., Weissman, MM., Drusoff, b.A., Carlos, R., Zwilling, I., and Klerman, G.L. Differential symptom reduction by drugs and psychotherapy in acute depression. *Archives of General Psychiatry,* **36**: 1450–1456 (1979).

Escobar, J.I. and Tuason, V.B. Antidepressant agents — A cross cultural study. *Psychopharmacological Bulletin.* **16**: 49–52 (1980).

Feighner, J. Diagnostic criteria for use in psychiatric research. *Archives of General Psychiatry.* **26**: 57–63 (1972).

Fenichel, O. *The psychoanalytic theory of neurosis.* New York: Norton, 1945.

Fiere, R.R., Kumbaraci, T. and Dunner, D.L. Lithium prophylaxis of depression in bipolar I, bipolar II and unipolar patients. *American Journal of Psychiatry.* **133**: 925–929 (1976).

Fink, M. Miansern — A new tetracyclic antidepressant. *Psychopharmacology Bulletin.* **15**: 27–29 (1979).

Freud, S. Mourning and melancholia. In: *Collected papers,* vol. IV. London: Hogarth Press, 1917.

Glass, R.M. Recent developments in the psychotherapy of depression. *Psychosomatics,* **2**: 110–113 (1981).

Gold, M.S., Pottash, A.L., Extein, I., & Sweeney, D.R. Diagnosis of depression in the 1980's. *JAMA,* **245**: 1562–1564 (1981).

Gordon, J.S. Holistic medicine: toward a new medical model. *Journal of Clinical Psychiatry,* **3**: 114–119 (1981).

Gonzalez, E.R. Beyond tricyclics: Outlook on antidepressive treatment. *Journal of the American Medical Association.* **243**: 1503–1505 (1980).

Guze, S. and Robins, E. Suicide and primary affective disorders. *British Journal of Psychiatry.* **117**: 437–438 (1970).

Harlow, H.F. Love in infant monkeys. *Scientific American.* **68**: 200–209 (1959).

Illaria, R. and Prange, A.J. Convulsive therapy and other biological treatments. In: Flach, F.F. and Draghi, S.C. (Eds.), *The nature and treatment of depression.* New York: John Wiley, 1975.

Itil, T.M., Michael, S.T. and Soldatos, C. Androgens as antidepressants. *Psychopharmacology Bulletin.* **15**: 31–33 (1979).

Jacobsen, E. *Depression.* New York: International Universities Press, 1971.

Jacobsen, E. *The self and the object world.* New York: International Universities Press, 1964.

Kanfer, F.H. and Phillips, J.S. *Learning foundations of behavior therapy.* New York: Wiley, 1970.

Kaplan, H.I., Freedman, A.M., and Sadock, B.J. *The comprehensive textbook of psychiatry,* Baltimore: Williams & Williams, 1982.

Katz, M.M. and Hirschfeld, R.M.A. Phenomenology and classification of depression. In: Lipton, M.A., DiMascio, A. and Lillam, K.F. (Eds.), *Psychopharmacology: A generation of progress.* New York: Raven Press, 1978.

Kendel, R.E. The classification of depressions. In: Burrows, G.D. (Ed.), *Handbook of studies on depression.* Amsterdam: Excerpta Medica, 1977.

Kendel, R.E. *The classification of depressive illness.* London: Oxford University Press, 1968.

Kiev, A. *Transcultural psychiatry.* New York: Free Press, 1977.

King, D. Sleep deprivation therapy in depressive syndromes. *Psychosomatics.* **21**: 404–416 (1980).

Klein, D.F. Endogenomorphic depression. *Archives of General Psychiatry.* **31**: 447–454 (1974).

Kline, M.S. *Factors in depression.* New York: Raven Press, 1974.

Klerman, G.L. Affective disorders. In: Kaplan, H.I., Freedman, A.M. and Sadock, B.J. (Eds.), *Comprehensive textbook of psychiatry,* vol. 2. Baltimore: Williams & Wilkins, 1980.

Klerman, G.H. and Barrett, H. The affective disorders: Clinical and epidemiological aspects. In: Gershon, S. and Shopsin, B. (Eds.), *Lithium: Its role in psychiatric treatment and research*. New York: Plenum Press, 1975.

→ Kline, N.S. *Depression: Its diagnosis and treatment*. Basel: S. Karger, 1969.

Kline, N.S. Drug therapy of depression. In: Cole, J.O., Schatzberg, A.F. and Frazier, S.H. (Eds.), *Depression: Biology, psychodynamics and treatment*. New York: Plenum Press, 1976.

→ Kovacs, M. Cognitive therapy in depression. *Journal of the American Academy of Psychoanalysis*. **118**: 127–149 (1980).

Lazarus, A. *The practice of multimodal therapy*. New York: McGraw-Hill, 1980.

Lazarus, A. Multimodal behavior therapy: Treating the basic id. *Journal of Nervous and Mental Disease*. **156**: 404–411 (1973).

Lessee, S. Tranylcypromine (parnate) – a study of 1000 patients with severe agitated depressions. *American Journal of Psychotherapy*, **32**: 220–247 (1978).

Lewinshon, P.M. The behavioral study and treatment of depression. In: Herson, M., Eisler, R.M. and Miller, P.M. (Eds.), *Progress in behavior modification*. New York: Academic Press, 1975.

Lieberman, M. *Survey and evaluation of the literature on the verbal psychotherapy of depressive disorders*. Washington, D.C.: Clinical Research Branch, N.I.M.H., 1975.

Luborsky, L., Singer, B. and Luborsky, L. Comparative studies of psychotherapies. *Archives of General Psychiatry*. **32**: 993–1005 (1975).

Marks, J. and Pare, C.M.B. (Eds.) *The scientific basis of drug therapy is psychiatry*. New York: Pergamon 1965.

Marmor, J. *The nature of the psychotherapeutic process*. New York: Brunner/Mazel, 1964.

Marshal, E. Psychotherapy works, but for whom? *Science*. **207**: 506–508 (1980).

Mendels, J. and Cochrane, C. The nosology of depression: The endogenous reactive concept. *American Journal of Psychiatry*. **124** (Suppl.): 1–11 (1968).

Mendelson, M. The psychotherapy of the depressed patient. In: T.B. Karasu & L. Bellak (Eds.), *Specialized techniques in individual psychotherapy*. New York: Brunner/Mazel, 1980.

Mendelson, M. Intrapersonal psychodynamics of depression. In: Flach, F.F. and Draghi, S.C. (Eds.), *The nature and treatment of depression*. New York: John Wiley, 1975.

Muller, J.L. & Ostroumova, M.N. Resistaence to inhibiting effect of dexamethasone in patients with endogenous depression. *ACTA Psychiatr. Scand.*, **61**: 169–177 (1980).

Myers, J.K. and Weissman, M.L. Use of a self-report symptom scale to detect depression in a community sample. *American Journal of Psychiatry*. **137**: 1081–1084 (1980).

Nelson, J.C. and Charney, D.S. Delusional and non delusional unipolar depression. *American Journal of Psychiatry*, **138**: 328–333 (1981).

Pare, C.M.B. Monoamine oxidase inhibitors: A personal account. In: Browns, G.D. (Ed.), *Handbook of studies on depression*. Amsterdam: Excerpta Medica, 1977.

Paykel, E.S. Atypology of depression. *British Journal of Psychiatry*. **118**: 275–288 (1971).

Paykel, E.S., DiMascio, A., Haskell, D. and Prusoff, B.A. Effects of maintenance amitriptyline and psychotherapy on symptoms of depression. *Psychological Medicine*. **5**: 67–77 (1975).

Prange, A.J. Pharmacotherapy of depression. In: Flach, F.F. and Draghi, S.C. (Eds.), *The nature and treatment of depression*. New York: John Wiley, 1975.

Quitkin, F., Rifkin, A. and Klein, D.F. Prophylaxis of depressive disorders: Current status of knowledge, *Archives of General Psychiatry*. **33**: 337–341 (1976).

→ Rapps, C.S., Reinhard, K.E. and Seligman, M.E.P. Reversal of cognitive and affective deficits associated with depression and learned helplessness by mood elevation. *Journal of Abnormal Psychology*. **89**: 342–349 (1980).

Robins, E. and Guze, S.B. Classification of affective disorders. The primary-secondary, the endogenous-reactive, and the neurotic-psychotic concepts. In: Williams, T.A., Katz, M.M. and Shields, J.A. (Eds.), *Recent advances in the psychobiology of the depressive illness*. Washington, D.C.: U.S. Government Printing Office, 1977.

Rounsalville, B.J., Klerman, G.L., and Weismann, M.M. Do psychotherapy and pharmacotherapy for depression conflict. *Archives of General Psychiatry*, **38**: 24–29 (1981).

→ Rush, A.J., Beck, A.T., Kovacs, M. and Hollon, S. Comparative efficacy of cognitive therapy and pharmacotherapy in the treatment of depressed outpatients. *Cognitive Therapy Research*. **1**: 17–37 (1977).

Sack, R. and Goodwin, F.K. The "pharmacological bridge": A view from the clinical shores. *Psychopharmacology Bulletin*. **10**: 52–52 (1974).

Salzman, L. Interpersonal factors in depression. In: Flach, F.F. and Draghi, S.C. (Eds.), *The treatment of depression*. New York: John Wiley, 1975.

Schildkraut, J.J. Norepinephrine metabolites as biochemical criteria for classifying depressive disorders and predicting responses to treatment: Preliminary findings. *American Journal of Psychiatry*. **130**: 695–699 (1973).

Seligman, M.E.P., Klein, D.C. and Miller, W.R. Depression. In: Leitenberg, H. (Ed.), *Handbook of behavior modification and behavior therapy*. Englewood Cliffs, N.J.: Prentice-Hall, 1976.

Silverman, C. The epidemiology of depression. *American Journal of Psychiatry*. **124**: 833–891 (1968).

Strayhorn, J.M. Foundations of Clinical Psychiatry. Chicago: *Yearbook Medical*, 1982.

→ Weissmann, M.M. The psychological treatment of depression: Evidence for the efficacy of psychotherapy alone, in comparison with and in combination with pharmacotherapy. *Archives of General Psychiatry*. **36**: 1269–1279 (1979).

West, E.D. and Dally, P.J. The MAO inhibitors. *British Medical Journal*. **1**: 1491–1494 (1959).

White, K., Pistole, T. and Boyd, J. Combined monamine oxidase inhibitors-tricyclic antidepressant treatment: A pilot study. *American Journal of Psychiatry*. **137**: 1422–1425 (1980).

Whitehead, A. Psychological treatment of depression: A review. *Behavior Research and Therapy*. **5**: 495–509 (1979).

Winokur, G. The types of affective disorders. *Journal of Nervous and Mental Disease*. **156**: 82–96 (1973).

Winokur, G., Clayton, P. and Reich, T. *Manic depressive illness*. St. Louis: C.V. Mosby, 1969.

Wolberg, L.R. *The technique of psychotherapy*. New York: Grune & Stratton, 1954.

Wolman, B.B. *Handbook of clinical psychology*. New York: McGraw-Hill, 1965

Wolpert, E.A. Manic-depressive illness: The relations of biology to psychology. In: Obioles, J., Ballos, C., Gonzalez Monclus, E. and Pujol, J. (Eds.), *Developments in psychiatry*, vol. II, *Biological psychiatry today*. Amsterdam: Elsevier, 1979.

Zilboorg, G. and Henry, W.A. *A history of medical psychology*. New York: Norton, 1941.

18 The Treatment of Neuroses and Borderline Cases

Richard D. Chessick

Two basic assumptions will be made about the reader of this chapter. The first is that he or she is familiar with the standard textbook symptom-based descriptions of the neuroses, and also at least superficially aware of the various and confusing descriptions of borderline cases. For those who wish to review these syndromes, Freedman and Kaplan (1980) present adequate descriptions of the classical neurotic syndromes; Grinker *et al.* (1968) and Chessick (1974a, 1977) present clinical descriptions of the borderline patient. At the same time, it is clear that confusion reigns in the nosology as evidenced by the shift in the classification from DSM-II to DSM-III[1]; the reader, if he was trained several years ago, *must* familiarize himself with this shift in nosology. The present chapter will refer to the current nosology (DSM-III), although in my opinion it represents a step backward from understanding the neurotic disorders because it de-emphasizes the important dynamic concepts of emotional illness. A complete review of conflicting nosological and conceptual views of the neuroses is presented by Gray (1978).

The second major assumption is that the reader is familiar with the basic definitions and techniques of intensive psychotherapy as have been presented in detail, for example, in texts by DeWald (1971), Chessick (1969, 1971, 1974, 1977, 1977a, 1980), and in papers by Strupp (1969, 1970, 1972). There is not space in this chapter to discuss in detail the essence of intensive psychotherapy as it applies to the treatment of the neuroses and borderline cases, and since I have discussed this elsewhere in the references already cited, it will be assumed

---

[1]*American Psychiatric Association diagnostic and statistical manual of mental disorders*, 3rd ed. (III).

that the reader is reasonably familiar with the definitions, basic concepts and also the current controversies in the field. If the reader is not familiar with this literature, it would be in his best interest to stop at this point and study the references cited before attempting to wade into highly controversial issues discussed in the present chapter.

ADMIXTURE OF OPINIONS

No better summary of the problems covered in this chapter, and slogan to characterize what is happening in the treatment of the neuroses and borderline cases, can be found than the title of Grinker's (1964) brief paper: "Psychiatry Rides Madly in All Directions." He writes:

> The public today holds an admixture of opinions. As magical helpers of nature's curative powers who know so much about the unknowable, who can interpret a glance, a gesture, a slipped word, or a phrase to mean so much, we are endowed with all the powers of the idealized or supernatural father. The press exemplifies this attitude by insisting on obtaining and even printing our comments off the cuff on any and all facets of life and even behavior . . . . The professional view held by psychiatrists is today mixed and confused. Psychoanalysis, for which many have sacrificed so much, has not become the therapeutic answer; it seems to be mired in a theoretical rut vigilantly guarded by the orthodox and, except for relatively few examples, prevented from commingling with science. The great breakthrough promised by the modern psychosomatic approach, with its concepts of specificity of psychological etiology of degenerative diseases, has succumbed to the hard facts of multiple causation and critical phases of development. Small wonder that with these disappointments a fertile soil has been created for new therapies — pharmacological, psychological, and social — each one rapidly exploited as a panacea (p. 228).

This situation has been described by Abrams (1969) as the new eclecticism. He considers it "a refreshing departure" that dynamic psychotherapy is not always recommended as the treatment of choice for every disorder. We now have the enormous advances of pharmacotherapy, electric shock therapy, the behavior therapies, hypnosis and suggestion techniques and group techniques such as psychodrama, role-playing, couple or family therapy, sensitivity or T-group training and milieu therapy, as additions to our treatment procedures. Abrams does recognize that "The dangers of this proposed technical eclecticism are many: dilettantism, superficiality, dehumanization."

Even within the field of psychotherapy itself many "innovations" have been proposed and brought together (see for example, Goldman and Milman, 1972). Among them are such intriguingly entitled procedures as rational-emotive psychotherapy, bioenergetic analysis, Gestalt therapy and multiple therapy, and less esoterically titled proposals such as crisis therapy, existential therapy, hypnotic therapy, the use of videotape playback and many other conceptualizations. Some of these procedures vastly wander away from and others deliberately deny many of the basic concepts and premises of psychoanalytically informed psychotherapy.

An important and extremely controversial subgroup of the therapeutic techniques used in the treatment of the neuroses and borderline cases today are the behavior therapies, accompanied by an impressive array of scientific-sounding terminologies and statistics. There are as many varieties of behavior therapy proposed as there are varieties of psychotherapies — as summarized, for example, by Kanfer and Phillips (1966). Quite significantly their paper has a subtitle: "A Panacea for All Ills or a Passing Fancy?" Whether or not the behavior therapies really simply represent another example of manipulation of the patient in a positive transference as basically suggested by Marmor (1971), it is certainly clear that, as he insists:

> In the final analysis, the technique of therapy that we choose to employ must depend on what aspect of man's complex psychic functioning we address ourselves to. If we choose to focus on the patient's overt symptoms or behavior patterns, some kind of behavior therapy may well be the treatment of choice. On the other hand, if the core of his problems rests in symbolic distortions of perception, cognition, affect or subtle disturbances in interpersonal relationships, the source and nature of which he may be totally unaware, then the more elaborate re-educational process of dynamic psychotherapy may be necessary (pp. 27–28).

THE PSYCHOTHERAPIST

To put this another and perhaps a simpler way, the basic decision about what form of therapy to use in the treatment of neuroses and borderline cases depends at least in part on the personality of the psychotherapist, his philosophy of life, his attitude toward people and his beliefs about the nature and etiology of emotional disorder, which are largely a function of his personality. Perhaps the most dramatic description of what is going on in this controversial field today is provided by Kubie's (1971) discussion of the retreat from patients. Kubie explains that an important factor in the choice of how to manage and treat emotional disorders is what he calls "maturity" as a psychiatrist. This maturity is a result of the meeting of three rivers in life:

> The individual has first to work his way out of many of the conflicts which he buried in early life and which tie him to his own childhood. In one way or another . . . an evolving series of therapeutic experiences must occur if man is to escape bondage to his own past in order to win his freedom and to grow toward maturity as a human being. Secondly,

maturity requires that he must have accepted such adult responsibilities as marriage and parenthood.   It is in coping with these that he will encounter and master the problems which confront every adult as he emerges from youth.   Emotional maturity of this kind is a necessary prerequisite for dealing with the problems of others from a mature basis . . . . (Third) Not reading, not diligent study, not psychological aptitude can supplant the experiences of sustained relationships with patients as they fall ill and fall well again.   Nothing can take the place of being a participant-observer of these fluctuating changes over weeks, months, and even years (pp. 99–100).

Kubie reviews a variety of reasons for the current "flight from patients," or more precisely for the current tendency to avoid involving patients with one's self in long-term intensive psychoanalytically informed psychotherapy.   What it boils down to is the tremendous demands that are made on the psychological structure of the therapist by the prolonged experience of doing a lot of intensive psychotherapy, for surely psychotherapeutic involvement imposes complex emotional stresses on all therapists, and especially on the novice.   As Kubie points out: "Every patient who is undergoing psychotherapy of any kind requires high investments of feeling and time: *time* because change and growing up take time and *feeling* because of the therapist's inescapable, mixed identifications with the patient, subtly masked though these may be . . . when we treat someone else we are also treating or at least defending ourselves.   This takes a great deal out of the therapist at any age, but especially when he is young."

The constant battering from the patients, their frequent overt or masked primitive demands and the continuous exposure to the hostility from patients and their families wear down the older therapist and tend to produce depression. Kubie calls this phenomenon "the late age drop-out" from clinical work.   These "drop-outs" often turn bitterly against their early activities and mislead younger men into following suit.   Kubie makes it clear that the score of a few complete successes, many partial successes and some partial failures and complete failures can breed depression and anger so that "A long life devoted to therapy in psychiatry may lead even the skillful, experienced, and successful among us to an ill-defined sense of mourning and a weariness of the spirit."

All these pressures tend to influence the young psychiatrist or the resident in psychiatry to retreat from work with individual patients and to work with groups or families.   Such a retreat often involves turning prematurely to teaching, research or administration of community services.   This seduction of the young therapist away from psychotherapy before he has developed the ability to deal with interaction between his own emotional problems and those of his individual patients, causes irreparable harm to the future of psychiatry.

All psychiatrists today are under enormous social pressure, the sources of which are manifold.   The practitioners of group therapy, behavior therapies, community psychiatry and statistical research, as well as the so-called directive and organic psychiatrists described by Hollingshead and Redlich (1958), exert a powerful pressure on the psychotherapist toward ostracism, loneliness and isolation from his colleagues.   Derogatory references often describe intensive psychotherapy as a religion, a mystic faith or sheer quackery, and especially attack it as a nonscientific technique that cannot provide the standard statistical proofs of its efficacy. Therefore the practitioners of intensive psychoanalytically informed psychotherapy become second-class citizens in the psychiatric and medical profession. They often react to such pressures with separatist tendencies, abandoning the white coat and the ordinary professional medical journals and forming groups, seminars and publications of their own.

In addition, every possible pressure from the rest of the medical profession is constantly present. There is an almost total lack of understanding of long-term psychotherapy among many in the medical profession itself. This is especially manifest in the insistence of the nonpsychiatrist physician that patients show rapid improvement in a few sessions, in a continual derogation of the long-term psychotherapist in jokes and comments made among nonpsychiatrist physicians and in a constant resentment of the psychotherapist who cannot take one patient after another on referral because he can only see so many patients in long-term therapy and there is very little turnover. Perhaps the most lethal of all criticisms is the direct expression of opinions by respected nonpsychiatrist physicians to their patients and at public meetings, accusing analytically oriented psychotherapists of at best being foolish and incompetent, and at worst as being seducers and exploiters of their patients. Third-party payers and insurance companies avidly leap on this situation to avoid or limit payment of claims, posing an increasing threat to the very livelihood of the psychiatrist practicing psychotherapy, and propelling her or him toward the use of drugs and electric shock for "fast-fast-fast relief."

SOCIOCULTURAL FACTORS

As if this were not enough, society itself has become increasingly inimical to a concentration on the unfolding of the individual. Kepecs (1968) explains that the style of psychoanalysis, once a revolutionary movement, has now become relatively conservative. "Much of its value system and orientation is in conflict with aims and aspects of contemporary society and of contemporary American psychiatry. . . . Its style, characterized by leisurely introspection and study of the function of the human mind and by minute self-conscious observations of the details of human interactions and transactions, is in many ways not compatible with current social circumstances. And adaptation to many social needs and pressures is probably not compatible with psychoanalysis."

One of the greatest psychoanalytic psychotherapists, Franz Alexander (1964), in the last paper written before his death, reminds us that:

The psychoanalyst who still holds on to the original goal, to understand each person on the basis of his highly specific life history, which may resemble grossly others in the same group, but which is still different, is looked upon by many as having an antiquated 19th century orientation. Mass civilization is not concerned with the unique person. . . . Psychoanalysis and psychotherapy in general are among the few still existing remedies against the relentlessly progressing levelization of industrial societies which tend to reduce the individual person to becoming an indistinguishable member of the faceless masses (pp. 238, 243).

This trend, which was already apparent to Alexander in the early 1960s, continued with a vengeance throughout the 1970s. Applebaum (1972), for example, explains how political, social and technological forces, with greater or lesser regard for scientific considerations, have lately impinged upon individual long-term psychotherapy. The goals of such forces include the delivery of health care on as wide a numerical or economic basis as possible, the use of community resources rather than private practice ones and the discovery of new means of treatment with which to achieve these goals. "Often these objectives are accompanied by skepticism as to the extent that insight into unconscious influence on behavior results in beneficially changed behavior . . . . In these contexts, the term 'long term treatment' is often used invidiously to suggest that it is old fashioned and wasteful as well as ineffective."

At this point the reader of this chapter will have to make up his own mind. This controversy is far from resolved. My opinion is that intensive psychoanalytically informed psychotherapy remains the most effective procedure available for both the understanding of and the amelioration or cure of the neuroses and borderline cases, and at the same time it affords one of the few opportunities left in our modern-day civilization for the full unfolding of the individual's potential for reason, love and creative work. Thus on philosophical, humanistic and theoretical psychiatric grounds, as well as from the vantage point of over twenty years of clinical experience in the practice of outpatient office intensive psychotherapy with the neuroses and borderline patients, I still choose to stand against the enormous pressures that have been described above toward abandoning intensive psychotherapy as our fundamental therapeutic technique. This does *not* imply that the whole variety of new treatment techniques developed in the past twenty-five years are useless or irrelevant, but it does relegate them to a secondary role, at least for the time being. In proceeding to review the neuroses and borderline cases, I will attempt to show, when appropriate, what the role of these secondary techniques might be.

PSYCHOANALYTIC CONCEPTS

If one accepts that a basic psychoanalytic orientation is necessary to understand and treat the neuroses and borderline cases effectively, then it is clear that no treatment of these disorders can be sensible without a thorough understanding of the psychodynamics and psychopathology of each individual patient. This cannot be provided by a chapter of this nature, but certain basic principles in approaching the psychodynamics of neuroses and borderline cases can be outlined. The pioneer attempt to establish a rational nosology based on understanding rather than symptom description was made by Freud (see Chessick, 1980), whose initial classification was very limited in that it was designed to separate the psychoneuroses that had definable content from the "actual neuroses" in which anxiety resulted from a transformation of more or less mechanically blocked libido (Freud, 1962a).

Sadow (1969) points out that currently this system appears crude, since today we rarely concern ourselves with Freud's concept of the actual neuroses. "However, it is at the same time an historically interesting idea because Freud separated structured from primitive and relatively unstructured disease entities." This problem in the nosology of the neuroses is still with us, as anyone who studies DSM-II and DSM-III will quickly discover. A typical modern psychoanalytically informed approach to the neuroses and borderline cases however is provided by Sadow, who attempts to classify these disorders not in terms of symptomatology but in terms of the functioning of the ego. He thinks of the ego axis as a developmental continuum and describes the borderline patient, for example, not as being characterized by any specific defense or ego defect but in terms of the range of movement along the ego axis. Thus the psychotic patient is unable to function even briefly at more structuralized levels of ego functioning, whereas the borderline patient shifts back and forth, which means that although much of his behavior is characterized by prestructuralized object relations, he frequently proves capable of rather highly developed functions as well. Sadow likes to place this group of disturbances developmentally in relation to the period of the transitional object.

Similarly, in the field of the transference neuroses, as they were originally described by Freud, the level of structuralization has grown to far greater proportions, and the range of ego states available is very large. In the neuroses, when regression takes place, recovery is generally prompt, complete and relatively independent of external intervention.

The point of all this, whether one agrees or disagrees about Sadow's particular depiction of the ego axis, is that important decisions regarding treatment method and goals may be made more reasonably if the ego pathology is recognized. To offer one's self to the patient as a long-term, stable, potentially unifying object is the general plan of the treatment of more severely disturbed or "preoedipal disorders." "The goal is to help stabilize the ego by way of identification with the therapist so that the more flexible defenses become possible." As one moves from the borderline area of ego functioning to the area of transference neuroses, the emphasis shifts from stabilization and building of ego structure to interpretation of unconscious motivations in order to relieve and free the ego's conflict-free functioning. In order for the latter to occur, a workable, relatively stable transference has to develop in the therapy (Chessick, 1969, 1974, 1977). This in turn is a function of the state of ego development and the position along the ego axis in which the patient happens to be living at any given time in the treatment.

It is therefore obviously incumbent upon the therapist at all times to assess as accurately as possible the state of ego functioning of the patient and to minister to the patient in a way that is appropriate and compatible with the patient's ego state. A number of guidelines for the assessment of a patient's ego functioning are offered by DeWald (1971). Thus if one accepts the intensive psychotherapy orientation in the treatment of the neuroses and borderline cases, one works primarily from assessment of ego states rather than from nosological classifications that have been developed on the basis of predominant symptomatology. It is obvious that the capacity to assess a patient's fluctuating ego states requires far more training and demands mandatory intensive psychotherapy of the therapist, whereas symptomatic descriptions are more easily observable and can be rated and assessed in a whole variety of statistical ways and rating procedures.

CLASSIFICATORY SYSTEM

From the point of view of clinical experience, the neuroses and borderline cases may be divided into four groups. The first of these groups contains the DSM-II diagnostic entities anxiety neurosis, hysterical neuroses (including hysterical neurosis, conversion type and hysterical neurosis, dissociative type) and phobic neurosis, as well as perhaps the depersonalization neurosis. In my experience these disorders rarely present in pure form, and we usually encounter a mixture of symptomatology. (These diagnostic labels are renamed and scattered over DSM-III; I will carefully indicate the new nosology below.)

The second group is the DSM-III Dysthymic disorders (DSM-II depressive neurosis), which often overlie a more basic emotional disorder of one kind or another (I will discuss this in detail below). The third group following DSM-III is Obsessive compulsive disorder, which frequently shades off into either the Borderline personality disorder, the Paranoid personality disorder or the frank Schizophrenic disorder. This shading-off has been discussed in an outstanding characterization by the world's foremost expert on the subject, Harry Stack Sullivan (1956), and cannot be covered in detail in this chapter.

Finally, we have the fourth group, DSM-III Hypochondriasis and also Atypical somatoform disorder, which commonly accompany the Borderline personality disorder and will be discussed with it, although they are a frequent accompaniment of Paranoid and Schizophrenic disorders also. There is no place in DSM-II for the Borderline personality disorder, as I have described it in previous publications (Chessick, 1969, 1974a, 1977). This has been remedied in DSM-III, but the distinction from other personality disorders is sometimes quite difficult.

As stated at the beginning of this chapter, no attempt will be made to describe in detail the clinical pictures of any of these disorders; it is assumed that the reader is already familiar with them.

ANXIETY NEUROSIS (DSM–III: PANIC DISORDER AND GENERALIZED ANXIETY DISORDER)

Let me now review the therapeutic strategies for each of these clinical groups. The kind of treatment presented to a patient complaining of anxiety must be completely dependent on the clinical assessment of the cause of the anxiety. Thus the ordinary appearance of anxiety or panic states very frequently is *not* and should not be diagnosed as a Generalized anxiety disorder, and requires crisis intervention, supportive treatment and psychopharmacologic therapy. Similarly, acute schizophrenic panics or serious adjustment disorders are best treated in a brief and eclectic fashion. The clinician must be clear when he is dealing with a Generalized anxiety disorder and when he is not, and this is usually not too difficult to discern if a *careful history* is obtained.

In one form of the Generalized anxiety disorder, the patient suffers chronically from acute flare-ups and anxiety – and he is well acquainted with this fact, has insight that his mental functioning is disturbed and is aware that the flare-ups subside pretty much regardless of what form of support is offered. When these flare-ups are extreme, we diagnose the DSM–III Panic disorder. In another form, the patient suffers from chronic "free-floating" anxiety, which does not cause him to deteriorate in terms of its intensity or associated disintegration of function, but in which he maintains a constant high level of anxiety, or tension associated with practically anything. The best diagnosis of Generalized anxiety disorder and Panic disorder is made from the patient's own description and opinion of what is going on. In these anxiety disorders, whether characterized by occasional flare-ups or free-floating anxiety, there are usually deep-seated problems in ego functioning, and very frequently phobic, conversion and dissociative disorders are resorted to when the anxiety becomes too overwhelming.

The techniques of support and modifying stress as well as medication and deconditioning may be used in these disorders if it is felt that the patient is not a suitable candidate for intensive psychotherapy, but the treatment of choice if this has been a chronic condition is intensive psychotherapy, and these patients often respond well to it. In the area of treatment of anxiety states, Dyrud (1971) has attempted to indicate the overlap between the behavior therapies and psychoanalytically oriented psychotherapy. He quotes Freud's famous dictum that "Anyone who wants to make a living from the treatment of nervous patients must clearly be able to do something to help them."

From time to time in clinical experience one is fooled by a patient with a Generalized anxiety disorder that proves to be absolutely refractory to intensive psychotherapy, although the acute flare-ups can be ameliorated by many varieties of supportive, psychopharmacologic or behavior techniques.   Usually such patients turn out to be schizophrenic or borderline cases who have been inaccurately assessed in terms of their ego states. The anxiety disorder in these cases protects the patient from further decompensation.

HYSTERIAS (DSM–III: CONVERSION DISORDER, DISSOCIATIVE DISORDERS)

In a similar fashion, the Conversion and Dissociative disorders have been treated by an infinite variety of techniques. Most of these techniques achieve symptomatic relief, for example, in the use of hypnosis or pentothal by intravenous drip to encourage abreaction and subsequent relief of symptoms. But often even as Freud's pioneering studies in hysteria (Freud and Breuer, 1962; Chessick, 1980) indicate, the patients come up with new symptoms often almost as fast as the old symptoms are removed (although this has been challenged by some proponents of behavioral therapy). The psychodynamic understanding of the Conversion disorders and the Histrionic personality disorders (DSM–III) is one of the most confused areas in all psychiatric and psychoanalytic theory. For example, Lazare (1971) writes: "The historical development of psychoanalytic theory, therefore, has made its current concept of the hysterical character confusing to many general psychiatrists. As a consequence (and for other reasons), analysts and nonanalysts rarely acknowledge each other in the literature, even when discussing the same subject."

Lazare presents a fine review of the concept of the Histrionic personality disorder in the literature and moves into a discussion of the so-called healthy hysteric in contrast to the sicker patient who shows more infantile manifestations and responds much more poorly to intensive uncovering psychotherapy. Again we are left fundamentally with the necessity to assess ego function. Thus it is not uncommon for the sick hysteric to experience considerable subjective relief and show dramatic objective changes following a relatively brief period of ego-supportive psychotherapy. The important factor is to determine whether the patient can tolerate intensive psychotherapy, or whether we must limit our goals and use supportive measures — or, as has been suggested by Kass (1972), use a behavioral group treatment of hospitalized patients with hysteria with little attention to the basic psychodynamic factors, and focus primarily on strengthening executive ego functions "on the assumption that the patient might then be in an advantageous position on his own to perform those integrative, synthetic ego functions with regard to his experience and his biological endowment."

Unfortunately it is often clinically very difficult to delineate those patients with hysteria who will best respond to intensive psychotherapy and those who will not. The first step is a very careful physical and psychological examination because a variety of organic medical disorders can produce the typical symptomatology of both the conversion and dissociative types of hysteria. It is a tragedy for the patient when these organic disorders are missed. I believe that whenever possible patients with hysteria with no discernable physical illness should receive a trial of intensive psychotherapy for at least six or eight months. No fixed date is chosen for making any decisions about further treatment because the tendency of such patients to simply stall and cling to their symptoms is very great.

After six or eight months the experienced clinician can usually judge if any progress is being made toward the development of a stable transference and the uncovering of significant material. If not, it is perhaps best to recommend to the patient that procedures be instituted to afford specific symptomatic relief. In a great many such cases, the patients have already undergone a whole variety of procedures for symptomatic relief, and they know what helps and what does not. Sometimes it is necessary to continue in primarily a supportive manner in order to help the patient adjust to the limitations in his ego function.

In the trial of psychotherapy it is very important for the therapist to try to assess carefully the potentials of the patient. If it seems that the potential exists for the formation of a workable transference neurosis, formal psychoanalysis is the treatment of choice. If, on the other hand, the patient shows no capacity to respond to uncovering treatment and little if anything can be done about the secondary gain, the therapeutic goals should be modified and kept as realistic as possible. It is just as tragic to come across a patient with hysteria who has had many years of formal psychoanalysis with several psychoanalysts with no improvement as it is to find a patient with hysteria who has never had a reasonable chance to work in intensive psychotherapy with anybody.

PHOBIAS (DSM–III: PHOBIC DISORDERS)

The Phobic disorder is of course the classic disorder to which the behavioral techniques have been applied, and a pure Phobic disorder is rare in clinical therapeutic practice. When one encounters a pure or almost pure Phobic disorder, especially in children, it is probably best to use brief psychotherapy and environmental manipulation and, in the case of adults, reassurance, group therapy, drugs and the behavioral therapies. As a matter of fact, Agras et al. (1972) provide evidence, in a five-year follow-up of thirty phobics, that even untreated phobia tends to improve. Children's phobias usually improve quickly if they do not mask serious underlying psychopathology. In the study of this group 100% showed improvement or recovery at the end of five years. Exposure to the feared object or situation seems to be the basic mechanism that brings about recovery in these cases, especially in the context of a supportive relationship in which the therapist lends authority to a realistic evaluation of the circumstances and assures the patient that no harm will come to him.

Frazer and Carr (in Freedman and Kaplan, 1975) indicate that "Even with classical psychoanalysis designed to accomplish major personality change it has been found that the phobia usually will not disappear simply by uncovering the original situation that led to its formation. Freud himself saw a necessity for the modification of psychoanalysis in the treatment of phobias, stressing the need for the psychoanalyst to intervene and insist that patients attempt to brave the anxiety-provoking situation. . . . 'and to struggle with their anxiety while they make the attempt'." In the context of a relationship with a guiding supportive figure, the patient is encouraged at the appropriate state of trans-ference into desensitization experiences, whether they are so labeled or not. These authors also point out, and I agree from clinical experience, that although a high degree of optimism is possible in the treatment of phobias, a certain small percentage appear quite resistive to therapeutic endeavors. This usually turns out again to be a misappraisal of ego functioning with the hidden presence of an underlying borderline or schizophrenic disorder.

It is important in discussing those cases of anxiety disorder, conversion disorder, dissociative disorder and phobic disorder that do not respond to in-tensive psychotherapy to make it clear that the diagnosis of an underlying borderline or schizophrenic disorder should not be based on the lack of re-sponse, but should be made at the beginning in the initial assessment of the patient, for example, by careful attention to what Knight (1954) has described as microscopic signs. The astute clinician will most of the time be able to spot the presence of an underlying schizophrenia or a borderline case, especially if it is possible to obtain a good history. One cannot sufficiently stress the im-portance of taking a thorough history and making a careful psychological examination of every patient at the beginning of every treatment.

DEPRESSIONS (DSM-III: MAJOR DEPRESSION, OTHER SPECIFIC AFFECTIVE DISORDERS)

The treatment of choice, once an accurate diagnosis of depressive *neurosis* (DSM-III: Dysthymic disorder) has been made, is psychotherapy. Careful distinction between a Dysthymic disorder and Major affective disorders is ab-solutely mandatory, and as a matter of fact the patient's life may depend on it. The first responsibility of the psychotherapist in the treatment of the Dysthy-mic disorder is the assessment of suicide risk. In those cases where it is judged that a serious suicide risk is present, precautions for the prevention of suicide must take precedence over everything else. In my clinical experience, if a Dysthymic disorder has been accurately diagnosed, and if the patient is being seen frequently enough and the lines of communication and contact between the patient and therapist are carefully preserved, the suicide risk is minimal. However, there is always a certain suicide risk in dealing with any depressive disorder, and this is a serious stress on the psychotherapist. Only those therapists who are willing to assume such a risk should work with depressed patients. It is necessary to assess carefully the suicidal problem because it is extremely disruptive to a psychotherapy for a patient to be going in and out of the hospital in revolving-door fashion every time he threatens suicide.

Davies (1964) reminds us that "Depressive illness is colored into almost innumerable shades by the personality and character of the individual in whom the disease occurs." Chodoff (1972) has attempted to review the enduring personality patterns that influence clinical depression and possibly predispose certain individuals to episodes of depressive illness. The situation at present is seriously compromised by methodological inadequacies. In my clinical experience, the Dysthymic disorder is frequently a secondary formation that appears when other forms of either neurotic defenses or characterologic defenses have failed to deal with the situation. Therefore, the therapist should be prepared for the fact that as the depression lifts, he will be dealing with a more basic underlying psychologic disorder.

It is extremely important for the clinician to realize that the lifting of a depression in a Dysthymic disorder is not a cure, and that a long period of psychotherapeutic work is ahead. Unfortunately it is exactly at this point that the patient considers leaving treatment because he feels better, and it is incumbent on the therapist to confront the patient with evidence of the underlying disorder in order to stimulate the patient's motivation to really work through the basic problem. This is frequently possible because the patient already has some experience with the therapist, and since there has been improvement, the transference at this point is often positive; on this basis the patient may proceed. One of the finest summaries of suggestions for treating the depressed patient that I have seen is presented by Levin (1965), and the reader is referred to this paper for details of the psychotherapy of the depressed patient.

The question of whether to use psychopharmacological agents in the treatment of Dysthymic disorders remains unsettled; definitely such patients ordinarily do not respond to electric shock treatment. In my experience it is rarely necessary to give patients with Dysthymic disorders mood-elevating drugs, and often when that is done, the patient bitterly complains of side-effects. The experience of my colleagues has not always been the same, and the practicing therapist will have to experiment and decide for himself.

I am personally inclined not to use drugs in the treatment of the psychoneuroses beyond occasional use of the minor tranquilizers or soporifics; for if the treatment is an intensive psychotherapy, then an enormous magical power is attributed to the therapist, and at times the treatment disintegrates around the issue of attempting to get the therapist to give more gratification in terms of medication. On the other hand, a patient who is suffering intensely from insomnia or from anxiety deserves the relief that medication can give if it is judiciously and carefully controlled. In my experience in supervising neophyte therapists, the vast majority of medication that is handed out to neurotic patients and borderline cases is dispensed in order to allay the anxiety of the therapist.

OBSESSIVE-COMPULSIVE NEUROSES (DSM-III: OBSESSIVE COMPULSIVE DISORDER)

Whereas patients with Dysthymic disorders have an excellent response rate to psychotherapy, the treatment of Obsessive compulsive disorders remains one of the thorniest and — if the reader will pardon the irony — stubborn and obstreperous problems in psychiatry. The decision about whether to use psychotherapy in the Obsessive compulsive disorders is especially important because many such patients quickly permit the therapy to degenerate into an endless obsessional debate, which leads to frustration for both the therapist and the patient. The utmost sensitivity is necessary on the part of the therapist to judge when the patient is really capable of insight into what the therapist and patient are experiencing in the treatment. If there are precipitating events and some evidence of good relationships with others, and the patient is not utterly paralyzed by the Obsessive compulsive disorder, then psychotherapy has possibilities. On the other end of the spectrum, there are patients who are so severely paralyzed with Obsessive compulsive disorders that leukotomy has been recommended. There is evidence that leukotomy can lessen the intensity of the disorder.

To get the flavor of the treatment of the Obsessive compulsive disorders, I have already suggested reading Sullivan (1956), and I also recommend Freud's famous case of the Rat-Man (1962b; see also Chapter 12 in Chessick, 1980). The psychotherapy of such disorders is invariably extremely long and difficult. Behavior therapy has been tried with some claims of symptomatic relief; at present there are no drugs or other somatic therapies that are generally agreed to be useful in the treatment of this disorder.

In my experience, the Obsessive compulsive disorder is a step backward on the ego axis and often shades off into schizophrenia; therefore the patient is actually vigorously protecting himself against a schizophrenic breakdown by clinging to a severe Obsessive compulsive disorder. For this reason the inner sense of protection causes the patient to stubbornly maintain a neurotic position in order to prevent disaster. Only those psychotherapists should work with the Obsessive compulsive disorders, who are willing to endure over a long period of time the very special kind of sticky relationship that takes place between the patient and the therapist in the treatment of such disorders. This has been described by Sullivan (1956) as the fly-paper pattern of interpersonal relations. Certainly therapists who need to see rapid changes should stay away from the treatment of such patients. At present, the treatment of choice, especially if the disorder has not been long-standing, is formal psychoanalysis. Of all the entities discussed in this chapter, the chronic long-standing Conversion disorder and Obsessive compulsive disorder, especially if the symptoms are of a fixed nature, are the most refractory to any form of treatment.

BORDERLINE CASES (DSM-III: BORDERLINE PERSONALITY DISORDER)

I turn finally to a discussion of the treatment of borderline cases. By this time it should be clear that a continuum exists between the various neurotic disorders and the borderline case and that the same considerations of the assessment of ego function upon which a rational psychotherapeutic plan is developed apply to all. Although the borderline case may be fragile and may have a vulnerable personality organization, "borderline regression can be understood as decompensation and defense, as regressive flight from more advanced tasks, and as enfeebled, deviant infantile adaptation. . . . Selective assessment of the regressed, distorted and intact ego functions is of fundamental importance in both diagnosis and treatment" (Blum, 1972).

One of the most common mistakes in the treatment of the neuroses is to mistake a borderline case for a classical neurosis as a result of an inadequate history and psychological examination. There are as many varieties of recommendations for the treatment of the borderline patient as there are for the neuroses, and general agreement is found only on a few basic issues. The distinction between Borderline personality disorders and Narcissistic personality disorders may be especially difficult; the controversial work of Kohut (1971, 1977) and discussion in Chessick (1977) should be consulted along with Kernberg (1975, 1976) on this unresolved and critical problem.

Ordinary encouragement or supportive therapy produces either no effect or a dramatic remission soon followed by a relapse into the same or new symptoms accompanied by the angry demand for more magic — especially if the supportive therapy primarily has been the administration of various psychopharmacological agents for symptomatic relief. These patients abuse the dosage instructions, and the side-effects produced complicate the picture tremendously; they may even collect medications from various physicians and make suicide attempts with them.

It is also generally agreed that the rapid shifts up and down the ego axis with all the excitement, storm and panic they cause the patient and those around him, usually accompanied by either missing appointments, failure to pay the bill or spending session after session in talking about symptoms and constantly introducing new problems, soon make the physician and the patient frustrated and discouraged. Typically there occurs an increasing exasperation on the part of the therapist as well as a developing barrage of complaints about the treatment from the patient, often leading to an impasse and a referral either for chronic hospitalization or to another form of treatment. A variety of ways are employed by psychotherapists to get rid of these patients.

FOUR APPROACHES

As I have previously written (1974a, 1977), four types of psychotherapy have been recommended for these patients. The first of these is an authoritative and directive approach with much psychological shoving of the patient to "get him moving." This is a total-push type of treatment often used for schizophrenics and deals mainly with the symptoms; so unless interminable contact is maintained with the patient, relapse is to be expected, especially when life stress arises. If this approach is made to work, it is certainly quicker and cheaper than long-term intensive psychotherapy.

At the other end of the spectrum is formal psychoanalysis, argued to be the treatment of choice, for example, by Boyer and Giovacchini (1967; Giovacchini, 1972). Most psychotherapists reject this approach out of clinical experience in which many borderline patients show a complete intolerance to the formal psychoanalytic situation, reacting with suicidal attempts, transitory psychosis or dramatic and chaotic symptoms and acting-out that finally interrupt the treatment.

The third approach attempts to combine supportive psychotherapy with providing a direct "corrective emotional experience" for the patient. This can range from minor gratifications such as taking the patient's hand to actually holding, rocking, feeding and having sexual intercourse with the patient. I have discussed the great danger of direct primary process interchange with patients in other publications (1969, 1971, 1974, 1977), and it is unnecessary to review that here.

The treatment that is coming to be most generally accepted for the borderline patient is what has been called psychoanalytically oriented psychotherapy or psychoanalysis with parameters – the latter a controversial term. The most complete and thorough review of psychoanalysis with parameters for borderline cases has been presented in a series of papers by Kernberg (1967, 1968, 1971) and two books by Kernberg (1975, 1976), and in Giovacchini (1972). These are excellent but very difficult works and require considerable knowledge on the part of the reader. In Wilson's summary (1971), Kernberg advises interpretation of the predominantly negative transference in the here and now, limit setting to block acting-out, and noninterpretations of the less primitive aspects of the positive transference to strengthen the therapeutic alliance. "Consistent transference interpretations of the primitive defensive operations which rigidly protect the borderline patient's weak ego can result in the resumption of ego growth. Clarification of interpretations to cope with the patient's distortions are an important component of Kernberg's interpretative approach."

My publications referred to above have presented a similar approach for the analytically oriented psychotherapist; a briefly stated practical approach may be found in Chessick (1979). The psychotherapy of the borderline case is very difficult and long, but is quite rewarding for both therapist and patient. The borderline case is being seen with increasing frequency in the offices of psycho-therapists. In fact, the borderline patient already constitutes a very substantial increment of patients seeking psychotherapy.

In the neuroses it is certainly possible to argue that somatic, or behavioral, or group therapies form a feasible alternative in the therapeutic armamentarium. At least they do harm a relatively small percentage of the time — perhaps no more often than psychotherapy. In the borderline cases, the psychopharma-cological and often the group approaches — especially if conducted by ama-teurs — may do serious harm. Although these patients tend to decompensate far less than was originally thought, and are not so fragile in the sense that they can easily become schizophrenic for a long period of time, they *are* impulsive and may be precipitated by the use of psychopharmacologic agents or intensive or marathon group or encounter maneuvers into actions that may be destructive or even fatal for them. Here again the essence of the choice of treatment for the neuroses and the borderline cases rests on a careful diagnostic evaluation of the patient by an alert and well-trained clinician with as thorough as possible an understanding of himself.

REFERENCES

Abrams, G. The new eclecticism. *Archives of General Psychiatry.* **20**: 514–523 (1969).

Alexander, F. Social significance of psychoanalysis and psychotherapy. *Archives of General Psychiatry.* **11**: 235–244 (1964).

Agras, W. *et al.* The natural history of phobia. *Archives of General Psychiatry.* **26**: 315–317 (1972).

Applebaum, S. How long is long term psychotherapy? *Bulletin of the Mennin-ger Clinic.* **36**: 651–655 (1972).

Blum, H. Borderline regression. *International Journal of Psychoanalytic Psycho-analytic Psychotherapy.* **1**: 46–60 (1972).

Boyer, L. and Giovacchini, P. *Psychoanalytic treatment of characterological and schizophrenic disorders.* New York: Science House, 1967.

Chessick, R. *How psychotherapy heals.* New York: Science House, 1969.

Chessick, R. *Why psychotherapists fail.* New York: Science House, 1971.

Chessick, R. *The technique and practice of intensive psychotherapy.* New York: Jason Aronson, 1974.

Chessick, R. The borderline patient. In: Arieti, S. (Ed.), *The American hand-book of psychiatry,* 2nd ed. New York: Basic Books, 1974a.

Chessick, R. *Intensive psychotherapy of the borderline patient.* New York: Jason Aronson, 1977.

Chessick, R. *Great ideas in psychotherapy.* New York: Jason Aronson, 1977a.

Chessick, R. A practical approach to the psychotherapy of the borderline patient. *American Journal of Psychotherapy* **33**: 532–546, 1979.

Chessick, R. *Freud teaches psychotherapy.* Indianapolis, Ind.: Hackett, 1980.

Chodoff, T. The depressive personality. *Archives of General Psychiatry.* 27: 666–667 (1972).

Davies, E. Some varieties of depression and their treatment. In: Davies, E. (Ed.), *Depression.* London: Cambridge University Press, 1964.

DeWald, P. *Psychotherapy*, 2nd ed. New York: Basic Books, 1971.

Dyrud, J. Treatment of anxiety states. *Archives of General Psychiatry.* 25: 298–305 (1971).

Freedman, A. and Kaplan, H. *Comprehensive textbook of psychiatry*, 2nd ed. Baltimore: Williams & Wilkins Co., 1975.

Freedman, A. and Kaplan, H. *Comprehensive textbook of psychiatry*, 3rd ed. Baltimore: Williams & Wilkins Co., 1980.

Freud, S. Early psychoanalytic publications. *Standard edition of the complete psychological works of Sigmund Freud,* vol. 3. London: Hogarth Press, 1962a.

Freud, S. Little Hans and the Rat-Man. *Standard edition of the complete psychological works of Sigmund Freud,* vol. 10. London: Hogarth Press, 1962b.

Freud, S. and Breuer, J. Studies on hysteria. *Standard edition of the complete psychological works of Sigmund Freud*, vol. 2. London: Hogarth Press, 1962.

Giovacchini, P. (Ed.) *Tactics and techniques in psychoanalytic therapy.* New York: Science House, 1972.

Goldman, G. and Milman, D. *Innovations in psychotherapy.* Springfield, Ill.: Charles C. Thomas, 1972.

Gray, M. *Neuroses.* New York: Van Nostrand Reinhold Co., 1978.

Grinker, R. Psychiatry rides madly in all directions. *Archives of General Psychiatry.* 10: 228–237 (1964).

Grinker, R. *et al. The borderline syndrome.* New York: Basic Books, 1968.

Hollingshead, A. and Redlich, F. *Social class and mental illness.* New York: John Wiley and Sons, 1958.

Kanfer, F. and Phillips, J. Behavior therapy. *Archives of General Psychiatry.* 15: 114–128 (1966).

Kass, D. Behavioral group treatment of hysteria. *Archives of General Psychiatry.* 26: 42–50 (1972).

Kepecs, J. Psychoanalysis today. *Archives of General Psychiatry.* 18: 161–167 (1968).

Kernberg, O. Borderline personality organization. *Journal of the American Psychoanalytic Association.* 15: 641–685 (1967).

Kernberg, O. The treatment of patients with borderline personality organization. *International Journal of Psychoanalysis.* 49: 600–619 (1968).

Kernberg, O. Prognostic considerations regarding borderline personality organization. *Journal of the American Psychoanalytic Association.* 19: 595–635 (1971).

Kernberg, O. *Borderline conditions and pathological narcissism.* New York: Jason Aronson, 1975.

Kernberg, O. *Object relations theory and clinical psychoanalysis.* New York: Jason Aronson, 1976.

Knight, R.P. *Psychoanalytic psychiatry and psychology.* New York: International Universities Press, 1954.

Kohut, H. *The analysis of the self.* New York: International Universities Press, 1971.

Kohut, H. *The restoration of the self.* New York: International Universities Press, 1977.

Kubie, L. The retreat from patients. *Archives of General Psychiatry.* **24:** 98–106 (1971).

Lazare, A. The hysterical character in psychoanalytic theory. *Archives of General Psychiatry.* **25:** 131–137 (1971).

Levin, S. Some suggestions for treating the depressed patient. *Psychoanalytic Quarterly.* **34:** 37–65 (1965).

Marmor, J. Dynamic psychotherapy and behavior therapy. *Archives of General Psychiatry.* **24:** 22–28 (1971).

Sadow, L. Ego axis in psychopathology. *Archives of General Psychiatry.* **21:** 15–24 (1969).

Strupp, H. Toward a specification of teaching and learning in psychotherapy. *Archives of General Psychiatry.* **21:** 203–212 (1969).

Strupp, H. Specific versus non-specific factors in psychotherapy and the problem of control. *Archives of General Psychiatry.* **23:** 393–401 (1970).

Strupp, H. On the technology of psychotherapy. *Archives of General Psychiatry.* **26:** 270–278 (1972).

Sullivan, H. *Clinical studies in psychiatry.* New York: W.W. Norton and Co., 1956.

Wilson, C. On the limits of the effectiveness of psychoanalysis. *Journal of the American Psychoanalytic Association.* **19:** 552–564 (1971).

19 The Treatment of Antisocial Behavior

Sanford Goldstone

We do not possess a causal therapy of the psychopathies; medicinal or organotherapeutic attempts are in their earliest stages. Final therapy setting out from the basis of intimate knowledge of the personality has always to strive toward a psychagogic effect. We are still unable and perhaps always will remain unable to change the constitutional structure of the psychopathic personalities but we can educate many of them to understand themselves, to come to terms with themselves, and to set themselves genuine goals which they may reach in spite of their psychopathic peculiarities. (Kahn, 1931)[1]

This began as a straightforward clinical discussion of the treatment of antisocial behavior by the mental health professions. Unfortunately, the eclectic eyes of this practitioner have become sufficiently clouded by simultaneously rewarding and frustrating experiences that the straightforward and the clinical were at first difficult, and at last impossible, to produce. What seems to have emerged is an essay derived from these experiences tied to prevailing ideas and knowledge about antisocial conduct from the standpoint of the clinician and behavioral scientist. Unless we limit our discussion of antisocial behavior to the few exotic actions that apparently respond to aversive conditioning, or unless we exaggerate the dangers to society of the consequences of those mental diseases

---

[1]This chapter is dedicated to Eugen Kahn, my teacher and colleague from 1955 to 1967. His many hours of patient discussion with a slowly developing young psychologist initiated an enduring interest in deviant personalities and their social consequences. It is too bad that Professor Kahn is not here to author this presentation since his wisdom, experience and perspective would have yielded a substantially greater contribution.

that can be treated chemically, there are no successful therapeutic handles upon this problem; confinement treats the effects, not the behavior. Such a limitation of the scope of discussion about antisocial behavior would be as unrealistic as a more general discourse accompanied by exaggerated treatment claims and hopes. Hence, these clouded eclectic eyes will present a clouded eclectic picture leaving little more than the plea for increased clarity of thinking and the challenge of accumulating additional knowledge for the behavioral scientist and clinician. It is too early in the development of our professions to hope, let alone claim, but it is not too early to continue our slow beginning.

INTRODUCTION

Although almost half a century has elapsed since Kahn (1931) published his *Psychopathic Personalities*[2], the summary of his views regarding treatment cited at the outset continues to represent the state of the art and science. Clinicians preceding Kahn as well as his contemporaries wrote prolifically about the "enemies of society" and in general shared his view about the limitations of the mental sciences in delivering relief to and from those deviant people who behaved antisocially. Our generation of mental health professionals in this last half of the twentieth century cannot point with the pride of noticeable progress to new discovery and greater control in the treatment of antisocial behavior, and if I could return and report 100 years from now, nothing would surprise me more than the happy discovery that things had changed; nothing would be more pleasing than to learn that this change had transpired with significant contribution from behavioral and clinical scientists.

Contemporary clinicians, while quarreling about etiology and technique are in general agreement about outcome. Antisocial behaviors of individuals and groups may be products of complex interacting endogenous and exogenous forces that are legion, but our scientific and clinical knowledge of these forces and our capacity to measure and control them are limited.

Perhaps this discussion of antisocial behavior and its treatment should be presented by an enthusiastic supporter of a therapeutic tool, a theory, an area of psychologic, biologic, or social research accompanied by the conviction of certain and significant success in some not too distant tomorrow. To suggest at the outset that we have not progressed noticeably during this golden century of the mental and social sciences may be viewed as destructively pessimistic and discouraging; to voice skepticism about probable future progress deriving predominantly from the mental sciences may be seen as cynical. To date we have had no shortage of technique, theory, social movement, and research sparks that promised progress and success with fanfare and failed the test of time and laboratory. Clinical realism about problems as complex as man and his nature

---

[2] This book was published first in 1928 as part of Oswald Bumke's *Hanbuch der Geisteskrankheiten.*

is neither discouraging nor pessimistic. Realism permits perspective and encourages the mental sciences to offer limited and modest assistance in coming to grips with antisocial behavior along with all others concerned with man's nature, suffering, healing, and survival. No single profession or discipline has earned the status of primacy in the search for knowledge about antisocial behavior, and none has a successful treatment. All in concert require their part in this effort to reduce man's action against man but none alone represents cause and promotes cure. Hence, it is a prime thesis of this presentation that antisocial behavior is *never* a psychiatric disease or illness, *never* a personality disorder, *never* a mental health problem alone; antisocial behavior may be symptomatic of disease or impaired health but is never a natural consequence of illness. This position eliminates the promise by mental health workers that treatment will eliminate or significantly reduce antisocial behavior, and may avoid pointless arguments between professions and persuasions which assign blame for the frustrating outcome of sincere and active efforts. Antisocial behavior as symptomatic of both normal and deviant people is part of the subject matter of the behavioral sciences, but does one treat the antisocial behavior directly?[3]

This presentation will review representative ideas about antisocial behavior and its treatment from a clinical and behavioral science point of view through the eyes of an observer who feels that the effort and struggle are worthwhile with possible progress impeded predominantly by prevailing mythologies and a failure to develop a rational approach to a science and philosophy of personality that is both clinically functional and logically sound. Such an approach may be feasible by combining the structural properties of *personality* (e.g., impulse, character, etc.) as seen by the clinician with those related areas of behavioral research (e.g., arousal, learning, etc.)

Antisocial behavior, its diagnosis or assessment and its treatment will be examined from the standpoint of the mental health professions. The frames of reference of psychiatry, clinical psychology, and social work have enough in common to be grouped together; these professions are linked to the clinico-scientific point of view which generally excludes moral judgment and public policy, and the focus will be upon individual functioning. The professions that represent man's morality, justice, and codes of conduct as well as the disciplines devoted to the study of society, culture, large groups and the nature of our species have a larger stake in the understanding and modification of antisocial behavior, but they will not be included here. These other professions ultimately define behavior as antisocial, not the mental health workers. Antisocial behavior will be considered here in a general sense as unacceptable conduct usually in violation of values, statutes and codes that reflect pervasive public policy (e.g., homicide, assault, theft, property destruction) and specific community standards (e.g., pornography, public drunkenness). Some antisocial behaviors are invariant, and consistent from time-to-time and place-to-place, while others are culturally

---

[3]Except with physical and chemical confinement.

judged and involve wider variations with time and content. Discussion will exclude (1) antisocial behavior which is a product of psychosis or where, for any reason, the individual is exempt from criminal responsibility,[4] (2) group behavior such as ghetto and student riots, (3) victimless behavior with consenting adults, and (4) the very infrequent or single antisocial act by an individual whose life-style is predominantly acceptable. In short, we are back by any name, to those *psychopathic personalities* which are presumed to increase vulnerability to antisocial behavior. Kahn's (1931) book will be used as a basic clinical resource since it describes graphically the varieties of the psychopathic personalities that we all see, and its non-theoretical orientation and age removes it from the battleground of contemporary controversy. Since Kahn's work is not generally known, his ideas will be summarized briefly as a tribute to this psychiatrist-scholar, and as a reflection of my point of view regarding the structure of personality and its deviations. The Kahn schema for personality structure and organization provides a classification schema with clinical merit, and permits the construction of delicate bridges to the theoretician and researcher who study the *psychopath.*[5] Other clinical references with merit (Cleckley, 1964; Craft, 1965; Maughs, 1941; McCord & McCord, 1964) warrant additional study for those who wish both historical perspective and comparison among ideas and experiences. A recent volume by Hare (1970) represents an excellent and detailed review of contemporary clinical, theoretical, and scientific work in this field, and the *Comprehensive Textbook of Psychiatry* (Freedman and Kaplan, 1967) reflects the views of a sufficient number of clinicians to reflect consensus among workers about etiology, diagnosis and the discouraging therapeutic picture.

This discussion will proceed from (1) a presentation of general issues, to (2) a summary of Kahn's views about the structure of personality and its capacity for deviation, to (3) a brief review of contemporary theory and research about *the psychopath,* concluding with (4) additional comment about hopeful possibilities and risky pitfalls confronting the mental health professions as they join the other professions in the treatment and control of antisocial behavior.

---

[4]We do not wish to complicate the picture further by incorporating that confusing interface between the mental sciences and law, *the insanity defense.*

[5]Schneider disliked the ambiguity associated with the term *psychopathy,* pointing out that it had been used previously in a more inclusive sense for all psychopathological phenomena; he preferred *deviate personalities* which were seen as "variations, deviations from the vaguely conceived but ill-defined, average of human personalities, deviations upwards or downwards, toward the more or toward the less, abnormal personalities in the most literal sense." This use of the *average man* is similar to the legal community standard based upon the *reasonable man* and emphasizes the cultural basis for defining the middle ground of psychopathic antisocial behavior. There are no absolute boundaries between the normal and the psychopathic, only fluid transitions. "In one point in history and environment much may be considered psychopathic which in another time or another locality or among other races were or are considered in no sense outside the pale of the normal" (Kahn, 1931).

ISSUES

A rational treatment is based upon a scientific approach to etiology, and an objective, empirical evaluation of outcome, not upon fashionable technique, social pressure, mythology, or evangelical zeal. At the very most we can hope for reasonable knowledge of origin and cause, and the therapy a rational product of etiology; at the very least, our techniques and outcomes should stand the empirical tests of clinical research to be retained as substantially true and effective. Hence, we must come to grips with fundamental issues which have received clinical comment, but are not dealt with via reason, rigor and clarity.

Rational diagnosis should precede rational treatment. *Who* are those psychopathic personalities[6] that behave antisocially? Is there a rational taxonomy with reliable and valid properties that can define useful classes? Upon which available frame of reference shall a functional schema be based? The most obvious and traditional point of departure has been to view the psychopathic personalities who behave antisocially from the standpoint of *disease,* a view rejected by Kahn and Schneider who emphatically refused to consider psychopathy from the standpoint of disease, preferring to see it as characterologic (Schneider) or personality (Kahn) variations. The psychopath differs quantitatively *(deviate)* not qualitatively *(disease)* from a norm. Although one rarely encounters the notion of psychopathy as disease at this juncture the implication of this position lingers on. While a diagnostic tag need not imply disease, it is difficult for the diagnostician to ignore tradition. An inspection of the relevant elements of the *Diagnostic and Statistical Manual of the American Psychiatric Association* (1952, 1968), an accepted classification schema for mental disease, reveals apparent contradiction, vagueness, and underscores this dilemma. Although labels pertaining to the psychoses, neuroses and brain syndromes change slightly from time to time, these modifications have been small reflecting conceptual, clinical and scientific progress. Relative consistency of these pathologies persists across time, and generations of professions, and they appear to be quite resistent to social pressure and change. However, this is not the case with the personality disorders. The 1952 *Manual* subcategory *sociopathic personality disturbance* was eliminated in 1968; three subtypes, *sexual deviation, alcoholism,* and *drug dependence* are now listed separately, while the *dyssocial reaction* is no longer viewed as a primary psychiatric disorder. Only the *antisocial personality* remains.

> This term is reserved for individuals who are basically unsocialized and whose behavior pattern brings them repeatedly into conflict with society. They are incapable of significant loyalty to individuals, groups, or social

---

[6]The label *psychopathic personality* is used here to represent any and all deviation, excesses, or insufficiencies of personality structure and function without psychotic, neurotic, or organic origin whether or not accompanied by antisocial behavior. However, the term *psychopathic* is retained to reflect a clinical or mental health orientation to the problem of deviant behavior as opposed to sinful or criminal; antisocial behavior is viewed as symptomatic of personality pathology.

values. They are grossly selfish, callous, irresponsible, impulsive, and unable to feel guilt or to learn from experience and punishment. Frustration tolerance is low. They tend to blame others or offer plausible rationalizations for their behavior. A mere history of repeated legal or social offenses is not sufficient to justify this diagnosis. (1968)

The description is clear, but as a diagnosis based upon a medical or mental health frame of reference it is absurd. First, it does not describe personality; it is a description of "enemies of society" and community irritants. Second, it defines a moral and social, not personality disorder. Finally, the concluding caveat[7] reveals the greatest measure of contradiction. The *mere history* should be a prime basis for any diagnosis, if there exists in fact an *antisocial personality.* Perhaps it would be more useful to speak of antisocial behavior as symptomatic of other disorders of personality, mental disease, and social deviance. The diagnosis, *antisocial personality* as a mental disorder does not conform to a rational diagnostic schema.

It is interesting to note that the personality disorders are so subject to social and cultural pressures that they may be voted in or out of existence as witnessed by the 1973–1974 decision of the American Psychiatric Association which eliminated homosexuality from the *Manual.*[8]

In rejecting the disease model as the basis for rational diagnostic and therapeutic schemata, other scientific and theoretic frames of reference that have been employed to study psychopathic personalities should be emphasized. Do the problems posed by antisocial behavior have any place in the scientific and clinical domains of the mental sciences? Can any aspect of antisocial behavior be understood and perhaps controlled with the conceptual and clinical tools of the behavioral sciences?

Antisocial behavior has been viewed as a learning disability subject to specific training procedures; as an insufficiency of arousal and stimulus deprivation requiring a continued infusion of motivational and affective supplies. It has been viewed from the standpoint of deviant memory, attention, or information processing; as a product of toxic families due to loss, separation, rejection, brutality, uncertainty, or defective genes; and as a structural or functional disorder of the brain. These distinctions are heuristically useful, and have been valuable in the scientific study of psychopathic personalities and antisocial behavior. Each provides a solid bedrock of tradition and technique for studying different aspects of life touching all strata from the molecular to the social. However, when concerned with a functional disorder of man's relation to man involving violations

---

[7]The caveat is useful when testimony involving exculpation or diminished criminal responsibility is an issue since it permits the expert witness to accept a life-style of antisocial behavior without the diagnosis of antisocial personality.

[8] At the time of this writing members of the Association have requested a new ballot because of unfair election practices.

of social codes of conduct, no approach that reduces the system to simple biologic and psychologic elements can provide more than a partial picture of the substrate.   Although this writer accepts the scientific necessity for studying personality and social behavior via biologic and psychologic research, these segments do not pool spontaneously to recreate the total person interacting with a dynamic environment. The clinical and social engineer must organize both scientific and descriptive data into a picture of human-world struggles and compromises. Antisocial behavior must be viewed as a disorder of design and function of the total personality interacting with an equally complex social environment. When we refer to a psychopathic personality who behaves anti-socially we speak of a purposive human with a unique personality subject to description and classification interacting with a purposive social environment equally subject to description and classification. The very concepts of *antisocial* and *personality* cannot be rendered meaningful if one excludes purpose and if one does not tackle the whole personality, the whole environment and the entirety of the interaction. It is likely that the psychopathic personalities *are* learning disabilities, *and* disorders of insufficient arousal or stimulation, *and* deviate information processing, *and* products of family experiences, *and* defective genes, *and* brain dysfunction. It is at once each and all of these combined and yet none separately. Just as one cannot describe the visual essence of a sunset to a congenitally blind person via the physical properties of the stimuli, so the antisocial behavior can be neither described nor classified by any system that is less than holistic. Hence, a compromise may be required in proposing a diagnostic and theoretical frame of reference; to be rational and functional it must be holistic and teleological which reduces the potential for direct scientific inquiry. At the same time it is possible for the elements of a holistic approach to personality to be studied scientifically and be integrated into the corpus of knowledge about the whole.   It may be useful to analyze scientifically a Rembrandt in terms of chromatic or chemical characteristics of the pigment; knowledge about the painter and painting is obtained although it does not define the nature of artistic truth and beauty which is less subject to laboratory study.

It would seem that the state of the art, the state of the science and the overpowering complexity of the problem might lead to the discouraging conclusion that the mental sciences have little if anything to contribute to a complex problem area. While understanding and knowledge is limited with treatment and control even less developed, we should continue to progress in our understanding of parts and pursue the ultimate challenge of the whole.

Kahn (1931) considered this challenge. As a psychiatrist he concerned himself with the whole and offered three definitions of psychopathic personalities. *First,* the causal or scientific definition: "By psychopathic personalities we understand those personalities which are characterized by quantitative peculiarities in the impulse, temperament, or character strata." This definition highlights his three-tiered approach to personality structure. Each tier (i.e., impulse, temperament, character) is clinically useful and at the same time subject to scientific study but the personality is the pooled state of all three strata. Since this definition defines statically the individual psychology of the person, it is incomplete functionally. Hence, the *second* teleological definition: "By psychopathic personalities we understand personalities whose unified goal striving activity is impaired by quantitative deviations in the ego and foreign valuation leading to the establishment of pseudovalues and the striving toward pseudogoals." This definition emphasizing purpose and philosophy describes general directions, fate, and destiny. Both combine in the *third* causal-teleological and, hence, clinical definition providing a holistic approach to the nature of man: "By psychopathic personalities we understand those discordant personalities which on the causal side are characterized by quantitative peculiarities in the impulse, temperament, or character strata, and in their unified goal striving activity are impaired by quantitative deviations in the ego and foreign valuations." This complex definition has both scientific and functional merit, viewing the personality as an integration of its biological, psychological and social properties with a will, a purpose and a destiny. Any lesser definition which attempts to cope with psychopathy and antisocial behavior represents an oversimplification. No one can take such complicated stuff as man's personality, man's social behavior and man's nature, and explain them in terms of any single frame of reference. Psychopathic antisocial behavior is at once biologic and social, a product of constitution and heredity and experience.

KAHN'S PSYCHOPATHIC PERSONALITIES

As a psychiatrist, Kahn's *personality* had to be potentially normal or deviate in its structural properties and in organization permitting the portrayal of the plethora of styles and sizes encountered by the clinician. He wanted building blocks and architecture that were clinically and scientifically useful. The structure consisted of three interacting properties, *impulse, temperament* and *character* pooled in harmonious or non-harmonious, concordant or discordant equilibrium. Each property was assessed separately in quality and magnitude, and the organized whole portrayed as the total personality in preparing a diagnostic formulation. Each property represents a researchable area for the behavioral scientist. As with Freud, the *personality* begins with impulses which are instinctual vital urges toward biologic need gratification dedicated to self and species preservation and development. Strong impulse is dominant in young children who proceed developmentally toward more voluntary (character) and compassionate (temperament) processes. Impulse is aimless "raw" arousal with intensity its only dimension, and with it begins the normal dynamic personality and the deviate personality with unmoving weak impulse or less controlled powerful urge. It is the *impulse* property of personality that is most closely and obviously linked to antisocial behavior, and it is this property that requires careful diagnostic attention and therapeutic control. From impulse develops the affective component of personality, *temperament* with both arousal intensity and quality (e.g., happy, or unhappy). The final dimension, *character* is the organizer, regulator, and steerage for the personality; it is the final cause and image of the personality perpetuating its aims, attitudes and purposes. It is the *character* that regulates interaction between the whole personality and the environment. *Impulse* and *temperament* are in constant contact with the environment but *character* controls the interaction between total personality and environment. The concordant personality involves harmony of impulse, temperament and character with all processes moving with minimal friction. No *impulse, temperament* or *character* component alone necessarily produces a psychopathic personality, only a system out of balance.

The reader is urged to study Kahn's (1931) book for more complete details of his views about the development and structure of personality and those deviations that increase the likelihood of antisocial behavior. It is of particular interest to note his meticulous clinical appraisal of *impulse, temperament,* and *character* as the basis for accounting for history and predicting course. Specifically, his graphic portrayal of clinically useful types and classes highlights the numerous qualitative and quantitative varieties of personality that emerge from the harmonious and the discordant pooling of impulse, temperament and character. There is no singular *psychopath* that reflects a simple and specific personality stereotype as outlined in the diagnosis *antisocial personality.* Indeed, the neuroses for Kahn were variations on the psychopathic theme involving anxiety and conflict; borderline states were also in this category involving extremes of poor adaptation, inadequacy, and incompetence.

Kahn describes 16 clinically useful classes of psychopathic personalities, adding three to Schneider's list: the nervous, the anxious, the sensitive, the compulsive, the excitable, the hyperthymic, the depressive, the moody, the affectively cold, the weak-willed, the impulsive, the sexually perverse, the hysterical, the fantastic, the cranks, and the eccentric. This was a pragmatic typology with all classes vulnerable to antisocial behavior, although some more than others. These classes of deviate personalities were developed conceptually from a predominant disorder of impulse alone, or temperament alone, or character alone, or the discordant balance among properties. From the standpoint of impulse one views normal development toward increased control from a charged, restless and tense state to voluntary directed behavior. The often noted relationship between psychological and biological immaturity on the one hand and deviate personality on the other may be associated with maturational lag of impulse controls. Very few psychopathic personalities derive alone from impulse of excessive intensity but more often from discordant balance between the regulating character and impulse producing in adults and more frequently in children stealing, fire-setting, wandering, sexual acting-out, and assault. The psychopaths weak in impulse with low vitality are commonly seen but rarely are antisocial.

From the standpoint of temperament alone, personalities may deviate from affective excess (e.g., vivacious, excitable, explosive, irritable, cheerful, etc.), insufficiency (e.g., phlegmatic, torpid, shallow, etc.) or instability and lability. Again, temperament alone rarely produces antisocial behavior.

It is from the standpoint of character alone that we being to approach the problem of antisocial behavior, since without disorder or deviance here, no such conduct is likely. Character is the combined attitudes and goals of the personality; it regulates and directs; it is the purposive component of personality; it is portrayed in the ego and is formed through contact with the environment. Kahn stresses five aspects of character important in the development of psychopathic personalities: (1) the excessive concern for ego or environment, (2) the over- or under-evaluation of ego, (3) the under- or over-evaluation of the foreign or non-ego, (4) the ability to establish goals and values, and (5) the negative effect of environment on the personality. There are two types of ego over-evaluation, the *active* autist who denies the environment, exaggerates ego strength and sees himself as conqueror of the enemy world, and the egocentric whose grandiosity is a protest against weakness. There are two types of ego under-evaluation, the *passive autist* whose weakness produces a yearning for the non-ego and a life on a protected island, and the *ego-searcher* whose style is devotion, sacrifice and self-surrender. These excesses and insufficiencies of *impulse, temperment,* and *character* combine to yield the predominant, non-adaptive, disordered, tormented and tormenting personalities, some especially disposed to antisocial behavior. Kahn described several such combinations: The passive *asocial personality weak in impulse* who is driven by the environment and because of poorly directed steerage is without goal or purpose producing potential parasites who are often habitually petty criminals. The *cold, affectively shallow passive autist weak in impulse* and *active autist strong in impulse* correspond to Kraepelin's antisocial psychopaths and Schneider's affectless morally blind and insane. The disorder is in the affect, not cognition. They are indifferent to the feelings of others without shame and remorse.

The *passive, cold autists, weak in impulse* show both affective torpidity and poverty and a lack of psychic activity. They are typically lazy and have no earnest endeavor and no interest. They are passively asocial and contribute largely to the ranks of the petty criminal. Although weak in impulse they are capable of sudden, explosive, ruthless animal urges but crumble in the face of strength.

The *active, cold autists, strong in impulse* show a poverty of affect and powerful urge to do battle with an enemy society. They are agile, mobile and autistically euphoric, at war with the environment as "picked troops of professional criminals"(Heindl*).They are ruthless, unyielding, tyrannical personalities, with leadership ability. Circumstances may allow them to be great pioneers and leaders but their courage, coldness and denial of the outside world leave them without pity and potential criminals at war with society. As for prognosis, they are uneducable and untreatable due to an absence of affective resonance.

The *hysterical psychopathic personality* as a role playing theatrical may

* Cited in Kahn (1931).

contribute fraud, swindling and quackery as well as some eccentric cranks. Their natural bearing is pose and lack of genuineness. Most are shallow in affect and egocentric in character.

These complex types have one thing in common, a relative lack of affective resonance which is seen as the basis for their poor prognosis. Regardless of theoretic persuasion or mode of practice, shallow affect and poor motivation reduce educability and the potential for behavior change.

CONTEMPORARY VIEWS

It would appear that the clinician can view antisocial behavior from the stand-point of disordered personality structure and organization. The diagnosis should emphasize impulse strength, temperament quality and magnitude, and character strength and direction with the total personality portrayed as an image of the integration and balance among these properties. Those psychopathic personalities most vulnerable or disposed to antisocial behavior have in common shallow, nonresonant emotion which reduces compassion, motivation, and the capacity for reinforcement of social learning. The *active,* alienated grandiose narcissist, and the *passive,* "as-if" narcissist searching for self in the reflected appraisals of others provide the characterologically determined leaders and followers. Finally, those affectively shallow and characterologically narcissistic people strong in impulse yield the more dangerous, potentially explosive, and persistent threats to society; those shallow narcissists weak in impulse may be troublesome but usually in a more petty less frightening fashion. The various combinations of quality and intensity of these properties of personality produce the various kinds of people most likely to do violence to prevailing social norms.

If we are to pursue treatment beyond confinement or detention in hospitals and prisons, there must be valid ideas and knowledge about impulse control, shallow effect, and character formation. Let us touch briefly on the state of the science.[9]

First we will deal with impulse, a fundamentally biologic concept studied physiologically through autonomic and cortical responsiveness and their corre-lations with impulse control. Writers and researchers have viewed this problem of impulse control from the standpoint of maturational retardation, reduced cortical arousal, and related excessive need for stimulation.

A second approach to the psychopathic personalities is through studies of learn-ing and learning deficiency as a possible product of reduced affective resonance.

The final and most popular area of study emphasizes character formation as a product of experience through family impact and socialization. Antisocial behavior derives from attitudes, values and behavioral styles conditioned by unfortunate family and social experiences such as deprivation, separation, rejec-tion, and discord during the critical years of personality development. The

[9] Hare (1970) has written a more complete review.

social and family impact hypothesis may derive its popularity from simplicity since blame is clear, and because it offers hope since prevention is possible. The impulse-arousal and shallow affect-learning hypotheses require complex research and provide less immediate hope for modification or prevention, the locus of blame is less clear, and they do not lend themselves to exploitation as rational foundations for social reform movements.

Impulse-Arousal Approach

The studies of cortical correlates (e.g., Bay-Rakal, 1965; Ellingson, 1954, Knott, *et al.*, 1953; Kurland, *et al.*, 1963; Schwade and Geiger, 1956; Hill and Watterson, 1942) which point to the kinds of EEG tracings frequently found in normal or minimal brain dysfunction children (e.g., excessive slow activity, 14 and 6 positive spikes, etc.) add credence to the *maturational retardation* hypothesis. Such characteristic psychopathic behavior as narcissism, impulsiveness, and reduced ability to delay gratification also point to maturational retardation. If psychopathy is related to slow cortical maturation, incidence should decrease with age. It has been suggested (e.g., Gibbens, *et al.*, 1955; Robins, 1966) that psychopaths with abnormal EEGs tend to outgrow both EEG and behavioral abnormality; also, psychopaths tend to become less antisocial with age. The slower recovery rate by both psychopaths and schizophrenics (Shagass and Schwartz, 1962) suggests reduced cortical excitability, which could relate to attenuation of sensory input magnitude, particularly input with disturbing consequences.

Early autonomic studies were equivocal or nondifferentiating, but a recent study by Hare (1968a) using Cleckley's (1964) strict criteria showed that psychopaths had lower levels of resting skin conductance and less nonspecific GSR (Galvanic Skin Response) activity indicating under-arousal. These results require cautious interpretation but in general when positive results appear, autonomic under-arousal and under-activity occur. Stimulation provides guidance and regulatory cues based upon effective information processing and prior learning. Stimuli also increase the level of activation or arousal, which is the physiological and psychological state of the organism proceeding from sleep through awareness to excitement. A prevailing view is that psychopathy is related to a lower state of cortical arousal and to a chronic need for stimulation as with Petrie (1967) who divides extremes of sensory modulation into reducers and augmenters. Studies (Hare, 1968b; Schoenherr, 1964) suggest a higher shock detection threshold in psychopaths; and psychopaths who are not anxious had higher pain tolerance thresholds than anxious nonpsychopathic delinquents. This important research is in an embryonic stage, but in general psychopathy appears related to a tendency to attenuate sensory input. If so, cues essential for social functioning may be too subtle and too weak; if near or below threshold, they may be ineffective. In an attempt to maintain optimum arousal the psychopath may seek more intense stimulation or exciting, arousing stimulation. In scanning the environment for exciting stimulation he may miss or ignore many social cues for the guidance and regulation of behavior.

This area of research is exciting and continues to provide essential clues about the nature of the psychopathic personality who behaves antisocially. It would seem that the psychopath compensates for low arousal and stimulus deprivation through high input intensity requirements.

The understanding of impulse-arousal through continued research may provide therapeutic handles for this part of the problem of antisocial behavior, but except for chemical and physical confinement, *no treatment modality is suggested that has worked.*

Shallow Affect-Learning Approach

The students of human learning focus upon psychopathy as a product of a specific kind of learning experience or deficiency in the ability to learn certain kinds of behavior. Eysenck (1964) views the psychopath as an extrovert with a nervous system predisposed to the rapid development of cortical inhibition. He acquires conditioned responses slowly and extinguishes them rapidly and this learning defect is viewed as a constitutional predisposition. In general, psychopaths do not develop conditioned fear responses readily; they learn responses poorly that are motivated by fear and reinforced by fear reduction (e.g., Lykken, 1955; Schacter and Latane, 1964; Schoenherr, 1964; Schmauk, 1968). Also, they tend to be less influenced by the relationship between past events and consequences of present behavior.

The behavior therapists have reported successful extinction of some sexual deviations (e.g., Barlow, *et al.,* 1969; Callahan and Leitenberg, 1973; Feldman, *et al.,* 1968; Fookes, 1969) but aversive conditioning models require the presence of fear and its reduction and, hence, the psychopath is not viewed as an appropriate candidate for this kind of therapy. Occasional dramatic claims for results in the office and on the cell block notwithstanding, it is generally accepted that *behavior therapy does not work* in correcting the learning defects of psychopathic personalities who behave antisocially.

Socialization-Character Formation Approach

The most popular and persistent view of all proposes to explain the psychopathic personalities and their antisocial behaviors on the basis of life-styles produced by social conditions and disturbed family relationships. This approach is both appealing and tempting because (1) it is simple and easily understood, (2) it assigns blame and permits the endorsement and support of personal prejudices in the name of science and health, (3) it provides a rational basis for social pressure and reform. Hence, this hypothesis has wide acceptance, blaming specific social conditions (e.g., poverty) and family friction (e.g., separation) for the development and formation of character patterns and life-styles that are psychopathic[10] and antisocial. Proponents inevitably accept predominant environmental causation. Blame is assigned to very specific social and family factors and, with minimal evidence, social reform and family styles are recommended as preventive treatment. This places the mental sciences in the center of potential mythology which attains truth value by appeal, assertion, and fiat. The need for social reform and intact families should not be supported without fact through mental health mythology.

The prevailing generalization that psychopathic personalities are produced by specific and nonspecific disturbances in family and social conditions has been supported by research and survey using retrospective methodology (e.g., Greer, 1964; Gregory, 1958) which is subject to substantial error and should be used to search for, not test hypotheses. Hence, these studies carry little more weight than the clinical convictions of Kahn (1931) and Cleckley (1964) who viewed family conditions as minor contributing and potentiating factors. The proponents of social and family causation cannot account rationally for the fact that most people survive deplorable family and social conditions without developing a psychopathic personality accompanied by antisocial behavior.

Importance of experience in character development and formation is an issue of such fundamental importance for the mental health professions that it cannot be sustained by a prevailing mythology. Epidemiologic research methods are appropriate in the determination of the effects of specific early social and family factors in the understanding of subsequent disordered personalities and antisocial behavior. Two such studies are worthy of mention since they offer useful facts.

The first by Robins (1966) and co-workers represents a landmark in social research about the conditions associated with the development of the psychopathic personalities and antisocial behavior. About 30 years after children appeared in a psychiatric clinic, they were studied in terms of their adult social and psychiatric characteristics; the sample included more than 500 patients and 100 healthy controls. The childhood predictors of adult psychopathic personality emphasizing antisocial behavior were enumerated and a profile drawn. The most important discoveries pertained to family background. While most of those who developed antisocial, psychopathic personalities came from low socioeconomic homes, the father emerged as the most significant figure. Fathers of psychopaths were more likely to have a history of antisocial or irresponsible behavior. Robin's work emphasizes the lack of available discipline and the presence of marital discord rather than parental loss or separation as predictors of adult psychopathic behavior.

The second study by Rutter (1971) and his co-workers on family factors and antisocial behavior found no significant long-term effects of permanent or

---

[10] Again, we are not referring to group behavior of obvious social origin such as campus and ghetto riots. Our psychopaths who behave antisocially have a nonharmonious balance of the personality factors *impulse, temperament,* and *character* producing a nonspecific behavioral disposition or vulnerability.

transient parent-child separation when considered in combination with parental discord and disharmony. Again, loss or separation was secondary to prevailing conditions prior to loss or separation.

The importance of social factors and parent-child relationships in personality development and character formation has been established. However, absolute positions that assert family and social causation of antisocial behavior are without foundation.

Robins and Rutter have provided the most substantial evidence to date about the relative importance of loss and separation on the one hand, and discord and disharmony on the other, yet the broken home myth remains. More research on the process of socialization and character formation will provide the facts necessary for a science of preventive intervention. However, *no treatment method based upon disordered character formation from disturbed social and family conditions has worked* in the modification or prevention of psychopathic personalities who behave antisocially.

COMMENTS ON TREATMENT

A realistic appraisal of clinical and scientific progress through 1974 demands the reaffirmation of Kahn's (1931) comment of more than four decades ago that was used to open this chapter. We still *do not possess a causal therapy* of the psychopathic personalities and efforts at biologic and psychologic intervention at the levels of treatment and prevention remain *in their earliest stages.* Therapeutic programs must emerge from *intimate knowledge of the personality* based upon combined psychological and educational procedures. While we are *still unable and perhaps always will remain unable to change the constitutional structure of the psychopathic personalities,* hope lies in increasing our capacity to *educate many of them to understand themselves, to come to terms with themselves, and to set themselves genuine goals which they may reach in spite of their psychopathic personalities.*

Unfortunately those combinations of strong or weak impulse, shallow emotion, and self-centered grandiose or impressionable characters most vulnerable to a life-style emphasizing antisocial behavior provide few assets that would permit the education and adaptation of these psychopathic personalities.

Again, mental health workers must emphasize knowledge of personality and its interaction with experience. When antisocial behavior is involved these professionals must join forces with other concerned disciplines. We have prime responsibility for learning to modify personality functioning, but we are one among many in the treatment of antisocial behavior. As suggested earlier, antisocial behavior and its reduction is not the province of the mental and behavioral sciences -- the study of biologic, psychologic, and social influences upon personality development and formation represents our domain.

Without credible exception, students of these antisocial psychopathic personalities continue to report poor results (e.g., Cleckley, 1964; McCord and McCord,

1964; Hare, 1970) with psychologic, biologic, and social therapies. Modest successes have been reported in authoritarian, highly disciplined and structured correctional settings (Arendsen Hein, 1959; Sturup, 1964) but these findings may be, in part, a product of the suggestion that the severity of antisocial behavior decreases spontaneously with age (Hare, 1970; Robins, 1966). Patterson (1966) has summarized possible bases for poor treatment results: *First,* psychotherapies assume the presence of pain and discomfort as motivating forces for change. Unfortunately, the antisocial psychopathic personality rarely experiences sufficient distress and does not recognize the wrongness of the conduct. *Second,* data suggests a defect in time orientation with a predominant focus upon the here and now, depriving the antisocial psychopath of an opportunity to profit from a past, and predict with concern the consequences in the future. *Three,* and, of fundamental importance, is the therapeutic requirement of an affective relationship with sufficient depth to provide a setting for corrective emotional experience. The shallow temperament precludes all but an intellectual therapeutic experience without personal, compassionate involvement. *Finally,* Patterson suggests that the pessimism of the therapist concerning the effectiveness of treatment for this group of people may produce a self-fulfilling prophesy.

Considering these difficulties and the complexity of the problem, Thorne (1959) delivered a prescription based upon Kahn's notion that the antisocial psychopathic personality might become more effective by educating him to the fact that the behavior is defeating, and extending time perspective from present orientation into the future through total command and control over reward and punishment. Thorne's model requires the mobilization of family, friends and the entire community in controlling reinforcement and modifying life-style. This theoretical model requires the following for successful treatment: The therapist must control all finances as formal trustee; family and friends must never rescue the antisocial psychopath from the consequences of his behavior; the therapist must be strict and persistent in setting limits and establishing controls; the therapist must never rescue from or stand in the way of legal and social consequences; the therapist must respond only to effective social action and not to verbal promises and commitments; the antisocial psychopath must be faced repeatedly with the self-defeating nature of his behavior; and, the therapist must be alert for reinforcing incentives which will promote more socially effective behavior, even if it requires bribery with the money he controls. In 1959, Thorne placed a conservative annual price-tag on this therapy at $15,000, and the effort and feasibility were highlighted. Indeed, the dollar cost would be much greater at this time but insignificant compared with the turmoil, chaos and exhaustion imposed upon family, friends, and therapist. The Thorne prescription may be viewed as a satiric effort to demonstrate the cost in time, money, effort, people, and community resources required to provide a treatment program with questionable likelihood of success. Even if the Herculean therapist and family, and Utopian community were located, Thorne's hope for locating effective reinforcing incentives and extending time perspective may represent an unrealistic dream. Needless to say, the Thorne prescription has not received a fair test.

Frustration tends to lead to the hope that some biologic magic is lurking offshore that will permit a chemical, surgical or genetic engineering solution to this problem; the tides do not seem favorable for fulfillment from these sources.

What we can do is very modest, but does represent a contribution. We can't treat antisocial behavior or change the psychopathic personality who behaves antisocially. We can offer a useful appraisal of personality as a whole and assess its distinct properties. We can provide clinical opinions regarding vulnerabilities and dispositions, and speculate about outcome in general and in relation to specific circumstances. I have accepted the role as supporting service to other agencies directly responsible for antisocial behavior, consulting about the nature of the individual, his psychopathology and personality with recommendations about biologic, psychologic, and social intervention that might reduce the probability of destructive conduct.

CONCLUSIONS

Economists are now regrouping behind their drawing boards after a disastrous decade of enthusiastic prediction and treatment; theories and methods were promoted and tried with a mildly arrogant certitude for success (Greene, 1974). No approach or point of view has produced change in what appears to have been the economic destiny of our times. The state of the science was insufficiently developed and too narrow for the complexity of man's economic nature to yield an art or technology that could alter significantly history's course.

The mental sciences are also given to promises, and our failures have been predominantly due to premature excessive and enthusiastic commitment, and the inability to deliver. Nowhere is this more evident than with the management and treatment of antisocial behavior. As with the economists, we are now witnessing an erosion of public trust and professional confidence.

It has been the thesis of this discussion that the mental health professions and behavioral sciences have no treatment for the antisocial behaviors of psychopathic personalities. However, these disciplines can contribute to the understanding of personality structure and function, thereby defining and classifying people who are most vulnerable and disposed to behaving antisocially. The point of view offered by the mental health professions adds another useful dimension to the complex matrix of disciplines concerned with man's relationships. A science and technology based upon the nature of our species utilizing the methodology of ethology (Tinbergen, 1968) must provide fundamental data on characteristics given by evolution, their function, and their modifiability. Are homicide and theft mere extensions of man's natural hunting, aggressive and predatory instincts becoming deviant only through an interaction of unfortunate personal characteristics and social circumstances? Can the properties of a psychopathic personality be harnessed through education and opportunity to reduce the likelihood of antisocial behavior? Can we learn to predict early enough in the formation of personality to modify direction prior to the development of the antisocial style? It is fair to state that the disposition for psychopathic antisocial behavior has roots in the development and formation of personality, but the antisocial life-style is conditioned by experience and circumstances. To date the mental health professions have not produced effective tools for prevention or treatment at the stage of development or at the interface with society. It is not discouraging to stipulate our ignorance, and to acknowledge slow progress early in man's most complex professional sport – *knowing himself.* We are still in the process of learning from deviance about man's nature, and are not yet ready to apply knowledge toward effective control.

Excessive promises and social pressures combined with a bit of narcissistic self-deception have placed the mental health professions in danger of becoming an instrument of public policy. In the name of diagnosis and treatment, people are often confined, detained, and medicated because of presumed dangerousness from mental illness and emotional disorder. These decisions, made by health professionals, represent a form of preventive detention using health facilities as arms of the Criminal Law, and provide convenient but abused resources for those responsible for the administration of justice.

This essay did not yield much useful information about the treatment of antisocial behavior for the health professional. Yet the health "mentality" is seen as quite useful in providing a supporting service to those responsible for representing public policy which defines and controls antisocial behavior.

> Since in psychopaths not everything is psychopathic it is possible to bring many of them to turn more and more toward their non-psychopathic *Anlagen,* and on this basis to deal successfully with their inner difficulties, at least to a certain degree. In such attempts it is expedient to call the psychopaths' attention to the fact that even *psychopathy lays responsibility on the individual. Psychopathy means not only aberration and difficulty but also differentiation and capacity for suffering.* The physician, however, and the psychotherapist in particular, may be confirmed by this insight in that which fundamentally every man owes to every other; respect for his fellowman. (Kahn, 1931)

REFERENCES

Arendsen, Hein, G. Group therapy with criminal psychopaths. *Acta Psychotherap.* (Suppl.). **7**: 6–16 (1959).

Barlow, D.H., Leitenberg, H. and Agras, W.S. Experimental control of sexual deviation through manipulation of the noxious scene in covert sensitization. *J. Abnorm. Psychol.* **74**: 597–601 (1969).

Bay-Rakal, S. The significance of EEG abnormality in behavior problem children. *Can. Psychiat. Assoc. J.* **10**: 387–391 (1965).

Callahan, E.J. and Leitenberg, H. Aversion therapy for sexual deviation: Contingent shock and covert sensitization. *J. Abnorm. Psychol.* 81: 60–73 (1973).

Cleckley, H. *The mask of sanity,* (4th edition). St. Louis: Mosby, 1964.

Craft, M.J. *Ten studies into psychopathic personality.* Bristol: John Wright, 1965.

Diagnostic and statistical manual of mental disorders, (first and second editions). Washington, D.C.: American Psychiatric Association, 1952, 1968.

Ellingson, R.J. Incidence of EEG abnormality among patients with mental disorders of apparently nonorganic origin: a criminal review. *Amer. J. Psychiat.,* 1954, 111: 263–275 (1954).

Eysenck, H.J. *Crime and personality.* London: Methuen, 1964.

Feldman, M.P., MacCulloch, M.J. and MacCulloch, M.L. The aversion therapy treatment of a heterogeneous group of five cases of sexual deviation. *Acta Psychiat. Scand.* 44: 113–123 (1968).

Fookes, B.H. Some experiences in the use of aversion therapy in male homosexuality, exhibitionism, and fetishism-transvestism. *Brit. J. Psychiat.* 115: 339–341 (1969).

Freedman, A. and Kaplan, *Comprehensive textbook of psychiatry.* Baltimore: Williams & Wilkins, 1967.

Gibbens, T.C.N., Pond, D.A. and Stafford-Clark, D. A follow-up study of criminal psychopaths. *Brit. J. Delinq.* 5: 126–136 (1955).

Greene, W. Economists in recession. *N.Y. Times Magazine.* May 12, 1974.

Greer, S. Study of parental loss in neurotics and sociopaths. *Arch. Gen. Psychiat.* 11: 177–180 (1964).

Gregory, I. Studies of parental deprivation in psychiatric patients. *Amer. J. Psychiat.* 115: 432–442 (1958).

Hare, R.D. Psychopathy, autonomic functioning, and the orienting response. *J. Abnorm. Psychol.,* (Mono. Suppl.). 73 (No. 3, Part 2): 1–24 (1968a).

Hare, R.D. Detection threshold for electric shock in psychopaths. *J. Abnorm. Psychol.* 73: 268–272 (1968b).

Hare, R.D. *Psychopathy: theory and research.* New York: John Wiley, 1970.

Hill, D. and Watterson, D. Electroencephalographic studies of the psychopathic personality. *J. Neurol. Psychiat.* 5: 47–64 (1942).

Kahn, E. *Psychopathic personalities.* New Haven: Yale University Press, 1931.

Knott, J.R., Platt, E.B., Ashby, M.C. and Gottlieb, J.S. A familiar evaluation of the electroencephalogram of patients with primary behavior disorder and psychopathic personality. *EEG Clin. Neurophysiol.* 5: 363–370 (1953).

Kurland, H.D., Yeager, C.T. and Arthur, R.J. Psychophysiologic aspects of severe behavior disorders. *Arch. Gen. Psychiat.* 8: 599–604 (1963).

Lykken, D.T. A study of anxiety in the sociopathic personality. Doctoral Dissertation, University of Minnesota, 1955.

Maughs, S.B. Concept of psychopathy and psychopathic personality: its evolution and historic development. *J. Crim. Psychopath.* 2: 329–356 (1941).

McCord, W. and McCord, J. *The psychopath: an essay on the criminal mind.* New York: Van Nostrand Reinhold, 1964.

Patterson, C.H. Theories of counseling and psychopathy. New York: Harper & Row, 1966.

Petrie, A. *Individuality in pain and suffering.* Chicago: University of Chicago Press, 1967.

Robins, L.N. *Deviant children grown up.* Baltimore: Williams & Wilkins, 1966.

Rutter, M. Parent-child separation: psychological effects on the children. *J. Child Psychol. & Psychiat.* **12**: 233–260 (1971).

Schachter, S. and Latane, B. Crime, cognition and the autonomic nervous system. In: Jones, M.R. (Ed.), *Nebraska symposium on motivation.* Lincoln: University of Nebraska Press, 1964.

Schmauk, F. A study of the relationship between kinds of punishment, autonomic arousal, subjective anxiety and avoidance learning in the primary sociopath. Doctoral Dissertation, Temple University, 1968.

Schoenherr, J.C. Avoidance of noxious stimulation in psychopathic personality. Doctoral Dissertation, University of California, Los Angeles, 1964.

Schwade, E.D. and Geiger, S.G. Abnormal electroencephalographic findings in severe behavior disorders. *Diseases Nervous System* **17**: 307–317 (1965).

Shagass, C. and Schwartz, M. Observations on somatosensory cortical reactivity in personality disorders. *J. Nervous Mental Disease.* **135**: 44–51 (1962).

Sturup, G.K. The treatment of chronic criminals. *Bull. Menninger Clin.* **28**: 229–243 (1964).

Thorne, F.C. The etiology of sociopathic reactions. *Amer. J. Psychotherapy.* **13**: 319–330 (1959).

Tinbergen, N. War and peace in animals and man: an ethologists approach to the biology of aggression. *Science.* **160**: 1410–1418 (1968).

20 The Treatment of Drug Addiction

James W. Dykens and Rogelio D. Bayog

Of the many individual, family and community problems confronting the professional dealing with mental disorders, none continues to present a greater challenge than drug addiction. Its prevalence is widespread, its incidence difficult to measure (Lavenhar, 1973) and its pattern shifting. The *National Survey on Drug Abuse* released by the Department of Health and Human Services (1979) showed the number of Americans who have used illicit drugs has increased dramatically in the past two decades. Between 1972 and 1979, experience with marijuana and cocaine doubled among 12- to 17-year-olds and among those 25 years of age. The use of inhalants and hallucinogens has shown a marked increase. Bachman, Johnston and O'Malley (1981), reporting on the patterns of drug use, note that the characteristics of the populations at risk have not changed significantly.

The urban epidemic of PCP use is reported by Yago *et al.* (1981). As many as 43.4% of 145 consecutive patients seen in a Los Angeles County psychiatric emergency room were positive for PCP. These 63 patients manifested a variety of psychotic clinical pictures.

An effective and concerted approach toward the many issues relating to drug addiction has yet to be attained. Broad legislative and law enforcement issues focusing upon sources of drug supply, the drug traffic and control of criminal behavior relating to addiction are apparently meeting questionable success. The comprehensive mental health worker is faced with a host of biopsychosocial factors that require integrated management in dealing with the individual addict, with his family and with addiction as a social issue.

To be addicted is to be "dedicated to" or "bound." It is being "fixed." There is a chemical bond with concomitant fixed feeling and cognitive states, repetitive behavior and a supporting and binding drug culture. Balanced attention to all aspects of the system of numb fixation is required in understanding and managing the prevention and treatment of drug addiction. It is intended here to scan issues of a social, psychological and biological nature that are pertinent in approaching the field of drug addiction.

BIOPSYCHOSOCIAL CONCEPTS IN DRUG ADDICTION

The social backdrop of the addict and the drug subculture helped create the ambience of the 1960s, in which there was increased awareness of the self and of the social milieu. Opening up of the mind through psychedelic experience for greater self-understanding as well as activism for social change occurred. Issues of civil rights, poverty, alienation, poor housing, environmental pollution, sexism and racism emerged. Rationalism gave way to the expression of feelings and actions. Reinforcement occurred in literature, art forms, including films, jazz, acid, rock music and street violence. The streetwalker was joined by the street user, the street pusher, the nomadic street sleeper — and the street worker. Meanwhile, in the homes lining the city streets as well as suburban and rural roads, the American adult public was ingesting psychotropic medication by the ton to deal with its anxieties, depressions and emotional crises. Double messages and double binds between the generations led to dissatisfaction and alienation — and in some instances, tragic deaths by overdosage.

Through identification with his primary group the addict finds common language and support from peers against what is perceived to be a Janus-faced family and establishment. Through habituation, the addict became increasingly isolated with social breakdown, anomie, isolation and psychosocial regression. Criminal behavior associated with the seeking of drug supplies or abandonment of the search through suicide has confounded the social problem.

A number of significant issues in treatment of the addict are clustered within the family situation. A concept of useful value to clinicians for understanding the addict's family comes from the work of Johnson and Szurek (1952), which is pertinent to all acting-out behavior. This model holds that the genesis of acting-out behavior in the child arises from unconscious wishes and impulses in the parent that are expressed vicariously through the child. Clinical experience, as pointed out by Seldin (1972), supports the idea that until and unless the family is considered in understanding and managing the addict, little progress is likely to be made. Parental inconsistency and communication disorders in the family may place the addicted member in a double bind. A commonly found family situation is a mother who alternates between overprotection and active rejection which generates ambivalence about love and nurturance. The absent, distant or passive father is unavailable for rescue operations, through identification for the male or for helping the female separate from a domineering mother. For the married addict, the marriage itself may emerge as the main target for therapy.

Through displacement from the primal family, the spouse may symbolically stand for the parent and vicariously gain gratification through the addict's addiction. It is to be noted, also, that within the street culture are figures who symbolically may represent family members. Thus, the pusher-supplier, the police-authority and the security-guaranteeing jail, can both cause and express suffering reminiscences for the addict.

Family crises relating to developmental or accidental life change events, described by Caplan (1964), are of signal importance in the management of the drug addict. Of special importance, here, is the idea that in dealing with the drug addict, the therapist deals with the addict's present life crisis and crisis coping mechanisms as well as the recurrent crisis of drug abuse.

In treating the addict, while it may not be easy to tackle problems within a resilient character armor, it is feasible to detail out a life change event that has brought the addict to the treatment situation. In approaching the addict-in-crisis, the therapist may profitably detail out the elements of the psychosocial crisis as carefully as he details out the detoxification procedure. While the addict appears to move in his life-style from one supply crisis to another, with constant yearning for need-satisfaction, there is always the straw that breaks the camel's back. An understanding of such a crisis situation can lead to greater understanding of the addict, especially of his perception of family role or its extension into his peer group.

Oceanic feelings of bliss in the addicted state represent both a physiological and a psychological escape from the helpless and hopeless feelings of depression. It is of major importance that in detoxifying the addict, the therapist be aware of clinical depression that may emerge as the drug is withdrawn. Substitute supplies are necessary through supporting interpersonal relationships from staff. The psychosocial dynamics of depression are those of the loss. In detoxification, the addict must work through the loss of his drug. In order to prevent recidivism, it is to be noted that feelings of loss occur when one makes voluntary renunciation as well as when something is "taken away." Thus, in helping the addict to remain drug-free, his feelings of loss in letting go of the drug require working through.

In treating and managing the addict, one must understand him or her as a person, and understanding, in a comprehensive sense, is facilitated by consideration of Erikson's (1963) work. Especially relevant in dealing with the addict is Erickson's elaboration of the oral phase of psycho-sexual development into the first incorporative mode of behavior, associated with "getting," and the second incorporative mode, associated with "taking." Depending on the mode or style of behavior developed through prior psycho-social transaction between mother and child, the infant learns a basic pattern of trusting or distrusting. In the addict this nuclear concept appears to be unsolved. In failing to establish a point of orientation in the trust–distrust behavior continuum, the addict swings between the extremes of gullible self-deceit and massive distrust of a nonsupplying milieu. His manipulation and acting-out against treatment, as well as society, require that treatment programs create the expectation of trust and, at the same time, do not get caught in the confidence game the addict may try to play.

The therapist may also consider the addict's use of the repetition compulsion in his addiction. Further regression into the use of early defenses such as denial and projection may require active management in order to deal with the meaning of his addictive behavior.

Vaillant (1978) lists several broad biopsychosocial factors that contribute to the development of alcoholism and drug abuse. These include availability, as evidenced by increased prevalence of heroin abuse among American troops in Vietnam where heroin was cheap and readily available; the slow or fast-acting capacity of the drug to alter consciousness and physical dependence; hereditary factor, well-documented among offspring of alcoholics, which remains to be determined among drug addicts; and cultural facts (i.e., whether or not a culture provides clear guidelines for nonabusive drug use is significant). Studies on personality type indicate the high incidence of sociopathy among drug abusers with acting-out, impulsivity and poor frustration tolerance. The final factor mentioned by Vaillant is symptom relief. Cocaine and amphetamines produce temporary mood elevation. PCP may produce findings similar to alcohol intoxication. Opiates act to soothe anger and hunger.

Bayog and Fisch (1979) describe a common "addictogenic" family: absent or aloof, passive father; a controlling, immature and very ambivalent mother; and a conflicted marital relationship causing emotional turmoil and poor role models.

In his study of a patient during experimental self-regulated readdiction to morphine, Wikler (1952) concluded that the ultimate determinant of the motivation to use morphine repeatedly appears to be the relative intensity of such anxiety as is consequent to the inadequate satisfaction of "primary" needs through "normal" or "neurotic" mechanisms. Primary needs are defined as subjective experiences that are related to adaptive responses of the organism to interpersonal aspects of changes in its internal and external environment. These include hunger, fear of pain, and sexual urges. Rado (1957) writes of drug dependence as a self-inflicted process resulting from an aggrandized self image that collapses under reality and thus stimulates hedonistic mechanisms to regain the grandiose picture of the self.

Winnicott (1953) observes the experiences of healthy infants and concludes in his studies on transitional objects and the transitional phenomenon that addiction can be stated in terms of regression at the early stage when the infant creates illusions unchallenged by reality testing. This does not allow the growth from the pleasure principle to the reality principle needed to get beyond primary identification.

The oral-narcissistic and regressive dynamic pattern is a consistent finding in the addict. In considering the oral nature of acting-out, Altman (1957) reinforces the belief that oral needs are characterized by their urgency and lack of capacity for gaining satisfaction from substitues.

Kohut (1977) writes of addicts as having a primary disorder of the self. A void exists that the addict tries to fill by sexual activity or by oral ingestion. Further, he writes, "It is the lack of self-esteem of the unmirrored self, the uncertainty about the very existence of the self that the addict tries to counteract by his addictive behavior." He notes that there is no pleasure in addictive eating, drinking or drug use. The primary disorder of the self develops as a result of persistent failure of the parents or their substitutes to mirror the grandiose and narcissistic wishes of the child during the pregenital period.

Wurmser (1974) states that compulsive drug use and the drug of choice by the addict represent a defense against overwhelming affects. He posits that narcotics and barbiturates calm intense feelings of rage, shame and loneliness and the anxiety evoked by these feelings. Psychedelic drugs attenuate affective states of boredom, meaninglessness and emptiness. Amphetamines and cocaine provide temporary relief from massive depression and feelings of weakness and unworthiness.

Thus far, there is no unitary theory that provides a comprehensive explanation of the etiology of drug addiction. It is important that clinicians view each patient as a unique susceptible individual with specific strengths and weaknesses. Biopsychosocial and pharmacological factors interact to cause a chronic disorder.

DRUG INTOXICATION AND DRUG WITHDRAWAL SYNDROMES

Opioids

This drug group includes natural opioids such as heroin and morphine as well as synthetics with morphine-like action such as meperidine and methadone.

Opioid Intoxication. This may be diagnosed by the following clinical features. 1) There is a history of recent use of opioids from the patient or collateral sources. 2) Depressed respiration, pinpoint pupils (in the absence of brain damage) and stupor or coma with findings of needle tracks are strongly suggestive. 3) Cyanosis may be present along with fall in body temperature, decreased urine formation and flaccid skeletal muscles. 4) Pulmonary edema is a common complication. 5) Testing of urine and gastric contents may help identify the specific opioid or other CNS depressant.

Treatment of Opioid Intoxication. Because of various factors influencing the purity of street drugs, accurate doses are not known by persons self-administering heroin. Because degree of tolerance affects response to a dose, a first-time user may accidentally overdose himself. The role of additives (i.e., quinine action) needs to be considered by the treating physician.

Hospitalization is indicated for the patient with overdose. It is vital to establish and maintain a patent airway. Drug treatment during the period of intoxication is with parenteral (preferably intravenous) administration of naloxone, 0.4 mg (1 ml). If the desired degree of counteraction and improvement in respiratory functions is not obtained immediately following naloxone administration, the dose may be repeated at 2- to 3-minute intervals. Lack of improvement after two to three doses suggests other causes. It is important to monitor patients receiving naloxone closely as the duration of action of this agent is brief in contrast to long-acting synthetic opioids such as methadone and *l*-acethymethadol (LAAM), which could persist for 24 to 72 hours.

Opioid Withdrawal Syndrome. Jaffee (1980) describes the typical withdrawal symptoms. Lacrimation, yawning, rhinorrhea and sweating appear 8 to 12 hours after the last dose. The addict may fall into a tossing, restless sleep after 12 to 14 hours and wake up more miserable. Additional signs and symptoms, which reach their peak at 48 to 72 hours, are anorexia, gooseflesh, restlessness, irritability and tremors. Weakness, depression, nausea and vomiting, intestinal spasm and diarrhea are common. Chills may occur, as do elevation of pulse and blood pressure. Patients often complain of pains in the bones and muscles of the back and extremeties. Abdominal cramps are common.

Methadone in decreasing doses is the drug of choice for the treatment of opioid withdrawal. The methadone equivalents for various opioids follow: 1 mg methadone for 2 mg heroin, for 4 mg morphine and for 0.5 mg hydromorphone. For withdrawal, it is recommended generally that methadone be administered initially in a single oral dose of 15 to 30 mg. This dose, or part of it, may be repeated when withdrawal symptoms recur. Usually after 36 hours a stabilizing dose is established at 10 to 40 mg, administered orally once daily. It is recommended that this dosage be reduced, 5 mg daily, until the methadone is discontinued. Some mild abstinence symptoms can occur a few days after completion of the detoxification schedule.

This type of rapid detoxification is recommended to prevent withdrawal symptoms. A slower detoxification process may lead the patient to become addicted to methadone. The amount of drug taken by an addict is rarely known to the clinician or addict. Therefore, great care is necessary in withdrawal programs. The administration of doses of methadone in these small amounts in the first 24–36 hours is especially recommended.

Raynes and Patch (1973) reported a different approach to the problem of detoxification. They compared a group of addicts who self-determined the reduction schedule of methadone. This was accomplished in an outpatient hospital setting that provided psychotherapy and other activities such as day care. They reported twice the success in this group of patients compared to a control group of hospitalized addicts, whose medication was doctor-controlled on a regular basis. Psychosocial support is also cited in the effective employment of this new method of detoxification.

During detoxification, the patient is treated medically according to symptoms. It has been found that prescribing psychotropic substances during the withdrawal period can cause untoward reactions.   Jarvik (1970) cites that phenothiazines have been shown to increase the sedative effects of morphine; monoamine oxidase inhibitors are suspected to interfere with the "detoxification mechanisms for other drugs."   There is also some question about the use of dibenzazepine derivatives with some drugs of abuse.

Controversy exists concerning the setting for detoxification. Some advocate that detoxification be done in the hospital. Others believe that detoxification should be done on an outpatient basis, provided that the same medical, social and psychological services are available as are afforded the inpatient.

An essential adjunct to any treatment program for the drug addict is urine monitoring.   Sensitive laboratory methods have been developed for detecting the major substances drug abusers and drug-dependent persons use (opioids, barbiturates, amphetamines, cocaine, PCP).   Random urine sampling is a definitive but less costly method to determine whether a patient is drug-free.   A "clean" or "dirty" urine has psychological implications in the treatment of the addict.

Barbiturates and Similarly Acting Sedative or Hypnotic Drugs

Barbiturate Intoxication.   The clinical features of this syndrome are: 1) There is a history of recent ingestion from the patient or collateral sources. 2)   Physical examination findings may include slurred speech, ataxia and nystagmus; stupor or coma may be present; and arrythmias are not uncommon. 3) Behavioral changes may include irritability, low frustration tolerance and impulsivity, and often patients become abusive.   Some patients describe a "high."

Treatment of Barbiturate Intoxication.   This is best done in a hospital setting.

Patients who took an overdose need aggressive supportive measures including respiration and blood pressure maintenance and prevention of aspiration.   Emetics and/or gastric lavage may be indicated.   Fluid and electrolyte balance are carefully monitored.

Death occurs by depression of the respiratory and cardiovascular systems.

After management of emergency states, detoxification from barbiturates requires determination of the level of tolerance.

Barbiturate Withdrawal Syndrome.   Patients in withdrawal may present with the following signs and symptoms: 1)   physical examination findings may include postural hypotension, tremulousness, nausea and vomiting, hyperpyrexia and seizures;   2)   psychological changes include disturbances of sleep patterns, irritability and anxiety, and withdrawal psychosis has been reported.

Wesson and Smith (1975) recommend a technique of barbiturate detoxification best done in a hospital setting.

For each 100 mg of short-acting barbiturate (secobarbital, pentobarbital, amobarbital) 32 mg of phenobarbital is substituted.

A careful history is obtained regarding the amount of barbiturate used. However, clinicians must keep in mind that barbiturate addicts may exaggerate or minimize the amount of drug use.

Two days of stabilization on the short-acting barbiturates is recommended before starting withdrawal with phenobarbital.

A recommended regime of phenobarbital for the person tolerant to 400 mg of pentobarbital follows:

	6 A.M.	12 Noon	6 P.M.	12 P.M.
Day 1	32 mg	32 mg	32 mg	32 mg
Day 2	32 mg	0	32 mg	32 mg
Day 3	32 mg	0	0	32 mg
Day 4	0	0	0	32 mg
Day 5	0	0	0	0

If signs of intoxication appear at any point, one dose of the daily dosage is omitted. Conversely, if withdrawal signs and symptoms are significant, a dose may be reinstituted or increased.

Amphetamines

Amphetamine Intoxication Syndromes.   These include intoxication, delirium and delusional disorder.

Intoxication may manifest with the following clinical findings: 1) There is a history of recent amphetamine ingestion from the patient or collateral sources. 2) Physical findings may include tremors, brisk reflexes, dilated pupils, dry mouth, tachycardia and hypertension. 3) Behavioral changes may include agitation, emotional lability, irritability, increased hostility and aggressiveness, overtalkativeness and hypervigilance.

Delirium may occur within 24 hours of use. The patient is confused and disoriented and may experience illusions and visual and auditory hallucinations. He may be incoherent. Some patients develop a panic reaction.

The delusional disorder or amphetamine psychosis presents a paranoid-schizophrenic-like picture. The following clinical features are seen: 1) history of weeks or months of abuse of amphetamines; 2) psychological symptoms characterized mainly by paranoid delusions while the patient is alert and oriented; 3) positive urine test for amphetamines.

Serious and potentially fatal complications known to occur with toxic doses of amphetamines are seizures, stroke and hyperpyrexia. Hepatitis, subacute bacterial endocarditis and malnutrition may also occur.

Treatment of Intoxication Syndrome. This is best carried out in a hospital setting. Careful evaluation and treatment of the medical complications are essential.

Supportive talking therapy in a nonthreatening, warm atmosphere is often useful.

Tinklenberg (1975) recommends the judicious use of diazepam, 20 to 30 mg orally (or 15 to 20 mg intramuscularly) for treatment of restlessness and agitation. Haloperidol or the more sedating neuroleptics are deemed to be the drugs of choice for the psychotic manifestations of amphetamine psychosis. Administration of intravenous Valium at a rate of 5 to 20 mg per minute initially repeated at 15- to 20-minute intervals is indicated in the management of seizures which generally are in the form of status epilepticus.

Amphetamine Withdrawal Syndrome. A well-recognized depressive syndrome is described by both Ellinwood (1975) and Schuckit (1979). It is characterized by apathy, lack of initiative, irritability, lowered mood and easy fatigability. Sleep pattern is impaired with increased dreaming. The depression may be severe leading to persistent suicidal ideations. Some patients actually attempt suicide.

This affective state may last for 3 to 4 weeks with waxing and waning of the symptoms.

Psychiatric hospitalization is indicated for the depressive syndrome. It is important to forewarn patients of the course of the illness and relate it to amphetamine withdrawal. When they have hypersomnia, they must be allowed to sleep it off.

Ellinwood (1975) recommends giving tricyclic antidepressants at the beginning of treatment to avoid or attenuate the depressive picture and continue this beyond a month after withdrawal. He notes that patients' attempt to manipulate physicians into giving them amphetamines to tide them over the acute painful stage should be resisted as counterproductive.

Phencyclidine (PCP)

Used as a veterinary anesthetic (Sernylan), it is also known as horse tranquilizer, hog, peace pill, crystal and angel dust.

Patients with PCP intoxication can present with anxiety reactions reaching panic proportions and an acute psychotic reaction.

Showalter and Thornton (1977) reviewed PCP toxicity and describe the following psychological changes: 1) distortions in body image; 2) depersonalization, isolation and depression; 3) severe anxiety; 4) negativism, hostility and apathy; 5) psychosis with disorganization of thought, concrete thinking, blocking and neologisms.

Severe impairment of symbolic cognition and sequential thinking occur along with anterograde amnesia.

Ingestion of low doses may produce a drunken feeling with euphoria, emotional outbursts, ataxia, slurred speech, tremulousness and nystagmus.

Delirium may occur as a result of this drug, or may occur 24 hours after use or following recovery from an overdose. Other complications of PCP use include seizures, severe hypertension, myoglobinuria, renal failure, coma and respiratory depression resulting in death.

The severity of the reaction is dose-related as found in the studies of Burns and Lerner (1978) and by Yesavage and Freman (1978).

Diagnosis can be established by a qualitative and quantitative urine drug screen for PCP. Gastric secretions may also be used for PCP determination. However, a negative urine test does not exclude PCP intoxication, as patients may smoke it.

In the treatment of PCP intoxication, Rotman, Bayog and Okeefe (1981) summarize the treatment approach. Support of respiratory and cardiac functions are crucial. Gastric lavage, activated charcoal and saline cathartics may be indicated, depending on the time of ingestion.

Low-dose intoxication is best handled by placing patients under observation in an isolated, warm, nonthreatening environment. Staff are advised not to "talk down" the patient. Supportive conversation, however, may be beneficial. Diazepam in intravenous doses of 10–15 mg appears to be the agent of choice for controlling the combative, agitated and anxious patient. When a nueroleptic medication is indicated, haloperidol is preferred over phenothiazines. Extreme care should be employed, as neuroleptics may worsen tachycardia and produce hypotension.

If intubation is indicated, use of succinylcholine is beneficial to induce skeletal muscle relaxation.

Patients should be kept well hydrated, and frequent suctioning may help. For hypertensive crisis, clinicians use diazoxide and hydralazine with success. Diazepam and phenytoin are effective in management of PCP-induced seizures.

Use of contant gastric suction is recommended to eliminate extensive amounts of PCP secreted into the gastric lumen. Acidification of the urine with ammonium chloride dissolved in saline produces a tenfold increase in clearance.

Cannabis (Marijuana, Hashish, T.H.C.)

Cannabis Intoxication Syndromes. Weil (1970) classifies the adverse reactions to marijuana as follows: 1) simple depressive reactions, 2) panic reactions and 3) toxic phychoses. Simple depressive reactions usually occur among ambivalent first-time users of the drug. Spontaneous remission occurs without treatment.

Panic reaction is the most common complication induced by this drug. It is characterized by physical findings including tachycardia, conjunctival injection, pallor, sweating and increased appetite. Psychological symptoms include marked anxiety with fear of "going crazy" or having a heart attack.

Marijuana psychosis is described by Talbott and Teague (1969). Patients complain of impaired coordination, aching of large muscles of the extremities, disorientation, severe impairment of recent memory and short attention span. Judgment and thinking processes are impaired.

The hallmark of this delusional disorder is the presence of paranoid symptoms ranging from suspiciousness to overt delusions and hallucinations. Some patients experience depersonalization and emotional lability.

Schuckit (1979) gives an excellent overview of the treatment of panic reactions, flashbacks and psychosis resulting from marijuana use. A careful diagnostic work-up is essential, including the use of toxic screening to rule out other drug use. Psychiatric evaluation is needed to identify preexisting psychopathology.

The patient is reassured that the panic and other symptoms will clear within the next four to eight hours. "Talking down" the patient in a quiet room is reassuring. For excessive anxiety, the benzodiazepines (Valium, 5 to 10 mg or Librium, 10 to 50 mg) are the drugs of choice. Simple reassurance suffices in the management of flashbacks.

To manage temporary delusional disorder with paranoia and hallucinations, brief hospitalization may be indicated if a supportive program is not immediately available. Use of neuroleptic medication such as haloperidol, 5 to 20 mg daily in divided doses is recommended when the patient becomes combative, agitated or out of control. If the syndrome lasts more than one day, the presence of other major mental illness should be suspected.

Hallucinogens (LSD — Lysergic acid diethylamine, Mescaline, Psilocybin; STP — 2-5 Dimethoxy-4 methyl amphetamine)

Intoxication Syndromes. These include hallucinosis, recurrent flashbacks, depression, toxic psychosis and persistent psychosis. Jaffee (1980) describes the various effects of hallucinogens. Initially there are dizziness, weakness, drowsiness, nausea and paresthesias. Illusions, hallucinations, synesthesia and sensation of slowed time are present. The mood becomes labile. Other disorders of perception include overlapping of past and present, prolonged after-images, micropsia or macropsia. There is fear of loss of boundaries and disintegration of the self so that a person may go into a panic.

Bowers (1977) reviewed the persistent psychosis ascribed to chronic hallucinogen use characterized by isolation and withdrawal, shallow affect and paranoid delusions. In a follow-up of 15 patients from 1.9 to 5.8 years later, these patients had a prolonged schizophreniform psychotic reaction.

An acute short-lived toxic reaction with anxiety, illusions, confusion, disorientation, clouded consciousness, distorted body images and paranoid delusions was described by Taylor, Maurer and Tinklenberg (1970).

Management of Hallucinogen-Induced Syndromes

1. Overdosed patients may present with convulsions and hyperthermia. The airway should be established, heart and vital signs monitored carefully and support given to respiration and blood pressure.
2. Convulsions are treated with dilantin and intravenous diazepam.
3. Ungerleider and Frank (1975) recommend treatment of panic reactions by taking the patient to a warm, comfortable and quiet room away from noise, anxious relatives or friends and other sources of disturbing stimuli. Consistent verbal contact with reality-orienting cues can communicate confident reassurence that the patient is not losing his mind. It is crucial not to leave the patient alone but to avoid physical restraint unless absolutely necessary.
4. Benzodiazepines, preferably Valium 15 to 30 mg orally or intramuscularly, are used for severe agitation.
5. Flashbacks from hallucinogen ingestion are time-limited and respond well to reassurance. While medication is not often required, benzodiazepines can be effective.
6. Delusional and affective disorders from the use of hallucinogens usually clear within hours to days. Such patients need a careful neurological and psychiatric work-up. In severe cases, hospital treatment is preferred.

Solursh and Clement (1968) point out that polydrug use often includes hallucinogens (specifically STP) and additives with atropine-like activity. Phenothiazines are contraindicated as they potentiate this anticholinergic action and may lead to cardiovascular shock and death.

Persistent psychosis needing pharmacological intervention may be managed with phenothiazines used judiciously and carefully monitored.

Cocaine

Like amphetamine, cocaine is a central nervous system sympathomimetic agent. A mild intoxication syndrome from cocaine ingestion may be characterized by confusion, anxiety and depression. Severe psychosis marked by agitation, hallucinations, paranoid delusions and violent behavior can develop.

These psychological changes may be accompanied by dyspnea, tachycardia, cardiac arrythmias, dilated pupils, hypo- or areflexia and convulsions. Death may be caused by respiratory arrest or cardiovascular collapse.

The principles of management of cocaine intoxication syndromes are similar to those of the amphetamines previously described.

Dependency is not acknowledged to occur, since physical effects of withdrawal are minor. A spectrum of depression varying in severity is a common psychological concomitant of cocaine withdrawal.

TREATMENT SYSTEMS IN DRUG ADDICTIONS

Meyer (1972) states that the rehabilitation of drug addicts involves four general kinds of services: 1) treatment of overdosage; 2) treatment of the withdrawal syndrome; 3) treatment of medical complications; 4) modification of chronic relapsing behaviors. The basic goal of rehabilitation is to limit the disability and to improve the psychological, social, vocational and physical health of the individual.

Costello (1975a,b) reviewed treatment systems for alcoholics that may be applied to drug rehabilitation programs. He found that effective treatment programs has the following characteristics: 1) a well-organized treatment philosophy implemented in a consistent and logical fashion; 2) inpatient resources for medical care and nonmedical rehabilitation; 3) an aggressive outreach linkage with community agencies, both to bring patients through community contacts and to effect transition back into community resources; 6) behaviorally oriented interventions in addition to purely verbal therapies.

The Drug Abuse Warning Network (DAWN) Program

In July 1972, the Drug Enforcement Administration, in response to section 201 of the Controlled Substances Act sponsored by the National Institute on Drug Abuse, instituted the drug abuse warning network program. The purpose of the program was to provide continuing information on patterns of drug abuse throughout the United States.

Ungerleider, Lundberg, Sunshine and Walberg (1980) reviewed 1008 emergency room patient records from the Los Angeles County University of Southern California Medical Center, reports that were contributed to the DAWN program, and found that the three most frequently reported drugs of abuse were alcohol, diazepam and barbiturates. They concluded that many drugs picked up in the laboratory were not picked up by the examining physician. Those authors recommend a prospective study to determine the reliability of the DAWN reports (Project Dawn III and Project Dawn IV reports; see References section).

Reliable and available information from programs like the DAWN program is important in raising the awareness of physicians treating cases of acute intoxication and overdose so that the level of suspicion is high and a correct diagnosis is established with laboratory confirmation.

The Therapeutic Community Program

Residential therapeutic communities have developed across the United States using the confrontation model. They incorporate therapeutic approaches in a group living situation, utilizing intensive group therapy with catharsis, corrective recapitulation of the family group, group cohesiveness, development of socializing techniques and imitative behavior as the major curative factors. Immediate feedback is given to group members, and intense feelings are exchanged and encouraged.

Leaders, who tend to be authoritarian and charismatic, are either ex-addicts or experienced rehabilitation technicians. Program directors claim a high degree of success rate. However, most centers also show a high dropout rate. Because of the intensive nature of therapy, it is important to carefully select patients who enter this kind of treatment program. Unfortunately, good outcome studies are lacking in this field. Such studies are crucial for measuring cost effectiveness, determining which kinds of patients are helped most by this approach and discovering how length of stay impacts on the overall treatment outcome.

Many patients who enter the therapeutic community program do so under court pressure. Deneault, Correira, Taveira and Andrews (1980) report that 80% of their admissions in a twelve-bed inpatient residential program have active legal charges, and that these patients elect to go through a treatment program rather than to jail. This practice to include rather than exclude patients with legal problems has been found to be beneficial. First, 95% of patients admitted under this procedure complete the program until the staff feels they have achieved maximum hospital benefits. Second, the patients follow through on a program of outpatient visits that include urine screenings for drugs. Failing to participate in the program (i.e., leaving against medical advice), failing to keep appointments, showing persistent "dirty" urines, constitute a basis for reporting to the court or its designee.

From a psychodynamic point of view, these patients are viewed as lacking in ego strengths that may be provided by staffs and peers in the therapeutic community.

Behaviorally, there is a high need for the patient to negotiate successfully in his living with a group of peers. Addicts need active encouragement to use people (i.e., staff and patients) as substitutes for the drugs they used to take.

A forum for open and honest communication of feelings is provided. Failure to participate is grounds to conclude that the patient is "not ready" to deal with his feelings and problems and to make necessary changes. Identification with the group leaders is an important corrective factor.

Methadone Maintenance Clinics

Methadone maintenance was introduced in the United States through the pioneering efforts of Vincent Dole, a pharmacologist from Rockefeller University, and his collaborator Marie Nyswander (1965).

Their clinical work indicated that methadone, a long-acting synthetic narcotic, is effective in treating opioid withdrawal syndrome. When given in adequate doses to opioid addicts, it produced satisfaction of "drug hunger" and prevented euphoria or a "high" when patients took other narcotics in addition to methadone.

This allowed clinic staff to help patients make changes in their life-style and deal with problems in various other health areas.

Early on, Dole hypothesized that heroin addicts, like diabetics, suffer from a deficiency of opioid-like substance and need prolonged administration of a substitue. Animal models did not appear to support this hypothesis. Further work is needed to clarify the issue. More than 4000 patients were treated in the Dole-Nyswander program. Results showed that 80% remained in treatment and showed successful adjustment in the community for the majority of patients.

Like many programs, the outcome study showed flawed methodology. While its usefulness is uncontested, the data do not give specifics on pre- and post-treatment findings as well as health areas in which improvements have been made, including: 1) drug-taking status; 2) vocational status; 3) interpersonal relationships; 4) psychological status; 5) physical health.

The question of methadone dosage has spurred a debate among proponents of methadone treatment. One school recommends high-dose maintenance (80-120 mg) to prevent relapse, whereas others suggest a range of 40-50 mg a day. The usual range of methadone maintenance in the United States is now between 40 and 100 mg daily.

Along with methadone maintenance, the Food and Drug Administration and the National Institute of Drug Abuse (see "Methadone for Treating Narcotic Addicts," 1980) recommend the provision of ancillary services, such as hospital affiliation, to provide needed medical services; facilities for urine screening (to be done at least twice weekly); assignment of a primary counselor to each patient to help define problems; and collaboration with the patient in making and implementing treatment plans. This comprehensive range of medical and rehabilitative services should be easily accessible to the patient.

Extreme care is needed in screening patients for entrance into methadone maintenance programs. The present regulation requires that a patient be physiologically addicted to qualify. Because of inherent complications, persons under 18 years old can be admitted only with prior approval from the state authority and the FDA. Pregnant patients desirous of methadone maintenance are also accepted on a case-by-case basis due to findings that newborns of mothers who continue to use illicit heroin are at higher risk for significant withdrawal syndrome and other complications.

In summary, methadone maintenance continues to be an effective approach in preventing illicit opioid use among narcotic addicts. It is a potentially powerful treatment component of drug rehabilitation. A minority of patients appear to continue to engage in illicit narcotic or polydrug use, but to an attenuated degree. Many reports indicate lowering of drug-related crimes when patients utilize methadone maintenance treatment.

Bale *et al.* (1980) made a prospective controlled study comparing the effects of therapeutic communities and methadone maintenance in a one-year follow-up of 585 opioid addicts. Their data analysis shows the following: subjects who spent less than 50 days in a therapeutic community did not function better at the one-year point than subjects who were only in the detoxification program. Those who spent more than 50 days, an average of four months, were significantly less likely to be using drugs, to get arrested or to be convicted and were more likely to be working or going to school than those in the detoxification-only group. There were no outcome differences between the total therapeutic community and the methadone subjects. The rate of retention of therapeutic communities was 17.9% of 340 patients compared with 29.4% for the methadone program. The central finding in their study is the positive correlation between length of stay in the program and good outcome.

Drug Outpatient and Aftercare Clinics

As a chronic relapsing disorder, drug addiction requires treatment in one form or another far beyond a period of inpatient care or from the beginning in lieu of inpatient care.

There are many forms of outpatient services. Clear distinctions are often made between methadone and "drug-free" clinics, the latter being a common component of residential treatment programs. The basic goal of outpatient and aftercare programs is to help the individual patient and his family in their rehabilitation efforts. This requires looking at the various health areas outlined by Pattison (1980).

Like methadone clinics, these services should include hospital or medical affiliation to provide evaluation and treatment, urine screening as a tool of therapy and follow-up, vocational rehabilitation (i.e., assessment, concrete help in job seeking), psychotherapeutic procedures that assist patients in healthy use of leisure time and work on conflicted relationships.

Traditionally, patients who go through inpatient and outpatient services and then return to the community are lost to follow-up. The use of collateral sources of information (e.g., parents, spouse, friends), has been found helpful on a proactive basis in keeping the patient in treatment. The establishment of rapport with the individual counselor, however, is the cornerstone upon which therapeutic progress is made.

The Halfway House

Though common for alcoholics, transitional care facilities for drug addicts in the community are rare. Those commonly referred to such agencies are patients who on completion of the inpatient phase of treatment are homeless, jobless or indigent.

The halfway house provides food, shelter, clothing and a well-structured living milieu. Residents are given responsibilities they are expected to keep.

Staff are usually ex-addicts who can serve as figures for identification as well as resource persons or counselors.   If patients are not subsidized by public financing, they are expected to go to work and pay their way.

The Police-Court System

The courts have become active referral sources for drug addicts who enter the treatment system.   Overcrowding in jails, an enlightened approach to drug addiction as a compulsive illness and the favorable results of enforced treatment have encouraged judges to offer treatment options in lieu of incarceration. The use of the police and the courts as helpful components in the treatment of addictions demands more attention and study.

TREATMENT APPROACHES IN DRUG ADDICTION

Psychotherapy and Behavior Therapy

Dynamic psychotherapy and behavior therapy are two scientific approaches that have evolved for the purpose of motivating, changing life-styles, modifying behavior, enhancing skills or getting relief from anxiety, depression and other forms of emotional turmoil.

Although dynamic psychotherapies based on psychoanalytic principles are widely practiced, the direct effect on the treatment of drug addiction has been disappointing.

Behavior therapy, rooted in Pavlovian and Skinnerian concepts, began to be applied in drug addiction treatment in the 1950s and 1960s. Removal of the symptom or symptoms through the use of reinforcement, aversion, desensitization, implosion, assertiveness training, role-playing, rehearsals and multiple other techniques appears to shown some promise.

Marmor (1980) writes that whether therapists use the psychoanalytic or behavioral approach — or one of the newer therapies — the basic matrix is a good patient-therapist relationship. This rests largely upon the trust and rapport engendered by the therapist's genuine interest, respect and empathy for the patient as much as upon the patient's motivation to be helped. Given this matrix, he adds, other important elements in the psychotherapeutic process are as follows: 1) release of emotional tension in the context of hope and expectation of receiving help;   2) cognitive learning about the basis of the patient's difficulties;   3) operant conditioning toward more adaptive patterns of behavior by means of explicit and implicit approval-disapproval cues with corrective emotional experiences in therapy;   4) suggestion and persuasion, overt or covert;   5) identification with the therapist or other group members;   6) repeated reality testing or rehearsal of the new adaptive techniques.

Rawson, Glazer, Callahan and Liberman (1979) compared behavior therapy alone, Naltrexone (a narcotic blocking agent) alone and combining Naltrexone and behavior therapy among a group of 181 outpatient heroin addicts. Their data show that Naltrexone is a promising new treatment approach. The behavior therapy program consisted of contingency contracting, relaxation training, sensitization, covert sensitization and self-control procedures in which patients stayed an average of 16.1 weeks. They did not show useful results. Twenty-eight percent of the behavior therapy clients were opiate-free at the end of 12 months, while 72% were opiate-positive or in jail. Forty-eight percent of the Naltrexone clients and 50% of the Naltrexone/behavior therapy clients were opiate-free at 12-month follow-up.

To help patients reinforce drug abstinence, Stitzer, Bigelow and Liebson (1979) used contingency management for their patients and concluded that in methadone maintenance the use of this approach may provide a method of enhancing their effectiveness by utilizing privileges that are already dispensed by the clinics in a more rational way to promote inspired therapeutic outcome among drug addict patients.

Family Therapies

The work of Seldin (1972) has identified the family both as a locus of pathology and as victims of the patient's maladaptive behavior. While there are inherent difficulties in involving the addict's family in treatment, innovative and active approaches have been described. Bayog and Fisch (1979) describe a brief active evaluation-intervention that focuses on the family as the patient for the identification and solving of problem areas. Marital couples, family network, and multiple family therapies have been described with empirical data. Treatment outcome results are scanty.

On the basis of current understanding of the role of the family as cause and consequence for the addict, more clinical experience urgently needs to be generated and documented. This can only add to our repertoire of approaches to the chronic relapsing behavior of addicts.

Drug Therapies

Except in methadone maintenance, no drug has consistently been recommended as treatment for the addict. Neuroleptic medications in low doses have been prescribed to alleviate anxiety and are sometimes preferred by physicians over benzodiazepines because of the strong addictive potential of the latter. Compliance is poor because of uncomfortable side-effects (i.e. restlessness, dryness of the mouth) that frequently occur. Neuroleptics do have a place in the management of the addict with psychotic symptoms.

Anti-anxiety drugs are of little value in the overall management. However, used judiciously and on a strict time-limited basis for adjustment disorders with anxious or depressed mood, these drugs may produce beneficial effects and prevent the patient from being lost from treatment.

Therapeutic communities and the majority of halfway houses often exclude patients on neuroleptics including antidepressants. The latter drugs are indicated in cases of major affective illness and are also used following an extended post-withdrawal period to ascertain that the mood is not a feature of the drug withdrawal syndrome.

Overall, a common philosophy is to avoid substitution of drugs to deal with underlying conflict and problems.

THE TREATMENT OF POLYDRUG ABUSE AND DEPENDENCE

During the last few years, the increasing incidence of polydrug abuse and dependence has stimulated more interest in the individual study of these patients. Benvenuto and Bourne (1975) report the high incidence of severe and significant psychopathology including depression, severe anxiety and psychosis.

McKenna and Khantzian (1980) administered the Psychiatric Status Schedule devised by Spitzer and Endicott to 97 patients admitted to an inpatient detoxification/treatment unit, and found drug users whose use is limited to a single substance to be rare. All the patients showed considerable symptoms of anxiety, depression and somatic concerns and were troubled by frequent thoughts of suicide. Feelings of social isolation and impairment of ego functions involved in maintaining a daily routine were common.

For the polydrug and combination polydrug/narcotics group, behavioral disturbance is elevated above the psychiatric inpatient level. Impulse control disturbance is very high, and reality-testing disturbance approaches or is above the inpatient group level.

The treatment of polydrug abuse is in its infancy; more understanding and experience are required.

When a patient abuses multiple drugs, clinicians need to manage withdrawal from each drug and make decisions on what to detoxify first. Generally opioid withdrawal is done first; and because of life-threatening potential, withdrawal from barbiturates, the benzodiazepines and other sedative-hypnotics (i.e., Quaalude, Doriden, Noludar, Placidyl) is done last.

The nature of the underlying psychopathology and the highly troubled families of polydrug abusers make treatment difficult.

Some cardinal principles mentioned in the preceding sections are worth repeating here. Vaillant (1978) emphasizes the importance of promoting a supportive group membership in a drug-free environment, substituting people (staff and peers) for drugs.

Those therapeutic community programs that are most successful adhere to the principle of combining confrontation, group therapy, opportunities for healthy identification, vocational assessment, rehabilitation and concrete help in restructuring a life-style that includes the use of leisure time.

The effective role of the police-court system in getting patients into treatment needs emphasis. Since the majority of addicted patients lack the ego capacity to organize and maintain a daily routine, the cognitive learning that goes on in a therapeutic community program is crucial for successful, long-term changes. Family meetings and family networks are useful. Spouses of addicts need help to examine noxious life-styles with the polydrug abuser, to help the addict spouse maintain the motivation to change and finally to continue the gains made in follow-up therapy.

Changes in the addict-spouse often lead to the breakup of the relationship as the addict becomes abstinent, more assertive and independent. Unconscious wishes of the nonaddict spouse to play a dominant, highly ambivalent role to the addict should be interpreted carefully. Helping the non-addicted female strive to be a "good-enough mother" (described by Winnicott, 1953) is an important goal in couples therapy.

Helping polydrug patients has emerged as one of the most difficult and challenging therapeutic endeavors. The risks are high, but successes do occur. Staff usually have high morale and are enthusiastic about their treatment approach. Anecdotal success stories are related with a sense of pride, accomplishment and encouragement. This pride should be nurtured. It can facilitate the implementation of more scientific outcome evaluation studies.

REFERENCES

Altman, L.L. On the oral nature of acting out. *Journal of the American Psychoanalytic Association.* **5**: 648–662 (1957).

Bachman, J.G., Johnston, L.D. and O'Malley, P.M. Smoking, drinking and drug use among American high school students: Correlates and trends, 1975–1979. *American Journal of Public Health.* **71**: 59–69 (1981).

Bale, R.N., Van Stone, W.W., Kuldan, J.M., Engelsing, T.M., Elashoff, R.M. and Zarcone, V.P. Therapeutic communities vs. methadone maintenance. *Archives of General Psychiatry.* **37**: 179–193 (1980).

Bayog, R.D. and Fisch, A. Family evaluation in a methadone maintenance clinic. *Transnational Mental Health Research.* **21**: 28–32 (1979).

Benvenuto, J. and Bourne, P.G. The federal polydrug abuse project: Initial report. *Journal of Psychedelic Drugs.* **7**: 115–120 (1975).

Bowers, M.B. Psychoses precipitated by psychotomimetic drugs. *Archives of General Psychiatry.* **34**: 832–835 (1977).

Burns, S.R. and Lerner, S.E. Phencyclidine deaths. *Clinical Toxicology.* **7** (4): 135-141 (1978).

Caplan, G., *Principles of preventive psychiatry.* New York: Basic Books, 1964.

Costello, R.M. Alcoholism treatment and evaluation, I. In search of methods. *International Journal of Addictions.* **10**: 251–275 (1975a).

Costello, R.M. Alcoholism treatment and evaluation, II, Collation of two year follow-up. *International Journal of the Addictions.* **10**: 857–868 (1975b).

Deneault, P., Correira, R., Taveira, A. and Andrew, R. Outcome study in a 12 bed therapeutic community program for polydrug abusers, unpublished report (1980).

Dole, V.P. and Nyswander, M. Medical treatment for heroin addiction. *Journal of the American Medical Association.* **193**: (8): 646–650 (1965).

Ellinwood, E.H. Emergency treatment of acute adverse reactions to CNS stimulants. In: Bourne, P.G. (Ed.), *A treatment manual for drug abuse emergencies.* Rockville, Md.: National Clearinghouse for Drug Abuse Information, 1975.

Erikson, E. *Childhood and society.* New York: W.W. Norton & Co., 1963.

Jaffee, J.H. Drug addiction and drug abuse. In: Goodman, L.S. and Gilman, A. (Eds.), *The pharmacological basis of therapeutics,* pp. 535–584. New York: The Macmillan Co., 1980.

Jarvick, M.D. Drugs used in the treatment of psychiatric disorders. In: Goodman, L.S. and Gilman, A. (Eds.), *The pharmacological basis of therapeutics.* New York: The Macmillan Co., 1970.

Johnson, A.L. and Szurek, S. The genesis of acting out in children and adults. *Psychoanalytic Quarterly.* **21**: 323–343 (1952).

Kohut, H. *The restoration of the self.* New York: International Universities Press, 1977.

Lavenhar, M.A. The drug abuse numbers game. *American Journal of Public Health.* **63**: (9): 807–809 (1973).

Marmor, J. Recent trends in psychotherapy. *American Journal of Psychiatry.* **137**: 409–416 (1980).

McKenna, G.J. and Khantzian, E.J. Ego functions and psychopathology in narcotics and polydrug users. *International Journal of the Addictions.* **15**: 259–268 (1980).

Methadone for treating narcotic addicts: Joint revision of conditions for use. *Federal Register.* **45**: 184 (1980).

Meyer, R.E. *Guide to drug rehabilitation, A public health response.* Boston: Beacon Press, 1972.

Pattison, E.M. The selection of treatment modalities. In: Mendelson, J.H. and Mello, N.K. (Eds.), *Diagnosis and treatment of alcoholism.* New York: McGraw-Hill, 1979.

Project DAWN III – April 1974–75 under BNDD contract no. 72–47, publication of DEA and NIDA. Ambler, Pa.: IMS America Ltd.

Project DAWN IV – 1978–79, publication of DEA and NIDA. Ambler, Pa.: IMS America Ltd.

National Survey on Drug Abuse. Rockville, Md.: Department of Health and Human Services, 1979.

Rado, S. Narcotic bondage: A general theory of the dependence on narcotic drugs. *American Journal of Psychiatry.* **114**: 165–170 (1957).

Rawson, R.A., Glazer, M., Callahan, E.J. and Liberman, R.P.   Naltrexone and behavior therapy for heroin addiction. In: Krasnegor, N. (Ed.), *Behavioral analysis and treatment of substance abuse.* Rockville, Md.:   National Institute on Drug Abuse, 1979.

Raynes, A.S., Patch, V.D.   An improved detoxification technique for heroin addicts. *Archives of General Psychiatry,* **29**: 417–419 (1973).

Rotman, E., Bayog, R. and Okeefe, A.   PCP – A new killer. *Physician Assistant Health Practitioner,* **5**: 8, 66–73 (1981).

Schuckit, M.A. *Drug and alcohol abuse.* New York: Plenum Publishing Corp. 1979.

Seldin, N.   The family of the addict: A review of the literature. *International Journal of the Addictions.* **7**: 97–107 (1972).

Showalter, C.V. and Thornton, W.E.   Clinical pharmacology of phencyclidine toxicity. *American Journal of Psychiatry.* **134**: 11 (1977).

Solursh, L.P.   Emergency treatment of acute adverse reactions to hallucinogenic drugs. In: Bourne, P.G. (Ed.), *A treatment manual for drug abuse emergencies.* Rockville, Md.: National Clearinghouse for Drug Abuse Information, 1975.

Stitzer, M.L., Bigelow, G.E. and Liebson, I.   Reinforcement of drug abstinence, a behavioral approach to drug abuse treatment. In: Krasnegor, N. (Ed.), *Behavioral analysis and treatment of substance abuse.*   Rockville, Md.: National Institute on Drug Abuse, 1979.

Talbott, J.A. and Teague, J.W.   Marijuana psychosis. *Journal of the American Medical Association.* **210**: 2 (1969).

Taylor, R.L., Maurer, J.I. and Tinklenberg, J.D.   Management of "bad trips" in an evolving drug scene. *Journal of the American Medical Association.* **213**: (3): 422–425 (1970).

Tinklenberg, J.R.   The treatment of acute amphetamine psychosis. In: Bourne, P.G. (Ed.), *A treatment manual for drug abuse emergencies.* Rockville, Md.: National Clearinghouse for Drug Abuse Information, 1975.

Ungerleider, J.T. and Frank, I.M.   Management of acute panic reactions and flashbacks from LSD ingestion. In: Bourne, P.G. (Ed.), *A treatment manual for drug abuse emergencies.* Rockville, Md.: National Clearinghouse for Drug Abuse Information, 1975.

Ungerleider, J., Lundberg, G., Sunshine, I. and Walberg, C.   The drug abuse warning network. *Archives of General Psychiatry.* **37**: 1 (1980).

Vaillant, G.   Alcoholism and drug dependence. In: Nicholi, A.M., Jr. (Ed.), *The Harvard guide to modern psychiatry.* Cambridge, Mass.: Harvard University Press, 1978.

Weil, A.T.   Adverse reactions to marijuana: Classification and treatment. *New England Journal of Medicine.* **282**: 18 (1970).

Wesson, D.R. and Smith, D.E.   Managing the barbiturate withdrawal syndrome. In: Bourne, P.G. (Ed.), *A treatment manual for drug abuse emergencies.* Rockville, Md.: National Clearinghouse for Drug Abuse Information, 1975.

Wikler, A.   A psychodynamic study of a patient during experimental self-regulated readdiction to morphine. *Psychiatric Quarterly.* **26**: 270–293 (1952).

Winnicott, D.W.   Transitional objects and transitional phenomenon. *International Journal of Psychoanalysis.* **34**: 89–97 (1953).

Wurmser, L. Psychoanalytic considerations of the etiology of compulsive drug use. *Journal of the American Psychoanalytic Association.* **22**: (4): 1974.

Yago, K.B., Pitts, F.N., Burgoyne, R.W., Aniline, O., Yago, L.S. and Pitts, A.F. The urban epidemic of PCP use: Clinical and laboratory evidence from a public psychiatric hospital emergency service. *Journal of Clinical Psychiatry.* **42** (5): 193–196 (1981).

Yesavage, J.A. and Freman, A.M. III. Acute PCP intoxication, psychopathology and prognosis. *Journal of Clinical Psychiatry.* **39**: 664–666 (1978).

21 Alcoholism

Morris E. Chafetz

There are many definitions of alcoholism. A widely quoted definition is used by the World Health Organization and states that "alcoholism is a chronic behavioral disorder manifested by repeated drinking of alcoholic beverages in excess of the dietary and social uses of the community and to an extent that interferes with the drinker's health or his social or economic function."

This definition is less than satisfactory because it is descriptive and symptomatic, rather than etiological. The physiological, psychological and social phenomena it embraces are integrated at varying levels, leading to qualification and often forcing the observer to act more as a moralist than as a scientist. The definition also implies a greater concern with group deviance than with individual discomfort, signifying that much destruction must occur before difficulties can be noted.

I believe instead that alcoholism is a chronic behavioral disorder manifested by an undue preoccupation with alcohol and its use to the detriment of physical, emotional and social function. In light of this thinking, the approach, understanding, therapy and evaluation of the alcoholic is holistic, although relief of specific symptoms may be of primary importance at a given moment (Chafetz, 1967a).

The patient in a state of acute alcohol intoxication is in pretty sad shape, and his appearance and manner are not conducive to sympathy. The intoxicated patient often is anxious and has little control over his body's actions. He may be obnoxiously demanding, even belligerent. He may be dressed sloppily and his hair may be uncombed. His red eyes stare out from a blotchy face; his mouth is dry; his breath reeks of ethanol. Frequently, his skin is clammy and cold. Just as common as these physical signs are his expressions of guilt. This is different from the guilt we psychiatrists usually see because it is accompanied by overt evidence that "I have been a bad person," which is the way both he and society look at alcoholic bouts serious enough to require medical attention. Complicating this sorry state may be various physiological, traumatic or psychological symptoms, such as pneumonia or head injuries.

An alcoholic patient is often greeted with displeasure and disgust. Hospital emergency room staffs usually look on him as a troublesome intruder. Unless he has a major surgical or medical complication, the alcoholic commonly is given a cursory examination, summarily treated, and sent away (Chafetz, 1967b).

To treat only the patient's acute intoxication and to ignore the need for rehabilitation is the poorest form of "half-practice", and the height of therapeutic folly. I believe that being concerned only with the acute state of alcoholism accomplishes little beyond temporary relief for the patient and provides the potential for generous multiplication of the physical, psychological and social problems of alcoholism.

Drug therapy can be employed both for relieving the acute bout of alcoholism and as a valuable adjunct in a rehabilitation program. It must be remembered throughout that therapy always should be individually tailored to meet each patient's needs.

Another important point should also be emphasized: No matter what the pharmacological action of a drug, its total effectiveness cannot be evaluated without knowing how, where, when and by whom the drug is given and in what manner countervailing forces to its effect are present in the therapeutic situation.

ACUTE ALCOHOLIC INTOXICATION

1. Patients who do not require hospitalization may be treated with a minor tranquilizer such as chlordiazepoxide (Librium), 10 to 25 mg four times per day for one to three days, or with hydroxyzine (Vistaril). In elderly alcoholic people, the least possible effective dose should be used and precaution is advised in suicidal patients. Because of their addiction potential, Librium and Vistaril should be used judiciously in treating alcoholics. They should not be used on a prolonged basis in these patients.

Syncope, drowsiness, ataxia and confusion are reported side effects of chlordiazepoxide. Also associated with its use have been skin eruptions, idiopathic jaundice, menstrual irregularities, extrapyramidal symptoms and nausea.

In agitated alcoholic states, chlordiazepoxide has been found to significantly alleviate agitation. A dose of 100 mg intravenously also eliminates gross, generalized tremors when these are present as the sole manifestation of alcoholic withdrawal. Librium appears to be more effective when the alcoholic state is uncomplicated by a major psychiatric disease.

Hydroxyzine (Vistaril) is useful in eliminating anxiety, tension, agitation, apprehension and confusion without impairing mental alertness. Oral dosage varies with individual requirements and ranges from 25 mg three times daily to

100 mg four times a day.

Drowsiness may accompany its use, and dryness of the mouth may occur when higher doses are used.

For rapid calming of the patient, hydroxyzine may be given intramuscularly 50-100 mg and repeated every 4-6 hours as required.

2. There has been recent interest in the use of propranolol (Inderal) as a possible "sobering pill." However, in a recent double-blind, crossover study with propranolol and a placebo, Dr. Ernest P. Noble and co-workers at the University of California, Irvine, found that, contrary to early reports that the drug counteracts the effects of alcohol, the effect was, in fact, the opposite (Noble *et al.*, 1973). In most tests, propranolol showed significant synergistic effects with alcohol. Thus these findings preclude propranolol's use as a "sobering up pill," and also point to the possible danger of alcohol ingestion by patients who have been prescribed the drug for treatment of arrhythmias.

3. Since alcohol acts as a diuretic, it has been common practice to administer electrolytes intravenously (Knott and Beard, 1970). However, it has been shown that alcohol acts as a diuretic only when its blood concentration is rising and stops when high levels are reached. In fact, the chronic alcoholic may be overhydrated, rather than in a state of dehydration. Therefore, fluid replacement should not automatically be started in the patient in withdrawal. If the patient has severe malnutrition, vomiting or diarrhea, replacement may be necessary.

4. Diphenylhydantoin (Dilantin) is useful in treating the convulsions that patients in withdrawal may experience. Patients may be started on 0.1 g (1 1/2 grains) three times daily, and the dose adjusted upward according to response.

Common side effects include nystagmus, dizziness, muscular incoordination, insomnia, diplopia, transient nervousness, motor twitchings, headache, nausea, vomiting and constipation. Hypersensitivity reactions manifested by rash and fever also occur. Most disappear with reduction in dosage. Prolonged convulsions may be treated with diazepam administered intravenously.

5. In addition, treatment of the acutely intoxicated individual should include adequate diet and vitamin supplements, proper nursing care, and medical management of other complications commonly associated with acute and chronic alcoholism.

REHABILITATION

Most treatment facilities stop their efforts on behalf of alcoholics when recovery from the acute state has occurred. As we showed when I was director of the Massachusetts General Hosptial's Alcohol Clinic and Acute Psychiatric Service, the acute stage of alcoholic intoxication may be the crucial event in initiating a rehabilitative program for sufferers from alcoholism. I again emphasize that: *Any and all rehabilitative endeavors must be tailored to the individual needs of the patient and his resources.* This requires a thorough evaluation of him physically, emotionally and socially. Drug treatment in the rehabilitation of the alcoholic must be combined with a total effort in the patient's behalf. It is senseless to believe that merely pushing some pills at a patient will produce an effective therapeutic response.

To use drugs effectively, the physician must first have established some sort of relationship with the patient. A practitioner who permits himself only a nodding acquaintance with his patient had better not try his hand at rehabilitating alcoholic persons. Interest, concern, respect and a desire to understand, rather than to judge, are requisites of effective treatment.

It must be remembered that alcohol is a drug which the person uses in abundant doses as a form of self-medication. If the physician merely offers him another drug in an impersonal way, the chances of his misusing the new drug are increased. Tailoring medication to the patient in itself implies the necessity of learning something about the person, which is the cornerstone of beginning relations.

There are many different reasons why people have alcoholic problems. Depression is common to most alcoholic patients. The pain of aloneness and hopelessness that most alcoholics suffer is intense enough to demand relief at any cost. Reason and moralism cannot deal with what the person must contend with within himself. To the patient, alcohol seems the only solace. Many alcoholics are aware that, for some, alcohol only intensifies depression, but they cannot give it up because there is no substitute. Since our goal of rehabilitation is to lessen or abolish the need for alcohol, drugs which combat depression are one part of total treatment. If the patient has symptomatic depression after he has dried out, antidepressants should be used.

1. The antidepressant imipramine (Tofranil) is a useful adjuvant. The drug's action appears to be specific to depressive states and its effect has been characterized as depressolytic, rather than stimulatory. Dosage range is usually 100–150 mg daily, most often administered orally. One hundred fifty milligrams is common as the average daily dose. Signs of improvement or response to the medication may be measured by a number of criteria: disappearance of psychomotor inhibition, disappearance of feelings of hopelessness and helplessness and lessening of self-destructive attitudes. Patients often will report that with relief of depression their desire for alcohol also diminishes. Imipramine also works by lessening feelings of guilt. Furthermore, the alleviation of depression turns the person from a preoccupation with his inner self to outer directedness, offering the potential for reaching the patient with other rehabilitative methods. The amenability of the patient, whose intense depression has been lessened, to respond to other measures is important. For some patients, symptom control may be all that can be hoped for, while for others a drug-free life may be well within reach.

Dryness of the mouth, slight tremor of the extremities, dizziness and blurred vision, pruritus and dermatitis, nausea and vomiting have been reported with imipramine. However, they are relatively infrequent and are usually readily controlled by lowering dosage. Rare cases of hypotension, exacerbation of eczema and ulcerative colitis have been reported.

While imipramine usually is effective in treatment of depression associated with alcoholism, there is a certain delay before therapeutic effectiveness is noted. The drug should be maintained for about three months with gradual weaning over ten days to prevent complications. Some investigators feel that prolonged maintenance may be indicated depending upon the expected course of the depression.

Clinical experience at the Massachusetts General Hospital showed that imipramine is effective in lowering the intensity of the depression commonly found among alcoholic persons.

2. Amitriptyline hydrochloride (Elavil) is also useful in treating depression. Like imipramine, amitriptyline's principal effect is a blocking of the re-uptake of norepinephrine at synapses within the central nervous system. It provides more of a sedative effect than does imipramine.

The usual daily dose is 100–150 mg. The expected response to therapeutic doses of both these drugs may require about three weeks, and the drug should be continued for two to three months after depression is alleviated. Amitriptyline usually is stopped after a maximum of six months as tolerances can be reached over long periods. In the event of relapse, reinstitution of the drug is possible.

Side effects are mild with amitriptyline. Drowsiness, dizziness, nausea, excitement, hypotension, tremulousness, weakness, headache, anorexia, perspiration and lack of coordination have been reported. In rare instances, dermatitis and peripheral neuropathy occur. High doses may bring acute psychotic reactions, temporary confusion and disturbed concentration. Tachycardia, urinary retention, constipation and dry mouth sometimes appear. Since the side effects appear to be an extension of the pharmacological activity of the drug, reduction of dosage will usually control them.

Use of amitriptyline is contraindicated for patients with glaucoma and urinary retention. Because of unpredictable potentiation effects, patients who have been receiving other antidepressants — especially those in the amine inhibitor group — should be allowed two weeks before amitriptyline is introduced, and even then it should be done cautiously and gradually.

In the use of antidepressant medication, the physician should be on guard for suicidal possibilities. In addition, since these drugs alter the electrocardiogram and may produce arrhythmias, especially with overdose, they should be used with caution in heart patients. The use of any drug in the treatment of alcoholism without the careful interest and observation of an interested physician may be the source of a fatal therapeutic encounter when *only* symptom removal is the goal.

3. Trifluoperazine (Stelazine) and/or chlorpromazine (Thorazine) is useful in treating thought disturbances and psychotic disorganization which may be associated with alcoholism. One to two milligrams of trifluoperazine twice a day and/or 25 to 50 mg of chlorpromazine three times a day may be prescribed.

Hypotensive responses, jaundice, dermatitis, agranulocytosis, dryness of the mouth, constipation and extrapyramidal symptoms have been reported as side effects of these drugs. They should be stopped immediately if jaundice or agranulocytosis appears. Dermatological complications can usually be counteracted by the administration of an antihistaminic drug, such as diphenhydramine hydrochloride (Benadryl), 50 mg three times a day or by switching to another phenothiazine. The antihistaminic may be given concurrently without interfering with the therapeutic effects of trifluoperazine and chlorpromazine. Reduction of dosage or the addition of an anticholinergic substance, such as benztropine (Cogentin) or trihexphenidyl hydrochloride (Artane) will usually control the other side effects. The possibility of a coexisting depression must also be borne in mind.

DETERRENCE

No discussion of drugs in the treatment of alcoholism would be complete without reference to drugs designed to deter drinking. These drugs have given much hope to those who worship at the altar of simple answers to complex problems, but on the whole they have been disappointing. However, when they are placed in proper perspective, their aid in the total treatment of the alcoholic problem can be marked.

Most experience, as well as most hope, rests with disulfiram [bis (diethylthiocarbamyl) disulfide], popularly known as Antabuse. Under ordinary circumstances, this substance is relatively inert in the body, but when alcohol is drunk, it interferes with its metabolism.

In an individual who has taken disulfiram, a toxic reaction begins moments after ingestion of alcohol. A rapidly deepening, lobster-red color develops from the head downward and spreads over the face, sclerae, upper limbs and chest. The intense redness is accompanied by a sensation of heat and the rising crescendo of a pounding headache, by feelings of constriction in the neck and an irritation of throat and trachea resulting in spasms of coughing. All of this unpleasantness is accompanied by a sudden steep rise in blood pressure for about 30 minutes to a point of maximum intensity. This is followed by a precipitous drop of blood pressure, the onset of nausea and the replacement of redness by pallor. If enough alcohol has been taken, nausea turns to violent vomiting. Breathing is difficult and gasping, precordial pain simulating a coronary attack is present; and a sense of uneasiness and fear of dying develops — so terrifying that many a patient has wished for what he feared. After the severe discomfort has lasted for two to four hours, the patient falls to sleep, ending the discomfort as well as the alcohol-disulfiram reaction.

Dizziness, head pressure, blurred vision, air hunger, palpitations, numbness of the hands and feet, and insomnia also have been reported.

Side effects to disulfiram alone have been minimal. Some patients complain of fatigue or impotence. Others occasionally develop mild dermatitis, malaise, headache or gastric distress, and a few have a characteristic "garlic odor" to the breath. Some therapists caution against use in the patient with incipient psychosis, severe coronary disorder, cirrhosis of the liver, kidney disease, diabetes, pregnancy, asthma and epilepsy; but most practitioners who are confident of their relationship and understanding of the individual have used disulfiram with people in these categories with caution and without harm.

One 500 mg tablet of disulfiram is administered daily upon arising for five days, starting 24 hours after the last drink, and then half a tablet (250 mg) daily is used as a maintenance dose. I suggest routinizing the taking of disulfiram, preferably upon awakening. This eliminates a day of decision making about drinking: Some practitioners maintain patients on 125 mg daily (1/4 of a tablet), but our experience at Massachusetts General Hospital showed this to be an unsatisfactory maintenance dose. Patients who are maintained on the large dose of 500 mg daily develop symptoms of polyneuritis. Patients who discontinue disulfiram are advised to wait at least four days, and preferably for one week, before resuming their alcohol intake.

TREATING THE DISULFIRAM-ALCOHOL REACTION

1. Place the patient in shock position and provide generous amounts of ascorbic acid intravenously.

2. Electrolytic balance can be maintained by dextrose and saline infusions and plasma and oxygen provided where indicated.

3. Antihistamine medication is useful intramuscularly or intravenously.

When disulfiram was introduced, it was believed that an "experience session" with the drug and alcohol would certainly "cure" the alcoholic person's desire for drink. Person after person was hustled off to the hospital, begun on disulfiram, and then given his half ounce of whiskey. However, in time, and after some deaths from cardiac and respiratory failure, it was judged an unnecessary and perhaps cruel experience for patients. Consequently, now the treating physician only describes the consequences and the occasional patient who tests out his disbelief does not usually require additional evidence.

Generally, those who have evaluated disulfiram's effectiveness have stressed its usefulness as ancillary to a total program of rehabilitation.

ALCOHOLISM: A CHRONIC DISEASE

There is no one single magic cure for alcoholism. Problems of alcoholism, like most behavioral disorders, are long-standing and chronic. To expect, as do many physicians, that the alcoholic patient should never relapse is as unrealistic as to expect the diabetic never to go out of control. Response to treatment should be judged on a multiple scale of altered drinking patterns and evidence of improved social, physical and emotional function, rather than against the single criterion of being alcohol-free.

REFERENCES

Chafetz, M.E.   Addictions.   III: alcoholism.   In: *Comprehensive Textbook of Psychiatry*.   Baltimore, Md.:   Williams & Wilkins Co., 1967a.

Chafetz, M.E.   Drugs in the treatment of alcoholism.   *Medical Clinics of North America*, **51**:   5 (1967b).

Knott, D.H. and Beard, J.D.   Diagnosis and therapy of acute withdrawal from alcohol.   *Current Psychiatric Therapies*, **10** (1970).

Noble, E.P., Parker, E., Alkana, R., Cohen, H. and Birch, H.   Propranololethanol interaction in man.   Paper presented at 1973 Federation of American Societies for Experimental Biology, Atlantic City, New Jersey.

22 Recent Developments in Psychosomatic Disorders

Thomas R. Garrick and Chase P. Kimball

Psychosomatics has traditionally involved an eclectic orientation toward diagnosis and treatment. Most recently, these various perspectives have been unified within the framework of a "biopsychosocial" model (Engel, 1980; Kimball, 1981). This model stresses a multidimensional analysis of the many biological, psychological and social factors affecting the organism and utilizes various types of therapeutic intervention to alter the course of illness, such as group therapy or psychoanalysis. Since the last edition of this book, psychiatry in general has moved in this direction as reflected in the third *Diagnostic and statistical manual* (DSM-III) (American Psychiatric Association, 1980). The manual attempts to: 1) provide a common language for researchers and clinicians irrespective of theoretical orientations; 2) incorporate diagnostic distinctions suggested by newer research data; 3) develop a descriptive phenomenology of mental illness; and 4) establish a multiaxial basis for identifying the different aspects of mental illness. Similar to the tradition of psychosomatics, it deemphasizes unitary etiology and constitutes a movement away from linear cause–effect models toward one of cyclical interaction among several factors. These factors operate at many levels within and between organisms, from subcellular to socio-historical. The psychosomatic diseases involve complex disturbances in the interactions of physiologic regulatory mechanisms, and these disturbances are different at different stages in the course of the illness. Research into their etiology is increasingly focused in identifying risk factors predisposing an individual's development of a diseased state at a specific time. Analogously, research into treatment has focused on altering a person's reaction to such stressors. As the various factors contributing to psychosomatic diseases are more explicitly demonstrated, multiple points of entry for treatment are also under exploration and evaluation for both specificity and efficacy.

Recent impetus for this approach developed largely out of the pioneering studies of Holmes and Rahe (1967). These researchers as well as others have demonstrated significant correlations between illness onset and the proximal occurrence of significant life stresses, ranging from death of a spouse to minor violations of the law (Minter and Kimball, 1980). Stresses of larger magnitude or cumulative stresses correlate better with subsequent onset of serious illness. Along similar conceptual lines, various researchers demonstrate illness predispositions in particular individuals made vulnerable by early relationship experiences with family (Thomas, 1981). Conversely, some factors have also been identified that are protective, such as being on a college athletic team or below a certain height/weight ratio (Thomas and Greenstreet, 1973). These factors seem to operate from moments to years following the significant life event(s). The factors may be clustered into four groups: genetic/biologic; environmental/social; psychologic/behavioral; and apparently autonomous habits. This clustering is suggested only as a pragmatic demonstration of the multi-leveled involvement. Many of the listed factors are serial links in a pathophysiologic chain (Weiner, 1977). For example, one patient may have experienced multiple personal stresses such as getting married and moving. This may have led to increased cigarette smoking, resulting in a bronchitic infection and asthmatic condition. Another patient's stresses may have led to depression and personal negligence. Such negligence may have led to contracting a cold, also resulting in an asthmatic condition. The possible inductive sequences are endless, despite the commonality of discrete factors. Moreover, such risk factors may only be indirectly involved in the inductive sequence leading to disease. In these examples it is equally possible that cigarette smoking or personal negligence is present but not important in the actual pathophysiologic induction of wheezing (bronchospasm). Cigarette smoking, similar to the asthma, may be the result of the patient's individual reaction to the stressors. Thus, such an approach of identifying risk factors correlating with illness allows for an analysis of discrete variables relating to disease onset without oversimplifying the process.

Table 22-1 exemplifies this approach for a few commonly labeled psychosomatic diseases. The admixture of biologic, psychologic and social predisposing factors is consistent with Alexander's notions of these illnesses as spectrum diseases. Individuals with similar disease may vary in the degree of vulnerability contributed from each of these areas. For example, some ulcer patients may have strongly expressed genetic factors placing them at risk for the development of peptic ulcer disease regardless of the stresses they encounter (Weiner, 1977), whereas others without such loading may develop ulcers as a result of their living style or coping strategies (Kimball, 1981). Much future research will be needed for accurate prediction of how various risk factors play a part in the manifestation of a specific disease.

This movement toward careful identification of discrete factors that may coalesce in time and place and result in illness is paralleled in the newer psychotherapeutic approaches that emphasize identification and change of discrete

Table 22-1. TYPICAL RISK FACTORS IN FOUR ILLNESSES WITH MULTIPLE ETIOLOGY.

Disease	Genetic/Biologic	Environmental/Social	Psychologic	Habits
			RISK FACTORS	
General susceptibility to illness*	Intrauterine environment (Hanson, Jones and Smith, 1976) Temperament (Thomas, 1973, 1981) Genetic predisposition Prior illness Age	Stress severity (Holmes and Rahe, 1967) Pathogens in environment	Early relationships (Thomas, 1973, 1981) Giving-up/given-up state (Engel, 1968)	Exercise (Thomas 1973, 1981) Nutritional state Alcohol, cigarette, drug use
Duodenal ulcers* (all subtypes)	Increased pepsinogen Gastrinomos, Z.E. syndrome Alcoholic cirrhosis, Chronic renal failure, Chronic obstructive pulmonary disease, Familial disease of tremor, ulcer + narcolepsy Sex	Induction into Army	Conflict between wishes to be fed and hostility	Cigarette smoking Coffee consumption Alcohol consumption
Coronary artery disease and essential hypertension*	Lower class Cultural determinants Age Race Sex Rapidly changing socio-cultural milieu Early death of a parent		Periods of high stress Type A personality Anger	Obesity Cigarette smoking Exercise Coffee (?) Salt intake
Asthma*	Familial ImmunoL. states Infection	Allergens Cleanliness of household White collar parents Stress Working environment	Emotional arousal Dependency conflicts	Smoking

*Unless otherwise noted, Weiner (1977) is the best reference source for integrating the importance of risk factors in disease.

illness-inducing behaviors. As a barometer of such changes relevant to psychosomatic medicine, DSM III has named the psychophysiologic illnesses: as 1) an Axis I diagnosis of psychological factors affecting physical condition, combined with 2) an Axis III diagnosis of the medical condition as listed in ICD 9 (World Health Organization, 1977). Those "psychosomatic" conditions without concurrent primary physiologic change (such as conversion or hypochondriasis) have been identified as somatoform disorders (American Psychiatric Association, 1980). In these newer approaches, therapeutic procedures are increasingly evaluated for their ability to alter target behaviors or conditions. Such procedures are currently combined to treat complex cases, often crossing the boundaries of psychologic ideology. For example, an ulcer patient may be treated with cimetidine to control acid secretion in the stomach, with readjustment of a working situation to minimize stressors, with behavior therapy to change smoking habits and with insight-oriented therapy to work out central conflicts around dependency needs. In another situation, marital therapy and minor tranquilizers may be combined to manage a chronically anxious patient with premature ejaculation. The boundary in such treatments between prevention, diagnosis and treatment is often indistinct. This is particularly the case in the psychosomatic diseases that are characterized by distinct exacerbations and remissions of physioanatomic malfunction; treatment is geared at reducing the quantity and severity of exacerbations rather than "cure." The treatment programs of patients with these disorders encompass smaller treatments at different levels: from drug therapy to issues of compliance; from alteration of illness-inducing habits to readjustment of maladaptive reactions to stress.

Exemplary methods are shown in Table 22-2. Treatment programs can be designed with interventions targeted at altering discrete behaviors that nonetheless are integral parts of a larger therapy involving the personality. Pragmatism guides therapy more than theory. We emphasize that no therapeutic procedure is pure. All therapy involves dynamics beyond those considered specific to a procedure that needs to be addressed at times. Even the rather mechanical application of biofeedback involves transference and countertransference reactions integrally important to the treatment outcome (Greenspan, 1979). Moreover, it is likely, although not carefully demonstrated yet, that any therapeutic change will profoundly affect one's interaction with the environment as well as one's biology. It is beyond the scope of this update to review the newer developments in all the different areas potentially applicable to treatment of psychosomatic disease, particularly the exciting developments in object relations theory and pharmacotherapy. In the former area significant fine tuning of the understanding of preoedipal dynamics often central in psychosomatic patients has occurred. In the latter area, fine tuning of biologic diagnosis, monitoring and specificity has led to greater sophistication in pharmacological approaches as well. The remainder of this chapter will focus, therefore, on the rising field of behavioral medicine.

Table 22-2. EXEMPLARY TREATMENT OPTIONS.

Risk Factor (disease)	Typical Therapeutic Approach
Known Genetic/Biologic Predisposition	
—glucose intolerance (diabetes)	—minimize effects on blood sugar via diet —insulin
—prior alcoholic cirrhosis (alcoholism)	—rearrange life-style to minimize drinking —behavioral alcoholic treatment
—increase Pepsinogen 1 (ulcers)	—monitor symptoms and signs for early disorder and palliate with antacids —become aware of situations occasioning symptoms and try to alter —cimetadine
Environmental/Social	
—known exposure to high environmental stress (disaster)	—examination of coping strategies to maximize adaptability/minimize stress —brief therapy to help work through the fears
—lower-class black male (hypertension)	—use efficient drug regimen to ensure compliance with medications —dietary training —self-control/biofeedback for blood pressure
Psychologic	
—chronic depression (other medical illnesses)	—insight-oriented therapy —cognitive therapy to counter negativistic thoughts —medical therapy to palliate symptoms
—Type A personality (coronary prone)	—life-style change —relaxation therapy —improve compliance with medications using easy regimens
—Emotionally induced wheezing (asthma)	—behavior analysis to pinpoint episodes occasioning attacks —appropriate psychotherapy to cope with these stressors —education regarding emotions, allergies and asthma
Habits	
—High calorie intake (obesity)	—behavioral therapy for obesity —nutritional education
—alcohol abuse (alcoholism)	—behavior analysis to define situations occasioning drinking —program to improve nondrinking coping strategies

Most psychological treatments are directed toward helping the patient explore and integrate relationships in order to achieve flexible and adaptive behavior patterns.   The introspective modalities such as psychoanalysis and dynamic psychotherapy stress the understanding of the genesis of feelings and cognition. The behavioral approaches stress the identification of the controlling variables affecting the individual's behavior. Behavioral medicine arose from the theoretical and treatment tradition of the "behaviorists." Those who identify themselves as behaviorists range from those who deny the importance of "cognition" to those who treat only those "cognitions." There are two primary schools, however, that guide behavioral thinking: the classical and radical.

Classical Conditioning

Classical conditioning is historically associated with the work of Ivan Pavlov and currently with Joseph Wolpe. In this approach, a previously neutral stimulus (conditioned stimulus, CS) becomes paired with a stimulus (unconditioned stimulus, US) that reliably elicits a behavioral or physiologic response (unconditioned response, UR) (Catania, 1979). Thereafter, the neutral stimulus (CS), in the absence of the unconditioned stimulus, elicits the response — now a conditioned response (CR). Pavlov studied salivation (UR) as it was reflexly elicited by food (US). Food was presented to a dog concurrent with the ringing of a bell on repetitive occasions. Subsequently, Pavlov found that presentation of the bell stimulus (CS) by itself resulted in salivation (CR) in the dog. Analogously, in the clinical psychophysiological disorders, a neutral stimulus may come to elicit an anxiety response in the patients. This process is clearly exemplified by cancer patients who get nauseated and begin vomiting (CR) at only the sight or smell of the hospital (CS) in which they had previously received chemotherapy (US), which has reliably induced vomiting (UR) chemically during their course of treatment. Such responses generally involve various admixtures of autonomic processes rather than voluntary motor and sensory pathways. Overactivity of selected organ systems in vulnerable individuals accounts for the development of altered physiology (Wolpe, 1980). The objective in classical behavioral therapy is the training of the individual to alter the undesired physiological response. Since it is hypothesized that anxiety (or other aversive emotions) triggered the undesired response, teaching the individual to use a response that is incompatible with anxiety results in its alleviation. Relaxation responses made in the presence of a previously anxiety-inducing (conditioned) stimulus seek to replace the undesired conditioned response (Wolpe, 1980).

Operant Conditioning

The operant approaches are associated with B.F. Skinner. The important focus of control in this system are the consequences of behavior (Catania, 1979). This is contradistinguished from the classical approaches in which governance of behavior is accorded to antecedent stimuli. In operant conditioning, the factors defining the operant are the discriminative stimulus, the behavior and the consequences of that behavior. The *discriminative stimulus* (S^D) defines the conditions under which the *consequences* (CSQ) are contingent upon the occurrence of a *specified behavior* (SB). Reinforcement is defined as those conditions in which presentation or elimination of a consequence leads to an increase in the probability of behavior. Punishment defines those situations in which presentation leads to a decrease in the probability of behavior. For example, assume a depressed patient is an S^D for the prescription of an antidepressant medication by the psychiatrist. The environmental event that maintains this behavior by the psychiatrist is improvement in the patient's condition (reward). Given an identical S^D (depressed patient), the behavior of prescribing a minor tranquilizer is not maintained by the environment (patient's condition). In fact, the depression may worsen, thus punishing the psychiatrist's behavior for using minor tranquilizers as sole treatment (SB) in clinically depressed patients (S^D) in that s/he will be less likely to repeat this behavior.

Central to the operant model is the learning history (Catania, 1979). It is crucial to understand what environmental events have been contingent upon the individual's past behavior, and what situations occasioned such behaviors. Usually operant procedures are future-oriented with the objective of teaching the individual how to obtain possible consequences and/or eliminate disturbing ones.

THERAPEUTIC APPROACHES OR BEHAVIORAL MODELS IN THERAPY

Several treatment strategies will illustrate the above models.

Systematic Desensitization

This is the primary technique derived from classical conditioning and is used to desensitize an individual reacting to an anxiety-inducing situation (Wolpe and Reigna, 1976). The subject is placed in a state of relaxation. This is performed through progressive relaxation exercises, a series of structured muscle relaxation exercises involving small and large muscle groups throughout the body. Other methods such as meditation, hypnosis-induced relaxation, biofeedback-assisted relaxation (see below) or autogenic training techniques may be used to achieve this state. In the relaxed state, the patient is instructed to imagine the anxiety-inducing stimuli or situations beginning with mild anxiety-inducing situations and gradually extending to more provocative imaginings. For example, in a graded hierarchy, an individual with a phobia of dogs (CR) is instructed first to visualize puppies (CS) in a cage. Later the individual visualizes a puppy playing with a bone on the floor. Still later, the individual may visualize his playing with the dog; and so on. Once comfortable with dogs in imagination, the individual may continue this structured procedure with real puppies and dogs until comfortable. The new CR to the presence of dogs is relaxation instead of anxiety.

Many psychophysiologic illnesses are noted to be situation-, or stimulus-, specific, often exacerbating under the stimulus of a particular stressor. Systematic desensitization can often help alleviate the anxiety evoked in such situations — particularly when the situations do not currently in reality threaten the individual as much as previously. Asthma is one example. Norah Moore (1965) used desensitization along three hierarchies to treat asthma: one based on the progression of an asthmatic attack; one on an allergic or infective situation; and one on a psychologically stressful situation. All were directed toward the anxiety or provoking situation present at the beginning of an attack. She found significant, objective and subjective, improvement in her patients. Follow-up studies over a two-year interval have demonstrated lasting effects resulting from such types of intervention.

Discrimination Training

These techniques are direct derivatives of the operant behavioral model. The approach identifies (and then often manipulates) those discriminative stimuli that occasion specific behaviors leading to specific consequences. Analysis of the functional relationship between the discriminative stimulus, behavior and its consequences is the foundation of several behavior therapies (Fordyce and Steger, 1979). For example, one treatment of obesity (consequence) involves identifying the characteristic situations (S^D) in which overeating occurs (SB), and then systematically altering those situations (Stunkard, 1979). A similar approach is useful in behavioral analysis of exacerbation of other illness and noncompliance behaviors.

Frequently, medical consultation requests concern patients in whom medical work-up fails to identify the presence of somatic disease. The consultee wishes to know if the symptom is a somatic expression of psychologic distress. This is one of the more difficult consultation requests. A behavioral approach in which characteristic patterns of onset of symptoms are identified often contributes to both an explanation of the behavior and to a method of therapeutic intervention. For example, consults for patients with complaints of debilitating abdominal pain and diarrhea (SB) are frequently requested by the gastrointestinal service. Extensive medical work-up has been negative; management has been frustrating. Careful exploration of the circumstances surrounding daily episodes of symptoms identifies recurrent stress situations (S^D) proximal to the development of the symptoms. A careful behavioral analysis may be aided by the patient filling out extensive daily diaries recording his/her activities, thoughts and feelings together with a record of the experience of symptoms. The repeated concurrence of symptoms and anxiety-inducing situations noted in the records is often striking to both patient and therapist. Frequently the situations occasioning anxiety or symptoms are only topographically similar to those situations that are functionally dangerous. This is similar to transference relationships where the present-day situations occasioning anxiety are only reminders of earlier dangerous (or perceived-dangerous) situations.

A behavioral analysis or discrimination training often is an initial phase within a larger therapy. Once the core situation(s) occasioning the physiologic event are identified, therapy may be refocused upon the situations themselves, the environments or behaviors. The cognitive therapies focus on examining a person's awareness (verbal report) of the whole situation occasioning his/her behavior. Cognitive therapists note faulty evaluations of the overall situation, and then systematically challenge these "faulty cognitions," hoping to change them in the process. In other cases, environmental manipulation alone may alter the course of physiologic disease (Beck, Rush and Shaw, 1979; Goldiamond, 1979). Altering a work situation or living arrangement can have profound effects on a person's biologic adaptation. Finally, behaviors themselves may be addressed, as in the next section.

Behavioral Skills Training

This strategy is used when the behavioral analysis or other diagnostic procedures suggest that the patient's disorder is due in part to poor interactional skills (SB): that is, illness behavior is used to adapt to his/her environment, rather than more direct techniques. Therapy focuses around helping the patient learn alternate, more adaptive repertoires (SB) to obtain the same outcome (Goldiamond, 1974, 1979; Skinner, 1953). This approach has had its foundation in teaching retarded and autistic children. More recently, skills training has been extended to the treatment of psychophysiologic disorders.

Physiologic symptoms may be viewed as behaviors or parts of behavioral clusters used by individuals to alter their environment and interpersonal relationships (Goldiamond, 1974, 1979). Asthmatic attacks (SB) in a child may serve to attenuate (CSQ) upsetting marital discord in the family. Another child in the same family may develop a different maladaptive behavior that also results in decreasing the marital discord. Accordingly, both behaviors, although topographically different, produce the same beneficial outcome for each of these children (Skinner, 1953). A third child thus may react with altered eating behavior, headaches, anxiety attacks or psychosis. The behavior "chosen" will in part depend on individual biologic, psychologic and social risk or vulnerability factors. Behavioral treatment may be directed toward teaching the patient and/or family other means (SB's) of decreasing discord without the use of somatic symptom formation. A behavioral management program is based on identifying the situations (S^D) and associated outcomes (CSQ) in which physiologic behaviors (SB) develop.   Unlearning of illness behaviors is not central to this approach.   It is found that once less costly behaviors are developed to get the same consequences (or better ones), the illness behaviors drop out.   This is an extension of the model developed by I. Goldiamond for the treatment of behavioral disorders (Goldiamond, 1974, 1979; Skinner, 1953).   Other examples of this approach might include: patients presenting with impotency (SB) who are taught acceptable and comfortable ways (SB) to approach intimacy and direct communication (the basis of much modern sex therapy), and patients with irritable bowel syndrome whose symptoms are concurrent with inadequate coping skills along with feelings of frustration and anger, who are taught assertiveness behaviors (SB) as a way of replacing episodes of anger, frustration and gastrointestinal symptoms (SB) (Garrick, 1981).   Emotions are seen as internal (subjective) indicators of the environmental contingencies rather than elicitors of behavior (Skinner, 1974).

Following is an unusual case application of such a treatment approach:

Mr. A is a 33 year old man who was seen by the psychiatric consultant to evaluate paroxysmal atrial tachycardia (P.A.T.) of four years' duration. Propranolol (120 mg/day) was helping to maintain his heart rate below 160 beats per minute.   However, the patient continued to have attacks in which anxiety was prominent.   The patient had been given Valium early in the course of his illness and was unable to decrease his daily 40 mg dose without precipitating P.A.T. and/or anxiety and/or withdrawal.

Significant present Hx revealed to Mr. A to be a successful businessman, from which he gained most of his pleasure.   He was married four years before for the second time and felt this present marriage to be difficult. He identified his propensity for extramarital affairs.   Neither he nor his wife was able to decide on a divorce.   He was the youngest of two boys of a distant father who was disliked by the patient for as long as he could remember.   He felt his mother to be intensely controlling, such that the patient could barely spend one day with her before needing to escape. The patient was thrown out of school at 15 years of age and has hustled his way since.

Behavioral analysis revealed two significant findings.   First, he demonstrated such poor writing and communication skills (in the face of clearly above average intelligence) that understanding him was difficult.   Second, nearly all attacks of P.A.T. (SB) occurred when the patient was on his way to meet his wife (S^D).   Therapy focused on pointing out the correlation between symptoms and intended behaviors and on teaching (SB) the patient new skills to more effectively communicate with his wife.   These skills included paying attention to subtle processes of verbal and nonverbal interactions.

Within three months of weekly therapy the P.A.T. resolved, allowing cessation of the propranolol.   The patient, at one year of treatment, was treating his anxiety attacks with planning and organized action. One year following treatment, the patient was also free of symptoms of P.A.T.

Physiologic symptoms in this section are seen as a "behavior" among several in a cluster of behaviors occurring in relation to identified contingencies. Alternatively, the classical conditioning model may be applied: the situations a person gets into leads to anxiety, which is reflected in physiologic dysfunction. Treatment could be to teach the person to alter the circumstances triggering the anxiety. Either model could lead to similar treatments.

Biofeedback: Consequential Control

In the psychophysiologic illnesses commonly treated by psychiatric consultants, the most popular strategy using consequential control is biofeedback training (Shapiro and Surwit, 1979). Instrumentation is used to amplify and display to the patient specific physiological signals related to their symptoms (SB). Using the feedback as an immediate consequence, the patient learns to alter and control the physiologic variable, thereby altering the experience of the symptom. The new physiologic response is the ultimate consequence. Biofeedback has been used to train individuals with epilepsy to control seizure activity (Calloway, 1980); patients with both tension and migraine headaches to alter these disorders (Budzynski, Stoyva, Adler and Mullaney, 1973; Shapiro and Surwit, 1979), patients with neurologic incontinence to use autonomically innervated sphincters to regain continence (Engel, Nikoomanesh and Schuster, 1974); patients with asthma to decrease airway resistance (Kahn, Staerk and Bonk, 1974); and patients with hypertension to decrease their systolic and diastolic blood pressure (Agras and Jacob, 1979). Although many studies have demonstrated effectiveness of the techniques (Ray, Raczynski, Rogers and Kimball, 1979), carefully designed and better controlled research is needed. Biofeedback alone, as well, has a limited role in the therapeutic armamentarium inasmuch as its effects are frequently short-lived and may be unrelated to symptom-triggering situations (S^D). When combined with behavioral analysis and treatment as above, these techniques can become a powerful therapeutic adjunct. Some have noted biofeedback to be particularly useful in the treatment of severely character-disordered psychosomatic patients (Rickles, 1981). The active involvement in self-regulation supports a sense of positive self-esteem and ego strength can help stabilize people with these disorders. However, other noninstrumented relaxation techniques are often just as useful (Silver and Blanchard, 1978).

Relaxation Techniques. Relaxation techniques teach people how to relax. Clinical efficacy depends on the daily practice of these techniques (as in biofeedback). In this approach the patient suppresses persistent anxiety responses (CR) (classical model) and learns to use body cues to relax (SB) (operant model).

Individuals using relaxation techniques also learn to monitor their levels of tension and relaxation, thereby potentially becoming more aware of the cues that cause tension (Benson, 1975; Jacobson, 1970). Relaxation exercises are central to many behavioral approaches to psychophysiologic illnesses. Often, however, less or no emphasis is put on identification of the provoking situation (S^D).

While research is still developing in this area, there has been some progress in evaluating some of the factors involved, most notably in the therapy of hypertension. Patients with hypertension, off and on medication, learn one of a combination of relaxation techniques that are practiced once or twice daily. Studies most frequently have involved progressive relaxation, meditation or biofeedback-assisted relaxation. Persistent and significant changes in systolic and diastolic blood pressure have been obtained in several studies (up to 36/23 mm Hg reduction from 184.5/109 mm Hg pretreatment) (Agras and Jacob, 1979; Patel, 1977).

Consequential Control. A therapist's giving direct rewards to a patient contingent upon the patient's emitting specific behaviors is a factor in most therapies and may be explicitly used in certain situations. This is often useful in the liaison context where the medical staff's behaviors are intertwined with the patient's disturbing behaviors. The following exemplifies one such case:

> Ms. B is a 40 year old child care worker who was unable to walk without the aid of a walker for two years. During that time a neurologic workup revealed marginal nerve conduction defects; an orthopedic work-up was positive for kyphoscoliosis. A gynecologist felt the patient had endometrosis impinging on the nerve roots and performed a hysterectomy. The patient, who had become clinically depressed following this procedure, developed diarrhea and profound dehydration. The psychiatric evaluation identified the illness (SB) as beginning one month following a major family argument (DS) in which the patient asserted herself (SB) for the first time. The family was very tight-knit, originating in rural Pennsylvania. Childish arguments, alcoholism and antagonism toward individuality characterized the interactions. In the hospital, the patient spent most of her time in bed, fetally positioned under the covers. The staff was attentive to this sick woman, but becoming frustrated. This seemed to increase her own withdrawal and anxiety. The psychiatrist noted her communicability increased with his parental caring (a reinforcing CSQ) and decreased with with autonomy-encouraging behavior (a punishing CSQ).
>
> A program was organized with the medical staff in which they spent increased regular periods of time with her contingent on her emitting healthy behaviors such as getting out of bed, sitting up eating, etc. Concurrently, the consultant psychiatrist spent time with the patient, giving

her "parental like, caring attention" contingent upon her getting out of bed walking without a walker. This time began with only 5–10 minutes daily but within 14 days rapidly increased up to one hour as the patient quickly increased the duration of her walking. (Antidepressant medications were used later in the treatment and effectively seemed to help her vegetative signs.) On the walks during the three-week hospitalization (often with other family members) the patient was taught some more effective ways to directly cope with her relatives. Three-year follow-up identified the patient as walking well without any hospitalization in the interim. She continued on once-monthly psychiatric monitoring. (It is interesting that her headaches persist and seem to serve similar functions in this disturbed family network.)

Although the consequential control (of in-hospital available consequences) was useful early in the therapy, teaching the patient to acquire similar rewards in her natural environment was central to the long-term successful outcome.

DISCUSSION

Most of the behaviorally oriented treatments can be classified into one or more of the above headings. Increasingly efforts are directed toward the identification of such discrete verifiable methods, a mode natural to science. This emphasis is reinforced by a society concerned with economic accountability and increasingly sensitized by mass media to a science and medicine that values measurable and replicable evidence of treatment efficacy. None of the actual treatments is pure, however. All involve the processes of deconditioning, discrimination training, skills training and attention to consequences governing behavior. The art of therapy thus involves the creative application of "generic" techniques — particularly in situations where scientific control and measurement are not feasible.

REFERENCES

Agras, S. and Jacob, R.   Hypertension. In: Pomerleau, O.F. and Brady, J.P. (Eds.), *Behavioral medicine*. Baltimore: Williams & Wilkins, 1979.

Beck, A.T., Rush, A.A. Shaw, B.F. and Emery, G. *Cognitive therapy of depression*. New York: Guilford Press, 1979.

Benson, H. *The relaxation response*. New York: William Morrow & Co., 1975.

Budzynski, T.H., Stoyva, J.M., Adler, C.S. and Mullaney, D.J. EMG biofeedback and tension headache: A controlled outcome study. *Psychosom. Med.* **35**: 484 (1973).

Calloway, E. Biofeedback of brain electrical activity. In: *Biofeedback*. APA Task Force, 1980.

Catania, A.C. *Learning*. Englewood Cliffs, N.J.: Prentice-Hall, 1979.

Diagnostic and statistical manual of mental disorders, 3rd ed. American Psychiatric Association, 1980.

Engel, B.T., Nikoomanesh, P. and Schuster, M.M.   Operant conditioning of rectosphincteric responses in the treatment of fecal incontinence. *N. E. J. M.* **290**: 646 (1974).

Engel, G.L.   A life setting conducive to illness: The giving-up, given-up complex. *Arch. Intern. Med.* **69**: 293 (1968).

Engel, G.L.   The clinical application of the biopsychosocial model. *Am. J. Psychiatry,* **137**: 535–544, 1980.

Fordyce, W.E. and Steger, J.C.   Chronic pain. In: Pomerleau, O.F. and Brady, J.P. (Eds.) *Behavioral medicine.* Baltimore: Williams & Wilkins, 1979.

Garrick, T.   Behavior therapy for irritable bowel syndrome. *Gen. Hosp. Psychiat.* **3**: 48–51, 1981.

Goldiamond, I.   Toward a constructional approach to social problems. *Behaviorism.* **2**: 1 (1974).

Goldiamond, I.   Behavioral approaches and liaison psychiatry. In: Kimball, C.P. (Ed.), *Psychiatric clinics of North America,* vol 2. Philadelphia: W.B. Saunders Co., 1979.

Greenspan, K. *Psychosomatics.* New York: Greene & Stratton, 1979.

Hanson, J.W., Jones, K.L. and Smith, D.W.   Fetal alcohol syndrome, experience with 41 children. *J. A. M. A.* **235**: 1485 (1976).

Holmes, T.H. and Rahe, R.H.   The social readjustment rating scale. *J. Psychosom. Res.* **11**: 213–218 (1967).

Jacobson, E. *Modern treatment of tense patients.* Springfield, Ill.: Charles C. Thomas, 1970.

Kahn, A.U., Staerk, M. and Bonk, C.   Role of counterconditioning in the treatment of asthma. *Psychosom. Res.* **18**: 89 (1974).

Kimball, C.R. *The biopsychosocial approach to the patient.* Philadelphia: Williams & Wilkins, 1981.

Minter, R.E. and Kimball, C.P.   Life events, personality traits and illness. In: Kutash, I. and Schlescugen, L.B. (Eds.), *Handbook on stress and anxiety.* San Francisco: Jossey-Bass, 1980.

Moore, N.   Behavior therapy in bronchial asthma: A controlled study. *J. Psychosomat. Res.* **9**: 257 (1965).

Patel, C.H.   Biofeedback-aided relaxation and meditation in the management of hypertension. *Biofeedback and Self Regulation* **2**: 1 (1977).

Rickles, W.H.   Biofeedback in the psychosomatic narcissistic disorders. *Psychiat. Ann.* **11**: 23–41 (1981).

Ray, W.J., Raczynski, J.M. Rogers, T. and Kimball, W.H. *Evaluation of clinical biofeedback.* New York: Plenum Press, 1979. (200 studies)

Shapiro, D. and Surwit, R.S.   Biofeedback. In: Pomerleau, O.F. and Brady J.P. (Eds.), *Behavioral medicine.* Baltimore: Williams & Wilkins, 1979.

Silver, B.V. and Blanchard, E.B.   Biofeedback and relaxation training in the treatment of psychophysiologic disorders: Or are the machines really necessary? *J. Behav. Med.* **1**: 217–239 (1978).

Skinner, B.F. *Science and human behavior.* New York: Free Press, 1953.

Skinner, B.F. *About behaviorism*. New York: Knopf, 1974.

Stunkard, A.J. Behavioral medicine and beyond: The example of obesity. In: Pomerleau, O.F. and Brady, J.P. (Eds.), *Behavioral medicine*. Baltimore: Williams & Wilkins, 1979.

Thomas, C.B. Stamina: The thread of human life. *J. Chron. Dis.* **34**: 41–44 (1981).

Thomas, C.B. and Greenstreet, R.L. Psychobiological characteristics in youth as predictors of five disease states: Suicide, mental illness, hypertension, coronary heart disease and tumor. *Johns Hopkins Med. J.* **132**: 16–43 (1973).

Weiner, H. *Psychobiology of human disease*. Amsterdam: Elsevier, North Holland, 1977.

Wolpe, J. and Reigna, I.J. (Eds.), *Behavior therapy in psychiatric practice*. New York: Pergamon Press, 1976.

Wolpe, J. Behavior therapy for psychosomatic disorders. *Psychosomatics* **21**: 379 (1980).

World Health Organization. *Manual of the international statistical classification of diseases, injuries and causes of death*, 9th rev. Geneva: World Health Organization, 1977.

23 Research in Psychotherapy

Sol L. Garfield

Research in psychotherapy covers a wide variety of topics and issues, and this chapter can only serve as an introduction to this important subject. An attempt is made, however, to acquaint the reader with some of the areas of investigation, as well as some of the methods and problems encountered in this research. It is hoped, also, that the reader will be able to appreciate the importance of this aspect of psychotherapy, for many of those interested in psychotherapy appear to show relatively little interest in research. They appear more interested in learning about certain approaches to psychotherapy and the associated theoretical formulations than they are in becoming acquainted with research data evaluating the effectiveness of the various psychotherapies. However, in the final analysis, discussions and debates concerning the effectiveness of the different forms of psychotherapy can only be settled by means of systematic empirical research.

It is of interest to speculate on the rather ambivalent or even critical attitude that some psychotherapists manifest with regard to the value of research in psychotherapy. Psychotherapists exhibit a diversity of professional and non-professional backgrounds, have a wide range of training experiences and engage in a variety of different forms of psychotherapy. Apart from a common belief in the efficacy of psychotherapy, or rather in the efficacy of their particular type of psychotherapy, psychotherapists do not necessarily have a common value system or set of beliefs. Behavior therapists, for example, generally tend to be research-oriented, whereas humanistic therapists are much less so. Thus, there is a wide variation in the views of psychotherapists concerning the role and signifi-cance of research in psychotherapy. Some psychotherapists feel very strongly that psychotherapy is an art and can never be a science. From such a perspective, research is an unnecessary and unproductive enterprise. A recent letter in the *American Psychological Association Monitor* is illustrative of this view:

> Psychotherapy is NOT a science; it is an art, and is dependent on and expressed through the personality of the psychotherapist. It cannot be objectively measured unless one only views psychotherapy and personality in the mechanical way that is so fashionable among many of our colleagues who are too frightened and too inept to establish an interpersonal relationship of a therapeutic variety with a patient.
>
> Psychotherapy is an art ... which cannot be quantified. (Lehrer, 1981)

Obviously, if one adheres to such a view, there is no sense whatsoever in attempting to conduct research on psychotherapy, nor is there any need for the psychotherapist to be familiar with the existing research literature. Clearly, research of a systematic character would be viewed as irrelevant, impossible and unnecessary. In many ways this might make life simpler, but whether this would be advantageous to the field of psychotherapy is extremely doubtful. There are a number of sound reasons for taking the position that research on psychotherapy is of critical importance for the field and its continued development. Some of these reasons can be mentioned here very briefly.

From both a practical and social point of view it is important to demonstrate that psychotherapy actually accomplishes what it is supposed to do. The goal of psychotherapeutic effort is to help ameliorate the pain and difficulties of individuals with psychological problems. However, both individual patients and society as a whole can reasonably ask: "Does psychotherapy actually help people? Is it an effective intervention or form of treatment?" Some type of meaningful answers to such questions should be given, and such answers are best secured by means of systematic research. To respond by saying the psychotherapy is an art, and therefore such answers are not required, will not be seen as really satisfactory or credible.

Apart from being sensitive to the increasing demands for accountability on the part of consumers, legislators and third-party payers (Garfield, 1981), there is the intrinsic need on the part of psychotherapists to demonstrate that they are indeed providing a useful and valid service. In fact, this can even be viewed as an ethical requirement. With over 200 forms of psychotherapy apparently being dispensed (Herink, 1980), some means of gauging and demonstrating their effectiveness would appear necessary. Again, the best way to accomplish this is through systematic research appraisal. Furthermore, if psychotherapists do not take the lead in evaluating their therapies, it is possible that they will find others taking on this task. Now, however, let me leave the role of research advocate and review some of the findings and problems in this area of psychotherapy.

AREAS OF INVESTIGATION

A large variety of topics and problems have been investigated and reported in the research literature on psychotherapy. In a bibliography of research on individual psychotherapy prepared by Strupp and Bergin and completed in December 1969, almost 3000 studies were listed. Approximately 98% of the studies listed were reported in the period 1940 to 1967. Thus, there was an impressive amount of research published during this period. The topics listed also covered a wide range. There were studies of therapy process, outcome, client characteristics, therapist personality and role in psychotherapy, as well as methodological investigations and comparative studies of different types of psychotherapy and behavior change. These broad categories, of course, include many different types of investigations, but they do indicate some of the major areas of study.

The different areas and topics investigated reflect the various interests and settings of the investigators as well as the relative popularity of a given area at certain periods. During the 1950s and 1960s there was considerable interest in studies of therapy process and in the client-centered therapeutic conditions of empathy, warmth and genuineness; at other times, a greater emphasis has been placed on evaluating the outcomes of psychotherapy. Over this period of time also, there was evident an increase in the quantity of research as well as its quality. For example, an analysis of outcome studies by Bergin (1971) indicated almost a fifteen-fold increase in the number of published studies in the five-year period 1966–1970 as compared with the period 1936–1940.

This pattern of an increase in the magnitude of research in psychotherapy has appeared to continue into the 1980s and has clearly been augmented by the popularity of behavioral and cognitive therapies in the past two decades. The number of journals reporting research in psychotherapy has also increased. As a result it has become increasingly difficult to keep up with the volume of reported research. However, perhaps in response to this need, as well as reflecting the increased importance of research in this area, a number of important handbooks and research reviews have appeared (Bergin and Garfield, 1971; Garfield and Bergin, 1978; Gurman and Razin, 1977; Kazdin and Wilson, 1978; Meltzoff and Kornreich, 1970; Smith, Glass and Miller, 1980).

Thus, it is apparent that research in psychotherapy has become an increasingly important and visible area of psychotherapy, even though some therapists may view it as lacking in clinical feasibility. Indeed, a tremendous variety of research projects have been conducted to explore and evaluate some of the diverse theories and methods of psychotherapy. Although this research is ofttimes beset with difficulties because of the problems and complexities encountered, the results obtained have increased our understanding of the psychotherapeutic process and have led us to question some of our previous beliefs. Before examining some illustrative research studies and findings, let us first consider some of the important variables in conducting research on psychotherapy.

METHODOLOGICAL ISSUES IN RESEARCH

In evaluating psychotherapy process or outcome a number of variables need to be considered in planning the research investigation. Let us take the matter of evaluating outcome for illustrative purposes. In this instance four basic variables most likely would be viewed as being of major importance. Clearly, one must evaluate the client or patient as a potentially important variable in research on psychotherapy, for clients vary on a number of dimensions that conceivably could influence the results obtained. Similarly, some appraisal must be made of the therapist. As these two individuals constitute the main participants in the psychotherapeutic process, there would appear to be little question concerning their importance. However, apart from their individual significance as potential variables influencing research on outcome, the interaction of such patient and therapist variables might also contribute something of unique value in understanding outcome. That is, some therapists may secure better results with some patients, and vice versa. Finally, the fourth variable is the criteria of outcome used.

The first three variables probably do not need much elaboration here. Clients obviously differ on a number of attributes that conceivably might effect outcome. These would include such aspects as age, education, intelligence, degree of disturbance, personality characteristics, motivation for therapy, current life situation and stress, and so forth. Therapists also might be expected to differ in terms of such attributes as theoretical orientation, age, sex, length of experience, personality, training, professional discipline, expectations and ethical concerns. To disregard such potentially important features of the main participants in psychotherapy would lead to the fostering of what have been called "uniformity myths" in psychotherapy — that is, viewing all clients or all therapists as comparable or interchangeable, and disregarding their variability (Kiesler, 1966, 1971). Although probably no one would take the position that all therapists and all patients are similar or comparable, many research studies in the past have essentially disregarded patient and therapist variability to a considerable degree. All of the patients available for study tended to be grouped in terms of rather crude classifications and treated as a homogeneous group or as specific subgroups. Therapists, on the other hand, have been differentiated mainly in terms of overall theoretical orientation and length of experience. The potentially more important factors of individual performance or personality have received less formal attention.

Even more complicated and difficult to appraise are the interactions that take place between therapist and client. A number of interesting but complex questions can be raised in this regard. For example, what kind of therapist using what kind of approach works best with specific kinds of patients? Does a passive patient improve more readily with an active or a nondirective therapist? Does an older male patient who is depressed respond better to a middle-aged male therapist than to a young female therapist? How does the reputation of the therapist influence how different kinds of patients respond?

The types of questions raised in the preceding paragraph can be multiplied easily, for there are many possible combinations of therapist and patient dyads. It can also be mentioned that very little research of this type has actually been carried out (Berzins, 1977). One may even question if such research really should be done, since there would appear to be an almost unlimited number of possible interactions, and such research seemingly could go on forever. However, if such interactions are deemed to influence the process and outcome of psychotherapy, can they be disregarded if research on psychotherapy is to produce clinically meaningful results? For the time being, let us leave such questions and examine the fourth major variable mentioned earlier — criteria of outcome.

A variety of outcome measures have been used in past research that has attempted to appraise the effects of psychotherapy. Although the matter is of the utmost importance for the field of psychotherapy, there is no real unanimity of opinion as to the best measures to use. Probably the most commonly used criterion in the past was the therapist's own evaluation of the patient's progress at the termination of therapy. This might consist of a brief statement placed in the patient's file, or a rating made by the therapist on a specific rating scale. The reasons for utilizing therapists' ratings are readily apparent. Therapists are available to provide such ratings, and their cooperation in providing ratings of this type usually can be secured without great difficulty. Furthermore, a case can be made for the fact that the therapist is more knowledgeable about the case than anyone else, and thus is in a good position to provide ratings of outcome. Nevertheless, there are some problems in relying solely on therapists' ratings as the criterion for evaluating outcome in psychotherapy.

One of the limiting factors in using therapists' ratings as a criterion of outcome is that therapists are not strictly objective evaluators. They are involved in a real sense in the therapeutic endeavor, and this involvement conceivably can influence their judgments of outcome. Moreover, therapists' formal ratings of outcome are usually made at the end of treatment, and the therapist must attempt to recall how the patient was functioning at the beginning of therapy. Such recall is also subject to possible distortion. Still another possible influence on the therapist's ratings of outcome is the patient's initial level of adjustment. Patients who have relatively minor difficulties or mild symptoms are more likely to be viewed at the end of treatment as having improved the most, since they are obviously functioning at a higher level than the majority of patients who were more seriously disturbed at the start of therapy. That is, the level of final functioning or adjustment may be confused with degree of improvement (Garfield, 1978a; Mintz, 1972). For example, if two patients show exactly the same *amount* or *degree* of improvement, the one who entered treatment at a higher level of adjustment is apt to be judged as the more improved at the end of treatment, even though the degree of improvement is theoretically the same.

Thus, there appears to be some basis for questioning the validity of therapists' ratings on outcome in psychotherapy. There is also some research evidence indicating that therapists' evaluations of treatment tend to be relatively more positive than some other outcome criteria (Garfield, Prager and Bergin, 1971; Sloane, Staples, Cristol, Yorkston and Whipple, 1975). In addition, therapists' ratings have shown rather low correlation with other types of outcome criteria. Sloane *et al.* (1975) reported that therapists' ratings correlated only .13 with ratings made by independent assessors, .21 with ratings made by patients and −.04 with ratings provided by informants. In a study by Horenstein, Houston and Holmes (1973), only a nonsignificant correlation of .10 was secured between therapists' and clients' ratings of change. Garfield *et al.* (1971) reported a correlation of .44 between global ratings of therapists and patients and a correlation of .38 between the ratings of the therapists and their supervisors. However, test measures of outcome did not correlate significantly with the therapists' ratings of outcome. It is of interest to note also that in some of these studies, the correlation between patients' ratings and judges' ratings were distinctly higher. Significant correlations of .54 and .65 were reported between patients' and judges' ratings of outcome by Horenstein *et al.* (1973) and Sloane *et al.* (1975), respectively. Ryan and Gizynski (1971) also reported a significant correlation of .66 between outcome ratings made by the experimenters and the patients, whereas the correlations between therapists and patients, and between therapists and experimenters, were not significant.

The research discussed above not only indicates possible limitations in relying on therapists' ratings as exclusive criteria of outcome, but indicates significant variability among the different outcome criteria used. With regard to ratings made by patients, therapists and impartial judges, it seems clear that each may view outcome with different expectations and from a quite different perspective. One study, for example, found that global ratings of change were influenced by the expectations of the observers (Kent, O'Leary, Diament and Dietz, 1974), although behavioral recordings made by these same observers were not similarly influenced. Consequently, one can reasonably raise some question about the utility and validity of evaluations of outcome in psychotherapy based solely or primarily on the ratings of therapists. Nevertheless, many research studies in the past have relied to a large extent on such ratings. Patients' ratings of outcome have also been used rather frequently, and it is worthwhile to discuss them briefly as well.

Since the patient seeks help with certain problems and is the recipient of psychotherapy, it seems quite reasonable to have the patient evaluate the therapy received. Should not the consumer of the service be in the best position to evaluate the service provided? While this position appears to have face validity, the issue actually may not be as simple as it appears. A number of factors may influence the ratings that patients make. In the first place, the expectations of patients may vary, with some perhaps expecting great transformations of their personality and life situation, and others having more modest expectations. Clients may attribute to therapy improvement that is actually due to significant changes occurring outside of treatment. Clients also may desire to please their therapists, or to justify their efforts and expense in securing therapy by providing positive ratings of outcome. In some instances, the client may even state he is very much improved in order to terminate therapy against the wishes of the therapist. Thus, a number of factors could influence the ratings provided by patients. But even though we recognize possible distorting influences on patients' ratings, we would not want to disregard these ratings completely. Patients' ratings are easy to secure, and, as mentioned previously, they have shown much higher correlations with those of supposedly objective observers than have the ratings of therapists.

More recently, ratings have been obtained from a separate evaluator or judge in the hope of obtaining more objective ratings of improvement or change. The evaluator generally interviews the patient prior to the beginning of therapy and again at termination, usually following a set of specific guidelines. Instead of merely providing an overall global judgment of improvement, a more recent trend has been to identify the three or so primary presenting symptoms of the patient and to rate each separately (Sloane et al., 1975; Strupp and Hadley, 1979). Another advantage in using impartial evaluators is that estimates of the evaluators' reliability can be obtained. Either two evaluators can be present during the interviews with each providing independent sets of ratings, or the interviews can be taped and a second rater can provide ratings based on the tapes.

Although ratings have been used widely in evaluating outcome, a number of other criteria have also been used. Among the more popular have been psychological tests and questionnaires, including tests of mental ability, self-report personality inventories and projective tests of personality. Unlike the usual situation with ratings scales, where they have tended to be employed primarily at the end of therapy, some type of pre–post difference score has usually been employed with tests. The patient is tested at the beginning and end of therapy, and the difference between the two sets of scores constitutes the amount of change. This is a more specific comparison of pre- and posttherapy functioning, and one might expect that the different methods of appraising change could produce different results — which, in fact, has been the case. In a study conducted by the author (Garfield et al., 1971), although ratings by patients and therapists indicated that about 80% of the patients had improved, difference scores obtained from the Minnesota Multiphasic Personality Inventory revealed very little change as a result of therapy. Clearly, the method of evaluating outcome is of some importance in terms of the kinds of results secured.

Difference scores based on standardized tests have some apparent advantages over at least many types of rating scales. The initial level and the final one are measured at the appropriate times, and the scores are potentially more objective.

However, there are also some problems with the use of difference scores. As I have stated the matter elsewhere: "They make no allowance for the initial level of scores and treat all differences of equal amount as equal in importance. Such statistical considerations as possible regression to the mean, inequality of measuring units, and the like, are not compensated for with this procedure. Consequently, other methods such as analysis of covariance and residual scores have been recommended by some investigators (Mintz, Luborsky and Christoph, 1979)" (Garfield, 1981, p. 173).

As has been indicated, evaluating outcome in psychotherapy is not quite the simple matter that it may appear, but there is no need at this point to elaborate further on the research problems mentioned. Enough has been said to give the reader some idea of the difficulties involved in psychotherapy research and how variations in assessing outcome may influence the results obtained. There are, however, some other important aspects of research in psychotherapy that also merit our attention.

CONTROLLED AND UNCONTROLLED RESEARCH

In the earlier reports of outcome research in psychotherapy, uncontrolled studies were relatively frequent and were an obvious target of criticism from scientifically oriented investigators (Eysenck, 1952). The limitations of these studies would appear obvious, yet such studies were conducted and some are still conducted from time to time (Bergin, 1971; Kernberg, Burstein, Coyne, Appelbaum, Horwitz and Voth, 1972; Malan, 1976). Consequently, it is worth emphasizing that no really valid conclusions can be drawn from such research. If a group of patients are treated by means of a specific form of therapy, and, let us say, 80% show some improvement on a reasonably adequate measure of change, can we conclude that the treatment is really effective? It may appear so, because an improvement rate of 80% seems quite impressive. However, without an adequate control group, one cannot be sure if the change is due to the treatment, or to some other variable such as the passage of time. For example, suppose a comparable group of patients to those treated are not given treatment but are followed for a similar length of time, and are evaluated in a similar fashion. At this time it is found that 80% of this group are judged to be improved — the same percentage as the treated group. How do we interpret the improvement rate of the psychotherapy group when such additional data are provided? Of course one can continue to say that psychotherapy helps 80% of the patients treated. However, what does this really mean if we can say also that *no therapy* helps 80% of similar patients? Clearly, such data would not be viewed as being strongly supportive of the effectiveness of psychotherapy.

As has been indicated, controlled research studies can provide more meaningful and definitive results than uncontrolled studies. For this reason most scientific research has utilized controlled procedures. The well-known placebo provides one example of a procedure developed for controlled research in medicine and pharmacology. The reason for its significance is that investigators of drugs and medications desire to know if it is really the pharmacological agent that produces treatment effects, or if the effects are produced by other possible variables. The mere taking of a pill, for example, has been known to produce positive (or negative) effects on some patients, even when it is an inert placebo (Shapiro and Morris, 1978). Seeing a physician and being spoken to in a kind and knowledgeable manner may also have positive treatment effects that may be ascribed to the medication given.

Consequently, in more recent years, there has been a much greater emphasis on the importance of controlled studies in research on psychotherapy. Furthermore, a greater sophistication is evident concerning what might be viewed as adequate control groups. It is not only necessary to have a control group for evaluating the effects of psychotherapy, but it is necessary to have an appropriate control group. This requires considering a number of potentially important variables.

First, the sample of subjects placed in the control group should be as similar or comparable to the control group as possible. If one is treating moderately severe depressives, then the control group should consist of comparably depressed subjects. Also, all other patient variables that conceivably might affect outcome should be comparable in the two groups of subjects. These might include some of the other patient variables mentioned previously, such as length of depressive incident, motivation for therapy, current life situation and the like. This, of course, makes the research much more difficult and complex. However, the chances of securing definitive or reliable results are increased. This is particularly important if one or more of the variables mentioned might influence outcome significantly. For example, if a control group is formed of patients who are more severely disturbed than the treated group, or of a group who refuse treatment, the results might be biased in favor of the treatment group.

The best procedure for obtaining comparable and unbiased groups of patients is random assignment. In this way there is no evident bias in assigning patients to the treatment or control groups. Furthermore, one can monitor the patients assigned in this manner so that if by chance some inequities do occur, corrections can be made in future assignments. In this way, the groups will be as similar as possible.

Although random assignment is the preferred procedure theoretically, it is recognized that it is usually difficult to carry it out when working with actual patients in a clinical situation. Patients come to a clinic because they seek help for their problems, and they are not particularly interested in being placed in a no-treatment control group. Some attempts have been made to get around this problem, but not always successfully. One procedure that has been used is what has been termed a wait-list control group. Patients who apply for treatment are assigned randomly to the treatment and control group. Those who are assigned to the control group are told that there will be some delay before they can be assigned to a therapist, but that they will be contacted when there is an opening. If the treatment being evaluated has a specific time limit, then the patients in the control group can be told that they will not have to wait any longer than the specified period. In the study by Sloane *et al.* (1975), for example, the therapies investigated were limited to four months. Thus, the patients were definitely promised therapy within four months.

Although the wait-list method has some advantages, there are also some problems with this procedure. Some patients will not wait for the specified period of time and will seek treatment elsewhere. Some will get better without treatment and refuse to show up for the evaluation procedures. Some will move or otherwise be lost to the research study. One possible way to avoid some of these problems is to maintain some regular contact with the patients in the control group, even though this may violate the conditions for a strictly no-treatment group. Such a procedure was used in the Sloane *et al.* (1975) study. In such a study comparing two different types of therapy, contact with the control patients might not be viewed as a critical problem. However, the conclusions would have to be limited mainly to the comparison of the two therapies, and no absolute claims could be made concerning the effectiveness of the treatments as compared to no treatment.

Some researchers in the field of psychotherapy have also stated that a no-treatment control group is not a really effective control in studying the effects of specific therapies (Paul, 1967). Their reasoning is that some of the effects of psychotherapy may be due simply to the attention received from the therapist and/or related factors, and thus may not be due to the specific procedures of the therapy. Consequently, what has been called an attention-placebo control group is deemed essential. In setting up such a control group, the investigator essentially attempts to devise a pseudo-therapy that may give the appearance of being an actual treatment. At the same time, this attention-placebo therapy must not include what are presumed to be the active ingredients of the therapy being evaluated, or for that matter, of any formal therapeutic procedure. If the latter efforts are not successful, the results will be confounded. Devising such an attention-placebo therapy control and having therapists perform their roles appropriately is not a simple task, particularly if the therapy extends for some time. Nevertheless, the rationale on which this type of control is based is not without merit. If one is seriously interested in demonstrating that the effectiveness of a given form of therapy is due to the specific and unique features of the therapy and not just to the opportunity to talk over one's problems with another human being, some sort of placebo control group would appear to be of great value, if not absolutely essential.

Probably enough has now been said about controlled research, and further discussion is not required. Individuals who plan research studies will have to go beyond this presentation and be familiar with experimental design and appropriate procedures for statistical analysis (Kazdin, 1980). Nevertheless, the major points stressed in this and the preceding section should help to make the psychotherapist more sensitive to the requirements of sound research and also help him/her to evaluate the adequacy of the reports in the research literature on psychotherapy. However, there is one additional related topic I would like to discuss before presenting the procedures and findings of a well-conducted actual research study of psychotherapy.

STATISTICAL VERSUS CLINICAL SIGNIFICANCE

I have discussed this topic elsewhere on several occasions (Garfield, 1978b, 1980) and therefore will only allude to it briefly here. Most published studies in psychology and related fields usually present the results of some statistical analysis made of the data secured, and most commonly there is a reference to the statistical significance of the findings obtained. There is no question that such analyses need to be performed. Otherwise the results secured could be due to chance. Statistical analyses of this type are thus required in order to indicate the probability that the findings are not due to chance.

So far so good. We note that the findings obtained in a given investigation are reported to be statistically significant. Thus, we can have some confidence that they are probably not due to chance. However, although we can draw this *statistical* conclusion, a conclusion as to the practical or clinical significance of the study also needs to be made. In other words, one can secure findings that are not random, but at the same time they may not be very significant for practical purposes. A hypothetical example may illustrate what is involved here.

We conduct a study of intensive psychotherapy with a group of patients suffering from severe anxiety. The therapists are analytically trained, and all have had at least fifteen years of professional experience. The patients are seen twice a week for a period of up to a year. The control subjects are seen by comparably experienced therapists once a month for up to one year. Our main measure of outcome is the "Freud–Jung Scale of Anxiety," which is a reliable and valid anxiety scale. Standard scores are obtained on this scale where the mean score is 50 and the standard deviation is 10. Because this is viewed as a very important study, there are 500 anxious patients in each group. Now, let us proceed to the results obtained and the statistical analysis.

Both groups of patients obtained very high scores on the F-J Scale at the beginning of therapy, with identical means of 79. After completion of therapy, the intensive treatment group has a mean of 70, whereas the control group has secured a mean of 74. We compare the two sets of differences and discover that they are significant at better than the .01 level of probability. This is a highly significant finding statistically, and if the research study were repeated with new groups of comparable patients, the probability is high that we would again secure comparable differences. We might then conclude that intensive psycho-analytically oriented psychotherapy is significantly more effective than less intensive therapy of this type.

This conclusion is correct if one speaks *only* of statistical significance. How-ever, this conclusion may be questioned if one is trying to determine if this intensive form of psychotherapy is clinically or economically worthwhile. It can be pointed out that the improvement of the intensively treated group is limited, for the mean scores after treatment are still quite high. In other words, although the intensively treated group shows a greater reduction in anxiety than the less intensively treated group, on the whole these patients remain very anxious. Furthermore, the difference at the end of treatment between the two groups is of relatively little clinical significance, and does not appear commen-surate with the much higher costs for the more intensive treatment. We might conclude, therefore, that although the intensive form of psychotherapy was superior to the control form of therapy at a statistically significant (.01) level, the actual results were disappointing, since most patients still showed rather marked anxiety at the end of treatment.

The hypothetical example presented above is not completely fanciful, and comparable examples can be found in the published literature (Garfield, 1978b, 1980). The interested reader should have little difficulty in finding such reports in the literature if he or she carefully inspects the actual data reported. If such data are not presented, then, of course, it is impossible to make a judgment concerning the clinical significance of the findings. For this reason as well as others, it is important that investigators report the basic data for the variables found to be significant, and not just the results of the statistical analyses alone. Although the latter are essential, they must be supplemented by data that allow the reader to appraise the clinical significance of the results secured.

AN ILLUSTRATIVE RESEARCH STUDY

Since a large number of psychotherapists may not keep close track of the research literature in this area, it may be worthwhile, for illustrative purposes, to consider in some detail a well conducted and reported research study.

Overview and Description

One of the best-known studies in the area of psychotherapy in recent years, and one to which we have already made some reference, is the study conducted by Sloane, Staples and their colleagues (1975). This was a study comparing the relative effectiveness of brief psychoanalytically oriented psychotherapy and behavior therapy. In contrast to many previous studies that tended to use relatively inexperienced psychotherapists and trainees, the Sloane *et al.* study used very experienced and well-known therapists. The group of three behavior therapists included Joseph Wolpe and Arnold Lazarus.   The senior psycho-analytically oriented therapist "had treated some 6000 patients over his 35 years of practice, some in classical psychoanalysis and many in psychoanalytically oriented psychotherapy" (p. 80); and the second analytically oriented psycho-therapist had twenty years of experience, having conducted both classical psychoanalysis and psychoanalytically oriented therapy.   The third therapist in each of the two groups was less experienced than the other two therapists, having had six to eight years of appropriate therapeutic experience.

The patients who constituted the subjects in this study were selected from those who sought outpatient treatment at a university medical center.   Four criteria were used in selecting patients.   The first was that the individual be a "psychiatric patient," but one whose disturbance was judged not to be ex-tremely severe.   The patient was defined as a person "who felt subjective dis-comfort, whose symptoms interfered with his proper functioning in work, social, or sexual life, and who was prompted to seek psychiatric help for these diffi-culties" (p. 56).   Thus, some individuals were rejected because they were viewed as essentially normal or because their problems were seen as situational and thus likely to change in the relatively immediate future.   At the other extreme were severely disturbed individuals who could not safely forgo the prospective waiting period of four months or whose prognosis for short-term therapy was very poor – for example, alcoholism or drug addiction, schizophrenia or organic brain damage.

A second condition for admission into the study was that the individual be willing to receive psychotherapy and not demand some other form of treat-ment.   The third condition was that the assessor in the study, a psychiatrist, con-sider psychotherapy to be the treatment of choice for the patient rather than some other treatment.   Finally, prospective patients for the study had to be between the ages of eighteen and forty-five.   Twenty-nine applicants were judged not to meet these requirements.   Consequently, they were excluded from the study and referred to other treatment outlets.

The patients considered appropriate for the study were then randomly assigned to one of the three treatment groups – psychoanalytically oriented psychotherapy, behavior therapy or the wait-list control.   Although ideally it would have been desirable to make all groups comparable on every variable that potentially might influence outcome, the number of such variables makes this type of group assignment practically impossible.   This is particularly true when patients must be assigned to the different treatments at the time they are accepted into the study.   Consequently, the groups were matched only on sex and severity of neurosis with the hope "that otherwise random assignment would equally distribute other characteristics among the three treatment groups" (Sloane et al., 1975, p. 74).

The treatment plan called for nine subgroups of ten patients each, with three for each treatment condition.   Thus, each therapist was to receive ten patients, and three of the subgroups would fall in the wait-list control group. The neuroticism scale of the Eysenck Personality Inventory was used to evaluate the degree of pathology. Because there were more female than male patients available, six females and four males eventually constituted each subgroup. These patients were also classified so that each subgroup received three females with high pathology, three females with low pathology, two males with high pathology and two males with low pathology. Once this arrangement was decided, the actual assignment to subgroups was made by recourse to a table of random numbers.

The three therapists in each group thus treated at least ten patients each. A time limit of four months was placed on each treatment for purposes of the research study. However, patients could be continued in treatment after this period if it seemed indicated. Each of the patients was interviewed by the psychiatric assessor at the time of initial assessment, after the four months treatment period and one year after the initial assessment. At these times, the severity of the patient's three main complaints or target symptoms was evaluated and rated by the assessor on a scale ranging from zero to 4. The second and third ratings were made by the assessor "without refreshing his memory as to the initial severity" (p. 53). The difference between the initial and posttreatment ratings defined the extent of improvement. In addition, the assessor also made a global rating of change on each symptom, utilizing a 13-point scale ranging from zero ("very much worse") to 12 ("completely recovered").

These evaluations of the primary complaints of the patients constituted the main criteria of outcome. However, a questionnaire, the Structured and Scaled Interview to Assess Maladjustment (SSIAM) was also used. The SSIAM consists of ten items for each of five separate areas of adjustment: work, social, sexual, relations with original family and relations with present family; each item is then rated on an 11-point scale. This instrument was administered to each patient and also to a significant other.

In addition to the outcome measures described, a number of diagnostic appraisals of the patients were made. The Minnesota Multiphasic Personality Inventory (MMPI) was administered prior to treatment and tended to show considerable pathology in the patient sample. Four of the nine clinical scales were well within the abnormal range, and the mean score for all clinical scales was 70.09, just within the abnormal range. Two other personality scales were administered as well, the Eysenck Personality Inventory and the California Psychological Inventory, and the results obtained were generally congruent with those from the MMPI. Finally, each patient received a formal diagnosis from the psychiatric assessors based on the then-current manual of the American Psychiatric Association, DSM-II. Approximately two-thirds of the patients received diagnoses of neurotic disorders with slightly less than a third being diagnosed as having personality disorders. It is of interest to mention also that

64% of the patients stated that they had previously participated in formal psychotherapy. Of this group, 41% had been in therapy for ten sessions or less, whereas 59% had had more extensive treatment.

A few other features of this study need to be mentioned before we discuss and evaluate the results. A research assistant played an important role throughout the study. She met the patient and his/her friend or relative before the patient was to see the assessor and obtained the patient's family and general medical history. She also administered the Eysenck Personality Inventory and then tried to prepare the patient for the psychiatric interview. She explained the use of the tape recorder and reassured the patient that confidentiality of the material would be observed. She also informed the patient that there sometimes was a waiting list for treatment, but that all patients who were accepted for treatment would eventually receive treatment within four months. This latter item was necessitated by the planned use of a wait-list control group. The research assistant answered any questions concerning the procedures pertaining to the psychiatric assessment, and then introduced the patient to the assessor.

The research assistant was also the key figure with regard to the wait-list control group. She was described as a "warm friendly person," and in addition to being the initial contact with each patient, she phoned each of the wait-list patients every few weeks. At these times, she asked how they were getting along, and reminded them that eventually they would be assigned to treatment. Although this type of personal contact would appear to make the wait-list group a "minimal contact" group rather than a "no-treatment" group, this procedure was deemed advisable for several reasons. The investigators felt a sense of responsibility for these patients because their treatment was being postponed by the research requirements. Also, such contact might increase the probability of the patients' remaining in the control group, a very important consideration − and in fact it appeared to do so. Patients on the wait-list were also permitted to call the assessor if ever a crisis arose.

As already indicated, measures of outcome were completed four and twelve months after the initial assessment. Those patients who actually received treatment were asked to complete the Truax Relationship Questionnaire and the Lorr Inventory. These two rating scales were included to evaluate the patient's attitude toward the therapist and his/her perception of the therapist's behavior. The fifth therapy session of all patients who remained in therapy to that point also was used as the source for selecting four four-minute therapy segments. These samples were independently scored by two raters according to Truax's criteria for five therapeutic conditions: Depth in Interpersonal Contact, Accurate Empathy, Therapist Self-Congruence, Unconditional Positive Regard and Depth of Interpersonal Exploration. The therapists also provided "ratings on work, social, sexual and overall change" and on a scale designed to measure attitudes toward the patient.

Sloane and his collaborators also attempted to provide at least some guides and checks on the therapies conducted to ensure that, in general, they were representative of the two types being compared. Because patients with a variety of symptoms were to be treated, it was not feasible to limit the therapists to the use of a specific therapeutic technique such as, for example, systematic desensitization. Thus, the therapists were allowed to use whatever procedures or techniques they deemed most appropriate for the individual case. Although this conceivably increases the possibility of error variance — for therapist variables will interact with treatment variables — the design does reflect the realities of clinical practice (Kazdin, 1980). Consequently, a list of definitions or criteria for each of the therapies was compiled and approved by the therapists in the study. The in-therapy behavior of the therapists for the fifth interview, which was recorded, was rated on a number of dimensions. Differences in the behaviors of the two groups of therapists were found, and in a general way conformed to the stated differences in the two therapies.

The preceding description of the overall plan of the Sloane *et al.* study, although concise, is reasonably complete and should give the reader some appreciation of the complexities inherent in such a study as well as the thoroughness and comprehensiveness of the general design. It required six trained and experienced therapists, three psychiatric assessors, a research assistant, raters and the like, and included ninety-four bona fide patients. Although the amount of time the investigation required is not indicated in the report, it is apparent that several years were required for planning and conducting the study. Now, however, let us proceed to a brief presentation of the results obtained.

Results

The results secured four months after the initial assessment will be the main outcome results discussed here. They essentially represent the posttreatment data and appear to be the most meaningful. The one-year assessments are limited because the wait-list control subjects were offered treatment after four months, and patients who had completed one form of therapy and showed little improvement were in some instances offered and given the other type of treatment.

In general, both treatment groups improved significantly more than the wait-list group on the ratings of the three target symptoms. However, there was no significant difference between these two different forms of psychotherapy in terms of these ratings of outcome. All groups were rated as having "moderately severe" symptoms prior to treatment. At the four-month assessment period, both treated groups showed an average decrease of one and one-half points on the ratings of target symptoms made by the assessors. These ratings fell between the mild and trivial categories of severity. The wait-list patients, on the other hand, showed a decrease of only one-half point on the five-point rating scale — that is, these ratings fell between the mild and moderate categories. Thus, it was shown that all three groups of patients had improved to some degree at the four-month assessment, but the extent of improvement was significantly greater for the two treated groups than for the control group. It can also be noted that the degree of improvement for the treated groups still indicated some degree of symptom discomfort at this appraisal.

The other main measure of outcome was the SSIAM, a measure of overall adjustment. Although ratings are secured on five areas of adjustment, for various reasons, which need not be elaborated upon here, ratings on only two areas were used: "Social Isolation" and "Work Inadequacy." The patients who received behavior therapy showed a statistically significant decrease in work inadequacy. The patients on the wait list and those treated by psychoanalytically oriented psychotherapy also showed improvement at the four-month assessment period. However, this difference was statistically significant only if a one-tailed test was used, and was marginally significant ($P < .10$) when a two-tailed test was used.[1]

Both the behavior therapy patients and the wait-list controls demonstrated a significant improvement on the scale measuring social adjustment. However, the group that received the psychoanalytically oriented therapy did not improve significantly on this variable.

The investigators point out that the amount of change secured on these two scales, while consistent and in most cases statistically significant, "did not reflect the major shift which seemed clinically apparent. This was no doubt due at least in part to outpatients' tendency to cluster toward the lower (better adjusted) end of the scale, leaving relatively little room for measurable improvement" (Sloane et al., 1975, p. 92).

In an additional comparison, the extent of improvement in work and social adjustment, and symptomatic improvement, were tested in $3 \times 2 \times 2$ analyses of variance with treatment, patient sex and severity of neuroticism as the third factor. Only with reference to symptomatic improvement were there differences between the treatment groups. As already mentioned, the behavior therapy and the psychotherapy groups both showed greater symptomatic improvement than did the wait-list control group. However, the differences between the three treatment groups on the work and social adjustment measures were not significant. The degree of improvement also appeared to be independent of sex of patient and degree of neuroticism as measured by the Eysenck Personality Inventory.

The results presented above constitute the major findings on outcome of treatment in this study which compared two well-known contemporary forms of psychotherapy. The description provided should enable the reader who has not engaged in research on psychotherapy to become more cognizant of what is involved in such an undertaking. However, before leaving the Sloane et al. study, a few other findings can be mentioned that may be of particular interest to psychotherapists.

---

[1] A fuller explanation of this problem can be found in Appendix 4 of the full report of the study (Sloane et al., 1975).

Other Findings

When the 13-point rating scale of symptomatic improvement used by the assessors is collapsed into a 5-point rating scale, the results can be viewed in terms of the percentage of patients improved. Although this procedure has limitations, the percentage of patients rated as improved has been reported in many previous studies of psychotherapy. In this way some crude observations and comparisons can be made. In the study under review, 80% of the patients in both active treatment groups were judged as improved or recovered on this basis. The wait-list patients only had 48% who were so rated, and the difference between treated and control groups was significant. However, the global ratings for overall adjustment were somewhat higher. Ninety-three percent of the behaviorally treated patients were rated as improved, whereas 77% of both of the other two groups of patients were rated as improved or recovered.

Another point of interest, referred to in our general discussion of criteria of outcome, concerns the agreement among different raters. As we indicated there, in the study by Sloane et al. the ratings of improvement made by patients and by assessors were correlated at a moderately high level ($r = .65$), whereas the correlations of the therapists' ratings with those of the other two sets of raters were not significant. Seventy-four percent of the patients in the behavior therapy group and 81% in the psychodynamic group rated themselves in the improved or recovered categories, as compared to 44% of the control patients, in terms of symptom change. These percentages are quite similar to the comparable ratings of the assessors mentioned earlier. With regard to the ratings of overall improvement, the patients' ratings indicated that 93% of those who received behavior therapy and 80% of the psychotherapy group considered themselves as improved. In contrast to this, 55% of the wait-list patients rated themselves as improved. This is perhaps understandable, since the wait-list individuals were still awaiting therapy. The behavior therapists generally gave somewhat higher ratings of improvement than did their patients or the assessors. It is interesting to note also that the ratings provided by a patient's family member or friend correlated only .25 with the ratings of the patients.

The tape recordings of the fifth therapy session also provided a means of comparing the therapy behaviors and interactions of the two groups of therapists. Behavior therapists more frequently gave advice, instructions and information. They presented their own value judgments and generally performed in a more directive manner, providing most of the verbalization in the therapy hour. The analytically oriented psychotherapists were more reflective, allowed their patients to select what they wanted to talk about and encouraged them to explore and express their thoughts and feelings. As might be expected, their speech content was much less than that of their patients. In their own descriptions of the therapy they conducted, these therapists also placed much greater emphasis on the therapeutic relationship than did their behavioral counterparts.

Nevertheless, and perhaps surprisingly, the behavior therapists showed higher levels on the Truax scales of depth of interpersonal contact, therapist self-congruence and accurate empathy as rated on the tapes of the fifth interview. The two groups of therapists were approximately equal in terms of ratings of unconditional positive regard or warmth. The patients' ratings on a comparable Relationship Questionnaire showed a higher mean score on one of four sub-scales (Genuineness) as well as on the overall score for the behavior therapists as compared with the other group of therapists.

Thus, although the two groups of therapists functioned differently and in line with the tenets of their respective orientations, they obtained essentially comparable outcomes on the criteria used. This is certainly an intriguing but not unusual finding. It is also one that I believe points to the probability of common factors in diverse forms of psychotherapy (Garfield, 1974, 1980). This is not the proper place, however, to speculate about such a research finding.

The results secured in terms of the ratings of therapists' empathy and similar attributes were also interesting, since some individuals have depicted behavior therapy as a somewhat cold and mechanical process. This, obviously, does not appear to be the case in this study, which illustrates how opinions about therapy may not always be supported by empirical investigation.

Discussion of Study

We have now reviewed in some detail a previously published study that attempted to compare the effectiveness of two well-known forms of psychotherapy. Attention was first paid to the overall design of the study, which included such important considerations as the selection of therapists and patients, the length of therapy, description and verification of the therapies provided, assignment of patients to treatment and control groups, selecting the type of control group, the use of several different measures of outcome and an adequate analysis of the data obtained. Because the original study was reported in book form, more detailed data were provided than are supplied in studies published as articles. Thus, more of the specific aspects of the study could be delineated.

It should be apparent, even from this condensed presentation, that planning and conducting a reasonably sound study is a complex undertaking. Consequently, it is very important to plan the project as carefully as possible and to anticipate the difficulties and problems that may arise. There is an old research maxim to the effect that "whatever can go wrong will go wrong," and there is more truth than poetry in this saying. One manner of reducing problems to a minimum is to be familiar with the previous research dealing with the problem to be investigated. In this way the potential investigator becomes aware of the variety of procedures and measures that have been used in comparable studies, and have been found to have some merit. An additional helpful activity is to become familiar with articles or books that specifically review research in psychotherapy and discuss limitations in past research as well as suggesting methodologically better procedures (Chassan, 1979; Garfield and Bergin 1978; Kazdin, 1980). Finally, it is frequently very worthwhile to conduct a pilot or preliminary study on a small number of subjects in order to see how adequate the research design is when put into practice. This latter procedure can help the investigator to discover deficiencies and problems in the research before the actual study is begun. In this way the necessary modifications and improvements can be made and the main study strengthened.

It is apparent that the Sloane *et al.* study reflected the familiarity of the investigators with the kind of problem they wanted to study. They appeared to show good judgment in the selection of therapists and patients, and used a variety of outcome measures so that the possible limitations of any single one would not detract seriously from the merit of the study. The findings they secured also appear to be clear-cut and reasonable. Other comparative studies have tended to report similar findings (Luborsky, Singer and Luborsky, 1975). Furthermore, the findings do have interesting and potential significance for the field. If very different forms of psychotherapy secure similar results, is this because they exert their influence in different ways, or are there common factors responsible for the gains found with both forms of therapy?

SUMMARY

This chapter has attempted to provide the reader with a brief introduction to the area of psychotherapy research. Reference has been made to the diverse attitudes that psychotherapists have expressed toward this topic. Although some feel strongly that adequate research of psychotherapy can never be carried out, others take the view that research is necessary for the advancement of the field. Social necessity and accountability would appear to emphasize the importance of research.

Some of the array of topics that have been researched were also mentioned briefly. Particular attention was devoted to methodological issues in research on psychotherapy, including the important matter of evaluating outcome. Discussed here were the importance of patient and therapist variables and their interactions in therapy, outcome measures, controlled and uncontrolled research and the distinction between statistical and clinical significance. The last section of the chapter was devoted to a presentation and discussion of a well-known and well-executed study of psychotherapy that compared behavioral therapy and psychoanalytically oriented psychotherapy. By actually examining a completed research investigation in this area, it was hoped that the complexities of research in psychotherapy would be illustrated and made more meaningful to psychotherapists whose actual participation in research may be limited.

REFERENCES

Bergin, A.E. The evaluation of therapeutic outcomes. In: Bergin, A.E. and Garfield, S.L. (Eds.) *Handbook of psychotherapy and behavior change.* New York: Wiley, 1971.

Bergin, A.E. and Garfield, S.L. (Eds.) *Handbook of psychotherapy and behavior change.* New York: Wiley, 1971.

Berzins, J.I. Therapist–patient matching. In: Gurman, A.S. and Razin, A.M.(Eds.), *Effective psychotherapy. A handbook of research.* Oxford: Pergamon, 1977.

Chassan, J.B. *Research design in clinical psychology and psychiatry*, 2nd ed. New York: Irvington, 1979.

Eysenck, H.J. The effects of psychotherapy: An evaluation. *Journal of Consulting Psychology.* **16**: 319–324 (1952).

Garfield, S.L. *Clinical psychology. The study of personality and behavior.* Chicago: Aldine, 1974.

Garfield, S.L. Research on client variables in psychotherapy. In: Garfield, S.L. and Bergin, A.E. (Eds.) *Handbook of psychotherapy and behavior change*, 2nd ed. New York: Wiley, 1978a.

Garfield, S.L. Research problems in clinical diagnosis. *Journal of Consulting and Clinical Psychology.* **46**: 596–607 (1978b).

Garfield, S.L. *Psychotherapy: An eclectic approach.* New York: Wiley, 1980.

Garfield, S.L. Critical issues in the effectiveness of psychotherapy. In: C.E. Walker (Ed.) *Clinical practice of psychology.* New York: Pergamon, 1981.

Garfield, S.L. Psychotherapy: A forty-year appraisal. *American Psychologist.* **36**: 174–183 (1981).

Garfield, S.L. and Bergin, A.E. (Eds.) *Handbook of psychotherapy and behavior change*, 2nd ed. New York: Wiley, 1978.

Garfield, S.L., Prager, R.A. and Bergin, A.E. Evaluation of outcome in psychotherapy. *Journal of Consulting and Clinical Psychology.* **37**: 307–313 (1971).

Gurman, A.S. and Razin, A.M. (Eds.) *Effective psychotherapy. A handbook of research.* Oxford: Pergamon, 1977.

Herink, R. (Ed.) *The psychotherapy handbook: The A to Z guide to more than 250 different therapies in use today.* New York: A Meridan Book, New American Library, 1980.

Horenstein, D., Houston, B. and Holmes, D. Clients', therapists', and judges' evaluations of psychotherapy. *Journal of Counseling Psychology.* **20**: 149–153 (1973).

Kazdin, A.E. *Research design in clinical psychology.* New York: Harper & Row, 1980.

Kazdin, A.E. and Wilson, G.T. Criteria for evaluating psychotherapy. *Archives of General Psychiatry.* **35**: 407–416 (1978).

Kent, R.N., O'Leary, K.D., Diament, C. and Dietz, A. Expectation biases in observational evaluation of therapeutic change. *Journal of Consulting and Clinical Psychology.* **42**: 774–780 (1974).

Kernberg, O.F., Bernstein, C.S., Coyne, R., Appelbaum, D.A., Horwitz, H., and Voth, T.J. Psychotherapy and psychoanalysis: Final report of the Menninger Foundation's psychotherapy research project. *Bulletin of the Menninger Clinic.* **36**: 1–276 (1972).

Kiesler, D.J.   Some myths of psychotherapy research and the search for a paradigm. *Psychological Bulletin*. **65**: 110–136 (1966).

Kiesler, D.J.   Experimental design in psychotherapy research. In: Bergin, A.E., and Garfield, S.L. (Eds.) *Handbook of psychotherapy and behavior change*. New York: Wiley, 1971.

Lehrer, A.   Letter. *APA Monitor*, p. 42 (February 1981).

Luborsky, L., Singer, B. and Luborsky, L.   Comparative studies of psychotherapies.   Is it true that "Everyone has won and all must have prizes"? *Archives of General Psychiatry*. **32**: 995–1007 (1975).

Malan, D.H.   *The frontier of brief psychotherapy: An example of the convergence of research and clinical practice*. New York: Plenum, 1976.

Meltzoff, J. and Kornreich, M.   *Research in psychotherapy*. New York: Atherton, 1970.

Mintz, J.   What is "success" in psychotherapy? *Journal of Abnormal Psychology*. **80**: 11–19 (1972).

Mintz, J., Luborsky, L. and Christoph, P.   Measuring the outcomes of psychotherapy: Findings of the Penn psychotherapy project. *Journal of Consulting and Clinical Psychology*. **47**: 319–334 (1979).

Paul, G.L.   Insight versus desensitization in psychotherapy two years after termination. *Journal of Consulting Psychology*. **31**: 333–348 (1967).

Ryan, V. and Gizynski, M.   Behavior therapy in retrospect: Patients' feelings about their behavior therapists. *Journal of Consulting and Clinical Psychology*. **37**: 1–9 (1971).

Shapiro, A.K. and Morris, L.A. The placebo effect in medical and psychological therapies. In: Garfield, S.L. and Bergin, A.E. (Eds.) *Handbook of psychotherapy and behavior change*, 2nd ed. New York: Wiley, 1978.

Sloane, R.B., Staples, F.R., Cristol, A.H., Yorkston, N.J., and Whipple, K. *Psychotherapy versus behavior therapy*. Cambridge, Mass.: Harvard University Press, 1975.

Smith, M.L., Glass, G.V. and Miller, T.I.   *The benefits of psychotherapy*. Baltimore: The Johns Hopkins University Press, 1980.

Strupp, H.H. and Bergin, A.E.   *A bibliography of research in psychotherapy*. Washington, D.C.: National Institute of Mental Health, 1969.

Strupp, H.H. and Hadley, S.W.   A tripartite model of mental health and therapeutic outcomes: With special reference to negative effects in psychotherapy. *American Psychologist*. **32**: 187–196 (1977).

Strupp, H.H. and Hadley, S.W. Specific vs. nonspecific factors in psychotherapy. A controlled study of outcome. *Archives of General Psychiatry*. **36**: 1125–1136 (1979).

Author Index

551

Subject Index